Albion's Glory

Albion's Glory

A Celebration of Twentieth Century English Composers

Stephen H. Smith

Matador
Unit E2 Airfield Business Park,
Harrison Road, Market Harborough,
Leicestershire. LE16 7UL
Tel: 0116 279 2299
Email: books@troubador.co.uk
Web: www.troubador.co.uk/matador
Twitter: @matadorbooks

ISBN 978 1800465 435

British Library Cataloguing in Publication Data.
A catalogue record for this book is available from the British Library.

Printed and bound in the UK by TJ Books LTD, Padstow, Cornwall
Typeset in 11pt Adobe Jenson Pro by Troubador Publishing Ltd, Leicester, UK

Matador is an imprint of Troubador Publishing Ltd

Contents

Chapter 1. **Setting the Scene**

Chapter 2. **The Composers**

Progenitors of the English Musical Renaissance

Ten of the Best

The Best of the Rest

Chapter 3. **Accessing the Music**

Abbreviations

BBC NOW	BBC National Orchestra of Wales
BBC PO	BBC Philharmonic Orchestra
BBC SO	BBC Symphony Orchestra
BBC Scottish SO	BBC Scottish Symphony Orchestra
BMS	British Music Society
CBSO	City of Birmingham Symphony Orchestra
CUMS	Cambridge University Music Society
DRP	Deutsche Radio Philharmonie
ECO	English Chamber Orchestra
ENO	English National Opera
ISCM	International Society for Contemporary Music
LFO	London Festival Orchestra
LPO	London Philharmonic Orchestra
LSO	London Symphony Orchestra
LSSO	Leicestershire Schools Symphony Orchestra
Malta PO	Malta Philharmonic Orchestra
NLO	New London Orchestra
Northern CO	Northern Chamber Orchestra
NPO	New Philharmonia Orchestra
Phil O	Philharmonia Orchestra
RAM	Royal Academy of Music
RCM	Royal College of Music
RLPO	Royal Liverpool Philharmonic Orchestra
RNCM	Royal Northern College of Music
RPO	Royal Philharmonic Orchestra
RSNO	Royal Scottish National Orchestra
Scottish CO	Scottish Chamber Orchestra
Scottish NO	Scottish National Orchestra
Welsh Nat Op O	Welsh National Opera Orchestra

One

Setting the Scene

1. What Makes a Composer "English"?

The vexed question of what makes a composer distinctively "English" is ever with us, for different people will answer it in different ways, and the arguments seem interminable. Some of those who made their name here and were happily absorbed into the English musical scene were born elsewhere. Arthur Benjamin (1893–1960), Hubert Clifford (1904–59), Percy Grainger (1882–1961), Frederick Kelly (1881–1916) and Malcolm Williamson (1931–2003) all hailed from Australia and in most cases came here to study, while John Joubert (1927–2019), born in South Africa, arrived in England in 1946 for the same purpose and remained here for the rest of his life. Do we still regard these composers as "colonials", or have we adopted them as our own? After all, one of them, Malcolm Williamson, eventually rose to receive that most British of accolades, Master of the Queen's Music (or is it still "Musick"?). And if we do choose to adopt such musicians, why not the New Zealander Douglas Milburn (1915–2001), who also joined the pilgrimage of budding musical talent to our shores? Do we exclude him from the list because he consciously sought to create a distinctively "New Zealand" style of music? If we do, we are surreptitiously bearing testimony to the view that it is not simply one's place of birth that counts; the aura of the music does too. But then, what do we do with composers like Colin Matthews (b. 1946), Peter Racine Fricker (1920–90), Harrison Birtwistle (b. 1934), Robert Simpson (1921–97) and Peter Maxwell Davies (1934–2014) (another former Master of the Queen's Music) who were all born in England, but whose music sounds far more cosmopolitan than that of English stalwarts like Elgar, Vaughan Williams and Holst?

The same dilemma embraces other composers who were born in this "sceptred isle" but who chose to ply their trade in foreign fields – W.H. Bell (1987–1946), Edgar Bainton (1880–1956), Eugene Goossens (1893–1962) and, most notably, Frederick Delius (1862–1934), among others. It happens that I have excluded the first three from consideration in this book (actually, economy of space has much to do with it), but eyebrows would certainly have been raised had I excluded dear old Frederick! Yet his initial training was undertaken in Florida, and his formal training in Leipzig, while his music was influenced by an eclectic mix of Negro spirituals, French cultural life, German literature and the mountains of Norway, with the merest deferential nod to the old country (as in *Brigg Fair* and the *North Country Sketches*, for example). It is easy – almost obligatory – to think of his exquisite miniaturist gems such as *On Hearing the First Cuckoo in Spring, A Summer Night on the River* and *In a Summer Garden* as depicting quintessentially English landscapes, but the cuckoo is likely to have spoken French, the garden to have been his own in the French village of Grez-sur-Loing, and the river the one which ran past the bottom of it.

The question of what makes music "English" even has repercussions for the work of wholly continental composers. The early output of the Portuguese composer Joly Braga Santos (1924–88) is a case in point. Listeners well-acquainted with the so-called English renaissance composers who have never heard a note of Braga Santos prior to hearing one of his first four symphonies (his style became more astringent following a period of study in Italy around 1960) could be forgiven for attributing the music to an English composer if they were unaware of its true source. It *sounds* so English, and comparisons with Vaughan Williams, Moeran and Walton are frequently made. Yet Braga Santos was the prodigy of his mentor, a Portuguese composer of the previous generation named Louis de Freitas Branco (1890–1955), the influences of whom can be found in the younger man's music. The reasons for Braga Santos's uncanny resemblances to the English renaissance composers are readily discernible in his use of Portuguese sixteenth century polyphonic techniques, and of modal inflections, buoyed by an intimate acquaintance with regional Portuguese folk music.

The question of what makes certain kinds of music distinctively "English", therefore, is far more complex than it might at first appear, and our choice of who to include in our survey and who to exclude from it must take account of many factors.

2. Choosing the Composers

My choice of composers to be included in this volume is an entirely personal (though not arbitrary) one; someone else's choice would no doubt look very different. It can safely be assumed, however, that the household names – Elgar, Vaughan Williams, Holst, Walton, Britten, Delius – would make everyone's list, as would – probably – many of the "second division" composers such as Alwyn, Bax, Bridge, Howells, Ireland and Moeran. I would hasten to add that the epithet "second division" (not my own term) is not meant to cast aspersions on the quality of their music, which is often as finely crafted as that of the "greats". It is simply that, for a variety of reasons, these composers have never enjoyed as much exposure as the "big six". This variety is well-exemplified in the range of composers I have just named.

William Alwyn is perhaps better known for his film music than for his well-wrought symphonic cycle and chamber works. Although he lived within a stone's throw of Benjamin Britten and his entourage in Aldeburgh on the Suffolk coast, he seems to have been snubbed by the Britten set and never enjoyed the recognition he may otherwise have had.

Bax was recognised as a major symphonist in his day, but he had the misfortune to die in 1953, just as the musical establishment, aided and abetted by Sir William Glock at the BBC, was beginning to embrace the "new music", namely serialism, almost to the exclusion of everything else. Thus, poor old Bax suffered an eclipse from which his reputation has never fully recovered, although more recently he has been well-served by the recording industry.

Bridge's fate was to some extent self-inflicted. His earlier music embraced a rich English romanticism, but later in his comparatively brief career he turned his hand to a modern, astringent style which, though it may have served him well in the heady 1950s, many listeners in the 1930s found impenetrable, so that his foray into experimentalism lost him many friends.

Herbert Howells was widely considered the most promising young English composer of his generation, and was dubbed "my son in music" by the formidable Sir Charles Villiers Stanford – high praise indeed, coming from him. This early promise is more than evident in his student pieces (the *Bs Suite for Orchestra*, for instance), but he was sensitive to criticism, and the cool reception received at the premiere performance of his Piano Concerto No. 2 in 1925 brought on composer's block. On recovering from this, he was dealt another blow in 1936 by the tragic death of his nine-year old son Michael, from polio, and again fell silent. His eventual response to this tragedy can be heard in his acknowledged masterpiece *Hymnus Paradisi*. From then on, he all but abandoned the composition of secular music and devoted himself to writing for the Anglican Church. Today, Howells's Evening Services, in particular, are regularly performed in cathedrals and churches throughout Britain and beyond, but his early secular works have never really recovered from their undeserved neglect, although, as with Bax, most have now been recorded.

John Ireland is known to have become embittered about what he perceived as a lack of recognition compared with young "upstarts" like Benjamin Britten, but his reticence in composing large-canvas works (the Piano Concerto of 1930 has been the most enduring) leaves the impression that he was primarily a miniaturist whose exquisite piano pieces and songs were caviare for the few. Perhaps his compositions were not ambitious enough for a general public.

Moeran's early promise was arrested by a disastrous three-year period of dissolution among the Warlock ménage at Eynsford in Kent (1925–28), during which he hardly wrote a note of music. Following that period, he seems to have been consumed with self-doubt, and although the works became steadily more ambitious, they appeared slowly (the Symphony in G minor, commissioned by Hamilton Harty in 1926, did not materialise until 1937). After his early death at the age of fifty-five, his music was all but forgotten, and was only kept alive at all thanks to champions like the conductor Vernon ("Tod") Handley.

These are just a few of the impediments to wider recognition that these composers, and others like them, have had to endure, if not in their own lifetimes, then after their deaths. However, the story is not quite that clear-cut. As I have hinted, these days, thanks to a vibrant recording industry, including enterprising companies like Lyrita, Chandos, Naxos, Dutton and Toccata, almost the entire output of these musicians is available on CD (as well as MP3 format for listeners so inclined). The problem now is rooted in the concert hall. The majority of programmes are so overloaded with the "classics" that there is precious little opportunity to hear anything English beyond the works – and even then, only the most popular works – of the household names. Of course, it may be argued that there are sound musical reasons why these have made it into the concert repertoire when those of "lesser" composers have not. Obviously, that may be true, in part. But there are some acknowledged top-drawer compositions out there which are hardly ever performed live. In the late 1930s, Moeran's Symphony in G minor was being mentioned in the same breath as Vaughan Williams's Symphony No. 4 and Walton's Symphony No. 1. How often is it performed today? I have only once heard a live airing (at a Promenade concert some years ago). Who can boast that they have heard a live performance of any of Havergal Brian's thirty-two symphonies? Yes, there was that grand occasion on 17th July 2011 when the great Gothic

Symphony was given a rousing performance under the baton of Martyn Brabbins to a packed Royal Albert Hall; and I can testify to a performance of the Symphony No. 10 at Sheffield City Hall given by James Loughran and the Hallé Orchestra back in 1973. Loughran just happened to have it in his locker, having recorded it with the Leicestershire Schools Symphony Orchestra the previous year. But two live performances (in my experience) over a period of nearly fifty years hardly constitutes a rich harvest. So, unfortunately, the vast bulk of English music is dependent on the recording studio and the commitment of conductors like Martyn Brabbins, Martin Yates and others to record neglected but worthwhile English works, and it is to be hoped that they can keep alive the torch handed down to them by conductors like Sir John Barbirolli, Sir Adrian Boult, Sir Charles Groves, Richard Hickox and Vernon Handley.

3. The Omissions

a) In General

By way of economy, I have reluctantly had to restrict this book, with one exception, to the composers who are English by birth, even though some of them may not sound English in the traditional or widely-acknowledged sense. This, unfortunately, disqualifies some outstanding figures from the other home countries: from Wales, William Mathias, Daniel Jones, Grace Williams and Alun Hoddinott; from Scotland, Hamish MacCunn, Alexander Mackenzie, John McEwan and James MacMillan; and from Ireland, Hamilton Harty, Howard Ferguson, Ina Boyle, Brian Boydell and John Kinsella – to name but a few. My one exception is Sir Charles Villiers Stanford who, although born in Dublin, was so much a prominent part of English musical life for so long (his tenure as Professor of Composition at the RCM extended to over thirty-five years), and launched so many quintessentially English composers on their careers, that a gaping hole would have been left in this survey had I not included him.

Also omitted are the abovementioned "colonial" composers, however significant their influence and contribution to the musical life of this country. We extend to the likes of Malcolm Williamson and John Joubert our gratitude and highest praise, but in a book which requires the strictest control in matters of selection, I am afraid they must be overlooked here. Lest I be accused of xenophobia, however, I have also omitted composers who were born in England but spent the greater part of their professional careers abroad – Bainton, Goossens and Bell, for example.

The final restriction is a chronological one: the working lives of the individuals included must generally occupy a sufficiently substantial part of the twentieth century in order to qualify for inclusion. 1848, the date of Parry's birth, marks the *terminus a quo*. Elgar, born in 1857, was staunchly Victorian, certainly, yet it would have been unthinkable to omit the grand old man of English music, even if he had been short-lived. And, given that virtually all his most important works date from 1900 (the *Enigma Variations* appeared just a year before this), there is no awkward dilemma to be faced.

With William Hurlstone (1876–1906) it is somewhat different. He was among that outstanding group of English composers who studied at the RCM towards the end of the nineteenth century, and was one of its brightest stars. Indeed, he was appointed a Professor of Composition there in 1905, at the tender age of twenty-nine, but soon afterwards succumbed to a lung disorder which deprived the musical world of an enormous talent. It would have been churlish, therefore, to have excluded him from consideration.

A more famous example of tragic brevity is the very English George Butterworth (1885–1916) who, during his painfully brief compositional career, made a highly significant contribution to the development of a peculiarly "English" style during the first decade or so of the twentieth century.

William Baines (1899–1922) is yet another example of tragically-stifled promise. Although only twenty-three at the time of his death from tuberculosis, his catalogue already numbered some two hundred works (counting juvenilia, presumably), including a substantial symphony. The best of his piano pieces, such as *Paradise Gardens* and the Seven Preludes, retain a place in the repertoire to this day.

Moving now to the end of the century, I have not included any composer born since 1960. Those born later in the century – Thomas Adés (b. 1971), for example – are likely to leave a legacy as twenty-first century composers, since this is when their most mature works will have been written. As it happens, the only living composers represented here are Harrison Birtwistle (b. 1934), Andrew Downes (b. 1950) and Ian Venables (b. 1955), whose compositional careers span over forty years. The latter two are firmly rooted in the English tradition. Downes shares Finzi's passion for the poetry of Thomas Hardy and betrays the influence of Vaughan Williams in both his Symphony No. 1 (for organ and orchestra) and his lovely overture *In the Cotswolds*, while Ian Venables has been described as "a worthy successor to those many art-song composers who, from the nineteenth century renaissance of British music to the present day – from Parry and Stanford, and continuing through to Finzi – have considered the setting of English words to music as central to their artistic creeds".[1]

b) Let's Hear it for the Ladies!

In these enlightened days of gender equality – or of working towards it (there is still some way to go) – it will not have passed unnoticed how comparatively few female composers have been included in this survey. To a large extent this is due to the nature of the project. Our review covers only twentieth century composers, and for much of that century composition was regarded as an overwhelmingly male occupation. Of course, even as far back as Victorian times, there were exceptions to the rule, as Alice Smith (1839–84), Ethel Smyth (1868–1944), Dora Bright (1862–1951) and the mysterious LH

1 Graham J. Lloyd, liner notes, *At Midnight*, Signum Classics, SIGCD 204.

of Liverpool (?) can testify[2], but none of these became household names like Elgar and Vaughan Williams. Until very recently, Masters of the King's/ Queen's Music have always been just that – Masters, not Mistresses[3], and this had much to do, no doubt, with prevailing twentieth century attitudes. Still, musical qualities count for something too. Elgar, Bax, Bliss, Williamson (a controversial choice, as it turned out), and Peter Maxwell Davies were all very well known as composers prior to their appointment, and were versatile enough to accommodate a more populist style for occasional pieces when required, so their credentials spoke for them, making their appointment a natural choice.

My choice of composers here obviously reflects the male bias of the twentieth century which, in the present case, is hardly avoidable. I have, however, managed to include Ethyl Smyth, Rebecca Clarke, Elizabeth Lutyens and Ruth Gipps. If I were asked to name at least ten English female composers, I could at least do what over 95% of the population could not – which does not say a great deal for current public awareness. Obviously, it is not incumbent on female composers to write attractive, tonal music which the public want to hear, rather than restrict themselves to an academic style based on strict musical theory. The best-loved music, however, has always been that with an emotional heart.

---

2 Two recordings provide an interesting survey of the music of nineteenth and twentieth century English women composers. The first, "In Praise of Women" (Helios CDH 55159), focuses on songs with piano, while the other, "A Cello Century of British Women Composers" (ASV CD QS 6245), consists of chamber works for cello and piano by figures including Rebecca Clarke, May Muckle, Margaret Hubicki, Imogen Holst, and Sheila Mary Power.

3 In 2014, however, following the death of Sir Peter Maxwell Davies, the first female holder of the office, Judith Weir, was appointed.

4. A Potted *Potted* History of Twentieth Century English Music

The question of Englishness in music is, of course, rooted in the struggle, from the late nineteenth century onwards, to escape Teutonic influences. As is well-known, the Germans had sneeringly dismissed England as "das Land ohne Musik", which may have been incentive enough to encourage composers of the younger generation – Elgar, Vaughan Williams, Holst and others – to respond. Parry and Stanford, who held court at the RCM for over thirty-five years, were undoubtedly two of the finest music teachers of their generation. The list of budding composers who passed through their hands – Vaughan Williams, Holst, Howells, Gurney, Ireland, Rebecca Clarke (Stanford's first female student) – sounds like a roll-call of Britain's finest. Yet their own symphonies, despite being labelled "English" (Parry's Third) and "Irish" (Stanford's Third), sound like imitations of Brahms who could no doubt have done it better. To be fair to Stanford, we do find the influence of Irish traditional music in his Irish Rhapsodies and the later songs, and, stickler though he was in his teaching methods, he clearly did not prevent his students from developing their own musical language. Even Vaughan Williams appreciated the value of learning from selected continental composers, having arranged private lessons with Bruch in 1897 and Ravel in 1908. After the latter foray, he complained of having returned home with a bad attack of French fever, but there is little doubt that Ravel's lessons helped him hone his orchestral technique, as is evident in works like *On Wenlock Edge* which, in turn, served as a model for younger composers such as George Butterworth, Herbert Howells and Ivor Gurney. Thus, Vaughan Williams's French studies were all grist to the English mill.

The question of who was the best English composer of the twentieth century is no doubt trite and pointless, yet it still rages. It is almost universally acknowledged that there are only two serious candidates – I hardly need name them. Even the precocious Benjamin Britten is out of the frame. In the view of the respective

Elgar and Vaughan Williams enthusiasts, there is little doubt that their man heads the field. Yet quintessentially English as their music (and lives) may have been, they were English in very different ways. Elgar, the senior of the two by some fifteen years, had already made a name for himself with the *Enigma Variations* and *The Dream of Gerontius* by 1900, while Vaughan Williams was yet a student at Cambridge and the RCM and was still some years from finding his mature voice. Of course, it would be inaccurate to say that Elgar was all "pomp and circumstance", representing only the ceremonial side of Britain – the Violin and Cello Concertos and the late chamber works teach us otherwise. He *was* a cheerleader for the British Empire (as in the *Pageant of Empire* of 1924), but much more. His large-scale choral works were informed by the late Victorian choral tradition in which he was steeped, and his Second Symphony is generally acknowledged to have tolled the death-knell for the era of Edwardian opulence. His post-war music became more rueful, more subdued, more personal – yet it was still quintessential Elgar. Indeed, during the First World War, when it was widely regarded as unpatriotic to embrace German music, Elgar became the people's champion, and by this time Vaughan Williams had become sufficiently well-established to be considered representative of identifiably English values and traditions. *The Lark Ascending*, written in 1914 but not premiered until after the end of hostilities, seemed to embody everything that English people held dear, and for which the nation had been fighting. Eventually, once the wounds of war had begun to heal, the German musical establishment was pardoned, and it became fashionable to listen to Beethoven and Brahms again, but by that time English music, boasting an indigenous language, had taken root.

The death of Elgar (along with Holst and Delius) in 1934 left the field to Vaughan Williams as the pre-eminent British composer. His essential influences were deeply rooted in the English soil – in the landscape, in Tudor polyphony and, of course, in English folksong – although, conversely, Bach never ceased to be his abiding passion. But if Vaughan Williams was firmly established on the throne by the mid-thirties, the music scene around him was in ferment. The young pretenders at the time were Walton (*Belshazzar's Feast* and the First Symphony), Britten (although the operatic side of his talent, for which he became celebrated, was yet to emerge), and – for his Symphony in G minor alone – E.J. Moeran. This was also the age of neo-romantics like Arnold Bax and, to some extent Edmund Rubbra, and of neo-classicists such as Arnold Cooke (1906–2005) and Lennox Berkeley (1903–89). There were quieter, more lyrical voices, too, like those of Julius Harrison (1885–1963), Walter Leigh (1905–42), Gerald Finzi (1901–56), and Robin Milford (1903–59). At around this time, too, the Emerald Isle was proving a rich source of inspiration, notably for Philip Heseltine (Peter Warlock), Bax and Moeran, although it seems to have been the glorious Irish landscape that beguiled above all. If there is any Irishness in the music itself, it is most evident in Moeran.

Other young composers sought their musical polish further afield – Kenneth Leighton in Italy, Elizabeth Maconchy in Czechoslovakia (as it was then), and Walter Leigh, Arnold Cooke, Roger Quilter, Balfour Gardiner, Cyril Scott and Norman O'Neill in Germany. The influence of these foreign adventures is obvious in the music of some (Leighton, Maconchy, Scott), while leaving others (Quilter and Leigh) virtually unaffected – at least superficially.

The 1950s was a time for the younger generation of composers to seize its chance. The deaths of Gerald Finzi (1956), and especially Vaughan Williams (1958), marked the end of an era. Societies for the promotion of new music sprang up, and, for a time, serialism became all the rage. Annual festivals like that at Cheltenham, provided a ready platform for performances, and conductors such as Barbirolli were keen to lay this new music before the public. It was during these years that William Alwyn, Arthur Butterworth, Alan Rawsthorne, Humphrey Searle and Peter Racine Fricker all flourished. The appointment of Sir William Glock as Director of Music at the BBC ensured an open avenue for broadcast performances, although, unfortunately, to the detriment of tonal composers with a penchant for melody and lyricism. Some of the more traditionalist composers – Edmund Rubbra, George Lloyd and Malcolm Arnold, for example – remained true to their own musical styles and principles, battening down the hatches in full confidence that serialism, much in vogue at the time, would be but a passing trend. Others, alas, were deeply affected by what they regarded as unjustifiable neglect. John Jeffreys destroyed a significant proportion of his manuscripts, including two violin concertos, while the deletion of many of Robin Milford's works from the catalogue of Oxford University Press (the Music Department of which his father, Sir Humphrey Milford, had been the founder) may well have contributed to his suicide in 1959.

As those who had stuck to their tonal guns had foreseen, the Glock era duly passed and it became fashionable to write tunes once more. The serialists did not simply disappear, but now they were required to share the spotlight with the more traditionalist composers and with others who were trying to develop techniques of their own which fell into neither category.

Today there exists an eclectic mix of styles in English music. The tonal, easy-listening tradition is maintained by Christopher Ball, Lionel Sainsbury and Christopher Wright, among others, while others, who might best be described as composers of light music – Matthew Curtis, Paul Carr, and Philip Lane, for example – keep alive the tradition maintained by those of an earlier generation as represented by Eric Coates, Ernest Tomlinson and Haydn Wood. Living symphonists writing in a variety of accessible styles include Christopher Gunning, David Matthews, Rodney Newton, and Philip Sawyers. There are composers celebrated for their film music who have turned their hand to classical forms – Richard Rodney Bennett and Michael Nyman, for instance; and for those who wish to sink their teeth into something seriously challenging, there is the music of Harrison Birtwistle, Colin Matthews, Mark-Anthony Turnage … the list goes on. The English choral tradition can be found ably represented in the work of Anthony Pitts, Francis Pott and Paul Spicer, along with the somewhat more eclectic styles of Jonathan Dove and Sir John Tavener (1944–2014), while the glories of English art-song are maintained by composers including Brian Blyth Daubney, Andrew Downes, Geoffrey Kimpton, John Pickard, John Williamson (1929–2015) and, especially, Ian Venables, among many others.[4]

5. The Survey

Even given the omissions on account of geography and chronology, explained above, this still leaves literally hundreds of English composers meeting the criteria for inclusion. I have therefore been in a Desert Island Discs situation regarding my selection. As already noted, the major composers have selected themselves, but the household names occupy a relatively small proportion of those chosen, and for the rest, my choice has necessarily had to be a personal one; someone else's list would no doubt look very different. I have tried to ensure that composers of differing styles are fairly represented. There are song and chamber music specialists as well as symphonists, and some who are equally at home in all the traditional genres.

I have sought to accord sufficient space to the lesser-known figures. After all, there are mountains of books and articles on Elgar, Vaughan Williams and Britten to which I can add nothing new. Of course, each of these major figures receives his due attention. But it is one of the chief purposes of this volume to provide a selection of unjustly neglected composers with their day in the sun. Some of these have interesting stories to tell and a catalogue of music well worth exploring.

Each entry concludes with a brief bibliography (where appropriate) and a select discography. I also include, where possible,

4 Apart from Birtwistle, Downes, Tavener and Venables, who are treated in the survey, the other names in this paragraph will not be mentioned again. This is not because they are not composers of merit, but simply because we are obliged to draw the line at some point. A glance at Amazon will show what works of theirs are available on record, and there will be plenty of examples posted on YouTube for those who want a taster of their sound-world.

the current web address of any society, trust or homepage relating to the individual composer. These vary enormously in range and quality, the best of them providing useful further information, links to other relevant sites and, occasionally, samples of the music. It is up to the interested reader to explore these and – who knows? – even enrol as a member of the society if the prospect is sufficiently attractive.

Following the survey itself, there is a short chapter detailing other ways, apart from CD, that the music can be accessed.

Two

The Composers

Progenitors of the English Musical Renaissance

1. Sir Charles Hubert Parry (1848–1918)

> The English Musical Renaissance... would no more be possible without Parry than the first Viennese School without Haydn or the second Viennese School without Schoenberg.[1]

No doubt these words are as true of Parry as they would be if applied to Sir George Grove (1820–1900) or Sir Charles Villiers Stanford. Yet, as we have seen, the music of Parry and Stanford, on the whole, was firmly rooted in the nineteenth century Germanic tradition. When Germany sneered at Britain as "a land without music", she meant without its *own* musical tradition, for Britain was steeped in the music of Brahms, Mendelssohn, Schumann, and latterly Wagner, while Bach and Beethoven who, along with Brahms, were the other members of the holy triumvirate, were also adored. Even Parry's Symphony No. 3, "English", is not really

1 Bernard Benoliel, liner notes, *Masters of the English Musical Renaissance*, Forlane, UCD 16724/25, p. 2.

so *very* English. If it is, it is the Englishness of a country squire, which is precisely what Parry was, as well as an MP and a JP at various times – a man of many parts; he was much more than music alone. Benoliel's pronouncement, above, can best be interpreted as meaning that Parry and Stanford were *facilitators* of the English Musical Renaissance. They left it to their students to put it into effect. An entire generation of truly English composers – Vaughan Williams, Holst, Bridge, Ireland, Howells, Gurney and Moeran, among others – came under the tutelage of these two giants.

Vaughan Williams, who was taught by both men, during two separate periods at the RCM, has left us a vivid picture of contrasting personalities: Stanford, the arch-conservative who would not allow a note of his students' music to pass unjustified, and could be as scathing as he was generous; Parry, the broad-minded yet sensitive liberal who was more open to his students pushing the boundaries as long as he could find something "characteristic" in the music itself. "Write choral music as befits an Englishman and a democrat", he told Vaughan Williams: something Stanford would – or could – never have said; although precisely what Parry meant by it is anyone's guess.

Parry was born in Bournemouth into an aristocratic family on 27th February 1848. His father was Thomas Gambier Parry (1816–88) whose wealth, which had been inherited from his grandfather, a director of the East India Company, had enabled him to purchase a country seat, Highnam Court in Gloucestershire. Hubert, the youngest of six children by his first wife, Isabella (1816–48), learned all too soon of the fragility of life. His mother died of consumption just five days after giving birth to him, and of his five siblings, three died in infancy, and a sister, Lucy (1841–61) was dead by the age of twenty. His only surviving brother, Clinton (1840–83), was also short-lived, but was closer to Hubert than anyone else in the family. They shared a keen interest in music, and by all accounts Clinton was an equally precocious talent. As was frequently the case among nineteenth century aristocrats, however, music was seen to be suitable only as a pastime, not as a profession.

Thus, the two brothers, who wanted to be professional musicians, suffered initially under their father's opposition, and Clinton went to the bad.

Parry's education began privately under a governess, progressing to preparatory school, first at Malvern (1856–58), and then at Twyford (1859–61) where music was encouraged. It was at this time that he came under the influence of the celebrated organist and composer Samuel Wesley (1810–76), from whom he acquired a lifelong love of Bach which ultimately found expression in a book on the composer, *Johann Sebastian Bach: The Story of the Development of a Great Composer* (1909). Another organist, Edward Brind, gave Parry the usual basic grounding in piano and harmony and, significantly, introduced him to the Three Choirs Festival scene.

In 1861 Parry's well-worn route through education for the upper crust took him to Eton where he remained for six years. At the time the college was not especially strong on music, given that its young gentlemen were expected to enter one of the "respectable" professions – the Church, the army, or the civil service. His path through Eton was smoothed considerably by the fact that he excelled at sport. For his continued musical education, however, he found a useful ally in George Elvey (1816–93), the organist at nearby St. George's Chapel, Windsor, who not only provided Parry with a thorough grounding in musical principles, but recognised his talent and was determined to see him into Oxford. He also oversaw Parry's compositional efforts and arranged for some of his anthems to be performed by the Chapel choir. Parry sat the Oxford BacMus examination while still at Eton, becoming the youngest recipient of the award.

Once he did go up to the University, it was to read law and modern history, as his father desired, and music had to take a back seat, although he did find time during one summer vacation to study with Henry Hugo Pierson (1816–73) in Stuttgart. Throughout these years his enthusiasms wavered according to the tastes of whoever his tutor happened to be; but although he was exposed to the music of a wide range of composers, they were almost exclusively of Austro-German origin – Bach, Beethoven, Handel, Haydn, Mendelssohn, Mozart, Schumann, Weber, Wagner – with one or two other continentals, notably Rossini, thrown into the melting pot. There is little wonder that Parry's own music, even in maturity, sounded so Teutonic.

On leaving Oxford in 1870, Parry still felt under obligation to his father and worked for seven years as an underwriter at Lloyd's of London while continuing with his music studies in his spare time, first with the English composer William Sterndale Bennett (1816–75), and then in Germany with Edward Dannreuther (1844–1905) from whom he acquired a taste for Wagner.

By 1875, when Parry was twenty-seven years of age, his compositions were becoming widely-known and admired, and came to the attention of George Grove, editor of the *Dictionary of Music and Musicians*. Grove had no hesitation in inviting him to be his assistant. Parry himself contributed no fewer than 123 articles, and Elgar, who never enjoyed Parry's educational privileges and was largely self-taught as a composer, testified to the fact that he had benefitted more from Parry's articles than from anything else. When Grove was appointed the first Director of the RCM in 1883, he took his valued assistant with him, appointing him Professor of Composition and Music History. From this point, Parry began composing some of his most celebrated pieces, including *Prometheus Unbound* (1880), sometimes considered to be the work that generated the English Musical Renaissance more than any other, and *Blest Pair of Sirens* (1887), one of Parry's most popular works, which was regarded by Vaughan Williams as the finest work in the English choral repertoire.

When George Grove retired as Director of the RCM in 1895, Parry was seen by many as his natural successor, and he retained the post until his death in 1918. He added to his workload by also accepting the post of Heather Professor at Oxford in succession to Sir John Stainer (1840–1901) in the year of Groves's death, 1900. He also took on the role of Music Examiner at London University for several years. And, as if all this were not enough, he published from books on music at frequent intervals. Apart from his work on Bach, other titles included: *Studies of Great Composers* (1886), *The Art of Music* (1893, exp. 1896), *The Music of the Seventeenth Century* (1902), and *Style in Musical Art* (1911) – a collection of his Oxford University lectures.

His personal life was also proceeding apace from one honour to another – in 1898 a knighthood, and three years later the baronetcy of Highnam Court, the family seat. Parry was a man of enormous energy, and had to be in order to cope with all his official duties and obligations – educational, political, judicial, not to mention familial. The music writer Robin Legge sounded a timely warning when he wrote:

> A composer who counts is rare enough anywhere, any time. Do not try to use him as a mixture of university don, cabinet minister, city magnate, useful hack, or a dozen things besides. A great blow was delivered against English music when Parry was appointed to succeed Sir George Grove as director of the RCM.[2]

The work of a cabinet politician, for most practitioners, is a full-time job, yet here we find Parry juggling his commitment with all his others like a master plate-spinner. In the midst of all this, what time was left for composition? In the above citation Legge was writing Parry's obituary, when his life's work was done. One wonders whether he was truly aware of the true extent of Parry's output. If, as is often averred, composition tends to be a case of 10% inspiration and 90% perspiration, Parry can hardly be said to have bucked the trend. After all, he continued to compose oratorios to commission, long after he had lost enthusiasm for the form itself, which must have required a peculiar form of tenacity.

When we turn to his catalogue, we find that he composed a good deal more in his lifetime, despite all his other commitments, than

2 Quoted in "Hubert Parry", https://en.wikipedia.org/wiki/Hubert_Parry, p. 5.

many composers without such commitments do in theirs. Apart from the five symphonies, there are a dozen or so other purely orchestral works, including a Piano Concerto (1879) and two of his best-known pieces, *Lady Radnor's Suite for Strings* (1894) and *Overture to an Unwritten Tragedy* (1893), as well as the *Elegy for Brahms* (1897) and the substantial *Symphonic Variations* (1897). There is also incidental music for the annual Oxbridge Greek play performances – *The Birds* (Cambridge), *The Frogs, The Clouds,* and *The Acharnians* (all Oxford). There was a single attempt at an opera, *Guinevere* (1885–86) whose production, however, proved less than successful, much to Parry's chagrin. Among the many choral works with orchestra are the oratorios *Judith* (1888), *Job* (1892) and *King Saul* (1894). Of the unaccompanied choral works, the best-known and most poignant are the six motets comprising the *Songs of Farewell* (1916–18), completed shortly before Parry's death from Spanish flu in 1918, and which concludes with the prescient *Lord, let me know mine end* (Psalm 39).

Other choral offerings are liturgical and include morning and evening services, anthems, motets and hymn tunes, the last of which include the ever-popular *Ye servants of God* (Laudate Dominium) and *Dear Lord and Father of mankind* (Repton).

In his choral settings, Parry preferred to set the words of recognised poets, old and new, rather than minor ones. Thus, we find Blake, Bridges (especially), Browning, Campion, Donne, Dryden, Dunbar, Herrick, Keats, Milton, Tennyson, and Vaughan much in evidence. Others, like A.C. Benson (1862–1925), had some currency at the time, but later fell from favour.

Parry was not only a "big work" composer in terms of length and size of the forces used; he could also turn his hand to chamber music, solo piano/ organ music, and songs – which he did throughout his career, although there are certain trends in evidence. For example, all the major chamber works, including three string quartets (1867, 1868, 1878–80), three string trios (1878, 1884, 1884–90), a piano quartet (1879), a violin sonata (1889) and a viola sonata (1893) had been written by the mid-nineties. With a few exceptions, the same is true of the solo piano pieces (including the substantial

Theme & Variations in D minor [1878–85]). The solo organ pieces, on the other hand, derive almost exclusively from the final decade of Parry's life. The songs, of which there is a considerable output, were composed throughout his career, from *Why does azure deck the sky?* (1866) to *English Lyrics, Set XII*, published posthumously in 1920. Here, in the *English Lyrics* (1881–1918), especially in the later sets, Parry is more liberal in his choice of poets, and includes many that are merely names to us today – Arthur Gray Butler, Julia Chatterton, Alan Cunningham, A.P. Graves (father of the better-known Robert Graves), Philip Massinger, Langdon Elwyn Mitchell, Julian Sturges, John Suckling, and Harry Warner.

Given that we have concluded this briefest of references to Parry's overall output with a mention of his songs, it may be worth pausing to consider their quality. I would certainly not presume to attempt this myself, even if there were sufficient space to do so, but if we take just the twelve sets of *English Lyrics*, written at various times over a period of forty years, we can hardly expect every one of the seventy-four individual items to be miniature masterpieces. Few today would compare these with the song output of Warlock, Gurney or Finzi on equal terms. In his book *Parry to Finzi*, Trevor Hold casts a critical but even-handed eye over Parry's song output and attempts to sort the wheat from the chaff.[3] He finds the songs distinctly uneven in quality, but singles out *Through the ivory gate*, *From a city window*, and *When the sun's great orb* as being among the more successful. Hold sums up Parry's song achievement in the following way:

> It was his deep love of English literature and his admiration for the German *Lieder* tradition that fired his imagination. He wanted to demonstrate that sympathetic, seriously considered musical setting could also enrich the wealth and heritage of English poetry. The breadth of range and eclecticism of his choice of poets and poetry is in itself an achievement. He was not afraid to choose poetry which

3 Hold, *Parry to Finzi*, pp. 17–40.

> many would have felt to be "too perfect" or "complete in itself" to need the addition of music... And he was quite prepared to choose poems by minor or obscure poets... when he felt that they were "apt for music". Very importantly, he used song... to express and charter his own intensely expressed feelings and spiritual and political beliefs: sometimes successfully, sometimes not, but always with commendably serious intention."[4]

For Hold, Parry's songs touch upon two aspects of his life – his Englishness and his political activities – both of which manifest themselves in a wide range of his music. In case anyone should be in any doubt as to his Englishness, he spells it out in some of his titles: his Symphony No. 3, "English"; *An English Suite for Strings*; the unison song *England*; *Characteristic Popular Tunes of the British Isles* (for piano duet, 1885); and, of course, the twelve sets of *English Lyrics*. Hold puts this down, at least in part, to his lyrical approach to music. His texts are taken almost exclusively from English poets throughout the ages. And why not? He was, after all, an English country squire with a voracious appetite for the literature of his homeland.

Perhaps, however, we can take Parry's Englishness only so far. When we listen to his most celebrated piece of all, *Jerusalem*, with its vision of Albion, as it is being played on the traditional Last Night of the Proms in front of hundreds of vociferous, patriotic, flag-waving Promenaders, we can hardly help but feel what wonderful English music it is. But take away the hype and listen to it as if at its premiere a century ago: would we have recognised it as English music then, or would we have acknowledged an underlying Teutonic influence? As we have seen, Parry was not ashamed to admit to the influence of the great Germanic musical tradition, although it was his aim to rework it within a purely English setting.

So to that other, non-musical aspect of Parry's life – his politics – which nevertheless may have found musical expression, as Hold

4 Hold, *Parry to Finzi*, p. 40.

suggests. Here, I use the term "politics" in its looser or broader sense rather than of party factionalism. Possibly one could not have perceived merely from observing Parry's bearing and behaviour what kind of party animal he was. One person who was better placed than anyone else to comment on Parry's social and political affiliations was his daughter Dorothea, who sought to scotch "the fantastic legend" about her father. The legend itself was perpetuated as clearly as anyone by Arnold Bax who wrote that Parry, Stanford and Mackenzie, the three great pedagogues of the RCM or RAM, "were all three solid reputable citizens... model husbands without a doubt, respected members of the most irreproachably Conservative clubs, and in Yeats's phrase had 'no strange friend.'"[5] George Bernard Shaw's comment about this triumvirate was even more dismissive. Writing in 1956, Dorothea countered this misapprehension, pointing out how unconventional and radical her father was. He "had a very strong bias against Conservativism... was a free-thinker, and did not [even] go to my christening".[6] In point of fact, he had something in common with his pupil Vaughan Williams. Both men came from privileged backgrounds and were raised in large, comfortable houses set in acres of glorious English countryside. Both were endowed with a generous spirit and broad, liberal sympathies. And both sought to develop a new English musical tradition, Parry as facilitator and Vaughan Williams as practitioner.[7] By way of contrast, we may consider Parry's relationship with his colleague at the RCM, Stanford (see directly below). A flamboyant and opinionated Irishman, he was in many respects the Yang to Parry's Yin. Stories abound of his testy humour and his unconventional

5 Arnold Bax, *Farewell My Youth* (London: Longmans, Green & Co., 1943, p. 28). One wonders how far this comment was provoked by Parry's regarding Bax's early songs as sounding like "a bevy of little devils" (quoted in *Farewell My Youth*), p. 27.

6 Dorothea Ponsonby, "Hubert Parry", *The Musical Times*, 97, no. 1359 (1956), p. 263.

7 Put like that, of course, the picture is too crude, but there is little room for expansion here. Perhaps the metaphor of standing on giants' shoulders will go some way to making the point.

approach to teaching, as we shall see, and his conservatism was self-evident; yet, like Yin and Yang, they complemented one another; the RCM would not have been the same – nor as effective – without those two in harness. Vaughan Williams studied under both, and although he sympathised with Parry's liberalism, it did not prevent him revering Stanford as a fine teacher in his own way, and Stanford could be just as generous in spirit. He rated Parry as the finest English composer since Purcell – some accolade – and he was eager to promote his students' work in public performance when he thought it showed promise, or even as a means of demonstrating where a work needed improving. As the years went by, however, their relationship deteriorated. Stanford's outspoken opposition to Parry was matched by the use of the latter's superior position at the college to provoke his colleague. Even so, it was Stanford who petitioned for Parry to be interred in St. Paul's Cathedral after his death.

Although Parry did not create a new national music out of his own compositions, he did, with the help of Stanford (and Mackenzie at the RAM), provide the means for others to do so, and to carry forward and complete the task; and for that alone, he deserves an enduring place in the history of English music.

a. Bibliography

Dibble, Jeremy, *C. Hubert H. Parry: His Life and Music* (Oxford: Oxford University Press, 1998)

Ponsonby, Dorothea, "Hubert Parry", *Musical Times*, 97, no. 1359 (1956), p. 263.

Trott, Michael, *Hubert Parry: A Life in Photographs* (Redditch, Worcestershire: Brewin Books, 2017)

b. Selected Discography

i) Symphonies

Symphonies Nos. 1–5	LPO, Bamert	Chandos	CHAN 9120-22

ii) Orchestral

Symphonic Variations	LPO, Bamert	Chandos	CHAN 6610
An English Suite	LSO, Boult	Lyrita	SRCD 220
Lady Radnor's Suite	LSO, Boult	Lyrita	SRCD 220

iii) Choral with Orchestra

Te Deum	BBC NOW & Chorus, Järvi	Chandos	CHAN 10740
Jerusalem	BBC NOW & Chorus, Järvi	Chandos	CHAN 10740
Magnificat	BBC NOW & Chorus, Järvi; Roocroft (sop)	Chandos	CHAN 10740
The Lotus Eaters	LPO & Choir; soloists; Bamert	Chandos	CHAN 241-3
Blest Pair of Sirens	LSO & Chorus, Hickox	Chandos	CHAN 241-3

iv) Choral

I was glad	Manchester Cathedral Choir, Stokes	Naxos	8.572104
Songs of Farewell	Manchester Cathedral Choir, Stokes	Naxos	8.572104

v) Chamber

String Quartets Nos. 1–3	Archaeus Quartet	MPR	MPR 102
Piano Trio No. 1	Leonore Piano Trio	Hyperion	CDA 68243
Piano Trio No. 2	Leonore Piano Trio	Hyperion	CDA 68276
Piano Trio No. 3	Leonore Piano Trio	Hyperion	CDA 68243
Piano Quartet in A flat major	Leonore Piano Trio, and Roberts (viola)	Hyperion	CDA 68276

2. Sir Charles Villiers Stanford (1852–1924)

Like Parry, Stanford's musical roots lay firmly in the soil of Germany where he spent some years in concentrated study and met some of the leading German musicians of the day, including Brahms. In later years, however, he made innovative use of traditional Irish melodies and inflections, especially in overtly Irish works such as the six *Irish Rhapsodies* for orchestra, the *Six Irish Folksongs* for unaccompanied chorus, and, among his songs with piano accompaniment, *A Sheaf of Songs from Leinster, Six Songs from The Glens of Antrim*, and *A Fire of Turf*. As early as 1887 he completed a third symphony which he labelled "Irish". Clearly, he was intensely proud of his Irish background.

Stanford was born into comfortable circumstances in Dublin on 30th September 1952. His father, John, was a lawyer of some prestige, and his mother, Mary, also came of legal stock. Both parents were cultured, and musical enough to perform in public to a competent standard. John Stanford, in fact, performed the title role in the Irish premiere of Mendelssohn's *Elijah* in 1847. As was so often the case in those days, although his parents encouraged their son's precocious musical talent, they did not envisage a professional career for him in that direction, although when he began to kick against the goad, his father offered only token resistance.

As a boy, Charles Stanford was exposed to a plethora of teachers for piano, organ, violin and composition studies. These comings and goings must have been confusing for a young lad, for every teacher deploys his or her own methods. However, young Charles was evidently a quick learner, for by the age of seven, not only was he able to give a competent piano recital of works by Beethoven, Mendelssohn, Mozart and Bach, but he was already showing signs of skill in composition. He spent the summer of 1863, aged ten, in London, taking the opportunity to augment his piano and composition studies with lessons from London-based teachers. On his return to Dublin, yet more teachers were added to the list, including Robert Stewart, then organist of St. Patrick's Cathedral.

In 1870, Stanford went up to Cambridge University on an organ scholarship, and also read for a Classics degree at Queen's College. However, with music as the absolute priority, Classics never stood a chance, and he only just managed to scrape through third-class, coming second bottom of his class. This proved immaterial, as it turned out, for, after performing as soloist in a CUMS concert, he was invited to become the society's assistant conductor under John Larkin Hopkins, who was also organist at Trinity College. Within the year Larkins fell terminally ill, and Stanford stood in as both conductor and organist – not a bad achievement for someone still only twenty years old. When the authorities at Trinity offered him a two-year fixed-term contract, he felt confident enough to strike a bargain in which his accepting the position was to be conditional on his being allowed the occasional sabbatical to enable him to study in Germany – a mark of the esteem in which he must have been held, despite his comparative youth.

In accordance with the terms of his contract, Stanford spent the following summer in Leipzig studying with Carl Reinecke, professor of both composition and piano. Although by this time Leipzig's star as a centre for musical excellence was beginning to wane, it was still the place to be for aspiring maestros. However, Stanford was disappointed with the instruction he received from Reinecke: "Of all the dry musicians I have even known he was the most desiccated… he loathed Wagner… sneered at Brahms and had no enthusiasm of any sort."[8]

This criticism from the "progressive" Stanford would ultimately turn out to be deeply ironical, for once he had his feet under the table at the RCM, it was Stanford himself against whom the charge of conservatism was frequently levelled. Certainly, it was not until comparatively late in his career that a distinctive Irish lilt began to infuse his diet of German romanticism, as we have noted. Be that as it may, he persisted with Reinecke's teaching the following year,

8 Quoted in "Charles Villiers Stanford", https://en.wikipedia.org/wiki/Charles_Villiers_Stanford, p. 4.

until Joachim suggested he try Friedrich Kiel in Berlin from whom he claimed to have learnt more in three months than from anyone else in three years.

On his return to Cambridge, Stanford resumed his contracted duties, and by now was beginning to compose large canvas works, including a violin concerto (later withdrawn), his First Symphony (1875), and an oratorio, *The Resurrection* (1875), which was performed by CUMS. He also wrote the incidental music to Tennyson's drama *Queen Mary* at the request of the poet himself. Next came Stanford's first attempt at opera, *The Veiled Prophet* (1878–79) which, although turned down by impresario Carl Rosa for performance in England, was eventually staged in Hanover in 1881. A further eight operas (plus an abandoned one) followed at regular intervals, ending with *The Travelling Companion* (1916), which has now been recorded. Opera, however, was not really Stanford's metier. He had to wait until 1893 for the English premiere of *The Veiled Prophet*. The 1883 production of *Savonarola* received lukewarm reviews at best, and some outright hostile ones. Even Parry was critical. *The Canterbury Pilgrims*, from the same year, was again panned by the critics, while George Grove pointed to its lack of sentiment. These negative comments from Stanford's own colleagues must have cut deeply, and may have contributed to the later ill feeling between them. Perhaps he might have enjoyed greater success had he not been attempting to juggle two operas simultaneously rather than channelling his whole attention into just one.

1883, however, was not all gloom, for it was in that year that Stanford accepted George Grove's invitation to become Professor of Composition at the newly-formed RCM, and to be joint conductor of the RCM orchestra. It was a position which he occupied until his death over forty years later. Teaching proceeded largely on the basis of one-to-one or small group tutorials, and over the years Stanford became legendary for his demanding instruction and his unorthodox methods. The list of students who benefitted (or suffered) under his tuition reads like a who's who of early twentieth century English composers: Edgar Bainton, Bliss, Bridge, George Butterworth (all too briefly), Rebecca Clarke, Coleridge-Taylor, Walford Davies, Thomas Dunhill, Goossens, Gurney, Dyson, Holst, Howells, Hurlstone, Ireland, Gordon Jacob, Moeran (very briefly), Rootham, Somervell and Vaughan Williams. The list is far from exhaustive. As for the unorthodox "methods", Bainton confessed:

> Stanford's teaching seemed to be without method or plan. His criticism consisted for the most part of "I like it, my boy", or "It's damned ugly, my boy" (the latter in most cases). In this, perhaps, lay its value. For in spite of his conservatism, and he was intensely and passionately conservative in music as in politics, his amazingly comprehensive knowledge of musical literature of all nations and ages made one feel that his opinions, however irritating, had weight.[9]

This reasonably balanced assessment is echoed by many others who came under his influence, including Vaughan Williams who noted that rather than pointing the way ahead directly, Stanford's comments were aimed at coaxing the young composition student to navigate his own way through the problems presented by any piece that he had written.[10]

Every Stanford student seems to have had his personal fund of stories.[11] Howells recalls an occasion when he and Gurney were jointly present at a Stanford tutorial, and the great man was examining a manuscript of the latter. Eventually, he made a minor alteration with his pencil. Gurney looked at the mark and replied,

9 Quoted in "Charles Villiers Stanford", https://en.wikipedia.org/wiki/Charles_Villiers_Stanford, p. 6

10 See also the similar assessment by Howells, quoted in Paul Spicer, *Herbert Howells* (Bridgend: Seren, 1998), p. 34

11 To access some of these, see Walford Davies, et al, "Charles Villiers Stanford by Some of His Pupils", *Music & Letters*, 5.3 (1924), pp. 193–207. The contributors include the composers Bainton, Bridge, Dunhill, Dyson, Friskin, Gurney, Howells, Ireland and Vaughan Williams, along with the conductor Leslie Heward and the pianist Harold Samuel.

"Well, Sir Charles, I see you've jiggered the whole show". Stanford threw him out of the room, closed the door, and turning to Howells said, "You know, I love him more each time".[12]

Another story concerns Arnold Bax who, while studying at the "other place" (the RAM) arrived at the RCM for a rehearsal by the RCM orchestra of an early orchestral piece of his, which he expected Stanford to be conducting. When he arrived shortly before the session was due to begin, he was met by Stanford with the words, "So there ye are, you're Bax aren't you? Well, now, you can go up there and work your wicked will on the orchestra". Protestations by Bax that he had never conducted an orchestra in his life were brushed aside, and he was made to endure forty-five minutes on the podium. The experience resolved him never to touch a baton again.[13]

Just as Stanford had once eschewed the arch-conservatism of Carl Reinecke, so now he found himself in much the same position, with his own composition students finding their own voice almost despite him. Yet he seems to have fostered and celebrated their achievement. Vaughan Williams's *Sea Symphony* must have sounded very modern at its premiere at the Leeds Festival on 12th October 1910 under the composer's baton; yet it was Stanford who had pulled the strings to get it performed. Some of Herbert Howells's early music sounded ultra-modern for the time, even Stravinskian in places (he was dazzled, like many other young English composers, by Diaghilev's *Ballet Russes*), yet Stanford could still refer to him affectionately as "my son in music". There were limits, however. Although Bridge's early romantic style yielded to experimentalism later on, he seems to not to have pressed this development until after the death of Stanford, perhaps in deference to his old mentor.

---

12 Michael Hurd, *The Ordeal of Ivor Gurney* (Oxford: Oxford University Press, 1978), p. 35.

13 See Lewis Foreman, *Bax: A Composer and His Times* (Woodbridge, Suffolk: Boydell Press, 2007), pp. 34–35.

No less than Parry, Stanford was imbued with tremendous energy, and one can only marvel how he managed to fit in all his commitments. On top of all his other activities, he succeeded Sir George Macfarren (1813–87) as Professor of Music at Cambridge in 1887. During his first six years in post he helped to establish the BMus at the University on a firmer footing than had been the case hitherto. From 1885–1902 he additionally served as conductor of the Bach Choir, and from 1898–1910 as conductor of the Leeds Philharmonic Society. Meanwhile – somehow – he still found time to compose. His Symphony No. 3, "Irish" (1887) was in vogue for a time and secured performances in Hamburg, Berlin, Vienna and New York. He also scored a rare success with his comic opera *Shamus O'Brien* (1895) which ran for eighty-two consecutive performances, and was additionally performed in translation in Germany, and revived by Thomas Beecham in London in 1910.

Elgar's rise to prominence as a composer from 1900 was counterbalanced by Stanford's decline, and it brought out the best and worst in the older man's dual personality – his generosity and his spitefulness. While Elgar had been a struggling provincial composer during the late nineteenth century, Stanford had generously promoted his cause by conducting his music and raising his profile socially; but it was a different matter now that he was taking precedence, and some unpleasantries were exchanged, at least in writing. As one commentator put it, "Stanford had his innings, but then Elgar bowled him out".

After World War I, the RCM must have seemed to Stanford, as to Parry, a place of ghosts, with so many former students dead or maimed – in particular the loss of George Butterworth on the Somme, and Ivor Gurney soon to be confined to a mental asylum for the remainder of his life. With the death of Hubert Parry in 1918, Stanford lost a long-standing colleague. Although he continued to teach and compose, his health began to decline, and in mid-March 1924 he suffered a stroke which resulted in his death, at the age of seventy-one, some two weeks later. After his cremation, his ashes were interred in Westminster Abbey.

Stanford's output stretched to almost two hundred opus-numbered items, plus a large body of other work, including juvenilia, which he excluded from his catalogue. Anything written prior to 1875 he consigned to the lumber room. What remained, however, included the nine completed operas, seven symphonies, six *Irish Rhapsodies*, three piano concertos (the last orchestrated by Geoffrey Bush), three violin concertos (the first withdrawn, the last orchestrated by Jeremy Dibble), and concertos for cello and clarinet, as well as the *Concert Piece for Organ & Orchestra* (op. 181). His chamber music includes eight string quartets, two string quintets, a piano quintet, two piano quartets, three piano trios, three violin sonatas, two cello sonatas, and a nonet, among many other pieces. For the Church, there are communion, morning and evening services in B flat major, A major, F major, G major, C major, D major, E flat major, and various anthems and motets. Among the works for choir/ soloist and orchestra is the *Requiem*, a *Te Deum*, the *Mass in G major*, the oratorio *The Resurrection*, the cantata *At the Abbey Gate*, the *Missa "Via Victrix" 1914–18*, the ever-popular *Songs of the Sea* and *Songs of the Fleet*, and the lesser-known *The Revenge: A Ballad of the Fleet*. There are some fifty songs for unaccompanied choir to texts ranging from anonymous Elizabethan poets, through Milton and Tennyson, to obvious favourites of Stanford's such as William Cory and Mary Coleridge; and in excess of seventy songs with piano accompaniment to texts by Dunbar, George Eliot, A.P. Graves, Heine, Letts, Keats, Moira O'Neill, Shakespeare, Stevenson, Whitman, and others. There are two sets of 24 piano preludes "in all the keys" (opp. 163, 179), and for organ five sonatas, and various preludes, postludes, toccatas, fugues and fantasias, most of them composed during or following World War I. It is a huge output for any composer, let alone for one who held so many administrative and teaching posts, and sat on so many committees, often simultaneously. He must have been a workaholic with a vengeance.

Stanford's busy schedule suggests that he cannot possibly have had the time to hone all the works that he produced, and he often suffered under the critics. He was accused of lacking in imagination or passion, especially in those dramatic works (opera, for example) that most required it. In one sense, composition came too easily for him. He was so well schooled in technique that he could dash off a technically near-flawless work at will – be it a symphony, a concerto, or a set of piano preludes. But technique itself is never enough. If composition is reduced merely to an academic exercise, it becomes dry and uninspiring. So it was with Stanford, generally-speaking. We have only to ask what advance his symphonies had on those of Brahms or Schumann. If they offer nothing more, or different, we might as well stick with the originals. Perhaps this was the root of his quarrels with his students. Vaughan Williams, Holst, Howells, Gurney, Bliss, Bridge – these were all seeking a way forward, a new language in which to express themselves, or, put bluntly, to leave Stanford behind. What was "damnably ugly" to Stanford may well have been the sound of their quest to find something "characteristic" in their efforts, as Parry would have said.

On the other hand, there can be no doubt whatsoever that without Stanford the face of English music today would look very different. Without him there would have been no Vaughan Williams, Holst, Howells – at least not in the sense in which they developed as composers of distinction. They did not write Stanford's music, and it is due largely to Stanford that they did not. Few, if any, of his students had no misgivings about him, but even fewer could deny that they had any respect for him, and some, like Herbert Howells, revered him. There can be no doubt, too, that without Stanford and Parry at the helm at the RCM, the English Musical Renaissance would never have been what it came to be. True, under Sir Alexander Mackenzie, the RAM played its part, turning out leading composers such as Bax, Bowen and Holbrooke, but of these only Bax emerged without speaking in a European tongue – hardly surprising, given the bias toward German staff members at the college. Under Grove and Parry, the RCM set out to break the shackles of Teutonic influence, although it was left to their students to bear the fruit of this enterprise. Under this regime, Stanford played his full part.

a. Bibliography

Davies, Walford, et al, "Charles Villiers Stanford by Some of His Pupils", *Music & Letters*, 5.3 (1924), pp. 193–207.

Dibble, Jeremy, *Charles Villiers Stanford: Man and Musician* (Oxford: Oxford University Press, 2002)

Greene, H.P., *Sir Charles Villiers Stanford* (London: Arnold, 1935)

Rodmell, Paul, *Charles Villiers Stanford* (London: Routledge, 2002)

b. Selected Discography

i) Symphonies

Symphonies Nos. 1–7	Ulster O., Handley	Chandos	CHAN 9279-82
	(Boxed set; also available separately)		

ii) Concertos

Piano Concerto No. 2	Ulster O., Handley; Fingerhut (piano)	Chandos	CHAN X10116
Violin Concerto No. 2	BBC Concert O., Arwel Hughes; Marshall-Luck (violin)	EM Rec.	EMR CD 023
Cello Concerto	RPO, Braithwaite; Baillie (cello)	Lyrita	SRCD321
Clarinet Concerto	Ulster O., Handley; Hilton (clar)	Chandos	CHAN 7002/3

iii) Orchestral

Irish Rhapsodies Nos 1–6	Ulster O., Handley	Chandos	CHAN 7002/3
Prelude: Oedipus Rex	Ulster O., Handley	Chandos	CHAN 7002/3

iv) Choral

Partsongs	Birmingham Cons. Chamber Choir,Somm Spicer	SOMMCD 0128

v) Songs

Songs, vols. 1 & 2	Varcoe (bar); Benson	Hyperion	CDA 67123/4

c. Website

The Stanford Society (www.thestanfordsociety.org)

Ten of the Best

1. Frank Bridge (1879–1941)

Ask people today what they know about Frank Bridge and, assuming they know anything at all, they will most likely identify him first and foremost as Benjamin Britten's mentor – as if he was a facilitator of composition in others rather than a composer in his own right. Yet he *was* a composer of the highest order, equally at home in orchestral and chamber music, who was able to earn a fairly meagre living in a financially unrewarding profession by composing songs and salon pieces for solo piano, while simultaneously attempting to set his own path in his more "serious" pieces.

He was born in Brighton in 1879, the tenth of twelve children, nurturing a lifelong love of the Sussex Downs nearby, and sharing it with the listening public in such pieces as *Enter Spring*. His father was a printer – and a frustrated musician – until he took the plunge by advertising his services as a violin teacher, also securing the post of Musical Director of the Empire Theatre in Brighton.

From 1896–1903, young Bridge studied at the RCM under the notoriously conservative Stanford. One needed a strong stomach to take Stanford's criticism, but Bridge had the right temperament, and was able to benefit. Goodness knows what Stanford would have made of his later experiments in the 1930s! No doubt Bridge's expediency in confining himself in the early years to romanticism placated his teacher, and even at this stage the fine craftsmanship that was to characterise his entire output was evident. The more astringent style adopted in works such as the String Quartet No. 3, did not begin to appear until after Stanford's death in 1924.

On leaving the RCM Bridge set about establishing his career. Rarely in the history of music can there have been a more consummate musician. Not only did his compositions boast a superb technique, but he seems to have developed the same qualities as both a conductor and a player. Having taken up the viola in preference to the violin, he established the English String Quartet which, by all accounts, was one of the finest on the circuit. As a conductor he was frequently the go-to choice when the appointed conductor was indisposed at short notice, and he often insisted on taking up the baton in performances of his own works.

By Britten's account, Bridge was also a stimulating teacher. He was as technically demanding as any teacher could be, making Britten fight for every note, playing back Britten's compositions to him on the piano, and then demanding to know whether the notes he heard represented precisely what he had meant. But there was more to his training than this. Bridge played his pupil records, often of the "moderns", and accompanied him to concerts. He also drove him around the Sussex countryside from his cottage in Friston, recognising that every composer is a product of his environment. In a sense, he treated him as an equal and expected an adult response.

Britten always had the highest regard for his mentor and his well-known string piece *Variations on a Theme of Frank Bridge* (1937) helped to keep Bridge's name alive long after it had suffered eclipse. It is a worthy and touching tribute. By contrast, Britten gave rather short shrift to the teaching he received at the RCM where he studied composition with John Ireland and piano with Arthur Benjamin – one lesson each per week. Part of the distaste might have resulted in Britten's comparing his RCM lessons with his stimulating experience with Bridge, but the portrait painted of a shambolic John Ireland with his general tardiness, slovenliness and even, on occasion, drunkenness, would not have commended itself to the sensitive young Britten.

Bridge's compositional career can be divided broadly into two parts: a largely pre-war period in which he wrote a number of chamber works (*Three Idylls, Phantasie Quartet, Novelletten*), most of his song output, and some significant orchestral scores, notably his *Suite for Strings* (1910) and *The Sea* (1911). Of the latter, it may be said that the highly descriptive nature of the sea in its various moods must have been facilitated by his being physically on hand to observe them. He must have been personally familiar with nearby Beachy Head. Coincidentally, those other great sea sketches of the period, Debussy's *La Mer,* were completed, at much the same time, at a hotel in Eastbourne. Debussy's work is, of course, impressionistic, while Bridge set out to write a vividly descriptive piece, commenting as follows:

> *Seascape* paints the sea on a summer morning. From high drifts is seen a great expanse of waters lying in the sunlight. Warm breezes play over the surface. *Sea-Foam* froths among the low-lying rocks and pools along the shore, playfully not stormy. *Moonlight* paints a calm sea at night. The first moonbeams are struggling to pierce through the dark clouds, which eventually pass over, leaving the sea shimmering in full moonlight. Finally, a raging *Storm.* Wind, rain and tempestuous seas, with the lulling of the storm an allusion to the first number is heard and which may be regarded as the sea-lover's dedication to the sea.[14]

The transition from Bridge's first period, with its tonalism and romanticism, to the second, more astringent one informed by the serialism of Berg in particular, is somewhat blurred, since some of the works, like the *Rhapsody-Trio* and perhaps *There is a Willow Grows Aslant a Brook,* while an advance on the former style, do not possess the defiant modernity of, say, the Third and Fourth String Quartets or the Second Piano Trio. If Bergian serialism is a starting point in some of these works, Bridge also

14 Quoted by Paul Hindmarsh, liner notes, *Frank Bridge, Vol. 2* (Chandos CHAN 10012).

presses beyond it to a sound-world entirely his own. It is one which did not prove popular with listeners at the time, and those who had exulted in the *Suite for Strings* and *The Sea* promptly deserted him. Why did Bridge make such a radical move? There might be two reasons – one idealistic and one practical. The first is that he wanted to preserve his integrity as a composer. It would have been easy enough to curry favour by continuing in his popularist vein. Holst's most famous work by a country mile was *The Planets*, and although he must have been pleased with its popularity initially, he soon became aware of the poisoned chalice he had created for himself when he attempted to develop his style into something much sparser. Everything he tried to achieve latterly was overshadowed by the popularity of *The Planets*. When composers maintain their integrity, they tend to forfeit their public reputations, and both Holst and Bridge opted to maintain their integrity.

The practical reason that Bridge continued to plough his lone furrow is that he had the good fortune, in 1922, to meet with the fabulously wealthy music patron Elizabeth Sprague Coolidge who patronised Bridge's work in particular. She established a trust fund in Bridge's name which was to support him and his family for the remainder of his life. As a token of their friendship and appreciation, Bridge dedicated several works to her, including the last two string quartets, the Second Piano Trio and the Second Violin Sonata – all modernist works in keeping with Mrs. Coolidge's passion for modern chamber music.

What I have called the second phase of Bridge's compositional career, the musicologist and composer Anthony Payne regards as his middle period which, had circumstances been otherwise, might have been followed by a final phase which, as it turned out, never transpired. Added to the other factors that brought about his neglect, says Payne,

> … was the poor health that dogged the final ten years of his life, a time when he might have been expected to forge ahead after establishing a radically original style in the splendid achievements of the previous five years. All in all this was not a settled or particularly happy time for Bridge and I think we may safely say that he was prevented from realising his full potential because of it. Composing time and creative momentum were lost at an absolutely crucial stage in his career and we lack what would surely have been an impressive and challenging final period in his life's work, something which his comparatively sporadic output over the final years can only hint at.[15]

Whatever the "might have beens", at least we have a fairly substantial body of music, in radically different styles, left for us to enjoy, and the hold of some of these works on the repertoire remains comparatively secure.

15 Anthony Payne, *Frank Bridge – Radical and Conservative* (London: Thames Publishing, 1999), p. 9.

a. Bibliography

Hindmarsh, Paul and Jessica Chan, *Frank Bridge – The Complete Works: Portrait of an English Composer in His Time* (PHM Publishing, 2nd edn, 2016)

Huss, Fabian, *The Music of Frank Bridge* (Woodbridge, Suffolk: Boydell Press, 2015)

Payne, Anthony, *Frank Bridge: Radical and Conservative* (London: Thames Publishing, 1986)

b. Selected Discography

i) Orchestral

Enter Spring	BBC NOW, Hickox	Chandos	CHAN 9950
Dance Rhapsody	BBC NOW, Hickox	Chandos	CHAN 10012
The Sea	BBC NOW, Hickox	Chandos	CHAN 10012
Suite for Strings	LPO, Boult	Lyrita	SRCD 242
Sally in Our Alley	LPO, Boult	Lyrita	SRCD 242
Cherry Ripe	LPO, Boult	Lyrita	SRCD 242
Sir Roger de Coverley	LPO, Boult	Lyrita	SRCD 242

ii) Chamber

String Quartet No. 3	Allegri Quartet	Lyrita	SRCD 302
String Quartet No. 4	Allegri Quartet	Lyrita	SRCD 302
Three Idylls	Maggini Quartet	Naxos	8.553718

2. Benjamin Britten (1913–76)

Without doubt Britten was a controversial figure. Tales abound of those who became known, facetiously, as "Britten's corpses" – people who had been of use to him in one way or another, but had been cut dead after somehow offending the great man. On the other hand, he attracted a great many lifelong acolytes, including Peter Pears and Britten's long-term assistant Imogen Holst. Among highly-esteemed Russian friends were fellow-composer Dmitri Shostakovich (1906–75) and cellist Mstislav Rostropovich (1927–2007). There is almost unanimous agreement, too, that with *Peter Grimes* (1945) he put English grand opera firmly on the map for the first time in 250 years. But in order to survive at the court of "King Ben", as it was sometimes termed, one had to buy into his ideas without reservation and pledge absolute loyalty to his goals. In this way, Britten achieved much of what he set out to achieve. This is not to say, however, that what he did achieve was always unquestionably fine, and the term "brilliant", like the word "genius", as with other composers, can at times be used much too liberally. Britten's "way" was not the only way on offer in Britain during the 1940s–50s, and his dismissal of the so-called pastoral school under Vaughan Williams, Holst and Moeran leaves a bitter taste.

In order to make sense of this most complex of characters, we need to go back to the beginning. He was born at Lowestoft on the Suffolk coast on 22nd November 1913. Although in later life he travelled widely, it was this short stretch of coastline between Lowestoft and Aldeburgh that became for him a lifelong muse. His father was a dentist with little interest in music, and even refused to have a radio in the house, so that in his early boyhood Britten had little opportunity to hear the sound of an orchestra. His mother, however, played the piano reasonably well and also had good musical connections. It was she, in fact, who had serious ambitions for her clever son, declaring rather grandly that he might become the fourth "B" after Bach, Beethoven and Brahms – surely a tall order, even for Britten! At the age of seven he was sent to a prep school in Lowestoft where he excelled in mathematics and enjoyed tennis and cricket, despite a weakened heart caused by his contracting pneumonia as a baby. Meanwhile he studied both piano and viola locally.

In 1928, still aged only thirteen, he transferred to the well-appointed Gresham's School at Holt in Norfolk as a boarder. Although it was in the adjoining county to his own, he felt terribly homesick initially, since it was the first time he had been separated from his family. Two years later he won a scholarship to the RCM, studying composition with John Ireland and piano with Arthur Benjamin, though only a lesson per week with each. Although Ireland was impressed with his student's innate abilities, the feeling was not reciprocated and, in that rather dismissive manner that was hardly calculated to endear one to Britten, considered that he learned little of use during his three-year spell at the college. It was quite otherwise, however, with Frank Bridge to whom Britten was introduced by his viola teacher Audrey Alston, and who agreed to take him as a private student. He had first been bowled over – or "knocked sideways", as he put it – by hearing a performance of Bridge's suite *The Sea* at the Norwich Triennial Festival in 1924, and so his confidence in his new mentor's abilities was established at the outset. Bridge set about widening Britten's experience both musically and more generally. They attended concerts together and toured Sussex – one of the chief sources of inspiration for Bridge's own works. But, of course, they also put in the hard yards too. Britten recalled how Bridge would send him across the room while he played one of Britten's compositions and then demand that he justify every note in the composition. Tears of exhaustion were often the result.

Britten's first opus-numbered composition, the *Sinfonietta*, appeared in 1932, and was joined the following year by the oboe quartet *Phantasy* (performed by Leon Goossens, no less) and the choral piece *A Boy was Born*. Otherwise, his early work involved writing scores for the BBC Film Unit, including the iconic *Night Mail* with words by W.H. Auden who become a close friend. In

1936 the two of them collaborated on a new project, *Our Hunting Fathers* which, on the surface, was a protest against fox-hunting, but at a deeper level had a more political message to impart. The following year was memorable for two reasons, one negative and one positive. Britten's mother died, an event which, given his close relationship with her, he felt keenly. More positively, however, he met the tenor Peter Pears who was to become his lifelong partner as well as an important muse.

In 1939 the pair of them decamped to the USA. The official reason given was the disenchantment felt by Britten and his fellow-artists over the apparent lack of opportunity to succeed in England. The fact that W.H. Auden and Christopher Isherwood had already departed for the States might have been a further incentive. The more cynical commentator suggested that it was a plain case of draft-dodging. However, Britten and Pears settled in with a local family who were in sympathy with their artistic agenda and the compositions began to flow. Among the works from this period are the *Seven Sonnets of Michelangelo*, *Les Illuminations* (both 1940), and two which came to be regarded as among his major works, the Violin Concerto (1939–40) and the *Sinfonia da Requiem* (1940). The second of these illustrates the potential hazards involved in writing to commission. It was the British Council that invited Britten to submit a score to commemorate the 2,600th anniversary of the foundation of the Mikado dynasty in Japan (the date being purely traditional). He was among a number of other composers, including Richard Strauss (1864–1949) and Ildebrando Pizzetti (1880–1968), invited to submit a work for the occasion. The Japanese were sent a copy of Britten's plan which they approved, but they rejected the completed work on the grounds that it was too grave in nature (they had expected something more celebratory). Moreover, somewhat curiously, it was dedicated not to the Japanese dynasty but to the memory of Britten's parents (his father had died in 1934) which was hardly appropriate for the commission. Further objections were raised about the specifically Christian titles of the various movements – Lacrymosa, Dies irae and Requiem aeternam.[16] As things transpired, the work was taken on board by John Barbirolli and the NYSO and performed in March 1941, only months prior to the Japanese attack on Pearl Harbour.

Although Britten's sojourn in the USA was reasonably productive, his work was not universally acclaimed. The influential critic Virgil Thomson, for instance, while warming to Stanley Bate's music, was just as scathing of Britten's efforts. He and Pears had, in any case, been contemplating a return to British shores, and in 1942 the home fires were well and truly lit when he read George Crabbe's narrative poem *The Borough* in which Peter Grimes is presented as the villain of the piece. The fact that the action is set on the Suffolk coast provided the decisive impulse for his and Pears's return, and in April they made the perilous Atlantic crossing.

On landing in Britain, he first had to convince the authorities of his genuine standing as a conscientious objector and was eventually allowed exemption on appeal. What Michael Tippett, who was imprisoned for airing similar views, thought of this is not on record, as far as I am aware. Britten used his mother's legacy to purchase and renovate the Old Mill at Snape as a base from which to work. Chief among his first projects, once he had settled there, was his opera *Peter Grimes*, based on Crabbe's story, although in his version Britten presents Grimes as victim rather than villain. Joan Cross, the artistic director of Sadler's Wells at the time, determined to bill *Peter Grimes* to reopen proceedings after the war, pulling rank in order to do so, as not everyone was in favour, some preferring a more traditional, well-established opera. Still, the performance went ahead. Later in the year, Britten, Cross and Pears parted company with Sadler's Wells to set up their own group which eventually became the English Opera Group. Things were going well for Britten at this time, as it was in 1945, too, that he wrote what was to become his most popular work, *A Young Person's Guide to the Orchestra*.

---

16 A fuller account of the Japanese anniversary commissions as a whole, and of Britten's role in the process, can be found in David Gallagher's liner notes to the Naxos CD of Pizzetti's *Symphony* (8.573613).

As the English Opera Group began to find its feet, Britten wrote new operas for the company to perform, including *The Rape of Lucretia* (1946), in conjunction with Glyndebourne, and *Albert Herring* (1947). At the same time, he and Pears hatched the idea of a local festival to be staged at Aldeburgh where Britten had recently moved from Snape. The Aldeburgh Festival was a success from the beginning, and throughout the 1950s Britten poured out operas to be staged at the event as well as elsewhere. Building on the success of *Peter Grimes,* he turned to Herman Melville for inspiration in creating *Billy Budd,* another story in which the chief character is an outcaste. It was first performed at Covent Garden in 1951. In 1953 came *Gloriana* to mark the Coronation of Queen Elizabeth II, a suitably lavish presentation although, oddly, it focused on the life of Elizabeth I. The following year saw *The Turn of the Screw,* after Henry James's ghost story, and still one of Britten's most performed operas.

Throughout the fifties, the operas performed in Aldeburgh were staged in existing buildings, mainly the Jubilee Hall and, for smaller productions, the local parish church. The latter was the venue for a new species of drama, the church parable, which typically required a minimum of instrumental forces and the participation of children in the choral roles. These included *Curlew River* (1964) and *The Prodigal Son* (1968).

As the Aldeburgh Festival continued to grow, a greater range of facilities was required than could be accommodated in the existing buildings and in the 1960s a new venue was found in some derelict maltings at Snape. The largest of these was converted into an 800-plus seat concert hall in which future performances could take place. It was opened by the Queen in the summer of 1967 (probably at the behest of Lord Harewood, the Queen's cousin, who was a patron of the arts and an enthusiastic supporter of the project). The fact that the building was gutted by fire just two years later proved no obstacle, and even provided an opportunity for the Queen to officiate at the reopening in 1970.

Another of Britten's highly-regarded works is the *War Requiem* which was commissioned for the opening of the new Coventry

Cathedral alongside the blitzed original in 1962. It is a setting of the Latin Mass interspersed with the poetry of Wilfred Owen and, given Britten's stance as a conscientious objector, is a great prayer for peace. As noted below, the unequal attention paid to it in rehearsal in comparison with Bliss's commission for the same event (*The Beatitudes*) rather crowded out the latter work and provided its performance with considerable difficulties.

In 1970 Britten began to turn his attention to what was to be his final opera, *A Death in Venice*, based on Thomas Mann's novella concerning an ailing novelist called Aschenbach who is tormented by a carnal beauty in the shape of an Adonis-like youth, Tadzio, who dances before him but is inaccessible to him. Like many of the lead characters in Britten's operas, from *Peter Grimes* and *Billy Budd* onwards, Aschenbach is depicted as a lonely outsider shunned by a society to which he can never fully belong. It is hard not to see Britten himself in some of these depictions, for as a homosexual he would have been shunned by "respectable" society at the time, and was even approached by the police on account of it after the home secretary urged them to enforce the existing laws against homosexual practice.

Shortly into his work on *Death in Venice*, Britten was told by his doctors that he would need a heart operation as a matter of some urgency if he hoped to survive for more than a couple of years. However, he decided to delay this until he had completed the opera by which time, he knew, it was likely to have little effect. In 1973 he did undergo the surgery, which was relatively successful, although during the operation he suffered a slight stroke which limited the use of one hand and prevented him from performing as an accompanist as he had been accustomed to doing, especially in his own works such as his songs and folksong arrangements. One of his last works, in fact, was an orchestral suite of English folksongs, *A Time There Was* (1974), the final movement of which is dominated by a lonely cor anglais solo, valedictory in nature. The official goodbye came on his sixty-third birthday when, with the help of his nurse Rita Thomson, he hosted a champagne party for family and friends. He died less than two weeks later in the arms of his long-standing partner Peter Pears. Although officialdom would have laid him to rest in Westminster Abbey, he was buried at his own request in the churchyard of Aldeburgh parish church which, given his lifelong love of the Suffolk coast, was surely appropriate.

During his lifetime and in the wake of his death, members of the Aldeburgh set sought to elevate Britten to cult-like status, as if he had the Midas touch on everything he composed. Now, over forty-five years since his demise, there has been sufficient time for honest reappraisal and, while there are still those who speak his name in hushed tones, others have sought to take a more objective view. Certainly, it would be rash to suggest that he fulfilled his mother's wish to have him installed in the musical pantheon as the fourth "B", and the general consensus now seems to be that his best work was done in the 1940s–50s, after which the ideas became less inspired and more repetitive. The plot of *Death in Venice*, for example, seems inadequate to sustain a full-length opera. On the other hand, his initial brilliance was widely recognised by friend and foe alike, and the reputation he built on the strength of the works conceived in his prime seems to have been well-earned. His major works – *Peter Grimes*, *Young Person's Guide*, Violin Concerto, *Variations on a Theme of Frank Bridge*, *War Requiem* – have all stood the test of time and are still regularly performed. There are less inspired works, but that is as true of Beethoven as it is of Britten. All in all, then, we are completely justified in ranking him alongside the elite – Elgar, Vaughan Williams, Walton and Tippett.

a. Bibliography

Carpenter, Humphrey, *Benjamin Britten: A Biography* (London: Faber & Faber, 1992)

Cooke, M., *The Cambridge Companion to Benjamin Britten* (Cambridge: Cambridge University Press, 1999)

Evans, Peter, *The Music of Benjamin Britten* (Oxford: Oxford University Press, 1996)

Evans, J., ed., *Journeying Boy: The Diaries of the Young Benjamin Britten, 1928–38* (London: Faber & Faber, 2009, 2010)

Headington, Christopher, *Britten*, Illustrated Lives of the Great Composers (London: Omnibus, 1996)

Hodgson, Peter J., *Benjamin Britten: A Guide to Research*, Routledge Music Biographies (London: Routledge, 1996)

Holst, Imogen, *Britten* (London: Faber & Faber, 1980)

Hurd, Michael, *Benjamin Britten* (Sevenoaks: Novello, 1966)

Kennedy, Michael, *Britten*, Master Musicians (London: J.M. Dent, 1981)

Kildea, Paul, *Benjamin Britten: A Life in the Twentieth Century* (London: Penguin, 2014)

Matthews, David, *Britten* (London: Haus Publishing, 2003)

Oliver, Michael, *Benjamin Britten*, Twentieth Century Composers (London: Phaidon, 1996)

Powell, Neil, *Benjamin Britten: A Life for Music* (London: Hutchinson, 2013)

b. Selected Discography

i) Concertos

Piano Concerto	Phil. O., Menges; Abram (piano)	EMI	5 74781 2
Violin Concerto	Hallé O., Barbirolli; Olof (violin)	EMI	5 66053 2

ii) **Orchestral**

Young Person's Guide to the Orchestra	CBSO, Rattle	EMI	5 55394 2
Sinfonia da Requiem	CBSO, Rattle	EMI	5 55394 2
Suite on English Folk Tunes, "A Time There Was"	CBSO, Rattle	EMI	5 55394 2
Variations on a Theme of Frank Bridge	ECO, Bedford	Naxos	8.557200

iii) **Opera**

Peter Grimes	City of London Sinfonia; Opera London; London Symphony Chorus; soloists; Hickox	Chandos	CHAN9447/8
Billy Budd	LSO & Chorus; Tiffin Boys Choir, soloists; Hickox	Chandos	CHAN 9826(3)
Death in Venice	City of London Sinfonia; BBC Singers; Langridge (ten); Hickox	Chandos	CHAN 10280

iv) Chorus with Orchestra

Spring Symphony	LSO & Chorus; Southend Boys Choir; Soloists; Hickox	Chandos	CHAN 8855
Psalm 150	Chorus & Orchestra of the City of London School; Hickox	Chandos	CHAN 8855

v) Choral

Rejoice in the Lamb	Choir of St. John's Coll., Camb., Robinson	Naxos	8.554791
Hymn to St. Cecilia	Choir of St. John's Coll., Camb., Robinson	Naxos	8. 554791
Ceremony of Carols	New London Children's Choir, Corp; Kanga (harp)	Naxos	8.553183

vi) Songs

Holy Sonnets of John Donne	Langridge (ten); Bedford (piano)	Naxos	8.557201
Seven Sonnets of Michaelangelo	Langridge (ten); Bedford (piano)	Naxos	8.557201
Winter Words	Langridge (ten); Bedford (piano)	Naxos	8.557201

c. DVDs

Benjamin Britten: A Time There Was (Tony Palmer, Isolde Films, 2008). TPDVD 125

Britten's Endgame: Benjamin Britten's Final Years (John Bridcut, Decca, 2013). 074 3861

The Hidden Heart: A Life of Benjamin Britten and Peter Pears (Teresa Griffiths, EMI, 2008). 2 16571 9

Peter Grimes (Joan Cross/ John Culshaw/ Brian Large, Decca, 2008). 074 3261

Billy Budd (Cedric Messina/ Basil Coleman, 2008). 074 3256

Death in Venice (Tony Palmer, Isolde Films, 2012). TPDVD 176

Young Person's Guide to the Orchestra (All-Star Orchestra, Schwartz). Naxos 2.110562

3. Frederick Delius (1862–1934)

When great men meet their end, bizarre circumstances occasionally accompany their passing. The writer Thomas Hardy had expressed a wish to be buried in Stinsford churchyard when the time came, but by then he had become such a notable figure in English life that the establishment insisted on interring his remains in Westminster Abbey. A typical English compromise was reached when a surgeon was engaged to remove Hardy's heart before the rest of his body was taken forward for cremation at Woking, and thence to London. Thus, his heart, at least, was interred at Stinsford, though with much less pomp and circumstance than the main ceremony at the Abbey.

Equally as bizarre, if not more so, were the circumstances surrounding the death of Frederick Delius on 10th June, 1934. Surely the most reliable account of these was given by Eric Fenby, Delius's faithful amanuensis from 1929 to the time of his death, and who was heavily involved with the funeral arrangements.[17] There are contradictory accounts of these affairs, and it is as well, all else being equal, to lean towards that of one who was directly involved. In John Bridcut's documentary, *The Pleasures of Delius*[18], the view is afforded that Delius had always wanted to be buried in the garden of his house in the French village of Grez-sur-Loing, which had been his home for thirty-five years, but that after his death Sir Thomas Beecham persuaded his ailing wife Jelka Rosen that he had expressed a wish to be interred in a churchyard somewhere in the south of England, and that as Beecham was on friendly terms with a churchwarden at St. Peter's Church, Limpsfield, arrangements were made for him to be re-interred there. The burial took place at midnight in order to avoid unwanted publicity.

---

17 Fenby provides a detailed account of proceedings in his *Delius as I Knew Him* (London: Quality Press Ltd., 1936), pp. 225–34.

18 Crux Productions, 2018; CRUXGZ003DVD. The film was originally broadcast as a BBC production under the title *Delius: Composer, Lover, Enigma.*

There is some element of truth to this, but there is more to it than meets the eye. It is generally agreed that Delius's preference was to be buried in his own garden at Grez, but French law forbade this. According to Fenby[19], Delius's second preference was to be buried "somewhere in the south of England" because such churchyards reminded him of those he had known in Norway as a young man. There, friends and members of the public could come and strew flowers on his grave. Although this explanation may sound plausible enough, it still seems somewhat incongruous with the fact that Delius was a lifelong and dedicated atheist who had nothing but contempt for the Church and delighted in deriding Fenby's own Christian faith. As to the choice of Grez as a domicile, Delius is on record as saying, "I would have hated [to live in] an English village with institutes of this and that and the vicar for ever on the doorstep".[20] It seems odd, therefore, that he should have consented to a Christian burial in one. Still, that is what happened, and the well-kept headstone is there for all to see. The choice of Limpsfield as Delius's final resting place is not explained by Fenby, and the alleged Beecham connection sounds plausible. The strange circumstances of the so-called midnight burial were determined, in his view, by the timing of the boat bearing Delius's remains from Boulogne to Folkestone which delayed the arrival of the coffin in Limpsfield until the witching hour. The impression given in Bridcut's film is that the entire funeral took place under flickering lamps with owls hooting, whereas in fact this part of the proceedings, in the presence of the vicar, was simply to mark the arrival of the coffin. The full funeral rite was deferred until the following afternoon, with the bulk of the mourners, including Vaughan Williams and Beecham, in attendance, and members of the LPO on hand to play some of Delius's shorter pieces during the service.[21]

---

19 Fenby, *Delius as I Knew Him*, p. 227.

20 Fenby, *Delius* (The Great Composers; London: Faber & Faber, 1971), p. 91.

21 Thomas Beecham, *Frederick Delius* (London: Severn House Publishers, 1975), pp. 212–13.

At the time all this was taking place, Delius's wife Jelka was in the final throes of terminal cancer. She insisted on making the crossing from France to be at the graveside, but on her arrival in England was too ill to attend. She died just a couple of days later and was buried with her husband.

Eric Fenby soon came to regret his part in the conspiracy to re-inter Delius's remains in England, writing eloquently about it in *Delius as I Knew Him*:

> For me it was all wrong. If the shade of Delius looked down from the Elysian fields, he too must have seen that it was all wrong and that he had blundered. Better that he had been left in that cold graveyard at Grez, over there by the wall amongst the peasants whom he had known, than that he should rest with strangers in a strange place even in his native land.[22]

Why have I chosen to introduce this entry by considering the circumstances of Delius's death and burial? – primarily because it illuminates several aspects of the composer's life. First, the extraordinary nature of these events reflects the extraordinary life of the man: as in life, so in death. Second, it raises questions about the composer's nationality. Having been born to German parents in England, he lived the latter half of his life in France. What does this tell us about Delius's true identity? Finally, it hints at his negative attitude to organised religion. A man who worshipped nature and Nietzsche, and yet could still entitle major works "Mass" and "Requiem": what might this tell us about his approach to life and faith? Was he wholly consistent in his views, and if not, did it much matter to him?

Fritz Theodore Albert Delius was born in Bradford to Julius Delius and his wife Elise, just one of fourteen children. The father, a prosperous wool merchant, had emigrated from Germany, and cut

---

22 Fenby, *Delius as I Knew Him*, p. 234.

the figure of an old-style patriarch who seems not to have spared the rod on any of his children when occasion demanded it, and whose word was law. Church attendance was compulsory, although Delius frequently absconded and had to be rescued by one of his sisters when, over Sunday lunch, his father questioned him on the content of the sermon. As far as Julius was concerned, Fritz – Frederick, as he would later prefer to be known – was destined for the family business. Music was certainly accepted as a form of home entertainment, and the children were encouraged to learn an instrument so that they could provide it. Fritz himself received tuition in violin from a member of the Hallé Orchestra, enabling him to play in the family quartet. Visitors to the family home included Joachim and other musical notables. However, Julius was firmly set against music as a career and, much against his will, on leaving Bradford Grammar School, where he was an indifferent student at best, Fritz was packed off to a business college in Isleworth with the aim of eventually managing the family business. Subsequently he was dispatched to various locations as the firm's representative – to Stroud in Gloucestershire, Sweden, France and elsewhere. But these trips were largely unsatisfactory from a business point of view. Instead, they simply served to broaden Delius's mind and made him resolve to go his own way in life. He was too much interested in the culture of the places he visited to advance his father's business interests.

Eventually, Julius despaired of his son making any progress in the family business, and the idea came about that he might make a better fist of managing an orange plantation in Florida. So, backed by his father's capital, he made the arduous journey to Solana Grove with a new business partner. This venture certainly proved to be a turning-point in Delius's life, though not in the manner his father would have expected or approved. The oranges were doomed from the beginning. What captivated him was the sound of Negro spirituals and folksongs sung by the black workers that floated to him from the surrounding orange groves. It was not long before he abandoned the oranges and travelled thirty-five miles to Jacksonville where he took lessons in harmony and composition from a local musician, Thomas Ward, from whom, by Delius's own account, he learned more than in any academy. In fact, he adopted a magpie approach to his musical education, imbibing just what he needed at the time from whoever was in a position to provide it.

In 1885 he left the orange plantation in the hands of a caretaker and moved to Danville, Virginia, where he advertised himself as a teacher of violin, piano and composition. It was during these years in the southern States that he apparently fathered a child by an African-American woman. His liberal attitude to sex, evident here, was eventually to be his undoing.

When father Julius saw that the orange venture had been as much of a flop as all the rest, he waved the white flag and paid for Fritz to study formally at the Leipzig conservatoire. But despite the presence of great conductors and composers like Mahler and the visits of Brahms and Tchaikovsky, his attention was drawn to other aspects of the city's cultural life. Certainly, he had little regard for his formal tuition at the conservatoire which was much too rigid for his tastes. Much more important to him was a first meeting with Grieg (1843–1907) who encouraged him in his efforts at composition and introduced him to the mountains of Norway. Both these influences were of vital importance to his development. In 1888 Grieg heard a private performance of one of Delius's first orchestral works to gain a foothold in the repertoire, namely the *Florida Suite*, very much influenced by his experiences at Solano Grove, on the strength of which he was convinced that his protégé, as he regarded him, was destined to become a composer of stature. He met with Julius Delius in London, and convinced him that this was where his son's future lay.

In the same year Delius left Leipzig and moved to Paris, immersing himself in the city's culture. He was financed initially by his Uncle Theodore who was living there. It was to the banks of the Seine that all kinds of artists flocked – poets, playwrights, painters, sculptors, as well as composers – and it was with writers like Strindberg and artists such as Gauguin[23] and Munch, rather than musicians, that Delius made influential relationships, although Grieg continued to be an important influence. Although he worked on his compositions (*Appalachia*, one of his best-loved works, was written during this period), he was also beguiled by the Parisian nightlife and soon began the promiscuous liaisons that probably caused the onset of his syphilis. One woman who did turn out to be good for him was the young Serbian-born artist Jelka Rosen who he met in 1897. She owned a riverside house in Grez-sur-Loing, some forty miles from Paris, where she had a studio, and as the relationship developed, Delius became a frequent visitor until, eventually he moved in with her and in 1903 they were married.

In his earlier life, Delius was widely acknowledged to have been an easy-going, affable character, well-liked by most of those who knew him, and not the difficult, crabby individual he later became as the result of his illness. Still, even in those days, he harboured an unpleasantly selfish streak. Jelka opened her home to him and virtually gave up her career to serve his interests, but he gave little in return. He openly continued seeking his own pleasures among Parisian prostitutes, and once advised Eric Fenby never to marry unless his intended was more in love with his art than with him. Even more reprehensible is the fact that Delius maintained his sexual indiscretions in the full knowledge that he was suffering from syphilis, and seems to have had no regard for anyone or anything but his own hedonistic pursuits. It is difficult to know whether his marriage to Jelka was ever consummated. He was certainly aware of his condition beforehand and may have refrained from sexual union in order to spare his wife the same ordeal as his Parisian prostitutes – at least one would like to think so.

Delius left in his music a legacy of the various stages in his life. His Florida experiences find expression in both the *Florida Suite*

23 Delius bought Gauguin's famous painting *Nevermore* from the artist himself. In later life, as funds began to dwindle, he had to sell the original, but before parting with it prevailed upon his wife Jelka to make a copy of it.

(1888) and *Appalachia* (1902), while the seductions of the Parisian nightlife he knew so well are brilliantly captured in *Paris – Song of a Great City* (1899). His love-affair with the mountains of Norway, is depicted in *Song of the High Hills* (1912). Once settled in Jelka's home in Grez, he began to produce some of the exquisite orchestral miniatures for which he is most celebrated: *In a Summer Garden* (1908), *Summer Night on the River* (1911), and *On Hearing the First Cuckoo in Spring* (1912). Although these sound quintessentially English, the garden, river and cuckoo are almost certainly French, although another orchestral work written during this same period, *Brigg Fair* (1907) is based on an English folksong that was introduced to him by Percy Grainger (1879–1961), who had produced his own choral setting.

The outbreak of World War One in many ways marked a transition from the rich and productive vein of form that Delius had enjoyed up to that point to a much leaner period which included not only a diminution of output, but – in Beecham's view, at least[24] – in quality too. To some extent this may have been due to the fact that the war rudely disrupted his incessant routine. In matters of work Delius was a man of habit, and as hostilities edged ever nearer to Grez, he and Jelka were forced to abandon their beloved home and flee to Britain. They hid their valuables in the garden, apart from Delius's most treasured possession, Gauguin's painting which went with them, and spent the next couple of years in various locations in the south of England, including a property near Watford on which Beecham has taken the lease. Two of Delius's shorter pieces, the *Dance Rhapsody No. 2* (1916) and the tone poem *Eventyr* (1917) were written during this period of exile, as was the Violin Concerto (1916) which sounds remarkably untouched by events in Europe and of which Yehudi Menuhin remarked, "It is hardly a concerto, but it is a lovely poem".[25] The most substantial work of the war years, the *Requiem*, however, tended to puzzle critics, and

24 Beecham, *Frederick Delius*, p. 173.

25 Quoted in Lyndon Jenkins's liner notes to Warner Classics' *Delius: 150th Anniversary Edition* (0 84175 2).

was certainly not calculated to win approval from the concert-going public. Following its premiere in 1922, it remained unperformed for over forty years. Although dedicated to "the memory of all young Artists fallen in the war" (in itself a testament to Delius's single-mindedness – why not simply "all"?) the text, which is now thought to have been penned by Delius's friend Heinrich Simon rather than by Delius himself, really amounts to a reiteration of the composer's manifesto on life – that as there is no God and no hereafter, life should be lived to the full from moment to moment. It is hardly a message that recently bereaved parents who had lost sons in the war would have welcomed, but the *Requiem* is at least consistent with the earlier (and indisputably greater) *Mass of Life*. Apart from a very early and unpretentious *Ave Maria* (1887), Delius's use of liturgical titles was always intended to highlight his own religionless philosophy. If he can be said to have had a religion at all, it was nature-worship. In the *Requiem* the message that death is oblivion is rammed home relentlessly. With spring comes life's renewal, but not for the deceased individual. It is an uncompromising and, in this work, metronomic statement, and one can well understand the offence it may have caused the unsuspecting listener who might have been expecting something conventionally liturgical. The chief problem, however, lies in the sub-standard quality of the text which sounds like warmed-up (and inferior) Nietzsche, with a pinch or two of Ecclesiastes thrown into the mix.

It was during the war years that the friendship between Delius and Philip Heseltine (Peter Warlock) was at its height. Heseltine's hot flush of enthusiasm for Delius's music occurred while he was still at Eton and he became a committed Delian simply on the strength of the scores he was able to access. It was some years later before he was able to hear any of the music itself. The young Heseltine sent his new hero a fan letter to which Delius responded, and a regular exchange of missives began. The relationship was, in effect, that of the father-son variety. Heseltine was a wayward soul, and the gist of the older man's advice to him was that success would be possible only through single-minded devotion to his art – which, of course, for Heseltine, was precisely the stumbling-block: "Do not begin to think, dear Phil, that luck is against you, because the real reason is that you do not push your ideas to their material end with sufficient energy ... You would succeed at anything you take up if you would concentrate on it and not diffuse your energies in so many things."[26] Delius was speaking from experience. He stuck tenaciously to the task of composition. As Heseltine himself wrote: "He holds no position in the musical life of [Britain]; he does not teach in any of the academies ... he never gives concerts ... he never conducts an orchestra, or plays an instrument in public ..."[27]

But this, of course is what Heseltine could never bring himself to do. In one sense, however, this very diffusion of energies proved beneficial to Delius's cause, since Heseltine took him up enthusiastically (along with other "lost" causes like the Dutch composer Bernard van Dieren [1880–1936]) and promoted his music, including assisting Beecham to organise the Delius Festival in London in 1929.

Throughout his life Delius was blessed with certain conductors who were captivated by his music and championed his cause. In his early days as a composer he was enthusiastically taken up by German conductors including Hans Haym, Fritz Cassirer and Alfred Herz at a time when he was little more than a name in England. His one great act of self-promotion in his homeland occurred in 1899 when, at his own expense, he put on a concert of his own works at St. James's Hall in London. There, for the first time, he was able to hear what his orchestral music sounded like when played professionally. The First World War rather put paid to the good will that had been shown him by the German people, and his insistence on being called Frederick instead of Fritz probably did not help. By this time, however, he had been discovered and taken up by the English conductor Thomas Beecham who conducted the premieres of *Paris: Song of a Great City* in 1908, and the *Mass of Life* the following year.

26 Quoted in Beecham, *Frederick Delius*, p. 180.

27 P. Heseltine, "Some Notes on Delius and His Music", *Musical Times*, 56 (1915), pp. 137–42.

From then on he became a lifelong champion of Delius's music and began recording it in the late 1920s onwards, while the composer was still alive. Delius was remarkably frugal about offering the usual directions regarding tempo, dynamics, and so on, but Beecham seemed to possess a telepathic instinct of what Delius wanted, and the latter soon came to regard his new champion as being the most reliable interpreter of his music.

By the end of the war Delius was beginning to feel the effects of the syphilis he had probably picked up in his Paris days. He had difficulty in walking and his eyesight was beginning to fail. By 1928 he was blind and virtually paralysed, and composition became impossible. However, a young Yorkshire musician, Eric Fenby (1906–97), read of the composer's plight and wrote to him offering his services as an unpaid amanuensis. Jelka replied, accepting the offer on Delius's behalf. Fenby soon found that he had to fit in around the daily routine, such as it was. Delius was frequently in no state to compose, and when he was, Fenby had to be ready at a moment's notice. A sensible method of dictation had to be worked out before any progress could be made, and Fenby provides a fascinating account of their working practices in his book *Delius as I Knew Him*.[28] Over a period of five years, thanks to Fenby's dedication and meticulous oversight, a late flowering of the composer's fertile imagination emerged, including the Violin Sonata No. 3, *A Song of Summer*, *Songs of Farewell*, the *Caprice and Elegy* for cello and chamber orchestra, and *Cynara*. Some of these entailed the completion of unfinished works, while others were completely new. *Songs of Farewell*, in particular, is a substantial work for large orchestra and double chorus, and the fact that it was composed in the way it was, by painstaking dictation, is astonishing.

Despite his debilitating illness, Delius still managed to receive the occasional visitor. May Harrison came to play through the

---

28 A valuable recording of a talk in which Fenby "acts out", as it were, the procedure involved can be found in the EMI recording of the opera *A Village Romeo and Juliet* (5 75785 2). The highly-acclaimed Ken Russell film *Song of Summer* (1968) also covers this period.

completed Violin Sonata No. 3, not a note of which had to be changed; and in 1933, when Elgar was in Paris to conduct his Violin Concerto, he took the opportunity to visit Delius at Grez. In their younger days they had been cool about each other's work, but this meeting was entirely cordial and initiated a belated friendship that was maintained through an exchange of letters that persisted until Elgar's death in February 1934. Fenby returned to England once his work as Delius's amanuensis was complete, but was recalled shortly before the latter's death when Jelka had to have an operation to remove a tumour. In effect, he was there to nurse the dying composer, and was at his bedside when he died.

Finally, how do we assess Delius as a composer? Everything about him seems to have aroused heated debate, and this is no less true of his music than of other matters. Much has been made of the fact that his music is inimitable. He composed after his own fashion to the complete disregard of other composers and their styles. But with Delius nothing is quite that simple. Critics have noted that he was in fact influenced in subtle ways by others – notably Wagner, Grieg, Strauss, Chopin, and even Debussy. But a composer who, certainly in later life, habitually lambasted the work of all and sundry, would hardly have been expected to acknowledge these, with, perhaps, the exception of Grieg. One musical influence he did acknowledge was that of the negro songs he heard at Solano Grove, and which in any case is plainly evident in the *Florida Suite* and *Appalachia*, as we have seen. Yet despite these influences, acknowledged or not, it is true that Delius's style remains staunchly idiosyncratic. This is to be explained in part by Fenby's observation that he tended to compose back-to-front. He formed in his mind the sound effects he wanted for a particular work, and then sought to reproduce them in score by whatever means were available to him, which is why, according to Beecham, "the best of Delius is undoubtedly to be found in those works where he disregarded classical traditions and created his own forms"[29], and why his concertos were either not the best of Delius,

29 Beecham, *Frederick Delius*, p. 217.

or not really concertos at all. It should be added that in later life he became increasingly isolationist, refusing to listen to the music of most other composers[30], especially that of his compatriots of which he was almost wholly dismissive. These traits certainly reinforced his unique style[31], for which he is hailed and harangued in equal measure.

In terms of personality, most people know Delius only as the crabby, cantankerous invalid of his final years, to which Eric Fenby provides eloquent witness.[32] Beecham, however, provides a rather more balanced assessment, comparing this picture with a younger, more magnanimous aspect of his personality.

> Abundant testimony is forthcoming as to what sort of person Frederick was up to his thirty-eighth or thirty-ninth year... [H]e took pleasure in performing little services for those around him, straightened out more than one complication troubling a friend who was not on the spot to handle it himself, and never thought twice about assisting impecunious fellow musicians out of his very modest resources. On one occasion he turned aside for weeks from his own works to organise the first Paris exhibition of the paintings of Edvard Munch.[33]

Finally, which nation can lay the best claim to Delius as one of its own? Naturally, as he was born in Bradford, he must be English by birth, and in *North Country Sketches* and *Brigg Fair*, there is evidence

30 According to Fenby (*Delius as I Knew Him*, p. 195), who on one occasion asked if he could listen to a Mozart piano concerto on the radio, Delius replied: "You needn't ask me to listen to the music of the Immortals. I can't abide 'em. I finished with them long ago!"

31 I say "style", but Fenby insists that Delius's music had no style, as "this is generally understood in the sense of precision and ease of manner ... and grace of gesture." (*Delius as I Knew Him*, pp. 206–07). Delius's "style" involves a kind of stylishness consisting of rhapsodic formlessness.

32 Fenby, *Delius as I Knew Him*, pp. 177–96.

33 Beecham, *Frederick Delius*, p. 218.

that he neither disdained the English landscape around his home city nor the beauties of English folksong. It should be remembered, however, that he was also suffused with German blood, and was adopted by Germany in a musical sense long before any great interest was shown in Britain. Then again, he lived well over half his life in France, and must have regarded that country as his permanent home. He was also captivated by the mountains of Norway where he had spent many a happy holiday. The texts he chose for his vocal works are equally multinational – Nietszsche (Germany), Dowson (England) and Whitman (America), among others. In this question, then, as in others, Delius continues to elude us.

In the final analysis, it is no doubt best to take the music as it comes, for better or for worse – and most critics agree that the quality is uneven: there are duds as well as masterpieces. Fenby suggested that Delius's music either elicits love on first hearing or complete indifference – there can be no grey areas. I cannot agree. My own introduction to Delius was through a recording of a selection of his miniatures played by the Hallé Orchestra under Sir John Barbirolli, along with a live performance, by the same forces, of *Appalachia* at Sheffield's City Hall in 1970. These pieces I have always loved. The concertos, the *Requiem*, and much of the chamber music, as well as most of the songs, I find less inspiring – but no doubt some will tell me that it is my ear which is at fault. What can be said is that in pursuit of beauty, the music of Delius, on the whole, is a very promising place to begin.

a. Bibliography

Beecham, Thomas, *Frederick Delius* (London: Severn House Publishers; 2nd edn; 1975)

Boyle, Andrew J., *Delius and Norway* (Woodbridge, Suffolk: Boydell & Brewer, 2017)

Carley, Lionel., ed., *Delius: A Life in Letters*, 2 vols (London: Scolar Press, 1983, 1988)

Carley, Lionel and Robert D. Threlfall eds., *Delius: A Life in Pictures* (Oxford: Oxford University Press, 1977)

Fenby, Eric, *Delius as I Knew Him* (rpr., nd, 1936)

----------, *Delius*, The Great Composers (London: Faber and Faber, 1971)

Heseltine, Philip, "Some Notes on Delius and His Music", *Musical Times*, 56 (1915), pp. 137–42.

----------, *Frederick Delius* (London: John Lane, 1923)

Huismann, Mary C., *Frederick Delius: A Research and Information Guide* (London: Routledge, 2005)

Jenkins, Lyndon, *While Spring and Summer Sang: Thomas Beecham and the Music of Frederick Delius* (Aldershot: Ashgate, 2005)

Lee-Browne, Martin and Paul Guinery, *Delius and His Music* (Woodbridge, Suffolk: Boydell Press, 2014)

Palmer, Christopher, *Delius: Portrait of a Cosmopolitan* (London: Duckworth, 1976)

Smith, Barry, *Frederick Delius and Peter Warlock: A Friendship Revealed* (Oxford: Oxford University Press, 2000)

b. Selected Discography

i) Concertos

Piano Concerto	LSO, Gibson; Kars (piano)	Decca	470 190-2
Violin Concerto	Welsh Nat. Op. O., Mackerras; Little (violin)	Decca	470 190-2
Cello Concerto	RLPO, Mackerras; Wallfisch (cello)	CFP	5 75803 2
Double Concerto	RLPO, Mackerras; Little (violin), Wallfisch (cello)	CFP	5 75803 2

ii) **Orchestral**

On Hearing the First In Spring	Hallé O., Barbirolli	EMI	5 65119 2
In a Summer Garden	Hallé O., Barbirolli	EMI	5 65119 2
Summer Night on the River	Hallé O., Barbirolli	EMI	5 65119 2
Brigg Fair	Hallé O., Barbirolli	EMI	5 65119 2
A Song of Summer	LSO, Barbirolli	EMI	5 65119 2
Walk to the Paradise Garden	LSO, Barbirolli	EMI	5 65119 2
Paris: Song of a Great City	LSO, Collins	Decca	470 375-2
Sleigh Ride	RSNO, Lloyd-Jones	Naxos	8.557143
Florida Suite	RSNO, Lloyd-Jones	Naxos	8.557143

iii) **Chorus with Orchestra**

Appalachia	Hallé O., Ambrosian Singers, Barbirolli	EMI	5 65119 2
Sea Drift	Bournemouth SO & Chorus, etc., Hickox	Chandos	CHAN 9214
Songs of Farewell	Bournemouth SO & Chorus, etc., Hickox	Chandos	CHAN 9214

Songs of Sunset	Bournemouth SO & Chorus, tec., Hickox	Chandos	CHAN 9214
Cynara	Hallé O., Elder; Williams (bar)	Hallé	CD HLL 7535
Mass of Life	Bournemouth SO & Chorus, Waynflete Singers; soloists; Hickox	Chandos	CHAN 9515

iv) Opera

A Village Romeo & Juliet	RPO, John Alldis Choir & soloists; M. Davies	EMI	5 75785 2

v) Chamber

Violin Sonata No. 1	Menuhin (violin); Fenby (piano)	EMI	3 70566 2
Violin Sonata No. 2	Menuhin (violin); Fenby (piano)	EMI	3 70566 2
Violin Sonata No. 3	Menuhin (violin); Fenby (piano)	EMI	3 70566 2
String Quartet	Villiers Quartet	Naxos	8. 573586

vi) Choral

Complete Part-Songs	Elysian Singers of London, Greenall	Somm	SOMMCD 210

vii) Songs

Songs	Kenny (sop); Lane (piano)	Hyperion	CDA 67594

c. DVDs

The Pleasures of Delius (John Bridcut, Crux Productions, 2018). CRUXGZ003
Delius: A Village Romeo and Juliet (Petr Weigl, Decca, 2003). 074 177-9
Delius: Walk to the Paradise Garden (Boston SO, Barbirolli, 1959). VAI 4304
Song of Summer (Ken Russell and Eric Fenby, BFI, 1968)

d. Webpage

The Delius Society (www.delius.org.uk)

4. Sir Edward Elgar (1857–1934)

So much literature has been written about Elgar, including numerous biographies, some of which are listed below, that it would be vain to simply repeat what has already been said more eloquently by others better qualified to do so. For the sake of completeness, however, I shall outline the bare biographical details the reader might expect, and then treat one or two particular issues which may be of interest. For example, what distinguishes great Elgar from the merely ordinary? Critics seem never to have reached a consensus on the issue. Again, how "English" is Elgar's music? Was Elgar truly innovative, writing music only an Englishman could have written, or was his work simply "second-hand Brahms", as Herbert von Karajan dismissively labelled the *Enigma Variations*? And how do we stand with regard to those scores which Elgar left incomplete at his death, some of them potentially substantial, and which were "elaborated" by others in order to produce a performing version? Should such practices be encouraged?

Elgar was born at Lower Broadheath, some three miles west of the centre of Worcester, on 2nd June 1857. The family was not super-rich, but Elgar, along with his brother and three sisters, enjoyed a comfortable upbringing. However, this did not include a privileged education, and he attended school locally until the age of fifteen. Crucially, what did exist in the household was music. Elgar senior, William (1821–1906), is generally described as a piano-tuner who also owned a music shop on the High Street in Worcester. But he was more than that. He was an excellent violinist, and organist of St. George's Roman Catholic Church in the city (although he seems not to have taken Catholic dogma very seriously), a post he held for forty years. He also appears to have had some influence over the programme of the Three Choirs Festival when it was held in Worcester, and must have been a well-known and respected musician in the city.

From an early age Elgar began taking piano and violin lessons from local teachers, and was sometimes taken by his father on his piano-tuning excursions to try out the piano when the job was done. Thus, young Elgar's facility with the piano came to the ears of some influential people in the locality, which is no doubt what his father wanted. Elgar was also in the ideal environment for self-tuition. He was able to borrow books on music theory and organ technique and, of course, there was the "immemorial sound of voices" in the cathedral on his doorstep. His musical training may not have been very formal, but it was effective. Even so, the budding musician had designs on furthering his studies in a more rigorous setting, and even began to learn German with this object in view, but the family purse would not stretch to that extent. Although Elgar was naturally disappointed – and he would suffer his fair share of disappointment during his career – we can now see, with hindsight, that this was probably a blessing in disguise. European, and especially Teutonic, influences already dominated in "das Land ohne Musik"[34], and three years in Leipzig would surely have confirmed Elgar's place in that time-honoured tradition. The fact that his musical upbringing did not involve studying at any of the academies, home or abroad, was key to his development.

---

34 This oft-quoted phrase has a long history which is worth a brief comment. The sentiment, though not the phrase itself, dates back at least as far as the German musicologist Carl Engel in a work of 1866, although, interestingly, Engel does refer to the apparent existence of English folksongs in the country areas of England. The phrase itself first occurs in the title of a book published at the turn of the century by a certain Oscar Adolf Hermann Schmitz (*Das Land ohne Musik: Englische Gesellschaftsprobleme* [München: George Müller, 1904), which extends to some three hundred pages, dealing not only with music but English culture in general as a "social problem". The offending passage reads as follows: "I have long tried to understand what kind of lack it is that manifests itself in so many English qualities [*Vorzügen*] which have such a deadening effect. I have asked myself what is missing from this nation… Finally, I have found something which distinguishes English people from all other cultures to quite an astonishing degree, a lack which everybody acknowledges … but has not been emphasised enough. *The English are the only cultured nation without its own music [Die engländer sind das einzige Kulturvolk ohne eigene Musik]*" (translation, with the exception of a single word, by Alexa Woolf).

Instead of Leipzig, then, he began work as a solicitor's clerk, but found the work so uncongenial that he preferred to assist in his father's shop. By this stage he was proficient enough on piano, organ and violin both to give public performances and offer himself as a private music teacher. He also joined his father in sessions at the Worcester Glee Club, which were held at the Crown Hotel (now Wetherspoons) on Broad Street. The glee was a gentleman's music society devoted to singing with or without accompaniment, and young Elgar was sometimes called upon to provide musical arrangements, and even to conduct, although he had little practical experience behind him.

One of his more unusual appointments at this time was the conductorship of the attendants' band at the Worcester and County Lunatic Asylum at Powick, a few miles outside the city, a post he held for five years (1879–84). It was an experience which proved invaluable to his formative steps as a composer, for he was obliged to arrange music according to the instruments available, and he also composed polkas and quadrilles of his own. Further useful experience was gained through his playing violin in William Stockley's Orchestra in Birmingham (1882–89), and in 1883 one of his own works, *Serenade mauresque*, was played, giving Elgar the opportunity of hearing an orchestral work of his played on a professional footing for the first time. Yet, ever the pessimist, he complained that he had no money (the asylum post was paying £32 per year) and no prospects. Since he also had several private pupils on his books, he must have been earning a reasonable, if uncertain, income.

One of his pupils was Alice Roberts, the daughter of a late major-general. After a three-year courtship, the couple were married (1889), although her family strongly disapproved of the match on both social and religious grounds (he was a Roman Catholic), and she was disinherited. Neither of them ever had cause to regret their marriage, however. She was an intelligent woman who was the driving force behind her husband's creative activity, and proved an excellent business manager. She knew, also, how to handle his frequent bouts of self-doubt and depression. She, in turn, was able to bask in Elgar's celebrity when recognition finally came. She was the muse behind *Salut d' Amour* for violin and piano, which even today remains one of Elgar's most popular and engaging pieces.

With Alice's encouragement, the (not so young) couple moved to London – for a while, at least (1889–91). His heart remained in Worcester and the surrounding countryside, but she was astute enough to realise that if he was to truly succeed, he would need to be more than a provincial composer. It was while he was in London, ironically, that he was commissioned to write an orchestral work for the Three Choirs Festival by the Worcester Festival Committee. The result was one of Elgar's first widely recognised works, the overture *Froissart*, which Elgar himself conducted at the Festival in 1890.

The next decade brought forth a number of works which, though they may not be Elgar's greatest, are nonetheless still remembered – *The Black Knight* (1892), *The Light of Life* (1896), *Caractacus* (1898), and the ever-popular *Serenade for Strings* (1892). But it was to be two works written toward the end of this period that were to establish his name on a permanent basis – the *Enigma Variations* (1899) and *The Dream of Gerontius* (1900). Regarding the first of these, the story goes that Elgar's wife Alice overheard the "original" theme as he was improvising on the piano, and remarked on its attractive quality. This gave him the idea of devising fourteen variations on it, each depicting the distinctive characteristics of his various friends, along with his wife and himself. The most famous variation of all, *Nimrod*, was dedicated to his publisher and friend August Jaeger.[35] The *Enigma Variations* was the first of Elgar's major works to go international. Part of the reason for its success, however, is that it *sounded* European, and lends more than a casual nod to Richard Strauss. It is to be wondered, therefore, how it subsequently came to be regarded as so English in tone.

---

35 Why Nimrod? The name Jaeger is German for "hunter", and Nimrod was the "mighty hunter" in the Bible (Gen. 10: 9) – hence the connection.

The Dream of Gerontius is considered by many to be the finest of all British oratorios, although it is perhaps more characteristic of the church tradition of its day than of Elgar himself. He drew on Cardinal John Henry Newman's text about the hard-won redemption of the dying Gerontius, but this failed to please everyone, and its performance was initially banned by the deans of some Anglican cathedrals, while others allowed it only subject to certain amendments to the text, such as the excision of references to the Virgin Mary. Still, these were religious rather than musical objections. From a personal viewpoint there are works of Elgar that I much prefer, but for many *Gerontius* remains the high watermark of his output.

The abovementioned compositions seem to have opened the floodgates to Elgar at his best. Next to appear, in 1901, was the *Pomp & Circumstance March No. 1* with its famous trio tune that was subsequently set to the words *Land of Hope and Glory*, eventually becoming a Last Night of the Proms tradition. Three more marches followed over the next six years, while a fifth in the series, which was probably sketched at the same time, appeared in 1930. Unknown to many, a sixth march was left unfinished and was "realised" by Anthony Payne.

In 1904 Elgar received a knighthood for his services to music – not a bad achievement for a lad who began his life in a music shop and whose symphonies and concertos had yet to be written. The following year he was appointed Peyton Professor of Music at the University of Birmingham, despite his never having attended a university or any music academies himself. It was a sign of the esteem in which he was now generally held. However, he used some of his lectures to score points against the music critics and to air his own prejudices, so it may have been a relief to all when he resigned his position three years later to be replaced by Sir Granville Bantock.

Elgar was a reluctant symphonist, probably because he fully understood what the word, in its classical sense, implied. Writing a symphony meant inviting comparison with the great symphonists of the past – Beethoven, Brahms, Bruckner and Mahler. Elgar's

First Symphony was simmering for a decade, and he was over fifty years old at the time of its completion in 1908. The first theme of the first movement is a winner, especially when, after its initial subdued presentation, it blossoms out into the full orchestra. Its nobility of bearing is hard to match and, if the earlier works had not already established the composer as an international celebrity, this one certainly did. Within a year of its premiere, it had received a hundred performances worldwide[36], including Leipzig, New York, Rome, St. Petersburg and Vienna.

Encouraged by the reception it received, Elgar set to work on a Second Symphony which appeared in 1911, but this time the public response was muted. Now, instead of the listener's being invited to bask in the glory of Empire, it was as if they were being asked to mourn its passing – at least the passing of a phase or era. The old opulence was at an end and the carnage of World War One was just three years away. Today, with the hindsight of over a century, we can assess the symphony through the lens of our modern values and recognise it, in musical terms, as a work of high quality. We can see that the ruminative, sorrowful side of it was to emerge more fully in the final flowering of Elgar's output immediately after the war, notably in the Cello Concerto and the major chamber works.

Between the two symphonies came the Violin Concerto (1910), commissioned and premiered by Fritz Kreisler, with Elgar himself at the helm of the LSO. It is a big-boned work lasting some fifty minutes, and may be in part modelled on the Brahms concerto. Its emotional heart lies in the slow central movement, with a meltingly beautiful theme that may have been inspired by Elgar's solitary walks on the Malverns, even though he had been living in Hereford for some years before he set to work on it. The result, in any case, is that the concerto drew similar public acclaim to that received for his First Symphony.

36 It took Vaughan Williams's Symphony No. 6 twice as long to reach that number.

After this, there is a sense in which Elgar could afford to bask in the sunlight of celebrity. He became something of a globe-trotter, visiting the USA three times between 1905–11, as well as various locations in Europe. He received honorary degrees from some of the world's most prestigious universities, including Oxford, Cambridge and Yale, and rather cultivated the image of a self-made man, although he was never completely satisfied with his lot.

We can now see, from our vantage point, that after the Violin Concerto, Elgar had three substantial works left in him, namely, the String Quartet, the Piano Quintet and the Cello Concerto, which followed nose-to-tail (opp. 83–85). The two chamber pieces were well-received and premiered together at the Wigmore Hall in 1919. A further chamber work, not generally regarded as the match of the other two, was the Violin Sonata, op. 82, composed in 1918 and first publicly performed by Elgar's great friend "Billy" Reed with Landon Ronald at the Aeolian Hall in London. All these works were composed at "Brinkwells", the cottage in East Sussex where Elgar spent much of his time in later years. The Cello Concerto was composed at much the same time and was also premiered in 1919 (and *not* following the death of his wife as is sometimes supposed). The first performance, however, did not go well, for the work had not been allowed sufficient rehearsal time, and Elgar, who was conducting, did not really possess the professional conductor's capacity to save the performance from disaster. Fortunately, critics generally saw through the problems to the inherent quality of the music. The Cello Concerto is not an instant crowd-pleaser in the sense of the Violin Concerto, but it has been recognised as one of the best, if not *the* best, in the cello concerto repertoire.

Following the death of his wife in 1920, Elgar lost much of the drive and direction that had been down to her, and although still supported by his daughter Carice, he tended to spend most of his time away from composition. He was often to be found at the races or cricket, and even dabbled in chemistry. Still, musical activities were not altogether curtailed. The *Empire March* and the orchestral song-set *Pageant of Empire* were written for the British Exhibition of 1924, and in the same year he was appointed Master of the King's Music. He was now very much the grand old man of English music, but this did not imply that he eschewed innovation. He was one of the first composers to realise the potential of the recording studio, and in his final decade made a number of invaluable recordings of his major works.

Elgar's stature as the pre-eminent figure of British music was recognised when the BBC organised a major festival in honour of his seventy-fifth birthday in 1932, and the following year, as we have seen, he visited Delius in his home at Grez-sur-Loing, the two composers showing a mutual respect for each other's achievements. Elgar died, following a relatively short battle with cancer, in February 1934, leaving a BBC commission for a Third Symphony in the early stages. He resisted the inevitable calls for him to be buried with full honours in Westminster Abbey, and was buried alongside his wife in St. Wulstan's Roman Catholic Church in the shadow of the Malverns he had so loved.

In order to complete this section on Elgar, it will be as well to briefly consider a few issues which have been raised regarding his work as a composer, and his abiding status as the pre-eminent composer in England in the twentieth century, or even all centuries. In what sense, indeed, is Elgar's music "English" at all? When critics ask that question of Vaughan Williams, they usually single out three distinct influences: Tudor polyphony, English folksong, and the English landscape. But, although Elgar respected the music of Purcell, he derided that of William Byrd and his contemporaries, and he had no time for folksong. On the other hand, German and French influences are widely evident. Brahms, Wagner and Strauss are regularly mentioned in this regard, while the lighter touches in his orchestration are frequently attributed to Berlioz and, perhaps Delibes who Elgar is known to have admired. Yet critics are largely agreed that there is an extra ingredient which makes Elgar's style distinctive, and if this cannot be explained by English music of an earlier age, nor by a love of folksong, then, by process of elimination, we are left with the English landscape. Elgar travelled far and wide across Europe and America, but he always professed the deepest love for his home county, for the Malverns and Severn side. On one occasion he wrote to his friend Sir Ivor Atkins, "If it is sunshiny just go round to the West end of [Worcester] Cathedral, look over the valley towards Malvern and bless the beloved country for me".[37] Worcester and the Malverns were in Elgar's blood, and it may well be that factor which ultimately inspired him to compose in a way that would have been impossible had he been recalling a German landscape.

The next issue concerns Elgar's choice of texts for his choral works and songs, excluding here the major oratorios. The question is whether or not a composer should select the best texts available from the most prestigious poets. Vaughan Williams never ceased to be impressed by Walt Whitman, and Holst, in his *Choral Symphony*, restricts his choice to Keats (although the text used in the scherzo is little more than doggerel). Britten makes use of Wilfred Owen's poetry in the *War Requiem*. It is argued by many that if the poems used are already masterpieces, like Keats's *Ode to a Grecian Urn*, used by Holst, no musical setting will further enhance the poem, and may even diminish its effect. On the other hand, the use of doggerel, even if written by Keats, seems incongruous with the remaining Keats texts as used by Holst in the aforementioned work, thereby weakening the effect of the work as a whole. This rather suggests that composers are best-served by seeking a happy medium – poems which, if they are not of the highest calibre, are not simply bad. Of the fifty-odd Hardy poems set by Gerald Finzi, it can hardly be said that they all belong to Hardy's best work, but that leaves the door open for Finzi to weave his magic and reveal to the listener truths that might not be immediately obvious, or even intended by the poet, in the spoken text.

Now, when we come to Elgar, it is generally recognised that song-writing was not his forte, and he was rarely at his most inspired when he wrote them; but then he must have received little inspiration from the texts he chose to set. Among his chosen

37 M. Grundy, *Elgar's Beloved Country*, p. 4

poets were Gilbert Parker, Arthur Salmon, Arthur C. Benson (who composed the words of *Land of Hope and Glory* when Elgar was prevailed upon to set his famous *Pomp & Circumstance* tune), and his wife Alice Roberts. None of these are household names, exactly, the reason for this being obvious – none of them were distinguished poets. On one occasion Elgar even set a poem by one Pietro d' Alba[38] – a pen name for himself. The first verse runs:

Come, O my love! Come, fly to me;
All my soul cries out for thee:
Haste to thy home, I long for thee,
Faint for thee, worship thee only, but come!

Yes – best stick to the music, Edu! The setting appears as the first of two orchestral songs, *The Torch* and *The River*, both of which have been recorded several times. In both cases, the music is heart-on-sleeve stuff, but it does not serve to save the texts from what would otherwise have been certain oblivion.

Wife Alice's occupation is sometimes given as poet (perhaps in much the same sense that Elgar once gave his occupation as "knight"), but her verse is at best mediocre, and sometimes embarrassing, as in her occasional poem *The King's Way*, written to commemorate the opening of the new Kingsway road in London:

The newest street in London town,
    The King's Way!
The newest street in London town,
Who'll pace it up and pace it down?
The brave, the strong, who strive and try,
And think and work, who fight and die
To make their England's royal way
    The King's Way!

38 The name was suggested to him by his daughter's white (*alba*) rabbit, Peter (*Pietro*).

Don't call us, Alice...

Some of Elgar's songs, such as those for *Pageant of Empire* (1924), may have gone down well at the time (though even here the words are undistinguished, despite their having been penned by Alfred Noyes [1880-1958]), but they are passé today, and simply sound anachronistic. They are still worth a listen, however, if only for their attractive tunes.

By far and away Elgar's best song-cycle, in my view, is *Sea Pictures* (1899) which really does provide some thrilling moments, especially when sung by a top-rank contralto. Among the "unknowns" contributing to the texts here, Alice puts in her customary appearance (*In Haven*), but, unusually for Elgar, he also sets a recognised poet, Elizabeth Barrett Browning (*Sabbath Morning at Sea*) whose text, unsurprisingly, is the best of the five. In this work, however, Elgar is inspirationally on fire. *Where Corals Lie* is understandably a favourite of many listeners, but Browning's *Sabbath Morning at Sea* also receives fine treatment.

Elgar's gravitation towards minor poets has long been recognised, and when the point was raised with him, he would simply reply, "The immortals need no help from me". That much is incontestable, but it does not justify setting inept verse, which is what Elgar undoubtedly did on occasion. Butterworth and Finzi, two of England's finest composers of art-song, took the "middle" approach of which I spoke earlier, choosing to set texts by recognised poets (Housman and Hardy respectively), though not necessarily their finest work. In so doing, they managed to forge a genuine partnership between poet and composer. The poems were worthy enough to be set, but not so self-contained as to preclude their being raised to another level by the music.

Finally, we come to the vexed question of contemporary composers and musicologists (Anthony Payne, Martin Yates and Graham Parlett spring to mind) who take it upon themselves to "elaborate" or "realise" the works earlier composers left incomplete at their deaths[39], and which has now become something of a cottage industry. The three chief instances of this practice in respect of Elgar are Payne's elaboration of Elgar's Third Symphony and his realisation of the *Pomp & Circumstance March No. 6*, and Robert Walker's realisation of the Piano Concerto. The whole saga of bringing the materials for the symphony to a performable state through the process of arranging and elaborating the sketches left by Elgar at his death is graphically told jointly by Payne and Colin Matthews in the liner notes for the NMC recording by Andrew Davies and the BBC SO.[40] It is for the interested reader to consult these in order to learn the full story. I will simply say here that Elgar, on his death bed, seems to have anticipated some kind of elaboration of the sketches, for he told his close friend W.H. (Billy) Reed, who had been working through the symphony with him, that he did not want anyone to "tinker" with it after his death, and that the sketches should be burned. Yet shortly afterwards he told his doctor that he expected someone would complete it. Clearly, the symphony was on Elgar's mind during his final weeks.

Far from burning the sketches, Reed published forty pages of them in facsimile as part of his 1936 biography of Elgar, thereby openly inviting musicologists to "tinker" with it against Elgar's express wishes. Anthony Payne was the first to take up the challenge seriously in 1972, but it took over twenty years for the project to bear fruit. One problem was purely logistical. Only the first few bars of the opening movement were as Elgar intended, fully orchestrated. The rest is in the form of haphazard sketches, with one or two indications for development here and there – rather like the pieces of a jigsaw which one must figure out. Yet unlike a jigsaw, in the case of the Elgar sketches, many of the pieces were missing and there could be no single solution. Anthony

39 Deryck Cooke's performing version of Mahler's Tenth Symphony seems to have set the trend.

40 Elgar: *Sketches for the Third Symphony, elaborated by Anthony Payne* (NMC D 053)

Payne chose his, but a different elaborator would necessarily have arrived at a different solution.[41] Of course, no solution, Payne's included, could perfectly replicate what Elgar himself would have written. We do not have Elgar's Third Symphony; we have Payne's symphony in which he makes copious use of the materials Elgar left behind. We can enjoy this work in its own right, and at the same time have valuable access to Elgar's last symphonic thoughts.

Payne also brought to realisation the *Pomp & Circumstance March no. 6*. The sketches for this work were assembled from two different sources, and although they presented as much of a puzzle as the sketches for the Third Symphony, Payne's experience of working on the latter piece, coupled with the fact that the march turned out to be less than nine minutes in length, meant that he was able to complete his task in six weeks rather than the twenty years that it took him to complete the symphony. Again, however, we should be aware that a good deal of guesswork is involved, and that the finished product cannot be what Elgar himself would have written.

The realisation of the Piano Concerto, this time by Robert Walker, is a different matter again. The remaining materials are, if anything, even more sketchy and fragmentary than those for the symphony. Elgar began the work in 1913, but made no attempt to get it done in one creative burst. As a result, it languished. The composer recorded five "improvisations" for HMV in 1929 which prove to have a family resemblance to the concerto, and Walker made use of these in his realisation, along with the pages of sketches. Once again, however, there is no telling how Elgar would have proceeded, and in places Walker is compelled to compose his own link passages in order to make the work performable. The overall result, in my view, is not as Elgarian as Payne's elaboration of the

41 As will be explained below, Martin Yates and Kris Russman both "realised" Butterworth's unfinished *Fantasia for Orchestra*, and although each is faithful to the Butterworth sound and style, the solutions they reach are quite different from one another.

Third Symphony. The spirit of Elgar is there, of course, but listeners will not find the quintessential Elgar sound that characterises the two string concertos of the period.[42]

42 A detailed account of the emergence of the Piano Concerto, as realised by Robert Walker, can be found in the liner notes of the Dutton recording of the work by David Lloyd-Jones and the BBC Concert Orchestra, with David Owen Norris at the piano (CDLX 7148).

a. Bibliography

Adams, Byron, *Elgar and His World* (Princeton, NJ: Princeton University Press)

Anderson, Robert, *Elgar* (London: J.M. Dent, 1993)

Collett, Barry, *Elgar Country* (London: Thames Publishing, 1986)

Collett, Pauline, *An Elgar Travelogue* (London: Thames Publishing, 1983)

Grimley, Daniel and Julian Rushton, eds., *The Cambridge Companion to Elgar* (Cambridge: Cambridge University Press, 2005)

Grundy, Michael, *Elgar's Beloved Country* (ND)

Hurd, Michael, *Elgar* (London: Faber & Faber, 1969)

Kennedy, Michael, *Elgar's Orchestral Music* (London: BBC, 1970)

----------, *Portrait of Elgar* (Oxford: Oxford University Press, 1993)

----------, *The Life of Elgar* (Cambridge: Cambridge University Press, 2004)

McVeagh, Diana, *Elgar the Music Maker* (Woodbridge, Suffolk: Boydell Press, 2007)

Messenger, Michael, *Edward Elgar* (London: Shire Publications, 2005)

Moore, Jerrold Northrop, *Spirit of England: Elgar and His World* (London: Heinemann, 1984)

----------, *Elgar: A Creative Life* (Oxford: Clarendon Press, 1999)

----------, *Elgar: Child of Dreams* (London: Faber & Faber, 2006)

Mundy, Simon, *Elgar* (London: Omnibus, 1984)

Reed, W.H., *Elgar* (Master Musicians; Claremont, CA: Pomona Press, 2008, orig. 1938)

Young, Percy, ed., *A Future for English Music and Other Lectures by Elgar* (London: Dennis Dobson, 1968)

b. Selected Discography

i) Symphonies

Symphony No. 1	LPO, Barenboim	Sony	SB2K 89976
Symphony No. 2	LPO, Barenboim	Sony	SB2K 89976
Symphony No. 3 (elab. Payne)	BBC SO, A. Davies	NMC	NMC DO53

ii) Concertos

Violin Concerto	LPO, Barenboim; Zukerman (violin)	Sony	SB2K 63247
Cello Concerto	Philadelphia O., Barenboim; Du Pré (cello)	Sony	SB2K 63247

iii) Orchestral

Enigma Variations	Philadelphia O., Ormandy	Sony	SB2K 63247
Cockaigne Overture	Philadelphia O., Ormandy	Sony	SB2K 63247
Pomp & Circumstance Marches	Philharmonia O., A. Davies	Sony	SB2K 63247
Serenade for Strings	ECO, Barenboim	Sony	SB2K 89976
Elegy for Strings	ECO, Barenboim	Sony	SB2K 89976
Overture: In the South	ECO, Goodwin	Harm. Mundi	HMU 907258
Sospiri	ECO, Goodwin	Harm. Mundi	HMU 907258

iv) Choral/ Solo with Orchestra

Dream of Gerontius	LSO & Chorus; soloists;	LSO	LSO 0083
The Music Makers	LSO & Chorus; Palmer (contr); Hickox	EMI	5 65126 2
Sea Pictures	LSO, Hickox; Palmer (contr)	EMI	5 65126 2

v) Songs with Orchestra

Songs with Orchestra	BBC Concert O.; Wordsworth; Rudge (mezz-sop); Neven (bar)	Somm	SOMM CD 271-2

vi) Chamber

Piano Quintet	Allegri Quartet; Ogden (piano)	HMV	5 73455 2
String Quartet	Music Group of London	HMV	5 73455 2

c. DVDs

Elgar: The man Behind the Mask (John Bridcut, Crux Productions, 2018). CRUXGZ002
Elgar's Tenth Muse (Susan Francis/ Paul Yule, Warner, 2007). 50 51442 857528
Enigma Variations (All-Star Orchestra, Schwartz, 2017). Naxos 2.110562

d. Website

The Elgar Society (www.elgar.org)

5. Gerald Finzi (1901–56)

Like Elgar and Vaughan Williams, Gerald Finzi is widely regarded as a quintessentially English composer, but although this "Englishness" is closer to that of the latter than the former, and the two became firm friends, it is an Englishness borne out of Finzi's individuality. With his preference for country living, his love of the English landscape and of English literature and the music of England's past, and his close association with the Three Choirs Festival, he seems to have been the perfect English gentleman. Yet Finzi was of Italian Jewish descent, even though his forebears had been living in Britain since the eighteenth century. Despite this, the name occasionally gave rise to snootiness among the music critics, especially when Finzi was still an unknown quantity as a composer.[43]

Gerald was the youngest of five children, including one sister, born to John (Jack) Finzi, a successful shipbroker, and his wife Eliza (Lizzie) who was a good pianist, and even composed a little. The family did not want for money. They lived on Hamilton Terrace in St. John's Wood where their close neighbours included the composers Frederic Cowen and Edward German, and the artist William Strang, as well as notables from other professions. It was a district "bristling with blue plaques", as Banfield puts it.[44] Following a spell of private education, Gerald was sent to Kingswood, a boarding school in Camberley, where he was profoundly unhappy. Indeed, he saw the whole of his childhood in much the same light. None of his siblings showed much interest in music, and he seems to have been left very much to his own pursuits.

His early years were materially comfortable, but it was not long before the clouds began to gather. His father contracted cancer and died in 1909, shortly before Gerald's eighth birthday, and by 1918

43 It is interesting that, in his biography of Finzi, Stephen Banfield (*Gerald Finzi: An English Composer* [London: Faber & Faber, 1997]) chooses to deal with Finzi's Italian origins from the outset. The title of the book suggests that it is part of his brief to justify the composer's deep-rooted Englishness.

44 Banfield, *Gerald Finzi*, p. 10.

his three brothers were dead too. Felix (1893–1913) committed suicide in India, Douglas (1897–1912) died of pneumonia at his boarding school, while Edgar (1898–1918), who had joined the Fleet Air Arm, was shot down and killed only a week before the Armistice.

In October 1915 Finzi moved with his mother to Harrogate, her reason being to escape the Zeppelin raids on London, and her choice of Harrogate being no more than that she considered it to be roughly in the centre of the country. However, she was no doubt aware that the town was an up-market place for the North of England and boasted a lively cultural life. It was here that Finzi met the young composer Ernest Farrer (1885–1918), who became his mentor in composition and who he soon came to idolise like an older brother – perhaps a surrogate for the ones he had lost. Farrer's free-and-easy style of tuition suited Finzi's temperament far more than the rigorous inflexibility of, say, the formidable Sir Charles Villiers Stanford, under whom Farrer himself had studied at the RCM. Still, the Stanford connection was fortuitous, for it meant that he could benefit from Farrer's tutorial style in full confidence that he himself had enjoyed a sound academic training and knew what he was talking about. Alas, the relationship was to be short-lived. Even as he accepted Finzi as a pupil, Farrer had applied for a regimental commission, and from 1916 spent long periods away on military service, so that tuition from that point became sporadic. Finally, Farrer suggested that the continuity of Finzi's studies would be best-served by regular tuition from Edward Bairstow, organist at York Minster, and the North of England's answer to Stanford. Terms were arranged, and Finzi joined Bairstow in the organ loft. The rigours of the teaching he received in harmony and counterpoint must have been excruciating for him, but he endured them for five years, and it can hardly be doubted that he parted from Bairstow a much more knowledgeable musician than when he had started.

In September 1918 the news that Finzi must have been dreading arrived – that Ernest Farrer had been killed in France. The date of his death was 18th September, less than a fortnight after that of Finzi's brother Edgar. The presence of so much death at an impressionable stage in Finzi's life undoubtedly left its mark on his later compositions and his choice of poets like Thomas Hardy who, in effect, became a kindred spirit, reflected in his own outlook on life. The brevity of life, the relentless passing of time, and the need to make an impression while there is still a chance to do so, are constant themes, not only in Finzi's songs but, inherently, in his instrumental works too.

From 1922, Finzi moved with his mother to Painswick in Gloucestershire, an area teeming with composers, artists and writers – just the kind of place that was likely to inspire the impressionable young man. Once settled, he composed two of his earliest works, the song-cycle *By Footpath and Stile* (op. 2) and the orchestral *A Severn Rhapsody* (op. 3). Even at this stage, Finzi's chosen poet for the song-cycle was Hardy. Three of the six settings are "churchyard" poems in which the writer calls on friends who turn out to be underground, or imagines the remains of people long buried to have suffused the earth that supports the growth of new life. The other poems ruminate on the passing of personal pleasures, or childhood memories and experiences. All dwell on the remorseless passing of time.[45] There would be many more such settings to come, if perhaps more refined than these early efforts. *A Severn Rhapsody* is an exquisite nature poem that might have been written by Butterworth. Critics generally remark on it as an apprentice piece, but the orchestration is beautifully conceived for a first attempt. Here is Finzi finding his voice. The delightful *Introit*, for violin and small orchestra was also written during this period.

It was in Gloucester that Finzi became acquainted with Herbert Howells (1892–1983), and a growing friendship was cemented when the Finzis spent five weeks with Howells at a property in Churchdown at the foot of Churchdown (locally "Chosen") Hill in the summer of 1925. Gerald had arrived in Gloucester too late to

45 The songs are: *Paying Calls*; *Where the picnic was*; *The Oxen*; *The Master and the Leaves*; *Voices from things growing in a churchyard*; and *Exeunt omnes*.

make the acquaintance of Howells's great friend Ivor Gurney who had been committed to the London Mental Asylum at Dartford in 1922. Chosen Hill had been an iconic muse for them both, and it eventually impressed Finzi also, since two of his works, one at either end of his career, have their roots in the place, namely *Nocturne (New Year's Music)* (1926) and *In Terra Pax* (1954). The latter was inspired by an experience Finzi had one Christmas Eve as a young man. Ursula Vaughan Williams takes up the story:

> We had a wonderful Sunday ... when the Finzis drove us out to Chosen Hill and Gerald described how he had been there as a young man on Christmas Eve at a party in the tiny house where the sexton lived and how they had all come out into the frosty midnight and heard bells ringing across Gloucestershire and beside the Severn to the hill villages of the Cotswolds.[46]

The earlier work, a purely orchestral one as opposed to *In Terra Pax*, was nevertheless inspired by literature. By his own admission, Finzi had in mind Charles Lamb's essay about New Year's Eve, as well as Bridge's lines referring to Christmas Eve: "... when the stars were shining/ Fared I forth alone". Banfield surmises that Finzi's experience probably occurred in 1925, on the eve of his departure to London, when he would no doubt have harboured mixed feelings. Moreover, Finzi confessed that New Year's Eve in particular always evoked in him a sadness regarding the passing of time.

The excursion up the hill with the Vaughan Williamses in 1956 had a tragic sequel. Finzi called on the sexton in his cottage to introduce his honoured guest at a time when his children were suffering from chicken pox. Finzi, who by this time was suffering from Hodgkin's Disease, caught the virus which exacerbated his already weakened state, and he died a week or so later.

46 Ursula Vaughan Williams, *RVW: A Biography of Ralph Vaughan Williams* (Oxford: Oxford University Press, 1964), p. 374.

Finzi duly decamped to London, ostensibly for lessons in counterpoint with R.O. Morris (1886–1948), although at the time of Finzi's arrival he was away in America. More valuable, for the purposes of raising his profile at least, were the connections he was able to make with fellow composers and other musicians. Among those in the Morris coterie were Howard Ferguson (1908–99) and Edmund Rubbra (1901–86), both of whom became staunch supporters and lifelong friends. He was also introduced to Vaughan Williams (another lifelong companion), Holst and Bliss. It was thanks to the good offices of Vaughan Williams, in fact, that Finzi was able to obtain a teaching post at the RAM, and although he was not a born teacher, he held the position until his departure from London in 1933.

At this point, the next stage of Finzi's career began to develop. In September 1933 he was married to Joyce (Joy) Black at Dorking Register Office. It was a quiet affair, with only a few, including the Vaughan Williams's, in attendance, but it initiated a largely idyllic and settled period of happy wedlock that lasted until Finzi's death. Joy Finzi was an outgoing, resourceful woman, good at taking the initiative, who was a fine artist in her own right, both as sculptor and portraitist. Her finely-wrought pencil portraits, some of which appear in the National Portrait Gallery, are beautifully judged, and regular visitors to their house, including several composers and writers, could usually count on getting themselves "done" unawares.[47]

The newly-weds had designs on having a house custom-built, but until such time as the plan could be realised they took possession of a large house in the Wiltshire downs at Aldbourne. The country life suited Finzi, but it was Joy who had urged him to move there from London. In time they were blessed with two sons, Christopher (1934–2019), known to all as Kiffer", and Nigel (1936–2010). Both developed musical abilities and played a large part in promoting their father's work after his death, although Nigel later poured more of his energies into managing a successful building business.

47 That is to say, she would not require them to "sit" formally, but would simply sketch them on the hoof, as it were.

By 1939, the new house, Church Farm, on the Hampshire downs at Ashmansworth, was ready to be inhabited. At first the trials, tribulations and privations of the Second World War had to be contended with, and Gerald took a job working in the Ministry of War Transport in London as his contribution to the war effort. The generosity of the Finzis can be seen in the way that, from the beginning, they made their new home a kind of open-house at which all and sundry were made welcome. Their first act of kindness was to open their doors to German and Czech refugees. It was during these years, too, that a contingent of German prisoners of war was sent to complete the walls and terraces around Church Farm, while the Finzis provided food and companionship.[48] Later, the house became a haven for all manner of composers and other artists, including Howard Ferguson, Malcolm Lipkin, Robin Milford, Arthur Bliss and his wife, Edmund Blunden and J.B. Priestley, to name but a few. Vaughan Williams was a frequent visitor and worked on his Eighth (and after Finzi's death Ninth) Symphony there.

Church Farm provided the opportunity for Gerald to expand his interests. He had an encyclopaedic knowledge of English literature and a library that stretched to over three thousand books. In addition, he amassed an enviable collection of around seven hundred books and manuscripts relating to the music of several eighteenth-century English composers, including William Boyce (1711–79), John Stanley (1712–86) and Capel Bond (1730–90). By 1940 he had established a local ensemble based at nearby Newbury which became known as the Newbury String Players. These reached a decent standard of proficiency and under Finzi's baton performed not only some works of the eighteenth-century composers in whom he had an interest, but the music of

48 According to a story told by Kiffer Finzi, on one occasion a German aircraft came down nearby, and he and Nigel cycled out to the wreckage, found the pilot, who had baled out, and brought him home to the house. Joy Finzi prepared him a hearty breakfast, and he allowed the boys to play with his unloaded revolver until the police came to take him away. The tale is typical of the Finzis' hospitality.

his friends, such as Howard Ferguson and Robin Milford. In the late forties Kenneth Leighton (1929–88) was added to Finzi's growing circle when his early piece *Veris Gratia* was performed by the Newbury Strings, an event which gave the young composer his first opening.

Away from music, Finzi, along with his wife, took an interest in the extensive garden at Church Farm, growing home produce, and establishing an orchard devoted to rare apple varieties which saved some of them from extinction.

On 26th December 1937, Ivor Gurney died from tuberculosis in the City of London Mental Hospital where he had spent the final fifteen years of his life. Ever since his seeing action during World War One, he had deposited his songs and poems with a trusted friend from his RCM days, Marion Scott, for safekeeping. Finzi, with the aid of Howard Ferguson, was called in to catalogue the songs and assess their potential value with a view to publication. According to Finzi's own account, Scott was more of a hindrance than a help, since she had done nothing to organise, even in perfunctory fashion, the manuscripts beforehand, and yet seemed reluctant to allow Finzi unrestricted access. During a three-day spell in which he was able to work on the materials, he was aghast to find that she waited until the final day to make available a sheaf of songs that Gurney had apparently written in his prime. After this ordeal, Finzi resorted to referring to Scott as "Maid Marion". However, we should perhaps balance Finzi's somewhat dismissive attitude with the fact that, in Gurney's lifetime, Scott had been the only one to fully believe in his genius, and had had the good sense to preserve intact everything he sent to her in full awareness of the fact that those best-placed to do so should eventually have the opportunity to make a full assessment of the materials available. Gurney had entrusted her with his manuscripts, so it was understandable that she would be somewhat guarded about them.[49]

49 A fascinating account of this relationship can be found in Pamela Blevins, *Ivor Gurney and Marion Scott: Song of Pain and Beauty* (Woodbridge, Suffolk: Boydell & Brewer, 2008).

In regard to Finzi's own compositions at this time, the key event took place in 1939 with the completion of what must be his best-known work, *Dies Natalis* (op. 8) for high voice and strings. There is much that is characteristic of Finzi here. The opus number bears testimony to its long gestation period – around fourteen years – a feature which was quite common in relation to Finzi's works, including some of the song-sets, which were sown early on and then allowed to germinate until such time as they were considered ripe for performance. His chosen text is, again, fairly typical, for it is the work of a seventeenth century writer Thomas Traherne (1638–74) who then, as now, was relatively obscure. Then, too, the theme of the text – seeing the world through the eyes of a new-born child as a place of wonder, and the loss of this vision through the inevitable experience of growing to adulthood – is also one that would have appealed to someone of Finzi's outlook. The five movements (the *Intrada* being purely orchestral) with their intimations of Bach, show Finzi at the height of his creative powers. The premiere of the work was scheduled for the Three Choirs Festival in September 1939, but the outbreak of war prevented it. A less high-profile debut took place at the Wigmore Hall the following year.

Finzi is frequently classed as an art-song composer and miniaturist who was reluctant to tackle larger canvases, a view that would carry considerable weight if we traced his career only as far as *Dies Natalis*. The final fifteen years of his life, however, finds him tackling the more extensive forms, notably the concerto, and it is during this period that the substantial *Intimations of Immortality* were written. The Clarinet Concerto (op. 31) was premiered at the Three Choirs Festival in 1949 by the legendary Frederick Thurston with Finzi conducting. It, too, is a substantial work lasting half-an-hour, with an extended slow central movement allowing the solo instrument to show off its dreamy, lyrical qualities.

In 1951 Finzi was diagnosed with Hodgkin's Disease and given between five and ten years to live. He had always had the uneasy impression that Father Time was against him and would prevent him from expressing all the music that was in him, but it was not a feeling that was reflected in his working practices. Many of his projects had been started in early or mid-career, only to be left aside for years, or even decades, until the urge or opportunity should arise for completion. Such was the case with the Cello Concerto (op. 40), Finzi's last numbered work, which was completed in 1955, although the sketches for the slow movement date back as far as the mid-thirties. A commission from Sir John Barbirolli and the Hallé Orchestra for a major work to perform at the Cheltenham Festival prompted Finzi to begin working on the outer movements early in 1955. Andrew Burn insists on linking the concerto with the composer's awareness that his days were numbered, suggesting that in the opening movement the listener is "plunged into music of turbulent and tragic emotions in which the composer seems to be railing against his fate"[50], but that the "life-enhancing" finale suggests that he was resigned to it. However, it is easy to make such assumptions with the benefit of hindsight, and to forget that something of this concerto had been conceived long before Finzi fell ill. Obviously, his condition would have been in his mind, but to what extent it affected the character of the piece is difficult to say. It is certainly the boldest, most ambitious concerto he attempted, and stands as a fitting memorial to him.

A much earlier concerto was for violin and small orchestra. It was in the usual three movements, but Finzi, dissatisfied with the opening movement, withdrew it, and the remaining two were premiered by Sybil Eaton and the British Women's Symphony Orchestra under Malcolm Sargent in 1927. By way of encouragement, Vaughan Williams announced his intention of programming it the following year, thereby prompting Finzi to rewrite the first movement. Thus, the premiere of the full concerto took place at the Queen's Hall with RVW conducting the LSO. Sybil Eaton was again the soloist. However, the performance received a lukewarm reception, and Finzi decided to retain the slow movement as an independent work, entitling it *Introit*. In 2001, however, the concerto was reassembled

50 Andrew Burn, liner notes, *Finzi: Cello Concerto*, Naxos (8.555766)

and recorded by Chandos (CHAN 9888), with Richard Hickox conducting the City of London Sinfonia, and Tasmin Little as soloist. Listeners can therefore judge for themselves the quality of the troublesome first movement.

Another aborted project was a piano concerto, the remains of which survived as two independent pieces. The slow movement was completed in 1929, becoming the lovely *Eclogue* for piano and strings (op. 10). The *Grand Fantasia,* written at much the same time, was to have been another movement of the concerto, but when this was abandoned, he added a toccata and entitled the piece *Grand Fantasia and Toccata* (op. 38) in which form it was premiered in 1953. This is a big-boned work with plenty of muscular piano writing, and the spirit of Bach is more alive in this piece than anywhere else in Finzi's output.

A further large-scale work to appear in these later years was Finzi's setting of Wordsworth's ode *Intimations of Immortality*. Here again, the composer was gnawing away at the project for most of his career, and it did not see the light of day until it was premiered at the Three Choirs Festival in 1950 under Herbert Sumsion in Gloucester Cathedral. The reaction was generally favourable, but some critics questioned the wisdom of setting such sublime poetry to music at all, since it was perfectly capable of standing on its own feet. But in a letter to Howard Ferguson, dated 1936, as if in anticipation of this objection, Finzi wrote: "I don't think everyone realizes the difference between choosing a text and being chosen by one."[51]

One gaping hole yet to be filled concerns Finzi as a writer of art-song, the genre in which he was most at home and in which he excelled more than in any other. As space is at a premium, I shall

---

51 Cited by Stephen Banfield, liner notes, *Finzi* (British Composers Series), EMI, 7 64720 2. More detailed comment on the critics' reaction, pro and con, can be found in Banfield, *Gerald Finzi*, pp. 371–75. Trevor Hold (*Parry to Finzi: Twenty English Song Composers* [Woodbridge, Suffolk: Boydell Press, 2002], p. 398) is certainly sympathetic to Finzi's belief that, for a song composer, no poem should off-limits.

restrict myself here to his Hardy settings. Finzi was a self-declared Hardy addict, admitting, "I have always loved him so much and from the earliest days responded, not so much to an influence, as to a kinship with him".[52] He set at least fifty of Hardy's poems, and intriguingly had marked a further fifty in his personal copy of the *Selected Poems* for further consideration. One of the main reasons for this close affinity was the shared philosophy of life held by poet and composer – the remorseless passing of time, the brevity of life, the tyranny of fate, and a dour agnosticism which nevertheless embraced more than a mere tolerance of the Church and its traditions. Finzi, therefore, had a sometimes near-telepathic sense of Hardy's nuances and meanings, even though the two never met.

None of the Finzi song-sets is a genuine song-cycle in the sense of its telling a story which progresses from point A to point B such as we find in, say, Vaughan Williams's *Songs of Travel* in which the vagabond sets out on the open road of life, lives and loves, and then "closes the door". The closest Finzi comes to this idea is in the early *By Footpath and Stile*[53], in which the six songs comprising the set are in close thematic unity, but without there being any real sense of progression – although the final number, *Exeunt omnes*, serves a similar purpose to *I have trod the upward and the downward slope*, which concludes Vaughan Williams's *Songs of Travel*.[54]

A Young Man's Exhortation is a set of ten songs, with piano accompaniment, sub-divided into two groups of five which have some thematic links, but also different emphases. The first group deals with "various moods of youth and love" and the second with

52 Andrew Burn, liner notes, *Finzi: Earth and Air and Rain*, Naxos, 8.557963.

53 Hold (*Parry to Finzi*, p. 404) inclines to the view that it is a song-cycle, although it is not a description used by Finzi himself.

54 John Francis ("'I have Trod the Upward and the Downward Slope': the End of the Journey?" *Ralph Vaughan Williams Society Journal*, 78 [2020], pp. 23–25) has recently pointed out, however, that the final song in the Vaughan Williams cycle, with which we are familiar today, was not reinstated until after the composer's death, which may suggest that he did not greatly value its position as valedictory song.

"philosophical retrospect under the shadow of age".[55] They were written and collected between 1926–29, a remarkably short period of time for Finzi. There are some very attractive songs in this set. The title poem is full of Hardy's mystifying archaisms[56] which make the meaning of the poem difficult to follow, and hence for the composer to set. Many of Hardy's (and Finzi's) perennial concerns are present – the fleetingness of life, the preciousness of the moment. When I first heard this song, I was arrested in particular by Finzi's setting of a couple of lines in the final stanza: "If I have seen one thing/ It is the passing preciousness of dreams" and the chord on the word "dreams" was a revelation to me. I was recently intrigued to discover that both Andrew Burn[57] and pianist and composer Martin Bussey[58] singled out this point in the song for special mention.

By contrast with the first song, *Budmouth Dears* is a rousing march with a winning tune depicting uniformed hussars eyeing up the pretty girls of the town. *The Comet at Yell'ham* introduces yet another mood. The remoteness of the comet in the vastness of the universe is evoked by unearthly sounds in the highest register of the piano, while the tenor represents the human element and the brevity of human life compared with the heavenly bodies. *Shortening Days* calls to mind two contrasting aspects of autumn: the one which spells decay and the onset of winter; the other as the cheery season of mellow fruitfulness. Here Finzi marks the contrast by setting the first verse in the minor keys, contrasting it with the hearty 'major' tread of the approaching cider-maker in the second. In *The Sigh*, a man in old age reflects on his married life and wonders why the girl

55 Banfield, *Gerald Finzi*, p. 144.

56 Try your hand at the first verse, for instance: "Call off your eyes from care/ By some determined deftness; put forth joys/ Dear as excess without the care that cloys/ And charm Life's lourings fair".

57 Andrew Burn, liner notes, *Gerald Finzi* (English Song Series 16), Naxos, 8.570414: "In the final stanza the 'passing preciousness of dreams' draws from Finzi a melodic phrase of tender wistfulness".

58 Martin Bussey discusses the song in a video on his website (https://www.martinbussey.com) and identifies the key of F# minor as being responsible for that arresting moment.

of his choice sighed at their first kiss. Finzi treats the refrain ("But she sighed") by means of subtle variation, thereby maintaining the listener's interest. The "market dames" in *Former Beauties* are what the "Budmouth dears" turn into with the passage of time. The third stanza adopts a lilting dance rhythm as the poet remembers these aging women as the "muslined pink young things" of long ago. *Transformations* resurrects the odd notion, first introduced in *By Footpath and Stile,* that the remains of the dead may somehow live again in the plants and trees that surround their graves: "So they are not underground/ But as nerves and veins abound/ in the growths of upper air ..." The mood of the final song, *The Dance Continued,* resembles that of *Life Laughs Onward* which concludes the song-set *Till Earth Outwears.* In both, the sentiment is expressed that the dead are not to be pitied. They may have had their hour in the sun, but now lie content while the current of life runs on as nature intended.

Another Hardy set, *Earth and Air and Rain* (1928–32), followed hard on the heels of *A Young Man's Exhortation.* It shows signs of development as a group in that it contains a wider variety of themes, moods and stylistic features. The high-spirited *When I set out for Lyonesse* and *Rollicum-rorum,* for example, contrast markedly with the wistfulness of *To Lizbie Browne,* or the declamatory *The Clock of the Years.* The opening song of the set, *Summer Schemes,* teaches that whatever plans we have are always susceptible to being overruled by fate. The frailty of life is underscored in *Proud Songsters.* Whatever tonal or other limitations there may be in this set, interest is maintained through the thematic variety of the texts to which Finzi responds with his customary attention to detail.

The ten songs in the set entitled *Before and After Summer* (1932–49) again embrace a range of moods, from the tender *Childhood among the Ferns,* in which the idyll of childhood innocence, with the wish that it could always be so, is contrasted with the inevitability of adult experience, to the dramatically ironic *Channel Firing* in which preparations for international conflict threaten to "make red war redder". Also included is the poem *The Best she Could,* which Finzi tellingly entitles *The Too Short Time*, for time is the constant factor in this set as in others. *Amabel*, like *Former Beauties* in *A Young Man's Exhortation*, is a reflection on the effect which time exerts on the pristine female form, while the final song, *He Abjures Love*, reflects on love's ultimate futility.

The final two Hardy sets (opp. 19a and 19b) were compiled by Howard Ferguson and members of the Finzi family from individual songs left by Finzi at his death. The first of these, quoting a line from the poem *In Years Defaced*, is entitled *Till Earth Outwears* (1927–55). The text just noted reflects on the ecstatic love of couples from long ago swept away by time, yet somehow the spirit of ecstasy remains, as is beautifully suggested in Finzi's setting. The following poem, *The Market Girl*, uncharacteristically ends in an upbeat mood, while in the next, *I look into my glass*, we are back with Hardy's usual depressive self as he reflects that, although the body decays, the feelings of love remain ever young, taunting and tantalising the decrepit physical form. The final song, *Life Laughs Onward*, embraces the natural order – that the old must be swept away in order for the flow of life to be maintained. This is a song of acceptance, written in 1955 under the shadow of Finzi's own mortality. Perhaps it signifies his coming to terms with his own fate.

The final set, *I Said to Love*, contains the usual broad range of moods and metres in the poetry and the equally broad range of Finzi's responses. At least three of the poems were set during the final year of the composer's life. The two earlier settings, *Two Lips* (1928) and *I need not go* (1936), are thematically related in that they contrast the poet's feelings towards, or neglect of a woman (probably Hardy's first wife, Emma, is in view) with her obliviousness to them now that she lies in her grave. *At Middle-Field Gate, February* (1956) is another poem of contrast. The dreary scene calls to mind another at the same spot when life was fair, but now beyond recovery. *In Five-Score Summers* (which Hardy entitles *1967*) perfectly captures the poet's much-vaunted meliorism ("If way to the better there be/ It exacts a good look at the worst"). The final poem in the set, *I said to love*, was Finzi's last Hardy setting, completed a few weeks before his death, and takes up the theme of love's ultimate futility encountered in *He Abjures Love*. Here, however, the mood has hardened into a bitter rant, underpinned by some furious outpourings in the piano accompaniment.

What about the legacy of Finzi's Hardy settings? Although Trevor Hold's review[59] makes some positive observations, he also offers some sharp criticisms. Comparing Finzi's technique with the likes of Vaughan Williams, Howells, Ireland and Britten, as if to suggest that Finzi is not up to the same mark, he castigates him for a lack of proper attention to tonality or key-change[60], and for being so besotted by the nuance of each word in the text that he neglects the overall sense of the poem – he cannot see the wood for the trees, as Hold puts it. Again, he says, there is little attention to rhythm, which tends to be dull and predictable (as an exception to this trend, Hold singles out *Channel Firing*), and finally, the lack of humour found fundamentally in Finzi as a person[61], and translated into the song settings, leads to a restricted range of moods (I imagine he means in the music rather than the range of texts set). Hold concludes:

> I write at length about these matters because Finzi has so often been held up as "one of the greatest figures in contemporary English song".[62] Despite the critical acclaim bestowed on him ... and the sincere enthusiasm which he inspires in his followers, I find a large number of his songs unmemorable, lacking in dynamism, zest and energy.[63]

---

59 Hold, *Parry to Finzi*, pp. 395–421.

60 Hold, *Parry to Finzi*, p. 399. Finzi's close friend Howard Ferguson also regarded this as a weakness (Banfield, *Gerald Finzi*, p. 151), but seems to have been tactful enough to keep his counsel until after Finzi's death.

61 It is true that, of the many photographs of Finzi in the public domain – both official and unofficial – one would be hard-put to find one of Finzi smiling, let alone laughing. His letters, however, generally give a less starchy impression, and many visitors to Church Farm speak warmly of the Finzis' hospitality.

62 S. Northcote, *Byrd to Britten: A Survey of English Song* (London: Baker, 1966), p. 111.

63 Hold, *Parry to Finzi*, p. 400.

He then mitigates this assessment by spending the next twenty pages discussing the songs he does like, though not without reserve. No doubt some of Hold's criticisms have some basis, but not all would share the charge that Finzi is lacking in melodic invention and rarely writes a memorable tune. Perhaps this can be said of some songs, but surely not of *Budmouth Dears* or *The Sigh*, among many others.

Music critics have their place, of course, but their task is to explain where and why a piece of music falls short, or what it is that makes another piece successful, and they normally do this in terms of specifics and technical language, referring to key relations, chordal progressions, and the like. But music is also supposed to communicate – to exert a desired effect upon the listener, and it sometimes manages to do that without recourse to rules and conventions. George Butterworth's song, *Fill a glass with golden wine*, from the song-cycle *Love Blows as the Wind Blows*, is widely held to be the weakest of the lot, yet it exerts on me the greatest emotional effect, which is surely what art-songs are supposed to do. Similarly, Finzi's sole setting of an Edward Thomas poem, *Tall Nettles*, written when he was just nineteen, has been dismissed as a derivative "prentice piece", as also the orchestral *A Severn Rhapsody*, but their effect on me (as on many others, no doubt) is magical. We should not judge music only in terms of crotchets and quavers.

Finzi holds a unique place in the history of English music. He is sometimes regarded as derivative of Vaughan Williams, yet the latter confessed to Arthur Butterworth that he himself had been the greatest cribber since Handel! Derivation, judiciously applied, strengthens rather than weakens a composer's style. For all the influences upon him, musical or otherwise, Finzi's voice is quintessentially English, yet unmistakeably his own. He may not be a composer who is always in the spotlight, but I have known people who have switched on their radio half-way through some musical offering and, having been suitably impressed, have been intrigued to discover at the end that a certain Gerald Finzi was the composer. Long may his still, small voice be heard.

a. Bibliography

Banfield, Stephen, *Gerald Finzi: An English Composer* (London: Faber & Faber, 1998)

Dressler, John C., *Gerald Finzi: A Bio-Bibiography* (Greenwood, 1997)

Ferguson, Howard and Michael Hurd, eds., *The Letters of Gerald Finzi and Howard Ferguson* (Woodbridge, Suffolk: Boydell Press; rev. edn; 2001)

Francis, John, "I Have Trod the Upward and the Downward Slope: The End of the Journey? *Ralph Vaughan Williams Society Journal*, 78 (2020), pp. 23–25.

Jordan, Rolf, ed., *The Clock of the Years: A Gerald and Joy Finzi Anthology* (Lichfield: Chosen Press, 2007)

McVeagh, Diana, *Gerald Finzi: His Life and Music* (Woodbridge, Suffolk: Boydell Press, 2013)

McCullough, Matthew, "A History and Analysis of Gerald Finzi's 'Dies Natalis'", *British Music Society Journal*, 41/1 (2019)

b. Selected Discography

i) Concertos

Violin Concerto	City of London Sinfonia, Hickox; Little (violin)	Chandos	CHAN 9888
Cello Concerto	RLPO, Handley; Wallfisch (cello)	Chandos	CHAN 8471
Clarinet Concerto	Guildhall String Ensemble, Salter	RCA	RD 60 437

ii) Orchestral

Orchestral Music	LPO, Boult; Friend (violin)	Lyrita	SRCD 239
Grand Fantasia & Toccata	NPO, Handley; Katin (piano)	Lyrita	SRCD 239
Eclogue	NPO, Handley; Katin (piano)	Lyrita	SRCD 239

iii) Chorus with Orchestra

Intimations of Immortality	RLPO & Choir; Langridge (ten); Hickox	EMI	7 64720 2
In Terra Pax	RPO, John Alldis Choir; Manning (sop); Noble (bar); Handley	Lyrita	SRCD 237

iv) Solo Voice with Orchestra

Dies Natalis	LSO, Langridge (ten); Hickox	Decca	468 807-2
For St. Cecilia	LSO, Langridge (ten); Hickox	Decca	468 807-2
Let Us Garlands Bring	NPO, Case (bar); Handley	Lyrita	SRCD 237
Farewell to Arms	NPO, Partridge (ten); Handley	Lyrita	SRCD 237

v) Choral

God is gone up	Choir of St. John's Coll., Camb., Robinson	Naxos	8.555792
Magnificat	Choir of St. John's Coll., Camb., Robinson	Naxos	8.555792
Lo, the full, final sacrifice	Choir of St. John's Coll., Camb., Robinson	Naxos	8.555792
Let us now praise famous Men	Choir of St. John's Coll., Camb., Robinson	Naxos	8.555792

vi) **Songs**

I Said to Love	Williams (bar); Burnside (piano)	Naxos	8.557644
Let Us Garlands Bring	Williams (bar); Burnside (piano)	Naxos	8.557644
Before and After Summer	Williams (bar); Burnside (piano)	Naxos	8.557644
Earth and Air and Rain	Williams (bar); Burnside (piano)	Naxos	8.557963
To a Poet	Williams (bar); Burnside (piano)	Naxos	8.557963
By Footpath and Stile	Williams (bar); Sacconi Quartet	Naxos	8.557963
A Young Man's Exhortation	Ainsley (ten); Burnside (piano)	Naxos	8.570414
Till Earth Outwears	Ainsley (ten); Burnside (piano)	Naxos	8.570414
Oh Fair to See	Ainsley (ten); Burnside (piano)	Naxos	8.570414

c. Website

Finzi Friends (https://www.finzifriends.org.uk)

6. Gustav Holst (1874–1943)

The Planets suite must surely rank as one of the most popular works in the history of English music. In the century since it was written, it has been programmed in concerts thousands of times, and has been recorded more than any other English work. There are currently over seventy recordings available in the catalogue, by a veritable Who's Who of conductors – Bernstein, Boult, Andrew Davis, Elder, Groves, Haitink, Handley, Hickox, Holst, Järvi, Maazel, Mehta, Ormandy, Previn, Rattle, Rozhdesvensky, Sargent, Stokowski, Svetlanov, von Karajan, and many others. Andrew Davis, Simon Rattle and Herbert von Karajan have each made three recordings.[64] Holst's own two-piano version has been recorded by Bennett & Bradshaw, Goldstone & Clemmow, Nettle & Markham, and Vorster & Chamberlain, while Peter Sykes's organ transcription has been recorded by Hansjorg Albrecht, Simon Johnson, and Peter Sykes himself.

The success of *The Planets* has been sensational. Whether this is due to the dynamism of *Mars*, the "big tune" in *Jupiter*, the colourful orchestration throughout, or a combination of these, is difficult to judge. Each listener will no doubt have his or her own reasons. One can only marvel how such an unassuming and anaemic-looking individual (to judge from the photographs) could have written such a piece. How could this seemingly mild-mannered man, who suffered from asthma, neuritis and poor eyesight, have turned out one of the most ferocious and uncompromising movements (*Mars*) in the whole of British music? More remarkable still is the fact that he was obliged to compose it in the little spare time he had as a music teacher at St. Paul's Girls School and Morley College. For unlike Vaughan Williams and Arnold Bax who both enjoyed

64 One distinguished name which, surprisingly, is missing from this eminent list is that of Sir John Barbirolli, who seems never to have recorded the work commercially, despite his reputation as a conductor of English music. He certainly conducted *The Planets* in the concert hall. I was present at a performance under his baton at the Sheffield City Hall in 1970.

private incomes, William Walton who enjoyed the patronage of the Sitwells at a crucial time in his budding career as a composer, and Armstrong Gibbs whose family made a fortune out of toothpaste, Holst had to rely on his teaching posts. The huge success of *The Planets*, however, proved to be an albatross around Holst's neck, for it outshone everything he wrote subsequently and led to the neglect of works which he considered to be equally, if not more worthy of attention.

Gustav Holst was of Swedish-Latvian descent, but the family had been living in England for over seventy years by the time he was born in Cheltenham on 21st September 1874. His father Adolph was an organist and choirmaster in the town, while his mother Clara, who died when Holst was eleven, was a singer and pianist. As a boy he was taught piano and violin, and at his father's instigation he took up the trombone, since Adolph thought that playing a wind instrument would help his son overcome his asthma. He began composing – mainly solo piano pieces, organ voluntaries and songs – from the age of about twelve, while his formal education took place at Cheltenham Grammar School (1886-91). On his departure from there he spent a few months, at his father's expense, studying counterpoint with George Frederick Sims, the organist at Oxford's Merton College. When he returned home, he took up a paid position as organist and choirmaster at Wyck Rissington, some twenty miles from Cheltenham, a journey he made either by bicycle or on foot.[65]

In 1892, while still only seventeen, Holst wrote an operetta entitled *Lansdown Castle, or the Sorcerer of Tewkesbury* which was performed the following year at the Cheltenham Corn Exchange to some acclaim, convincing him that his efforts at composition were not being wasted. Later that year he entered the RCM where his

65 F. Partridge, *The Gustav Holst Way* (Cheltenham: Reardon Publishing, 2014), p. 60. Actually, one needs to see Holst's physical fragility in proportion, for he was a legendary walker. In 1932, at the age of fifty-eight, he spent a couple of days walking from Burford, via Wick Rissington, Bourton-on-the-Water, and Winchcombe to Worcester – a distance of around forty miles.

studies included piano, organ and music history (with Sir Hubert Parry). But it was his studies in composition with Stanford which proved to be of the greatest benefit. As a non-scholarship student, Holst's day-to-day existence in London was a frugal one, but he was able to take full advantage of the musical life of the metropolis, including visits to orchestral concerts and the opera. He maintained an income of sorts by hiring out as a trombone player in the London theatres and, during summer vacations, seaside resorts where musical ensembles of all shapes and sizes were constantly in demand.

It was during his years as a student at the RCM that Holst met with the three chief influences that were to direct his personal and musical life. The first was the music of Wagner which he heard at Covent Garden and which infused nearly everything he wrote prior to about 1905. The second was his friendship with Vaughan Williams who he first met at the college in 1895, and where they developed the lifelong habit of critiquing each other's works while they were still in progress. Both men were of the view that this arrangement taught them more about their music than any amount of formal training could have done. The third influence was the socialist William Morris whose ideals were expounded in lectures by George Bernard Shaw and Morris himself at the Socialist Club whose venue was Morris's own home, Kelmscott House in Hammersmith. Like Vaughan Williams, Holst recognised that Morris's principles could be applied to the arts by a process of inclusion. Not everyone had the means or the talent to become a professional musician, but everyone, regardless of these, had the capacity for music-making. With this in mind, Holst spent as much time as possible putting these principles into practice, first taking up the conductorship of the Hammersmith Socialist Choir, and later teaching at Morley College which was devoted to advancing the education of ordinary working-class people.

Holst left the RCM in 1898, and in order to keep afloat became a jobbing musician, hiring out to all kinds of orchestras and playing the organ in various London churches. Although he regretted this kind of existence, which he knew was borne out of necessity, he was in fact learning the art of composition inside out. From his position as a trombonist, he gained invaluable experience of what was possible for a classical orchestra. Nowhere is this more evident than in the astounding orchestral effects he achieves in *The Planets.*

Further developments in Holst's life came around the turn of the century. In 1901 he married Isobel Harrison (1876-1969), a soprano he had met in his capacity as conductor of the Hammersmith Socialist Choir, with whom he had an only child, Imogen (1907-84) who became a noted composer and musicologist in her own right. A couple of years later his father died, leaving him a small legacy, and in 1903 Holst made the momentous decision to abandon orchestral playing in favour of composing. Possibly this turn was prompted by the successful premiere of his *Cotswold Symphony* by Dan Godfrey and his Bournemouth Municipal Orchestra the previous year. This work is not only a celebration of the Cotswolds, the landscape with which he was most familiar, but of the life of William Morris who had died in 1896, and to whose memory the slow movement is dedicated. Understandably, the music bears a heavy Teutonic influence, Wagner or otherwise, but within four years this was to change.

At this point Holst had not sufficient means to be a full-time composer, and he resorted to a number of teaching posts, some of which he held simultaneously. The most long-standing of these were at James Allen's Girls School, Dulwich (1903-21), St. Paul's Girls School, Hammersmith (1905-34), and Morley College (1907-24). At each of these establishments he transformed the music department and maintained the highest of standards. Two of his most popular works, the *St. Paul's Suite* (1912-13) and the *Brook Green Suite* (1933) were written for his students to play. In both these works, little concession is made to the youth of the performers. By all accounts Holst was a gifted teacher. Wherever he taught, whether at his various girls' schools, Morley College, or later at the RCM, stories abound of his encouragement and gentle persuasion. His methods were focused on getting his students to think through their own musical problems, and were a million miles away from the inflexible prescriptivism of his own teacher, Stanford.

To some degree, Holst's output was dictated by whatever happened to be influencing him at the time. Two enduring influences were literature (Whitman, Hardy and Bridges, in particular) and English folksong. Whitman's poetry inspired the purely orchestral *Walt Whitman Overture* of 1899. *The Mystic Trumpeter* (1904) seems to have been Holst's first choral setting of the poet, and a couple of years later, according to Vaughan Williams, the two composers set some words from Whitman's *Whispers of Heavenly Death* in friendly rivalry with one another which, in Vaughan Williams's case, resulted in *Towards the Unknown Region*, which was jointly declared the winner, while Holst's effort seems to have descended into obscurity. Still, he was not yet finished with the poet. At the outbreak of the First World War, he produced a setting from *Drum Taps* entitled *A Dirge for Two Veterans*, followed, at the end of the conflict, by *Ode to Death*, a setting of "When lilacs last in the dooryard bloom'd". Both these pieces can be said to reflect Holst's abhorrence of war, as well as his somewhat morbid fascination with death.

Holst's overt dalliance with English folksong is largely confined to the period of his first maturity immediately preceding the First World War. He was not an avid collector of folksong like Vaughan Williams and George Butterworth, but made use of material found in existing collections. The firstfruits of this enterprise was *A Somerset Rhapsody* (1906) which was written more or less simultaneously with Vaughan Williams's *Norfolk Rhapsody No. 1*. It was composed at the behest of the well-known folksong revivalist Cecil Sharp (1859–1924) and incorporates the tunes *A Lover's Farewell*, *Sheepshearing Song* and *High Germany*. The *Suite No. 2*, for military band (1911) incorporates folksongs from Hampshire, while the *Suite No. 1* (1909) is folksy in character, as is *Marching Song* (1906), although the themes are Holst's own.

Unlike many other composers influenced by the English folksong revival, Holst was able to lay himself open to other, disparate influences simultaneously to produce works of a completely different character. Thus, around the turn of the century and up until the outbreak of the First World War, Holst became interested in what would then have been considered off-beat religious and philosophical ideas. He was never conventionally religious, but he did develop an interest in theosophy, and began to read widely in Hindu philosophy. Thus began a period of setting some of the classic Hindu texts in various forms, ranging from a full-scale three-act opera, *Sita* (1899–1906), to four sets of *Choral Hymns from the Rig Veda* (1908–12). In between came the chamber opera *Savitri* (1908), a large-scale cantata *The Cloud-Messenger* (1910–12) to a text by the poet Kālidāsa, and *Two Eastern Pictures* (1911) – Kālidāsa again. There was also a symphonic poem, *Indra* (1903). Never one to do things by halves, Holst set about learning the Sanskrit language in which the texts were written in order to produce his own translations. He even enrolled, in 1909, with University College, London, in order to assist him in this. Although he considered the existing translations unsatisfactory, he never became fluent himself, and even his own daughter, Imogen, thought some of his efforts rather naïve, but his business was music, and it was the rhythm rather than the accuracy of translation which was paramount for him. Incongruously, however, while Holst was striving to evoke the flavour of the East in these works, the influence of Wagner, who Holst idolised more than any Hindu deity, was everywhere evident, especially in the earlier pieces such as *Sita* and *Indra*. Holst's musical depictions of Hindu themes were essentially an indulgence in which he was happy to pour out his energies for purely personal reasons. They certainly did not capture the public imagination.

Looking back over more than a century, we can see that Holst's Sanskrit period was a passing phase which really came to an end with the disastrous first performance of *The Cloud-Messenger* in 1913. Whatever happened on the night, the music is, in any case, not of Holst's best, and even his daughter was not prepared to defend it. Perhaps the best product of this phase is the least ambitious – from the various settings of Hymns from the Rig Veda which do at least evoke an airy, ethereal atmosphere quite different from what might be expected in traditional Christian spirituality.

It was not only the East which elicited a musical response from Holst. Always on the edge of hardship, it was Vaughan Williams's generous gift of £50 which enabled Holst to take a holiday in Algeria in 1908. There he absorbed the sights, sounds and smells of a culture very different from India which, despite his fascination for its religious traditions, he never visited. The work which was borne out of Holst's Algerian holiday was the *Oriental Suite – Beni Mora* (1910), which has an intimacy and a vitality missing from most of the Sanskrit works. Naturally, "being there" makes all the difference to a creative artist. But back in the land of cool British reserve, the reaction was lukewarm. One critic wrote: "We do not ask for Biskra dancing girls in Langham Place".[66] Fortunately posterity has been kinder than this. It is worth pointing out, however, that of England's foremost composers, Holst probably suffered more rejections than any other. None of his many operas met with lasting success, and in some cases the music was saved from total oblivion only by presenting it in the form of short orchestral pieces, as in the case of *The Perfect Fool*. The chief reason for this neglect seems to have been Holst's persistence in exploring exotic themes of which the average British concert-goer had no experience and was not in sympathy.

In 1914 a chance discovery during a leisurely ramble through Essex initiated another phase in Holst's life. One of the places he stumbled across was the pretty village of Thaxted with its quaint thatched cottages and olde-worlde atmosphere. The guild hall and the church were particular attractions. While he was there, he met the vicar of St. John's Church, Conrad Noel (1869–1942), a revolutionary character known locally as the Red Vicar on account of his socialist sympathies. Naturally, this endeared him to Holst whose own views were entirely compatible. From that day, he kept

66 Langham Place was the location of the Queen's Hall where the first performance of *Beni Mora* took place. It was destroyed in the Blitz in 1941.

an eye out for a suitable property to rent or purchase as a possible *pied-a-terre* which he could use for composing at weekends and vacations. Eventually a suitable cottage was found, and Holst became integrated into the life of the village. Conrad Noel had an interest in ancient Christian symbolism and traditions, especially in dance as a form of worship. In this connection he introduced Holst to a medieval carol, "This have I done for my true love" (or "Tomorrow shall be my dancing day") which the composer set for *a capella* choir. Holst served as choirmaster at St. John's Church whenever he was available, and with Noel's help established, from Whitsuntide 1916, an annual music festival, inviting his students from St. Paul's and Morley College to participate in it. Eventually, however, the vicar's outspoken communist sympathies (he hailed the Russian Revolution) in the heart of sleepy conservative Thaxted caused such controversy and offence among the genteel girls of St. Paul's that Holst felt obliged to relocate to a less divisive venue, which he found at James Allen's Girls School, Dulwich.

At the outbreak of war, Holst tried to enlist, but, unsurprisingly, considering his many ailments, was turned down as medically unfit. In any case, the prospect of the forty-year old composer scuttling around in the trenches always seemed highly unlikely. His teaching continued, and it was during the period of hostilities that he produced two of his most celebrated works – *The Planets,* which eventually put him on the map internationally, and *The Hymn of Jesus,* considered by many to be his most accomplished work. It is tempting to regard the ferocious opening movement of *The Planets* (*Mars*) as a reaction to the war raging in Europe, and the second, *Venus,* as a heartfelt plea for peace, but the significance of *The Planets* is astrological, Holst's interest in astrology having been kindled by Clifford Bax just prior to the war.

The Hymn of Jesus is a setting of a text from the Apocryphal Acts of John, 95, purportedly the record of a hymn sung by Jesus in the presence of his disciples just prior to his arrest, and begins with an orchestral prelude based on two well-known plainsong chants, *Pange lingua* and *Vexilla regis.* As with his Sanskrit settings, he picked up enough of the original language, Greek on this occasion, to enable him to produce his own translation.

As the war began to draw to its close, Holst finally got the chance to help the war effort in a more practical way when he was invited by the YMCA to serve as Musical Organiser to the British troops in Salonica who were awaiting demobilisation. As a parting gift to his friend, Balfour Gardiner paid for a private performance of *The Planets* to be conducted at the Queen's Hall by the young Adrian Boult. The first public performance came in 1919, again conducted by Boult, while Holst was still on duty in Greece. By all accounts, Holst was exhilarated by his time in Salonica. He enjoyed the work and had ample free time for sight-seeing, including Athens.

On his return from Greece in 1919, Holst assumed his old routine. In addition to his teaching at St. Paul's and Morley College, he accepted lectureships at Reading University and the RCM. Although these were very much part-time posts, they added to his overall teaching commitments. The heavy workload was exacting for a man whose health was far from robust, and the strain would soon begin to tell. He also returned to an unexpected and unwanted celebrity status, for *The Planets* had bowled over the British public. Attempts were made to shower him with honours, but he refused all but the Gold Medal of the Royal Philharmonic Society which was rather foisted on him (there is a photograph of him scowling at it).[67] This meteoric rise to stardom, however, was (for him happily) mitigated by his absolute musical integrity. He never once sought to repeat the success of *The Planets* by deliberately writing something in the same vein, but followed his instincts. There may be echoes of *Uranus* in some of the ballet music that opens his opera *The Perfect Fool* (the plot of which puzzled critics and audiences alike), but generally his music became sparer and more frigid. As ever, he wrote precisely the kind of music that pleased him, feeling no obligation to public taste or acclaim.

---

67 P. Holmes, *Holst* (Illustrated Lives of the Great Composers; London: Omnibus Press, 1997), p. 117.

In 1923 he followed in Vaughan Williams's footsteps by accepting an invitation to lecture and conduct his music in the United States – specifically at the University of Michigan. On his return to England, however, the pace of his professional life finally overwhelmed him and, on his doctor's advice, he cancelled all engagements, including his teaching commitments, throughout 1924, retreating to his house in Thaxted where he could recover in peace and quiet while working at leisure on a major *Choral Symphony*, set to texts by Keats. This is another work, however, that attracted mixed reviews. Some critics questioned what music could contribute to poems such as *Ode to a Grecian Urn* – one of the finest in the English language – which seemed wholly satisfying in itself. And was it really wise to set *Folly's Song* (a piece of doggerel, even if it is by Keats) alongside an undoubted masterpiece?

During the final decade of his life, Holst's creative imagination showed no signs of waning. In 1924 he set himself the challenge of setting the Falstaff scenes from Shakespeare's *Henry IV* to traditional folk and country tunes, drawn largely from Playford's *Dancing Master* of 1651, in the form of a one-act opera entitled *At the Boar's Head*. It was a private indulgence which was not appreciated by the general public and was soon forgotten. But by this time Holst had become used to mixed or hostile reviews and public indifference, and determined to write largely according to personal whim. By those standards, Holst's personal aims were successfully met. As Colin Matthews has written, "... the music flows effortlessly, without any sign of 'joins' between the tunes, and with no feeling that the setting of words to music is anything less than spontaneous".[68] Fortunately, the opera was recorded in 1975 by the RLPO & Chorus (men only) under David Atherton.[69]

The companion piece on the disc is Holst's final opera, again in one act, *The Wandering Scholar*. This was written in 1929–30 to a

68 C. Matthews, liner notes to *At the Boar's Head*, EMI 5 65127 2, p. 3.

69 It was recorded more recently on the Dux label by Warsaw Chamber Opera Sinfonietta conducted by Lukasz Borowicz, with Jonathan Lemalu as Falstaff.

libretto by Clifford Bax.[70] It is a perfect example of Holst's late frugal style in which everything is pared to the bone. There are just four soloists (bass, baritone, tenor and soprano) and a modest chamber orchestra (ECO on this recording) is used. It was eventually staged in 1934, by which time Holst was too ill to hear it, and it was left unrevised at his death.

Even at this late stage, Holst continued to accept commissions. One of these was the sombre *Egdon Heath* (1927), Holst's answer to a request on behalf of the NYSO for a symphony. Once again, the critical reception was cool. The reviewer in the *New York Times* judged it to be "long and undistinguished" (what would he have said if Holst *had* written a symphony!). Such criticism was surely undeserved and may well have overlooked the specific inspiration of the work, namely the opening pages of Hardy's *The Return of the Native* in which Egdon Heath – Hardy's name for the extensive region of scrubland stretching between Swanage and Dorchester – is meticulously described, almost as a character in itself, looming over the lives of the local inhabitants. In that context, the dark, brooding nature of the music corresponds perfectly well to the feel of Hardy's text. Author and composer were already well-acquainted by the time this work was written, and it is a pity that Hardy died in January 1928, just a month before its first performance.

Two further commissions at this time prompted Holst to turn his attention to the brass or military band. *A Moorside Suite* was written as a test piece for the National Brass Band Championships of 1928 (and later orchestrated by Gordon Jacob). In a letter to the editor of *The British Bandsman*, Holst expressed his delight over the commission and his willingness to serve again, if required. Perhaps, after having heard fifteen consecutive performances of the piece on the day of the finals, however, Holst was happy to give his ears a rest from the piece for some time afterwards. Be that as it may, Holst succeeds in combining winning melodies with technical challenge.

70 The amusing plot, which does not perplex the listener in the way that most of Holst's previous operas had done, is outlined by Colin Matthews (liner notes to the *Wandering Scholar*, EMI 5 65127 2, p. 2).

In its orchestral guise, the lovely *Nocturne* at the heart of the work is often performed as an independent item.

A commission by the BBC to write a work for military band resulted in the *Prelude & Scherzo: Hammersmith* (1930-31). Key to this piece is the interaction between the lively music of the Scherzo, depicting the *joie de vivre* of common life in this part of London and the sombre Prelude music representing the Thames as it flows unobtrusively and unconcernedly on its way. It is as if the river, which has the first and final say, and which alone will endure, is the one fixed point around which the transience of human activity revolves. Holst did not live to hear the work in its original form, but he prepared an orchestral version in 1931 which was performed under Adrian Boult in November of that year.

One of the most substantial works written by Holst towards the end of his life was the *Choral Fantasia* (1930) to a text by Robert Bridges (his *Ode to Music*), which he produced for the 1931 Three Choirs Festival in Gloucester at the behest of the cathedral organist Herbert Sumsion. In this connection Holst included an important part for the organ which makes considerable demands on the soloist. Once again, however, the work was misunderstood by audience and critics alike, although Vaughan Williams approved which, as Holst remarked, was all that really mattered. The modern listener may, in any case, be hard put to appreciate how this piece is really so very different from the earlier *Hymn of Jesus* with which Holst enjoyed considerable success.

In 1932, despite deteriorating health, Holst accepted an invitation from the syndics of Harvard University to undertake a six-month lectureship. Apart from the agreeable work (Holst always enjoyed lecturing), it provided him with an opportunity to be reunited with his brother Emil, who was an actor on Broadway. During his visit, however, Holst was taken ill with a duodenal ulcer (although some have speculated that cancer was diagnosed), which necessitated a change to his itinerary. When he returned to England he shed much of his official workload, retaining only his position at St. Paul's. He was advised that unless he had an operation on his ulcer, he would become a semi-invalid. He opted for the operation without hesitation, but the ordeal was too much for his frail constitution, and he died of heart failure on 25th May 1934, still four months shy of his sixtieth birthday. He was cremated, and his ashes were interred in Chichester Cathedral, close to the remains of Thomas Weelkes (1575–1623), a composer whose music he had especially admired. At the memorial service Vaughan Williams, Holst's greatest friend, conducted music by Holst and himself, which was surely as he would have wished.

At the time of his death, Holst had been planning a symphony, the scherzo of which he had already sketched. Subsequently, this was edited, and performed under the title *Scherzo* by Adrian Boult in 1935. Other short works from the last year of Holst's life include the darkly beautiful *Lyric Movement* for viola and small orchestra, the jazz-inspired *Capriccio*[71], and the abovementioned *Brook Green Suite*, written for the junior orchestra at St. Paul's.

As a composer Holst was never prepared to let the grass grow under his feet. Once he had overcome his undivided passion for Wagner, he opened himself up to all manner of musical influences and set his choral works to a broad range of texts – notably ancient Sanskrit writings, Bridges, Keats and Whitman, but also lesser-known writers such as Humbert Wolf, and even the Apocryphal New Testament. From the moment he acquired a distinctive voice, around 1905, his style, although always recognisable, was in a continually transformative state until, by the end of his career, many of his works were pared down to the bone, leaving nothing extraneous. Holst never courted popularity, and it is perhaps for this reason that the few works which did appeal took on a greater significance at the expense of others which, in reality, were equally as accomplished. To the casual listener, unfortunately, Holst remains a one-work wonder, a position exacerbated by the huge number of recordings of *The Planets* in comparison with any of his other works

71 The work was left untitled at Holst's death, and it was Holst's daughter Imogen who chose the name *Capriccio*.

(do we really need so many?).[72] And how many people, I wonder, are aware that the ever-popular carol tune *In the Bleak Midwinter* was written by Holst?[73]

If we are really to appreciate Holst's achievement as a composer, we need to regard his more popular works, including *The Planets*, in the context of his entire output – an aim which the recently-formed Holst Society will no doubt be eager to promote.[74]

72 The current number of recordings of each of Holst's more popular or frequently-performed works are as follows: *The Planets* – 70-plus; *St. Paul's Suite* – 15; *Perfect Fool* – 15; *Hammersmith* – 10 (4 orch.); *Brook Green Suite* – 9; *Egdon Heath* – 7; *Somerset Rhapsody* – 6; *Moorside Suite* – 5 (1 orch.); *Beni Mora* – 4; *Fugal Concerto* – 4. In some cases, the numbers are approximate, and include deletions of both CDs and LPs available on Amazon at the time of writing.

73 The words are by Christina Rossetti (1830–94).

74 The Holst Society was formed as recently as 2017 – an astonishing revelation, given that other societies devoted to less prestigious composers than Holst have been in existence for decades. The Havergal Brian Society, for example, was formed in 1975, and the original Granville Bantock Society prior to 1946, during the composer's lifetime.

a. Bibliography

Dickinson, A.E.F., *Holst's Music: A Guide* (London: Thames Publishing, 1998)

Grogan, Christopher, ed., *Imogen Holst: A Life in Music* (Woodbridge, Suffolk: Boydell Press, rev. edn, 2010)

Holmes, Paul, *Holst* (London: Omnibus Press, 1997)

Holst, Imogen, *The Music of Gustav Holst and Holst's Music Reconsidered* (Oxford: Oxford University Press, 3rd. edn, 1986)

----------, *Gustav Holst: A Biography* (London: Faber & Faber, rev. edn, 2011)

Huismann, Mary C., *Gustav Holst: A Research and Information Guide* (London: Routledge, 2011)

Partridge, Frank, *The Gustav Holst Way* (Cheltenham: Reardon Publishing, 2014)

Short, Michael, *Gustav Holst: The Man and His Music* (Hastings: Circaidy Gregory Press, 2014)

b. Selected Discography

i) Orchestral

The Planets	Hallé O., Elder	Hyperion	CDA 67270
Fugal Overture, etc.	LSO, Boult	Lyrita	SRCD 222
Brook Green Suite, etc.	ECO, Imogen Holst	Lyrita	SRCD 223
St. Paul's Suite	ECO, Menuhin	CFP	5 75981 2
The Perfect Fool	ECO, Menuhin	CFP	5 75981 2
Egdon Heath	LPO, Boult	Decca	470 191-2

ii) Concertos

Fugal Concerto	ECO, I. Holst; Bennett (flute); Graeme (oboe)	Lyrita	SRCD 223
Double Violin Concerto	ECO, I. Holst; Hurwitz & Sillito (violins)	Lyrita	SRCD 223

iii) Chorus with Orchestra

Choral Symphony	LPO & Choir, Boult; Palmer (sop)	EMI	5 65128 2
Hymn of Jesus	BBC SO & Chorus, Boult	Decca	470 191-2
A Choral Fantasia	City of London Sinfonia, Joyful Co. of Singers; Rozario (sop); Hickox	Chandos	CHAN 241-6
Dirge for Two Veterans	City of London Sinfonia, Joyful Co. of Singers, Hickox	Chandos	CHAN 241-6
Ode to Death	City of London Sinfonia; London Symphony Chorus, Hickox	Chandos	CHAN 241-6
Choral Hymns from the Rig Veda	RPO, RCM Chamber Choir, Willcocks	Unicorn	DKP(CD) 9046
Psalms 86 & 148	City of London Sinfonia, Britten Singers, Alley (org), Hickox	Chandos	CHAN 8997
Six Choruses for Male	ECO, Baccholian Singers of London, Menuhin	CFP	5 75981 2
Seven Partsongs	ECO, Purcell Singers Longfield (sop); I. Holst	Decca	470 191-2

iv) Operas

Savitri	City of London Sinfonia; Richard Hickox Singers; Soloists; Hickox	Helios	CDH 55042
The Wandering Scholar	ECO; English Opera Group soloists; Bedford	EMI	5 65127 2
At the Boar's Head	RLPO & Choir; soloists; Atherton	EMI	5 65127 2
The Perfect Food	BBC Northern SO & Singers; Soloists; Groves	Lyrita	REAM. 1143

v) Choral

The Evening Watch	Finzi Singers, Spicer	Chandos	CHAN 241-6
This Have I Done for my for True Love	Finzi Singers, Spicer	Chandos	CHAN 241-6
Six Choral Folksongs, etc.	The Holst Singers, Layton	Hyperion	CDA 66705

vi) Songs

Vedic Hymns	Maltman (bar); Bedford (piano)	Naxos	8.557117
Twelve Humbert Wolf Settings	Langridge (ten); Bedford (piano)	Naxos	8.557117

c. DVD

Holst: In the Bleak Midwinter (Tony Palmer, Isolde Films, 2011). TPDVD 173
Holst: The Planets (Philadelphia Orchestra, Ormandy, 1977). Euroarts

d. *Website*

The Holst Society (www.holstsociety.org)

7. Herbert Howells (1892–1983)

In the third week of September 1910, Herbert Howells and his close friend Ivor Gurney attended Gloucester Cathedral for "Elgar night" at the Three Choirs Festival. The main event, *The Dream of Gerontius*, however, was "held up", as Howells put it, for some twenty minutes by a new work composed by what Herbert Brewer called "some strange man" from Chelsea. The "strange man" was Vaughan Williams, and the new work was the ground-breaking *Fantasia on a Theme of Thomas Tallis*, conducted by the composer. Afterwards, he sat beside the seventeen-year old "music-bewildered" youth, sharing his copy of the Elgar score, and even signing his autograph. It was an overwhelming experience for Howells and Gurney, and one that they never forgot. The two young friends paced the streets of Gloucester all night, unable to get the music out of their head.

Howells was a Gloucestershire man himself, born above his father's business premises on the High Street in Lydney on the north bank of the Severn estuary on 17th October 1892. His father was a painter and decorator who played the organ (badly, according to Howells) at a local church on Sundays, and young Howells followed in his footsteps, being capable of deputising for his father by the age of eleven.

In 1904 the family business went bankrupt, but luckily for Howells, his progress as a young musician had been noted by a wealthy member of the Bathurst family who became a patron. It meant that in 1905 he was able to take up lessons with the organist of Gloucester Cathedral, Hebert Brewer, becoming an articled pupil three years later. He was joined by Gurney and a third pupil, Ivor Davies (later to find fame as Ivor Novello).

In 1911, Gurney enrolled at the RCM, followed by Howells a year later. It was a heady time to be studying at the college. Stanford was in his pomp, and among the students with whom the two Gloucestershire lads became closely acquainted were Arthur Bliss, Arthur Benjamin and Francis Purcell Warren. Howells even celebrated his new friends in a striking orchestral suite entitled *The*

Bs, each of the five movements focusing on a different character – "Bublum" (Howells himself), Bartholomew (Gurney), "Blissy", "Bunny" (Warren), and "Benjee" (Benjamin). The opening overture is gloriously fresh, and the kind of music only a young man could have written. Gurney is assigned a movement entitled *Lament*, the muted character of which seems somehow prescient of Gurney's tragic fate.

Unlike Gurney, who Stanford pronounced "the least teachable" of his students, Howells seems to have shown huge promise, being dubbed "my son in music" by the great man. Certainly, he settled into the London scene more readily than Gurney.[75] Although the Gloucestershire landscape inspired him, it was not an absolute requirement, and there were to be other influences such as the music of Stravinsky and Diaghalev's *Ballet Russes*. All looked set fair for Howells until, in 1915, he was stopped in his tracks by the news that he was suffering from Graves disease, which was then incurable, and was given an estimated six months to live. It must have been cold comfort to know that this meant he would not be conscripted into the army with the possibility of his being lost on the Western front. Remarkably, despite the shadow hanging over him, he continued to compose. Since his outlook seemed hopeless, he realised he had nothing to lose and agreed to undergo a brand-new radium treatment, by his account the first patient to do so.

Eventually, more by luck than by judgement, Howells recovered, but it was a protracted business, and when, early in 1917, he accepted the post of Assistant Organist at Salisbury Cathedral under Sir Walter Alcock, he found that he was obliged to relinquish it after a few months because his treatment for his illness necessitated too much travelling to and fro to St. Thomas's Hospital in London. However, with the help of a grant from the Carnegie Trust, he was able to assist Richard Terry in reviving and editing

75 This is not to say, however, that he never felt homesick in London. According to Paul Spicer (*Herbert Howells*, p. 33), Howells, unable to afford the train fare home, would sometimes buy a platform ticket and sit on Paddington station watching the trains leave for Gloucester. Gurney solved his homesickness simply by walking all the way home.

the Latin Tudor choral repertoire at Westminster Cathedral, which became an influence on his own early church music. It was also more convenient for his hospital visits.

At this point in his career, Howells was not the composer of sacred music for which he was later to become celebrated. Instead, he was concentrating his efforts on orchestral and chamber works. Alongside *The Bs* (1914), other orchestral pieces included the *Three Dances for Violin & Orchestra* (1915), with the rhapsodic slow movement at its heart, and the *Elegy for viola, string quartet & string orchestra* (1917) written in memory of one of the "Bs", Francis Purcell Warren, who went off to war and never returned. The use of the viola as the solo instrument is poignant in that Warren himself was noted as a highly promising violist, and the dark tones of the instrument were ideal for conveying the tragedy of his loss. The use of a separate quartet is likely to have been suggested by Vaughan Williams's Tallis Fantasia which would still have been fresh in Howells's mind at this time.

A further work which originates from this early period, but was revised and expanded in 1928, is the song-set (not strictly a cycle) with orchestra, *In Green Ways*. The long but unusually short-lined poem *The Goat Paths* by James Stephens was added during revision. The other songs are *Under the Greenwood Tree* (Shakespeare), *Merry Margaret* (Skelton), *The Wanderer's Night Song* (Goethe), and *On the Merry First of May* (Burkitt Parker & Claude Aveling). The settings are as wide-ranging as the texts themselves.

Howells's handling of the orchestra in these comparatively early pieces oozes confidence, but in turning to the chamber works of this period, we find that his touch is equally as sure. Not only this, but his output of such works was prolific between 1915–20, and included the *Piano Quartet*, the *Phantasy String Quartet*, the *Rhapsodic Quintet for Clarinet & String Quartet*, *Lady Audrey's Suite* for string quartet[76], sonatas for violin & piano Nos. 1 and 2[77], and *Three Pieces*

76 The "lady" in question was the young niece of Marion Scott, one of Howells's acquaintances.

77 There is in addition an ambitious B minor Violin Sonata extending over forty minutes, written in 1911 when Howells was still only eighteen years old.

for Violin & Piano. A String Quartet No. 3, *In Gloucestershire,* was in progress at this time but extensively revised later.[78]

Many of these works incorporate landscape music. The title of the *Third Quartet* makes this obvious, but it is there in other pieces too. The *Piano Quartet in A minor* (1916) is dedicated "to the hill called Chosen, and to Ivor Gurney who knows it". "Chosen", properly Churchdown Hill, is an outlier of the Cotswolds between Cheltenham and Gloucester, from which fine views could be had looking out to the Malverns. Marion Scott, the confidante of both men, vividly describes the associations of each of the three movements, seemingly with Howells's approval, in terms of Chosen Hill at particular times of day or year.[79]

The *Phantasy String Quartet* (1917) was written specifically as an entry for the Cobbett Folksong Phantasy Competition, gaining first prize. Again, images of Howells's beloved Gloucestershire come to the fore. The *Rhapsodic Quintet for Clarinet & String Quartet* (1919), which won a Carnegie Award, adopts the same fluid, lyrical approach as the works just mentioned.

We noted above the set of songs entitled *In Green Ways.* As well as the version for soprano and orchestra, Howells also prepared another with solo piano accompaniment, perhaps with performance opportunities in view. The name Herbert Howells is not the first to spring to mind in any consideration of English art-song, but in fact he contributed over sixty items to the genre throughout his long career, and with his *King David* produced what was undoubtedly his finest song, and one of the finest in the entire repertoire. It is a setting of a text by Howells's favourite poet, Walter de la Mare (1873–1956), and one that the composer once said he was prouder to have written than anything else in his output. The poet himself

78 Like Vaughan Williams, Howells was a compulsive tinkerer with his own works, but the revision on this occasion was necessary, in part, because he lost the original score on a train. He seems to have had bad luck in this regard, since a similar fate later befell part of his score for his *Missa Sabrinensis.*

79 The full description is quoted in Paul Spicer's liner notes to the CD *To Chosen Hill,* Metier, MSV CD92003.

expressed the wish that no other composer should set the work.[80] Howells and de la Mare, in fact, seem to have had a near-telepathic rapport[81], and, apart from *King David,* he produced two substantial song-sets using de la Mare's poetry – *A Garland for de la Mare* (11 songs), which occupied him, intermittently, for some fifty years, and *Peacock Pie* (6 songs). Both poet and composer were attracted by the fleeting, gossamer world of childhood, its clear-eyed innocence and its fantasies. Palmer suggests that Howells himself was the epitome of the qualities he sought to cultivate in his de la Mare songs – small and slender (he was only 5'–5" tall), quick and agile in his movements, and somewhat elfin in his features. It is not only in the songs that these are manifested; they are evident in some of his short orchestral scores, notably *Puck's Minuet, Merry-Eye, Corydon's Dance,* and *Scherzo in Arden,* for instance.

Rarely does Howells tackle the great existential conundrums of humanity or the high affairs of state. His songs, like de la Mare's poems, are cocooned in their own private world with which the listener or reader may nevertheless empathise. As for his choice of other poets, Wilfrid Gibson comes high on the list, but he tends to avoid the great poets of the past (there is a short setting of Shelley, *The Widow Bird*), preferring near-contemporaries such as James Stephens, Henry Newbolt, F.W. Harvey and Clifford Bax. It is perhaps surprising that he never seems to have set anything by his great friend Ivor Gurney, although he did undertake to orchestrate a couple of Gurney's own settings, namely *By a Bierside* and *In Flanders.*

Howells's organ and church music is generally associated with his later life, but the seeds had already been sown by 1918. The first three organ rhapsodies (Opus 17) were written between 1915–18. The most frequently performed of these is the stormy *Rhapsody No. 3* which is said to have been composed one sleepless night during

80 Spicer, *Herbert Howells,* p. 68; quoting C. Palmer, *Herbert Howells: A Study* (London: Novello, 1978), p. 16.

81 One that is explained in some detail in Palmer's liner notes for *Herbert Howells: Songs,* Chandos, CHAN 9185/86, pp. 5–9.

a Zeppelin raid while Howells was staying in York with Edward Bairstow (1874–1946), the Minster organist at that time. The first set of *Psalm Preludes* also dates from this period, as does a *Magnificat & Nunc dimittis in* G (1918), and the exquisite, ever-popular *Three Carol Anthems* (1918–20) – *Here is the little door, A Spotless Rose* and *Sing Lullaby*.

1920 was a red-letter year for Howells. In April he was appointed to the staff of the RCM where he remained for almost sixty years. The long roll-call of his students includes Madeleine Dring, Imogen Holst, Gordon Jacob, and Robert Simpson (all of whom were to become fellow composers of some merit), and much later the choral director Paul Spicer whose biography of his former mentor is both engaging and revealing.[82] Then, in August, he married the singer Dorothy Dawe (1891–1975) at St. Matthew's Church, Twigworth, a few miles to the north of Gloucester, where Canon Alfred Cheeseman (Gurney's old confidante) officiated. The marriage survived until Dorothy's death, despite Howells's habitual philandering.

For Herbert Howells, the art of composition was almost too easy. Blessed with a brilliant technique, his progression as a composer to date had been unrelentingly serene. He was regarded by Stanford, and others too, as the blue-eyed boy of English music. But, as 1925 loomed, all that was about to change. Back in 1914 Howells had written a piano concerto for Arthur Benjamin, one of the "Bs", who was a brilliant pianist as well as a composer, one of the bright young things of his generation. The premiere took place in July of that year at the Queens' Hall with Benjamin, the dedicatee, as soloist and Stanford conducting. The work is not without its flaws (Howells withdrew it following the first performance), but for a twenty-one-year old composer producing his first major orchestral score, it was impressive enough. When he came to write his *Piano Concerto No. 2,* in response to a commission from the Royal Philharmonic society, therefore, he cannot have had any

82 P. Spicer, *Herbert Howells* (Bridgend: Seren, 1998).

particular reason for thinking it would not be a success. Initially it seemed to have been so. The final cadence was met with hearty applause. But one critic, Robert Lorenz, stood up and shouted, "Well, thank God that's over!" After a stunned silence, applause was renewed with added vigour by Howells's supporters. The knee-jerk reaction of a single bigot should not have made any difference, but Howells was notoriously sensitive to criticism and immediately withdrew the work, even though the score was at the proof stage at the publisher. On reflection Howells conjectured, rightly or wrongly, that the critic's reaction had been politically motivated, that he was a member of the Heseltine "clique", and that he had been irked by the fact that the commission had not been offered to E.J. Moeran instead. On the other hand, it has to be said that for 1925 the structure of the work was anything but traditional. In effect it took the form of an extended sonata incorporating all three movements, which must have puzzled some listeners. Then, too, the influence of "moderns" such as Stravinsky, whose music had dazzled Howells as a student, was evident and not wholly appreciated by traditionalists. It has also been suggested that the soloist, Harold Samuel, best-known for his interpretations of Bach, was unsympathetic to the work, and that the conductor, Malcolm Sargent, misunderstood it.[83]

Whatever the precise reasons for the "failure" of the work, it dented Howells's self-confidence to such an extent that he was unable to compose anything of significance for several years. There were compositions: *Lambert's Clavichord* (1928)[84], the *Organ Sonata No.* 2 (1932), *A Kent Yeoman's Wooing Song* (1933), and *Pageantry* (1934), written for the annual National Brass Band Contest. None of these, however, required a symphony orchestra. Even the *Wooing Song*, which was eventually orchestrated in 1953, was left in short score for twenty years. It was not until 1938, with the composition of

83 Spicer, *Herbert Howells*, p. 80; idem., liner notes, Chandos, CHAN 9874, p. 6

84 The title of this work, a series of solo clavichord pieces, is meant literally. Herbert Lambert was an instrument maker from Bath who owned a clavichord which he loaned out to Howells.

the *Concerto for Strings*, that he returned to orchestral composition, and even then, not the full orchestra. The incident in 1925, in fact, seems to have engendered a distinct change in direction in which choral music came to the fore in place of the orchestral and chamber works with which he had made his name.

A second, even heavier, blow befell Howells in 1935 with the loss of his only son Michael to polio at the tender age of nine.[85] Both parents were devastated, and Howells never really recovered. The anniversary of Michael's death, 6th September, was revered year after year, and his spirit haunts much of the music Howells wrote subsequently. In *A Sequence for St. Michael*, written as late as 1961, the anguished choral cry of "Michael" that opens the work is clearly directed at someone other than the archangel, and the outpouring of emotion in the *Concerto for Strings* is charged with Howells's personal grief. Then, too, the familiar tune Howells wrote for the hymn *All our hope on God is founded*, was given the name "Michael" when it was included in the Clarendon Hymn Book of 1936, the year following the boy's death.

The work which is most closely associated with Michael's death, however, and is widely considered to be Howells's masterpiece, *Hymnus Paradisi*, is actually rooted in the *Requiem* of 1932, which at that stage remained unperformed. Howells himself regarded *Hymnus Paradisi* effectively as a revision of this work. If so, it is a far-reaching one, since the *Hymnus* is three times the length of the *Requiem*. It is perhaps more accurate to say that he mined the earlier piece for material he considered appropriate to the new one. At first, Howells was paralysed with grief and could not compose at all. It was at his daughter's suggestion that he took up his pen specifically to compose something in his son's memory. Even then, he consigned the finished article to the drawer until, fourteen years later, at the joint instigation of Herbert Sumsion and Vaughan Williams, he consented to have it performed at the 1950 Three Choirs Festival held in Gloucester.

85 There was also a daughter, Ursula (1922–2008), who became an actress.

Another potentially important work which seems to have had some connection with Michael's death, but which never fully saw the light of day in the composer's lifetime, was what seems to have been intended as a cello concerto. Like *Hymnus Paradisi*, it had its origins in the early thirties, before this tragedy, but was worked on afterwards and so was informed by it. It is known that he had been sketching the first movement as early as 1933, and also that he had worked it up into a complete entity by 1937 when he submitted it as an individual piece entitled *Fantasia* (reflecting the free, rhapsodic nature of the music) in part requirement for his D. Mus. Degree at Queen's College, Oxford. It turned out to be a substantial piece lasting over seventeen minutes. What became the slow movement of the concerto was completed in short score, and in 1992 was orchestrated by Christopher Palmer to be performed at Howells's Centenary Concert given at Westminster Abbey in the November of that year, under the title *Threnody for Cello & Orchestra*. This is the movement in which Howells's heart-wringing over his son's death is most in evidence.[86] The final movement existed only in the form of disordered sketches until Jonathan Clinch took them up and "realised" a performing version of the Finale. The Dutton Recording Company, enterprising as ever, then recorded all three movements as Howells's now complete *Cello Concerto* (Dutton CDLX 7317). Given the circumstances that beset the composer at the time, the Finale is remarkably upbeat, showing little sign of his emotional state in the wake of his son's death.

From 1940, Howells entered a new phase in which he focused almost (but not quite) entirely on church and organ music. In contrast to the brief earlier period of his association with Richard Terry at Westminster Cathedral, he became eagerly sought after by the Anglican Church, in particular by the dignitaries of various cathedrals who were anxious to commission new music to supplement their traditional repertoire. The staple diet provided

86 The *Threnody* was recorded by Murray Walsh and the LSO under Richard Hickox in 1995 (CHAN 9410).

by Howells consisted of Morning (Te Deum, Benedictus, Jubilate) and Evening (Magnificat, Nunc dimittis) Canticles which, along with a few additional items such as hymns and related pieces, occupy five volumes of Howell's sacred works in the Priory series.[87] Dating from 1940 onwards, there are Evening Canticle sets for Chichester, Gloucester, Hereford, Salisbury, St. Paul's, Winchester, Worcester Cathedrals and York Minster, as well as King's College and St. John's Cambridge, and Magdalen College and New College Oxford. Morning Canticles exist, in whole or in part, for Canterbury and Washington Cathedrals, St. George's Chapel Windsor, King's College Cambridge, St. Mary Redcliffe (Bristol), and the Chapel Royal, Tower of London. The untrained ear (like mine) may be under the impression that most of these settings sound remarkably similar to one another, but Howells took his commissions extremely seriously. It was not unknown for him to travel long distances to the cathedral or chapel for which he happened to be writing simply to sit quietly in its sacred space and absorb its unique acoustic.

What was it that so attracted Howells to writing for the church? He was certainly not conventionally religious and seems not to have held any belief in the traditional Christian doctrines. His daughter Ursula, in conversation with Paul Spicer, declared that, about a year before his death, he confessed to not believing in an afterlife.[88] His engagement with religion was perhaps similar to that of Vaughan Williams and Finzi. All three seem to have been agnostics with a spiritual sense that did not crystalize into doctrine. Religious buildings and rites could be beautiful in themselves and rouse the human spirit with their beauty without demanding anything by way of traditional belief. Doctrine, indeed, for these composers, may well have been detrimental to their aesthetic which consisted in a sense of the spiritual as a muse, and had no place for distinct articles of faith.

---

87 Priory Records: PRCD 745, 759, 782, 783, 784.

88 Spicer, *Herbert Howells*, p. 98.

The two outstanding works of Howells's latter years are *Missa Sabrinensis* – or *Mass of the Severn* (1954) – and *Stabat Mater* (1959–65). The first of these is a huge work for chorus, soloists and full orchestra. The reference to the River Severn in the title of the work is meant to highlight the link between the composer's birthplace at Lydney and Worcester where it was premiered. It has certainly never attained the popularity of *Hymnus Paradisi,* and the reason for this is not difficult to discern. The contrapuntal complexity of the work, along with the heavy orchestration and the problems posed, even for choirs of the highest calibre, make it virtually impossible to produce a near-flawless performance, and for the listener the words, which after all should have *some* importance in a choral composition, are lost in the textural layers which are piled up one on top of the other. Howells was too good a composer not to have been aware of all this, but he seems to have placed a greater emphasis on atmosphere, colour and emotional impact than on textural clarity. It is not a work which is likely to attract frequent performances, and yet it is precisely this which is required if critics are to establish its true value as a work of art.

The *Stabat Mater,* although yet another lengthy major choral work with tenor soloist and orchestra, is markedly different in character to *Missa Sabrinensis.* This is no doubt due in part to the fact that Howells was responding to a different text – a thirteenth century poem about Mary standing (hence the title) at the foot of the cross. Although the forces required are still substantial, and the demands on the chorus are as great as in the *Missa,* the writing is sparer and the musical contours are determined by the shape of the text. The theme of the poem, with its image of Mary's Son dying on the cross, would surely have brought to Howells's mind the death of his own son – thirty years ago by the time the work was completed. One wonders whether this was his prime reason for setting the poem in the first place, for it was his last extended work. It certainly cost him some effort to compose, for during the six years he was at work on it, he laid it aside several times. He was seventy-three by the time he finished it, and from then on, he focused on the short canticles and anthems which were his bread and butter.

One important work which was written while Howells was labouring over the *Stabat Mater*, and which has become one of his best-known pieces, was the motet *Take him, earth, for cherishing*, written in response to a commission for a memorial work in the wake of John F. Kennedy's assassination in 1963. It was completed the following year in time for Kennedy's memorial service at Washington Cathedral, and is considered to rank as one of the finest motets by any English composer. Always meticulous about his choice of texts, Howells opted for Helen Waddell's translation of a Latin poem by Prudentius.

Herbert Howells died in a Putney nursing home on 23rd February 1983, aged ninety, just a day after the death of Sir Adrian Boult (1889–1983) who had conducted and recorded so much of his music. Howells was cremated and his ashes were interred in the north aisle of Westminster Abbey alongside other composers of stature, including Stanford, Elgar, and Vaughan Williams. It would no doubt have given Howells great pride to know that he, the impoverished working-class lad from down-at-heel Lydney, had been laid to rest with two of those he had most respected – his teacher Stanford, and his great friend Vaughan Williams whose acquaintance he had first made on that magical evening in Gloucester Cathedral back in September 1910.

Howells's legacy today can be heard in any cathedral the length and breadth of the country, and in many abroad, for there can be hardly a week that passes without one of his canticle settings or anthems being performed somewhere in Britain and beyond. However, his work in this field must not be allowed to overshadow his achievement in composing secular music. His chamber music, with its rhapsodic qualities, is still rewarding to hear, and no doubt rewarding to play, and although his orchestral works have been recorded by the leading companies, they can never quite substitute for their being heard in the concert hall. Let us hope that the powers that be provide us with the opportunity to do so.

a. Bibliography

Clinch, Jonathan, "Shaping the Living and the Dead – Herbert Howells", *British Music Society Journal*, 39/1 (2017)

Cooke, Phillip A. and David Maw, eds., *The Music of Herbert Howells* (Woodbridge, Suffolk: Boydell Press, 2013)

Palmer, Christopher, *Herbert Howells: A Study* (Sevenoaks: Novello, 1978)

----------, *Herbert Howells: A Celebration* (2nd edn, London: Thames & Hudson, 1996)

Spicer, Paul, *Herbert Howells* (Bridgend: Seren, 1998)

b. Selected Discography

i) Concertos

Piano Concerto Nos. 1 & 2	BBC SO, Hickox; Shelley (piano)	Chandos	CHAN 9874
Cello Concerto	RSNO, Corp; Neary (cello)	Dutton	CDLX 7317
Concerto for Strings	RLPO, Handley	Hyperion	CDA 66610

ii) Orchestral

Three Dances	RLPO, Handley; Stewart (violin)	Hyperion	CDA 66610
Puck's Minuet	RSNO, Corp	Dutton	CDLX 7317
Merry-Eye	RSNO, Corp	Dutton	CDLX 7317
Elegy for Viola, String Quartet & Strings	City of London Sinfonia, Hickox	Chandos	CHAN 9161
Suite for String Orchestra	City of London Sinfonia, Hickox	Chandos	CHAN 9161

Serenade for Strings	City of London Sinfonia, Hickox	Chandos	CHAN 9161
The B's Suite	LSO, Hickox	Chandos	CHAN 9557

iii) **Choral/ Vocal with Orchestra**

In Green Ways	LSO, Hickox; Kenny (sop)	Chandos	CHAN 9557
Hymnus Paradisi	RLPO & Choir, Handley;Kennard (sop); Ainsley (ten)	Hyperion	CDA 66488
An English Mass	RLPO & Choir, Handley; Kennard (sop); Ainsley (ten)	Hyperion	CDA 66488
Stabat Mater	LSO & Chorus; Archer (ten); Rozhdesvensky	Chandos	CHAN 9314
Missa Sabrinensis	LSO & Chorus; soloists; Rozhdesvensky	Chandos	CHAN 9874

iv) **Chamber**

Piano Quartet	Lyric Quartet; West (piano)	Metier	MSV 92003
Phantasy String Quartet	Lyric Quartet	Metier	MSV 92003
Rhapsodic Quintet	Lyric Quartet; Collins (clar)	Metier	MSV 92003
String Quartet No. 3: "In Gloucestershire"	Danté Quartet	Naxos	8.573913
Violin Sonata No. 1	Barritt (violin); Edwards (piano)	Hyperion	CDA 66665

Violin Sonata No. 2	Barritt (violin); Edwards (piano)	Hyperion	CDA 66665
Violin Sonata No. 3	Barritt (violin); Edwards (piano)	Hyperion	CDA 66665

v) Choral

Take him, earth, for cherishing	Choir of King's Coll., Camb., Cleobury	Decca	470 194-2
Like as the Hart	Choir of St. John's Coll., Camb., Robinson	Naxos	8.554659
Long, Long Ago	Choir of St. John's Coll., Camb., Robinson	Naxos	8.554659
Behold, O God our Defender	Choir of New Coll., Oxford, Higginbottom	CRD	CRD 3455
Three Carol Anthems, etc.	Finzi Singers, Spicer	Chandos	CHAN 9458

vi) Services

Collegium Regale	Collegiate Singers, Millinger, Moorhouse (org)	Priory	PRCD 745
Worcester Service	Collegiate Singers, Millinger Moorhouse (org)	Priory	PRCD 759
Gloucester Service	Collegiate Singers, Millinger Moorhouse (org)	Priory	PRCD 759

Winchester Service	Collegiate Singers, Millinger Moorhouse (org)	Priory	PRCD 782
St. Paul's Service	Collegiate Singers, Millinger Moorhouse (org)	Priory	PRCD 782

vii) *Organ Solo*

Psalm Preludes, Sets 1 & 2	Cleobury (organ)	Priory	PRCD 480
Rhapsodies Nos. 1–4	Cleobury (organ)	Priory	PRCD 480
Sonata for Organ	Barber (organ)	Priory	PRCD 524

viii) *Solo Songs*

Complete Songs	Dawson, Pierard (sops); Ainsley (ten); Luxon (bar); Drake (piano)	Chandos	CHAN 9185

c. Website

The Herbert Howells Society (https://www.herberthowellssociety.com)

8. Sir Michael Tippett (1905–98)

From the days of his youth, Michael Tippett was a lover of causes which he expressed with a flair for the dramatic. His atheism, his pacifism, his feel for social justice, even his homosexuality, once he had come to terms with it himself, were expressed in the same forthright manner – by word (he was never short of these), by deed, and, of course, in his music. Havergal Brian, in old age, once told Robert Simpson that nothing mattered; for Tippett, by stark contrast, everything mattered, and it was all expressed with his customary eloquence – typically in what is arguably his best-known work, *A Child of OurTime* – which Tippet certainly was. His quest to find the best means of expression for his passionately-held views resulted in his preference for the more dramatic forms such as opera, although he was equally adept at purely symphonic writing and chamber music, even if the human voice reigned supreme in his output. Overall, he was a somewhat fussy individual (remember, everything mattered for him), and this, too, is reflected in the style of his music with its frequent cascades of notes (too many, some might say, as Emperor Joseph II of Austria is supposed to have told Mozart).

Michael Kemp Tippett was born into a progressive-thinking and well-heeled family at Eastcote (in what is now Greater London) on 2nd January 1905. His father, Henry, was a lawyer and businessman, while his mother, Isabel, possessed an artistic and liberal temperament, and had once been briefly imprisoned as a practicing suffragette. Tippett's heart-on-sleeve interest in social causes may well have been inherited from her. As was common with families of means at that time, his primary education took place at home under the watchful eye of a governess and specialist tutors who introduced young Tippett to the piano on which he enjoyed improvising. There followed a succession of private schools: first in Swanage (1914–18) where he astounded his teachers by writing an essay on the non-existence of God; then at Fettes College, Edinburgh (1918–20) where his homosexual activities with one of the other boys led to his removal; and finally at Stamford School in Lincolnshire (1920–22), where Malcolm Sargent had been a student and still had connections. In fact, he was in the audience at a school concert in which Tippett and a fellow student performed Bach's Concerto for Two Harpsichords in a version for piano. Although he did well musically at the college, his rebellious streak, not least his atheism, resulted in his expulsion.

The following year, with the blessing (and financial resources) of his father, he was admitted to the RCM, despite not having the formal entrance requirements. He was taught composition by Sir Charles Wood and, following his death in 1926, C.H. Kitson, a teacher very much in the pedantic Stanford mould, with whom the precocious Tippett experienced strained relations. The story is often told (including by Tippett himself) that he could have chosen to study with Vaughan Williams, who had recently joined the RCM as Professor of Composition, but decided against it on the grounds that his musical style had become so well-established that it would have led Tippett into imitating his teacher rather than finding his own voice.

In addition to composition, he also studied conducting with Sargent and Boult, and was introduced to contemporary music through the pieces they conducted. He soon had an opportunity to practice his new skill when, in 1924, and still only nineteen, he took up the conductorship of an amateur choir in Oxted, Surrey, staying in post after leaving the RCM and supporting himself by teaching French at a preparatory school in nearby Limpsfield (whose churchyard was soon to be the final resting place of Delius).

The years 1928–30 were quite productive for Tippett the composer. Among his works from that period were a string quartet, a concerto for flutes, oboe, horns and strings, a piano sonata, an overture and incidental music to the James Elroy Flecker play *Don Juan*, performed by the Oxted and Limpsfield theatrical group, and *The Undying Fire* for baritone, chorus and orchestra, to a text by H.G. Wells. Some of these pieces were included in a concert composed entirely of his own works which was given in Oxted in 1930.

Although these were subsequently withdrawn from his catalogue, they did give him a chance to hear his own compositions and to develop his technique. In the light of this experience, he re-enrolled with the RCM in order to study counterpoint with R.O. Morris, the pre-eminent counterpoint teacher of the day, and orchestration with Gordon Jacob, again one of the best in the business.

For a few years in the early thirties Tippett became a political activist on the far left, peddling the ideology of Trotsky in particular. He became involved in providing musical opportunities for unemployed miners in the North East, and running the South London Orchestra for unemployed musicians. Although he retained these political sentiments throughout his life, he realised the need to live essentially for his art, and his String Quartet No. 1 (1934–35) set him on the path to recognition.

It was the period 1938–39, however, in which Tippett's career took off alongside an upheaval in his personal circumstances, both of which must be seen against the backcloth of political events in Europe. Briefly, the personal upheaval was caused by the acrimonious end to a six-year homosexual relationship he had been having with an artist by the name of Wilfred Franks, which seems to have brought Tippett near to nervous collapse. In response, he consulted a psychotherapist who introduced him to Jungian psychoanalysis in which patients were encouraged to acknowledge two conflicting aspects of their personality – the light and shadow – and reconcile them in order to arrive at a fully rounded personality. By this means, Tippett began to come to terms with his unique individuality, including his homosexuality which at the time was not accepted by society in general, and about which even Tippett himself was ambivalent.

The parlous situation in Europe was also weighing heavily on Tippett's mind at the time, in particular the *Kristallnacht* pogrom of 9th–10th November 1938, involving the massacre of Jews in Germany in reprisal for the murder by a seventeen-year-old Jewish refugee of a German official in Paris. The first orchestral work in which Tippett found his mature voice and announced himself as a force to be reckoned with – namely, the Concerto for Double String Orchestra – was written under the shadow of these events, and yet, given the buoyancy of the outer music and the lyrical warmth of the slow movement, they seem nowhere evident in the music itself. It appears almost to be an antidote to the political events of the time, and perhaps it is the evident absence of *angst* in a time of *angst* that made the work an instant success when it was premiered in April 1940 by Tippett's own South London Orchestra under his baton at Morley College.

Regardless of whether this work can be seen as a piece of escapism, Tippett's other landmark work of the period, the oratorio *A Child of Our Time*, certainly cannot, for it faces events head on, and unapologetically so.[89] Personal and political events are taken up into both the libretto, produced by Tippett himself, and the music. The score is headed by a typically Jungian quotation from T.S. Eliot's play *Murder in the Cathedral*: "... the darkness declares the glory of light".[90] The Jungian analysis is even clearer in the libretto, notably where the soloists sing: "I would know my shadow and my light, so shall I at last be whole", which can be applied both individually and collectively.

The structure of the piece reflects Tippett's musical interests. It follows the tripartite layout of Handel's *Messiah*, which blew him away when he first encountered it, and which he had first conducted with his Oxted choir back in 1931. From that point he confessed preferring Handel to Bach owing to his greater dramatic qualities, yet Bach is also emulated in the structure of Tippett's piece, for the sequence of narrative recitative, dramatic choruses and scenas are suggested by their arrangement in the Bach Passions. In place of the Lutheran chorales, however, Tippett substitutes five negro spirituals which, although ostensibly commenting on eighteenth

---

89 Coincidentally (or not?), the composer began work on the piece on the day that Britain declared war on Germany – 3rd September 1939.

90 Tippett had approached Eliot with a view to his writing the libretto, but when the latter examined the scenario of the work, he suggested that this would serve Tippett's purpose just as it stood.

and nineteenth century black slavery, are broad enough to resonate through time as a reaction to all situations of oppression. Thus, *A Child of Our Time* becomes a child of any time and any place, wherever oppression is rife. We can all fill in the blanks.

In October 1940, with the war in full swing, Tippett was offered the post of Director of Music at Morley College which, prior to his death in 1934, had been occupied by Holst. As the buildings of the college had recently been blitzed, temporary accommodation had to be found, and Tippett had the task of reorganising the college choir and orchestra. Soon, however, he was presenting varied programmes that included music stretching from the sixteenth to the twentieth century. Among the staff recruited by the college were European refugees, including Mátyás Seiber and Walter Goehr.

In regard to active service during the war, Tippett declared himself a pacifist, and in 1942 he was summoned to appear before the authorities to explain his position. The committee exempted him from active service and assigned him to non-combat duties. However, he considered even this to be a compromise of his pacifist principles and refused the order. Consequently, he spent a two-month prison term in Wormwood Scrubs, returning to teaching duties at Morley College at the end of that period.

Tippett's penchant for the dramatic suggests that it would be only a matter of time before he tried his hand at opera, and although he was well into his forties before he did so, his first, and perhaps most successful effort, *The Midsummer Marriage* (1946–52), turned out to be the first of five.[91] The plot concerns the marriage of two couples and the interaction between ancient ritual and contemporary life, but the underlying symbolism is likely to evade understanding without an appreciation of Jungian psychoanalysis. It is also advisable to be familiar with Mozart's opera, *The Magic Flute*, since *The Midsummer Marriage* is modelled upon it, and to have a knowledge of T.S. Eliot's poetry, especially *The Wasteland* in

91 The others, all full-length three-act operas, were *King Priam* (1958–61), *The Knot Garden* (1966–69), *The Ice-Break* (1973–76), and *New Year* (1985–88).

which two of the characters, Madame Sosostris and the Fisher King inform characters in the opera. As in the case of *A Child of Our Time*, Tippett approached Eliot for a libretto, but again he turned down the offer, Tippett himself providing it as before. He was astute in the matter of self-promotion, and recognised that it would be advisable to draw a suite of music from the opera that could be heard on its own terms. He therefore selected the music he wrote for the four ritual dances, making it available separately in deference to listeners who might appreciate the music but not the opera.

In 1951 Tippett resigned his position at Morley College, sold his house in Limpsfield, and moved to Tidebrook Manor near Wadhurst, East Sussex. The works he wrote in the decade following completion of *The Midsummer Marriage* included one of his best-known, *Fantasia on a Theme of Corelli*, written in 1953 to mark the three-hundredth anniversary of Corelli's birth. But although it has entered the mainstream repertoire, it also represents the increasing complexity of Tippett's style. The casual listener, it is true, may find it pleasing enough if the music is simply allowed to wash over him/ her; the meticulous detail, however, is almost impossible to pick up – and must be extremely challenging to play, especially in the quicker passages. After hearing the premiere, *The Times* critic wrote: "... there was so much going on that the perplexed ear knew not where to turn or fasten itself."[92] The Sonata for Four Horns (1955) had to be transposed to a lower key before it was deemed playable; prior to the premiere of the Piano Concerto (1955), the scheduled soloist Julius Katchen declared it unplayable and had to be replaced; and at the premiere of the Second Symphony (1956–57) by the BBC Symphony Orchestra, conducted by Sir Adrian Boult, no less, the work broke down after a few minutes and had to be restarted. The fact that so many musicians were experiencing difficulties with Tippett's music at this time speaks volumes for the complexity of the music itself. He seems to have been writing on the

92 Quoted in *Michael Tippett*, https://en.wikipedia.org/wiki/Michael_Tippett, p. 8.

very edge of what was possible. Yet, for most people, music, like any form of art, is there to communicate and should not simply serve as an academic exercise in technique.

The 1960s began with another change of location – this time to Wiltshire. The major work from this decade was his third opera, *The Knot Garden* (1966), the story of a highly disfunctional family told with bemusing complexity and, somewhat in the manner of *Hamlet*, incorporates reference to a drama within the drama – in this case, *The Tempest*, in which the characters of the opera become characters in the Shakespeare play. Not, perhaps, one of Tippett's "winners". Another opera, *King Priam*, based on the legend of the King of Troy as depicted by Homer, which had been composed in the late fifties, was premiered in Coventry in 1962 as part of the celebrations for the opening of the new Coventry Cathedral (other commissions for the same event had been Britten's *War Requiem* and Bliss's *The Beatitudes*). Otherwise, Tippett was less prolific than hitherto, although his *Concerto for Orchestra*, written in celebration of Britten's fiftieth birthday, saw the light of day in 1963, as did *The Vision of St. Augustine* (1962–65), a large-scale work for baritone, chorus and orchestra, commissioned by the BBC. It was also a decade in which Tippett's efforts began to reap rewards in terms of honours: CBE (1959); HonFRCM (1961), an honorary doctorate from Cambridge University (1964), and ultimately a knighthood (1966). The Gold Medal of the Royal Philharmonic Society (1976), the CH (1979) and the OM (1983) were added subsequently.

From 1965, Tippett began to travel widely, first visiting the Aspen Music Festival in Colorado. He was rapidly gathering a devoted fan-base in the USA, and in 1974 was the honoured recipient of a Michael Tippett Festival devoted to his works, and also saw the first American production of one of his operas, the abovementioned *The Knot Garden*. He was present, too, at a performance of *A Child of Our Time* in Lusaka, for which President Kaunda was also in attendance. Other destinations during these years were Bali and Java where he was particularly captivated by Gamelan music and sought thereafter to incorporate it into some of his own works. Later, on a trip to

Australia, he conducted his recently composed Symphony No. 4 (1977). A further opera, *The Ice-Break* (1973–76), the *Triple Concerto* (1978–79) and the String Quartet No. 4 (1977–78) – his first foray into this medium for over thirty years – followed in quick succession.

By 1980, Tippett was seventy-five years old and becoming a little less prolific, but he was still fit enough, despite blindness in one eye, to travel abroad to Australia and Senegal (his orchestral work *The Rose Lake* [1991–93] was inspired by a visit he made to Lake Retba). Other major late works from this final period include his last opera, *New Year* (1985–88); the oratorio *The Mask of Time* (1980–82), commissioned for the centenary of the Boston Symphony Orchestra, and inspired by Jacob Bronowski's 1970s TV series *The Ascent of Man*, which examines man's relationship to time and his environment; and the String Quartet No. 5 (1990–91).

Tippett was still travelling in his ninety-third year, and it was on his final trip abroad, to Stockholm for a festival of his music, in November 1997 that he was taken ill with a stroke. He was taken home where he died on 8th January 1998, six days after his ninety-third birthday. His funeral, at Hanworth crematorium, Greater London, was a secular one in accordance with his wishes.

Like all leading composers, Tippett takes us on a musical journey. Like Vaughan Williams, whose teaching he rejected as a student, but whose work he grew to admire, his career in composition was one of restless exploration. No-one has accused him, as some critics have accused Britten, of recycling old music and dressing it in new clothes. He was always looking for new ways of expression. Most critics regard his work as falling broadly into three phases. The first mature phase takes us from his String Quartet No. 1 to his first opera *The Midsummer Marriage* (1935–52). Here, the many influences that shaped his music – Handel, Bach, Beethoven, and the madrigalists like Weelkes, Dowland and Monteverdi; and, among contemporaries, Stravinsky, Debussy and Sibelius, as well as more popularist sources such as jazz, ragtime, blues – and even folk music, at the outset – are at their most evident. Most works of this period are generally lyrical in nature and founded on home keys.

The second period stretches roughly from 1953–76, and includes the Symphony No. 2, and his fourth opera, *The Ice-Break.* Most works in this phase are characterised by increased dissonance and polytonality – changes which, it is claimed, were driven by the expansion of personal and political issues which the composer wished to address in his music. The final period (1977–95) moves forward from the experimentalism of 1953–76 towards a synthesis of the previous phases, reintroducing something of the lyricism of the first phase in a transformative way. There are also direct citations of his earlier works, as in the *Triple Concerto* in which he briefly quotes from *The Midsummer Marriage*. Tippett's glancing over his shoulder in this way does not imply that he had lost his power to surprise. His one-movement Symphony No. 4, for example, which describes the human life-cycle, is enveloped with the sound of breathing, using a wind-machine, or, perhaps, an amplified recording of real breathing – whichever is the more effective.

Whatever stylistic changes took place in his music during his sixty-year career, he never forsook the traditional genres. There were five operas, four symphonies (plus another from 1933 which he discarded from his official catalogue), concertos for orchestra and piano, as well as the *Triple Concerto* (for violin, viola and cello), five string quartets, and four piano sonatas. There were also oratorios, cantatas, madrigals, song cycles (*The Heart's Assurance, Songs for Ariel*), a Magnificat & Nunc Dimittis – even a hymn tune, "Wadhurst" – regardless of Tippett's atheist views.

Tippett was to some extent a controversial figure who held firm political and moral views and was not afraid to express them. No doubt it made him enemies as well as friends (of which he had many). Critics are equally as divided over his musical legacy, as the following citations will show. In a 1982 study of Tippett and Britten, Arnold Whittall rated them as "the two best composers of [the] generation born between 1900 and the First World War[93],

93 We should remember that this includes Finzi (1901), Rubbra (1901), Walton (1902), Berkeley (1903), Rawsthorne (1905), Lambert (1905), Cooke (1906), and Lutyens (1906)

and among the best of all composers born in the first two decades of the twentieth century". Against this accolade, compare the devastating judgement of Norman Lebrecht, writing in the year of Tippett's centenary: "I cannot begin to assess the damage to British music that will ensue from the coming year's purblind promotion of a composer who failed so insistently to observe the rules of his craft".[94] As it happens, the centenary celebrations were much more muted than Lebrecht feared, probably because the composer's death was still so fresh in the memory.

The consensus view lies between these extremes. The majority of critics argue that Tippett's best work was composed before 1960. The *Concerto for Double String Orchestra, A Child of Our Time, The Midsummer Marriage*, and the *Fantasia Concertante on a Theme of Corelli* are always mentioned, and have found a secure place in the repertoire. For many of his later works, the jury is still out. Much of Tippett's music includes very quick passages which shower notes too rapidly for the ear to assimilate. There is a kind of breathless vitality which may reflect his public persona as a restless, somewhat fussy individual, full of nervous energy, who was never lost for words. The general concert-going public is relatively conservative in its taste, and looks for tunes or themes to latch on to, and these are often in short supply in Tippett's music. His more abstruse works, therefore, will never be the flavour of the month. These are music for the connoisseur who is prepared to wrestle with the musical argument and plumb the depths for elusive meanings, and it is hardly surprising that those works which have gained a degree of popularity are the most immediately accessible, those which do not expect the listener to share the composer's *angst* – and in some cases his personal *angst* at that. His continued reputation is likely to rest on these populist works rather than on those tough-minded pieces which wear their heart on their sleeve in a world in which people have quite enough real-life *angst* of their own.

94 Both citations from *Michael Tippett*, https://en.wikipedia.org/wiki/Michael_Tippett, p. 16.

a. Bibliography

Bowen, Meirion, ed., *Tippett on Music* (Oxford: Oxford University Press, 1995)
Kemp, Ian, *Tippett: The Composer and His Music* (Ernst Eulenburg Ltd., 1984)
Soden, Oliver, *Michael Tippett: The Biography* (London: Weidenfeld & Nicolson, 2019)

b. Selected Discography

i) Symphonies

Symphony No. 1	BBC Scottish SO, Brabbins	Hyperion	CDA 68203
Symphony No. 2	BBC Scottish SO, Brabbins	Hyperion	CDA 68203
Symphony No. 3	BBC Scottish SO, Brabbins; Nicholls (sop)	Hyperion	CDA 68231
Symphony No. 4	BBC Scottish SO, Brabbins	Hyperion	CDA 68231

ii) Concertos

Concerto for Double String Orchestra	Moscow Chamber O.; Bath Festival O., Barshai	HMV	5 73049 2
Triple Concerto	Bournemouth SO; Chilingirian (violin); Rowland-Jones (viola); De Groote (cello), Hickox	Chandos	CHAN 9384

iii) Orchestral

Fantasia Concertante on a Theme of Corelli	Bath Festival O.; Menuhin and Masters (violins); Simpson (cello); Tippett	HMV	5 73049 2
Ritual Dances	BBC Scottish SO, Hurst	Naxos	8.553591

iv) Choral with Orchestra

A Child of Our Time	LSO & Chorus; soloists; C. Davies		LSO Live 0670

v) Opera

The Midsummer Marriage	Chorus & Orchestra of the Royal Opera House; soloists; C. Davis	Lyrita	SRCD 2217

vi) Chamber

String Quartets Nos. 1–5	Lindsay String Quartet	ASV	CD DCS 231

9. Ralph Vaughan Williams (1872–1958)

Along with Elgar, Vaughan Williams was undoubtedly the pre-eminent English composer throughout the first half of the twentieth century, and after Elgar's death in 1934 bore the palm alone, becoming the undisputed grand old man of English music. Folksong collector, editor of the English Hymnal, conductor of the Leith Hill Festival for almost fifty years, professor of composition at the RCM, member of umpteen committees, including the English Folksong and Dance Society and, later, of the Council for the Encouragement of Music and the Arts (CEMA), leading figure in the Society for the Promotion of New Music, promoter of music in schools, competition adjudicator – there were few areas of British musical life where Vaughan Williams's influence was not felt.

Elgar had been the local tradesman's son, largely self-taught as a composer, who rose to become Master of the King's Music. It is almost certain that Vaughan Williams was offered the honour following Elgar's death, but declined (as he also declined a knighthood). Elgar basked in the pomp and circumstance of his hard-won celebrity; Vaughan Williams, on the other hand, although born into privilege, also grew up in an atmosphere of progressive socialism which touched all areas of his life, including his religious views (Elgar was a lifelong Roman Catholic), and his years at Cambridge University certainly broadened his field of vision. Given his background, it is not particularly surprising that he regarded English music as the property of the people rather than of the privileged few, and he expended as much effort on amateur music-making as on the professional scene. After all, if nothing else, everyone can sing, and he recognised the importance of the amateur choir tradition for the future of music in Britain, often writing works within the compass of the amateur singer. Elgar was often aloof; Vaughan Williams was a man of the people.

He was born in the small Gloucestershire village of Down Ampney, a few miles south-east of Cirencester, on 12th October 1872. His father was the vicar of the local parish church, while his paternal grandfather and uncle were respected judges, both of whom had been knighted for their services. His mother Margaret was not only the great-granddaughter of Josiah Wedgwood, the famous potter, but the niece of Charles Darwin. As a young lad, Ralph (he always insisted on the pronunciation "Rafe") asked his mother about Darwin's theory of evolution, to which she replied, "The Bible says that God made the world in six days. Great Uncle Charles thinks it took longer; but we need not worry about it, for it is equally wonderful either way".

When he was just two years old, his father died suddenly, and his mother took the children to live in the family home, Leith Hill Place near Dorking in Surrey. He began receiving piano lessons from his Aunt Sophy (Wedgwood) at the age of five, and even made his first effort at composition, a simple four-bar piano piece which he entitled *The Robin's Nest*. He soon added violin studies to his musical curriculum, and by the age of eight had passed the associated music exams of Edinburgh University, having taken a correspondence course. Vaughan Williams may have been a late developer, but he was not a slow learner.

After home tuition, his formal education began in 1883 at preparatory school in Rottingdean near Brighton, and in 1887 he progressed to Charterhouse, Godalming, where his musical interests were encouraged, and, still only fifteen years old, he was allowed to organise a concert in which he played the violin in his own Piano Trio in G major. On leaving Charterhouse, the traditional course for someone of Vaughan Williams's background would have been to progress directly to Oxbridge. Eventually, he followed suit, but prior to this he enrolled for the first of two spells at the RCM, then quite recently established, where he studied under Sir Charles Hubert Parry (1890–92). As we have seen, Parry always encouraged his composition students to find at least something "characteristic" to say, which marked out their work as something that only they could have written, no matter how derivative the piece as a whole. Vaughan Williams would certainly have empathised with Parry's broad-minded liberalism which allowed for individual exploration.

When Vaughan Williams returned to the college after three years at Cambridge, his studies in composition were with Stanford, whose methods were very different. Gone was Parry's "woolly-minded" liberalism. Stanford was strictly conservative in music as in politics, and for him music could be only one of two things – beautiful or ugly. Vaughan Williams, like all Stanford's students, was made to justify every note of the exercises or compositions he presented. "All rot, my boy", is all he could get from Stanford on one occasion. Still, he did succeed in filing away some of his student's rough edges, especially with regard to orchestration.

It was during this second spell at the college that Vaughan Williams met a fellow student who was to become a lifelong friend, namely Gustav Holst. Their common interests included walking and folksong. From the first, they fell into the habit of discussing and critiquing one another's work while it was still in progress, which they found to be mutually beneficial, to the extent that Vaughan Williams felt he was able to learn more from this process than from his formal tutorials with Stanford which were often wasted on arguing over whether a student effort was "damnably ugly" or not.

In between these spells at the RCM, Vaughan Williams went up to Trinity College, Cambridge, to read history, although he kept up with his music by continuing his studies with Parry on a weekly basis, as well as with Sir Charles Wood (1866–1926). He was, however, able to focus sufficiently on his history to obtain a respectable BA degree in 1895, but also took and passed the BMus examination. Later, in 1899, he followed this up with a doctorate in music, for which he had submitted, as his chief composition, the extensive *Cambridge Mass* (recently recorded by Albion). Vaughan Williams certainly benefitted from the idyll that was late Victorian Cambridge, not least from his interaction with those from other disciplines such as the philosopher Bertrand Russell (1872–1970). It was under Russell's influence, so it is claimed, that he declared himself and atheist for a while, although he soon lapsed into an easy-going agnosticism. Of greater musical significance is the fact that Russell also introduced him to the poetry of Walt Whitman which inspired several key works, especially the ground-breaking *Towards the Unknown Region* (1905) and, most extensively, *A Sea Symphony* (1910).

Another significant acquaintance made during these years was Adeline Fisher whose ancestry was characterised by Anglican bishops and other church hierarchy. A well-known painting by John Constable (1776–1837) shows one of these Fishers, an archdeacon of Salisbury, strolling with his wife in front of his cathedral. Following a short engagement, Adeline and Ralph were married in October 1897 and honeymooned for several months in Berlin where he availed himself of the opportunity to study under Max Bruch. On their return to England they set up home in the shadow of Westminster Abbey before moving in 1905 to a house on Cheyne Walk, Chelsea, overlooking the Thames, where they remained for the next twenty-four years.

During the first decade of the twentieth century, Vaughan Williams ripened to maturity. At the start of it, he had still to have a work of his published, a deficiency which was rectified in 1902 with the publication of what turned out to be his most popular song, *Linden Lea*. Ironically, it is said to have earned him more money in royalties than anything else he wrote. At much the same time, his interest in the English folksong movement began to blossom, a development which had incalculable consequences for the discovery of his mature voice. He was not simply content to follow where others, like Cecil Sharp, were leading, but was determined to take the initiative. The opportunity came, somewhat fortuitously, at a church tea party at Ingrave in Essex where he met an elderly Mr. Potiphar who sang to him the folksong *Bushes and Briars*. It was a revelation. From then on, for the next decade, he set about scouring the country in search of folksongs and carols from counties stretching from Norfolk to Sussex to Herefordshire. The urgency of the task was not lost on him, for the feeling was that the oral tradition was dying out with the last generation of singers, and that the songs had to be committed to paper before it was too late. Vaughan Williams sometimes worked alone, but at others with fellow collectors, notably his younger contemporary George Butterworth. By the time the First World War brought the process to an abrupt halt, he had collected eight hundred songs – probably more than anyone other than Cecil Sharp. The fruits of his endeavours soon became evident in the works of his early maturity – the three *Norfolk Rhapsodies* (1905–06), most overtly. Other pre-war works, such as *The Lark Ascending* and *A London Symphony*, if they did not quote folksongs directly, were at least imbued with folksong inflections, including their characteristic modalism. Folksong was an abiding enthusiasm for Vaughan Williams, continuing to inform later compositions such as the *English Folksong Suite* (1923), *Six Studies in English Folksong* (1926), *Five Variants on Dives and Lazarus* (1939), and *Folk Songs of the Four Seasons* (1950).

Another important event at this time was his appointment as music editor of the new *English Hymnal* (1904–06) at the behest of the progressive Rev. Percy Dearmer (1867–1936), the literary editor of the project. According to Vaughan Williams's account he turned up unannounced one day in 1904 to make the request, telling him that it would entail about two months work. In the event it took two years, but he never regretted accepting the job, since it taught him so much about the art of writing good tunes: "I know now that two years of close association with some of the best (as well as some of the worst) tunes in the world was a better musical education than any amount of sonatas and fugues".[95] His work had some fortunate and lasting consequences. As editor, he was allowed the latitude to involve other composers who were asked to supply their own tunes to hymns or carols where required. His friend Gustav Holst, for instance, wrote the beautiful melody for *In the Bleak Midwinter*. Vaughan Williams supplied several tunes of his own, the best-known being *Down Ampney* ("Come down, O Love divine") and *Sine Nomine* ("For all the saints"). Other hymns and carols, such as Bunyan's "He who would valiant

95 Michael Kennedy, *The Works of Ralph Vaughan Williams* (2nd edn; Oxford: Oxford University Press, 1980), p. 74.

be" and Phillips Brooks's "O little town of Bethlehem" were set to existing folk tunes where suitable. It was in the course of his work on the *English Hymnal*, too, that he stumbled across Thomas Tallis's haunting tune to the words "When rising from the bed of death", which was to become the focus of Vaughan Williams's first indisputable masterpiece, the *Fantasia on a Theme of Thomas Tallis* (1910).

An incidental consequence of his work on the hymnal was the composition of one of his finest songs, *The sky above the roof* (1907). Percy Dearmer's wife, Mabel, had written a production for a local drama group, the script of which included her own translation of Paul Verlaine's French poem, and approached Vaughan Williams with a view to his setting it. He was not keen to do so, having little sympathy with the poet, but one day, according to his account, he entered his study and saw how untidy it was. He felt that he was faced with a stark choice – tidying up, or writing the song. Fortunately, for posterity, he decided on the latter.

Yet another important occasion during this formative decade for Vaughan Williams was the three months he spent during the winter of 1907–08 studying with Ravel in Paris. The French composer was three years his pupil's junior, but he was known to be a master orchestrator, and Vaughan Williams felt that it was time to apply some "French polish" to his own, sometimes stodgy orchestration. He baulked at Ravel's initial suggestion that he should write a minuet á la Mozart, but once an understanding had been reached a warm friendship developed. Ravel paid Vaughan Williams the compliment that he was the only student of his who did not write his (Ravel's) music. In any case, he imbibed from Ravel what he needed, and a new lightness of touch is discernible in the works written in the immediate aftermath of this period, particularly in the String Quartet No. 1 (1908) and the song-cycle *On Wenlock Edge* (1909), with its innovative string quartet and piano accompaniment.

The crowning glory of the decade, Vaughan Williams's red-letter year, occurred in 1910 with the premieres of the two works that made his name – the *Fantasia on a Theme of Thomas Tallis* at the Three Choirs Festival in Gloucester in September, and *A Sea Symphony* at the Leeds Festival just a month later. Following these successes, other significant compositions began to pour from his pen, including *A London Symphony* (1913) and *The Lark Ascending* (1914) – initially written for violin and piano, but orchestrated after the First World War. It has been suggested, perhaps rightly, that the latter work, with its exquisitely idyllic mood, could not have been written after the carnage of 1914–18.

Although he was forty-two years old by the time war was declared, Vaughan Williams had no hesitation about enlisting in the army. He joined the Royal Army Medical Corps as a private, serving in France and, later, in Greece. Like many soldiers involved in the hostilities, he revealed very little of the horrors he must have encountered and the discomforts he endured. In 1917 he was commissioned as a lieutenant in the Royal Artillery, and at one point was even left in charge of two hundred horses! It was out of his experience of the conflict that *A Pastoral Symphony* was born. Vaughan Williams describes how he took his ambulance wagon up a hill near Ecoivres and witnessed a Corot-like sunset which helped inspire the music. Thus, if the symphony was suggestive of landscape at all, it was a French one, regardless of how "English" the music may sound. When hostilities ended in November 1918, he was appointed Director of Music for the British First Army until his demobilisation three months later.

After his return to England, he found that the conditions of life had changed radically. He had lost many good friends during the war, and wrote to his friend Holst, "I sometimes dread coming back to normal life with so many gaps – especially of course George Butterworth…."[96] Gradually, however, he began to pick up the threads of his composing career. He completed his *Pastoral Symphony* which was premiered in 1922, the same year as he composed his starkly beautiful *Mass in G minor*. Other important works from this decade

96 Paul Holmes, *Vaughan Williams* (London: Omnibus Press, 1997), p. 52.

include the exotically-scored *Flos Campi* (1925), the operas *Sir John in Love* (based on Shakespeare's *The Merry Wives of Windsor*) and the desolate one-act *Riders to the Sea* (1925–32) which uses the text of J.M. Synge's play, and the ballet *Old King Cole* (1923). His music generally began to become less "folksy" and develop a harder edge, perhaps anticipating the kind of pieces he would write throughout the 1930s.

Away from composing, he began to take on conducting and teaching duties, succeeding Sir Hugh Allen as conductor of the Bach Choir (from 1921), and becoming a professor of composition at the RCM in 1919, remaining in post for twenty years. His composition students included Ivor Gurney, Gordon Jacob, Constant Lambert, Grace Williams, Ruth Gipps, and Elizabeth Maconchy, as well as others, such as Ina Boyle and Arthur Butterworth, who consulted him on a more informal basis.

On the domestic front, his wife Adeline began to suffer from progressive arthritis to the extent that she could no longer manage the stairs at their Cheyne Walk home, and they made the decision to move to a more accessible house on the edge of Dorking known as White Gates. Vaughan Williams certainly missed the convenience of his London home, despite the frequent rail services to the capital, but at least he was on hand to rehearse and conduct the massed amateur choirs performing at the Leith Hill Festival whose activities took place chiefly in the Dorking Halls.

The 1930s saw further changes, both musically and personally. His major works from that decade were dark-hued, gritty and sometimes violent in mood. In 1930 he produced his percussive Piano Concerto, a big-boned work written specifically for Harriet Cohen (Bax's long time mistress), although her comparatively small hands struggled to cope with the demands made on them, for the work was more suited to the muscular, octave-spreading fingers of a Busoni.[97] The music is sinister and explosive by turns, and in some

97 The difficulty of the solo part is perhaps acknowledged by the fact that in 1946 the composer sanctioned a two-piano version of the work, prepared by Joseph Cooper.

ways foreshadows the powerful Fourth Symphony of 1934 which took the musical world by storm.

Two other important works from this decade were *Job: A Masque for Dancing* (1930) and the anti-war cantata *Dona Nobis Pacem* (1936). The brainchild of the ballet *Job* was the economist Geoffrey Keynes, an old friend from Vaughan Williams's Cambridge days, and the composer, who shared his enthusiasm for the project, set to work on the score even before the precise details had been settled. *Dona Nobis Pacem,* with texts drawn from RVW's favourite poet Walt Whitman, John Bright, the Mass, and various Bible passages, may best be seen as a protest against the deteriorating political situation in Europe, and in particular the rise of Fascism.

Throughout the thirties, Adeline's arthritic condition continued to deteriorate. Meanwhile, another woman entered Vaughan Williams's life. In 1938 Ursula Wood (1911–2007), the wife of Captain Michael Forrester Wood, sent him some ideas she had for a ballet scenario, hoping that he would write the music. He seems to have been lukewarm about the proposal, but he did invite her to meet him to discuss it, and became rather more interested in her than in her ballet. She came back with a different scenario based on Spencer's *Epithalamion* about which he was more enthusiastic. The personal relationship which developed alongside the working one was a somewhat strange affair. One can understand how the sixty-five year old composer with a sick wife might have fallen for a woman thirty-eight years his junior; but it is more difficult to appreciate how she could have been sexually attracted to him – yet, by her own admission, she was.

In 1942, Ursula's husband died suddenly of a heart attack, which gave her the freedom to remarry when opportunity allowed, but Vaughan Williams remained attached and still committed to caring for the ailing Adeline. It is not entirely clear whether there was a sexual relationship during her lifetime. Vaughan Williams aficionado and music critic Michael Kennedy, who was acquainted with the composer, suggested that there was. However, he was entirely open with Adeline about this new woman in his life, and Ursula became a frequent visitor at White Gates with Adeline's blessing. In fact, a warm relationship seems to have developed between them. Ralph continued to care for his wife until her death in 1951, and in February 1953 he and Ursula were married.

There was no doubt that she was good for him. She opened up new vistas for the now octogenarian composer. They travelled all over Europe, and mixed business with pleasure when Ralph was invited to various universities in the USA, including Cornell and Yale, to lecture and conduct his music.[98] There were frequent visits to the opera and the theatre, and a general sense of *joie de vivre*. She kept him feeling younger than his years and served as his muse. The *Four Last Songs* (1954–58), for instance, were settings of her poems, and she doubled as his personal secretary.

But let us now retrace our steps back to the 1940s. At the beginning of World War II, we find him still keen to do his bit for king and country. He was not above engaging in the daily round and common task, such as collecting scrap from his neighbourhood for the war effort. He also served on a committee for refugees from Europe. Unsurprisingly, however, his chief contribution was a musical one. When, in 1940, he was invited to produce the score for the propaganda film *The 49th Parallel*, he jumped at the chance. Although the writing of film music requires a singular technique and a peculiar precision, he found it no obstacle, and during the remainder of his life virtually reinvented himself as a film composer, producing vivid scores for feature films including *A Flemish Farm* (1943), *The Loves of Joanna Godden* (1946), *Scott of the Antarctic* (1948), and (with Ernest Irving) *Bitter Springs* (1950), and documentaries such as *Coastal Command* (1942), *The People's Land* (1943), *The Dim Little Island* (1949) and *The England of Elizabeth* (1955). Music from *Scott of the Antarctic* found its way five years later into his seventh symphony, *Sinfonia Antarctica*.

98 His first visit to the USA had been in 1932 when he was invited to give a series of lectures at Bryn Mawr College, Pennsylvania.

The 1940s brought forth several important classical scores, too, notably the visionary Fifth Symphony (1938–43) and the tumultuous Sixth (1944–47) with its eerie finale. There was an Oboe Concerto (1944), written for Leon Goossens, which tended to revert to the pastoralism associated with the composer's earlier years, and *An Oxford Elegy* (1949) for small orchestra, chorus and narrator, to texts by Matthew Arnold, which shares the world of *Flos Campi.*

As the composer entered his eightieth year, he showed no signs of letting up. On the contrary, his ideas became even more imaginative and experimental. His Symphony No. 8, for example, includes a huge battery of tuned and untuned percussion – in his own words, "all the 'phones and 'spiels known to the composer", while the Symphony No. 9 seems to be a summation of his life's work, with quotations from pieces such as the orchestral impression *The Solent,* written over fifty years previously. Another work of long gestation was his opera – or "morality", as he called it – *The Pilgrim's Progress* on which he had been labouring, on and off, for over forty years, and which was finally brought to performance – not entirely successfully in the first instance – in 1951. He was at work on yet another opera, *Thomas the Rhymer,* at the time of his death on 26th August 1958. His final completed work, as far as I can discover, was the *Three Vocalises* for soprano and clarinet.

Vaughan Williams's funeral took place at Golder's Green followed by cremation. On 19th September a memorial service was held in Westminster Abbey where, amid great ceremony, his ashes were interred adjacent to those of Purcell and of his old teacher Stanford.Vaughan Williams composed a huge amount of music in all the traditional – and some not so traditional – genres during his long life, and it would be impossible here to comment on any of it in detail. The nine symphonies, however, each with its own individuality, remain the backbone of his work and represent the ongoing development of his style throughout the forty-five-year period during which they were written. It will be appropriate, therefore, to make some brief comment on them.

Symphony No. 1: A Sea Symphony

> *"Ah who shall soothe these feverish children?*
> *Who justify these restless explorations?"*

These words, taken from the Finale of *A Sea Symphony,* could easily describe the seven-year gestation period of the symphony itself. That Vaughan Williams was working up to a substantial work about "the sea itself" is clear from his composing activity around the turn of the century. In 1903 he was working on a Whitman-based piece entitled *Songs of the Sea,* which seems not to have gone beyond the preliminary sketches; but in the same year he completed his orchestral impression *The Solent* which did receive a run-through at the RCM, and in which the fingerprints of the mature composer are clearly evident. Although it was not performed again in his lifetime, he must have retained an affection for it, because the opening theme was quoted in subsequent works, notably in *The England of Elizabeth* and the Symphony No. 9, both of which were written in the last few years of his life. It is also quoted in *A Sea Symphony* at the line "And on its limitless, heaving breast, the ships". In 1906, he was off to sea again with *The Steersman,* a movement for baritone and women's chorus which he abandoned. Thus, by the time *A Sea Symphony* came to fruition in 1910, it already had a good deal of history behind it, and at its premiere at the Leeds Festival that year, it helped establish Vaughan Williams as one of Britain's leading composers.

The four-movement form of the work, with its slow second movement followed by a scherzo, suggests that it is truly symphonic in structure, but the substantial use of chorus and soloists in all four movements (and not, as in Beethoven's Symphony No. 9, only in the Finale) was entirely innovative, and some critics have regarded it as something of a hybrid – a kind of symphony-cantata, for the text inevitably has some effect on the shape of the musical argument. It is noticeable, too, that when Butterworth sowed the seeds of *A London Symphony* in Vaughan Williams's mind one evening in 1911, his precise words were: "You know, you ought to write a symphony" – as if he did not regard *A Sea Symphony* to be genuinely symphonic. Be that as it may, no-one these days seems to baulk at the title.

The symphony works at two levels: first, it is suggestive of the sea in its various moods, especially in the first and third movements; but, particularly in the second and fourth movements, the sea becomes a metaphor for the journey of the soul, and we enter the depths of contemplation in the mind of man. At last, we are invited to "sail forth" and "steer for the deep waters only" to be lost in the mysteries of the universe. In Michael Kennedy's words, "the music recedes from our hearing like a ship disappearing over the horizon".[99]

In this work, perhaps for the first time, all the familiar RVW fingerprints come together: his love of Walt Whitman's poetry, which he never outgrew; his predilection for modalism; his skill in writing *noblimente* passages for the brass; and his suggestion, and sometimes citation, of folksongs (snatches of both *The Golden Vanity* and *The Bold Princess Royal* appear in the scherzo). After the premiere of this work, there was to be no looking back.

Symphony No. 2: A London Symphony

Like its predecessor, *A London Symphony* grew out of earlier material on which the composer had been working, namely a symphonic poem about London. This, no doubt, was in Vaughan Williams's mind when Butterworth prompted him to write a symphony. However, this may not have been the sole motivation. Robin Matthew-Walker[100] has made a strong technical case for the view that Delius's then recent work, *Paris – Song of a Great City*, was the chief spur. The opening ten bars of each work, in which the city in question seems to be rousing from slumber, are almost identical, and Matthew-Walker speculates that Vaughan Williams may well

99 M. Kennedy, liner notes, *Vaughan Williams: A Sea Symphony*, Chandos, CHSA 5047, p. 8.

100 R. Matthew-Walker, liner notes, *Vaughan Williams: A London Symphony*, Hyperion, CDA 68190, pp. 2–3.

have been in attendance at the Queen's Hall in London in 1908 when *Paris* received its second British performance under Beecham.

In its original form, the symphony was a substantial work lasting an hour in performance, and somewhat Mahlerian in scope, in as much as everything seems to be cast into the melting pot to produce a vivid cross-section of – in this case – London life. It was extensively revised in 1918, when some fifteen minutes of music was cut, and then less drastically, twice more in 1920 and 1933. There is no doubt that the major 1918 revision tightened the structure of the symphony, though at the expense of losing some very attractive music, in particular an exquisite "Elizabethan"-style melody in the slow movement which Vaughan Williams might have done well to accommodate elsewhere – perhaps in a short orchestral rhapsody.[101]

How descriptive – or programmatic – is the symphony supposed to be? Some composers seem to delight in tantalising their listeners by hinting at images that *might* be suggested by the music, while simultaneously affirming that it may – or even *should* – be heard as pure music. Bax beguiled in just this way in respect to his symphonic poem *The Garden of Fand*, and Vaughan Williams does the same here. He allows that *A London Symphony* might better be called "Symphony by a Londoner" without suggesting that this was his own idea. Then he draws the listener's attention to the Westminster chimes, which are as obvious as the cuckoo in Delius's *On Hearing the First Cuckoo in Spring*. These strike the half-hour in the first movement, but, significantly, the three-quarters at the end of the scherzo: the musical argument has moved on. He suggests, further, the idea of the lavender seller's cries in the slow movement, along with the jingle of the cab-horses' bridles. This movement has been called "Bloomsbury Square on a November afternoon", the composer informs us – but again, he does not claim it to be *his* title. The scherzo may be regarded as echoing the distant sounds of the Strand as heard from the Embankment after dark. And yet, he says,

101 Fortunately for us, a recording of *A London Symphony* in its original form is available on the Chandos label, CHAN 9902, with the LSO conducted by Richard Hickox.

with a twinkle in his eye, although this "may serve as a clue to the music, ... it is not necessary". "Make whatever you want of it" seems to be his ultimate advice to the listener.

If a clue to the meaning of the symphony is to be sought, perhaps we should look to the Epilogue, a device used by the composer more than once, but which is more closely associated with the Bax Symphonies. Stealing in after the three-quarter chimes of Big Ben, its rippling quavers suggest the ceaseless flow of the river as it passes unobtrusively through the metropolis[102] and out towards the sea – out into history. Vaughan Williams himself declared that this Epilogue was suggested by a passage from H.G. Wells's *Tono-Bungay* in which London is seen from the vantage point of a warship sailing down the Thames and out towards the sea. The relevant passage runs:

> To run down the Thames so is to run one's hand over the pages in the book of England from end to end. The old cries and the old devotions glide abeam, astern, sink down upon the horizon, pass – pass. The river passes – London passes – England passes...

Vaughan Williams completed his symphony in 1913, at a time when the war clouds were beginning to gather. The sounds depicted in the symphony – the lavender-seller's cries, the jingle of the cab-horses' harnesses, and so on – were those with which the composer had been familiar when he had first arrived in the capital, and they would soon be gone forever to be replaced by new, more ominous sounds. If *A London Symphony* is about more than pure music, perhaps it is as much about the passing of Edwardian London as is Elgar's Second Symphony.

Symphony No. 3: A Pastoral Symphony

A few British composers have followed Beethoven in naming one of their symphonies *Pastoral*. Alan Rawsthorne's Second Symphony

---

102 Perhaps in much the same way as Holst's *Hammersmith* (1930–31).

is so-named. But by far the best-known is Vaughan Williams's Third Symphony. The term "pastoral" normally evokes images of the countryside, as it does in Beethoven, but RVW's use of the title, we have now come to understand, tends to lead his listeners off the scent, as does the music itself, to some extent. The music, in fact, could not sound more English, and yet we now know that this symphony was conceived in France during the First World War, and is essentially a requiem for the fallen in a conflict in which the composer played an active part, and in which he lost many friends. One clue to his intention lies in the dark undercurrent created by the lower strings which informs much of the first movement.

The second movement features the celebrated "Last Post" passage played first on solo trumpet, and later on solo horn, which is the clearest indication of the true nature of the work. We are told that the inspiration for its inclusion was a commonplace experience in which Vaughan Williams heard a bugler playing the Last Post and landing on the seventh instead of the octave, hence the slightly out-of-tune feel at this point. The composer, in fact, instructed the trumpeter to play only natural notes, since these are all that can be played on a bugle.

If we jump to the final movement, we note that its most singular feature is the wordless solo voice that opens and closes it, and virtually everything in between relates to this. The composer was open regarding whether the soloist should be a soprano or a tenor, and even allowed for a clarinet should no vocalist be available. However, a vocalist is the intention, and a soprano has become the norm. Might this be interpreted as a soldier's fiancée or wife mourning for her dead lover or husband? For the listener, at least, this scenario is hardly avoidable. A tenor voice might suggest a soldier's lament for his lost comrades or for the loved ones he has left behind him.[103]

The three movements mentioned so far are all predominantly slow, so the brief scherzo introduces some needed contrast. Even so, the marking *moderato pesante* leaves room for interpretation,

103 In recent times, Andrew Manze has taken up the case for the role of tenor. Listeners can now judge the effect for themselves in Manze's recording of the symphony (Onyx: 4161).

and many conductors prefer a less than full-blown scherzo. More important than tempo, perhaps, is orchestral texture which seems intent on suggesting a fleet-footed approach. William Hedley wonders what this movement has to do with any wartime experiences, but equally refuses to accept that it was included for purely musical reasons.[104] Vaughan Williams himself cautioned against reading meaning into it. But surely, for an audience that has been subjected to two deeply-felt, keening movements, the third must come as light relief before the keening is renewed by the soprano/ tenor solo. Hedley sums up the symphony as follows:

> I hear the composer telling us that the unspeakable horror that was the First World War has left its mark, and that mark can never be erased, but that the human soul is resolute, possessed of a nobility of strength and purpose that will transcend that.[105]

Many critics regard Symphonies Nos. 1–3 as a loose trilogy. Like all Vaughan Williams's symphonies, each is distinctive in itself, both structurally and thematically, but there are also similarities. The composer decided on suggestive titles for these three, a practice that, with the exception of *Sinfonia Antarctica,* he henceforth discontinued. Moreover, they all belong stylistically to the period of his early maturity. Thirteen years were to elapse before his next exercise in symphonic form. Then comes another three-symphony burst between 1934–47, two angry, dissonant symphonies (Nos. 4 and 6) separated by the visionary Fifth.

Symphony No. 4 in F minor

Vaughan Williams's symphonic reaction to the First World War might so easily have been one of rage and heartfelt protest, as

104 W. Hedley, "Vaughan Williams's Pastoral Vision", *Ralph Vaughan Williams Society Journal,* 78 (2020), pp. 10–19 (13).

105 Hedley, "Pastoral Vision", p. 14.

Bax's First Symphony, appearing in the same year as the Pastoral, certainly was, even though for Bax the Easter Rising may have been as much in mind as the war in Europe. But Vaughan Williams preferred a mood of dignified grief. The violence and dissonance of his Symphony No. 4 in F minor (the first in which a particular key is stipulated) must have hit its first audience like a bolt from the blue. Of course, Hitler's rise in Europe was continuing unabated, and many must have been wondering if all the sacrifice in the First World War had been for nothing. With the benefit of hindsight, critics seem to have been united in adjudging this to be the composer's "war" symphony, or at least a warning of the threat in much the manner that Wilfred Owen's poems had been intended to warn. Michael Kennedy, however, felt that there was something much more personal behind it. By 1934, when the symphony was completed, Adeline's arthritis had virtually incapacitated her, and the relief of the composer's friendship with Ursula Wood was still four years away. Kennedy believed that it was the personal frustration Vaughan Williams was feeling at the time that found vent in the symphony. Yet, with his customary elusiveness, he disowned any programmatic associations: "I wrote it, not as a definite picture of anything external, e.g. the state of Europe, but simply because it occurred to me like that ... it's what I meant".

Symphony No. 5 in D major

A couple of years after the first performance of the Fourth Symphony, Vaughan Williams began work on his next. It had a gestation period of some six years, being completed in the midst of the Second World War (1943). Again, the composer had a surprise in store for his audience. Whereas, given the world situation at the time, listeners might have expected a violent, dissonant work to match the Fourth Symphony, what emerged was a serene, visionary symphony reaching moments of supreme radiance. Clashing cymbals and rattling side drums are nowhere to be heard. The tranquil mood of this symphony is in fact informed by music from

Vaughan Williams's unfinished opera *The Pilgrim's Progress*, from which it borrows directly, notably in the third movement. When he began work on the symphony, the opera was still thirteen years away from seeing the light of day, and he had his doubts as to whether it would be completed (he was already sixty-six in 1938).

The quiet horn call which opens the work sets the tone for the serene opening movement, *Preludio*. This is followed by a light, skittish scherzo, much of it marked *pp* or *ppp*, leading eventually to a chorale-like passage with an "oompah" undercurrent (a RVW hallmark). The heart of the symphony is undoubtedly the *Romanza* with its wonderful hushed opening in the strings. The term *romanza*, or "romance", was customarily reserved by the composer for his most deeply-felt music. The finale is a passacaglia which works up to a climax before ending in tranquillity – Pilgrim's entry into the Celestial City, perhaps – and on a note of resolution which is decidedly absent from the previous symphony, just as it would be from the next.

Symphony No. 6 in E minor

And so to the Sixth Symphony. Its violence and grinding dissonance are every bit the match of the Fourth Symphony, and yet it is not simply more of the same – it never is with Vaughan Williams. For here there are new elements with which to contend, not least the eerie, mysterious finale which the composer instructs should be played pianissimo throughout. The symphony erupts with three rising notes, plunging straight into a world of chaos which is maintained throughout until, seemingly without warning, the storm abates, giving way to a beautiful romantic melody led by the strings and then repeated by the full orchestra (the theme became popular as the theme tune for the 1970s TV series *A Family at War* – for those of us who can remember that far back). This dies away to be replaced by a second movement dominated by a three-note motif in which trumpets and drums grow ever more menacing the louder they become (the first movement of Shostakovich's *Leningrad*

Symphony springs to mind). The impression is of an advancing army that cannot be repelled. The martial mood (at least there is a semblance of order here) in its turn gives way to the tumult of the scherzo, described by Michael Kennedy as "a hell's kitchen of wailing saxophones".[106] This, too, fragments into nothing, leaving the stage to a finale of eerie stillness in which nothing much appears to happen at all. There is no sense of direction, and the music, which hardly rises above a whisper, seems to have been deconstructed. Even the desolate oboe that rises from the musical wasteland cannot bring hope or comfort, and the work ends *niente* – in nothingness. Vaughan Williams described it as "whiffs of theme drifting about" and quoted Prospero's words in *The Tempest*: "We are such stuff as dreams are made on, and our little life is rounded with a sleep".

The symphony was premiered by Sir Adrian Boult and the BBC Symphony Orchestra on 21st April 1948, and it certainly caused a sensation, with a hundred performances in its first two years. Naturally, the meaning of the work was hotly debated with many critics noting that it had been written at the onset of the nuclear age and speculating that the desolate finale presented an image of a landscape laid waste by nuclear conflict. One critic spoke openly of the work as a war symphony. Vaughan Williams himself was irritated by such comments, retorting: "Why can't a chap simply write a piece of music?" Perhaps this is a little disingenuous, however. Composers are often reluctant to explain the meaning of a work in detail, but it is virtually impossible to write a piece of music *purely* in the abstract – that is to say, just the notes, without having any image in one's head relating to the music at all. Vaughan Williams's reference to the text from *The Tempest* is, in itself, an image of sorts.

Although the final three symphonies are not formally or thematically related, their one point of contact lies in the composer's experiments with orchestral colour. All make liberal use

106 M. Kennedy, liner notes, *Vaughan Williams: Symphony No. 6*, Chandos, CHAN 10103, p. 5.

of percussion and include instruments not often associated with the standard orchestra – the organ in the *Sinfonia Antarctica*, the battery of tuned and untuned percussion in the Symphony No. 8, and the flugelhorn and saxophone in the Symphony No. 9. All these works were completed after the composer had attained the age of eighty, yet here he was, continuing to quest and explore.

Symphony No. 7: Sinfonia Antarctica

In 1947, Vaughan Williams was invited by the music director of Ealing Studios, Ernest Irving, to write a score for the forthcoming film *Scott of the Antarctic*. The theme of man against nature appealed to him, and, armed with a draft script, he set to work right away, even before the film had been produced. It took him little more than two weeks to complete a score which takes about eighty minutes in performance – almost as long as the run-time of the film itself.[107] Although Vaughan Williams was customarily a slow, meticulous worker, his previous experience in writing film music taught him that time was of the essence. Thus, things were well on schedule when he sent the score to Irving for editing. The result was one of the finest film scores not only of its day, but of any period, and was far in advance of any film music that the composer had written to date. He must himself have valued it highly and realised its symphonic potential, because he decided to use this music as the basis of a new symphony, *Sinfonia Antarctica*, completed in 1952 and premiered by John Barbirolli and the Hallé Orchestra in the following year.

Vaughan Williams cast his material into five movements, each of which was headed by a literary quotation which in some performances is recited by a narrator.[108] The bleak, inhuman

107 The full eighty minutes of the original score has been recorded on Dutton, CDLX 7340. This includes material that was cut from the score as heard in the film.

108 The citations are taken from Shelley, *Prometheus Unbound*; Psalm 104; Coleridge, *Hymn Before Sunrise in the Vale of Chamouni*; Donne, *The Sun Rising*; and Captain Scott's last journal.

landscape of the Antarctic is represented by a wordless women's chorus, solo soprano and wind machine, while the towering cliffs of ice at the edge of the ice shelf are depicted by the organ. Lighter moments include a quirky trumpet theme in the scherzo to depict the antics of the penguins. The centrepiece of the symphony is *Landscape*, an evocation of the bleak, white immensity of the vast continent, while the short *intermezzo* that follows introduces a brief spell of warmth and lyricism. In the film, this music depicts thoughts of home and of loved ones as the doomed men lie in their tent pinned down by a storm just eleven miles from their base. In the *Epilogue* the march theme from the *Prelude* returns, suggesting the heroism and bravery of Scott's party as they battle against the odds, but the solo soprano returns with her impassive vocalise, and the wind machine has the final word.

Symphony No. 8 in D minor

Still Vaughan Williams was not done with the symphony. Three years later he was at it again with his Eighth. It is his shortest, at under half-an-hour, and arguably his most experimental. The first movement is effectively in the form of a theme and variations, but Vaughan Williams explained that it would be more accurate to describe it as a set of variations in search of a theme, since there is no theme as such. Instead, we are advised to look for motifs. The jaunty *scherzo alla marcia* that follows is scored for winds alone, while in the third movement *Cavatina*, it is the turn of strings alone. In the final *Toccata*, "all the 'phones and 'spiels known to the composer" are unleashed, along with the tuned gongs he decided to add after attending a Puccini opera in London. They certainly make a joyful noise unto the listener if not unto the Lord! There are few shadows in this uplifting symphony, and the critic is denied the excuse to find hidden meanings as in most of the previous symphonies. The work was dedicated to, and first performed by, "glorious" Sir John Barbirolli with the Hallé Orchestra in Manchester on 2nd May 1956.

Symphony No. 9 in E minor

The exploration of orchestral colour and use of exotic instruments that characterises the previous two symphonies is taken up once more in Vaughan Williams's ninth and final essay in the genre. There is something valedictory about this work – he completed it less than a year before his death – and critics delight in comparing this or that passage with similar ones in one or other of his previous symphonies or other works. Some of these may have originated in the critics' imagination rather than the composer's, but there are some obvious influences Vaughan Williams himself acknowledges. One of these is a theme which appears on the flugelhorn in the second movement that can be traced all the way back to the opening of the orchestral impression *The Solent*, from 1903. As for the flugelhorn itself, we are told that the composer had the idea for its inclusion after a boat trip during a holiday in Austria and Germany when the pilot stopped the engine, produced a flugelhorn and began to play.

Another influence on the symphony was Vaughan Williams's favourite Thomas Hardy novel *Tess of the d' Urbevilles* which had earlier inspired him to sketch out some music depicting various scenes in the novel, particularly the climactic one involving Tess's arrest for murder at Stonehenge. The third movement scherzo, in which the side drum features prominently, has been said to evoke the legend of a ghostly drummer who haunts Salisbury Plain. It must be emphasised, of course, that no matter how programmatic this "Tess" music was meant to be in its original form, it loses all programmatic identity in the symphony. As the composer himself admits in a highly-entertaining and informative note written in 1958, "It is quite true that [the second] movement started off with a programme, but it got lost on the journey – so now, oh no, we never mention it – and the music must be left to speak for itself…".[109]

---

109 This citation is part of a substantial portion of Vaughan Williams's original note, reprinted in the liner notes to Everest's reproduction of Boult's recording of the symphony in the wake of the composer's death on 26th August 1958 (Everest, EVC 9001).

The three great crashing chords that conclude this work, each leaving a trail of harp glissandi in its wake, with the final chord fading into oblivion, is unlike the ending of anything else that Vaughan Williams wrote, and it is surely not too fanciful to suggest that this was in effect his farewell to the symphony. On hearing the second performance of the work, his widow, Ursula, seemed to agree: "I thought, well, that is the end of Ralph's life, and I can see a turning point. It is leading out into another place. It is extraordinary".[110] Certainly, this final symphony could be seen as representing Vaughan Williams the visionary gazing forth resolutely "towards the unknown region"; but, given the self-citations, it is equally a life review laid out from the perspective of calm detachment.

110 Cited in Stephen Connock's liner notes for *Vaughan Williams: Symphony No. 9*, Chandos, CHSA 5180, p. 14.

a. Bibliography

Adams, Byron and Robin Wells, eds., *Vaughan Williams Essays* (London: Routledge, 2016)

Alldritt, Keith, *Vaughan Williams: Composer, Radical, Patriot – A Biography* (Robert Hale, 2015)

Cobbe, Hugh, ed., *The Letters of Ralph Vaughan Williams 1895–1958* (Oxford: Oxford University Press, 2010)

Day, James, *Vaughan Williams* (Oxford: Oxford University Press, 3rd. edn, 1998)

Douglas, Roy, *Working with RVW* (Oxford: Oxford University Press, 1978)

Foreman, Lewis, ed., *Ralph Vaughan Williams in Perspective* (Albion Music, 1998)

Foss, Hubert, *Ralph Vaughan Williams: A Study* (London: Harrap, 1950)

Francis, John, "'I Have Trod the Upward and the Downward Slope': The End of the Journey?", *Ralph Vaughan Williams Society Journal*, 78 (June, 2020), pp. 23–25

Frogley, Alain, ed., *Vaughan Williams Studies* (Cambridge: Cambridge University Press, 2009)

Frogley, Alain and Aidan Thomson, eds., *The Cambridge Companion to Vaughan Williams* (Cambridge: Cambridge University Press, 2013)

Hedley, William, "Vaughan Williams's Pastoral Vision", *Ralph Vaughan Williams Society Journal*, 78 (2020), pp. 10–19.

Heffer, Simon, *Vaughan Williams* (London: Faber & Faber, 2009)

Holmes, Paul, *Vaughan Williams*, Illustrated Lives of the Great Composers (London: Omnibus, 1997)

Hurd, Michael, *Vaughan Williams* (London, Faber & Faber, 1970)

Kennedy, Michael, *The Works of Ralph Vaughan Williams* (Oxford: Clarendon Press, 2nd edn, 1994)

----------, *A Catalogue of the Works of Ralph Vaughan Williams* (Oxford: Oxford University Press, 2nd edn, 1996)

Lunn, John E., Ursula Vaughan Williams, et al., *Ralph Vaughan Williams: A Pictorial Biography* (Oxford: Oxford University Press, 1971)

Manning, David, ed., *Vaughan Williams on Music* (Oxford: Oxford University Press, 2007)

Mellers, Wilfrid, *Vaughan Williams and the Vision of Albion* (Albion Music, 1996)

Moore, Jerrold Northrop, *Vaughan Williams: A Life in Photographs* (Oxford: Oxford University Press, 1992)

Ottoway, Hugh, *Vaughan Williams*, Novello Short Biographies (Sevenoaks: Novello, 1978)

----------, *Vaughan Williams Symphonies* (London: BBC Books, 1987)

Pakenham, Simona, *Ralph Vaughan Williams: A Discovery of His Music* (London: Macmillan, 1957)

Palmer, R., *Folk Songs Collected by Vaughan Williams* (London: J.M. Dent, 1983)

Pike, Lionel, *Vaughan Williams and the Symphony* (London: Toccata, 2003)

Ross, Ryan, *Ralph Vaughan Williams: A Research and Information Guide* (London: Routledge, 2016)

Vaughan Williams, Ralph, *Heirs and Rebels: Letters Written to Each Other and Occasional Writings on Music* (Oxford: Oxford University Press, 1959)

----------, *National Music and Other Essays* (Oxford: Clarendon Press, rev. edn, 1996)

Vaughan Williams, Ursula, *RVW: A Biography of Vaughan Williams* (Oxford: Oxford University Press, 1964)

----------, *Paradise Remembered: Ursula Vaughan Williams – An Autobiography* (Albion Music Ltd., 2002)

b. Selected Discography

i) Symphonies

Complete Symphonies	RLPO & Chorus/ LPO, Handley	EMI (CFP)	5 75760 2

There are many RVW symphonic cycles available for those who like to compare the various interpretations, including the classic Adrian Boult cycle (EMI); Bernard Haitink and the LPO (Warner Classics); Andrew Davies with the BBC SO (Warner); Previn with the LSO (RCA); Bryden Thomson and the LSO (Chandos), and Richard Hickox with the LSO (Chandos). The two most recent cycles are Andrew Manze with the RLPO (Onyx), and Martyn Brabbins and the BBC SO (Hyperion), which is still in progress as I write.

ii) Concertos

Piano Concerto	LSO, Thomson; Shelley (piano)	Chandos	CHAN 8941
Violin Concerto	O. of the Swan, Curtis; Waley-Cohen (violin)	Signum	SIGCD 399
Oboe Concerto	LSO, Barbirolli; Rothwell (oboe)	EMI	5 66543 2
Tuba Concerto	LSO, Barbirolli; Catelinet (tuba)	EMI	5 66543 2

iii) Orchestral

Fantasia on a Theme of Thomas Tallis	LPO, Boult	EMI	7 64017 2
The Lark Ascending	Northern Sinfonia, Hickox Creswick (violin)	EMI	7 49770 2
Five Variants on Dives & Lazarus	Hallé O., Barbirolli	EMI	5 66543 2
Fantasia on Greensleeves	Hallé O., Barbirolli	EMI	5 66543 2
Overture: The Wasps	Hallé O., Barbirolli	EM	5 66543 2
Job: A Masque for Dancing	Bergen PO, A. Davies	Chandos	CHSA 5180
Norfolk Rhapsody No. 1	LSO, Hickox	Chandos	CHAN10001
English Folksong Suite	Acad. St. Martin-in-the-Fields, Marriner	Decca	460 357-2
Concerto Grosso	Acad. St. Martin-in-the-Fields, Marriner	Decca	460 357-2
In the Fen Country	New Queen's Hall O., Wordsworth	Decca	460 357-2
Serenade to Music	BBC SO, Wood (with original 1938 soloists)	Dutton	CDAX 8004

iv) Film Music

Scott of the Antarctic, etc.	BBC PO, Gamba	Chandos	CHAN10007
49th Parallel, etc	BBC PO, Gamba	Chandos	CHAN10244

Story of a Flemish Farm, etc.	BBC PO, Gamba	Chandos	CHAN10368

v) **Chorus/ Voice with Orchestra**

Five Tudor Portraits	LSO & Chorus, Hickox Rigby (mezz-sop); Shirley-Quirk (bar)	Chandos	CHAN 9453
Flos Campi	BBC NOW & Chorus; Brabbins Power (viola)	Hyperion	CDA 67839
Epithalamion	Britten Sinfonia; Joyful Co. of Singers, Tongue; Smith (bar)	Albion	ALBCD 025
Dona Nobis Pacem	LSO & Chorus; Langridge (ten), Terfel (bar); Hickox	EMI	7 54788 2
Sancta Civitas	LSO & Chorus; Langridge (ten),Terfel (bar); Hickox Company of Singers, Hickox	EMI	7 54788 2
Toward the Unknown Region	RLPO & Choir, Lloyd-Jones	Naxos	8.557798
Fantasia on the Old 104th Psalm Tune	LPO & Choir, Boult	EMI	5 74782 2
Oxford Elegy	Jacques O., Choir of King's Coll., Camb.; Westbrook (speaker); Willcocks	EMI	5 67221 2

vi) Opera

Hugh the Drover	RPO, Ambrosian Opera Chorus, St. Paul's Cath. Choir; soloists; Groves	EMI	5 65224 2
Riders to the Sea	O. Nova of London; Ambrosian Singers; soloists; M. Davies	EMI	7 64730 2
Sir John in Love	NPO, John Alldis Choir; soloists; M. Davies	EMI	5 66123 2
The Pilgrim's Progress	LPO & Choir; soloists; Boult	EMI	7 64212 2
The Poisoned Kiss	BBC NOW; Adrian Partington Singers; soloists; Hickox	Chandos	CHAN10120

vii) Chamber

String Quartet No. 1	Britten Quartet	EMI	5 85155 2
String Quartet No. 2	Music Group of London	EMI	5 65100 2
Phantasy Quintet	Music Group of London	EMI	5 65100 2
Violin Sonata	Bean (violin); Parkhouse (piano)	EMI	5 65100 2
Six Studies in English Folksong	Croxford (cello); Parkhouse (piano)	EMI	5 65100 2
The Lark Ascending	Mordkovitch (violin); Milford (piano)	Carlton	30366 00132

viii) Piano Solo

The Lake in the Mountains	Bebbington (piano)	Somm	SOMMCD 0164
Hymn Tune Prelude on Gibbons' "Song 13"	Bebbington (piano)	Somm	SOMMCD 0164

ix) Choral

Mass in G minor	Choir of Westminster Cath., Baker	Hyperion	CDA 67503
Valiant-for-Truth	Choir of Westminster Cath., Baker	Hyperion	CDA 67503
A Vision of Aeroplanes	Choir of Westminster Cath., Baker	Hyperion	CDA 67503
O clap your hands	Rochester Cath. Choir, Sayer	Lantern	
Come down, O Love divine	Rochester Cath. Choir, Sayer	Lantern	

xi) Songs

α) With Orchestra

On Wenlock Edge	Britten Sinfonia, Padmore (ten); Shave	Har. Mun	HMU807566
Songs of Travel	CBSO; Allen (bar); Rattle	EMI	7 64731 2

Four Hymns	LPO; Langridge (ten); Gunes (viola); Willcocks	EMI	5 85155 2

β) **With Piano, String Quartet, or Solo Instrument**

On Wenlock Edge	Langridge (ten); Britten Quartet	EMI	5 85155 2
Songs of Travel	Rolf-Johnson (ten); Willison (piano)	EMI	5 47485 2
Four Hymns	Padmore (ten); Outram (viola); Rolton (piano)	Albion	ALBCD 036
Five Mystical Songs	Keenlyside (bar); Johnson (piano)	Naxos	8.557114
Merciless Beauty	Langridge (ten); Endellion Quartet	EMI	5 85155 2
The House of Life	Rolf-Johnson (ten); Willison (piano)	EMI	5 74785 2
Four Poems by Fredegond Shove	Golden (sop); Rothfuss (piano)	Koch	3-7168-2H1
Four Last Songs	Golden (sop); Rothfuss (piano)	Koch	3-7168-2H1
Linden Lea	Golden (sop); Rothfuss (piano)	Koch	3-7168-2H1
The Sky above the Roof	Williams (sop); Burnside (piano)	Albion	ALBCD 002

xii) **Folksong and Carol Arrangements**

Five English Folksongs, etc.	Holst Singers, Layton	Hyperion	CDA 66777
Loch Lomond, etc.	London Madrigal Singers, Bishop	EMI	2 16155 2

The Captain's Apprentice, etc.	Tear (ten); Ledger (piano)	EMI	2 16156 2
Folksong Arrangements (4 vols)	Bevan (sop); Spence (ten) Williams (bar); Vann (piano); Liebeck (violin)	Albion	ALBCD 042/5

c. DVDs

O Thou Transcendent: The Life of Ralph Vaughan Williams (Tony Palmer, Isolde Films, 2007). TPDVD 106

The Passions of Vaughan Williams (John Bridcut, Crux Productions, 2018). CRUXGZ001

Riders to the Sea (Louis Lentin, Warner, 2008). 50 51442 978421

d. Website

The Ralph Vaughan Williams Society (https//:www.rvwsociety.com)

10. Sir William Walton (1902–83)

We have suggested that the foundations of the English musical renaissance were laid by Parry and Stanford, and built upon initially by Elgar, Vaughan Williams and Holst. Others then lent weight to this enterprise in various ways – some reinforcing what the pioneers had done by using language similar to, or at least not too far removed from theirs (we may mention Bax, Ireland, Bridge, Finzi, Hadley, Milford, Moeran, and Rootham), while others regarded these developments as a liberating force that legitimised the composer's pursuit of his or her personal goals. Having been released from the shackles of German romanticism, it would have been pointless to have fallen under the influence of a home-grown tyranny. Thus, once the renaissance had taken root, some composers wasted little time in forging new paths in neo-classicism (Berkeley, Cook, Rawsthorne) or atonalism (Lutyens), ironically taking their cue from recent developments on the continent rather than in England. Even many of the more traditional tonalists – Arnold, Lambert and Warlock, for instance – showed little interest in Tudor polyphony and/ or folksong which had been dear to the hearts of Vaughan Williams and Holst.

Out of this ferment in the early decades of the twentieth century, William Walton is often considered to be the bridge between the pioneers of the English musical renaissance and Benjamin Britten whose senior he was by eleven years. When Walton burst onto the scene in the early twenties with *Façade*, he was deemed an *enfant terrible*; by the end of the Second World War he was being dismissed as passé, and Britten had replaced him as the blue-eyed boy of English music.

Walton was born in Oldham (a town he vowed never to return to once he had escaped from it – although he did, very briefly) on 29th March 1902. Music was in the family, his father being a music teacher who had trained under Charles Hallé at the Royal Manchester College of Music, while his mother had been a professional singer prior to her marriage. From quite an early age he sang in his father's choir and proved to have a good voice. Exposure to the standard choral repertoire of the day – by Handel, Haydn, Mendelssohn and others – provided a decent grounding for what was to come. Piano and violin lessons were attempted, but Walton lacked the application to progress very far – a problem with which he was afflicted throughout his life. However, he does seem to have been blessed with a lucky star, situations turning up fortuitously just at the right moment. In 1912 his father spotted quite by chance a newspaper advertisement for choirboys at Christ Church Cathedral School, Oxford. Walton and his mother duly made the journey down, although they arrived late for the audition because they found at the last minute that his father had spent the money for the train fare in his local pub, and the money had to be borrowed from a friendly greengrocer. By the time they arrived the auditions were over, but in consideration of the distance they had travelled, the relevant authorities relented and heard Walton sing. The upshot was that he was accepted and remained at the choir school for the next six years. During this time he began to try his hand at composition, and a surviving part-song, *Litany* ("Drop, drop, slow tears"), written when he was fifteen years old, gives an indication of his true potential. Writing of a performance of the piece in 1970, the critic William Mann wrote:

> The technical fluency of the choral writing is explicable though still remarkable; the creative boldness and poetic feeling of the music are much more astounding. It is a real piece of music, no student exercise, and 55 years later it provided a genuine moving experience, even in the company of mature Walton.[111]

At the end of his time at the cathedral school, he enrolled as an undergraduate at the university, at sixteen years of age, being one of

---

111 Quoted in M. Kennedy, *Portrait of Walton* (Oxford: Oxford University Press, 1990), p. 251.

the youngest ever to do so (though probably not the youngest since Henry VIII, as is sometimes claimed). He progressed well enough with his music studies, but found the compulsory Greek and algebra a burden and failed these exams. Unfortunately, since they were required for graduation, he went down from Oxford without a degree. However, his predilection for good fortune prevailed. One of the friends he made at Oxford was Sacheverell Sitwell, sibling of Osbert and Edith. On discovering Walton's plight, he invited him to stay with them in London. As Walton was to recall, he accepted the invitation, intending to stay for a few weeks, but was still in residence fifteen years later. In effect, he became a composer-in-residence. At a stroke, Walton was relieved of any financial worries and was provided with a first-class cultural education. The Sitwells took him on their jaunts around Europe, during which he had the opportunity of meeting prestigious musical personalities including Stravinsky, Schoenberg, Berg and Gershwin. Walton and his hosts stayed at the best hotels when abroad, and ate at the most exclusive restaurants in London. He was moving in high society.

Although Walton was never to be truly prolific as a composer, he was expected, while staying with the Sitwells, to make some contribution. His early efforts were decidedly modernist, including a serialist-inspired string quartet (1919–22), which, while bringing him notoriety, also invited welcome publicity. Given that the Sitwells were writers, it was almost inevitable that they would eventually devise a collaborative project involving their personal composer. This took the form of *Façade* (1923), an "entertainment" in which Walton set a group of experimental poems by Edith Sitwell, scoring the music to be performed, initially, for six players. The verses were written primarily as studies in word-rhythms and onomatopeia[112], and the words are not sung so much as delivered in accentuated speech. The premiere, consisting of eighteen numbers, took place before an invited audience in the privacy of the Sitwells' drawing room, with Edith herself declaiming her poems through

112 See Kennedy's note in *Walton: Façade*, EMI, 5 73998 2, p. 10.

a megaphone fitted to a curtain designed by Frank Dobson. The precocious Walton was still nineteen years of age at the time.

The first public performance took place the following year at the Aeolian Hall, by which time the number of items had increased to twenty-four. The critics were present and made some cutting remarks about the whole enterprise. "Drivel They Paid to Hear" was the heading of one column. However, the intrepid Sitwells persisted, no doubt pleased with the notoriety they were attracting, and put on a further performance in Chelsea in 1926. Other reciters (including Walton's fellow composer Constant Lambert) were added, and the number of items reached twenty-eight. From this point the piece became a success, having apparently caught the mood of the "roaring twenties". It was taken to the ISCM festival in Siena, now reduced to twenty-two items, when Lambert was reciter-in-chief. The flexibility of the work enabled Walton to tinker with it for the rest of his life, adding and subtracting items at will, although the most popular numbers, such as *Black Mrs. Behemoth, Popular Song* and *Old Sir Faulk,* were ever-present. Twenty-one items were used in Sir Neville Marriner's 1972 recording with his Academy of St. Martin-in-the-Fields. A further innovation was introduced in 1926 when Walton arranged six of the items for orchestra alone (Suite No. 1), followed in 1938 by a second suite.

Walton's first purely orchestral work, from 1925, was the lively overture *Portsmouth Point,* inspired by a painting of the Portsmouth quayside, filled with broiling activity, by Thomas Rowlandson (1756–1827), and dedicated to the poet Siegfried Sassoon (1888–1965) who Walton had befriended at Oxford. Next came the short orchestral impression, *Siesta* (1926), a reminiscence, perhaps, of his earlier excursions to Italy. It was dedicated to Stephen Tennant, another friend from his Oxford days who, according to Michael Kennedy[113], was the model for the dissolute Sebastian Flyte in Evelyn Waugh's novel *Brideshead Revisited.* When asked about the piece in old age, Walton admitted that he had forgotten ever having

113 Kennedy, liner notes, *Walton Symphonies*, Hyperion, CDA 67794, p. 5.

written it. The brilliant *Sinfonia Concertante* for piano and orchestra was written in 1928. But none of these works really prepared the public for the sudden outburst of creativity on a large scale which took place between 1929–35.

The first of these substantial pieces, the Viola Concerto, was written in 1929, at a time when Walton was embarking on a series of high-profile love affairs, and his liaison with Imma von Doernberg, the widow of a German baron, seems to have found its way into this piece. For a first concerto, with only a few short orchestral pieces to his credit, his judgement of balance between viola and orchestra was most impressive. Christopher Palmer later commented:

> The violin is a multi-faceted personality; it can always ride on top of the orchestra. The luscious *cantabile* and expressive power of the cello can command attention at most times. But the viola is more of an introvert, a poet-philosopher, conspicuously lacking in brilliance of tone and ever liable to be blotted out by an unheeding orchestra. Yet in Walton's concerto we are never aware of any of these limitations.[114]

Regardless of its technical brilliance, however, it also sounded conspicuously modernist for the time it was written. Echoes of Brahms and Elgar there may be, but even more of Prokofiev, who Walton is known to have admired. Elgar himself heard an early performance but was unimpressed, marvelling how such music could possibly have been thought fit for a stringed instrument. More hurtful to Walton, however, was its out-of-hand rejection by the work's intended performer, Lionel Tertis, then the pre-eminent viola soloist. As it turned out, a more than capable substitute was engaged for the premiere, namely Paul Hindemith (1895–1963).[115] The score was dedicated to Christabel McLaren (later Lady

114 C. Palmer, liner notes, *Walton: Viola Concerto*, EMI, 7 49628 2, p. 3

115 It was not long, however, before Tertis changed his mind about Walton's concerto and decided to include it in his repertoire. There is a reference to his performing it with Ernest Ansermet as early as March 1931.

Aberconwy), Walton's latest girlfriend, who must have been vying with Imma von Doernberg for his attentions at the time.

The second major work of the period, *Belshazzar's Feast*, was first performed at the Leeds Festival under Malcolm Sargent in October 1931. It had been commissioned by the BBC with the stipulation that the forces should be limited to an orchestra not exceeding fifteen players, a small chorus and soloist. As work progressed – slowly – it soon became evident that these would be vastly exceeded. At one point, the Director of the Leeds Festival, Thomas Beecham, remarked to Walton, "As you'll never hear the thing again, my boy, why not throw in a couple of brass bands?" He took up the suggestion by adding two brass choirs, each consisting of three trumpets, three trombones and tuba. The work as it turned out was no longer suitable for the BBC commission, nor did a promised substitute in lieu ever materialise. Much of the work took shape in Amalfi, Italy, in 1930, where Walton was wintering with the Sitwells, and from where he extended his visit to include a spell in Switzerland with his lady of the moment, Baroness von Doernberg – somewhat to the Sitwells's displeasure.

Ostensibly billed as an oratorio, based largely on Daniel 5, but topped and tailed by passages from Isaiah, Psalms 137 and 81, with the addition of Revelation 18 to describe the fall of Babylon from its former glory – all selected by Osbert Sitwell (Walton admitted that he was unfamiliar with the biblical account) – the work was unlike anything that had emanated from the pen of a British composer. There was certainly nothing conventionally religious about it, and the organisers of the Three Choirs Festival banned the work from being performed in their respective cathedrals (Gloucester, Worcester and Hereford) until 1957, on the grounds that its secular interpretation of the biblical texts made it unsuitable for performance there. Despite this, it made a huge impact at the Leeds Festival in 1931, and was considered to be the most groundbreaking work heard there since Vaughan Williams's *Sea Symphony*, or even Elgar's *The Dream of Gerontius*. For originality, it certainly sat comfortably with these works.

Much of its success is due to its dramatic impact, and to the orchestral colour which paints so vividly the details provided by the texts (note, for instance, the use of the anvil to underscore the words "Praise ye the god of iron"). The baritone soloist (bass-baritone is especially effective) is given a declamatory role, appearing at intervals to mark out the contours of the narrative, while the chorus fills in the mood and emotional content, lamenting and rejoicing in equal measure. There is certainly no danger of nodding off during this work. Even if it is disliked (and it is not to everyone's taste), it demands attention. If Walton had not been noticed previously, he certainly was now.

In his book on Walton, Michael Kennedy[116] draws attention to the remarkable fact that *Belshazzar's Feast* was his first attempt at a choral work of any kind since he wrote *Litany* as a fifteen-year-old at Christ Church Cathedral School, and here the complexity of the choral writing far surpasses that of the earlier work. It is true that his musical upbringing in Oldham was full of brass bands and choirs, but hearing them was a far cry from composing for them. The impression received from hearing *Belshazzar's Feast* is that he had been doing it all his life.

At one point, Walton seems to have suffered a bout of composer's block which lasted for some months. He tells us that (for some odd reason) he got stuck on the word "gold" ("Praise ye the god of gold", presumably). Whether or not this had anything to do with the vagaries of his tangled love-affairs, it is impossible for us to say. What can be said is that he was a painstaking, meticulous composer for whom getting stuck was all part and parcel of the process. It happened during the composition of the Second Symphony (1956–60), and again, famously, in the case of his First Symphony (1932–35) to the extent that he was persuaded to allow a performance of the first three movements while the finale was still at the drawing board stage.

The Symphony No. 1 was commissioned in 1932 by Sir Hamilton Harty, then the conductor of the Hallé Orchestra. Harty

116 Kennedy, *Portrait of Walton*, p. 60.

seems to have been somewhat luckless in the matter of commissions – his request in 1924 for a symphony from E.J. Moeran did not bear fruit until 1937. He did not have to wait so long for Walton's effort, but he did have to do his share of chivying. For much of the gestation period, Walton was living in Switzerland with Baroness von Doernberg, and after one deadline had passed and another began to loom, Harty wrote despairingly to Hubert Foss at Oxford University Press: "Why don't you go over to Switzerland and wrest poor W. W.'s Baroness away from him so that he can stop making overtures to her and do a symphony for me instead?" As a matter of fact, there was a more pecuniary reason for the delay: in the summer of 1934 Walton was engaged in writing a film score – his first – for *Escape Me Never*, for which keeping to the deadline was essential for his pocket.

The symphony dragged on throughout 1934, but there were issues other than the film score which impeded progress. It was in this year that Walton's six-year relationship with Baroness von Doernberg came to an acrimonious end when she found another lover, and within months another woman had entered his life, namely Lady Alice Wimborne (1880–1948) whose husband, Lord Wimborne, was fabulously rich. This new relationship was a strange one, since Alice's husband, who was aware of what was happening, seems to have been remarkably cordial towards Walton, as were other members of the Wimborne family. Walton was also twenty-two years Alice's junior. Despite this new woman in his life, his split with Imma Doernberg had been a terrible wrench, and he was frequently ill throughout this period. None of this did anything for the progress of the symphony, but at last Walton reached the stage of having completed the first three movements in full score. A decision was then made, with his approval, to perform these movements as they stood, which duly occurred in December 1934, Harty conducting the LSO. To some extent, this was a risky enterprise, since the slow, dreamy third movement, coming after the nervous energy of the first and the whirlwind dynamism of the second must have sounded somewhat anticlimactic to an audience at that time. As things turned out, however, it was well-received.

The finale, which suffered from the same prevarication as the rest of the symphony, was eventually completed in late August 1935, by which time Vaughan Williams's Fourth Symphony had been premiered (10th April 1935). This might have taken the shine off the first performance of Walton's symphony in its complete form (again by Harty, this time with the BBC SO, on 6th November), but it seems not to have done, although the finale did become a bone of contention among critics. Some considered it to have been tagged on as a crowd-pleaser, assuming that it was conceived only after the first three movements had been completed – which was not, in fact, the case. Others, including Walton, considered it to be the best movement of all.

Having dealt with Walton's three major works of the period 1929–35 in some detail, I shall note other highlights of his output more briefly. His next high-profile project was in answer to an official commission to write a coronation march for the coronation of the new king, Edward VIII, although, by the time of its completion, the well-known abdication had occurred in favour of King George VI. Elgar, who would almost certainly have been approached, had died two years previously, and Walton was seen to be the most likely living composer to rise to the occasion, which he did superbly, for the march, *Crown Imperial*, was the equal of any of Elgar's *Pomp & Circumstance* marches. It is no surprise, therefore, that he was the composer of choice for the next coronation, that of Queen Elizabeth II in 1953, for which he composed *Orb & Sceptre*. He mined a passage from Shakespeare's *Henry V*, Act IV, Scene I for these titles and, with typical dry Waltonian wit, promised that his march for the future King Charles III would be the *Bed Majestical*!

In 1939, as war clouds loomed once more, Walton wrote, for Jascha Heifetz, a violin concerto which undoubtedly became the most popular of his three string concertos. It is suffused with Italian light in a manner that would not have been possible with the viola and cello concertos. There are shades of the Elgar concerto here and there; these could hardly have been avoided, given the cult-status of that work, yet still Walton's personal style wins through, and it quickly became acknowledged as one of his finest creations. Certainly, it was eagerly anticipated. For a while, it was the object of a tug-of-war between Heifetz and the British Council who wanted a violin concerto from Walton to be performed at the New York World Fair. Ultimately, he kept faith with Heifetz, trusting that he would like the work enough to add it to his repertoire which, after some reservations, he did. Walton later confided that, regardless of whatever other influences lay behind the concerto, the heart of it was inspired by the new love of his life, Alice Wimborne. Her husband had died that year, which left Walton and Alice free to live as partners, an arrangement which persisted until her own death in 1948.

During the war he was excused active service, but was attached to the Army Film Unit as music advisor, and was expected to compose for propaganda films and films of "national importance" (there was a difference). The best-known of these was *The First of the Few* (1942), starring Leslie Howard[117], about Reginald Mitchell, the designer of the Spitfire. Later, Walton arranged some of the music from the film as a concert work, *Spitfire: Prelude & Fugue*.

From 1941, when Walton's London home was bombed in the Blitz, he spent much of the war based at the home of Alice Wimborne in Ashby St. Ledger's, midway between Northampton and Coventry. For the remainder of the war he was kept busy composing film scores and incidental music. Some of these, such as *Next of Kin* (1941), *The Foreman Went to France* (1942) and

117 The tragic story of Leslie Howard's death in 1943 is related by Michael Kennedy (*Barbirolli: Conductor Laureate* [London: MacGibbon & Lee, 1971], p. 169). On his way home from America to take charge of the Hallé Orchestra (or what remained of it), John Barbirolli found himself stranded in Lisbon, waiting for an air passage to England. He was able to get an earlier flight than anticipated by swapping places with Leslie Howard who had been filming in Portugal and wanted to stay on in Lisbon for a few more days. Barbirolli was therefore able to take the Saturday flight, while Howard took the next plane available, which was shot down by the Germans with the loss of all on board.

Went the Day Well? (1942), are little remembered today, the music more or less dying with the film. Walton's collaborations with John Gielgud and Laurence Olivier, however, fared a good deal better. In 1941 Gielgud invited Walton to provide the score for his production of *Macbeth*. The music was composed for full orchestra and pre-recorded by the RPO under Ernest Irving, after which the recording accompanied the production on tour. It was on the set of *Macbeth* that Walton and Olivier first met. Thus, when the latter undertook to produce a film of *Henry V* in 1943, he had no hesitation in turning to Walton for the film score. The secret of the film's success lay in the extent to which the two men collaborated in marrying the film images with the music, and the famous battle scene at Agincourt is still talked about today. Other numbers, such as the interlude *Touch her soft lips and part*, have found a life of their own.

The success of this collaboration prompted several others. Two of these – film versions of *Romeo & Juliet* and *Macbeth*, for various reasons – largely financial – never came off, but two others, *Hamlet* (1947) and *Richard III* (1955) were completed successfully. Once again, Olivier recognised the importance of the musical score, giving Walton every consideration to spread his wings, as the composer acknowledged. The *Hamlet* score, which, of course, required plenty of heartfelt, tragic music, coincided with the death, after much suffering, of Walton's partner of twelve years, Alice Wimborne, and it is hard not to believe that his grief fed into the music he was writing.

The final film of the Olivier trilogy, *Richard III*, boasted a star-studded cast and, once more, Walton rose to the occasion. The music from all these films remains among Walton's most popular, due largely to the practice, adopted from the outset, of recasting the music in the form of suites which could be enjoyed irrespective of the plays. For this we have to thank, in the first instance, Malcolm Sargent (*Henry V*, 1945) and Muir Mathieson (*Henry V*, 1963; *Richard III*, 1963). Latterly, the late Christopher Palmer (1946–95) produced "scenarios" (music, along with some of the significant speeches) for all three plays, as well as an arrangement of music from Walton's first Shakespeare film score, *As You Like It* (1936). All the film work taken on by Walton throughout the war (there was also incidental music for a radio play, *Christopher Columbus*) left him little time for any "serious" music, but in 1944 he did embark on a new string quartet, reverting to the slow, meticulous method of composition which had come to be associated with all his major works. It finally saw the light of day in 1947. In the year of its completion, he began work on another long-term project, his only full-length opera, *Troilus & Cressida* (1947–54).[118] However, it had to be slotted in between other commitments, and ground to a halt altogether with the death of Alice Wimborne. As fortune would have it, however, Walton's personal life was about to take a welcome upturn. He was asked by the music publisher Leonard Boosey to join a British delegation to a copyright conference to be held in Buenos Aires. Present at the conference was an Argentinian girl, Susana Gil Passo (1926–2010), some twenty-four years Walton's junior, who was working as a secretary for the British Council. According to Walton's account, as soon as he spotted her, he determined to marry her. He proposed almost at once, and although she rebuffed his overtures, he persisted until, three weeks later, they were married in a civil ceremony, much to the displeasure of the girl's father, a lawyer. A month later, she was on her way to Britain to begin a new life with Walton. He dutifully introduced her to his friends and family, which even necessitated a trip to Oldham. When he had been living with the Sitwells, he had developed a taste for wintering in Italy, and now he determined to do the same with his wife. They were able to find rented accommodation on the Isle of Ischia in the Bay of Naples, not far from Amalfi which Walton knew and loved.

The fact that the marriage lasted until Walton's death thirty-five years later bears testimony to the fact that it must have been a tolerably happy one, although his initial ground-rules might

118 He later produced a one-act opera, *The Bear* (1964–67), which was staged by Britten at the Aldeburgh Festival.

have raised a few eyebrows. He insisted on not having children, which must surely have been hard for a twenty-two year-old girl to accept, and when she did become pregnant (owing, probably, to his carelessness) he prevailed on her to have an abortion. He even threatened to divorce her should there be any issue. Most of us would regard such behaviour as wholly unreasonable, and would hardly accept the excuse so often given in such cases that an artist must live for his art.[119]

Once the dust had settled, Walton took up *Troilus & Cressida* once more, just occasionally pausing to fulfil various commissions such as his 1953 Coronation pieces *Orb & Sceptre* and the *Te Deum* for chorus and orchestra. The opera was finished, after much soul-searching, in 1954, but it required a huge number of personnel to stage and the road to the first night was a rocky one. The role of Cressida had been written for Elisabeth Schwarzkopf, but she struggled with it and declined to perform it. Meanwhile, Laurence Olivier who had been earmarked to produce the opera backed out, as did the designer, Henry Moore. Schwarzkopf's replacement, the Hungarian Magda Lásló, struggled to master the English, and to cap it all, the conductor Malcolm Sargent took a doctrinaire approach which endeared him to neither cast nor chorus. For instance, the chorus's plea that he should beat time for them when they were singing unaccompanied fell on deaf ears. He also made cuts to the score and to the instrumentation in places, wherever he felt it appropriate to do so, much to Walton's consternation.

Despite the chaotic build-up to the premiere on 3rd December 1954, the performance passed off reasonably well, but it divided opinion, some regarding it as a grand opera in the true operatic tradition, while others thought it conservative and passé compared to Britten's *Peter Grimes*. *Troilus & Cressida* was certainly given its chance, with numerous performances around the world's opera

119 Kennedy (*Portrait of Walton*, p. 144) comments on Walton's possible motives in greater detail. Whatever they were, they were almost certainly borne out of self-interest. The same attitude can certainly be applied to Delius, and probably to Gurney as well.

houses within the first few years, but it has never really established itself in the repertoire long-term.

In 1956 Walton and his wife moved permanently to Ischia, having had a house built to his personal specifications. The hillside site commanded a gorgeous sea-view prospect, and an adjacent abandoned quarry was slowly transformed by Susana Walton into a magnificent garden. As he grew older and less inclined to travel, he invited old friends like Malcolm Arnold and Julian Bream (for whom he wrote *Five Bagatelles* for guitar [1970–71]) and many others, somewhat like a king holding court. One of the firstfruits of this move was the completion of his third and final concertante work, the Cello Concerto, written for Gregor Piatigorsky. Stylistically, it is no real advance on his previous concertos, and some critics said as much, but this in itself does not make it a poor concerto, and it has entered the repertoire and received several fine recordings.[120]

Throughout the 1960s, Walton continued to compose from his hillside retreat in Ischia. Never one of the more prolific composers, he was showing signs of slowing down, but every piece he did produce was worthwhile. There were two studies of themes by other composers: *Variations on a Theme by Hindemith* (1963), and *Impressions on an Impromptu of Benjamin Britten* (1969) – a long-standing friend. There were also two last film scores – for *Battle of Britain*, and *Three Sisters*, after the Chekov play, directed by Olivier. The first of these was a source of rancour between composer and film company. The company, United Artists, turned down Walton's score and turned to John Barry who declined. In the end, the new score was written by Ron Goodwin. Walton, naturally, was aggrieved, as was Laurence Olivier who was starring in the film and threatened to have his name withdrawn from the credits in protest. Eventually, United Artists relented to the extent of retaining Walton's music for

120 By Robert Cohen (London 443-450 2); Tim Hugh (Naxos 8.554325); Steven Isserlis (Hyperion CDA 68077); Yo-Yo Ma (Sony); Gregor Piatigorsky (RCA Victor 09026-61498-2); Janos Starker (RCA Victor 09026-61695-2); Paul Tortelier (EMI 5 73371 2); Raphael Wallfisch (Chandos CHAN 8959), among a number of others.

the sequence *Battle in the Air*. The remainder of Walton's score had to wait for a commercial recording before it could be heard.[121]

The pre-eminent work of the sixties was the Second Symphony. Although the outer two of its three movements contain some of the nervous energy found in the scherzo of the First Symphony, it is over all a slighter, less monumental work, and critical reaction to it was generally muted. One wonders if this would have been the case had this work been written without the First Symphony to afford a comparison. Michael Kennedy suggests that it might better have been called a sinfonietta, which could have allayed some of the negative comment, but, in any case, it is the quality of the music which is important rather than the title given to it. Here, Walton demonstrates that he is still capable of turning out a well-composed work for orchestra extending over just under half-an-hour. Indeed, his technique, if anything, is more finely-honed than in the First Symphony. It was, after all, completed twenty-five years later.

Discussion of the Second Symphony prompts me at this point to mention Walton's aborted Symphony No. 3. After hearing André Previn conduct in London, he offered to write a symphony for him. It must have been in a moment of rare – and perhaps rash – optimism, for the older Walton became, the harder he found it to compose. In the following eight years, he managed just one page of score, which he sent to Previn, who is supposed to have framed it. Perhaps he realised by then that it was the nearest he was likely to come to ever hearing the symphony! In the last few years of his life, Walton was often in poor health, and was taken into intensive care on more than one occasion. Nothing more was heard of the work.

The sixties was a decade of mixed fortunes for Walton personally. On the credit side he was awarded the Order of Merit to go with the knighthood he had received as early as 1951. Of British composers, only Elgar, Vaughan Williams and Britten had previously been so honoured. On the other hand, as just noted, there were times when

121 The *Battle of Britain Suite* is available along with some of Walton's other film music (including *Escape Me Never* and *The Three Sisters*) on Chandos CHAN 8870.

he was seriously unwell. As early as 1937 he underwent a hernia operation; another operation followed in 1954; three years later he was involved in a car accident in Rome and spent three months in hospital recovering from a broken hip. More serious than all these, however, was the discovery in 1966 that he was suffering from lung cancer (he had been a heavy pipe smoker throughout his adult life). The fate of Alice Wimborne, who had died from lung cancer, must have been preying on his mind at this time. He underwent an aggressive course of radiotherapy which, happily, did the trick. Wisely, he gave up smoking for good.

Walton's seventieth birthday year was marked by all kinds of celebrations, the centrepiece of which was on the day itself when the Prime Minister of the day, Edward Heath, himself an amateur musician who had been known to wield the baton, hosted a reception for him at No. 10 Downing Street. Guests ranged from the Queen and the Queen Mother, through the composers Malcolm Arnold, Arthur Bliss, Benjamin Britten and Herbert Howells (who had composed *A Grace* for the occasion), and, from the literary world, his old friend Laurence Olivier, to Walton's brother Alan. Anyone would have thought he was not expected to reach his eightieth birthday! In fact, he did – just. He died at his home in Ischia, and was cremated. His ashes were interred, according to his wishes, above the garden that his wife had so lovingly created over many years, and a memorial service was held at Westminster Abbey during which a memorial stone was unveiled, fittingly adjacent to those of Elgar, Vaughan Williams and Britten.

In the history of English music, Walton is in many ways a one-off. As commentators have noted, he hailed from unpretentious Oldham, yet ended up at Oxford University, via Christ Church Cathedral School, not because he was academically gifted, but because he could sing. He went down from Oxford without a degree, not because he was lacking musically (we have only to hear *Litany*), but because he had no enthusiasm for Greek and algebra. Yet honours were heaped upon him in later life in recognition of his achievements as a composer. He could conduct after a fashion –

generally his own music – but could play no instrument to concert performance standard. He wrote no books or learned papers, held no academic posts, and had no pupils – not even on a private basis. His sole business was composition, and about that he was as single-minded as Delius. He had an instinct for spotting those who could help him progress and cultivated their friendship, yet he was not above forsaking them once they had outlived their purpose. He was self-deprecating and could accept the criticism of others better than most, but he was grieved if he felt that his talents were not being sufficiently appreciated. There can be little doubt that in his final years his composers' block, which occasionally obtruded even in his prime, became terminal. He was writing effectively into his sixties, but in the public estimation, his reputation as one of Britain's top five composers rests heavily on that rash of key works written within a few years either side of 1930 – the Viola Concerto, *Belshazzar's Feast* and the Symphony No. 1 – and, we might add, the Violin Concerto of 1939. Had Walton composed these alone, his standing as a composer of the highest order would be assured.

a. Bibliography

Burton, Humphrey, et al., eds., *William Walton – The Romantic Loner: A Centenary Portrait* (Oxford: Oxford University Press, 2002)

Howes, Frank, *The Music of William Walton* (Oxford: Oxford University Press, 2nd edn, 1973)

Kennedy, Michael, *Portrait of Walton* (Oxford: Oxford University Press, 1990)

Lloyd, Stephen, *William Walton: Muse of Fire* (Woodbridge, Suffolk: Boydell Press, 2002)

Ottoway, Hugh, *William Walton* (Sevenoaks: Novello, 1972)

Tierney, Neil, *Sir William Walton* (London: Robert Hale, 1984)

Walton, Susana, *William Walton: Behind the Façade* (Oxford: Oxford University Press, 1989)

b. Select Discography

i) Symphonies

Symphony No. 1	Philharmonia O., Walton	EMI	5 65004 2
Symphony No. 2	English Northern Phil., Daniel	Naxos	8.553402

ii) Concertos

Violin Concerto	LSO, Walton; Menuhin (violin)	EMI	5 65005 2
Viola Concerto	LPO, Walton; Menuhin (viola)	EMI	5 65005 2
Cello Concerto	Bournemouth SO, Litton; Cohen (cello)	Decca	443 450-2

iii) Orchestral

Partita for Orchestra	Philharmonia O., Walton	EMI	5 65005 2
Overture: Scapino	LSO, Prévin	EMI	7 64723 2
Overture: Portsmouth Point	LSO, Prévin	EMI	7 64723 2
March: Orb & Sceptre	CBSO, Frémaux	EMI	7 64201 2
March: Crown Imperial	CBSO, Frémaux	EMI	7 64201 2
Façade: Suites for Orchestra	CBSO, Frémaux	EMI	7 64201 2
Spitfire: Prelude & Fugue	Philharmonia O., Walton	EMI	5 65007 2

iv) Film Music

Richard III, etc.	Acad. of St. Martin-in-the-Fields, Marriner; Gielgud (narr.)	Chan.	CHAN 8841
Hamlet: A Shakespearian Scenario, etc.	Acad. of St. Martin-in-the-Fields; Marriner; Gielgud (narr.)	Chan.	CHAN 8842
Battle of Britain, etc.	Acad. of St. Martin-in-the-Fields; Marriner	Chan.	CHAN 8870
Henry V, etc.	Orch. & Choir of St. Martin-in-the-Fields, Marriner; Plummer (narr.)	Chan.	CHAN 8892

v) Choral/ Vocal with Orchestra

Belshazzar's Feast	Philharmonia O. & Chorus; Walton Bell (bar)	EMI	5 65004 2
Façade	Acad. of St. Martin-in-the-Fields, Fielding and Flanders (narrs.). Marriner	EMI	5 73998 2
Gloria	CBSO & Chorus, soloists; Frémaux	EMI	7 64201 2
Te Deum	CBSO & Chorus, Choristers of Worcester Cath.; Grier (organ); Frémaux	EMI	7 64201 2

vi) Chamber

Piano Quartet	Maggini Quartet; Donohoe (piano)	Naxos	8.554646
String Quartet	Maggini Quartet	Naxos	8.554646
Violin Sonata	Thorsen (violin); Brown (piano)	Hyper.	CDA 67340

vii) Choral

Coronation Te Deum	Choir of St. John's Coll., Camb., Robinson	Naxos	8.555793
Jubilate Deo	Choir of St, John's Coll., Camb., Robinson	Naxos	8.555793

Drop, Drop, Slow Tears	Choir of St. John's Coll., Camb., Robinson	Naxos	8.555793
Where does the uttered music go?	Choir of St. John's Coll., Camb., Robinson	Naxos	8.555793
Set me as a seal upon thine heart	Choir of St. John's Coll., Camb., Robinson	Naxos	8.555793

c. DVDs

At the Haunted End of the Day: William Walton (Tony Palmer, Isolde Films, 2008). TPDVD 113

Partita for Orchestra (Boston SO, Barbirolli, 1959). VAI 4304

d. Website

The William Walton Trust (www.waltontrust.org)

The Best of the Rest

1. William Alwyn (1905–85)

William Alwyn was a creative artist to the point of compulsion. For him, life was little else but the expression of beauty, and he availed himself of every artistic medium available to him in order to achieve this aim. He was firmly of the view that whereas some things could be expressed in music, others could be communicated only in words, and yet others only in some form of visual art. Thus, he found the means to express himself in bold, colourful oil paintings (as is evident from the covers of the liner notes provided for the series of Chandos recordings), and his ideas concerning beauty are translated into words in his epic poem *Daphne, or the Pursuit of Beauty*. Other literary works include a journal, entitled *Ariel to Miranda*, which contains some valuable insights into his working methods at the time of his composition of the Third Symphony, and there is even a novel, *All Things Corruptible*. Alwyn sums up his thoughts on the role of art in *Daphne*:

> … I burn with the longing
> for self-justification, with the urge to express
> in words all that finds expression in my art,
> give substance to my thoughts, clarify objectives,
> seek conviction, search for consolation,
> track down beauty, if beauty is the end-all
> of my chase.[122]

---

122 Alwyn, *Daphne* (Southwold: Southwold Press), p. 1; cited in Adrian Wright, *The Life and Work of William Alwyn* (Woodbridge, Suffolk: Boydell Press, 2008), p. 216.

Not bad for someone who began his education at the local council school at the age of five, and was caned by the headmaster for being late on his first day. True, his painting and literature have long-since been forgotten, but his music has endured. He was, in his day, undoubtedly the complete artist.

William Alwyn Smith first saw the light of day in Northampton on 7th November 1905. His father was a grocer with an insatiable appetite for literature, especially that of the Bard – an interest that clearly rubbed off on young William. Yet there was little music in the family, apart from the suggestion that his mother, Ada, could play the piano to some extent. Alwyn's exposure to music derived largely from two sources: the hymns he sang in Sunday School, and the brass bands he heard in the local park. His father was perceptive enough to recognise his son's passion for music and bought him a rudimentary piccolo, while his mother arranged for him to have lessons with a local cobbler. Thus, it was in these early years that the course of his life was set. His father might have hoped that his son would follow him into the grocery business, but was astute enough not to stand in the way of his personal ambitions.

The next stage of his education took place at the local grammar school, and by 1920, still two months shy of his fifteenth birthday, he enrolled at the RAM, commuting there for twice-weekly lessons. By this time, he had progressed from piccolo to the flute, which formed the backbone of his studies, with piano and harmony as the other components of his course. But Alwyn also wanted to compose, a desire that was accommodated at the RAM by John Blackwell McEwan (1868–1948). Thus, he was developing on several fronts at once. He carried off several prizes during his period of study, but when the time came for him to leave the college, he was practical enough to realise that his first obligation was to pay his way. McEwan, while supportive of his student's ambitions, had pointed out that most professional composers were those who had access to private incomes – Bax, Lord Berners, Vaughan Williams – and Alwyn, the grocer's son, was not in that company. So, flute in hand, he found work wherever he could as a jobbing musician – first in the pit of the Carlton Theatre in London, and then with the local band in Broadstairs – just to keep body and soul together.

Such was Alwyn's life until 1927 which turned out to be a red-letter year for him. His reputation as a flautist must have preceded him because one morning he received a letter inviting him to take up the position of third flute with the LSO at that year's Three Choirs Festival in Hereford. Moreover, it was the year in which he scored his first notable success as a composer with his *Five Preludes for Orchestra* at a Henry Wood Promenade concert, alongside Vaughan Williams's *London Symphony*. Then he was invited to take up the position of Professor of Flute at his old *alma mater*, the RAM, at the remarkably tender age of twenty-one. To cap everything, on New Year's Day 1928, Alwyn was married to his fiancée Olive Pull. It had been a momentous year.

From this point Alwyn's compositional career really started to take off, and he began to attempt works on a larger canvas, including the Piano Concerto No. 1 of 1930. He wrote in every conceivable medium – from piano solos, songs, chamber music, film and radio music, through to symphonies and opera. Despite his impressive output, however, he was, like many leading composers, ruthlessly self-critical. His early series of thirteen string quartets (1920-36) he later rejected from his catalogue as unsatisfactory, deeming his quartet of 1953 to be his first successful work in the genre and labelling it No. 1. Two others were to follow. Thanks to a Somm Records release of the final four of these "failures" (SOMMCD 0165) and a Lyrita release of Nos. 6–9 inclusive (SRCD 366), listeners now have the opportunity to judge for themselves whether or not Alwyn was being fair to himself in this regard. Similarly, although he drafted some symphonic sketches, possibly while still in his teens, he later declared that he did not feel competent enough to tackle the symphonic form until middle-life. When, eventually, the First Symphony came (1949), it was apparently conceived as the genesis of a more extensive project in which No. 1 was intended as a symphony within a symphony, as Alwyn explains:

> I started work on a long-cherished scheme, grandiose in scale, but a project that I hoped might constitute a major contribution to the development of the symphony. I planned four symphonies as a sequence – No. 1 was the exposition; No. 2 was the slow movement; No. 3 a march-scherzo with coda; No. 4 the epilogue. You will find the thematic material for all four in No. 1. But essentially each work had to be a satisfactory entity in itself.[123]

I am not aware that all four symphonies were ever performed in sequence as intended, but as both Lyrita and Chandos recorded the full cycle some years ago, the avid listener can judge for him/herself the effectiveness of this enterprise. The first four symphonies were composed between 1949–59, while the stand-alone single movement fifth, *Hydriotaphia*, was added in 1973.

As we have seen, Alwyn had many strings to his bow, one of the most significant being his involvement with the film industry which provided him with a valuable source of income. Between the years 1937–63 he produced scores for over one hundred documentaries (including such pragmatic subjects as *Your Children's Teeth*) and some seventy feature films. Alwyn, expended the same professional care on these as he did on his "serious" music. Among the scores generally accredited to be among his best are those for *The History of Mr. Polly* (once described as "the finest film score ever written"), *The Winslow Boy, Odd Man Out, Desert Victory* and *The Ship that Died of Shame*. In addition, there were scores for radio and television. Professionally, this work offered a different kind of musical challenge to his classical scores, one in which firm discipline and punctuality was required, and in which one had to work to a budget under the instruction of the film director. The composer, therefore, needed to be quick-witted and pragmatic. The fact that Alwyn wrote so much film music suggests that his work in this genre was widely appreciated.

---

123 Quoted in Mary Alwyn's liner notes to the Chandos recording of Alwyn's Symphony No. 1 (CHAN 9155).

The beginning of the 1960s saw a turning-point in Alwyn's life, both maritally and geographically. One of Alwyn's students at the RAM during the 1940s was Doreen Mary Carwithen (1922–2003). Before long, there had grown an "understanding" between them, and by 1947 they were secret lovers. It was not until 1961, however, that they eloped to Suffolk, and a further thirteen years before his wife Olive granted him a divorce. He and Doreen were married the following year and she became Mrs. Mary Alwyn. The village to which they fled in 1961 was Blythburgh, and initially they had to find accommodation where they could, but in 1964 they moved into a purpose-built house with imposing views across the Suffolk levels. The move did not bring the couple unadulterated happiness, however. No sooner had Alwyn settled into his new home than he suffered a nervous breakdown (possibly incurred by his marital tensions), the effects of which lasted some two years. Although he found it difficult to compose at this time, he obtained a degree of relief through drawing and painting. For the remainder of his life he was susceptible to moods of black depression, and in the early eighties also suffered a serious stroke and the onset of myeloma (bone cancer). The cancer spread to his brain (the cause of his father's death) and to his lungs which was given as the cause of death.

The story of Alwyn's final years is a sad one. Although he lived little more than ten miles away from Benjamin Britten's home in Aldeburgh, he seems to have been shunned by the Britten "set" as well as by the "Establishment" (he was eventually awarded a CBE, thanks to the petitions of fellow composers such as Elizabeth Lutyens), and there is little doubt that he felt these sleights keenly. There were no more symphonies after 1973, and his association with the film industry ended in the 1960s. He did, however, embark on some new ventures, including a number of finely-wrought song-cycles and two full operas (*Miss Julie* and *Juan, or the Libertine* – neither of which was performed in his lifetime); and there was a final string quartet (1984) which Alwyn considered to be among his best works, and which he *did* hear a few months before his death.

Alwyn's feeling of neglect may possibly have been exaggerated, as is to be expected from one suffering chronic depression, but it is no doubt true to say that, by the time he died, he was already in the process of being forgotten as a leading composer of his day. It is a fate which is, unfortunately, all too frequently shared by those considered in the pages of this book.

a. Bibliography

Alwyn, William, *Composing in Words: William Alwyn and His Art* (London: Toccata Press, 2009)

Alwyn, William, *Daphne, or the Pursuit of Beauty* (Southwold: Southwold Press, 1972)

Culot, Hubert, "William Alwyn: A Memorial Tribute", *British Music Society Journal*, 7 (1985), pp. 17–29

----------, "William Alwyn at 100", *British Music Society Journal*, 27 (2005)

Johnson, Ian, "Music in the Shadows: A Tribute to Film Composer William Alwyn", *British Music Society Journal*, 38/2 (2016)

Johnson, Ian, *William Alwyn: The Art of Film Music* (Woodbridge, Suffolk: Boydell Press, 2006)

Wright, Adrian, *The Innumerable Dance: The Life and Work of William Alwyn* (Woodbridge, Suffolk: Boydell Press, 2008)

b. Selected Discography

i) Symphonies

Symphonies Nos. 1 & 4	LPO, Alwyn	Lyrita	SRCD 227
Symphonies Nos. 2, 3, 5	LPO, Alwyn	Lyrita	SRCD 228

These symphonies have also been recorded by Richard Hickox with the LSO on the Chandos label, and David Lloyd-Jones with the RLPO on Naxos.

ii) Concertos

Piano Concerto No. 1	LSO, Hickox; Shelley (piano)	Chandos	CHAN 9935
Piano Concerto No. 2	LSO, Hickox; Shelley (piano)	Chandos	CHAN 9935
Violin Concerto	RLPO, Lloyd-Jones McAslan (violin)	Naxos	8.570705

Lyra Angelica	City of London Sinfonia, Hickox; Masters (harp)	Chandos	CHAN 9065
Oboe Concerto	City of London Sinfonia, Hickox; Daniel (oboe)	Chandos	CHAN 8866

iii) **Orchestral**

Autumn Legend	City of London Sinfonia; Hickox; Daniel (cor anglais)	Chandos	CHAN 9065
Pastoral Fantasia	City of London Sinfonia, Hickox; Tees (viola)	Chandos	CHAN 9065
Tragic Interlude	City of London Sinfonia, Hickox	Chandos	CHAN 9065
Elizabethan Dances	LSO, Hickox	Chandos	CHAN 9935

iv) **Chamber**

String Quartet No. 1	Quartet of London	Chandos	CHAN 9219
String Quartet No. 2	Quartet of London	Chandos	CHAN 9219
Clarinet Sonata	Plane (clar.); Rahman (piano)	Naxos	8.572425
Oboe Sonata	Francis (oboe); Rahman (piano)	Naxos	8.572425

c. Website

The William Alwyn Website (www.williamalwyn.co.uk)

2. Richard Arnell (1917–2009)

The photographs depicting Richard Arnell in the early stages of his career might suggest that he was little different from any other young professional at that time. Clean-shaven, clean-cut, wearing a smart but plain suit and tie, he might easily be passed off as a bank manager, an estate agent, or a salesman. There is no visible sign of manic instability as with, say, Ivor Gurney, or quirkiness as with Peter Warlock. There is nothing to suggest anything other than a cool, debonair individual who just happened to make music his choice of career. Even his social life – what little is known of it – seems to have been perfectly regular, with the odd exception that he ran through wives like a knife through butter (he was married eight times). But what has that to do with composition?

Like many an aspiring artist he was born in London to well-to-do parents who, like many parents of aspiring artists, strongly disapproved of his choice of career. However, Arnell fought against such opposition and secured a place at the RCM where, over a four-year period (1935–39), he studied composition with John Ireland and piano with St. John Dykes. He proved to be a more than capable student and won the Farrer Prize for composition during his final year at the college. In 1939, while attending the New York World Fair, war broke out and Arnell found himself stranded in the USA (along with others, including Britten, Bliss and Stanley Bate), with no immediate hope of return. He had therefore to work as a jobbing musician in New York in order to pay his way, and was soon employed by the BBC North American service. He began to compose copiously in a variety of genres and had the good fortune at this early stage to meet the kind of people who could help his career progress, including film composer Bernard Herrmann (1911–75), the influential music critic and fellow-composer Virgil Thomson, and the conductors Leon Barzin and Sir Thomas Beecham. The latter was to be especially important, since, as he was only a visitor to the States, he would eventually be in the ideal position to carry his endorsement of Arnell's music back to Britain.

Arnell's early compositions were regularly performed in America, since the attitude of the musical establishment there was less stuffy towards new music than in conservative Britain. On his return in 1947, however, he did have one champion in Beecham, and was able to make a respectable living by taking up a teaching post in composition at Trinity College of Music, an association which was to last for the next forty years.

During his time in New York, Arnell had written a quantity of film music – chiefly for documentaries – and a ballet score, *Punch and the Child*, which turned out to be his most popular composition in this form. On his return to England, he wrote three further ballet scores: *Harlequin in April* (1951), *The Great Detective* (1953), based on Sherlock Holmes, and *The Angels* (1957).

Like a number of other composers – Shostakovich (1906–75) in Russia, Robert Simpson (1921–97) in England, and Daniel Jones (1912–93) in Wales, for instance – Arnell seems to have considered the symphony and the string quartet to have comprised the backbone of his output. The six numbered symphonies completed by the time of his death were composed between 1943–94. A seventh symphony, *Mandela*, was begun in 1996 but left unfinished. It was realised, completed and recorded on the Dutton label by Martin Yates with the RSNO, along with the rest of Arnell's symphonic output. Apart from these seven, a few other works are of symphonic proportions, including the early *Sinfonia Quasi Variazioni* (1941), and the ballet music for *The Angels* which Arnell himself declared was, in effect, a symphony. Of these, the Symphony No. 3 is now becoming generally recognised as his finest achievement in symphonic form. Martin Yates has written:

> What is so incomprehensible is that we are, in 2005, recording the most important works of his huge output for the first time. Since first looking at the score of the mighty Third Symphony, I have wanted to conduct it; more importantly, I just wanted to hear it. Recording it was a total joy, not only for myself, but for the orchestra and

> everyone involved with it, and to have been part of the event of playing this music for the first time in fifty years has been amazing.[124]

The emergence of the Seventh Symphony is a long story which Yates intriguingly summarises.[125] The piece was begun in 1996 but left incomplete at Arnell's death some thirteen years later. He had entitled it *Mandela* after the South African president, and had even contacted Mandela's office seeking his approval for the dedication, which was given. One might think that this would have provided the necessary impetus to proceed but, for reasons not fully understood, the work lay dormant, and in his final years, Arnell's failing eyesight meant that he was not able to compose at all. He did, however, ask Martin Yates to examine the sketches, which he did, and after the composer's death organised them in such a way as to provide a performing version. Obviously, a good deal of calculated guesswork was required to achieve this and, as Yates concedes, "What it cannot be ... is a symphony exactly as he would have written it". The completion, or "elaboration" of the unfinished works of deceased composers has become almost a cottage industry in recent years. But we shall reserve comment on the pros and cons of this process until later.

As already noted, the cycle of string quartets, written over a period of fifty-five years (1939–94), represents another important string to Arnell's bow, and there are in addition a couple of violin sonatas, a piano trio, quartets for piano and for horn, and quintets for strings and for brass. Other genres, notably solo piano pieces and art-song, seem to have been less important to him. Despite impediments to both sight and hearing in old age, he maintained an interest in musical activities generally, and Martin Yates was in contact with him until just a couple of weeks before Arnell's death at the age of ninety-one. One would like to think that the composer

---

124 Martin Yates, liner notes, Arnell: Symphony No. 3; Dutton, CDLX 7161.

125 Martin Yates, liner notes, Arnell: Symphony No. 7; Dutton, CDLX 7255.

would have approved of Yates's efforts in bringing the *Mandela* symphony to a state of performance. It is a pity that neither Arnell nor Mandela ever heard the fruits of it.

We earlier noted Yates's surprise about the sparsity of important works, including the symphonies, that had been brought to the recording studio prior to the combined enterprise of the Dutton recording company and Yates himself. Certainly, if these works are not disseminated through recordings, they are hardly likely to be made available in the concert hall. During his own lifetime Arnell faired relatively well in receiving performances of his work, especially during his sojourn in America. In his latter years he was more neglected and, like many composers, largely forgotten in the wake of his death. The fault may lie both with his personal circumstances and with his chosen direction in later years. It was his good fortune that he should have reached his musical maturity during his period in the USA (1939–47), where his music was eagerly taken up; but it was also a mixed blessing since, on returning to England after eight years absence, he found that his initial reputation as a promising young composer of the new generation had foundered. Moreover, musical tastes were beginning to change, threatening to leave the tonal idiom of Arnell behind. Sir Thomas Beecham continued manfully to champion his work, but with his death in 1962, Arnell lost his most important British advocate. He also tended to dissipate his own energies in various ways. In the first place, he ensured financial stability by teaching for forty years at the Trinity College of Music which, while gaining him wide respect as a teacher, left him less time to compose than he might otherwise have had. Further, he began to experiment in the field of electronic music which, although no doubt fascinating in itself, was hardly likely to have endeared him to a general public whose interest lay in the traditional repertoire. Still, for those willing to explore, the means of listening to a wide range of Arnell's output is now available, thanks to the Dutton recordings, as well as the postings on YouTube.

a. Bibliography

Dawney, Michael, "Richard Arnell at 75", *British Music Society Journal*, 14 (1992), pp. 3–6

b. Selected Discography

i) Symphonies

No. 1	RSNO, Yates	Dutton	CDLX 7217
No. 2, "Rufus"	RSNO, Yates	Dutton	CDLX 7184
No. 3	RSNO, Yates	Dutton	CDLX 7161
No. 4	RSNO, Yates	Dutton	CDLX 7194
No. 5	RSNO, Yates	Dutton	CDLX 7194
No. 6, "The Anvil"	RSNO, Yates	Dutton	CDLX 7217
No. 7, "Mandela"	RSNO, Yates	Dutton	CDLX 7255

ii) Orchestral

Overture: New Age	RSNO, Yates	Dutton	CDLX 7161
Prelude: Black Mountain	RSNO, Yates	Dutton	CDLX 7239

iii) Chamber

String Quintet	Locrian Ensemble	Dutton	CDLX 7123

3. Malcolm Arnold (1921–2006)

If we wish to understand the nature of Malcolm Arnold's music, we must endeavour to understand the nature of the man himself which, given the contradictions involved, is by no means easy. What can be said at the outset is that in no other English composer is the man more clearly mirrored in his music.

Arnold was born on 21st October 1921 to middle class parents in Northampton (also the birthplace of Alwyn and Rubbra) and, by his own admission, enjoyed a comfortable upbringing with, perhaps, rather more mollycoddling than was good for him. The family was involved in the footwear business, but both parents were musical and their son's talents were spotted at an early age. Despite the existence of four older children, money seems to have been no object, and Malcolm was privately educated, including studies in piano, violin and trumpet. It was this last instrument that caught his imagination. He went up to the RCM in 1938, studying trumpet with the legendary Ernest Hall, while also enrolling on courses in piano and, significantly, composition.

Even at this comparatively early stage, Arnold showed signs of an impulsive and headstrong nature, and was not entirely suited to the discipline of college life. In the end he remained for two years without taking his final examinations, but by then his ability on the trumpet was such that he was able to join the LPO, and in 1943, still only twenty-one years old, he was appointed principal trumpet. He later considered that what he learned about the orchestra as a performing member was more valuable to his compositional technique than any amount of training in theory he received, or could have received, at the RCM, although he always retained the highest respect for Ernest Hall.

Arnold's first spell as a trumpeter was cut short when, in 1944, he felt he should "do his bit" for the war effort by joining the army. For a man of his temperament, however, the discipline was intolerable. Once enrolled, there were no "get-out" clauses, so his course of action was to "accidentally" shoot himself in the foot. It was an action that could have incurred dire consequences, but in the event, he was discharged as medically unfit for service.

During these years, developments had been taking place in his personal life. He had married, in 1941, Sheila Nicholson, and had two children by her, Katherine and Robert (both of whom were to appear in Tony Palmer's documentary film of the composer). He resumed his position as a trumpeter, briefly with the LSO and then back with the LPO, but in 1948, notwithstanding his uneven relations with the college, the RCM awarded him a Mendelssohn Scholarship to study in Italy. When he returned, it was with the determination to become a full-time composer. Arnold's first efforts in this direction date from 1936, when he was still fourteen, and for the next five years he composed solo piano pieces, chamber works and a few songs. However, the first piece about which he felt confident enough to attach an opus number was a Divertimento for Orchestra (op. 1 – now lost). His first surviving orchestral work (op. 3) is a short tone poem, *Larch Trees* (1943), but in the same year he produced his sprightly overture *Beckus the Dandipratt* (op. 5) which received highly favourable reviews, and from that point his career as a composer was assured.

Arnold was astute enough to realise that most forms of composition do not provide a sustainable income, and knew that he would need to write music to commission. The obvious source in this regard was film and television, and he was fortunate enough to get in on the act at the beginning of his career. Indeed, he was soon in constant demand. Between the years 1948–50 alone, he wrote the music for some thirty documentaries on such riveting topics as water supply, oil, cotton and health & safety. Soon, the feature film scores began to appear, including those that were to make him a household name: *The Sound Barrier* (1952), *Hobson's Choice* (1953), *The Belles of St. Trinian's* (1954), *The Inn of the Sixth Happiness* (1958) and, of course, *The Bridge on the River Kwai* (1957).

With the financial security that his work for the film industry brought him, he was able now to turn his attention to weightier matters, writing the symphonic music into which he could pour his heart and soul. The first thing to notice about his symphonies is how disconcerting they can sound. Melting lyricism and serenity can give way to grinding dissonance within a few bars, a tendency that persists throughout his symphonic oeuvre. Slow movements can be permeated by an eerie or unworldly quality (as in Nos. 2 & 6, for instance), or sometimes by a limpid wistfulness, while passages of naked dissonance seem to scream at the listener, almost in an agony of sound. But then again, in stark contrast, there are skittish, light-spirited scherzos. It is difficult not to believe that all this is primarily the expression of Arnold's manic-depressive temperament which became aggravated by alcohol abuse. In later life, particularly following his move from Cornwall to Ireland in 1972, there were suicide attempts and, on his return to Northampton, incarceration in mental hospitals.

There is no doubt that Arnold could be a difficult man to live with. His first marriage ended in divorce, and in 1963 Isobel Gray became his second wife. They had a son, Edward, who was born autistic. But Arnold's demeanour was by no means wholly negative. He was hugely popular with his fellow musicians and cultivated a wide circle of friends. He could be generous to a fault with his money, and spent a good deal of time writing concertos for his musical colleagues – a clarinet concerto for Benny Goodman, a horn concerto for Dennis Brain, a guitar concerto for Julian Bream, a harmonica concerto for Larry Adler, and a flute concerto for his old friend from the RCM, Richard Adeney. There was even a piano concerto for three hands, written for Phyllis Sellick and Cyril Smith who had lost the use of an arm following a stroke, which caused a sensation when it was premiered at the Proms in 1969. These pieces were not generally commissions as such but gifts written with the specific qualities of each soloist in view. Arnold could also be great fun when he was on form, a quality which manifests itself in *A Grand, Grand Overture*, written for another friend, Gerard Hoffnung, and including roles for four vacuum cleaners, a floor polisher and a shotgun.

By 1980 Arnold was a spent force. The only works of any note that he produced in the period 1979–85 was the Trumpet Concerto (1982), the work on film scores having long since been abandoned. He had more or less rejected his wife and children, and in any case his increasingly erratic behaviour was becoming too much for them to handle. He had taken up with a couple, Brian and Sally Charlton, who ran a local pub in Northampton, and lodged with them in their bungalow. In one sense the pub was not the best place for him since his drinking bouts (he was a binge-drinker rather than a hopeless alcoholic) were legendary.[126] However, the Charltons appeared to understand him. They provided for his needs and took him out for meals as well as to musical events, and even on holidays. Within a couple of years, however, Sally Charlton died and Brian remarried a few months later. Brian's new wife, Mary, took to Malcolm, and for a while, arrangements went on as before. Unfortunately, his behaviour became ever more unpredictable and sometimes quite belligerent. He damaged property and on one occasion set fire to his room. After one such episode Brian Charlton could stand it no longer and threw him out onto the street. As he staggered round wondering what to do, he had the good fortune to bump into an acquaintance, and the next phase of his life began.

There is no room here for details[127], but to cut a long story short, various contacts were made which resulted in professional carer Anthony Day taking charge of Malcolm, initially for a trial period of six months. In the event, the partnership lasted for twenty years until the composer's death. At the time that Anthony Day took responsibility for him, the doctor with whom Malcolm was enrolled examined him and told Anthony that, in his view, he was so far-gone that he would not last more than a couple of years. The impression given is that the professional care he received was the main reason for his defying the odds. No doubt this had a good deal

126 He had been known to consume several bottles of wine over lunch, and then crack open a bottle of whisky in the evening.

127 The whole saga is discussed in detail in Anthony Meredith and Paul Harris, *Malcolm Arnold: Rogue Genius* (Norwich: Thames/ Elkin, 2004), chs. 16–17

to do with it, especially Anthony's insistence on barring his charge from alcoholic beverages. Malcolm was given a structured regime into which was built a variety of activities and, most important, a purpose to a life that had lost its way. It was an arrangement that bore immediate creative fruit in the form of the Ninth Symphony (1986), Arnold's most extended work in the genre. It caused some surprise among music critics when it was first performed in 1991 because it stood out stylistically from all his other symphonies. Some ascribed this to the fact that after years of mental illness and alcohol abuse, his technique had deserted him. Certainly, there are only occasional flashes of the orchestral brilliance which made his name. On the other hand, he had just been through five years of "hell", as he put it, and the symphony may have been an attempt to express this period in music. On another level, however, he describes it as "an amalgam of all my knowledge of humanity".[128] The symphony is cast in the traditional four movements, with the extensive finale lasting as long as the others combined. The first is distinctive for its extremely sparse scoring, frequently reduced to just one or two instruments. The second movement consists, almost in its entirety, of an engaging melody repeated sixteen times in various guises, while the third is full of manic high spirits whose mood seems somewhat forced – humour through gritted teeth, perhaps. All this leads to a huge, bleak lento finale which never rises above pianissimo, and is the epitome of despair, even with the D major ending, as the composer himself affirms.

The symphony does not quite mark the end of the composer as a creative artist. Subsequent works include a *Manx Suite* for orchestra, a set of *Welsh Dances*, and concertos for cello and for recorder, as well as a quantity of chamber music, but by 1990 he seems to have fallen silent. He continued to live quietly under the devoted care of Anthony Day at their Norfolk home until his death in 2006 at the age of eighty-four.

128 In interview with Andrew Penny. See Track 5 of the Naxos recording of the Ninth Symphony (8.553540)

Despite the many ills of his later years, Arnold has established a firm place in the pantheon of English twentieth century composers. His nine symphonies form the backbone of his serious music, but he is also remembered for his crowd-pleasing lighter works – the overtures and the dances (especially the two English sets and the Scottish) – and, of course, for his very fine film scores. He was a man of stark contrasts and contradictions, and since these are all reflected in his music, we shall only be able to appreciate the *real* Malcolm Arnold if we are prepared to acknowledge them all.

a. Bibliography

Burton-Page, Piers, *Philharmonic Concerto: The Life and Music of Sir Malcolm Arnold* (Lime Tree, 1994)

Cole, Hugo, *Malcolm Arnold: An Introduction to His Music* (London: Faber Music, 1989)

Culot, Hubert, "Malcolm Arnold at 80", *British Music Society Journal*, 23 (2001), pp. 77–83

Meredith, Anthony and Paul Harris, *Malcolm Arnold – Rogue Genius: The Life and Music of Britain's Most Misunderstood Composer* (London: Thames Publishing, 2004)

b. Selected Discography

i) Symphonies

Nos. 1–6	LSO, Hickox	Chandos	10853(4)X
Nos. 7–9	BBC Philharmonic, Gamba	Chandos	10853(4)X

Other interpretations of Arnold's symphonic cycle, either in part or whole, can be found on the Conifer, Naxos and Lyrita labels.

ii) Concertos

Seventeen Concertos	Various performers	Decca	476 5343

iii) Orchestral

English Dances	LPO, Boult	Decca	468 803-2
Scottish Dances	Philharmonia Orchestra, Irving	HMV	5 72480 2
Overture: Peterloo	CBSO, Arnold	HMV	5 72480 2
Overture: Tam O'Shanter	Philharmonia Orchestra, Arnold	HMV	5 72480 2
A Grand, Grand Overture	RPO, Arnold	HMV	5 72480 2

iv) Chamber

Quintet for Brass	Philip Jones Brass Ensemble, Howarth	Decca	468 803-2
String Quartets Nos. 1 & 2	McCapra Quartet	Chandos	CHAN 9112
Three Shanties	Members of the Nash Ensemble	Helios	CDH55073

c. DVD

Towards the Unknown Region: Malcolm Arnold – A Story of Survival (Tony Palmer, Isolde Films, 2004). TPDVD 112.

d. Website

The Malcolm Arnold Society (www.malcolmarnoldsociety.co.uk)

4. William Baines (1899–1922)

If George Butterworth's death at the age of thirty-one during the Battle of the Somme was considered a tragedy for English music, the case of William Baines might be regarded as an even more extreme example. The first clear signs of Butterworth's maturity date from around 1910 when he was twenty-five years old; Baines, on the other hand, never reached that age. Butterworth's legacy was a handful of finely-wrought song cycles and orchestral miniatures; by the time of his death at the age of just twenty-three, Baines already had over two hundred works to his name. True, most of these were piano miniatures, but there were also a few chamber works and others for full orchestra, including a substantial symphony written at the tender age of eighteen. Butterworth was a restless individual who scoured the country in search of folksongs and morris dances, and, of course, he died in France; Baines rarely stepped outside his native Yorkshire. These are the essential comparisons and contrasts between two aspiring yet short-lived composers. Who was this man, the never-wholly-forgotten musician whose flame was lovingly kept alive like a Yahrzeit candle by family and friends, and later by concert pianists like Eric Parkin?

William Baines was born into a musical family on 26th March 1899 at Horbury, West Yorkshire, a few miles south-west of Wakefield. His father worked as a cinema pianist and also played the organ at the local Methodist chapel. From the first he took charge of William's musical education. For his general education he went to the local elementary school in Horbury, the only formal education he ever had. Soon, it was clear that he was making such progress with his musical studies that some kind of college-based education would be required. Despite financial constraints, William's father was able to find him a place at the Yorkshire Training College of Music in Leeds where studies in counterpoint, harmony and piano technique were placed on a professional footing. It was around this time, at the age of twelve, that Baines made his first rudimentary attempts at composition.

In 1913 Baines's father found a new post as a cinema pianist in Cleckheaton near Bradford, and by 1917 the family was on the move again, this time to York, where father George had found advancement as musical director of the Fossgate Cinema. 91 Albermarle Road was William's home for the remainder of his short life.

In the autumn of 1918 Baines received his call-up papers to be drafted into the army and was dispatched to Blandford, Dorset, for military training. He had never been physically robust, and his sensitive artistic temperament was completely unsuited to army discipline (as was the case with Robin Milford, as we shall discover). The conditions at the camp were atrocious, and within two weeks Baines had contracted sceptic poisoning and was in a life-threatening condition. He might have died there and then had it not been for the help of a local vicar who, in league with William's parents, managed to secure his transfer to a military hospital in York. He hung on and recovered – in the immediate term, at least. However, his military experiences had incurred terminal damage, and for the remainder of his life he was never to weigh more than eight stone, although he was six feet tall. Tuberculosis set in and, for his final years, he was a doomed man.

Baines's chronic health problems largely explain why the vast majority of his compositions from 1919 onwards are individual piano miniatures, or sets made up of short movements. The pieces which represent his maturity and which secured his reputation were all written between 1918–22, and by which the modern listener – thanks to the recordings by Lyrita and Priory Records – can assess the quality of his output. His piano miniatures were influenced to some degree by the French impressionists, but in particular by Scriabin. Comment has been passed about Baines's unusually large hands and long fingers, enabling him to stretch across the octave with ease, and his piano works often have this kind of range in view. Temperamentally, he was a nature painter. There is little evidence that Delius ever heard any of his compositions, but if he had he would surely have approved. The titles Baines gives to his compositions –

Twilight Woods, Thoughtdrift, Glancing Sunlight, Drift-Light, Ebbing-Tide, Tides, and *Poppies Gleaming in the Moonlight* – bear testimony to the moods that he was aiming to express.

We do know something about his specific inspirations, since he kept a diary from the beginning of 1918 to the end of his life (health permitting). This is an interesting social document in itself, since it comments on both the life *and times* of the composer, and is written in somewhat flamboyant language. His sensitivity to his natural surroundings is everywhere to be found. He tells us, for instance, that the piece entitled *Paradise Gardens* (1919) was inspired by the effect of a particularly fine sunset over the gardens outside the Station Hotel in York.[129] We learn, too, that his holidays were taken in and around Bridlington, within reach of Flamborough Head – probably an inspiration for such works as *The Lone Wreck, Goodnight to Flamboro',* and *Labyrinth (A Deep Sea Cave).* Other works were cast in traditional classical form – the *Seven Preludes,* for instance. The story behind this work is that Baines originally composed *six* preludes, but was prevailed upon by his publisher, Elkin, to supply a more forceful conclusion, which he did with gusto!

Although in some respects the fates were against Baines, and his musical career was undoubtedly hampered by his poor state of health (he often had to turn down concert engagements which would have enhanced his reputation as a performer), in all other respects he had some loyal and influential promoters. His parents, of course, were very much behind his early development, as was Albert Jowett, principle of the Yorkshire Training College of Music, who seems to have privately supplemented the fees paid by William's parents when they could no longer afford to pay in full. Two other figures who tirelessly promoted his career were Frederick Dawson and Eaglefield Hull. The former was a Leeds-based concert pianist to whom Baines wrote asking if he might dedicate a work to him. This led to a close and enduring friendship, and to many happy visits

129 The relevant diary entry is cited by Roger Carpenter, *Goodnight to Flamboro': The Life and Music of William Baines* (BMS Monograph No. 4; 2nd edn; Upminster, Essex: BMS, 1999), p. 15

by Baines to the Dawson family home, Nun Appleton, adjacent to the River Wharfe. Here it was that Baines was inspired to compose *Twilight Woods* and *Glancing Sunlight*. Frederick Dawson fell in love with his friend's compositions and sought to promote them in his concert engagements.

Eaglefield Hull in effect became Baines's official promoter. At the time of their first acquaintance he was Principle of the Huddersfield College of Music and one of the chief instigators of the original British Music Society which was established in 1918. Baines was already building himself a reputation, and the dynamic Hull not only enrolled him in the newly-formed society, but organised concert tours for Baines as far afield as London, and negotiated terms with publishers for the promotion of his works. Certainly, the publicity seems to have worked. He had his name in lights, both locally and internationally, and the offers of publication began to roll in. However, fame and fortune persist only for as long as the artist is able to deliver, and as time passed and Baines's TB grew steadily worse, this became increasingly difficult for him to maintain. After his death, those who had sought to promote his interests did so for as long as they could. His devoted mother lovingly preserved all his manuscripts, and Eaglefield Hull wrote articles bearing titles such as "A New Yorkshire Musical Genius"[130], even prior to Baines's death, while Dawson continued to promote his works in concert. However, the older generation was passing away, and it was inevitable that the composer would eventually slip into obscurity. So it remained for some forty years until, in 1972, the enterprising Lyrita recording company engaged Eric Parkin to record a recital of Baines's piano works. Parkin later reminisced:

> For many years William Baines was just a name to me... Then in the sixties I was asked by Lyrita to make first recordings. Later came the 1972 Harrogate Festival where I met several of Baines's contemporaries. This was a moving

130 *The Bookman*, April, 1922.

> experience, for some of them had not heard a full Baines recital since William himself had played... He was a natural musician – a born pianist who would surely have gone on to greater heights.[131]

How might we assess Baines's output today? Clearly, the fact that half his catalogue dates prior to 1918, when he would have been nineteen years of age, suggests that we shall not find his mature achievement prior to that date. Silly comments have been made about his Symphony in C minor (op. 10), written when he was just eighteen. It is an extensive four-movement work and his first attempt at an orchestral score. Of course, it is a remarkable effort for a teenager of limited background and circumstances, but it was surely rash of Peter Pirie to rate it above Moeran's Symphony in G minor, which has itself been set alongside Walton's First (with what justification I am not competent to judge). Had he lived, Baines would in all likelihood have cultivated a sense of self-criticism equal to that of Vaughan Williams and Butterworth, which would have impelled him to cull his pre-1918 catalogue, including – who knows? – the Symphony.[132]

Again, Eaglefield Hull was no doubt over-ebullient in labelling Baines a genius, and the music critic of the *Daily Mail* more soberly writes: "'Genius' is perhaps a tall word to use merely on the strength of ... 28 pages of sometimes derivative, sometimes so freshly poetic music..."[133] In a way, the proof of the pudding is in the eating. There seems to be no evidence that any of Baines's manuscripts were lost or destroyed, so we must assume that the works recorded by Lyrita

131 Eric Parkin, liner notes, Priory CD, *Piano Music of William Baines* (PRCD 550), recorded in 1995.

132 Readers with sufficient musical expertise are, in any case, now at liberty to decide for themselves, given that the celebrated Grassington Festival performance of the Symphony in 1991 is now available on YouTube. Further discussion and musical examples are to be found in Carpenter, *Goodnight to Flamboro'*, pp. 63–67.

133 Cited in Carpenter, *Goodnight to Flamboro'*, p. 33.

and Priory, which overlap to some extent, are those considered to be among his finest. It would certainly not enhance Baines's reputation to commercially record the Symphony or any other work simply on account of their novelty, and the pieces that are before us today are probably those by which Baines himself would wish to be remembered.

a. Bibliography

Bell, Richard, "At the Grave of William Baines", *Wild West Yorkshire Nature Diary*, 22nd January, 2000

Carpenter, Roger, *Goodnight to Flamboro': The Life and Music of William Baines* (British Music Society, 1999)

Hull, Eaglefield, "A New Yorkshire Musical Genius", *The Bookman*, April 1922.

Walker, Robin, "William Baines: Past and Present", *British Music Society Journal*, 21 (1999)

b. Selected Discography

Paradise Gardens	Parkin (piano)	Priory	PRCD 550
Seven Preludes	Parkin (piano)	Priory	PRCD 550
Coloured Leaves	Parkin (piano)	Priory	PRCD 550
Silverpoints	Parkin (piano)	Priory	PRCD 550
Idyll	Parkin (piano)	Priory	PRCD 550
Tides	Parkin (piano)	Priory	PRCD 550
The Naiad	Parkin (piano)	Priory	PRCD 550
Twilight Pieces	Parkin (piano)	Priory	PRCD 550
Etude in F sharp minor	Parkin (piano)	Priory	PRCD 550

5. Sir Granville Bantock (1868–1946)

Historians have noted that one of the defining characteristics of Victorian Britain was its opulence and supreme confidence as expressed in its architectural and engineering achievements as well as its art. After all, given that a quarter of the world map was coloured pink, there was little room for doubt. This "can do" attitude certainly rubbed off on the music of Granville Bantock who thought nothing of launching into ambitious operatic projects, often based on Celtic and Oriental themes, and nothing seemed to faze him. He set the entire Song of Solomon to music, and his setting of Edward Fitzgerald's translation of the *Ruba'iyat of Omar Khayyám,* in three parts, is almost three hours in length. The scoring of Bantock's music is often opulent and Wagnerian, rather like a rich feast, but he was also capable of some deeply-felt chamber music and songs with piano. He was, indeed, a man of many parts.

Bantock was born in London, the son of a distinguished Scottish surgeon, and there were parental ambitions for him to take up a career in the Indian Civil Service. His own heart, however, was set on a career in music and, following the almost mandatory period of friction between father and son, he eventually got his way, studying with Frederick Corder at the RAM and winning the Macfarren prize in the first year of the award. His restive and ambitious nature was evident from the first, both in composition and in other musical activities. He projected a cycle of twenty-four tone poems based on Robert Southey's poem *The Curse of Kehana* (which, however, was never completed), and toured the world with George Edwardes's *The Gaiety Girl,* as well as founding a short-lived musical journal, the *New Quarterly Musical Review.* In 1897, only four years after leaving the RAM, he was appointed Musical Director of the Tower, New Brighton, transforming the orchestra there, with its standard repertoire of marches and waltzes, into one which specialised not only in "serious" music, but in modern works by British composers, including Parry, Stanford, Holbrooke, Cowen, Edward German, and others. His growing reputation as composer–conductor soon saw him rubbing shoulders with big names like Elgar and Sibelius, the latter dedicating his Third Symphony to him.

Bantock's successes in New Brighton, along with the recommendation of Elgar, soon led him on to greater things, and in 1900 he was appointed Principal of the Midland Institute of Music in Birmingham, adding the post of Peyton Professor of Music at the University of Birmingham, in succession to Elgar, eight years later. He tackled these ventures as energetically as he did everything else, and was soon busy at the Midland Institute trying to recruit the most talented musicians of the day, including, for a short while, Joseph Holbrooke and Rutland Boughton. He developed his conducting skills and began presenting works which were, in time, to become English classics, giving a notable performance of Elgar's *The Dream of Gerontius* in Wolverhampton in 1903.

Like a number of other composers – Arnold Bax and Havergal Brian spring to mind – Bantock was a veritable nomad, living at literally dozens of addresses throughout his life, including at least seven properties in the Birmingham area alone. In addition, there were moves back to London and Buckinghamshire, and holiday homes dotted around Bantock's favourite holiday spots in rural Wales, including a ramshackle dwelling amidst old slate quarry workings above Tan-y-Bwlch on the narrow gauge Ffestiniog Railway, which he shared with his friend Holbrooke.[134]

Bantock's 431-day world tour (1894–95) with George Edwardes's *The Gaiety Girl* is an indication of how much he loved to travel, both home and abroad, and the various cultural influences he imbibed were readily absorbed into his music. His wanderings in the Middle East, for example, inspired the opera *The Pearl of Iran* (1894), *The Ruba'iyat of Omar Khayyám* (1906–09), and (courtesy of James Elroy Flecker) *The Golden Journey to Samarkand* (1922). The Middle East is also implied in the great biblical settings: *Christus: A Festive Symphony* (1907) – a hugely ambitious ten-part

134 Particular interest in Bantock's various locations can be found in Em Marshall's *Music in the Landscape* (London: Robert Hale, 2011), pp. 52–64.

representation of the life of Christ which was never fully realised; the equally ambitious *Song of Songs* (1912–22); King Solomon (1937); *Vanity of Vanities* (1914) – a setting of Ecclesiastes; and *The Burden of Babylon* (1927). It has been said, somewhat facetiously, that Bantock would have set the entire Bible to music, given time! Further notable works, inspired by Greek myth and legend, include: *The Great God Pan* (1920); *The Cyprian Goddess* (Symphony No. 3, 1938–39); *Sappho*, for voice & orchestra (1906) – a setting of nine fragments from the enigmatic Greek poetess, in a translation by Bantock's wife Helena; and (courtesy of Shelley's great poem) *Prometheus Unbound* for chorus & orchestra (1936).

But it is Celtic lore and legend that surely inspired the greatest variety of Bantock's output, particularly in the latter stages of his career. Many of the works in this regard were purely orchestral, including: the *Hebridean Symphony* (1913); the *Celtic Symphony* (1940) – scored for strings and six harps, no less; *The Sea Reivers* (1920) – a movement discarded from the original *Hebridean Symphony*; Scottish Rhapsody (1913); *The Legend of Gael* (1915); *Scenes from the Scottish Highlands* (1913); and *Caristiona: A Hebridean Seascape* (1920). The most substantial of the Celtic works is *The Seal Woman* (1924), a folk opera with a libretto provided by Marjory Kennedy-Fraser, the well-known collector of Hebridean folksongs, some of the melodies of which are used by Bantock in the opera. In other works, however, Bantock was content to allow these songs to speak for themselves and without adornment, as in *Three Songs of the Hebrides* (1913–15), which includes arrangements of "The Mermaid's Croon", "Milking Song", and "Death Croon", for unaccompanied chorus (Meridian CDE 84570).

One has only to note the dates of the various works mentioned above, some of them on a huge scale, to infer than Bantock must have been working at fever heat during the middle decades of his life. The task of composition on its own must have occupied the lion's share of his time, but we have then to consider all the teaching and conducting in addition, not to mention his penchant for befriending and supporting fellow composers such as Joseph Holbrooke and

Havergal Brian, and his family responsibilities (he eventually had four children). Perhaps this adds to the suspicion that, even in the case of the most exalted composers, their success depends on 10% inspiration and 90% perspiration.[135]

Where does Bantock's reputation as a composer lie today? Thanks to his promotion in the recording studios of Hyperion, Chandos, Lyrita, Naxos and others, and the advocacy of conductors such as the late Vernon Handley (1930–2007) in particular, the major orchestral works seem fairly secure, and of course there is the superb Chandos recording of *Omar Khayyám* in an *almost* complete version, and a complete rendition on the Lyrita label. Of course, live concert performances remain a problem, as they do for the great majority of the composers we are considering. As for the remainder of Bantock's huge output, cash-strapped recording companies must understandably consider whether it is really worth recording any more of the composer's gargantuan operas and other choral works at huge expense, some of which, despite their exotic titles, are written in a familiar late nineteenth-century European tongue. It must be admitted that the Greek and Oriental themes chosen by Bantock, as well as the biblical epics and cantatas, probably struck a chord with audiences at the time in a way that they no longer do with today's public, and since recording companies are locked in a competitive market, they must manage their resources astutely if they are to survive. Would a lavish recording of, say, *The Song of Songs*, for soloists, double chorus and orchestra, be the most profitable way of expending a company's assets? There is in existence a Sir Granville Bantock Society whose members may vehemently disagree with this assessment, but we need to take a balanced view with regard to conditions as we find them in the present era. Perhaps, in any case, we already have excellent recordings of the majority of Bantock's most significant works.

---

135 A view not shared by the late John Taverner (1944–2014), however, who affirmed that in his own case, these figures were to be transposed.

a. Bibliography

Anderton, H.O., *Granville Bantock*, Living Masters of Music (London: Bodley Head, 1915)

Bantock, Cuillin, *Never Lukewarm: Recollections of Granville and Helena Bantock* (London: EM Publishing, 2012)

Bantock, Myrhha, *Granville Bantock: A Personal Portrait* (London: J.M. Dent, 1972)

Budd, Vincent, *An Introduction to the Life and Work of Sir Granville Bantock* (Gnosis Press, 2000)

Dressler, John C., *Granville Bantock (1868–1946): A Guide to Research* (Clemson, SC: Clemson University Press, 2020).

b. Selected Discography

i) Symphonies

A Hebridean Symphony	RPO, Handley	Hyperion	CDA 66450
A Celtic Symphony	RPO, Handley	Hyperion	CDA 66450
A Pagan Symphony	RPO, Handley	Hyperion	CDA 66630

ii) *Orchestral*

The Witch of Atlas	RPO, Handley	Hyperion	CDA 66630
The Sea Reivers	RPO, Handley	Hyperion	CDA 66630
Sapphic Poem	RPO, Handley; Lloyd-Webber (cello)	Hyperion	CDA 66899

iii) Choral with Orchestra

Omar Khayyám	BBC SO & Chorus, Wyn-Rogers (mezz-sop); Williams (bar); Spence (ten); Handley	Chandos	CHSA 5051
Sappho	RPO, Handley; Bickley (mezz-sop)	Hyperion	CDA 66899

c. Website

The Bantock Society (http://granvillebantock.com)

6. Stanley Bate (1911–59)

Of all the English composers to whom the epithet "forgotten composer" applies, none fits the bill more aptly than Stanley Bate. There are several reasons why a composer may be forgotten after his or her death. The age and output of the individual are two of the most common factors involved, but in some cases the amount of time spent abroad may be an issue too. Let us consider these factors in respect of Stanley Bate. He died (perhaps from natural causes, although there is a suggestion that substance abuse may have been a factor) at the age of forty-seven – not a great age, but certainly much older than twenty-three year-old William Baines and thirty-one year-old George Butterworth; yet Butterworth has never been out of favour, while Baines has made something of a revival in more recent years.

What about output? Here we face two issues: quantity and quality, and Bate scores on both counts. Some composers are forgotten because their oeuvre is simply too small to allow posterity to make a qualitative judgement about them. This is undoubtedly the case with C.W. Orr (1893–1976) and Janet Hamilton (1898–1979)[136], for example. Despite the fact that both composers survived into their eighties, their output was restricted to a handful of songs and instrumental pieces. Bate never reached fifty. It is a sobering thought that had Havergal Brian (1876–1972) died at Bate's age instead of living more than twice as long, not one of his thirty-two symphonies would have seen the light of day. Yet throughout his relatively short career, Bate was prolific in virtually every genre, producing four symphonies, four piano concertos, a viola concerto, many other orchestral works, film scores, ballet and incidental music, and a large quantity of chamber music, as well as piano solo pieces and songs. Although the quality of his output was not uniformly

136 For information on Janet Hamilton, see Rolf Jordan, "The Life and Works of Janet Hamilton", *British Music*, 32 (2010), pp. 62–76; John France, "The Music of Janet Hamilton: A Preliminary Survey", *British Music*, 32 (2010), pp. 78–81.

impressive, his best efforts were of sufficiently high quality to be played by Britain's leading orchestras, conducted by figures including Barbirolli and Boult, and at one point, Yehudi Menuhin expressed the wish that Bate should write a concerto for him.

It seems, then, that neither of these factors sufficiently explains Bate's neglect. It is true that, simply by dying, all but those English composers in the highest echelon fade into comparative obscurity – at least in the short term. This was as true of Alwyn, Arnold, Bax, Bliss, Rubbra and many others, as it was of Bate, and like some of those just noted, he achieved a fair degree of celebrity during his lifetime. His works were performed relatively frequently, and some of his symphonies and concertos found a place in the concert repertoire. Possibly the overriding factor that told against Bate was his absence from Britain, especially during the Second World War at a time when he was eligible for military service. As it happened, he was aboard the same America-bound ship as Britten and Pears. But whereas the latter pair returned before the end of the war, it was not until 1949 that Bate set foot in Britain again. In the meantime, his music had gained much more popularity in the States than on home soil. (The same was true of Richard Arnell).

Whatever recognition Bate gained during his lifetime, however, very soon evaporated after his death. Had it not been for the relatively recent intervention of the Dutton recording company, it is likely that he would be little better-known today than the aforementioned Janet Hamilton and others with far less to show for their compositional careers than Bate.

Born in Plymouth in 1911, Bate showed an early aptitude for music. His first composing efforts occurred when he was seven years old, and by the age of twelve he was proficient enough on the organ to play during services at a couple of local Methodist churches. While still in his teens he produced a couple of operas/ operettas, one of them to his own libretto, and although he required some help with orchestration, both were given successful local premieres.

In 1932 he won an open scholarship to attend the RCM and studied there with Vaughan Williams (composition), Arthur

Benjamin (piano), R.O. Morris (counterpoint) and Gordon Jacob (orchestration) – all studies which would stand him in good stead as a composer and concert pianist. It was during his time at college that he became enamoured of a fellow student, the Australian pianist and composer Peggy Glanville-Hicks (best known today for her Etruscan Concerto)[137] who he later married. After winning the Octavia Travelling Scholarship in 1936, Bate opted to study with Nadia Boulanger in Paris, and later with Hindemith in Berlin. Boulanger, in particular, thought highly of her student's abilities and conducted some of his works. On his return to London in 1937 Bate found paid work with a couple of London theatres, the Phoenix and the Lyric, writing incidental music for various plays and ballet music for "Les Trois Arts". His assistants on these occasions were his wife and Elizabeth Lutyens.

By 1940 he was beginning to spread his wings as a composer, as well as courting the great and the good. He completed his Symphony No. 3, widely considered to be the finest of the four he wrote, and was commissioned by Sir Henry Wood to write his Piano Concerto No. 2 for a Proms performance, although in the event, given the war situation, this never took place. Under the auspices of the British Council, Bate and his wife spent 1939–41 promoting British music in Australia, after which they moved to the USA where his composing career received a shot in the arm. Certainly, his work was appreciated more there than in Britain. Among other highlights, his Piano Concerto No. 2 was finally given its premiere by the NYSO under Thomas Beecham. Other notable conductors to show interest in Bate's compositions at this time were Serge Koussevitzky and Bruno Walter. Towards the end of the war Bate took time to visit Brazil where a number of his chamber works were performed. During this visit he met a diplomat, Margarida Guedes Nogueira, who was later to become his second wife following his

137 Available on ABC Classics Australian Composers Series (ABC 476 3222). Further information on the composer can be found in S. Robinson, *Peggy Glanville-Hicks: Composer and Critic* (Music in American Life; Chicago: University of Illinois Press, 2019).

divorce from Glanville-Hicks in 1948. Once back in the USA he composed his substantial Viola Concerto, much admired by the violist *par excellence* Lionel Tertis, although it was premiered by William Primrose.

Bate returned to England with his Brazilian wife in 1949, but successes in his homeland were far fewer than they had been in the States. One welcome triumph occurred in the summer of 1954 when his Third Symphony was premiered at the Cheltenham Festival by Barbirolli and the Hallé Orchestra. The following year, the Fourth Symphony was performed at the Royal Festival Hall and later broadcast; but apart from this brief interest Bate's best days were behind him.

Photographs of the composer are difficult to obtain, and the few that do exist show him in a rather gloomy pose, always dressed in a dark suit and in a sunless atmosphere, his face never quite in focus. The most familiar of these is an enlargement (hence the blurring effect) from what is actually a group photograph taken at the 1954 Cheltenham Festival in the presence of Vaughan Williams and his wife Ursula, with Michael Kennedy and his wife along with others, with Bate hovering somewhat on the periphery of the group. Ultimately, this probably sums him up – a rather shadowy figure who moved in exalted circles, but was always the bridesmaid and never quite the bride. He could have succeeded supremely well as a concert pianist, for he was blessed with a fine pianistic technique, but he tended to focus on playing his own works rather than the classics. He saw himself primarily as a composer, and when everything clicked, he was capable of some very fine work. His Third Symphony, for instance, ranks with the best that any other English composer was producing during the 1940s–50s, and he deserves to be ranked alongside the best of the so-called Cheltenham composers – Alwyn, Arnell, Alan and Geoffrey Bush, Arthur Butterworth, Peter Racine Fricker, Rawsthorne, Rubbra, William Wordsworth and others.

There may be a case for arguing that he tried to spread himself too thinly, for he got through an enormous amount of work – not simply composition – within his twenty years or so of active musical life. It is said that, shortly before his death, he had begun writing a book, presumably on music, completing some five hundred pages of it within just ten days.[138] He was found dead in bed on 19th October 1959. His elderly mother opined that it was overwork that killed him, while the coroner specified alcoholism as a contributory factor. The likelihood is that a combination of factors was involved. He may have been taking sleeping tablets. If so, their combination with alcohol could have proved fatal. We shall never know for certain.

Despite the best efforts of Dutton, Bate's position in the pantheon of English composers is tenuous indeed. To mix metaphors, he is on the list of endangered species. The likelihood of his being taken up in the concert hall today is practically zero, and unless his music can be heard in sufficient quantities, it will be impossible to form any meaningful judgement about the quality of his output, although what little can be heard demonstrates that he was capable of very good things. We really need individuals and small ensembles to perform some of the solo piano and chamber works before we can build a more general picture about the composer who, as both man and musician, will otherwise remain an enigma.

138 I am unable to confirm any specific source other than those which simply perpetuate the rumour.

a. Bibliography

Barlow, M. and R. Bennett, "Stanley Bate – Forgotten International Composer", *British Music*, 13 (1991), pp. 16–36

b. Selected Discography

Symphony No. 3	RSNO, Yates	Dutton	CDLX 7239
Symphony No. 4	RSNO, Yates	Dutton	CDLX 7255
Piano Concerto No. 2	RSNO, Yates; Sangiorgio	Dutton	CDLX 7282
Viola Concerto	BBC Concert O., Bell; Chase (viola)	Dutton	CDLX 7216
Cello Concerto	RSNO, Yates	Lyrita	SRCD 351

7. Sir Arnold Bax (1883–1953)

> I find it very annoying that Bax's comprehensive musical technique is not recognised. His eye and ear were so superbly developed. His gifts are astonishing; he releases us into an entirely different world, for nobody, in the whole of music, approaches the range of Bax's moods, or their type. He has given us something that is different from that of all other composers.[139]

Vernon Handley was one of the finest of all interpreters of Bax's music, so the fact that he has such a high regard for a composer whose works are so rarely heard in the concert hall today should make us sit up and take note. He was prolific, composing in every genre other than opera, and, from 1921–39 produced one of the finest symphonic cycles of any English composer in the twentieth century. His Symphony No. 6 must be mentioned in the same breath as Walton's First and Vaughan Williams's Fourth, and his body of mature chamber music is without compare. This is all the more astonishing, given that there was no need for him to work for a living at all. He was born in Streatham to upper middle-class parents (his father was a barrister) who were well able to provide for his every need and set him up with a private income. When Bax was ten years old he and his family moved to a large house called Ivy Bank near Hampstead Heath. It was set in extensive grounds where Arnold and his brother Clifford, who became a playwright, could indulge themselves in games of various kinds – both lads were enthusiastic cricketers. Bax enjoyed a private education at home, but his interest and obvious aptitude in music eventually required some professional guidance, so, at the age of sixteen, he applied to the RAM and was accepted. There, under Tobias Matthay, he developed a formidable piano technique, as is apparent from his

139 Vernon Handley, conductor, in the liner notes accompanying his Bax symphonic cycle (Chandos CHAN 10122).

series of demanding piano sonatas which can be brought off only by pianists of the highest calibre.

The wide range of moods in Bax's music, of which Vernon Handley speaks, is no doubt a reflection of the man himself. His behaviour was, to say the least, mercurial, and the accounts of his romantic attachments are legendary. Bax's marriage to a Spanish girl, Elsita Sobrino, in January 1911 was doomed from the start, notwithstanding the arrival of two children. Only months before the marriage, he had decamped all the way to the Ukraine in pursuit of a Ukrainian girl he had met in London and who had returned at short notice to the land of her birth. Most men would have let matters lie, but Bax, a man of means, as well as impulsive temperament, was determined to give chase. In the event, by the time he caught up with his quarry, she had become engaged to another. He did not leave entirely empty-handed, however. During the time that he was there, he absorbed the local cultural life, visiting St. Petersburg and Moscow among other places, and returned to England with a burning admiration for all things Russian – notably music and ballet – which was to influence his own compositions.

A less than commendable feature of Bax's relationships was their duplicitous nature. Foremost of these was his extended affair with the pianist Harriet Cohen (1895–1967), twelve years Bax's junior. In pursuit of her he abandoned his family in London, and from then on lived a nomadic existence, staying at hotels and residences throughout Britain and Europe. He supported his mistress financially for over three decades, allowing her to make concert appearances all over the world, and to stay at the most exclusive hotels while on tour. In return she promoted Bax's cause by playing his piano compositions, and became his creative muse, inspiring him to write further works for her.

While this amorous affair endured, however, both parties felt free to indulge in liaisons of their own, even reaching some measure of agreement about it. One affair that did cause rancour, once it came to light, was Bax's lengthy liaison with Mary Gleaves, twenty years his junior, who he first met in 1926. Between the wars Bax adopted the custom of spending part of the winter in Morar, seeking inspiration for his symphonies from the wild Scottish landscape. Unknown to Harriet Cohen, Mary Gleaves joined him on these expeditions as well as on other occasions. It was only when Bax's wife Elsita (who had always refused to grant him a divorce) died in 1947, at which point Harriet expected him to propose marriage to her, that the truth about his duplicitous behaviour emerged.[140]

There can be no doubt that Bax's liaisons with women fed into his life as a composer. Harriet Cohen was not only a creative muse but his publicity agent. He wrote for her and she showcased his works, even negotiating exclusive performing rights in some cases. Another significant influence, however, predating any of his more serious relationships, was his lifelong love of Ireland. A chance encounter with W.B. Yeats's *The Wanderings of Oisin* unleashed the Celt in him and, in his usual impulsive manner, he set out in search of the *real* Ireland in 1902. Of course, Ireland then would have been a good deal more romantic than it is today, but the important thing for Bax is that its landscape should have inspired the lore and legends encapsulated in the poetry of Yeats.

For the remainder of his life he returned again and again to the Emerald Isle, seeking inspiration that even his women were unable to provide. He toured the country extensively, establishing important *pieds a terre* in Rathgar (a suburb of Dublin) and Glencolumbcille (or Gleann Cholm Cille) in County Donegal. Soon, he was making the acquaintance of important creative artists such as George Russell (Æ) and those who would subsequently become the leading lights in the Easter Rising of 1916. He taught himself the ancient Irish language, Erse, and became proficient enough to write poetry and short stories in it, for which purpose he created for himself the pseudonym Dermot O'Byrne. (Amusingly, it was even claimed in one Dublin journal that "Arnold Bax was a pseudonym of the writer

---

140 Readers who want all the lurid details of these affairs through the exchange of letters written by the various parties concerned, can find them uncensored in Helen Fry's *Music and Men: The Life and Loves of Harriet Cohen* (London: Thistle Publishing, 2015).

Dermot O'Byrne[141], and there were many who were convinced that Bax had been born in Ireland). Perhaps it was only fitting that he should have been in Ireland (staying at the home of fellow composer Aloys Fleischmann in Cork) when he died.

The Irishness of Bax emerges from his music in both subtle and more obvious ways. Yeats was undoubtedly the inspiration for some of his tone poems, including *Into the Twilight* and *Cathleen-ni-Houlihan*, while two more (*Roscatha* and *In the Faery Hills*) formed a trilogy with *Into the Twilight* under the collective title *Eire*. Another Yeats-inspired tone poem, this time concerning the sage Cuchulain, is *The Garden of Fand*, his best-known work in the genre, with the obvious exception of *Tintagel*. The tone poems, written between 1905–17, were in a sense preparatory to the composition of Bax's First Symphony. This, too, certainly has an Irish flavour, if in a more subtle sense, and, if so, its theme, now, is no longer concerned with the sagas and legends of Ireland, inspired by literature, but with Ireland's politics. The symphony was completed in 1921, only three years after the end of the First World War (which may well have been in Bax's mind at the time), and five years after the Easter Rising of 1916. Bax lost friends in both these conflicts, and he made no secret of the fact that his sympathies lay with the Republicans. Indeed, one of the first pieces of his to emerge following their defeat at the hands of the British forces, was *In Memoriam, Padraig Pearse*, even the title of which was written in Erse. As Lewis Foreman[142] remarks, Bax had met Pearse on only one occasion, but in this elegiac work, his name comes to represent the heroic Republican cause as a whole.

We have referred to Bax's England and Bax's Ireland, but when we come to consider his symphonic cycle, we need to mention

141 Marshall, *Music in the Landscape*, p. 153. For those curious to know what "Dermot O'Byrne's" poetry sounds like, try consulting Lewis Foreman, ed., *Dermot O'Byrne: Selected Poems of Arnold Bax* (London: Thames Publishing, 1979). A few fragments can also be found in Marshall's book (pp. 153–78).

142 See Lewis Foreman, *Bax: A Composer and His Times* (Woodbridge, Suffolk: Boydell Press; 3rd edn, 2007), p. 148.

Bax's Scotland too. After completing the first two symphonies, the second of which is a tense affair which probably reflected his personal circumstances at the time (1924–26), the remainder of the cycle emerged over a relatively concentrated period (1929–39) according to a fairly predictable pattern. Bax would spend the midwinter months at Morar, a few miles from Mallaig (usually accompanied by Mary Gleaves) where he would put up at the Station Hotel, working in an unheated room on his symphonies. He would work out the themes and produce a short score in these surroundings, completing the orchestration on returning south in the spring. Much has been made of the view that Bax conceived his symphonies in terms of a projected cycle, evidence for which lies in the efforts he made to adopt the same working pattern for each one – the place (Morar), the working conditions, and the chosen form of the symphonies themselves – all three-movement works, usually with epilogue (Nos. 3, 5, 6, 7). Vernon Handley was of the view that Nos. 1–3 in effect form a trilogy, with the epilogue of No. 3 doubling as the epilogue of the trilogy as a whole. No. 4 stands alone as a happy, blustery work, and is sometimes regarded as his "sea symphony". Nos. 5 and 6 get to grips with more serious matters again, with the latter commonly regarded as Bax's symphonic masterpiece. In No. 7, there is some release of previous tensions, and a valedictory mood, as if Bax is signalling his intentions to wind down as a composer, although he still had thirteen years left to him.

The symphonies are certainly to be set apart from anything else Bax wrote. The tone poems provided the necessary preparation, but in the symphonies he attempted to create a sound world which is found nowhere else in his oeuvre, nor in anyone else's either. One has only to listen to the epilogue of the Symphony No. 3, with its vision of unworldly beauty, to appreciate that.

Although the final symphony was completed in 1939, Bax was not yet quite spent as a creative force. In 1942, following the death of Henry Walford Davies, he was appointed the new Master of the King's Music – much to the surprise of some and the relief of Walton! Perhaps he was not wholly suited to the post. After all, it was one thing to write to commission, but quite another to write to command, and he professed himself somewhat dubious about wearing silk breeches and sword for ceremonial occasions. Given that he was in post for over ten years, his royal duties seem not to have borne much fruit. The most substantial work was the Coronation March of 1952, although this was not officially commissioned. Otherwise, there are two Fanfares for the Royal Wedding (1947), and a contribution to a collaboration by several British composers, *Garland for the Queen* ("What is it like to be young and fair?") (1953), and little else.

On the other hand, like Vaughan Williams at much the same time, Bax made a late foray into the world of film music with a couple of highly evocative scores for *Malta GC* (1942) and *Oliver Twist* (1948) respectively. There was also incidental music to a play, *The Golden Eagle*, written by his brother Clifford, and late pieces for piano, both with and without orchestra, which Harriet Cohen continued to premiere.

Given his privileged financial position, Bax might have chosen to spend his life abroad lounging in the sun. He was indeed widely travelled, and his various liaisons with the most desirable beauties of the day are legendary. Yet he was hugely industrious, using his formidable skills to the utmost. Lewis Foreman's catalogue of his works stretches to almost forty pages, and many of these items are large-canvas orchestral scores which must have cost him a huge effort to produce. Some of them, such as *Spring Fire* (1913) – a symphony in all but name – were never performed in his lifetime.

Bax spent his final years (1941–53) based at the White Hart pub in Storrington at the foot of the Sussex downs, mixing with the locals as easily as a local farmer. But he died – of heart failure – where he would have wished, in his beloved Ireland, and was buried in St. Finbarr's cemetery in Cork.

As living composers go, Bax received reasonable acclaim during his lifetime, and was considered to be among the leading British composers of the 1920s–30s. But, in Britain at least, dead composers are soon forgotten, and Bax's music saw temporary neglect in the wake of his death. Fortunately, in the modern age, the recording industry can do an enormous amount to restore reputations, in which regard companies including Chandos and Naxos have done Bax proud, recording the bulk of his huge output in all its genres. Music really comes alive in the concert hall, and here Bax is all too seldomly performed. But then, that is the unfortunate fate of most British composers.

a. Bibliography

Bax, Arnold, *Farewell My Youth* (ed. Lewis Foreman: London: Routledge, 1992)

Bye, Christopher, "On the Highland Trail of Sir Arnold Bax", *British Music Society Journal*, 40/1 (2018)

Foreman, Lewis, ed., *Dermot Byrne: Selected Poems of Arnold Bax* (London: Thames Publishing, 1979)

----------, *Bax: A Composer and His Times* (Woodbridge, Suffolk: Boydell Press, 2007)

Fry, Helen, *Music and Men: The Life and Loves of Harriet Cohen* (London: Thistle Publishing, 2015)

Hannam, William B., "A Bax by any other Name would be ... Dermot O'Byrne", *British Music Society Journal*, 32 (2010), pp. 5–11

Scott-Sutherland, Colin, *Arnold Bax* (London; J.M. Dent, 1973)

----------, ed., *Ideala: Love Letters and Poems of Arnold Bax* (Petersfield, Hants: Fand Music Press, 2001)

b. Selected Discography

i) Symphonies

Symphonies Nos. 1–7	BBC PO, Handley	Chandos	CHAN 10122(5)

(Boxed set, including a one-hour interview with Vernon Handley. Other complete cycles include Bryden Thomson with the LPO and Ulster orchestras – also for Chandos; and David-Lloyd-Jones with the RSNO for Naxos).

ii) Concertos

Violin Concerto	LPO, Thomson; Mordkovitch (violin)	Chandos	CHAN X10154
Cello Concerto	RSNO, Yates; Handy (cello)	Lyrita	SRCD 351

iii) **Orchestral**

November Woods	Ulster Orchestra, Thomson	Chandos	CHAN X10156
The Happy Forest	Ulster Orchestra, Thomson	Chandos	CHAN X10156
The Garden of Fand	Ulster Orchestra, Thomson	Chandos	CHAN X10156
Tintagel	Ulster Orchestra, Thomson	Chandos	CHAN X10156
Nympholept	LPO, Thomson	Chandos	CHAN 9168
Dance of Wild Irravel	LPO, Thomson	Chandos	CHAN 9168
Into the Twilight	Ulster Orchestra, Thomson	Chandos	CHAN 8367
In the Faery Hills	Ulster Orchestra, Thomson	Chandos	CHAN 8367
Roscatha	Ulster Orchestra, Thomson	Chandos	CHAN 8367
Tale the Pine Trees Knew	Ulster Orchestra, Thomson	Chandos	CHAN 8367
Spring Fire	RPO, Handley	Chandos	CHAN X10155
Northern Ballad No. 1	LPO, Boult	Lyrita	SRCD 231
Northern Ballad No. 2	RPO, Handley	Chandos	CHAN X10155
Northern Ballad No. 3	LPO, Thomson	Chandos	CHAN X10155
Mediterranean	LPO, Thomson	Chandos	CHAN X10155
In Memoriam	BBC PO, Handley	Chandos	CHAN X10155

iv) Choral

Mater Ora Filium	Finzi Singers, Spicer	Chandos	CHAN 9139
This Worldes Joie	Finzi Singers, Spicer	Chandos	CHAN 9139
I Sing of a Maiden	Finzi Singers, Spicer	Chandos	CHAN 9139

v) Chamber

String Quartet No. 1	Maggini Quartet	Naxos	8.555282
String Quartet No. 2	Maggini Quartet	Naxos	8.555282
String Quartet No. 3	Maggini Quartet	Naxos	8.555953
Violin Sonata No. 1	Jackson (violin); Wass (piano)	Naxos	8.557540
Violin Sonata No. 3	Jackson (violin); Wass (piano)	Naxos	8.557540
Viola Sonata	Outram (viola); Rolton (piano)	Naxos	8.557784
Nonet	Nash Ensemble	Hyperion	CDA 66807
Oboe Quintet	Nash Ensemble	Hyperion	CDA 66807
Harp Quintet	Nash Ensemble	Hyperion	CDA 66807

vi) Piano Solo

Piano Sonata No. 3	Wass (piano)	Naxos	8.557592
Piano Sonata No. 4	Wass (piano)	Naxos	8.557592
Water Music	Wass (piano)	Naxos	8.557592
Winter Waters	Wass (piano)	Naxos	8.557592
What the Minstrel Told Us	Wass (piano)	Naxos	8.557769

c. Website

The Arnold Bax Website (www.arnoldbax.com)

8. Lennox Berkeley (1903–89)

If anyone was born with a silver spoon in his mouth it was Lennox Berkeley. His family, on both sides, was stuffed with aristocrats and, had circumstances been otherwise, he would have inherited the earldom of Berkeley, along with its imposing castle in Gloucestershire; but his father had been born out of wedlock which disqualified him and his descendants from inheriting the title. Still, Lennox did not fare too badly. There was French blood on both sides of the family, and he became a notable Francophile, composing many of his songs in French. He was sent to a reputable public school, Gresham's in Norfolk (attended later by both Britten and W.H. Auden), and in 1922 went up to Merton College, Oxford, to read French and philology. Although a man of some reserve, Berkeley attracted a number of influential friends, one of whom, thanks to his French connections, was Maurice Ravel (1875–1937), despite the twenty-eight-year age gap. It was he, in fact, who suggested that Berkeley should study composition with Nadia Boulanger (1887–1979), who consequently became another key influence on his development, helping to feed an already developing cosmopolitanism into his musical language.

Berkeley remained in Paris until 1932, soaking up the lively cultural atmosphere, and falling under the spell of the leading French composers of the day including Ravel and "Les Six" (whose best-known members were Poulenc and Milhaud), as well as Stravinsky who had made Paris his base some years earlier. It was during this period that Berkeley became a practising Roman Catholic – yet another factor that was to feed into his music, later inspiring important religious works such as the *Four Poems of St. Teresa of Avila* (1947), *Stabat Mater* (1960), *Missa Brevis* (1960), and the *Magnificat* (1968).

In 1936, at the Festival of the ISCM in Barcelona, Berkeley met Benjamin Britten for the first time. He was immediately impressed by the younger man, and Britten reciprocated, leading to a collaboration in the shape of an orchestral suite based on

Catalan folk tunes and entitled *Mont Juic*. Soon afterwards, for a short while, Berkeley moved in with Britten to the newly-restored Old Mill at Snape in Suffolk, sharing the costs of its upkeep, until the latter sailed with Peter Pears to the USA in 1939. During the war years Berkeley remained in England, working in the music department at the BBC. It was here that he met his wife-to-be, Elisabeth Bernstein, who he married in 1946. Among the three sons they produced was Michael (b. 1948), who became a composer in his own right. It seemed appropriate, therefore, that at the turn of the century Chandos Records should have produced a series of four CDs entitled "The Berkeley Edition" in which the music of father and son were showcased together.

1946 was also the year in which Lennox Berkeley began his twenty-two-year association with the RAM as Professor of Composition, teaching students including David Bedford, Richard Rodney Bennett, Peter Dickinson, William Mathias, Nicholas Maw, and John Tavener. Many of these attested to Berkeley's attractive personal qualities, and in particular to his fine qualities as a teacher. Given the meticulous attention he paid to his own works, one would hardly have expected less.

His undoubted "god" was Mozart, and the same command of form is to be found in his own music as in that of the Master. The forces used in his orchestral music are nearly always of classical proportions, without exoticism or extravagance, and consisting only of those instruments he considers sufficient to make the statement for which he is striving. The result is perfect clarity of sound, with nothing muddy about the orchestration, and his preferred genres are the traditional ones – the symphony, the concerto, the serenade, the divertimento, and among chamber works the string quartet. As for the sound world of the music, it is cosmopolitan, with a leaning towards France rather than England, and there is always an admirable restraint, as becomes the man himself.

Of the earlier works, the two that are best-remembered today are the *Serenade for Strings* (1938–39) and the *Divertimento* (1943), both eloquently scored, with not a hair out of place in either of them. Of the symphonies, the Third is generally agreed to be the pick of them. It is a concentrated work of fifteen minutes' duration consisting of several contrasting sections and containing elements of serialism while retaining the composer's distinctive voice. As noted, his quiet Catholic faith inspired several significant religious works. To those mentioned above we may add the *Mass for Five Voices* (1964) and the *Three Latin Motets* (1972). These, in common with his other religious works, keep well within the bounds of traditional Christian expectations in musical terms. He does, however, allow himself more indulgence in solo organ works such as the *Toccata* (one of the *Three Pieces* from 1968), which appears on the Naxos selection of his sacred choral music (8.557277), much of which has become well-established in the repertoire, and is frequently programmed as part of the sung services in churches and cathedrals up and down the country.

The year following his appointment to the staff of the RAM in 1946, Berkeley moved into a house on Warwick Avenue in the Little Venice district of London, where he remained until his death over forty years later. During that period honours were heaped on him, including honorary doctorates (Oxford, 1970), fellowships (Merton College, 1974; RNCM, 1975), the CBE (1957), and ultimately a knighthood (1974). He was an honorary member of various music institutions, both at home and abroad, and was President of the Cheltenham Festival between the years 1977–83. During his final decade, Berkeley began to suffer progressive dementia and was unable to compose after 1983. He died on Boxing Day, 1989.

It is difficult to place Berkeley's achievement within any line of descent. He certainly did not belong to the English pastoral school of composers, and although he enjoyed a close friendship with Britten, they were not alike stylistically, and in any case, Berkeley was the senior of the two by thirteen years. He had a great admiration for the music of Sibelius, and it is tempting to attribute the compact Symphony No. 3 to the influence of the Finnish composer's single-movement Symphony No. 7, but the sound world is not his. There may be a touch of French polish, as Vaughan Williams would have called it, not only through his mentor Nadia Boulanger, but also through the composers he met during his spell in Paris. In the end, we must accept Berkeley's music for what it is – a personal voice delivered in a refined, urbane, largely neo-classical manner. Why not fill a glass of the best claret, turn down the lights, put your feet up, and listen?

a. Bibliography

Dickinson, Peter, *The Music of Lennox Berkeley* (Woodbridge, Suffolk: Boydell Press, 2003)

----------, ed., *Lennox Berkeley and Friends: Writings, Letters and Interviews* (Woodbridge, Suffolk: Boydell Press, 2012)

Wordsworth, David, "Sir Lennox Berkeley: A Tribute", *British Music Society Journal*, 12 (1990)

b. Selected Discography

i) Symphonies

Symphony No. 1	BBC NOW, Hickox	Chandos	CHAN 9981
Symphony No. 2	BBC NOW, Hickox	Chandos	CHAN 10167
Symphony No. 3	BBC NOW, Hickox	Chandos	CHAN 10022
Symphony No. 4	BBC NOW, Hickox	Chandos	CHAN 10080

ii) Orchestral

Sinfonia Concertante	BBC NOW, Hickox; Daniel (oboe)	Chandos	CHAN 10167
Serenade	LPO, Berkeley	Lyrita	SRCD 226
Divertimento	LPO, Berkeley	Lyrita	SRCD 226
Partita	LPO, Berkeley	Lyrita	SRCD 226
Mont Juic (coll. Britten)	LPO, Berkeley	Lyrita	SRCD 226

iii) Choral

Stabat Mater	ECO, Ambrosian Singers; Del Mar	Lyrita	REAM 1129
Magnificat	LSO; Choirs of St. Paul's Cathedral, Westminster Abbey, and Westminster Cathedral; Berkeley	Lyrita	REAM 1129
Missa Brevis	Choir of St. John's College, Cambridge; Robinson; Vaughn (organ)	Naxos	8.557277

c. Website

The Lennox Berkeley Society (www.lennoxberkeley.org.uk)

9. Sir Harrison Birtwistle (b. 1934)

It is not known whether John Tavener's barb concerning the "po-faced music" emanating from Manchester during the 1950s–60s[143] was meant to be inclusive of Harrison Birtwistle, who studied at the Royal Manchester College of Music, along with Peter Maxwell Davies and Alexander Goehr, but, in the company of Elgar Howarth and the pianist John Ogden, he was associated with what became known as the Manchester set, or "Gang of Five"[144] – the English equivalent of the Frankfurt gang of mainly English composers (Balfour Gardiner, Walter Leigh, Norman O'Neill, Roger Quilter, Percy Grainger). In neither case were these composers linked stylistically, but simply because they emerged as the brightest prospects from the same musical establishment at the same time. Unlike the earlier Frankfurt group, however, Birtwistle, Davies and Goehr supported each other and undertook various projects together for some years following their college association, as we shall see.

Harrison ("Harry") Birtwistle was born in the Lancashire mill town of Accrington on 15th July 1934. When he was seven years old his mother bought him a clarinet and arranged for him to have lessons with a local band master, and he soon became sufficiently proficient to play in the band. His first efforts at composition came soon afterwards. Looking back on his first serious efforts, he described their style as being "sub-Vaughan Williams", and although he never studied with the great man formally, he did get the opportunity to submit some of his work for his considered judgement. His period at the RMCM stretched from 1952–55, after which he undertook his mandatory two-years National Service which he spent with the Royal Artillery Band based in Oswestry.

On leaving the army, one of Birtwistle's first steady jobs was the post of Director of Music at the exclusive Cranborne School (1962–

143 See below, p. 556

144 Mike Seabrook, *Max: The Life and Music of Peter Maxwell Davies* (London: Victor Gollancz, 1994), pp. 33–50.

65), for which purpose he moved to nearby Shaftesbury. While he was there, he conceived the idea of setting up a summer school of music in the grounds which included both the school building and the ruins of Wardour Castle. His old Manchester friends, Alexander Goehr and Peter Maxwell Davies, were enlisted to help with arrangements. There were composition courses taught by these three, instrumental classes, and chamber concerts performed by the acclaimed Melos Ensemble. Essentially, the event was modelled on the better-known Dartington Summer School. The venture was accounted a rousing success, prompting the organisation of another summer school at the same venue the following year, 1965. This time, however, it became more of a platform for the performance of new compositions by the organisers. Birtwistle's *Tragoedia* for ten players (flute/ piccolo, oboe, bassoon, horn, harp and string quartet) received its first performance, as did Maxwell Davies's *Ecce Manus Tradentis*. Unfortunately, the last-night celebrations got out of hand. Alcohol flowed freely, and damage was caused to property, resulting in the venture having to be discontinued. Still, the chief protagonists derived a number of positives from the experience. Their music had been heard by sympathetic ears, and their ability to organise such events had been honed. It was not long before Birtwistle would be masterminding another idea.

Almost immediately following the demise of the Wardour Summer School of Music, Birtwistle and his associates, along with a new member, Steve Pruslin, and the clarinettist Alan Hacker, formed a new group with the intention of securing well-rehearsed professional performances of contemporary works, not least their own. Maxwell Davies was away in Australia at the time the group was taking shape, but joined formally on his arrival back in Britain. It fell to Pruslin to suggest a name for the ensemble, and he decided on the Pierrot Players, after Schoenberg's iconic chamber work *Pierrot Lunaire*, and the group comprised precisely the instrumentalists Schoenberg had used in his piece: flute/ piccolo, clarinet, violin/ viola, cello, piano, and female singer. Members were chosen for their ability and commitment. Although a range of aspiring young composers benefitted from the Pierrot Players' concerts, it became something of a platform for its two principal composing members, Birtwistle and Davies.

In 1970, after three years with the group, Birtwistle abruptly terminated his membership following what seems to have been a rift with Maxwell Davies. The latter's official biographer, Mike Seabrook, later interviewed both men regarding the incident, but only got so far as to form a speculation. Davies contended that he was non-plussed as to the cause, whereas Birtwistle was evasive but somewhat bitter. The root of the problem seems to have lain in the contrasting personalities of the two men – Davies, outgoing and flamboyant; Birtwistle, undemonstrative and reticent. Moreover, the manager of the Pierrot Players, an outgoing Australian called James Murdoch, did not see eye to eye with Birtwistle, and vice versa, Murdoch was very much a Davies devotee, and Birtwistle may have been sore about the fact that Max seemed more sympathetic to Murdoch than to himself. A further factor, however, which has been confirmed by various knowledgeable sources, is that while Davies was producing a lot of work for the Pierrot Players to perform, Birtwistle was not. According to Murdoch, any antagonism between the two of them amounted to this failure to produce work for what, after all, was a theatre group which required feeding with new material in order to remain a going concern. Birtwistle was a much slower worker than Davies, and although the latter was able to write for the group while producing music for much larger forces, too, Birtwistle found this difficult to manage and felt constrained by his obligations.[145] After his departure, a clean break was made by renaming the ensemble the Fires of London.

From this time on, Birtwistle went his own way, and over the years has established a reputation as one of the most imaginative composers in the history of English music. Although in recent years he has produced a piano concerto, *Responses* (2013–14), a violin

145 Seabrook's assessment of this rift, and of the reasons behind it, are presented in *Max*, pp. 120–23.

concerto (2009–10) and a string quartet, *Tree of Strings* (2007), one would not generally look to him for the traditional forms. His main interest has always been in musical drama, the backbone of which is his series of seven operas (including chamber operas). There are other works, however, some of them purely instrumental, whose titles betray a dramatic interest – *Tragoedia* (1965) and *Secret Theatre* (1984), for example; and even the non-vocal works can create a visual impact – perhaps through the movement or the arrangement of the players on stage, or some apparent anomaly. *Theseus Game* (2002), for large ensemble, for instance, requires two conductors.[146]

A further feature of Birtwistle's music is his fascination for myth and legend, clearly evident in works such as the operas *The Mask of Orpheus* (1973–84), *Gawain* (1990), and *The Minotaur* (2008). He often treats these subjects in innovative ways rather than simply telling the story in linear fashion as most operas do. In *Gawain*, for example, the Arthurian legend is told from different perspectives, involving not only elements of chronological order, but the retelling of the narrative from a different angle, using some of the same thematic material. Something similar happens in *The Mask of Orpheus* in which the Greek myth is treated simultaneously in contradictory ways by two sets of singers and actors competing to present their particular versions of the myth. This kind of technique has been likened by Birtwistle himself to exploring a small provincial town by beginning from the square (the basic thematic material, as it were), and then fanning out into the various side streets, from some of which can be caught glimpses of the square from different perspectives, while from others the square is not visible at all. Ultimately, however, the square and streets are all part of the same town.

Naturally, all operas are meant to be seen as well as heard, although in the case of the more traditional examples – Mozart,

---

146 Although unusual, this is not unique. Charles Ives's Symphony No. 4, with its highly complex textual layering, also requires two conductors at one point.

Wagner, Verdi, Puccini, Britten, and so on – one can still derive pleasure from listening to the music on a recording, especially when in possession of a set of liner notes which includes an explanation of the plot and a full libretto. In Birtwistle's case, however, we are lost without the visual element, for his operas must be seen to be understood. In *Gawain*, the point at which the initial, chronological tale is concluded is marked by the blacking-out of the stage – a point which might pass unnoticed if the opera is only heard.

There is no sense in which Birtwistle's style can be pigeon-holed. His music is unlike that of any other composer, and the casual listener will find it difficult to relate one piece to another, or even to recognise it as the work of the same composer. The fact that he has always had such a fertile imagination and creative impulse makes him totally unpredictable; one never knows what is coming next. It is his boundless ability to surprise that explains his continued potential to fascinate the listener.

In the 1960s, along with his fellow firebrand Peter Maxwell Davies, Birtwistle was the *enfant terrible* of English music. Like Davies's *Eight Songs for a Mad King* (1969), with its theatrical elements and its intention to shock, Birtwistle's *Punch and Judy* (1967), with its translation of puppet violence into the real human world caused shock and divided opinion, with emotions ranging from adulation to derision – even disgust. But, once having established a platform for his unique manner of expression, Birtwistle showed that he was here to stay. Today, as so often happens in such cases, he has become the grand old man of English music (although he has never regarded himself as an "English" composer, and questions whether we can even know what such a phenomenon is). Again, because he has been on stage for so long (sixty years, and counting), he has been drawn into the bosom of the music establishment. His list of honours and awards would be the envy of all but a select few – Knight Bachelor (1988), Companion of Honour (2001), Fellow of the RAM (1986), RNCM (1989) and Royal Academy of Arts (1994), with honorary doctorates awarded by the Universities of Sussex, London, Cambridge and Oxford, among others.

Despite all this, he remains a somewhat diffident, unassuming individual, with the traces of a Lancastrian accent betraying his comparatively humble origins. He tends to be hesitant in interview, and may not even enjoy the experience very much. But those who have met him as strangers often remark on his kindness, warmth and humour. Still, at the age of eighty-six, his business is composition. His catalogue to date, if we include his incidental music to various classic plays and his sole film score (*The Offence*, 1972), stretches to some two hundred works, ranging from substantial operas and orchestral pieces, though chamber music to individual songs, with or without accompaniment. Birtwistle's music may continue to divide opinion, but it cannot be ignored, and has established itself as an indelible feature on the English musical landscape.

a. Bibliography

Jonathan Cross, *Harrison Birtwistle: Man, Mind, Music* (London: Faber & Faber, 2000).

Michael Hall, *Harrison Birtwistle* (London: Robson Books, 1984)

Michael Hall, *Harrison Birtwistle in Recent Years* (London: Robson Books, 1998)

b. Select Discography

i) Opera

Punch and Judy	Solists, London Sinfonietta	NMC
The Mask of Orpheus	Solists, BBC Singers, BBC SO; Davis & Brabbins (conductors)	NMC
Gawain	Soloists, Royal Opera Chorus, Orchestra of the Royal Opera House, Howarth	NMC

ii) Orchestral/ Ensemble

The Triumph of Time	Philharmonia O., Howarth	NMC
Ritual Fragment	London Sinfonietta	NMC
Secret Theatre	London Sinfonietta	NMC
Carmen Arcadiae Mechanicae Perpetuum	London Sinfonietta	NMC
Silbury Air	London Sinfonietta	NMC
Tragoedia	Ensemble Intercontemporain, Boulez	Deutsch Gram.

Endless Parade	BBC Philharmonic (Hardenberger, trump.)	NMC
Earth Dances	BBC SO, Eötvös	Collins

iii) **Chamber**

String Quartet, "The Tree of Strings"	Arditti Quartet	Aeon
Nine Movements for String Quartet	Arditti Quartet	Aeon

iv) **Vocal**

26 Orpheus Elegies	Maxwell (oboe); Tunstall (harp); Watts (countertenor)	Oboe Classics

c. DVD

The Minotaur	Soloists, Royal Opera Chorus, Orchestra of Opus Arte The Royal Opera House, Pappano

10. Sir Arthur Bliss (1891–1975)

When Arthur Bliss first came to prominence as a composer, he was very much a willing participant in the roaring twenties. Christopher Palmer once upbraided those who referred to him as the *enfant terrible* of British music at that time, but perhaps that had more to do with the fact that the majority of critics were already doing so. Inspired by Stravinsky and developments in France before and following the First World War, he experimented with writing for unusual combinations of instruments, including the use of the wordless voice as an instrument in itself. Incidental music written for a production of *The Tempest* in 1921 required an ensemble including piano, trumpet, trombone, gongs and other percussion, along with male voices. The most enduring composition to emerge from this experimental period was *Rout*, for wordless soprano and chamber ensemble. The defining moment for Bliss came in 1922 when his *Colour Symphony* was premiered at the Three Choirs Festival. It marked the end of his first phase as a composer and pointed ahead to the "things to come". He was thirty-one years old.

Arthur Bliss was born in London to Francis Edward Bliss and his second wife, Agnes Kennard, who died in 1895 while still in her thirties, when Arthur was just four years old. The family did not lack for money, since Bliss's father was a successful American businessman. After a formative education, Bliss was sent to Rugby, and from there went up to Pembroke College, Cambridge, where he studied classics, along with music under the legendary Sir Charles Wood. Having graduated from Cambridge in 1913, he continued his music studies at the RCM under Stanford, Vaughan Williams and Holst. Among his fellow students were Herbert Howells, Eugene Goossens and the Australian composer and pianist Arthur Benjamin. New music was in the air – Stravinsky, Debussy, Ravel – and Diaghilev's Ballet Russes was dazzling everyone. It must have been an exhilarating time for him. But his studies were interrupted by the onset of the First World War, and Bliss, along with his younger brother Kennard, enrolled as members of the officer class.

The horrific experiences he endured and witnessed haunted him for the rest of his days. Kennard was killed in battle, and Bliss himself was twice wounded and once gassed. His conversion to the Roman Catholic faith in 1918 may well have been prompted by his wartime ordeal.

The end of the war also marked the end of Bliss's initial experimental phase and the beginning of his explorations into the possibilities offered by the orchestra. Although he never showed much interest in extending the symphonic tradition represented by Elgar and Vaughan Williams, there is little doubt that his first significant orchestral work, *A Colour Symphony*, was a symphony in form as well as in name, and showed a remarkable facility with the orchestral forces. The idea of basing each of the four movements on different colours is symptomatic of the imaginative approach adopted by Bliss throughout his career. Who else would have thought of basing a ballet on a game of chess as in *Checkmate*, or setting to music a medieval text of riddles (*A Knot of Riddles*)? The various colours to which each movement of the symphony refers is based on their natural and symbolic associations. Purple, according to Bliss (or to his source, a book on heraldic symbolism), is the colour of amethysts, pageantry, royalty and death; red suggests rubies, wine, revelry, furnaces, courage and magic; blue is indicative of sapphires, deep water, skies, loyalty and melancholy; and green represents emeralds, hope, youth, joy, spring and victory. Reaction to the symphony was generally positive. Elgar damned it with faint praise, pronouncing it "disconcertingly modern", and yet his influence, as well as that of Stravinsky, is incorporated in it. Certainly, it put Bliss firmly on the map as a composer.

In 1923, Bliss accompanied his father, who had remarried, back to the land of his birth, and it was there, in California, that he met the girl who was to be his own wife, Gertrude Hoffmann (1904–2008). They were married in 1925 and were blessed with lifelong marital contentment. Soon afterwards he returned with his spouse to England. At this time he was still haunted by his war experiences on the Somme and the loss of his brother, but in 1930 he set about facing up to his demons in a powerful work for chorus, orchestra and orator entitled *Morning Heroes*. This, too, Bliss regarded as a "symphony", but it was of a very different timbre to *A Colour Symphony* of eight years earlier. Since it was completed some twelve years after the armistice, some might say that it had missed the boat as a meaningful response to those events, but it was never intended as a public requiem, but rather a personal statement addressing Bliss's own condition. He speaks of a recurring nightmare in which he finds himself once more with his battalion in the trenches facing a German battalion. Although the armistice has been signed, they seem to have been overlooked and are doomed to fight on to extinction.[147] Before he began work on the piece, he paid homage at the grave of his brother Kennard with whom he had been extremely close.

Bliss's choice of title (after the poem by Robert Nichols) was in deference to his emphasis on war as an opportunity for man to display heroic qualities which somehow mitigate the losses sustained. The first section opens with a calm but sorrowful introduction, with rumblings of war, before the orator breaks in with Hector's farewell to his wife Andromache (Homer, *Iliad*, VI). Andromache attempts to dissuade her husband from the path on which he is set, but he replies that valour and courage must take precedence over personal considerations. The text for the second section is taken from Walt Whitman's poem *The City Arming*, which presages the mood of optimism and patriotic fervour rife among those enlisting at the outbreak of war in 1914. Part Three consists of two texts contrasting in mood. A Chinese poem by Li-Tai-Po depicts a maiden pining after her lover away at war through the symbolism of a white rose she is embroidering and which becomes stained with blood from her pricked finger. This is followed by another poem of Whitman's, *The Bivouak's Flame*, which depicts a young American soldier, shortly to be pitched into battle, musing regretfully on the loved ones he has left behind him. In the fourth

147 Arthur Bliss, *As I Remember* (London: Faber & Faber, 1970), p. 96.

section, we return to the *Iliad* (Book XIX) and the fate of Hector who now engages with Achilles in single combat and is slain. Significantly, the section of the poem chosen by Bliss describes the visual resplendence of Hector's opponent, omitting any reference to the actual engagement. Instead, Hector's valour is implicit in the list of the slain Trojan heroes which follows.

Up to this point, all the texts have been about war in general or wars fought prior to 1914. Now, in the final section, Wilfred Owen's *Spring Offensive*, recited by the orator, brings matters within the direct experience of Bliss himself and the generation of young men who joined him in battle. The idealism of the vision seemingly adopted here is summed up in the oft-quoted lines, "Some say God caught them even before they fell", although, in the context of the poem as a whole, it is doubtful that such feelings were left untempered by those of a darker hue. After all, the poet who wrote that line, which itself is qualified ("*some* say"), could also speak of "the pity of war". Bliss, no doubt, had equally mixed feelings. Nevertheless, in conclusion to his work he chooses to reaffirm the theme of heroism by setting Robert Nichols's *Dawn on the Somme* which depicts the crater pools gleaming in the sun after a night of rain in terms of the "morning heroes" receiving laurels of victory from the sun god Apollo.

Whatever the precise meaning of this work for Bliss himself, he never attempted the like again, and so, if it was meant primarily as a means of self-exorcism, we may conclude that it was a success, and it is, at the wider level, all-embracing, as significant for us today as when it was first written – if only we would take notice.

Later in the thirties Bliss turned his attention to ballet with the music for *Checkmate*, noted above, and made an early foray into film music with his score for H.G. Wells's *The Shape of Things to Come*, both of which have remained firmly rooted in the repertoire and been recorded several times. Two further ballet scores, *Miracle in the Gorbals* and *Adam Zero*, followed in the 1940s. Less successful was his only attempt at opera, *The Olympians*[148], on which he collaborated with J.B. Priestley as his librettist. The plot, to be sure, was a somewhat improbable one, involving the pantheon of Greek gods who lose their divinity and wander around as a troupe of actors. It was praised by some critics, but generally received a lukewarm reception and has never been taken up into the repertoire.

Also in the 1940s, Bliss briefly became Director of Music for the BBC (1942–44), taking over the role from Adrian Boult and regarding it as his contribution to the war effort. By 1950, when he was knighted for his services to music, he had become one of the elder statesmen of his profession, along with Vaughan Williams and William Walton, and when the Master of the Queen's Music, Sir Arnold Bax, died in 1953, Bliss was offered and accepted the post. His ability to turn his hand to a good fanfare thus became especially useful. He faithfully produced all the ceremonial and occasional pieces expected of him, and certainly paid more than lip service to the post. In addition to this and other official roles, Bliss was also invited, in 1956, to join a delegation of British musicians to the Soviet Union in a welcome expression of friendship at a time when political relations were becoming increasingly strained.

Among the significant works of Bliss's later years were the *Meditations on a Theme of John Blow* (1955), a cantata *The Beatitudes* (1961), and the Cello Concerto (1970). The *Variations* contain some of the composer's most deeply-felt and spiritual music. Using a theme from an anthem by the eighteenth-century composer John Blow, each meditation is headed by a phrase from Psalm 23, the theme itself not being heard in full until the finale.

The Beatitudes is not, as might be imagined, merely a setting of Matthew 5: 3–11. Although, obviously, they are included, they are interspersed with a wide range of other texts, including Isaiah 2: 17–19, and poems by the seventeenth-century divines Henry Vaughan, George Herbert and Jeremy Taylor. There is even an

148 There was, in fact, also a television opera on the story of Tobias and the angel (1959–60), his librettist on this occasion being Christopher Hassall.

imaginative appearance of Dylan Thomas's *And Death Shall Have No Dominion*. The aim is to use these disparate sources to make a powerfully coherent statement, somewhat akin to what we find in George Dyson's *Quo Vadis*. The occasion for writing the work was a commission for a piece to be performed at the opening of the new Coventry Cathedral in 1962, but, through no fault of Bliss's, things did not go according to plan. Britten's *War Requiem* had also been commissioned for the same event, and rehearsals for this, along with the various other activities in the cathedral on the day of its consecration meant that the venue for Bliss's new work, written for the spaciousness of a cathedral setting, had to be rearranged at short notice. The performance eventually took place in a local theatre, but the use of a Hammond organ was no substitute for the new cathedral organ for which Bliss had written a substantial part. In the end he never heard his work performed in its intended venue. It was first heard there in 2012, fifty years after its intended performance.[149]

The Cello Concerto of 1970 was requested by the world-famous cellist Mstislav Rostropovich, and was premiered by him with the English Chamber Orchestra, conducted by Benjamin Britten, at the Aldeburgh Festival. It was Britten, in fact, who suggested to Bliss that he felt the work was substantial enough to be labelled "concerto" (rather than "concertino"). The work has a foothold in the cello repertoire, and has been recorded by both Robert Cohen (EMI) and Raphael Wallfisch (Chandos).

In discussing Bliss's orchestral and large-scale choral works, we should not neglect to mention that he was equally adept in the chamber music genre and wrote such music throughout his career, from the early String Quartet and the Piano Quartet, both of 1915, to the late String Quartet No. 2 (1950). There was also a clarinet quintet, dedicated to the Dutch composer Bernard van Dieren (1887–1936), and a viola sonata, inspired and performed by Lionel Tertis.

149 See Paul Conway, liner notes to the Lyrita recording of the work (REAM 1115).

Sir Arthur Bliss's music has been comparatively well-served by the various recording companies and seems not to have suffered the neglect, temporary or terminal, of many English composers. His star retains its place in the firmament, partly though circumstances – he was, after all, a figure of the musical establishment for some forty years, no less than Elgar and Vaughan Williams were – but essentially through the quality and craftsmanship of the music itself.

a. Bibliography

Bliss, Arthur, *As I Remember* (London: Faber & Faber, 1970)
Guyatt, Andrew, "Sir Arthur Bliss", *British Music Society Journal*, 1 (1979)
Sugden, John, *Bliss*, Illustrated Lives of the Great Composers (London: Omnibus Press, 1997)

b. Selected Discography

i) Orchestral

A Colour Symphony	Ulster Orchestra, Handley	Chandos	CHAN 10221X
Checkmate Suite	Ulster Orchestra, Handley	Chandos	CHAN 241-1
Suite: Things to Come	NPO, Herrman	Decca	470 186-2
Meditations on a Theme of John Blow	RPO, Wordsworth	Decca	470 186-2
Introduction & Allegro	RPO, Wordsworth	Decca	470 186-2
Hymn to Apollo	Ulster Orchestra, Handley	Chandos	CHAN 241-1

ii) Concertos

Piano Concerto	RSNO, Lloyd-Jones; Donohoe (piano)	Naxos	8.557146
Concerto for Two Pianos	RSNO, Lloyd-Jones; Donohoe & Roscoe (pianos)	Naxos	8.557146
Cello Concerto	Ulster Orchestra, Handley, Wallfisch (cello)	Chandos	CHAN 10221X

iii) Chorus with Orchestra

Morning Heroes	RLPO & Choir, Groves; Westbrook (orator)	EMI	7 63906 2
The Enchantress	Ulster Orchestra, Handley; Finnie (mezz-sop)	Chandos	CHAN 10221X
Pastoral: "Lie Strewn the White Flocks"	Northern Sinfonia & Chorus, Hickox	Chandos	CHAN 241-1
The Beatitudes	BBC SO & Chorus, Bliss; Harper (sop); English (ten)	Lyrita	REAM 1115

iv) Chamber

String Quartet No. 1	Maggini Quartet	Naxos	8.557108
Piano Quartet	Maggini Quartet; Donohoe	Naxos	8.555931
Oboe Quintet	Maggini Quartet; Daniel	Naxos	8.555931
Clarinet Quintet	Lindsay String Quartet; Hilton (clar)	Chandos	CHAN 241-1
Viola Sonata	Outram (viola); Rolton (piano)	Naxos	8.555931

c. Website

The Arthur Bliss Society (www.arthurbliss.org)

11. Rutland Boughton (1878–1960)

Mention the Glastonbury Festival today, and most people will think of the great annual summer gathering of rock bands and pop idols, and perhaps unseasonal (or seasonal?) rain and fields turned into a quagmire. Rather fewer will realise that the *original* Glastonbury Festival began over a century ago and hosted, not pop music, but a unique brand of English opera. It was all masterminded by a thirty-six year-old unassuming looking individual called Rutland Boughton. He had been born in 1878 to parents who had no particular interest in music. His father was a greengrocer in Aylesbury. Somehow, however, Boughton began to show a precocious musical talent. In 1892 he began work for a concert agency, but soon his flair for music was noticed, and he was fortunate that the wealthy Rothschild family took him under its wing and helped him raise funds for a three-year spell at the RCM where he studied under the notoriously demanding Stanford, as well as Walford Davies. This was during the golden age of the college when students Vaughan Williams, Holst, Ireland, and other leading composers-to-be all passed through its portals.

By 1905, just three years after leaving the RCM, Boughton was attempting his First Symphony, *Oliver Cromwell* (available on the Dutton label), and in the same year, his reputation having gone before him, he was invited by the Principal of the Birmingham and Midland Institute of Music, Granville Bantock, to teach there, and he remained until 1911. During the first decade of the twentieth century, Boughton made all sorts of contacts that would help him set the future course of his career. For a while he served as the piano accompanist to baritone David Ffrangcon-Davis whose daughter, also a singer, was to become invaluable to Boughton's ambitions within the next few years. He was also drawn, somewhat fatally as it turned out, into the socialist movement under the influence of John Ruskin, William Morris and George Bernard Shaw.

It has often been remarked that with the death of Purcell (1659–95), English opera entered a dark age lasting 250 years, which was ended only by the appearance of Britten's *Peter Grimes* in 1945; but thirty years prior to this, Boughton was conceiving something on an even more ambitious scale. His idea was to devise a series of operas – or musical dramas, as he preferred to label them – along the lines of Wagner's Ring Cycle at Bayreuth, but these would be distinctively *English* operas with peculiarly English themes. The centrepiece of these productions would be Arthurian legend, and Glastonbury was chosen as the location, no doubt because it was already associated with these legends. The Arthurian cycle eventually numbered five operas, although only two of these – *The Birth of Arthur* (1909) and *The Round Table* (1914–15) – were produced up to and including the Glastonbury years. Later ones included *The Lily Maid* (1932–33), *Galahad* (1943–44), and *Avalon* (1944–45). Boughton's Glastonbury project included assembling a commune of like-minded and committed people, one of whom was Gwen Ffrangcon-Davies who was to play a significant singing role.

The Festival was inaugurated not with the performance of an Arthurian music-drama, but one based on a play by Fiona MacLeod (the pseudonym of William Sharp) centred on Celtic lore and legend, *The Immortal Hour.* The first performance was staged on 26th August 1914 with a cast that included the well-known baritone and composer Frederic Austin and Boughton himself singing a bass role. It had a successful run in Glastonbury, but what happened next was phenomenal. The production moved on to the Birmingham Repertory Theatre where it enjoyed another successful run, which prompted the director there, Barry Jackson, to suggest a London season. Apparently Boughton expressed his doubts, but the plan went ahead. It opened at the Regent Theatre in 1922 and notched up 216 consecutive performances, a feat unrivalled, before or since, in the annals of English opera. The following year saw a run of 160 performances, and there was a further revival as late as 1953. In 1926 there was also a successful run in New York. One can only assume that Boughton, if not by design then by sheer good fortune, had caught the mood of the moment. Possibly the escapist nature of *The Immortal Hour* is just what people were looking for in the wake of the First World War. Perhaps it was the *Lord of the Rings* or the *Harry Potter* of its time!

Other Boughton music-dramas, including some of the Arthurian ones, had successful runs, too, but never on the scale of *The Immortal Hour*. One of these successes, *Bethlehem*, however, was also the cause of his downfall. It was based on a medieval Nativity play and was first performed in the village of Street near Glastonbury in December 1915. Its inclusion of traditional carols certainly added to its popularity. Naturally it was reprised in subsequent years, and all went well until, in 1926, Boughton's socialist sympathies got the better of him. In that year, with the world entering the Great Depression, and the miners' lock-out and General Strike in Britain, he chose to present the performance that Christmas as a modern-dress production, casting Mary as giving birth to Jesus in a miner's cottage, and Herod as the unacceptable face of Western capitalism. Given that the production had been scheduled for Church House, Westminster, the furore can well be imagined. The Glastonbury Festival was wound up, and an imaginative twelve-year venture came to an ignominious end. It was also the end of Boughton's brief period of celebrity. He decamped to the village of Kilcot in Gloucestershire where he acquired a smallholding and worked the land, although he continued to compose until the last decade of his life.

Boughton was by no means a composer of little else but musical dramas. He wrote three symphonies (the third of which is highly regarded), and concertos for oboe (two), flute, trumpet, and strings, as well as two string quartets and two oboe quartets. He has been relatively well-served by the recording companies; CDs of the symphonies and the string quartets have been available for some years, and there is a recording of one of his final orchestral works, the suite *Aylesbury Games* (1952), to remind us of his roots.

Boughton was still writing musical dramas into the 1940s, including the final two of the Arthurian cycle, but these still await performance. He seems to have been glancing back longingly to the period of his greatest successes, but by the time of the Second World War the world had moved on to other things, leaving Boughton in its wake. Still, there is no doubt that his most successful work, *The Immortal Hour*, has won him an imperishable place in the history of English music.

a. Bibliography

Hurd, Michael, *Immortal Hour: The Life and Period of Rutland Boughton* (London: Routledge & Kegan Paul, 1962)

----------, *Rutland Boughton and the Glastonbury Festivals* (Oxford: Clarendon Press, 2nd edn, 1993)

b. Selected Discography

i) Symphonies

Symphony No. 1 "Oliver Cromwell"	BBC Concert O., Handley; Williams (bar.)	Dutton	CDLX 7185
Symphony No. 3	RPO, Handley	Helios	CDH 55019

ii) Concertos

Oboe Concerto No. 1	RPO, Handley; Francis (oboe)	Helios	CDH 55019
Flute Concerto	NLO, Corp; Benyon (flute)	Hyperion	CDA 67185
Concerto for Strings	NLO, Corp	Hyperion	CDA 67185

iii) **Music Dramas**

The Immortal Hour	ECO, Geoffrey Mitchell Choir, various soloists, Melville	Hyperion	CDD 22040
Bethlehem	City of London Sinfonia; Holst Singers; New London Children's Choir; soloists; Melville	Hyperion	CDA 66690
The Queen of Cornwall	NLO, London Choir, Corp	Dutton	CDLX 7256

iv) **Chamber**

String Quartet in F major	Rasumovsky Quartet	Helios	CDH 55174
String Quartet in A major	Rasumovsky Quartet	Helios	CDH 55174
Oboe Quartet	Rasumovsky Quartet; Francis (oboe)	Helios	CDH 55174

c. Website

The Rutland Boughton Music Trust (https://rutlandboughtonmusictrust.org)

12. Havergal Brian (1876–1972)

On 17th July 2011, I was lucky enough to be in attendance at a packed Royal Albert Hall to hear a Proms performance of Havergal Brian's huge Gothic Symphony. Also in attendance were: the BBC National Orchestra of Wales, the BBC Concert Orchestra, the Bach Choir, the BBC National Chorus of Wales, Brighton Festival Chorus, CBSO Youth Chorus, Côr Caerdydd, Eltham College Boys Choir, Huddersfield Choral Society, London Symphony Chorus, Southend Boys and Girls Choirs, Susan Gritton (soprano), Christine Rice (mezzo-soprano), Peter Auty (tenor), Alastair Miles (bass), David Goode (organ), and Martyn Brabbins (conductor) – a grand total of nine hundred performers (give or take one or two!). Apart from the augmented orchestra on stage, there were four brass choirs, each consisting of two horns, two trumpets, two trombones two tubas and timpani, not to mention eight off-stage trumpets. Yet only once during the entire length of the symphony (approximately one hour and forty minutes) is the full strength of the orchestral forces employed. This Proms performance was the first professional airing of the Gothic for at least thirty years, and one can readily appreciate why.

My only other experience of hearing a Brian symphony in live performance was at Sheffield's City Hall back in 1973 when James Loughran and the Hallé Orchestra presented the Symphony No. 10, which he had recently recorded with the Leicestershire Schools Symphony Orchestra during the final year of the composer's long life. This work also requires a large orchestra, but no choral forces, and its duration is less than twenty minutes, in common with the majority of his later symphonies. Indeed, the Sinfonia Brevis (Symphony No. 22) is precisely that, at just over nine minutes in length.

One might think that Havergal Brian became a legend in his own lifetime, and there are further facts (not apocryphal stories) to support this claim. Of his final tally of thirty-two symphonies (an early effort entitled *Fantastic Symphony* was soon dismantled, and two of the movements pressed into service as short independent works), all but the first five were written after he had attained the age of sixty-five – an age when most people have retired. He was still composing into his ninety-third year. Yet apart from the aborted Fantastic Symphony, he was a comparatively late starter in symphonic terms. The Gothic occupied him for the eight years between 1919–27, at which point he was already fifty-one years old.

But the story becomes even more bizarre. Surely a man capable of producing the Gothic Symphony must have been a super-educated university graduate who sat at the feet of Parry, Stanford or Wood? Not a bit of it. He was born into a staunchly working-class family in the grimy Potteries town of Dresden, attending the local infant school and, from the age of ten, St. James Parish School, Langton, Stoke-on-Trent. However, his formal education ended at the age of twelve when he found employment as a surface worker at a local colliery. A year later he became an apprentice joiner, and then an office boy. And so the pattern of his early life was set as he drifted from place to place, and from one job to another. The omens were hardly auspicious, but, despite the straitened circumstances, Brian's interest in music was fostered by the lively choral tradition he found in his part of Victorian England. He sang, and proved intelligent enough to learn from both the standard choral repertoire and from those conducting it, and had soon developed sufficient musical ability to be appointed assistant organist at a local church. He also learned to play the violin, while a local music teacher provided some basic theoretical training. As a composer, however, he was virtually self-taught, no doubt learning valuable lessons from the music he heard. By the turn of the century, he had become sufficiently accomplished to begin composing for orchestra.

Alongside these musical developments, Brian's personal life continued apace. He married his first wife, Isobel Priestley, in 1899, and sired four children by her. He adopted the habit of naming the boys after composers or conductors he admired – Sterndale (after William Sterndale Bennett), and Hector (after Berlioz), for example.

During the first decade of the twentieth century things began to move purposefully in the right direction. While working as a timber merchant, Brian secured a post as music critic for the journal *Musical World* (from 1905 to 1908, when it folded), while at the same time his name came to the attention of Sir Edward Elgar, then in his pomp, who began to express an interest in his music, even asking to see some of his work. In 1909 the wealthy Herbert Minton Robinson, from the Minton china firm, sponsored Brian to the tune of £500 per year for the next four years, so that his financial worries were considerably eased. During these years, a steady stream of orchestral works began to emerge: *Fantastic Variations on an Old Rhyme*, *Festal Dance* (both of these the surviving remnants of the *Fantastic Symphony* of 1907), *In Memoriam* (1910), *English Suite No. 1* (1903–04), the overtures *For Valour* (1902), *Dr. Merryheart* (1912), and others. Then the advent of the First World War put a sudden stop to his progress. He enlisted as a private as early as 25th August 1914, although he was already thirty-eight years old, but a year later was discharged from the army, the reason being – of all things – flat feet! He spent the remainder of the war "doing his bit" in various clerking jobs. Post-war, he reverted to a series of part-time or short-lived jobs, though usually with a musical theme – a couple of months as a clerk at the Inland revenue (1920), followed by work as a music copyist with the publisher Godwin & Tabb, and then a more permanent post as assistant musical editor of *Musical Opinion* (1927–39). He even found time to spend a year (1925) teaching at the RCM, when he must have become acquainted with some of the leading names of his day.

Throughout this period, he was still finding time to compose substantial scores. One has only to note the dates of these works to realise how prolific he was. For instance, he began his Symphony No. 2 in June 1930, completing it on 6th April 1931. Six days later, he began work on the Symphony No. 3 and completed that on 5th June. Almost immediately he started on his Symphony No. 4 (*Das Siegesleid*, with chorus) – during the writing of which his first wife died, and he married his second wife Hilda Hayward – completing the work in December 1933. All these are substantial compositions for large orchestra, each lasting around fifty minutes.

The Symphony No. 5, *Wine of Summer* (1937) is a setting of the poem of that name by Alfred Lord Douglas (1870–1945).[150] It was the first of Brian's shorter symphonies, lasting for some twenty minutes. Following this there was a ten-year lull in his symphonic writing, which is often put down to his running out of inspiration. Brian himself intimated as much, writing that "in January 1948, the muse returned with a rush", the immediate fruits of which were the Symphony No. 6 (*Sinfonia Tragica*) and an overture, *The Tinker's Wedding*. But this can hardly have been the whole story since, between 1937 and 1944 he had been occupied on his vast four-hour setting for chorus and orchestra of Shelley's *Prometheus Unbound*, the greater part of it being undertaken when he was working as a clerk throughout the war years and beyond.

From that time on the symphonies began to come thick and fast. The Seventh (1948) was inspired by Brian's old love of all things Gothic, and was the last full-length example of the form that he wrote, the remainder lasting twenty-five minutes or less. These later symphonies take on a much more condensed, terser style than hitherto. At the time, however, he was writing without much hope that any of them would come to performance. His most valuable advocate, Elgar, had died in 1934, and another, Sir Granville Bantock, in 1946. However, a young music producer at the BBC, Robert Simpson (1921–97), stumbled across Brian's music and came to the rescue. For the remainder of the composer's life, he worked tirelessly to secure radio broadcasts of the symphonies so that, in his final years, he was able to hear some of what he had written, including, in 1966, a performance of the great Gothic Symphony by the BBC Symphony Orchestra and Chorus (etc.), conducted by Sir Adrian Boult. No doubt this renewed, if belated, attention prompted Brian to persist with his compositions. A final move to Shoreham-by-

150 Douglas (or "Bosie", as he was known) was the man involved in a homosexual relationship with Oscar Wilde (1851–1900) which resulted in the latter's imprisonment.

Sea in 1958 (he had lived at dozens of addresses throughout his life – mainly in Staffordshire, London and Sussex) produced a rich Indian summer of music over the next decade, including his last twenty symphonies. Although his final symphony was the last work he wrote, the one which immediately preceded it, *Legend for Orchestra: Ave Atque Vale,* seems to have signalled his intention to fall silent, which he did for the final four years of his life – by his own account without any regrets. He had said all that he wanted to.

Yet still there is a twist in the tale. In 1972, the composer's last year, and at the instigation of Robert Simpson, no doubt, the impressive Leicestershire Schools Symphony Orchestra made the first commercial recording of any of the composer's symphonies. Nos. 10 and 21 were selected, these being conducted by James Loughran (the conductor of the Hallé Orchestra in succession to Barbirolli) and Eric Pinkett (Music Director of the LSSO) respectively. In connection with this venture, Granada Television produced a documentary (still available on YouTube at the time of writing) which traced the course of events, including scenes of the young musicians endeavouring to come to grips with this strange, new music. The results can be heard on the recording itself. What a pity that the composer never lived to hear it. Even after the lapse of more than forty-five years, I am still firmly of the view that no work of Brian's provides a better introduction to his output than the Tenth Symphony. It is short enough, and contains all the stylistic fingerprints that have come to characterise his mature work as a whole.

At the end of the Granada documentary, there is a poignant scene in which members of the LSSO are bussed down from Leicestershire to Shoreham to visit the ninety-six year-old composer. It is a lovely summer afternoon, and they gather on the lawn outside the composer's humble council flat where the youngsters chat with him on an informal basis. His champion Robert Simpson is present, and Brian looks a contented man.

What about Havergal Brian's legacy? Most people remember him, if at all, for his Gothic symphony, which at one time enjoyed a place in the Guinness Book of Records under the heading "largest symphony" (which is probably true if its length and required number of performers are yoked together). Many who have never heard the work itself are aware of it by reputation. To some extent, however, Brian was his own worst enemy because he showed little interest in marketing his work. Most composers set their sights on performance because, after all, a composition is of little value to anyone unless it can be heard; it must be performed in order to live. Yet in an interview in 1966, when he was in the middle of composing his Symphony No. 26, he confessed that his abiding interest lay in getting his ideas down in score; performance seemed to be a secondary consideration in his view.

As with so many other English composers, alas, Brian's reputation today rests almost entirely on the record companies – notably Marco Polo/ Naxos, Dutton and Toccata, by which he has been well-served. Marco Polo's grandiose plan to record the entire symphonic cycle fell through at a relatively early stage, presumably due to financial constraints, but over the years other companies rallied round, with the result that the project has now been realised. Since then, efforts have been made to showcase other aspects of his output – songs, piano solos, concertos[151], and music from one or two of the operas. The only genre in which Brian seems to have expressed little interest (other than film scores) is chamber music.

All composers are necessarily individuals and must be unique in that obvious sense, but in certain cases the life and work of such individuals are without precedent and are in that more particular sense unique. We have seen that this was true of Rutland Boughton, and it is also the case with Havergal Brian. His life seems to have been made up of contradictions, and the uniqueness of his style is

151 Brian completed three string concertos – for violin (1935), for cello (1964), and for orchestra (1964). He lost the short score of the Violin Concerto on a train on his way in to London, but determined to rewrite it, as best he could, from what he remembered of the themes. He labelled the new piece Violin Concerto No. 2, but, as the original never turned up, later dropped the numeration.

due largely to the fact that he had no formal training in composition. Perhaps, like blue cheese or a certain wine, it is not to everyone's taste, but to those it catches by the throat, it can become a lifelong obsession, as members of the Havergal Brian Society will testify. His place in the history of English music is thus assured, and the composition of his Gothic Symphony is an achievement that will probably never be surpassed.

a. Bibliography

Eastaugh, Kenneth, *Havergal Brian: The Making of a Composer* (London: George Harrap & Co., 1976)

MacDonald, Malcolm, *The Symphonies of Havergal Brian*, 3 vols. (London: Kahn & Averill, 1974–78)

----------, *Havergal Brian on Music*, 3 vols. (London: Toccata, 1986–2009)

Matthew-Walker, Robert, *Havergal Brian: Reminiscences and Observations* (DGR Books, 1995)

Nettel, Reginald, *Ordeal by Music: The Strange Experience of Havergal Brian* (Oxford: Oxford University Press, 1945)

----------, *Havergal Brian and His Music* (London: Dobson Books, 1976)

Schaarwachter, Jurgen and David J. Brown, *HB: Aspects of Havergal Brian* (Aldershot, Hants.: Ashgate Publishing, 1997)

b. Selected Discography

i) Symphonies

Havergal Brian wrote thirty-two symphonies, all of which have now been recorded. The selection below is intended to reflect the wide range of these compositions, from the huge Gothic Symphony down to the minute Sinfonia Brevis. The listener unfamiliar with Brian's works would do well to begin with the Symphony No. 10, which formed my own introduction to his music and, as I came to recognise subsequently, contains all the typical Brian hallmarks.

Symphony No. 1, "Gothic"	BBC SO & Chorus; BBC ChoralSociety; City of London Choir; Hampstead Choral Society; Emmanuel Schools Choir; Orpington Junior Singers, Boult	Testament	SBT2 1454
Symphony No. 3	BBC SO, Friend	Helios	CDH 55029
Symphony No. 5 "Wine of Summer"	RSNO, Brabbins	Dutton	CDLX 7314

Symphony No. 6 "Sinfonia Tragica"	LPO, Fredman	Lyrita	SRCD 295
Symphony No. 7	RLPO, Mackerras	EMI	5 75782 2
Symphony No. 8	RLPO, Groves	EMI	5 75782 2
Symphony No. 9	RLPO, Groves	EMI	5 75782 2
Symphony No. 10	RSNO, Brabbins	Dutton	CDLX 7267
Symphony No. 16	LPO, Fredman	Lyrita	SRCD 295
Symphony No. 21	New Russia SSO, Walker	Naxos	8.573752
Symphony No. 22 "Sinfonia Brevis"	New Russia SSO, Walker	Naxos	8.572833

ii) **Concertos**

Cello Concerto	BBC Concert O., Yates; Wallfisch (cello)	Dutton	CDLX 7263
Violin Concerto	BBC Scottish SO, Friend; Bisengaliev (violin)	Marco Polo	8.223479

iii) **Orchestral**

English Suite No. 3	RSNO, Brabbins	Dutton	CDLX 7267
English Suite No. 5	BBC Scottish SO, Walker	Toccata	TOCC 0110
Legend: Ave atque vale	BBC Scottish SO, Walker	Toccata	TOCC 0110
Elegy	BBC Scottish SO, Walker	Toccata	TOCC 0110
Festal Dance	RSNO, Brabbins	Dutton	CDLX 7267

Overture: Tinker's Wedding	RLPO, Mackerras	EMI	5 75782 2
Overture: For Valour	Orchestra of ENO, Brabbins	Dutton	CDLX 7348
Overture: The Jolly Miller	BBC Scottish SO, Friend	Marco Polo	8.223479
The Tigers	Luxembourg RSO, Hager	Forlane	UCD 16724

c. Website

The Havergal Brian Society (www.havergalbrian.org)

13. Arthur Butterworth (1923–2014)

Draw a line from the Severn to the Humber estuaries, and nearly all of England's leading composers – Elgar, Vaughan Williams, Britten – would be accounted "southerners". Of those generally numbered among the top six, only Walton and Delius (Oldham and Bradford respectively) buck the trend, and they both sought their straw in more exotic climes as soon as they were able. Arthur Butterworth, on the other hand, loved all things northern, a fact which is evident from the landscapes and composers which inspired his music.

Butterworth was born into a musical family in Manchester on 4th August 1923. His mother played the piano, while his father was secretary of a local church choir. Butterworth had plenty of opportunity to explore music. The Hallé Orchestra was right on his doorstep, and he learned to play the trombone sufficiently well to earn a place with the famous Besses o' the Barn brass band. He also learned the rudiments of conducting. As was quite common in those days, however, although his parents were happy for him to make music in his spare time, they did not consider it appropriate as a career. Nevertheless, when he left grammar school, he managed to secure a place at the Royal Manchester College of Music (now the RNCM) where he studied the trumpet and composition which, even at this stage, it was clear was to become an abiding passion.

After college, he joined the Scottish National Orchestra (now the RSNO) as a trumpeter, and in 1950 wrote to Vaughan Williams asking for private lessons in composition. The elder composer's positive reply seems, more than anything, to have been dictated by the fact that Butterworth shared a surname with his late friend George, who had been killed in the First World War. At one of their earliest sessions, Butterworth presented his mentor with a few of his songs, apologising for the fact that they were rather derivative of Vaughan Williams's own style. "Oh, you mustn't worry about that, my boy", he replied reassuringly. "I've been the biggest cribber since Handel!"[152]

From 1955 Butterworth spent seven years as a trumpeter with the Hallé Orchestra under Sir John Barbirolli. This coincided with the completion of his Symphony No. 1, and in July 1957 Barbirolli undertook to conduct it with the Hallé at the Cheltenham Festival. Butterworth's breakthrough had arrived. The symphony is a full-blooded work of thirty-five minutes, full of the rugged northern landscape he had experienced for himself while still a member of the Scottish National Orchestra and, by his own admission, strongly influenced by the music of Sibelius – in particular his Symphony No. 6. Butterworth's love of northern landscapes is evident also in several other works, including *The Moors: Suite for Large Orchestra and Organ* (1962), *The Path Across the Moors* (1964), *A Dales Suite (Embsay)* (1965), *A Moorland Symphony*, for bass solo, chorus & orchestra (1967), Symphony No. 3 (*Sinfonia Borealis*, 1979), *Tundra: Boreal Suite for Large Wind Band* (1979), *Northern Light: A Symphonic Study* (1991), and *Grey Moorland: Concert March* (c. 2008).

Although some of Butterworth's miniatures, such as *The Path Across the Moors*, are simply structured and tuneful, with a popular appeal, his symphonies are vessels for personal expression. They are not written to please, but aim to create an atmosphere and an emotive force which cannot be expressed in words or any other form of art but music. At one point in his talk to the BMS, Butterworth quotes the last lines of Wordsworth's *Intimations of Immortality*: "[To me the meanest flower that blows can give]/ Thoughts that [do often] lie too deep for tears", paraphrasing it as: "Music that lies too deep for words".

In 1962 Butterworth relinquished his post with the Hallé Orchestra in order to devote more time to composition, but in order to make ends meet accepted a teaching post at the Huddersfield School of Music, and became principal conductor of

152 An anecdote reported by Butterworth himself during a talk given to the BMS at the New Cavendish Club, London, in 2008. See Dutton, CDLX 7212.

the Huddersfield Philharmonic Orchestra. Eventually he settled in the village of Embsay a few miles west of Skipton, on the edge of the Yorkshire Dales where he died on 20th November 2014, having lost his wife in the previous year.

Butterworth's other lifelong interests are also reflected in his output. For some thirty years he wrote widely for brass band, and his commitment to the chamber music medium lasted even longer, from the late forties to the end of his life. He was less interested in the choral medium, his most substantial piece being the *Moorland Symphony* for bass solo, chorus & orchestra.

What about Butterworth's place in the musical pantheon today? He did receive some recognition in his lifetime, being awarded the MBE in 1995, but, as ever, his reputation will rest with the recording companies. The brass bands, for all his love of them, do not seem to have taken him up, and amateur orchestras, which have occasionally played his pieces, are generally not really capable of tackling his more demanding music. The Symphony No. 1 has been the most widely disseminated of the seven he composed, and the only one to have been recorded more than once. Barbirolli's 1958 recording with the Hallé (Dutton CDLX 7212) was followed in 1998 by Douglas Bostock's interpretation with the München Symphoniker (Classico CLASS CD 274). Dutton have recorded Symphonies Nos. 4 and 5 (CDLX 7212, 7253), along with the substantial Viola Concerto (RSNO; Bradley, viola; Butterworth; CDLX 7212), and several shorter works (CDLX 7253). Finally, there is the Lyrita recording of Symphonies Nos. 1, 2 and 4 (REAM 1127). The chamber music has fared less well, but there is a Dutton recording of the Piano Trios Nos. 1 & 2, plus the Viola Sonata.

a. Bibliography

Conway, Paul, "Arthur Butterworth: A Life in Music", *British Music*, 37/1 (2015), pp. 33–45

France, John, "Arthur Butterworth: North Country Impressionist", *British Music*, 37/2 (2015)

b. Selected Discography

i) Symphonies

Symphony No. 1	Hallé O., Barbirolli	Dutton	CDLX 7212
Symphony No. 2	BBC Scottish SO, Adey	Lyrita	REAM 1127
Symphony No. 4	RSNO, Butterworth	Dutton	CDLX 7212
Symphony No. 5	RSNO, Butterworth	Dutton	CDLX 7253

ii) Orchestral

Viola Concerto	RSNO, Butterworth Bradley (viola)	Dutton	CDLX 7212
The Quiet Tarn	RSNO, Butterworth	Dutton	CDLX 7253
The Green Wind	RSNO, Butterworth	Dutton	CDLX 7253
Three Nocturnes	RSNO, Butterworth	Dutton	CDLX 7253
The Path across the Moors	Royal Ballet Sinfonia; Sutherland	ASV	CD WHL 2126

iii) Chamber

Piano Trio No. 1	Terroni Piano Trio	Dutton	CDLX 7164
Piano Trio No. 2	Terroni Piano Trio	Dutton	CDLX 7164
Viola Sonata	Geoff (viola); Terroni (piano)	Dutton	CDLX 7164

14. George Butterworth (1885–1916)

When Lt. George Kaye Sainton Butterworth fell to a sniper's bullet in Munster Alley at the Battle of the Somme in the early hours of 5th August 1916, England lost one of her most promising and aspiring young composers. He had already begun to make a name for himself with orchestral rhapsodies and idylls in a quintessentially English idiom – *A Shropshire Lad* and *The Banks of Green Willow* among them – and, of course, there were two exquisite song-cycles with texts from Housman's *Shropshire Lad* poems. There are those today who still lament the fact that fate never allowed Butterworth to develop into the flower of English music he would surely have become. Would he have turned into a symphonist like his close friend Vaughan Williams? Others, however, are of the view that we should be grateful for the few works we do have. Composers who die at the age of thirty-one, leaving such a precariously small output, are usually soon forgotten. At least Butterworth's works are distinctive enough to have secured him a place in the annals of English music, and today he can still, occasionally, be enjoyed in our concert halls as well as on record.

George Butterworth was born in London on 12th July 1885 to upper middle-class parents and enjoyed a comfortable upbringing. His father, Alexander Kaye Butterworth (1854–1946) worked as a solicitor on the Great Western Railway, and when in 1891 he took up a similar post with the North Eastern Railway, he decamped with his family to York. Later he was to become the railway's General Manager. Butterworth's mother, Julia Wigan (1849–1911) came of a musical family from Portishead near Bristol. She was proficient on the piano and became a fine career soprano. It was no doubt she who encouraged her son's musical gifts.

The course of Butterworth's early life followed that of many boys in a similar social position – prep school (at Aysgarth), followed by one of the traditional public establishments – in his case Eton. These in turn served to provide the Oxbridge colleges with their staple diet of young men whose careers would be made in the army, the church or the civil service. Few in those days "succeeded" in life without they were Oxbridge graduates. Yet Butterworth was no model scholar. The frequent reports of his housemaster at Eton reveal him to have been a somewhat wayward and indifferent student who was a constant worry to those charged with his academic progress. One reason for this is that he tended to dissipate his energies among a wide variety of interests and causes rather than focusing on a select few. Gradually, however, music became an overriding passion, and George's earliest efforts in composition date back to 1903 or earlier. In fact, he had tried his hand at writing hymn tunes while still at Aysgarth, and his experiments in composition continued apace at Eton.

Time and again, this early period of Butterworth's development, according to those who knew him, is characterised by his abruptness of manner – probably precipitated by an innate shyness. By all accounts he was a good sportsman, cricket being his chief interest here, and he took a keen interest in the various clubs and societies on offer, both at Eton and, later, when he went up to Oxford. On the other hand, he seems to have had few academic aspirations. At each institution through which he passed – Aysgarth, Eton, Oxford – he imbibed just what he needed, and quickly became bored with that in which he had no interest. Soon, it became obvious that Butterworth was gravitating towards a life in music – a tendency which was no doubt encouraged by his music-loving mother but resisted by his father whose plan was that his son should follow him in the legal profession. Once bitten by the music bug, however, there was little chance of his complying with that wish. The modest results obtained in "Mods" and "Greats" at Oxford bear clear witness to where his interests really lay. He might have succeeded in anything to which he put his mind, but clearly this did not include academia, even of the musical variety. Music for him was of the heart rather than the head.

After leaving Oxford he spent a year (1909–10) as a teacher at nearby Radley College, where he found the standard of music somewhat indifferent, and set about making improvements, including the formation of a choir. Even at Radley, however, he seems to have been more enthused by the sporting activities, and a lifelong career as a music master was never a realistic prospect. It was during this period that Butterworth's earliest published songs were composed, and within a couple of years he would reach his high-water mark, composing, between 1911–14, all the works which made him a household name and ensured his posterity.

One particularly fruitful outcome of Butterworth's Oxford and Radley years was the opportunity they afforded him to indulge his interest in folksong collecting and morris dance hunting. The English Folk Dance and Song Society had been established by Cecil Sharp and kindred spirits in 1898, with the object of saving for posterity the centuries-old traditional folksongs of England which it was feared would be lost forever if action was not taken to retrieve them from the dying breed of old singers. Butterworth joined the Society in 1906, entering into its activities with all the enthusiasm he could muster in what he considered to be a worthwhile cause. Between this year and 1913 he collected over 300 examples – mainly from Sussex, but also from various other counties, including Norfolk, Herefordshire and Yorkshire. Others may have collected more (Cecil Sharp, c. 3,000; Vaughan Williams, c. 800), but not in so concentrated a space of time. Furthermore, Butterworth had other irons in the fire. He spent a good deal of time not only researching morris dancing but also demonstrating the art, for he became a leading practitioner, as can be seen on a set of old Kinora spools (a kind of primitive cine device) which have, happily, been preserved for public viewing.[153] Just as valuable is a journal entry documenting a ten-day long morris-hunting expedition in the Bicester area of Oxfordshire in which Butterworth bemoans the trials and tribulations of trying to ascertain an accurate record of the dance movements from the few aged dancers who could hardly remember the details from so long ago.

153 These brief clips are available on the DVD *All My Life's Buried Here: The Story of George Butterworth*, available from the Butterworth Society web site (www.georgebutterworth.co.uk)

The position of Alexander Butterworth as General Manager of the North Eastern Railway necessitated, in July 1910, a move with his family back from York to London. Desirable accommodation was found at 19 Cheyne Gardens, Chelsea (Vaughan Williams was a close neighbour), but only six months later George's mother Julia died, having been ill for some years with Hodgkin's Disease. As he had always been especially close to her, he felt the bereavement deeply, and the composition of the song *Requiescat* two months later was probably prompted by his personal loss. The text was taken from a poem by Oscar Wilde (1854–1900) who had written the words in response to the death of his own sister in 1867. Certainly, the elegiac mood and the sparse piano accompaniment suggest a keenly-felt personal experience.

Possibly it was this event that released in Butterworth the concentrated burst of creativity over the following three years. The songs comprising the two Housman cycles – eleven in all – were composed at intervals between 1909–11, and were performed either individually or in various orders at first, only assuming their present form as *Six Songs from "A Shropshire Lad"* and *Bredon Hill and Other Songs* when they were prepared for publication in 1912. The *Orchestral Rhapsody: A Shropshire Lad* (Butterworth prevaricated over the title) was completed in 1911 and described by the composer as being "in the nature of an orchestral epilogue" to the two Housman cycles, the most obvious clue being that it is based primarily on "Loveliest of Trees", the opening item in *Six Songs*, and there is a hint also of "With Rue My Heart is Laden" at the end.

There are no folksong quotations in the Rhapsody, but the remaining orchestral works written during this highly productive spell are based unashamedly on folksongs, mainly from the composer's personal collection. The *English Idyll No. 1* is based on three Sussex tunes: "Dabbling in the Dew", "Henry Martin", and "Just as the Tide was Flowing", of which there are several versions in Butterworth's collection, with details of the singer and place duly noted. *English Idyll No. 2* is based on the tune "Phoebe and the Dark-Eyed Sailor", also collected in Sussex. The third "idyll",

The Banks of Green Willow, includes not only the folksong of the title, but also "Green Bushes". Again, Butterworth had more than one version of these songs in his collection. All these pieces were blessed with performances within a couple of years of completion. Indeed, the young Adrian Boult (1889–1983) chose to give the first performance of *The Banks of Green Willow* as part of his own debut programme as a professional conductor in 1913.

Other works from this period include a Suite for String Quartette [sic] and a song-cycle setting poems by W.E. Henley (1849–1903), *Love Blows as the Wind Blows* (1912). Music critics generally opine that the Suite does not represent Butterworth at his most inspired. Michael Barlow[154] is of the view that in each of the five movements "folksong influence is apparent", while Anthony Murphy[155] demurs, except for the first movement. Certainly, the piece as a whole is a departure from the orchestral rhapsody and idylls, although it does not necessarily post-date them. Continental influence (Brahms?) is not so very far away. There are passages of symphonic potential, and Kriss Russman recently prepared a version for string orchestra which is available on CD (BIS-2195).

Love Blows as the Wind Blows (1912; orch. 1914) is a setting of four Henley poems arranged as a genuine song-cycle, whose original scoring for string quartet accompaniment may well have been suggested by Vaughan Williams's cycle *On Wenlock Edge* (1909) which Butterworth is known to have admired. The poems included are: "In the Year that's Come and Gone", "Life in her Creaking Shoes" (which contains the work's title), "Fill a Glass with Golden Wine", and – the most accomplished of the four – "On the Way to Kew". A *leitmotiv*, heard at the outset, unifies the work as a whole, although it does not appear in the third song. In 1914 Butterworth himself prepared an orchestral version, taking the opportunity to omit "Fill a Glass". Several commentators have dismissed this song as the

154 Michael Barlow, *Whom the Gods Love: The Life and Music of George Butterworth* (London: Toccata Press, 2009), p. 43.

155 Anthony Murphy, *The Banks of Green Willow: The Life and Times of George Butterworth* (Malvern: Capella Archive, 2015), pp. 104–05.

weak link in the piece, but it is not known whether Butterworth recognised it as such and omitted it for that reason. Speaking personally (rather than musically), I think it is an exquisite little gem which works best in the original quartet version because the words require the kind of intimacy one would expect of lovers in a timeless moment of rapture, and this is best achieved with a string quartet. Of course, it requires a sympathetic performance from artists of the highest calibre for best effect.

As the war clouds gathered, Butterworth's inspiration showed no signs of abating, but, once having taken the king's shilling at the beginning of September 1914, he would have been aware that his chances of survival were very much in the balance. Consequently, ever self-critical of his own works, he destroyed at the earliest opportunity everything he considered sub-standard, including a solo piano piece, *Firle Beacon*, which had been much admired by Vaughan Williams – speaking of whom, it may be of interest to mention at this point that the two of them had a close professional rapport, and that any influence exerted by one on the other by no means passed only in one direction. Although Vaughan Williams was the elder man by some thirteen years, he had a high regard for Butterworth's opinions and took entirely to heart his parting shot, when leaving after a visit one evening in 1913, that "you ought to write a symphony". The result was *A London Symphony*. Nor did Butterworth's input end there. Following the first performance of the symphony, Vaughan Williams set about finding a publisher and was advised, on Donald Tovey's recommendation, to try a particular German firm, to which the full autograph score was sent. Nothing more was heard for the next few months and Butterworth realised that, with war looming, it might never be seen again. So, with his customary energy, he organised himself and a few others to copy the full score from the orchestral parts which, happily, were still available in London. Without his prompt action on that occasion, the *London Symphony*, in its 1913 state (there was a major revision of the score in 1918) might well have been lost. As far as I am aware the autograph score never did resurface.

One final work of Butterworth's which escaped the abovementioned cull, was the *Fantasia for Orchestra* which was found incomplete after his death. Clearly, this was a work in progress which he would have taken up again had he survived hostilities. As it stands it consists of some ninety-two bars fully-scored (lasting around three or four minutes in performance), and then breaks off with a trumpet figure and an accompanying note directing attention to a short score of which there is now no trace. Tantalisingly, this note may suggest that Butterworth had completed the piece and that it only remained for him to orchestrate the remainder. We can learn from the score as it stands that Butterworth was attempting something more ambitious than his previous works. The orchestra envisaged was a large one, but minus harp and timpani – usually a trademark of Butterworth's orchestration. There are signs of stylistic development, but resemblances to the Rhapsody and the Idylls, with their folksong inflections and modalism, are still evident.

In the present climate in which musicologists, composers and conductors set themselves the task of completing – or "elaborating" – the unfinished works of deceased composers, it is hardly surprising to find the *Fantasia* having been subject to such treatment – indeed, not once but twice (surely a "first" for British music!). The "elaborators" in this case are Kriss Russman (on BIS-2195) and Martin Yates (on Dutton CDLX 7326). Both, thankfully, allow Butterworth to speak for himself for the ninety-two bars of full score, thereafter using the ideas therein, along with the known compositional traits found in Butterworth's existing orchestral works, to arrive at a satisfying apotheosis. The dimensions of Russman's effort are roughly in line with those of the *Shropshire Lad* rhapsody, while Yates's elaboration is of over fifteen minutes' duration – although, as he admits, it is not possible now to know what the composer's original intention might have been. Yates concludes with the haunting little trumpet phrase with which Butterworth falls silent – and that, to my mind, is entirely appropriate.

a. Bibliography

Barlow, Michael, *Whom the Gods Love: The Life and Music of George Butterworth* (London: Toccata Press, 2009)

Murphy, Anthony, *The Banks of Green Willow: The Life and Times of George Butterworth* (Malvern, Worcestershire: Cappella Archive, 2015)

Smith, Wayne, *George Butterworth: Memorial Volume* (Shrewsbury: YouCaxton Publishers, 2015)

b. Selected Discography

i) Orchestral

A Shropshire Lad (Rhapsody)	Academy of St. Martin-in-the-Fields, Marriner	Decca	468 802-2
The Banks of Green Willow	Academy of St. Martin-in-the-Fields, Marriner	Decca	468 802-2
Two English Idylls	Academy of St. Martin-in-the-Fields, Marriner	Decca	468 802-2
Fantasia (Compl. Yates).	RSNO, Yates	Dutton	CDLX 7326

[An alternative "completion" of this work has been made by Karl Russman, and can be accessed on BIS-2195]

ii) Songs with Orchestra

Love Blows as the Wind Blows	BBC NOW, Russman,	BIS	BIS-2195
Six Songs from "A Shropshire Lad" (orch. Russman)	BBC NOW, Russman	BIS	BIS-2195

iii) Songs

Six Songs from "A Shropshire Lad"	Luxon (bar); Willison (piano)	Decca	468 802-2
Bredon Hill and Other Songs	Luxon (bar); Willison (piano)	Decca	468 802-2
Folk Songs from Sussex	Williams (bar); Burnside (piano)	Naxos	8.572426
Love Blows as the Wind Blows	Depuis (bar); Quator Claudel-Canimex	Atma	ACD2 2701
I will make you brooches	Stone (bar); Barlow (piano)	Stone	5060192780024
I fear thy kisses	Stone (bar); Barlow (piano)	Stone	5060192780024
Requiescat	Stone (bar); Barlow (piano)	Stone	5060192780024

c. DVD

All My Life's Buried Here: The Story of George Butterworth (HajduKino Productions, 2019).

Limited edition. For details, and to purchase, see www.georgebutterworth.co.uk.

15. Rebecca Clarke (1886–1979)

> [W]hen I had that one little whiff of success that I've had in my life, with the Viola Sonata, the rumour went round ... that I hadn't written the stuff myself, that somebody had done it for me. And I even got one or two bits of press clippings saying that it was impossible, that I couldn't have written it myself. And the funniest of all was that I had a clipping once which said that I didn't exist, there wasn't any such person as Rebecca Clarke, and that it was a pseudonym for Ernest Bloch![156]

This revelation, provided by Rebecca Clarke in an interview she gave at the age of ninety, bears eloquent testimony to the discrimination suffered by female composers even as late as the 1920s.[157] The Viola Sonata of which she speaks was her most extensive work, written in 1919, and her reference to Ernest Bloch (1880–1959) is part of the story of how it came about. Clarke was acquainted with the great American patron of the arts Elizabeth Sprague Coolidge (1864–1953) who ran an annual chamber music festival and competition, for which she invited Clarke to submit a piece. There were seventy-three entries for that year, and a double-blind judging process was adopted. In the end, the six judges were evenly split between Clarke's sonata and an entry by Ernest Bloch. Coolidge was called upon to cast the deciding vote which went in Bloch's favour. Nevertheless, the sonata was performed and gained a reputation as one of Clarke's most accomplished pieces. Yet her beginnings were anything but auspicious.

---

156 Cited by Liane Curtis in the liner notes to the Naxos recording of Rebecca Clarke's chamber music (8.557934).

157 Another example concerns a concert given by Clarke and May Muckle in which she presented two of her own works under her proper name and another under the pen-name Anthony Trent. While most of the critics commented favourably on the work by "Trent", they largely ignored the two works under Clarke's own name.

Rebecca Clarke was born in Harrow on 27th August 1886 to an American father and German mother. The father was something of a tyrant who was not averse to beating his children, and he kept a mistress in one wing of his extensive property, much to the dismay of his wife. On the other hand, he had musical interests and encouraged home music-making. He also facilitated Rebecca's musical education, enabling her to study initially at the RAM. After two years there, however, she was withdrawn by her father after her harmony teacher, Percy Hilder Miles, proposed marriage to her.[158] All was not lost, however. In 1907 her father submitted some of her songs to Stanford for his assessment. Seeing that they showed promise, he agreed to take her on as his first female student, and so she spent the next three years (1907–10) at the RCM. It was Stanford who suggested that she transfer from her instrument of choice, the violin, to the viola so that she could be in the "middle of the sound" when she played in an ensemble. She took his advice, seeking out the great Lionel Tertis for tuition, and eventually composed most of her most significant works for the instrument.

At the end of her spell at the RCM, she was unceremoniously ejected from the family home after openly protesting against her father's philandering, and suddenly found herself with her own way to make in the world. Initially, she arranged to make ends meet by playing the viola in various chamber ensembles in and around London, and then in 1912 joined Henry Wood's Queen's Hall Orchestra, one of the first women orchestral players in the capital. She also founded her own quartet with May Muckle, Marjorie Haywood and Kathleen Long.

From 1916 Clarke spent the next eight years in the land of her father's birth, the USA, developing her performing career. It was during this period that her most significant compositions emerged. The Viola Sonata (1919) has been mentioned. Two years later the impressive Piano Trio was submitted for consideration in Coolidge's

158 He must have retained his affections for her, since he bequeathed to her his Stradivarius.

competition, and although it did not win first prize, it did make its mark. Other pieces of this productive period include the substantial Cello Rhapsody (1923) and *Morpheus* for viola and piano which gained some popularity.

In 1924 she returned to London to continue her performing career, and from this time her compositions became more sporadic. For some years, from 1927, she was emotionally involved with the tenor John Goss (1894–1953) – perhaps best-known for his advocacy of Peter Warlock's songs in the 1920s. This lasted until 1933, and as she claimed that she could never compose when she was in love, the decline in her output is understandable. One work she did compose, however, *The Seal Man,* was dedicated to and sung by Goss, and seems to have been entirely a product of their relationship. Based on a prose-poem by John Masefield (1878–1967), it tells the familiar story of a woman (in some versions it is a man) who falls in love with a merman and drowns when she attempts to follow her lover into the sea. Perhaps the story was prophetic of her doomed relationship with Goss.

In 1939 she returned to the USA to visit her brothers, at which time war broke out, leaving her stranded. Unlike many other artists caught in the same net (Britten, Pears, Bate, Auden), however, she took the decision to remain there for the remainder of her life. One likely reason for this is that, while in New York, she bumped into Scottish pianist and composer James Friskin (1886–1967), an old acquaintance from her RCM days, whom she married in 1944. Despite her new husband's encouragement, however, she allowed her composing to more or less fizzle out. This seems to have been a half-conscious decision in any case, since, from 1942 she took up a position as a nanny. Of the works by which she is known today, the song *God Made a Tree* (1954) appears to be the only one from the period of her married life. She did not abandon music entirely, however, continuing to make arrangements of previous works, and establishing a May Muckle Cello Prize at the RAM, which is still awarded annually. After her husband's death she also wrote her memoir *I Had a Father Too,* which remains unpublished.

As we have seen, Rebecca Clarke was never a prolific composer at the best of times. Although her total output amounted to about eighty-five separate works, fifty-two of these were individual songs (there were no song-cycles), while the remainder were choral pieces and chamber works, nearly all of less than ten minutes duration. Many of these were written for herself and her friends to play. Her three major works – those on which her reputation was established and still rests – are the Viola Sonata, the Piano Trio and the Cello Rhapsody, all of which have been recorded on several occasions, and have some connection with Elizabeth Sprague Coolidge, either as entries to her competition, or (in the case of the Rhapsody) as a commission. It is in these pieces that Clarke finds her deepest expression and modes of development. Although she never tried her hand at composing for orchestra, some of the passages in her major works have symphonic potential, and the Viola Sonata has been arranged as a viola concerto by Ruth Lomon. Stylistically there is some affinity with the so-called French impressionists, particularly Debussy, but Clarke never allows these influences to drown out her individual voice.

It is to be hoped that, by now, society has become enlightened enough to assess Rebecca Clarke's output on the basis of its quality rather than on the gender of the composer. The Rebecca Clarke Society, founded in 2000, has done valuable work in securing her reputation and encouraging performances of her works. Those who hear them will surely find there a powerful individual voice whose merits are self-evident in the music.

a. Bibliography

Curtis, Liane, *A Rebecca Clarke Reader* (Bloomington, IN: Indiana University Press, 2004)

Ponder, Michael, "Rebecca Clarke", *British Music*, 5 (1983), pp. 82–88

b. Selected Discography

i) Chamber

Rhapsody for Cello & Piano	Wallfisch (cello); York (piano)	Lyrita	SRCD 354
Sonata for Cello & Piano	Wallfisch (cello); York (piano)	Lyrita	SRCD 354
Sonata for Violin & Piano	McAslan (violin); Jones (piano)	Dutton	CDLX 7132
Midsummer Moon	McAslan (violin); Jones (piano)	Dutton	CDLX 7105
Morpheus	Ponder (viola); Jones (piano)	Dutton	CDLX 7105
Dumka	Hope (violin); Dukes (Viola); Rahman (piano)	Naxos	8.557934

ii) Choral

Choral Music,	Choir of Gonville & Caius Coll., Camb., Webber	ASV	CDDCA 1139

iii) **Songs**

June Twilight, etc.	Wright (sop); Rees (violin); Sturrock (piano)	Gamut	GAM CD 534

c. Website

The Rebecca Clarke Society (www.rebeccaclarke.org)

16. Arnold Cooke (1906–2005)

Arnold Atkinson Cooke died on 13th August 2005 in a care home in Five Oak Green, Kent, some three months short of his ninety-ninth birthday, making him one of the longest-lived composers in English musical history. His final work, *Song of Innocence*, a Blake setting for voice and recorder in memory of the soprano Tracey Chadwell, was composed in 1996, leaving his last decade silent, but he had been a prolific composer well into his eighties, trying his hand at nearly all the traditional genres. He was even called upon, on one occasion, to provide a score for a film on the Colorado beetle – almost (but not quite) trumping Vaughan Williams's boast to have described foot-and-mouth disease in music (in the film *The Loves of Joanna Godden*)!

Cooke was born at Gomersall in West Yorkshire where his father ran a carpet business but was keen on home music-making. Arnold was introduced to the piano from an early age, and by the age of eight was beginning to compose. Later, he gained a place at Repton School in Derbyshire where all forms of musical activities were encouraged. By the age of fourteen he had composed a piano sonata, and was learning the cello as well as developing his piano skills. Moving on to Cambridge (1925–28) he took a BA in history, after which he transferred to music under Edward Dent who proved enormously helpful in a number of ways when it came to Cooke's establishing his career. After Cambridge he enjoyed a three-year spell in Berlin (1929–32), studying under Paul Hindemith whose influence can be detected in many of Cooke's compositions. Thus, when he returned to England, he was well-placed to develop his craft. The first thing he had to do, of course, was to provide a secure living for himself, which he did in the first instance by spending time as Musical Director of the Festival Theatre in Cambridge for which he wrote some incidental music. In 1933, Dent recommended him for the post of Professor of Composition at the (then) Manchester College of Music, which he retained until 1938 when he moved to London.

Cooke's early compositions were taken up by some prestigious musicians. Sir Henry Wood performed his Concert Overture No. 1 at a Queen's Hall Promenade Concert, while the celebrated Griller Quartet performed his String Quartet No. 1. In 1941, however, these initial successes were interrupted by war service with the Royal Navy in which Cooke was involved with some vital preparations for the D-Day landings. After hostilities were over, he managed to secure a post – again on Dent's recommendation – at the Trinity College of Music, London, where Richard Arnell was a colleague, and remained there until his retirement in 1978.

In 1963 he moved to Five Oak Green in Kent, commuting as necessary to London, and was musically active in the local community. He adopted the *gebrauchsmusik* principle of his teacher Hindemith – that music is not just for the elite, or for its own sake, but is meant for use by the people as a whole. Thus, many of Cooke's works are accessible to musicians of varying proficiency, and in some cases are written for unusual combinations. Among the accompaniments to his vocal works, for instance are horn and piano (*Nocturnes*), clarinet and piano (*Songs of Innocence*), flute, oboe and string quartet (*The Seamew*), and treble recorder and piano (*Five Songs of William Blake*). The recorder, in fact, was taken very seriously by Cooke, and he wrote extensively for it, including a concerto with strings (1957), and a divertimento for the same forces (1959). There are also several other works involving the instrument, including the Suite for Treble Recorder and Piano (1961), the Suite for Recorder Quartet (1965), and the *Six Pieces* for treble and tenor recorders (1976).

Cooke wrote more extensively for chamber forces than for any other genre. The backbone of his output in this regard is his set of five string quartets (1933–78), but he seems always to have been happy to tailor his instrumental forces to the requirements of the performers. Thus, there are quartets for piano and string trio (1948–49), flute, clarinet, cello and piano (1964), and a *Quartet-Sonata* for recorder, violin, cello and harpsichord (1964–65), as well as trios for clarinet, cello and piano (1965), and oboe, clarinet and bassoon (1984). There is even a suite for three viols (1978–79).

Among a quantity of solo organ music are two full-scale sonatas (1971, 1980), and a *Tudeley Prelude* (1989), the latter being written for the organ at the little church of Tudeley near Tonbridge, famous for its set of Chagall windows.

The pillars of Cooke's orchestral output are his six symphonies. Four of these (Nos. 1, 3, 4, 5) have been recorded, while No. 6 awaits its first performance. His symphonic technique is informed by the principles laid out by his teacher Hindemith. Notable in all these works are the economy of the forces used, the clarity of musical argument and the lack of excess. There are no preliminaries or note-spinning, and the listener is pitched into the argument without ceremony.

There are concertos for piano (1940), violin (1958), oboe (1954), clarinet (1956, 1982), treble recorder (1957), and orchestra (1986) – his last orchestral work. Unfortunately, there is so little opportunity to hear any of these works that further comment is pointless. Given the extent of Cooke's oeuvre, the amount of recorded music is woefully meagre. Of his sizeable chamber output, there are three string sonatas (Naxos), a clarinet quintet (Helios), a bassoon sonata (Sanctus), and very little else. Again, his most extensive work, the opera *Mary Barton* (1949–54), which must have cost him a huge effort to produce, still awaits its first performance. Sadly, it is an all-too familiar picture in respect of a large majority of English composers.

Cooke's compositions have quality written all over them, and should be heard for that alone. He was not an advocate of any particular "school" or fad of the moment, and as a result may have suffered a degree of neglect during the Glock era at the BBC. He had the integrity to forge his own path according to the principles he had inherited during his apprenticeship under Dent and Hindemith, and he applied them in a manner which was wholly characteristic. It is to be hoped that, in due course, record companies will have the imagination to dip into the large number of Cooke's works that remain to be explored.

a. Selected Discography

i) Symphonies

Symphony No. 1	LPO, Braithwaite	Lyrita	SRCD 203
Symphony No. 3	LPO, Braithwaite	Lyrita	SRCD 295
Symphony No. 4	BBC SO, Pritchard	Lyrita	REAM 1123
Symphony No. 5	BBC Northern SO, Keefe	Lyrita	REAM 1123

ii) Orchestral

Suite: Jabez and the Devil	LPO, Braithwaite	Lyrita	SRCD 203
Concerto for Orchestra	LPO, Braithwaite	Lyrita	SRCD 203
Divertimento	Manchester Camerta Mackenzie; Turner (rec)	Dutton	CDLX 7191

iii) *Chamber*

Violin Sonata No. 2	Stanzeleit (violin); Terroni (piano)	Naxos	8.571362
Viola Sonata	Goff (viola); Terroni (piano)	Naxos	8.571362
Cello Sonata No. 2	Wallfisch (cello); Terroni (piano)	Naxos	8.571362
Clarinet Quintet	Britten String Quartet; King (clar)	Helios	CDH 55105
Bassoon Sonata	Birnstingl (bassn); Haywood (piano)	Sanctus	SCS 022

17. Sir Peter Maxwell Davies (1934–2016)

At the age of fourteen, when he had already been attempting composition for some years, Peter Maxwell Davies submitted a piece entitled *Blue Ice* to the BBC radio programme *Children's Hour*. The producer showed it to Violet Carson (later to be immortalised as *Coronation Street's* Ena Sharples) who opined: "He's either quite brilliant or mad". Posterity has not allowed us to discover which of these alternatives she eventually decided upon, but there were definitely aspects of "Max's" personality, reflected in his hypnotic gaze, which gave the impression of a man on the edge of sanity, particularly in his formative period, and works from the iconic *Eight Songs for a Mad King* (1967) to the chamber opera *The Lighthouse* (1980) (based on the Flannan Isle mystery) reveal a keen interest in exploring madness and the extremities of human endurance. In many other respects, however, Davies shared in many of the concerns of sane society. He was, for instance, a keen environmentalist, an interest which resulted in works of very different timbres such as the vocal symphony *Black Pentecost* (1979), and the piano (or guitar) solo *Farewell to Stromness* (1979) inspired by the threat of plans to mine uranium in the Orkneys where Davies had settled.

Peter Maxwell Davies was born in Salford in 1934, and during his boyhood lived at several addresses in the area. One of his lighter orchestral pieces, *Cross Lane Fair* (1994), was inspired by memories of his visit as a small boy to a fair at Cross Lane in Salford. The use of the bodhran (a traditional Irish drum) and the Northumbrian pipes adds a suitably atmospheric touch, and the end of the piece is supposed to represent the young lad's falling asleep in his father's arms and being carried home. Perhaps this was one of the roots of his later interest in music theatre.

It was obvious from the first that music was to become an all-consuming interest, and after attending grammar school in Leigh, he studied at the University of Manchester and the Royal Manchester College of Music (later the RNCM) where his fellow students included the pianist John Ogden, the conductor Elgar Howarth, and composers Alexander Goehr and Harrison Birtwistle. The last-named shared with Davies an interest in music theatre and in 1967 the two of them co-founded the Pierrot Players, specifically for the purpose of playing their works.[159] Following his studies in Manchester, Davies spent a further year under the tutelage of Goffredo Petrassi (1904–2003) in Italy, returning with all the credentials required to make his name as an *avant garde* composer.

In 1959 he joined the music staff at Cirencester Grammar School for a brief period where he proved to be an innovative teacher, leaving in 1962 to take up a Harkness Fellowship at Princeton University where he studied with Roger Sessions (1896–85). Three years later he spent a year as composer-in-residence at the University of Adelaide.

It is safe to say that, during this early period of his career, Davies's music took no prisoners. Serialism was much in evidence and melody was conspicuous by its absence. His music theatre pieces were full of dissonance and violence, and he experimented with subverting music of an earlier period and applying it to the modern age. For example, the *Eight Songs for a Mad King* is a parody of Handel's *Messiah* which Davies uses to explore the madness of King George III. Pieces inspired by other composers of an earlier age, including the opera *Taverner* (1968) and *St. Thomas Wake* (based on a pavane by John Bull), are also treated on the basis of an eclectic mix of styles to form something entirely novel.

In 1970 Davies visited the Orkneys for the first time, an experience which was to determine his future course. He found a remote croft on Hoy and renovated it to make a home and studio, and the seascapes around the island began to colour his music. He was fortunate, too, to become acquainted with local poet George Mackay Brown (1921–96) with whom he worked closely on several

159 The project later went sour owing to a disagreement between the composers which has never been fully explained, and the group was relaunched by Davies alone and renamed *The Fires of London*. For a balanced account of this episode, see Michael Seabrook, *Max: The Life and Music of Peter Maxwell Davies* (London: Victor Gollancz, 1994), pp. 119–23.

projects. The beginning of Davies's life in Orkney coincided with a change of direction in his music, as it was from that time that he turned decisively to exploring the more traditional genres, including symphonies, concertos and string quartets. Although he was over forty years of age when he wrote his First Symphony (1976), he had ten to his name at the time of his death forty years later, a body of symphonic work as important in its own way as the symphonic cycles of Shostakovich and Robert Simpson. He responded not only to the Orcadian environment and traditions in particular, but to all things Scottish, and he began to write some works in a more approachable style. Although the symphonies do not make for particularly easy listening, it helps to know that they are generally borne out of the great seascapes in which Davies found himself, and the sound of the sea, in all its various moods, is to be found in them.

A further aspect of Davies's music-making from this time is his deep involvement with the Orcadian community. In partnership with George Mackay Brown and other like-minded souls, he founded the St. Magnus Festival in 1977, seeking as far as possible to involve local amateur musicians as well as professionals, and writing new works for the occasion. Like Britten, he delighted in writing for children, one of his final works being a children's opera entitled *The Hogboon* (2015). In addition, there were works inspired by personal friendships. The ever-popular *Orkney Wedding with Sunrise*, complete with the (actually un-Orcadian) Highland bagpipes, although commissioned by the Boston Pops Orchestra, was inspired by an actual Orkney wedding – that of Jack and Dorothy Randall – the "sunrise" music accompanying the inebriated guests back home next morning. Later, for the birth of the couple's daughter, Lucy, he wrote the touching *Lullabye for Lucy* to the words of George Mackay Brown. *Seven Songs Home*, for unaccompanied children's choir, and *Jimmack the Postie* are two examples of Maxwell Davies's musical portraits of day-to-day Orcadian life which made him such a popular and valued member of the community.

The composer's influence in the North, however, ranged far more widely than the Orkneys alone. He struck up a very productive partnership with the Scottish Chamber Orchestra, and over a ten-year period (1987–96) worked on a series of ten concertos, each showcasing a different instrument or instruments. These became known as the Strathclyde Concertos and included works for horn & trumpet, clarinet, bassoon, and double bass – many of the instruments, in fact, which have been rather neglected in the concerto repertoire.

The idea of an extended project of this kind seems to have fired Davies's imagination, because he embarked on a similar one with regard to chamber music, striking a deal with the Maggini String Quartet and the Naxos recording company to produce a series of ten "Naxos" string quartets (2002–07). Chamber music, in fact, became an abiding passion during the latter stages of the composer's career, and he was working on another string quartet (op. 338!) when he succumbed to leukaemia in 2016.

There are few, if any, musical genres that Maxwell Davies's pen left untouched. Operas, symphonies, concertos, overtures, choral – accompanied and unaccompanied, songs, chamber music – all are represented. Film scores were not a significant part of his output, but he did write the music for two Ken Russell films, *The Devils* and *The Boyfriend*. Given that he is often labelled an atheist[160], his lifelong interest in writing sacred music, including music for the Christian liturgy, may suggest a man of contradictions. However, the tradition of agnostics, if not outright atheists, composing liturgical and other religious music has a long and distinguished history in Britain, and includes the works of Vaughan Williams, Holst, Howells, Finzi, Britten and Bernard Stevens, none of whom were conventional Christians, or Christians at all. Maxwell Davies is worthy to be added to this list. While not subscribing to traditional Christian doctrine, he had a keen sense of the spirituality that underpins its

160 The relationship between Maxwell Davies's religious views and his sacred works is no doubt a complex one, and it is likely that there is more to his reputed atheism than meets the eye. Some useful discussion can be found in the admirably detailed liner notes by Roderick Dunnett in Hyperion's recording of the two Masses and other sacred works (CDA 67454).

musical traditions. Early instrumental works like *Alma Redemptoris Mater* and *St. Michael*, as well as *Seven in Nomine*, betray through their titles a certain residual spirituality, and plainsong has been an influence in his work throughout his career. As far back as the 1950s he was composing motets and carols at regular intervals. His move to the Orkneys, with its iconic St. Magnus Cathedral and the solid, simple piety of many of its people, as well as its pagan past, only served to enhance the innate spirituality in many of Maxwell Davies's compositions. Before settling on Hoy, however, the sacred nature of these works was by implication. Following this transition, he began writing for the liturgy itself. At the beginning of the present century, in fact, he embarked on a veritable glut of such pieces, including a Mass for full choir and, ideally, *two* organs (although one will serve). Simultaneously, he produced a further Mass for children's choir ("upper voices") and organ. Both were commissioned by the Choir of Westminster Cathedral. He also wrote a number of organ solos based on ancient Christian hymns or plainsong, including *Reliqui Domum Meum* (1996) and *Veni Creator Spiritus* (2002).

Naturally, as befitted someone of his stature, Davies was showered throughout his career with the usual accolades and honours, even though he also courted controversy at times, both in his music and his personal life. He was awarded the CBE in 1981 and knighted six years later, and, of course, there were the usual honorary doctorates and fellowships of prestigious universities. In addition, he was awarded the Companion of Honour (2014) and (belatedly, perhaps) the Gold Medal of the Royal Philharmonic Society (2015). His most celebrated honour, however, was surely his ten-year fixed-term tenure as Master of the Queen's Music. In one sense, Maxwell Davies may have seemed a strange choice, since he was known to be a somewhat lukewarm royalist at best, but he warmed to his task and fulfilled his duties, later confessing that his views on the monarchy had moderated over time.

There is little doubt that Maxwell Davies lived a colourful and eventful life, both on and off the field, as we might say of a sports personality. Musically, we cannot pin him down to one particular style, and it would be difficult for most people to identify any one of his works as being by him had they not heard the piece before. We must simply take each work as it comes and assess it on its own musical basis. What may be said of him, however, is that he bestrode the world of British music like a colossus in a manner not seen since the days of Vaughan Williams. His fingerprints were everywhere – in the world of children's music, music for the amateur, and, of course, that of the professional musician. He was performer, conductor and administrator as well as composer, and his output was as huge as it was varied. This present cameo of his life and work can hardly do him justice, and the reader who wishes to explore further will need to consult one of the authoritative biographies on the composer.

a. Bibliography

Griffiths, Paul, *Peter Maxwell Davies* (Robson Books, 1985)

Jones, Nicholas and Richard McGregor, *The Music of Peter Maxwell Davies* (Woodbridge, Suffolk: Boydell & Brewer, 2020)

Seabrook, Mike, *Max: The Life and Music of Peter Maxwell Davies* (London: Victor Gollancz, 1994)

Smith, Carolyn J., *Peter Maxwell Davies: A Bio-Biography* (Westport, CT: Greenwood, 1995)

b. Selected Discography

i) Symphonies

Symphony No. 1	BBC PO, Davies	Naxos	8.572348
Symphony No. 2	BBC PO, Davies	Naxos	8.572349
Symphony No. 3	BBC PO, Davies	Naxos	8.572350
Symphony No. 4	Scottish CO, Davies	Naxos	8.572351
Symphony No. 5	Philharmonia O., Davies	Naxos	8.572351
Symphony No. 6	RPO, Davies	Naxos	8.572352
Symphony No. 10	LSO, Poppano	LSO	LS 00767

ii) Concertos

Strathclyde Concertos:			
No. 3, for Horn & Trumpet	Scottish CO, Davies; Cook (horn); Franks (trumpet)	Naxos	8.572353
No. 4, for Clarinet	Scottish CO, Davies; Morrison (clar)	Naxos	8.572353

No. 7, for Double Bass	Scottish CO, Davies McTier (double bass)	Naxos	8.572355
No. 8, for Bassoon	Scottish CO, Davies; Levereaux (bassoon)	Naxos	8.572355
Piano Concerto	RPO, Davies; Stott (piano)	Naxos	8.572357
Trumpet Concerto	RSNO, Davies; Wallace (trumpet)	Naxos	8.572363
Piccolo Concerto	RPO, Davies; McIlwham (piccolo)	Naxos	8.572363

iii) **Orchestral**

Orkney Wedding with Sunrise	RPO, Davies; McIlwham, (bagpipes)	Naxos	8.572352
Cross Lane Fair	BBC PO, Davies	Naxos	8.572350
Caroline Mathilde	BBC PO, Davies	Naxos	8.572358
The Beltane Fire	BBC PO, Davies	Naxos	8.572362
Renaissance Scottish Dances	Scottish CO, Davies	Unicorn	DKP (CD) 9070

iv) *Opera*

The Lighthouse	BBC PO, Davies; Mackie (ten); Keyte (bar); Comboy (bass)	Naxos	8.660354

v) *Chamber*

String Quartets:

Nos. 1–10	Maggini Quartet	Naxos	8.557396-400

vi) **Choral**

Missa Parvula	Choir of Westminster Cath., Baker; Quinney (organ)	Hyperion	CDA 67454
Mass	Choir of Westminster Cath., Baker; Quinney, Houssart (organs)	Hyperion	CDA 67454

vii) **Organ/ Piano**

Organ Sonata	Bowyer (organ)	Nimbus	NI 5509
Farewell to Stromness	Davies (piano)	Unicorn	DKP(CD) 9070

18. Andrew Downes (b. 1950)

Andrew Downes was born in the Handsworth district of Birmingham and has been based in the area for most of his life. He went up to St. John's College Cambridge in 1969 to read music and gained a Masters degree in composition. In 1974 he moved on to the RCM, studying there with Herbert Howells, and the following year joined the staff of the Birmingham Conservatoire as lecturer in composition, remaining in one capacity or another for the next thirty years. He and his wife Cynthia have two daughters, Anna and Paula, both of whom have maintained the family musical tradition. Some years ago, Downes suffered a spinal injury which severely impaired his mobility.

Andrew Downes, now entering on his seventieth year as I write, is what one might call a musician's composer. Ask members of the general public – even the concert-going public – who he is, and the majority would not be able to say. Yet among fellow musicians he is very widely-known and much respected, and a large proportion of his output has come about through commissions from orchestras, conductors and performers.[161] His symphonic works have been championed by the Czech conductor Ondřej Vrabec and the Czech Philharmonic Orchestra, while the pianist Duncan Honeybourne has showcased his solo piano works[162], and continues to do so. He also premiered Downes's Piano Concerto with the Central England Ensemble in 2009.

---

161 Downes is as celebrated among the musical fraternity abroad as he is at home. He has written music for various ensembles and individuals, attended premieres, and been interviewed in a host of countries around the world, including the USA, Japan, France, Italy, the Czech Republic, Austria, India and Israel. In addition, his works have been performed in Australia, China, Mexico and Venezuela. His work has been widely broadcast by the BBC, as well as Italian television, and on Chinese and Dutch radio. How such an internationally celebrated composer is not better-known among the musical public in his homeland is a mystery.

162 Note especially the recording of Downes's complete works for solo piano by Duncan Honeybourne (*Daybreak in the Fields*, EM Records, EMR CD 040–41).

As a self-promoter, Downes must be one of the best in the business. His personal website is full of innovative ideas, and users are invited to share their experiences of playing or listening to his music. There are regular posts detailing upcoming concerts featuring his music and imminent premieres, video clips of Downes in interview, sound samples of some of his compositions, and a video recording of his full-length opera *Far from the Madding Crowd.* Lynwood Music is his personal recording company run by his wife and younger daughter Paula, the latter of whom is often featured in her capacity as soprano promoting her father's songs.

The fertility of mind that facilitates his efforts at self-promotion is applied equally effectively to his compositions. Most of the traditional genres are represented in an output numbering over 115 works. One particular fascination for him over the years has been his exploration of the possibilities of deploying specific instruments in ensembles of varying size. One of his best-known efforts in this regard is a Sonata for Eight Horns (1994). There is also a Sonata for Four Horns (1981), and a Suite for Six Horns (1999). The flute comes in for similar treatment with a Sonata for Eight Flutes, and even an entire symphony (No. 5) for flute ensemble (2001). There is yet another Sonata for Eight Pianos (2000), an early piece for eight cellos and five timpani (1969) and, surely most improbable of all, Five Dramatic Pieces for Eight Wagner Tubas (2005).

Downes has written a quantity of sacred music, usually to commission, including the Runnymede Service (Magnificat & Nunc Dimittis, along with Psalms 23, 121, 122, Preces & Responses), and a St. Luke's Passion. The style of these works is generally conservative, abiding by the usual expectations of music intended for the traditional liturgy. One of his most unusual commissions was *Fanfare for Madam Speaker* to celebrate Betty Boothroyd's appointment as Chancellor of the Open University in 1995.

It would be impossible here to comment in depth on the huge variety of works comprising Downes's output, so I will restrict myself to a few brief remarks on those major works which have been recorded and are accessible to the general listener. One of the earliest large-scale works to put the composer firmly on the map was his cantata *The Marshes of Glynn,* commissioned for the opening of the Adrian Boult Hall in Birmingham in 1986. The text, by the nineteenth-century American poet Sidney Lanier (1842–81), contains the flexibility in rhythm and metre which often attracts composers because they do not feel themselves straitjacketed as they can be in the case of the more traditional forms such as regular iambic pentameter, for instance. Most of the lines are long on the page, suggesting the breadth of the marshes against the sea and the sky. Cynthia Downes remarks that the poem extols the beauty of nature, which is certainly true at surface level, but there is also a deeper, metaphorical sense of the human spirit's striving for ultimate freedom and release from what inhibits it. All this is beautifully reflected in Downes's setting, one of the highlights of which, for me, is the marvellously luminous passage that brings Part 1 to a close. Eventually, the sea, which ebbs from the marshes in the morning, flows back to cover them as night falls, and a day on the marshes of Glynn, as well as man's spiritual journey, reaches its apotheosis. There is, indeed, a spirituality about the poem, and about Downes's interpretation of it, and the music adheres firmly to the great English choral tradition represented by Parry, Stanford, Elgar and Vaughan Williams. The spirituality of the piece seems to be closer to *A Sea Symphony* than to *The Dream of Gerontius*. It is an impressive work which would benefit from a fresh recording by professional forces, since the only one to date has been that of the premiere by the Birmingham School of Music Chorus and Orchestra, conducted by Damian Cranmer, some thirty-five years ago.

Andrew Downes has written six symphonies to date, each of which is refreshingly individual. Nos. 2 (1984) and 6 (2018) are both scored for chamber orchestra, while No. 1 (1982) is scored for organ, brass, percussion and strings. No. 3 (1992) is for large symphony orchestra, No. 4 (1996) for wind band, and No. 5 (2001) for flute ensemble. The particular forces used in each case help to dictate the symphony's character. The First Symphony is altogether a serious matter, with some profound writing and plenty of forte passages for the organ. The Second is not quite on the same scale, and is in effect a chamber symphony with some effective writing for woodwind. The Third Symphony is notable for its blend of cultures and styles, with both African and native American influences in evidence, especially in the use of the marimba. By contrast, the fourth movement, entitled *Belas Knap*, the name of a long barrow on the Cotswolds above Cheltenham, is largely reflective in mood, bringing us back onto home turf. The Symphony expresses musically the ideal that all cultures, peoples, and even ages should be in harmony. The Fourth Symphony, scored for wind band, was commissioned on behalf of the Albuquerque Concert Band, in deference to which each of the five movements explores various aspects of the city and its surrounding landscape and people – the mountains, the desert, the Rio Grande, and the Pueblo Indians.

These four symphonies have been recorded by Ondřej Vrabek and the Czech Philharmonic Orchestra, along with two concert overtures – the Vaughan Williams-influenced *In the Cotswolds* (1986), and *Towards a New Age* (1996), and a twenty-minute video about the recording of these works, resulting in an excellent package showcasing some of Downes's best pieces. His partnership with these Czech musicians has certainly been a fruitful one, for the same forces have further recorded a quantity of the composer's horn music, including a horn concerto.

Another thread in Andrew Downes's work is his evident love of Hardy's poems and novels. His very first acknowledged work, *Casterbridge Fair* (op. 1, 1973) was a setting of five Hardy poems.[163] This was followed in due course by two further sets, *Lost Love* (1977)[164] and *Old Love's Domain* (1985)[165], both of which were recorded by Paula Downes and friends in 2000. Since then, she has

163 The texts chosen are: *The Ballad Singer, Former Beauties, A Wife Waits, After the Club Dance*, and *After the Fair.*

164 The texts are: *The Walk, Lost Love, A Night in November, Last Love Word.*

165 The texts are: *The Division, Something Tapped, Where the Picnic Was, At Castle Boterel, The Curtains are Now Drawn.*

created a film setting of these songs to appropriate images (*Songs of Love and War*, Lynwood Music, 2012). A much more ambitious Hardy Project was the opera *Far from the Madding Crowd* which, again, has been filmed (Lynwood Music, 2007). Unfortunately, the performance is in the restricted space of a church, and the filming is done from a single static camera rostrum, so that the effect of the work is seriously compromised. Of all operas, surely one based on *Far from the Madding Crowd* requires breadth and space in order to achieve its full potential. A well-funded professional performance without such restrictions would reap dividends.

As we have seen, Andrew Downes is a highly inventive composer with a fertile imagination, whose creative impulse shows no sign of abating. At the time of writing, he was working on a violin concerto for Rupert Marshall-Luck, whose connections with the English Music Festival and the EM record company, directed by his wife, may lead us to expect a recording of the piece in due course. Downes's music has led to something of a cottage promotion industry, involving his wife and both daughters working in various capacities. And, as we have seen, he has staunch and faithful performance champions such as Ondřej Vrabec and Duncan Honeybourne, and the resources of the Birmingham musical establishment at his disposal. So, as he reaches seventy, perhaps we can anticipate further fruits to come.

a. Selected Discography

i) Symphonies

Symphonies Nos. 1–4	Czech PO, Vrabec	Artesmon	AS 744-2

ii) Orchestral

Piano Concerto	Central England Ensemble, Bradbury; Honeybourne (piano)	Lynwood	LYNW CD 005
Overture: In the Cotswolds	Czech PO, Vrabec	Artesmon	AS 744-2
Overture: Towards a NewAge	Czech PO, Vrabec	Artesmon	AS 744-2

ii) Choral

The Lord is my Shepherd, etc.	Royal Holloway Chapel Choir; Pike; Moles (organ)	Classicprint	CPVPO14

iii) Songs

Lost Love	P. Downes (sop); Martin (flute); Parsons (cello); Trippett (piano)	Lynwood	LYNWCD 001
Old Love's Domain	P. Downes (sop); Trippett (piano)	Lynwood	LYNWCD 001
Songs from Spoon River	P. Downes (sop); Trippett (piano)	Lynwood	LYNWCD 001

b. DVD

Far from the Madding Crowd (Lynwood, 2007)

c. Website

https://www.andrewdownes.com

19. Sir George Dyson (1883–1964)

Composers occasionally write books or articles. Vaughan Williams contributed fairly regularly to the music journals, while Philip Heseltine (Peter Warlock) wrote the first biography of Delius, and Anthony Payne penned a technical study of Frank Bridge. But how many produced an authoritative manual on grenade warfare? Among George Dyson's claims to fame, that was one. At the outbreak of the First World War, he joined the Royal Fusiliers and was soon appointed grenade officer of the 99th infantry brigade, so his manual was borne out of personal experience and became required reading for the troops. How did he manage to progress from this role to his ultimate appointment as Director of the RCM? All will be revealed.

Dyson came of humble stock. He was born in Halifax, West Yorkshire, where his father was a blacksmith and his mother a weaver. He found himself in the heart of good, honest choir country where the majority of churches had their choir master, and both Dyson's parents were musical in this respect. His own talent was evident from an early age and he was appointed a local church organist at the tender age of thirteen. He made rapid progress, becoming a Fellow of the Royal College of Organists at sixteen and, in 1900, became one of a large crop of aspiring composers under the tutelage of Stanford at the RCM. While there, he carried off the usual prizes, and a Mendelssohn Scholarship enabled further study in Italy, Austria and Germany where he met Richard Strauss.

On his return to Britain in 1907 he was appointed Director of Music at the Royal Naval College, Osborne, but left in 1911 to teach at Marlborough College. The war years were a mixed bag for Dyson. A year after publishing his grenade manual in 1915, he was invalided out of the army with shell-shock. By 1917 he had recovered sufficiently to marry Mildred Atkey, a solicitor's daughter, and in due course they had a daughter, Alice, and a son, Freeman, who became a celebrated physicist. In that year, too, he was awarded the DMus from Oxford, and took up a post as a major in the RAF in charge of organising the military bands.

Dyson's career now began to move apace. In 1920 the Carnegie Trust published one of his first significant compositions, the *Three Rhapsodies* for string quartet. Although hardly vintage Dyson, these pieces are well-crafted and show signs of promise.[166] In the following year he took up the dual posts of Professor of Composition at the RCM and music master at Wellington College, exchanging one school for another when, in 1924, he moved to Winchester. In addition, there were visiting lectureships at Liverpool and Glasgow universities. Clearly, composition at this stage had to be put on the back-burner. Nevertheless, in 1928 he produced his most successful piece to date, the cantata *In Honour of the City*, to the text of that title by the Scottish poet William Dunbar (c. 1469–c. 1520). Dyson was particularly concerned to write choral works which would be within the scope of amateur as well as professional choirs, and this cantata is direct and eminently singable, which no doubt accounted for its immediate popularity. The city in question, of course, is London, "the flower of cities all". The terms "tuneful", "virile" and "vigorous" have all been used to describe the work, and not without reason.

Flush with his success, Dyson set out to compose a more ambitious work along much the same lines, and in 1931 *The Canterbury Pilgrims* appeared, a large-scale setting of Chaucer's *Prologue*. Here we are introduced to some wonderfully entertaining musical depictions of the many colourful characters who wend their way from Southwark to Canterbury, including the knight, the squire, the nun, the wife of Bath, the poor parson, and all the motley crew. This work must be among his most approachable and entertaining compositions, each character being so vividly drawn. It remains Dyson's most popular large-scale composition, again within the range of many amateur choirs, and is still occasionally performed.

During the next decade Dyson produced a string of works on which his reputation came to rest, including *St. Paul's Voyage*

166 They can be heard on Hyperion CDA 66139, along with Howells's string quartet *In Gloucestershire*.

to Melita (1933), *The Blacksmiths* (1934), *Nebuchadnezzar* (1935), the Symphony (1937), *Quo Vadis* (1939), and the Violin Concerto (1942). Of the spiritually-inspired works, *Quo Vadis*, with its eclectic mix of texts ranging from Thomas Campion (1567–1620), Robert Herrick (1591–1674) and Henry Vaughan (1621–95), to William Wordsworth (1770–1850), John Keeble (1792–1866) and John Henry Newman (1801–90), comes nearest to donning Victorian clothes. It "takes us on a voyage of the spirit comparable with the great choral works of Elgar, Walford Davies, Howells and Vaughan Williams"[167], although it comes closer to the former two composers than the latter. Indeed, one of the criticisms of Dyson in his own day, and a major reason for his neglect after his death, is that he was too much of a traditionalist with regard to his choral writing. Sometimes, when he mined the Bible for inspiration, he came up with some surprising choices: who else would have thought of setting the story of Paul's shipwreck (Acts 27) to music? Dyson seems intent on exploiting dramatic effect, as also in his setting of the fiery furnace (Daniel 3, supplemented by the apocryphal Song of the Three Holy Children). The imaginatively-scored *The Blacksmiths*, for tenor, chorus, piano and orchestra, might well have been suggested by the fact that Dyson's father had been a blacksmith, while the Symphony seems to have been the crown of his purely orchestral output. It was completed more or less simultaneously with Moeran's Symphony in G minor at a time when symphonies by Vaughan Williams, Walton and Bax were also in the offing. It is tempting to compare Dyson's work with these, and although it is in exalted company, it should not be regarded as significantly inferior.

A year after the completion of his Symphony, Dyson succeeded Sir Hugh Allen as Director of the RCM, the first former student of the establishment to receive this accolade. He threw himself energetically into the administrative life of the college, overhauling its facilities and reorganising the curriculum. During the war years,

167 Lewis Foreman, liner notes for the Chandos recording of *Quo Vadis* (CHAN 10061(2)), p. 7.

despite the threat of German bombing, he insisted that the college remain *in situ* in its South Kensington home rather than decamping to a safer environment, which ensured a sense of continuity. Following hostilities, the RCM was faced with a glut of applicants, both from those whose studies had been interrupted by military service, and from aspiring new entrants. Hard choices had to be made, and the standard of entrants in general was higher than it had been for years.

Dyson's well-earned reputation as one of Britain's leading musical figures earned him a knighthood (1941) and appointment as Knight Commander of the Royal Victorian Order (1953). In 1952, at the age of sixty-nine, he retired to Winchester where he had spent thirteen years as a teacher at the college there. This move afforded him new freedom to concentrate on composition. From this final decade came the *Three Choral Hymns* (1952), *Sweet Thames, Run Softly* (1955), *Agincourt* (1956), and *Hierusalem* (1956), and he continued composing until a couple of years before his death. He had come a long way since his boyhood in Halifax.

Considering that Dyson was primarily a teacher and an administrator throughout his career, the size of his output is impressive. He turned out some substantial works, and was probably most at home with choral music, both accompanied and unaccompanied, although he was already forty-five when he composed *In Honour of the City*, his first substantial work in this genre. Among his most impressive achievements must be included *The Canterbury Pilgrims*, one of his most colourful efforts, and *Quo Vadis*, the first with a run-time of one-and-a-half hours, the other two hours. All Dyson's music bears the stamp of fine craftsmanship, with hardly – if ever – a note out of place (a la Dyson's own hairstyle!) – which is not to say that he did not have his critics, even among his fellow composers. At the beginning of Paul Spicer's excellent biography of the man and his music, he quotes from a letter by E.J. Moeran to his friend Lionel Hill whose father-in-law happened to be the celebrated concert violinist Albert Sammons:

> If only your respected parent-in-law would not have wasted so much time over such stuff as Sir G. Dyson's Concerto! ... But he has recently been playing it all over the place ... Why? If it were Walton's or the Bloch or Bartok I could understand it and applaud it ... But Dyson! – words fail me".[168]

There is no doubt that Dyson was a conservative among English composers of the time. He was well aware of it and made no apology for it: "My reputation is that of a good technician ... [I am] not markedly original. I am familiar with modern idioms, but they are outside the vocabulary of what I want to say".[169] Thus, those who are looking for the kind of musical thrill often engendered by the pyrotechnics of modernist works, with their exotic instruments, will need to look elsewhere, for Dyson, throughout his career, stuck doggedly to his conservative principles, and latterly at a time when doing so did him no favours. Nevertheless, his personal integrity forbade any departure from these principles. His music was all good, honest stuff, firmly rooted in the soil of the English tradition in which he had been brought up, and it is good that the very best of his choral work is well-established in the repertoire, and that his major pieces are well-represented on record.

168 P. Spicer, *Sir George Dyson: His Life and Music* (Woodbridge, Suffolk: Boydell Press, 2014), p. 1. Spicer is quoting from a lengthy missive by Moeran in Lionel Hill, *Lonely Waters: The Diary of a Friendship with E.J. Moeran* (London: Thames Publishing, 1985), pp. 40–42, which makes it clear than Moeran was making strenuous efforts to get Sammons to pay his own Violin Concerto, but at the time of writing with little success. This may have had more than a little to do with his vitriolic approach to Dyson's concerto. Certainly, there is no rationale presented as to why he should have found it so offensive.

169 "Obituary: Sir George Dyson", *The Times*, 30th September 1964; quoted from the Wikipedia entry on the composer.

a. Bibliography

Dyson, Alice and Christopher Palmer, eds., *Dyson's Delight: An Anthology of Sir George Dyson's Writings and Talks on Music* (London: Thames Publishing, 1989)

Palmer, Christopher, *George Dyson: A Centenary Celebration* (Sevenoaks: Novello, 1984)

----------, *George Dyson: Man and Music* (London: Thames Publishing, 1996)

Spicer, Paul, *Sir George Dyson: His Life and Music* (Woodbridge, Suffolk: Boydell Press, 2014)

b. Selected Discography

i) Orchestral

Symphony in G	City of London Sinfonia, Hickox	Chandos	CHAN 9200
Concerto Leggiero	City of London Sinfonia, Hickox	Chandos	CHAN 9076
Concerto de Camera	City of London Sinfonia, Hickox	Chandos	CHAN 9076
Concerto de Chiesa	City of London Sinfonia, Hickox	Chandos	CHAN 9076
Overture: At the Tabard Inn	LSO, Hickox	Chandos	CHAN 9531

ii) Choral with Orchestra

The Canterbury Pilgrims	LSO & Chorus; soloists; Hickox	Chandos	CHAN 9531
Quo Vadis	BBC NOW & Chorus; Chamber Choir of the Royal Welsh College of Music & Drama; soloists; Hickox	Chandos	CHAN 10061

Nebuchadnezzar	BBC SO & Chorus; Padmore (ten); Davies (bass-bar); Hickox	Chandos	CHAN 10439
St. Paul's Voyage to Melita	Bournemouth SO & Chorus; Mackie (ten); Handley	Somm	SOMMCD234
Agincourt	Bournemouth SO & Chorus, Handley	Somm	SOMMCD234
Hierusalem	RPO; St. Michael's Singers; Hill (sop); Trotter (organ); Rennert	Helios	CDH 55046
The Blacksmiths	RPO, RCM Chamber Choir, Willcocks	Somm	SOMMCD014
In Honour of the City	RPO, RCM Chamber Choir, Willcocks	Somm	SOMMCD014
Sweet Thames, Run Softly	RPO, RCM Chamber Choir,Roberts (bar); Willcocks	Somm	SOMMCD014

c. Website

The Sir George Dyson Trust (www.dysontrust.org.uk)

20. John Foulds (1880–1939)

It is difficult to know quite where to begin with John Foulds, for he was a composer of enormous energy and diverse musical interests. In a sense, he pursued several careers simultaneously – on the one hand a cellist with the Hallé Orchestra (in which his father was a bassoonist) in the heady days of Hans Richter, on the other a serious composer who pioneered the use of quarter tones in some of his works, and experimented with the use of Indian instruments in a Western musical setting. In addition to these activities, he paid his way by writing scores for theatre productions and popular light music pieces.

John Foulds was born in Manchester and began composing in childhood. In this, he was largely self-taught, but his years as an orchestral player in theatre ensembles and promenade orchestras, along with his elevation to the Hallé in 1900 when he was still only twenty, served him well. Many composers – Malcolm Arnold, for instance – have learned their trade in that way. Richter gave him valuable lessons in conducting, and soon he was on the way to a stellar career.

Foulds never lacked confidence in his abilities. Between 1905-07 he was at work on a huge "concert opera", *The Vision of Dante*, based on the poet's *Divine Comedy*. However, despite no less a person than Elgar trying to pull the strings, no performance was ever secured. Undeterred, he later embarked on another substantial project. Although he never served in the First World War, he produced a gigantic *World Requiem* (1919-21) in memory of all who had suffered in the conflict, and for a few years, from 1923-26, it became the work of choice to be performed on Armistice Day and was sponsored by the British Legion. At its premiere it was performed by an orchestra, massed choirs and soloists numbering over 1,200 members, a huge undertaking which even rivalled Havergal Brian's mighty Gothic Symphony. This annual event suddenly came to an end after 1926, the official reason being that the British Legion had decided to end its sponsorship of the work, though some have suggested that Foulds had incurred the displeasure of certain authority figures, either because the work was not jingoistic enough, or because it had come to their attention that he had not served in the war he was commemorating.

Following this setback, Foulds turned his back on England, spending the next three years (1927-30) based in Paris along with his second wife Maud MacCarthy, who he had met in London. Fould's first marriage had been to a librarian with whom he had little in common. With Maud it was different. She might have been attracted by his good looks (Foulds was as photogenic as Percy Grainger), but what really bonded them was their shared philosophy and musical interests. Both were keen theosophists and interested in Indian musical instruments. The house was full of strange, heady odours and aids to meditation. Their son Patrick described the scene: "... my sense of smell was early stimulated by roses, oil paint, *batik* wax smoking, and joss-sticks burning on 'The Shrine', an enormous hand-crafted piece of furniture, which held mother's *vina* and *table*, and where she meditated".[170] Foulds was one of those composers who firmly believed that, in the case of serious music, at least, he had to tap into the sounds out there in the ether; they did not come from his own mind, but simply passed through him.

It was during his Paris years that Foulds completed some of his most important and characteristic works, including the *Three Mantras* (1919-30), the *Dynamic Triptych* (1929), and the delightfully engaging *April – England* (he had not quite forgotten the old country). The *Mantras* began life as preludes to a projected three-act opera, *Avatara*, which Foulds abandoned. The outer two *Mantras*, *Mantra of Action* and *Mantra of Will*, are fuelled by enormous dynamic energy which gives the large orchestra full rein. By contrast, the central *Mantra of Bliss*, with its wordless female chorus, creates an airy, ethereal atmosphere.

170 Patrick Foulds (b. 1916) in the liner notes to Warner Classics CD of Foulds's orchestral music (2564 61525-2).

The *Dynamic Triptych* is in effect a piano concerto. Like the *Three Mantras,* there are two dynamic outer movements, toccata-like in conception, separated by a slow, romantic central movement which makes use of quarter-tones with which Foulds had been experimenting since the 1890s.

In his own day, Foulds was better-known as a composer of light music rather than as a classical composer, with works such as the overture *Le Cabaret* and *Suite Fantastique;* but it was the *Keltic Lament* which really made his name in the field and was probably played more than anything else he wrote. He contributed to the theatre with scores for plays including Shaw's *St. Joan* and Shakespeare's *Henry VIII.* Foulds complained that this kind of "hack work" obstructed his progress as a composer of "serious" music, but it did bring him an income without which he would not have been free to write his more substantial works at all.

Although he is most associated with orchestral works, he also wrote a quantity of chamber music, including at least nine string quartets. Not all of these have survived, but of those that have, the *Quartetto Intimo* (again using quarter-tones) is the most familiar. Among his works for piano solo are *Essays in the Modes,* and *Five Recollections of Ancient Greek Music* (later to be orchestrated as the *Hellas Suite*), in which he develops his interest in the traditional Greek modes.

In 1935 Foulds made what turned out to be a fateful move, with his family, to India where he took up the post of Director of European Music for All-India Radio. Here he was able to indulge his interests in Indian music and instruments, writing pieces which combined these with a traditional European orchestra. His success with his radio station, based in Delhi, led to his being asked to open a branch in Calcutta, and it was here that he contracted cholera and died on 25th April 1939. While in India, he is known to have written an ambitious *Symphony of East and West* in which he attempted a synthesis of musical styles, but this score, along with several others, was lost after his death.

Like so many of the composers covered in the present volume, Foulds's star sank fairly rapidly once he was no longer around, but, thanks largely to the tireless campaign of musicologist Malcolm MacDonald, he was rescued from oblivion.[171] Today Warner Classics and Lyrita have recorded important examples of his "serious" music, including the *Three Mantras* and *Dynamic Triptych*, and there is a splendid Chandos recording of the *World Requiem*, while Dutton has produced a four-volume series of Foulds's light music and theatre pieces. There is also a recording of some of the string quartets, including the *Quartetto Intimo*. The earliest extant recording of a Foulds piece – if it can still be tracked down – is an old Forlane disc recorded in 1981 in which his suite *St. Joan*, *Pasquinade Symphonique No. 1*, and *Mirage* rub shoulders with Parry and Havergal Brian. The liner notes describe these three as "masters of the English musical renaissance", with Brian and Foulds presented as heirs of Parry and Elgar. Foulds is said to have expressed an admiration for the music of Bartok, Busoni and Scriabin. However, the influences to be heard in his own music are more German and French, though these are distilled through his own stylistic traits, and his music is wholly characteristic; no-one else quite matches his dynamism, and his climaxes can be shattering. Now that his major works have been recorded, critics have a better chance of assessing his achievement. The next task must be to get them performed in the concert hall.

171 With the independent assistance of Robert Simpson, MacDonald did much the same for Havergal Brian.

a. Bibliography

MacDonald, Malcolm, *John Foulds* (Rickmansworth, Herts: Triad, 1975)

----------, *John Foulds and His Music: An Introduction* (London: Kahn & Averill, 2006)

Tufnell, Lance, "John Herbert Foulds (1880–1939): An Appreciation", *British Music*, 10 (1989)

b. Selected Discography

i) *Orchestral*

Dynamic Triptych	CBSO; Oramo; Donohoe (piano)	Warner	2564 62999-2
April, England	CBSO, Oramo	Warner	2564 62999-2
Song of Ram Dass	CBSO, Oramo	Warner	2564 62999-2
Keltic Lament	CBSO, Oramo	Warner	2564 62999-2
Three Mantras	CBSO, Oramo	Warner	2564 61525-2
Mirage	CBSO, Oramo	Warner	2564 61525-2
Overture: Le Cabaret	LPO, Wordsworth	Lyrita	SRCD 212
Hellas Suite	LPO, Wordsworth	Lyrita	SRCD 212
Pasquinade Symphonique No. 2	LPO, Wordsworth	Lyrita	SRCD 212
Keltic Overture	BBC Concert O., Corp	Dutton	CDLX 7252
Keltic Suite	BBC Concert O., Corp	Dutton	CDLX 7252

ii) **Chamber**

Cello Sonata	P. Watkins (cello); H. Watkins (piano)	Chandos	CHAN 10741
Quartetto Intimo	Endemion String Quartet	Pearl	SHE 564
Quartetto Geniale	Endemion String Quartet	Pearl	SHE 564
Aquarelles	Endemion String Quartet	Pearl	SHE 564

21. Peter Racine Fricker (1920–90)

Today, Peter Racine Fricker is perhaps best-known for his unusual name – Racine being taken from his association, by line of descent, with the French playwright of that name. However, in his day he was highly regarded as a composer and the style of his music chimed in with current trends in the 1960s–70s. He was born in Ealing, London, and educated at St. Paul's School before entering the RCM in 1937 to study composition with R.O. Morris and organ with Ernest Bullock. During the Second World War he joined the RAF as a radio operator (1941-46), and on his demobilisation resumed his studies with the Hungarian émigré Mátyás Seiber (1905–60) at Morley College. He began to make his mark as a composer, winning the A.J. Clements Prize for his Wind Quintet (op. 5), and the Koussevitzky Prize for his Symphony No. 1 (op. 9). In 1951 he added to these by winning the Arts Council of Great Britain composing competition with his Violin Concerto.

In 1952 Fricker succeeded Michael Tippett as Director of Music at Morley College where he remained for the next twelve years. From 1955 he combined his duties there with a professorship of music at the RCM. In 1964 he took up the post of Visiting Professor of Music at the University of California, Santa Barbara, becoming Chair of Music there six years later, and finally, in 1989, composer-in-residence of the Santa Barbara Symphony Orchestra, for which he composed his final orchestral work, *Walk by Quiet Waters*. He was working on a further commission when illness struck, and he died the following year.

These are the bare facts about Fricker's biography[172], and they make for rather arid reading. We do not find in it the histrionics of Peter Warlock, or the human tragedy of Ivor Gurney, but the somewhat unexceptional story of an academic composer whose basic atonalism, especially in his earlier works, reflects these biographical

172 They are conveniently assembled by Paul Conway in the liner notes to Lyrita's recording of the first four Fricker symphonies (REAM. 2136).

facts as we know them. There has never been an "official" biography, nor, to my knowledge, has a biography of any kind yet been written. Thus, we are left to fall back on the music itself, which is perhaps as it should be.

Although little is heard of Fricker's music in the concert hall today, his output was a reasonably prolific one, and his major orchestral works have been recorded, including all five of his symphonies and the Violin Concerto of 1950, along with the major cantata *The Vision of Judgement* (all on the Lyrita label), while his complete string quartets have been recorded by Naxos. These works suggest a predilection for the traditional forms. There is a second violin concerto and further concertos for piano (1954), viola (1953) and orchestra (1986), as well as two violin sonatas and a cello sonata. Fricker's facility with the organ led to several pieces for that instrument (recorded on the Toccata label), and both the Fifth Symphony and *The Vision of Judgement* include important organ parts.

The general style of Fricker's music is modernist and continental, owing something to composers such as Schoenberg, Bartok and Stravinsky. The music commentator John France, writing for MusicWeb International in celebration of the centenary of the composer's birth, says: "... his prevailing aesthetic was far removed from the pastoralism of Vaughan Williams and the post-Elgarian bombast of William Walton". In general, this is obviously true; Fricker's major works – the first four symphonies in particular – are not for the faint-hearted or for lovers of melody. Perhaps Vaughan Williams might have said to him, as he is reported to have remarked to one of his students: "If a tune should occur to you, my boy, don't hesitate to write it down". Still, as France has noted, perhaps Fricker's style floats in limbo between sounding too *avant garde* for traditionalists and not *avant garde* enough for progressives. The more recent revival of lyricism and tonality following the atonalism and experimentation of the 1950s–70s, may not have done Fricker's reputation any favours.

It is difficult to arrive at a general assessment of Fricker's achievement when so much of his music lies festering in the archives. John France, under the heading "If you have time to hear only one [Fricker] work ...", nominates the *Litany* for double-string orchestra (1956), which has attracted superficial comparisons with the Tallis Fantasia of Vaughan Williams and Tippett's Concerto for Double String Orchestra. Although this work has never been commercially recorded, it can be accessed on YouTube.[173] Of those works that have been released by reputable recording companies, my personal favourite is *The Vision of Judgement* (Lyrita REAM. 1124), a thunderous cantata setting a long poem by the eighth-century Anglo-Saxon poet Cynewulf. The orchestra is an extensive one, with the organ playing a pivotal role, while a large chorus is required (the piece was a Leeds Triennial Festival commission), along with soprano and tenor soloists. The work is highly dramatic, conveying stark emotions, as befits a text which contrasts the fates of the blessed and the damned, and Fricker draws suitably apocalyptic sounds from his choral and instrumental forces. Despite France's comments regarding the differences between the music of Fricker and Walton, noted above, there are certainly shades of Belshazzar's Feast here and there, although this may be, in part, because both are designed as dramatic cantatas on religious subjects which make use of large orchestras to create dazzling colour effects. Given that this cantata was Fricker's first attempt at a choral work on this scale, it is a remarkable tour de force, and well worth a place in the choral repertoire.

Fricker's music will certainly not be to everyone's taste. Much of it sounds austere, and when one glances at the official photographs of the composer, perhaps one can understand why. It is not recognisable English music as traditionally conceived, yet the composer *was* English and supremely accomplished in his art – hence his place in this volume. His music reminds us that Englishness is not *all* about landscape or ceremony; it embodies a rich tapestry of styles and a long cavalcade of influences.

173 Having listened to this piece myself, I agree with France that it is an impressive work, eminently accessible, and well-worth hearing.

a. Selected Discography

i) Symphonies

Symphony No. 1	BBC Northern SO, Thomson	Lyrita	REAM 2136
Symphony No. 2	BBC Northern SO, Rosen	Lyrita	REAM 2136
Symphony No. 3	BBC Northern SO, Downes	Lyrita	REAM 2136
Symphony No. 4	BBC Northern SO, Handford	Lyrita	REAM 2136
Symphony No. 5	BBC SO, C. Davis; Weir (org)	Lyrita	REAM 1124

ii) Orchestral

Violin Concerto	RPO, Del Mar; Neaman (violin)	Lyrita	SRCD 276
Rondo Scherzoso	BBC Northern SO, Thomson	Lyrita	REAM 2136
Comedy Overture	BBC Northern SO, Thomson	Lyrita	REAM 2136

iii) Choral with Orchestra

The Vision of Judgement	RLPO, Leeds Festival Chorus; Manning (sop); Tear (ten); Groves	Lyrita	REAM 1124

iv) Chamber

String Quartet No. 1	Villiers Quartet	Naxos	8.571374
String Quartet No. 2	Villiers Quartet	Naxos	8.571374
String Quartet No. 3	Villiers Quartet	Naxos	8.571374
Adagio & Scherzo	Villiers Quartet	Naxos	8.571374

22. Ruth Gipps (1921-99)

Like many other female composers of her generation, Ruth Gipps's musical life was one of achievement frustrated by gender prejudice in a profession overwhelmingly dominated by men. Yet she demonstrated a precocious talent from a very young age and developed into an outstanding all-round musician – composer, conductor and concert pianist, oboist and teacher.

Ruth Gipps was born in Bexhill on 20th February 1921. Both parents were musical: her father, Bryan, was a violinist, while her mother was a piano teacher who ran a local school of music, and it was from her that Ruth received her rudimentary training. She made such good progress that by the age of ten she was engaged to perform the Haydn piano concerto with the Hastings Municipal Orchestra under its principal conductor Julius Harrison. She was even younger when she completed her first composition, *The Fairy Shoemaker* for solo piano Op. 1, 1929). It was even bought by a publisher for one-and-a-half guineas.

Formal training continued with her entry into the RCM at the age of sixteen, where she studied composition with Gordon Jacob and Vaughan Williams, piano with Arthur Alexander, and oboe with Leon Goossens. She later continued her studies at the University of Durham where she met her future husband, the clarinettist Robert Baker and was awarded her PhD (1948) for a choral/ orchestral work entitled *The Cat* (op. 32). At this time, she was more celebrated as a concert pianist than as a composer, but in 1954 a cycling accident in which she sustained a shoulder injury curtailed this aspect of her musical life, after which she focused on composition and conducting. Her breakthrough as a composer came at the Last Night of the Proms in 1942 when Henry Wood conducted her tone poem *Knight in Armour*.

For some years during the later forties and early fifties she was based in the Birmingham area. Her husband was principal clarinettist with the CBSO, while she became conductor of both the City of Birmingham Choir and the Birmingham Co-op Amateur Orchestra.

During the period of her maturity, she became involved in teaching and administration. From 1959-66 she was a faculty member of Trinity College, London, and spent ten years (1967-77) teaching at the RCM. Finally, she took up a post as lecturer in music at Kingston Polytechnic (1971-79). Among her many other activities she founded two orchestras, namely the London Repertoire Orchestra (1955) and the Chanticleer orchestra (1961). Her programmes were always thoughtful and imaginative, often including works by living composers who had yet to be brought to public attention, as well as the more recognised names in Britain and abroad, and she provided debut opportunities to young performers who were to go on to enjoy stellar careers, including the pianist Philip Fowke, the violinist Iona Brown, and the cellists Julian Lloyd Webber and Alexander Baillie.

Despite all these achievements, however, she continued to suffer sexual discrimination. No less a person than Sir Thomas Beecham once infamously declared: "There are no women composers, never have been, and possibly never will be". However, Ruth Gipps learned from an early age to be strong-willed and override these prejudices. In any case, not all men in the musical establishment shared Beecham's views. While in Birmingham she struck up a fruitful working relationship with the conductor George Weldon, and it was during a holiday with her husband and Weldon that she began to conceive her Second Symphony. In 1967 she was appointed as Chairwoman of the Composers' Guild of Great Britain, an indication, perhaps, that the musical world had finally accepted her for her innate musical abilities and her achievements, regardless of gender.

On her retirement from teaching, Gipps returned to her native Sussex, settling in the village of Framfield. In her final years she was beset by ill-health and passed away in 1999, three days after her seventy-eighth birthday.

Throughout her life Ruth Gipps was a busy, active musician with irons in a number of fires, as we have seen. However, composition was a key aspect of her career, and she produced works at a steady rate over a period of some fifty years. The bulk of her output consisted of orchestral and chamber pieces, although there was also a small body of vocal and choral work, and a few solo piano pieces. Her final tally extended to some eighty opus numbers.

The backbone of her orchestral output was the five symphonies, although there are also concertos for piano, violin, horn, clarinet and oboe, and even a piece for contra-bassoon and chamber orchestra entitled *Leviathan* (1969). As regards the symphonies, the First was written in 1942 when the composer was just twenty-one. Naturally, the music of her RCM teachers, Jacob and, particularly, Vaughan Williams, looms fairly large here. Reviews of the work were mixed, but by no means wholly discouraging. The Symphony No. 2, written three years later, marked the composer's first real maturity and is one of her first major works to be genuinely characteristic. Here, the traditional four-movement structure of the First Symphony, with its classical layout, gives way to an experimentation with form – a one-movement work cast in several short sections, developed around a winsome theme which really wears its heart on its sleeve in the melting adagio.

It was another twenty years before the Symphony No. 3 appeared. In this Gipps returns to the traditional four-movement structure, although the second movement is a Theme & Variations rather than the usual slow movement. The Symphony No. 4 of 1972 is another large-scale work and has been dubbed by David C.F. Wright as a "masterpiece" with "as good an Adagio as you could wish for". Indeed, it is "arguably the best symphony written by a woman composer"[174] – high praise indeed! – although it should be added that women symphonists, especially in Britain, are a rare species.

The largest of all Gipp's symphonies, at least in respect of the forces required, is her last, the Fifth (1982). Unusually, if not uniquely, the Finale is an orchestral depiction of the traditional

174 David C.F. Wright, www.musicweb.uk.net/gipps/, pp. 9-10.

sections of the Roman Catholic Mass.[175] Gipps seems not to have been a particularly religious composer (although there are a few settings among her limited body of choral works, including a *Gloria*, a *Magnificat & Nunc Dimittis*, and a service for Holy Communion). It is fascinating to speculate why she should have chosen this form to include as a symphonic movement and how successfully it fits into the Symphony as a whole. The only way of hearing this work at present is via a very scratchy YouTube recording by the London Repertoire Orchestra. Let us hope that it will inspire some enterprising record company to produce a modern state-of-the-art rendition.

Among Gipps's chamber music are sonatas for violin, oboe, clarinet, and a late horn (or trombone) sonata (op. 80). She seems to have been more attracted to wind instruments than to strings, although there is a string quartet (1956). There are also one or two works that explore wind instruments of different pitches, notably *A Wealden Suite* for E*b*, B*b*, A and Bass Clarinets.

Although there are commercial recordings of the Symphonies Nos. 2 & 4, and the piano, horn and clarinet concertos, along with one or two shorter orchestral works, there is nothing from her extensive chamber corpus, a deficiency which needs to be rectified before a fair assessment of her overall output can be attempted.

175 The American composer Arnold Rosner's Symphony No. 5 (1973) explores the same idea, but in his case, he devotes each of the five movements to a different section of the Mass in Ordinary: Kyrie, Gloria, Credo, Sanctus, Agnus Dei.

a. Bibliography

Halstead, Jill, *Ruth Gipps: Anti-Modernism, Nationalism and Difference in English Music* (London: Routledge, 2016)
Wright, David C.F., "Ruth Gipps", *British Music*, 13 (1991), pp. 3–13.

b. Selected Discography

i) Symphonies

Symphony No. 2	BBC NOW, Gamba	Chandos	CHAN 20078
Symphony No. 4	BBC NOW, Gamba	Chandos	CHAN 20078

ii) Concertos

Piano Concerto	RLPO, Peebles; McLachlan (piano)	Somm	SOMMCD 273
Horn Concerto	LPO, Braithwaite; Pyatt (horn)	Lyrita	SRCD 316
Clarinet Concerto	BBC Scottish SO, Brabbins; Plane (clar.)	Champs Hill	CHRCD 160

iii) Orchestral

Knight in Armour	BBC NOW, Gamba	Chandos	CHAN 20078
Song for Orchestra	BBC NOW, Gamba	Chandos	CHAN 20078
Ambarvalia	RLPO Peebles	Somm	SOMMCD 273

iv) Piano Solo

Theme & Variations	Brownridge (piano)	Cameo	CC 9046 CD
Opalescence	Brownridge (piano)	Cameo	CC 9046 CD

23. Ivor Gurney (1890–1937)

Ivor Gurney – Bertie, as he was known to the family – was equally celebrated as a composer and poet and was widely regarded as the greatest dual practitioner of these arts since Thomas Campion (1567–1620). He was born in the city of Gloucester on 28th August 1890, where his father was a tailor and his mother a seamstress. For Gurney, close friendships were crucial for his artistic development, and he seems to have had an uncanny knack of cultivating these just at the right moment at every stage in his career. When his parents presented him for baptism at All Saints Church, they had neglected to provide any godparents, and so the vicar and his curate stepped in to do the honours. The latter was a certain Alfred Cheeseman, a well-read young man of twenty-five who took his role seriously, nurturing Gurney through his boyhood years and introducing him to books. It was probably through Cheeseman that he later met the Hunt sisters, Emily and Margaret, who not only encouraged his interest in literature but also in music. At this stage, Gurney seems to have been spending as much time with Cheeseman and the Hunts as in his own home where conditions were somewhat cramped (there were three siblings, which meant that he could not be the centre of attention), and his family had little sympathy with the boy's artistic pretensions.

The musical side of his life, however, took formal shape when he was enrolled as a chorister at Gloucester Cathedral and he began to attend the King's School (one of the buildings of which is named Gurney Hall in his honour). After spending six years there (1900–06) he became an articled pupil of the cathedral organist, Dr. Herbert Brewer, who provided some much-needed disciplined training. Two fellow pupils became famous in their own right. One was Herbert Howells who became a close, lifelong friend; the other was Ivor Davies, later to find fame as Ivor Novello.

It was while he was studying with Brewer that Gurney (along with Howells) experienced one of the formative moments of his musical life when, during the Three Choirs Festival of 1910 he heard the premiere of Vaughan Williams's *Fantasia on a Theme of Thomas Tallis* conducted by the composer.

The following year, Gurney went up to the RCM in London. In this connection there is a story, which may or may not be apocryphal, that the interviewing committee for entry to the college had already heard something about the young man from Gloucester with his exquisite Schubertian songs. When he walked in wearing his wire-framed spectacles and Severn pilot's coat, with a sheaf of songs under his arm, Parry is supposed to have exclaimed, "My God, it *is* Schubert!" Yet Gurney found it hard to settle into college life. For one thing, his compositions depended on inspiration and spontaneity. Grinding away at counterpoint and harmony was not something that appealed. But technique is precisely what the formidable Charles Stanford demanded. Stories about their quarrels are legendary, and on at least one occasion, Stanford forcibly ejected him from the room. He confided to Howells that he found Gurney to be one of his most brilliant students, but the least teachable. On another occasion, perhaps speaking with more prescience than he knew, he declared, "Mark my words, that boy will end up mad".

A further reason for Gurney's unhappiness was his exile from his beloved Gloucestershire with its ancient city, its "high blue hills" and quiet lanes, and the broad, winding Severn. London, by contrast, despite its many concert-going opportunities, was claustrophobic. It was not unknown for Gurney to walk all the way back from London to Gloucester, dossing down under hedges overnight. He may not have been able to afford the rail journey, but in any case, walking twenty or thirty miles a day was no obstacle to him.

In 1913 he suffered a serious nervous breakdown and was sent down from the RCM to recover. Once back in Gloucester his condition began to improve, but it was the harbinger of worse to come. He was showing signs of bipolar disorder which, although it may have been exacerbated by conditions in London, was not the cause of them. His strange behaviour, such as his all-night walking in the Cotswolds followed by his waking the household by playing the piano in the early hours, and his erratic eating habits, turned out to be due to more than his artistic temperament.

After a while he returned to the RCM to resume his studies, but by now the clouds of war were gathering, and at the beginning of 1915, despite his shortsightedness, he was allowed to enlist as a private in the 2/5th Gloucesters with whom he eventually arrived at the Western front. The camaraderie he found there, about which he wrote in some of his poems, seems to have lifted his spirits. In his poems and letters, he documented the day to day trench life of the ordinary "Tommy" in a plain, frank manner which had eluded many of his fellow war poets who had focused on the pity and futility of war. As he wrote, often under appalling conditions, he dispatched his work to yet another valuable friend, Marion Scott, for safekeeping. Scott and Gurney had met at the RCM where she was secretary of the Student Union. Her loyalty to Gurney proved invaluable, because she preserved everything he sent her, regardless of its aesthetic value. Without her help it is likely that Gurney's name today would be a mere footnote in the history of music and poetry. She effectively became his business manager, working tirelessly on his behalf for the remainder of his life and beyond. One of the first significant fruits of this partnership was the publication in 1917 of Gurney's first volume of poetry, *Severn and Somme*, in which he not only describes life in the trenches, but reflects on his beloved Gloucestershire that he so longs to see again.

Remarkably, he was not only sending drafts of his poems from the front, but even a few songs, among which are some of his best-known: *In Flanders*, *By a Bierside*, *Severn Meadows*, and *Even such is time*. The text for *In Flanders* was supplied by yet another invaluable friend, F.W. (Will) Harvey, a fellow Gloucestercian who he had first met on a tram in 1908. Gurney had spent many happy hours at his home in Minsterworth, and roaming the orchards and lanes on Severnside. Harvey, a solicitor by profession, also enlisted and saw action, but was taken prisoner. His poem *In Flanders*, which begins, "I'm homesick for my hills again" was borne out of his incarceration, and its nostalgic tone is empathetically treated in Gurney's setting.

At first, Gurney assumed that his missing friend had been killed, which prompted the elegiac poem *To His Love*.[176]

By a Bierside, to a text by John Masefield (1878–1967) begins in sombre mood but arrives at a stirring conclusion with the words "it is most grand to die". Along with *In Flanders*, it was later orchestrated by Herbert Howells. *Severn Meadows* is a rare instance of Gurney's setting his own poetry, and is full of nostalgia for his native county:

> Only the wanderer
> Knows England's graces,
> Or can anew see clear
> Familiar faces.
>
> And who loves joy as he
> That dwells in shadows?
> Do not forget me quite,
> O Severn meadows.

Even such is time sets Sir Walter Raleigh's famous text which he is thought to have written on the night before his execution.

From Good Friday 1917, Gurney's personal life began to go downhill. On that day he was wounded in the shoulder and sent for treatment in Rouen. It was not a "Blighty", but it did get him out of the fighting for a while. After his recovery, he was assigned to a machine gun company, though still with the Gloucesters, and was sent to Ypres where the infamous battle of Passchendaele was to take place. However, Gurney missed the worst of it because, in September, he suffered the effects of gas – a mild dose, according to his own account – and was dispatched to Bangour War Hospital in Edinburgh where he fell hopelessly in love with one of the VAD nurses, Annie Nelson Drummond. For a time, Gurney was in raptures about her, writing

176 This view, however, has recently been challenged by Kate Kennedy (*Dweller in Shadows* pp. 180-85), who argues that, by the time Gurney wrote the poem, he had already learned that Harvey was not dead after all, and that the poem must have had more general application.

movingly to Herbert Howells about her "pretty" features and "resolute little mouth"; but her kindness, and willingness to spend her free time with him seems to have been misinterpreted as a more passionate affair, and it was not long before the relationship was dissolved.

There was talk of sending Gurney for retraining and then back to the front, but his mental condition deteriorated and he was eventually transferred to Lord Derby's War Hospital in Warrington. "Deferred shell-shock" was diagnosed and in 1918 he was invalided out of the army with an honourable discharge and a modest war pension. Worrying signs of delusional insanity began to emerge. In a letter to Marion Scott, he declared that he had been conversing with the spirit of Beethoven. Shortly afterwards he wrote her another, even more worrying letter: "… this is a good-bye letter, and written because I am afraid of slipping down and becoming a mere wreck – and I know you would rather know me dead than mad…". Gurney did not carry out his threat, and the next day wrote Scott a note of apology. In October 1918 he was discharged from hospital and returned to Gloucester, but his reacquaintance with familiar surroundings did nothing to improve his mental condition.

We often hear that Gurney's mental trauma was caused by his experiences in the army (other sensitive artists, notably Malcolm Arnold and Robin Milford, were invalided out within weeks of their joining up), and these cannot have helped; but signs of instability had emerged during adolescence, and it seems likely that the war merely exacerbated a pre-existing condition. Further, in the year 1917-18, Gurney had been knocked from pillar to post, from one hospital to another, interspersed with periods of military retraining and threats of being sent back to the front. By now, he was unable to sustain any kind of normal life. His RCM scholarship had been held open for him, and in 1919 he returned to London to study there with Vaughan Williams, but by now long periods of concentration were impossible. He would take off to Gloucester without warning, re-emerging weeks later, and he attempted to supplement his war pension with a paid job as organist at Christ Church, High Wycombe. He was already acquainted with the town, and in particular with the

Chapman family who opened their home to him. While he was with them, he was able to enjoy some much-needed peace and quiet. But, as Michael Hurd[177] puts it, "he was in reality a Super-Tramp", always on the move from place to place and job to job. At various times he worked in a munitions factory, as a cinema pianist in Plumstead and Bude, in a cold storage depot in London, in the tax office in Gloucester, and as a farm-labourer at Dryhill Farm at the foot of Crickley Hill, one of his favourite haunts. Each of these lasted only a few weeks or months. Gurney was simply unsuited to the disciplined life in which commitment to the common task was essential.

Yet, astonishingly, despite all this, the years 1919–22 proved to be the most productive of his creative life. Hundreds of poems and songs were written, along with chamber pieces (there were probably twenty string quartets alone) and piano solos. Some of these, admittedly, were the products of a chaotic mind and were not fit for purpose, but in his lucid periods he produced some of his most inspired work. From this period come Gurney's only two existing orchestral scores, the *War Elegy* (1920) and *A Gloucestershire Rhapsody* (1919–21). Both sound attractive and coherent in their current state[178], but this is due only to the dedicated and painstaking restorative work carried out by Philip Lancaster and Ian Venables.

Despite all this creative activity, Gurney's delusional insanity deepened. He began to complain that he was being tormented by electricity, and pestered the local police by asking them to lend him a gun with which to shoot himself. His behaviour became ever more impulsive and erratic. He made the lives of his family members a misery. The Gurneys were at that time in straitened circumstances, and the father, David, was suffering from terminal cancer. They could not cope with Ivor's outbreaks on top of it all. He moved out of the family home and foisted himself on his newly-wed brother Ronald. He locked himself away in his room, shouted and raved,

177 M. Hurd, *The Ordeal of Ivor Gurney* (Oxford: Oxford University Press, 1978), p. 139.

178 They can be heard on Dutton CDLX 7172 and Chandos CHAN 10939 respectively.

and damaged the furniture. At last, magistrates were called, and in September 1922 he was committed to Barnwood Asylum in Gloucester. He absconded from there by throwing a large clock through a window and clambering through, cutting his hand badly in the process. He was soon apprehended and returned to Barnwood, but in order to prevent any repeat of this incident it was felt wise to a transfer him to a different asylum well beyond Gloucester, and he was taken to the City of London Mental Hospital at Dartford. Here his condition was assessed and monitored, and he was well-treated by doctors and attendants who did their very best for him. His many friends, poets as well as musicians, rallied round and visited when they could, as well as raising funds to keep him supplied with score-paper, writing materials and home comforts.

The most loyal friend of all was Marion Scott who went to enormous lengths to keep him as happy as possible. She was able to take him on day trips to places around Kent – Canterbury, Dover, Rochester. On one occasion she was allowed to take him to see *A Midsummer Night's Dream* at the Old Vic (Gurney had begun to identify himself with Shakespeare, believing himself to have written the plays), and she arranged for a performance of one of his quartets, even copying out the parts herself.[179] Her most valuable contribution, however, was to ensure the collection of as many of his manuscripts, both poetry and music, as possible. She took charge of those he produced in the asylum and wrote to his long-suffering brother Ronald who sent a further batch that had been left with him in Gloucester.

Another visitor to the asylum was Helen Thomas, widow of the poet Edward Thomas (1878–1917) who had been killed in the war. On one occasion, with characteristic thoughtfulness, she hit on the idea of taking her late husband's ordnance survey maps of Gloucestershire and, having opened them on his bed, he was able to trace the highways and byways he knew so well and walk again that beloved country in his mind.

179 Hurd, *Ordeal of Ivor Gurney*, p. 160.

Gurney's letters from the asylum are heart-breaking. He pleads to be taken away back to Gloucestershire, or to be allowed to die. Apart from a final luminescent burst of fifty songs between 1925–26, the music ceased, and although the poems continued to flow for a while longer, most of them were marred by the confusion of mind caused by his schizophrenia. Gurney fell completely silent during the last few years of his life. His physical health declined and he was eventually diagnosed with tuberculosis. He died on Boxing Day 1937, aged forty-seven, and was buried at Twigworth where his old mentor Alfred Cheeseman officiated, and Herbert Howells played the organ.

As I do not possess the competence to assess Gurney's achievement, I will not attempt to do so. Even Gerald Finzi, who was engaged to evaluate and prepare for publication those manuscripts which he considered to be of merit noted the difficulty of the task, remarking: "The sorting has been more difficult than expected, chiefly because there is comparatively little that one can be really sure is bad. Even the 1925 asylum songs … have a curious coherence about them somewhere which makes it difficult to know when they really are over the border".[180]

Finzi rather derided Gurney's family, particularly his brother Ronald[181] who pleaded with his brother's musical and poetic friends to allow him to devise some kind of disciplined regime for Ivor to adhere to rather than simply giving him free rein. The plea fell on deaf ears, and in retrospect Finzi intimated that Ivor Gurney was the one bright spark in an otherwise dull family who did not understand the artistic temperament. The latter comment might be true, but Ronald was genuinely trying to help his brother as best he could, and only meant to propose creating a structured environment in which Ivor would be free to pursue his art. Perhaps if that had happened, it would have been for the best. It should be noted, too,

180 Quoted in Banfield, *Gerald Finzi*, p. 395.

181 "I am afraid that it never has been, nor ever will be, possible to avoid such misunderstandings, when a radiant mind is born amongst sterile, unimaginative minds" (Quoted in Hurd, *Ordeal of Ivor Gurney*, p. 182).

that he did co-operate, if sometimes grudgingly, with those such as Vaughan Williams, Finzi, Howard Ferguson and Marion Scott who were endeavouring to bring Gurney's work to a wider public, and after Scott's death placed all the manuscripts at his disposal with the Gloucestershire Reference Library on permanent loan.

A sense of proportion needs to be maintained when talking about Gurney, whether as poet or composer. On many occasions the word "genius" has been applied without much attempt to justify that assessment. People of Gurney's temperament, whose art carries them to the very edge of sanity, and sometimes over it, are hailed as geniuses *ipso facto*, regardless of the quality of their work; yet only the work itself can determine whether the term is appropriate of Gurney, or any other artist.

Michael Hurd is clearly of the view that Gurney's true métier was as a song composer. Even though he is undoubtedly an admirer, he is honest enough to dismiss virtually the entire corpus of the composer's instrumental pieces. It is certainly the case that the individual quartet movements that Gurney left behind suggest that he could rarely muster sufficient concentration to produce coherent multi-movement works. As in his poetry, Gurney was best at the "short sprint". But even the solo piano music, according to Hurd, lacks distinction, on the whole. To this may be added the two orchestral works. In their recent edited form, they sound pleasing enough without being especially distinctive. *A Gloucestershire Rhapsody*, for instance, is a passable example of the short landscape-inspired rhapsodies and tone poems much in vogue at the time, and exemplified by Vaughan Williams, Holst, Delius, Moeran and Hadley, among others. In their original state, however, the scores were too chaotic for performance.

The songs are a different matter. Although even they are uneven in quality, the best of them are among the finest in the genre. Significantly, even while still a student at the RCM, Gurney seems to have had an instinct for knowing when he had written a work of merit. About the *Five Elizabethan Songs* (1914) – the "Elizas", as he dubbed them – he wrote excitedly to his friend Will Harvey:

> Willy, Willy, I have done 5 of the most delightful and beautiful songs you ever cast your beaming eyes upon. They are all Elizabethan – the words – and blister my kidneys, bisurate my magnesia if the music is not as English, as joyful, as tender as any lyric of all that noble host… How did such an undigested clod as I make them?[182]

The letter goes on to reveal that the accompaniment was originally intended for chamber ensemble rather than the solo piano which usually does the honours in modern performances. The most famous, and possibly best, of the set is *Sleep*, to a text by John Fletcher, and is rightly regarded as a miniature masterpiece.

As for the remainder of Gurney's song output, the range is wide with regard to both subject and mood – from the warm and earthy *I will go with my father a-ploughing* and the hearty *Captain Stratton's Fancy*, through to the exquisite miniature, *Severn Meadows* with its yearning for the landscapes of Gloucestershire.

Perhaps the final word of assessment should be left to Michael Hurd, who writes:

> We are left, then, with a song composer: somewhat flawed, but undeniably individual and certainly touched with genius. His finest songs have a rightness that cannot be challenged, and because of this he must be admitted to the galaxy of great British song composers and take his place, where, we may suppose, he would have wished, alongside such names as Dowland, Parry, Warlock, Finzi, and Britten. For a man whose life and work was played out against such appalling difficulties, it is no small achievement.[183]

182 Quoted in P. Blevins, *Ivor Gurney and Marion Scott: Song of Pain and Beauty* (Woodbridge, Suffolk: Boydell, 2008), p.84

183 Hurd, *Ordeal of Ivor Gurney*, p. 210.

a. Bibliography

Blevins, Pamela, *Ivor Gurney and Marion Scott: Song of Pain and Beauty* (Woodbridge, Suffolk: Boydell Press, 2008)

Boden, Anthony, *Stars in a Dark Night: The Letters of Ivor Gurney to the Chapman Family* (Stroud, Gloucestershire: Sutton Publishing, 1986)

----------, *F.W. Harvey: Soldier, Poet* (Stroud, Gloucestershire: History Press, 2016)

Hurd, Michael, *The Ordeal of Ivor Gurney* (London: Faber & Faber, rev. edn, 2011)

Kavanagh, P.J., ed., *Ivor Gurney: Collected Poems* (Manchester: Fyfield Books, 2004)

Kennedy, Kate *Dweller in Shadows: A Life of Ivor Gurney* (Princeton and Oxford: Princeton University Press, 2021).

Lucas, John, *Ivor Gurney* (Liverpool: Liverpool University Press, 2001)

Thornton, R.K.R., ed., *Ivor Gurney: War Letters* (Guildford, Surrey: MidNAG Publications, 1983)

----------, ed., *Ivor Gurney: Collected Letters* (Manchester: Carcanet, 1991)

b. Selected Discography

i) Orchestral

Gloucestershire Rhapsody	BBC NOW, Gamba	Chandos	CHAN10939
War Elegy	BBC SO, Lloyd-Jones	Dutton	CDLX 7172

ii) Chorus/ solo with Orchestra

Lights Out (orch. Yates)	BBC Concert O., Yates; Williams (bar)	Dutton	CDLX 7243
The Trumpet (orch. Lancaster)	London Mozart Players; City of London Choir, Wetton	Naxos	8.573426

iii) Chamber

Violin Sonata	Marshall-Luck (violin); Rickard (piano)	EM Records	EMR CD011
Adagio	Bridge Quartet	EM Records	EMR CD011

iv) Songs

Western Playland	Delmé String Quartet; Burnside (piano); Varcoe (bar)	Hyperion	CDA 66385
Ludlow and Teme	Delmé String Quartet; Burnside (piano); Thomson (ten)	Hyperion	CDA 66385
Five Elizabethan Songs	Bickley (mezz-sop); Burnside (piano)	Naxos	8.572151
Ha'nacker Mill	Bickley (mezz-sop); Burnside (piano)	Naxos	8.572151
By a Bierside	Bickley (mezz-sop); Burnside (piano)	Naxos	8.572151
All Night Under the Moon	Bickley (mezz-sop); Burnside (piano)	Naxos	8.572151
I will go with my father a-ploughing	Bickley (mezz-sop); Burnside (piano)	Naxos	8.572151
Severn Meadows	Agnew (ten); Drake (piano)	Hyperion	CDA 67243
Down by the Salley Gardens	Agnew (ten); Drake (piano)	Hyperion	CDA 67243
The Cloths of Heaven	Agnew (ten); Drake (piano)	Hyperion	CDA 67243

In Flanders	Williams (bar); Allan (piano)	Somm	SOMMCD 057
Edward, Edward	Williams (bar); Allan (piano)	Somm	SOMMCD 057

v) **Solo Piano**

Preludes Nos. 1–9	Bebbington (piano)	Somm	SOMMCD 038
Nocturne in B	Bebbington (piano)	Somm	SOMMCD 038
Nocturne in A flat	Bebbington (piano)	Somm	SOMMCD 038

c. Website

The Ivor Gurney Society (https://ivorgurney.co.uk)

24. Patrick Hadley (1899–1973)

Like his friend E.J. Moeran, Patrick Hadley had connections with both Norfolk and Ireland. Although he was born in Cambridge, where his father Sheldon was a lecturer in Classics (and from 1912 Master) at Pembroke College, the family moved in 1900 to a property near Heacham in Norfolk, which is where Hadley was based for most of his life. The Irish connection was on his mother Edith's side. She was the daughter of an Irish Protestant minister, and was born in County Athlone where he had been a curate. Their first son, Peyton, was born in 1895, followed by Patrick in 1899.

After prep school, Patrick – or Paddy, as he became widely-known – was sent to Winchester College, spending five years there from 1912-17. Throughout his school career, reports suggest that he was never suited for academia, and his progress was moderate at best. He enjoyed most games – football, rugby, cricket, tennis, athletics – but did not particularly excel, although his record for running the 200 yards remained unbroken for a couple of years.

On leaving Winchester, he was pitched straight into what remained of World War I. His brother Peyton had been in the thick of it from the outset. Double tragedy struck only weeks before the armistice. Peyton was wounded and invalided out, and then Patrick suffered a leg wound which necessitated an amputation below the knee. This was to trouble him for the remainder of his life, although he never allowed it to get the better of him. He continued to play tennis until well into middle age, and he was a good swimmer and a keen hill walker (there is a photograph of him standing on the summit of Great Gable). Peyton was not so fortunate. He never fully recovered from his wound and died of pneumonia only a week or so after Patrick himself had been wounded.

Despite Hadley's indifferent academic record, in 1919 he enrolled at Pembroke College to study music with Charles Wood and Cyril Rootham who he was eventually to succeed as Professor of Music. He was awarded his BMus in 1922, followed by his MA in 1925. Meanwhile, he had also enrolled at the RCM where

Vaughan Williams became his composition teacher and Adrian Boult and Malcolm Sargent taught him conducting, a skill which was to come in handy later on. At the end of his time as a student he was asked to stay on at the college as Professor of Composition, a role he retained, with a brief break, until his retirement in 1962.[184]

In 1930 Hadley was encouraged to apply for the vacant position of lecturer in music at Armstrong College, Newcastle-on-Tyne. It seems that he did the job for six months or so, although the facilities there were sadly lacking. The main bone of contention, however, was Hadley's request that he be allowed sufficient time for composition, which was not forthcoming, and despite having made a good start and being popular with the students, he resigned in June of that year. At least this freed him to focus on what turned out to be his best-known and most impressive work, *The Trees so High*.

In 1938 he was elected Fellow of Gonville & Caius College, Cambridge. One of his first tasks was to help the ailing Cyril Rootham, Chair of Music, to complete his Second Symphony. Rootham was suffering the effects of progressive muscular atrophy, and a small band of devoted students was engaged to take down the notes of the work at Rootham's dictation. It fell to Hadley to orchestrate the final movement subsequent to Rootham's death that year. As conductor of the Cambridge University Music Society (CUMS), deputising for Boris Ord during the Second World War, Hadley introduced varied programmes, from Bach and Mozart to Gilbert and Sullivan. Contemporary English composers were not neglected and included works by Bax, Delius (a Hadley favourite), Rawsthorne and Rootham. He also introduced one of his own works, *The Travellers* (1940; orch. 1942), dedicated "to those who have gone forth, and are going forth from these walls to travel on a hard road".

In 1946 Hadley was appointed Chair of Music at Cambridge University and settled into a life of lecturing and administration. Although opportunities for composition were restricted, works of

184 For those wondering how Hadley managed to fit this in with all his other commitments, it should be explained that the teaching load at the RCM could be very light, amounting to just two or three lessons a week in some cases.

one kind or another continued to flow from Hadley's pen. There was incidental music for student performances of Shakespeare's *Twelfth Night* (1949), Sophocles' *Antigone* (1939), and Aeschylus' *Agamemnon* (1953) – this latter for the unusual combination of male voices, two clarinets, harp and timpani) – and two more substantial works: *Fen & Flood* and *Connemara*. In 1962, Hadley retired from Cambridge to his family home in Heacham. Strangely, now that he had the leisure to compose, his output appears to have dried up almost entirely, with just one work on record, *A babe in Bethlehem's manger laid*, and that dated to the last year of his life. This is not to say that he did not enjoy a fulfilling retirement, nor that he was without music. He was involved in arrangements for the King's Lynn Festival, attended concerts, including performances of his own music, and had his trusty VHF radio to hand. He had a lifelong love of Ireland and a passion for cars and trains, interests which he was now able to combine in his regular motoring and rail tours in the Emerald Isle. As he grew older, however, he found these increasingly exhausting, and sometimes had to curtail his itinerary. His ever-faithful housekeeper, Myra Trundley, attended to his home comforts at Heacham. Always a heavy drinker and smoker, he died of throat cancer on 17th December 1973.

Hadley was a colourful character about whom anecdotes abound. By all accounts he was a kindly and helpful, if eccentric man. His many friends and acquaintances became used to receiving telegrams at all times of the day and night, which often began "I say –", and included all the punctuation printed out in full. Some of his eccentricities, however, could be rather more trying, especially for his long-suffering housekeeper who had family commitments of her own. On one occasion, she was enjoying a well-earned evening off at the local cinema when a message flashed on the screen requesting that she take a phone call in the manager's office. Fearing the worst, she rushed out of the auditorium, only to hear Hadley's voice at the other end of the line asking her if she had remembered to post a certain letter to the BBC. On another occasion, even more alarmingly, she received a knock on her door at 2.00 a.m. and opened it to find two policemen standing there. They told her that they had received a 999 call and that Dr. Hadley needed her urgently. She was taken in the police car to Hadley's home, about half a mile distant, let herself in with her own key, and found him in bed, as might be expected at that hour. When she asked what the trouble was, he explained that he had forgotten her home number and had to contact her via 999. When she asked what he needed, he replied, "Would you turn my pillow over for me, please?"[185]

His former students have their own fund of stories. Many remember him as a genial and generous man, a sort of kind uncle, perhaps, but certainly not a born teacher. Although generally buoyant and good natured, he was liable to fits of depression, and was not beyond telling his charges to xxxx-off if the fit was on him.

What about the music? Several influences are brought to bear on it, including folksong (*The Trees so High*; *One Morning in Spring*) and a strong sense of place (*Kinder Scout*; *The Hills*; *Fen & Flood*; *Connemara*). There are few works for orchestra alone, and Hadley's association with the Choir of Gonville & Caius ("the chaps", as he affectionately called them) and others, ensured that the human voice was of the first importance to him. There is very little by way of chamber music, but a string quartet exists from 1933 which, alas, remains unpublished and unrecorded. His sacred choral music with organ has fared rather better, and includes familiar and frequently performed gems such as *I sing of a maiden*, *The cup of blessing* (both 1936), and his most substantial work in the genre, *A Lenten Cantata* (1962).

I shall end with some comment on three of Hadley's key works, all of which have been recorded. Nearly all commentators agree that his masterpiece is the symphonic ballad *The Trees so High* (1931) which, to all intents and purposes, is a symphony. It is cast in four linked movements which are based on the Somerset folksong named in the title. It tells the tale of a lad who is bound in wedlock before he is fully-grown – married at sixteen, a father at seventeen,

185 E. Wetherall, *Paddy: The Life and Music of Patrick Hadley* (London: Thames Publishing, 1997), pp. 151, 156.

and mouldering in his grave at eighteen. Hadley's work makes the most of the haunting quality of the original tune. He compares the structure of the work to three independent brooks (movements 1-3) flowing into a single stream (movement 4). The first three are based on phrases from the folksong – the trio of the third movement is especially lovely – and are given to the orchestra alone. In the final movement, to a murmuring orchestral accompaniment, the baritone sings the first verse of the song, the melody of which is heard in full for the first time. The following verses are taken up by the chorus in various guises to create a truly haunting atmosphere. The baritone returns for the final verse, and his vocal line, against a broadening tempo, is magically underpinned by the chorus and orchestra, leading to three radiant chords – B minor, D minor and A flat – after which the music dies away. Although at one level, this work embodies a finely-judged treatment of the words and melody of the folksong, one wonders whether Hadley had in mind the many other young lads who also died tragically in the conflict in which he himself did not escape unscathed.

The Hills, for chorus, soloists and orchestra (1944), had a personal significance for Hadley, as he explains:

> I lost my mother in 1940 and that set my mind to the Derbyshire hills where she met my father in his old home on the hill above Whaleybridge [sic] … [T]hey became engaged in Taxal Woods and were married soon after in Dublin. Then I vivdly remembered that old Buxton – Manchester coach road, now just a track, and the moment when the magical panorama opens across the Chapel Valley with Kinder Scout towering up in the distance"[186]

Hadley's parents bought the house in Heacham shortly after their marriage and named it Shallcross, after Shallcross Hall near Buxton, where they had first met at a musical party.

186 Christopher Palmer, liner notes, *The Hills*, EMI 5 67118 2.

In *The Hills*, Hadley wears his heart on his sleeve, and is not coy about doing so, providing a detailed synopsis of the work. In the Prologue, he imagines himself as a prodigal son returning to the old haunts of his parents and, looking out to the Derbyshire hills, implores them to tell the tale of their courtship long ago. In the next section, *The Hills in Spring*, a vivid picture is painted of the Derbyshire moors at this time of year, with its grouse and curlew, "galloping clouds and fitful sunlight ... rollicking waterfalls spraying the fellside, whistling crags, billowing heather". Familiar topographical names set us firmly in the Peak around the great bastion of Kinder Scout. Into this landscape come the lost lovers, as if re-entering the days of their old courtship. It is as if the hills themselves are calling them to return, and they obey the summons. The tender third section, *In Taxal Woods*, recalls the lovers making their eternal vows. Next, the wedding celebrations are depicted, complete with intoxicated guests, while the Epilogue depicts the hills by moonlight. Once more they speak to the prodigal son, assuring him that his parents have returned and are now in their eternal keeping.

Although *The Hills* is an intensely personal work, it may nevertheless speak to a wider audience of their own early family memories, and has certainly been well-regarded musically by most critics, although it had to wait until 1947 for its first performance

Fen & Flood, described as a cantata, is really a series of tableaux tracing the history of the Fens from primeval times up to the disastrous floods of the night of 31st January 1953 which severely affected Norfolk and Holland alike, and which inspired the work in the first place. In between the depictions of these events, reference is made to the monks of Ely, the dissolution of the monasteries, the drainage of the Fens by the Dutch and public reaction to it, and the busy shipping trade of Lynn. Along the way there are Norfolk folksongs (*The Painful Plough*, *The Lynn* [or *Captain's*] *Apprentice*) and hymn tunes. It all makes for a lively musical extravaganza. Hadley secured the services of Charles Cudworth (1908-77), music librarian at Cambridge University Library, as a librettist. In the flood scene he uses the actual alarm call issued by the chief constable of Lynn on the night of the disaster, and in the 1956 performance of the work at King's Lynn, it was he who took on the baritone role, thus quoting his own words.

The original version of the work was written for baritone and soprano soloists, male chorus, violin, two clarinets and percussion – clearly with a performance at Gonville & Caius College in mind. However, Vaughan Williams, having been sent a copy of the score, was so impressed that he persuaded Hadley to allow him to produce a setting for full SATB chorus, and it was this version, with orchestra, that came to be regarded as the standard score, and which was recorded by Albion in 2010.

Patrick Hadley wrote a great deal of occasional or functional music in connection with his work with Gonville & Caius Choir. This included arrangements of anything from Purcell's *Faery Queen* and Verdi's *Stabat Mater* to *Waltzing Matilda*. Obviously, none of this was meant to be heard beyond the college. The fact remains, however, that over 50% of the compositions intended for public consumption remain unpublished. There is, for example, *Ephemera*, a setting of Yeats for tenor (or soprano) and chamber ensemble (1924); *The Last Memory* a rhapsody for solo cello, off-stage soprano and orchestra (1929); and *Connemara* for soloists, chorus and orchestra (1958), which is commonly mentioned among Hadley's chief works, but which the public currently have no chance of hearing. It is to be hoped that this deficiency will be rectified in the future.

a. Bibliography

Wetherell, Eric, "Patrick Hadley", *British Music*, 18 (1996), pp. 29–33

----------, *Paddy: The Life and Music of Patrick Hadley* (London: Thames Publishing, 1997)

Todds, Walter, *Patrick Hadley: A Memoir* (Triad Press, 1974)

b. Selected Discography

i) Orchestral

One Morning in Spring	Philharmonia O., Bamert	Chandos	CHAN 9539
Kinder Scout	BBC PO, Gamba	Chandos	CHAN 10981

ii) Choral with Orchestra

The Trees So High	Philharmonia O. & Chorus; Bamert; Wilson-Johnson (bar)	Chandos	CHAN 9181
La belle dame sans merci	Philharmonia O. & Chorus; Bamert; Archer (ten)	Chandos	CHAN 9539
Lenten Meditations	Philharmonia O. & Chorus	Chandos	CHAN 9539
The Hills	LPO; CUMS Chorus; Soloists; Ledger	EMI	5 67118 2
Fen & Flood (orch. Vaughan Williams)	Bournemouth SO; Joyful Co. Singers; Bevan (sop); Melrose (bar); Daniel	Albion	ALBCD 012

iii) **Choral**

Lenten Cantata	Choir of Gonville & Caius Coll., Camb.	ASV CD DCA 881
I Sing of a Maiden	Choir of Gonville & Caius Coll., Camb.	ASV CD DCA 881
My Beloved Spake	Choir of Gonville & Caius Coll. Camb.	ASV CD DCA 881

25. Julius Harrison (1885–1963)

Julius Harrison was born at Stourport-on-Severn in Worcestershire and, although he travelled countrywide, never severed links with his home county. His father was a greengrocer while his mother was of German origin and had been a governess. Both parents were musical. His father conducted the Stourport Glee Union, while his mother provided him with his first piano lessons. Organ and violin tuition were given by a local organist, and Harrison sang in the church choir. His general education, too, was local, beginning with a spell at a dame school in Stourport, followed by some years at Queen Elizabeth's Grammar School in nearby Hartlebury.

While still a teenager, he was appointed organist at a local church, and had the satisfaction of directing the Worcester Musical Society in his own *Ballade for Strings*. He went on to study composition and conducting with Granville Bantock at the Birmingham and Midland Institute of Music, and made his mark as a composer with a setting of Gerald Cumberland's poem *Cleopatra* which won first prize at the Norwich Festival in 1908, beating Havergal Brian into second place. One of the judges on that occasion was a certain Frederick Delius. The work received mixed reviews, but it was generally agreed that the young composer showed promise. In the same year he took up employment with the Orchestrelle Company, a maker of piano rolls, which necessitated a move to London. He was appointed as organist of the Upper Chapel in Islington, which provided him with an opportunity to compose pieces for the choir.

Harrison's big break as a composer came at this time when, at the behest of Hans Richter, he conducted his symphonic poem *Night on the Mountains* with the London Symphony Orchestra at the Queen's Hall. The general consensus regarding his orchestral music at this point is that it was too thickly textured and over-orchestrated – a flaw which he sought to redress as he became more experienced.

From 1913, Harrison was heavily involved in opera. He became répétiteur at Covent Garden under Arthur Nikisch (1855–1922) and in the following year was appointed Nikisch's assistant conductor for the season. In 1915, when Thomas Beecham presented a series of opera at the Shaftesbury Theatre, he joined a pool of conductors which included Hamish MacCunn (1868–1916) and Landon Ronald (1873–1938). In 1916, Harrison enrolled in the Royal Flying Corps, but his job was a technical one, based in London, and he was able to continue conducting for Beecham when off duty. After the war, he resumed his full-time conducting career, but now added concert music to his repertoire. He became co-conductor, with Landon Ronald, of the Scottish Orchestra (1920–23), and was also in charge of the Bradford Permanent Orchestra (1920–27). For a five-year spell from 1924-29, he cut down his conducting commitments in order to join the staff of the RAM, where he was Professor of Composition and Director of Opera.

From 1930 he took up the conducting appointment with which he is now most closely associated – that of the Hastings Municipal Orchestra. He brought an enormous amount of energy to the post, running an annual festival, and conducting up to twelve concerts per week during the summer season. He raised the standard and reputation of the orchestra until it rivalled Dan Godfrey's Bournemouth Municipal Orchestra, and invited high-profile figures such as Adrian Boult and Sir Henry Wood to guest-conduct. It was under Harrison's conductorship of the orchestra that a very young Ruth Gipps first came to public attention.

At the outbreak of the Second World War, the orchestra had to be disbanded, and Harrison was obliged to seek other employment. He became Director of Music at Malvern College (1940–42), and from then on was associated with the Malvern Festival, which was the occasion of Harrison's final public appearance as a conductor in 1947.[187] Towards the end of the decade he left Malvern to settle in Harpenden in Hertfordshire where he died in 1963.

Harrison's busy conducting schedule left him limited time for composition. His best-known work today is the rhapsody for violin

187 His conducting career had to be curtailed owing to incipient deafness.

and orchestra, *Bredon Hill,* an exquisite piece which is genuinely rhapsodic in nature and not merely by description, and which has rightly been labelled "a latter-day *Lark Ascending*".[188] Splendid though the Vaughan Williams piece is, with its timeless beauty, it would be refreshing to hear the Harrison alternative more often in the concert hall. Harrison is known to have visited the familiar Worcestershire landmark in the early 1940s while he was living at Malvern, although, as a Worcestershire man himself, he must have seen it from a distance many times. The connection of this work with the well-known Housman poem is confirmed by the appearance of the first verse as a preface to the score, and the gentle tolling of a bell at the end of the piece seems to represent the bell in the poem that calls the girl to her own funeral "when the snows at Christmas on Bredon top are strown". Harrison must have been aware that he had created a work after Vaughan Williams's own heart. Even more remarkable is the fact that he wrote it in the midst of the Second World War, and when it was broadcast in the summer of 1941, it must have provided solace to many in Britain.

Harrison celebrates his own beloved county in the *Worcestershire Suite* (1918) which is composed of four short movements: The *Shrawley Round* is named after a small village near Stourport where, as a boy, Harrison saw some children dancing, a memory depicted in the lively music. *Redstone Rock* is located on the River Severn and is said to have been the home of a local priest in the thirteenth century, as well as being inhabited by a host of sand martins. *Pershore Plums* celebrates the fruit-growing tradition associated with the Vale of Evesham. Harrison remembers, in particular, the beautiful pink and white blossoms that adorned the region each spring. The familiar strains of *The Ledbury Parson* draw the suite to a rollicking conclusion.

A later piece of similar ilk is the *Troubadour Suite* (1944). This four-movement work is based on the thirteenth century melodies of the wandering minstrels familiar throughout Europe at that time.

188 Lewis Foreman, liner notes, Dutton CDLX 7174.

Three of the melodies used are attributable to Thibaut IV, King of Navarre (1201–53).

The lovely Viola Sonata of 1945 is one of Harrison's larger-scale pieces and is cast in three movements. The first, although labelled *allegro energico*, is actually quite rhapsodic overall, bearing comparison with *Bredon Hill* in mood. The slow central movement extends the idyllic nature of the work, while the *vivace* finale provides the viola soloist with an opportunity to display the instrument's more agile character. The dark undertones of the work no doubt reflect the dark times in which it was written.

Harrison's voice as a composer can be numbered with pastoralists like Vaughan Williams, Finzi, Moeran and Milford, who abounded during the first half of the twentieth century. He is perhaps the least well-known because he was the least prolific. However, he was more than a one-work wonder, and his admirable Viola Sonata deserves to find a lasting place in the repertoire.

a. Bibliography

Self, Geoffrey, *Julius Harrison and the Importunate Muse* (Scolar Press, 1993)

b. Selected Discography

Worcester Suite	BBC Concert O., Wordsworth	Dutton	CDLX 7174
Troubadour Suite	BBC Concert O., Wordsworth	Dutton	CDLX 7174
Bredon Hill: Rhapsody	BBC Concert O. Wordsworth; Trusler (violin)	Dutton	CDLX 7174
Prelude Music for Harp & Strings	BBC Concert O., Wordsworth; Knight (harp)	Dutton	CDLX 7174

26. Joseph Holbrooke (1878–1958)

Whatever the merits of Joseph Holbrooke in any other regard, no-one can accuse him of hiding his light under a bushel or taking a self-effacing approach to his music. The well-known conductor of the Bournemouth Municipal Orchestra, Dan Godfrey, on one occasion was obliged to insert the following note of explanation into the programmes for one of his concerts:

> Mr. Dan Godfrey begs to announce that Mr. Joseph Holbrooke declines to play today, at this concert, because his name is not announced on the bills in large enough type, consequently the programme will be changed. The Piano Concerto and Dreamland Suite will be substituted by Violin Concerto, Paganini ... [and] Scènes Pittoresques, Massenet.[189]

Holbrooke himself lambasts the music critics for promoting the works of European composers at the expense of British ones, and even the concert-going public do not escape his barbs:

> While our good English musicians in power with fine orchestras and much money are pummelling to their utmost ability the down-trodden and unrecognised gifts (!) of Richard Strauss and his brethren abroad, we, in our small way ... try to leaven matters by writing out cheques and playing our own music to recalcitrant audiences[190] ... [and] the despicable members of the music profession are encouraged to play German music by an absolutely indifferent audience. One wonders if any such people have

189 S. Lloyd, *Sir Dan Godfrey – Champion of British Composers* (London: Thames Publishing, 1995), p. 152

190 Holbrooke programme note for a concert given at the Aeolian Hall on 28th February 1913.

> lost their sons or husbands at the front, or is it that the bulk of our music lovers "do not fight"?[191]

Holbrooke was certainly an angry young man, and unsurprisingly it made him enemies. One critic wrote: "I am tempted to think that Mr. Holbrooke is only discussing his own grievances against the English public, and that the real heading of his articles should be: 'Holbrooke's v. German or any other music'."[192] And another:

> Josef[193] Holbrooke [is] an excitable, deaf, talkative, combative musician, who lives in a solitary house in North London surrounded by ordinary Villadom, and writes there music which no-one can play. It is much Wagner-like in form and Strauss-like in its intricate orchestration... And Holbrooke, who composes it, is the enemy of the critics, the terror of publishers, and the intolerant hater of all that is commonplace in music. "Holbrooke's sauce", they call him.[194]

It is possible to learn a good deal from these spicy exchanges. Holbrooke certainly had a bone to pick with the great British public and the music establishment over their apparent preference for the traditional continental repertoire over any home-grown product. This position was generally recognised at the beginning of the twentieth century. But whereas Elgar, Vaughan Williams and Holst, in particular, sought to redress the balance by *writing* in a recognisably English idiom, Holbrooke simply harangued audiences

191 Holbrooke, "British Music Versus German Music, Part 4", *The New Age*, 16(4), 1914, p. 102.

192 G. Clutsam, Letter to the Editor, *The New Age*, 16(4), 1914, p. 110.

193 Holbrooke took to spelling his first name with an "f" in order to distinguish himself from his father who was also called Joseph and like his son worked in various music halls.

194 H. Swaffer, in *Josef Holbrooke – Various Appreciations by Many Authors* (London: Rudall Carte, 1937), pp. 19-24.

and critics alike as "enemies of the people". Ironically, his own music, as noted above, was clearly influenced by the European tradition. He was a close contemporary of Vaughan Williams, but their music could not have been more different. It hardly takes much perception to recognise that the music that concerned Holbrooke above all was his own, and his abrasive remarks concerning German music, considering when they were made, were political in tone, a fact that Holbrooke hardly cared to disguise.

Enough has been said to suggest that Holbrooke was an interesting individual. Let us now outline his biography. He was born into a musical family in Croydon on 5th July 1878. His father, also called Joseph, was a music hall musician and his mother a singer, although she died of tuberculosis in 1880 when Holbrooke was only two years old. The father was ambitious for his son and undertook to teach him the piano and violin, sometimes resorting to the rod as an incentive. Before long, young Holbrooke began joining his father in his music hall engagements, subsequently enrolling at the RAM where his principal teachers were Frederick Corder (composition) and Frederick Westlake (piano). During these years he composed a quantity of piano and chamber music, some of which was performed in student concerts, and he was sometimes called upon to give piano recitals. True to form, at one of these he substituted one of his own works for the scheduled Schumann *Toccata*, much to the displeasure of the college principal, Sir Alexander Mackenzie. Holbrooke did well in his studies, however, and carried off several prizes, both for piano performance and composition.

On leaving the college, his efforts to secure steady work, first in the music hall and then as a music teacher, proved fruitless. Indeed, he was often destitute, on one occasion lacking even the money for the rail fare back to London. By contrast, a few of his compositions were beginning to come to public attention. At the turn of the century his orchestral poem *The Raven* was conducted by August Manns, while his variations on *Three Blind Mice* was performed at a Henry Wood Promenade Concert at the Queen's Hall. At the same time, Granville Bantock, who became a lifelong friend, offered him a post at the Birmingham and Midland Institute of Music, but Holbrooke was never a stay-put sort of person, and after a couple of years in post moved back to London. Still, Bantock was an influential man to have as a friend, and the two stayed in touch, sometimes holidaying together in rural Wales, Harlech being a favourite haunt.

By now, Holbrooke's compositions were coming thick and fast. Henry Wood continued to promote his work, and his pieces were aired at various music festivals countrywide – Norwich, Leeds, Birmingham and Bristol, for instance. He also won the 1905 Cobbett Prize for his *Fantasie Quartet*.

A good deal of Holbrooke's music was influenced by literary sources, one of which, the poems and tales of Edgar Allen Poe, became something of an obsession – possibly to an even greater extent than Finzi's association with Thomas Hardy and C.W. Orr's focus on Housman. Over thirty of Holbrooke's works owed their origin to Poe. These included not only direct settings such as the choral symphony *Homage to E.A. Poe* and *The Bells*, but orchestral works (*The Raven, Ulalume, The Pit and the Pendulum*), concertos (*Tamerlane*, for clarinet, bassoon and orchestra), a ballet (*The Masque of the Red Death*), and even chamber music (*Ligeia*, a clarinet quintet; and *Irene*, a nonet). There were, in addition, other literary sources closer to home which led, indirectly, to an upturn in his financial fortunes. In 1907 Herbert Trench asked Holbrooke to set one of his own poems, *Apollo and the Seaman*. He obliged, and when the work was performed the following year at the Queen's Hall under Thomas Beecham, Thomas Scott-Ellis, 8th Baron Howard de Walden, happened to be in the audience, and was sufficiently impressed to invite Holbrooke to set one of his poems, *Dylan – Son of the Wave*. Out of this emerged not only a full opera, but the baron's lifelong patronage which put a permanent end to the composer's financial worries. The initial collaboration extended ultimately to an operatic trilogy: *Dylan*, *The Children of Don*, and *Bronwen*, under the collective title *The Cauldron of Annwn*.

Composition did not occupy the whole of Holbrooke's time. As a pianist with a formidable technique, he was frequently in demand, not only for performances of his own works, but to play the various concertos included in the standard repertoire.

As we have seen, Holbrooke harangued the musical establishment over the lack of opportunities for English composers, and although some regarded this as a thinly-veiled attempt to promote his own music, he did support his rhetoric with action by running a series of annual chamber concerts stretching over a period of more than thirty-five years (1899–1936) in which he ensured that the works of all manner of English composers of the day were given a voice, the beneficiaries ranging from Delius to those whose names were unfamiliar to the concert-going public.

It is perhaps true to say that Holbrooke's heyday occupied a relatively brief period stretching from 1900 to the outbreak of the First World War. The Armistice marked a change in the conditions of life in Britain, and a corresponding change in the direction of musical tastes. The inter-war years were a time for the young pretenders – Tippett, Britten, Walton and Rawsthorne, among others – and the kind of romantic, chromatically-rich fayre served up by Holbrooke was no longer in fashion. He attempted to move with the times, turning to light music, and even jazz, in order to court the public's attention, but the music which had established his reputation as a composer was no longer in vogue. A further blow to his fortunes came with the onset of deafness which eventually curtailed his career as a concert pianist.

He continued to promote his own music by buying back the copyright of many of his existing works and establishing his own company, the Modern Music Library, devoted to keeping his works in print and promoting recording where possible. He badgered the BBC for greater broadcasting opportunities, but his abrasive manner did not commend itself to this enterprise. Then, in 1946, Holbrooke lost, through death, his two greatest promoters, his patron Scott-Ellis, and fellow composer and friend Sir Granville Bantock. After this, composition became less frequent and he spent rather more time revising earlier works. His method of arranging his catalogue, however, was haphazard. In some cases, the music from one work was inserted into another, movements were composed for one set of instruments, only to be assigned later to a different set, and opus numbers were reassigned at will. Thus, there are two versions of the Clarinet Quintet in G, distinguished by opus numbers (opp. 15 and 27).

Holbrooke died in London on 5th August 1958, only three weeks before Vaughan Williams, by which time he was an almost totally forgotten figure. Not for him the interment in Westminster Abbey amid great ceremony. For many years thereafter this state of affairs remained unaltered, but, thanks to the advent of the CD in the early 1980s, things gradually began to change, and today many of Holbrooke's works, especially his tone poems and chamber music, can be heard once more, although the bulk of his work remains unrecorded.

Holbrooke's output was prolific. There are at least ten stage works, including opera and ballet; eight numbered symphonies; concertos for piano, violin, saxophone, and cello; some ten tone poems, including *The Raven*, *Ulalume*, *Byron*, *Queen Mab* and *The Birds of Rhiannon*; and a fair quantity of chamber music, including string quartets, violin sonatas, quintets for piano, clarinet and bassoon, trios, sextets, an octet and a nonet. In addition, there are piano solos and a few songs – not a bad yield for a forty-year compositional career. Holbrooke was in the habit of distinguishing his works by titles. For instance, there are symphonies entitled *Apollo and the Seaman* (No. 2), *The Ships* (No. 3), and *The Little One – Homage to Schubert* (No. 4), while the Piano Concerto No. 1 is called *The Song of Gwyn-ap-Nudd*, and his Violin Concerto is named *The Grasshopper*.

Today, Holbrooke is reasonably well-served by the recording companies. One of the pioneers was Marco Polo which issued two CDs of his tone poems and one of his chamber music, while CPO tackled some of the symphonies and the Violin Concerto. He is also represented on the Lyrita, Hyperion, Dutton and Naxos labels, and there are excerpts from historic recordings made during the composer's lifetime on Symposium. The tale of the concert hall is less encouraging. For practical reasons, live performances of the chamber music are far likelier than the symphonic works and concertos. There is irony in the fact that, despite the evocative titles he gave to many of his works, and his much-vaunted preferences for British music over European, much of his own output sounds distinctly Teutonic – a factor which largely contributed to his later neglect. By the twenties and thirties, audiences who wanted to hear *real* British music were flocking to Elgar, Vaughan Williams, or, in the case of the more adventurous, to Walton, Tippett and Britten. Those like Parry, Stanford and Holbrooke were regarded as relics of a former age and fell into neglect. If Holbrooke had written the kind of music that was being written by the contemporaries whose music he was seeking to promote, he would no doubt have fared better.

a. Bibliography

Ryan, Hubert, et al., eds, *Josef Holbrooke: Various Appreciations by Many Authors* (Rudall Carte & Co., 1937)

Watt, Paul and Anne-Marie Forbes, eds., *Joseph Holbrooke: Composer, Critic and Musical Patriot* (Lanham, MD: Rowman & Littlefield, 2014)

b. Selected Discography

i) Symphonies

Symphony No. 3, "Ships"	DRP, Griffiths	CPO	CPO 555 041-2
Symphony No. 4, "Homage to Schubert"	RLPO, Vass	Dutton	CDLX7251

ii) Concertos

Piano Concerto No. 1	BBC Scottish SO, Brabbins, Milne (piano)	Hyperion	CDA 67127
Cello Concerto	RSNO, Vass; Wallfisch (cello)	Dutton	CDLX 7251
Saxophone Concerto	RSNO, Vass; Dickson (sax)	Dutton	CDLX 7277

iii) Orchestral

Ulalume	Czecho-Slovak RSO, Leaper	Marco Polo	8.223446
Bronwen	Czecho-Slovak RSO, Leaper	Marco Polo	8.223446
The Raven	Czecho-Slovak RSO, Leaper	Marco Polo	8.223446

Byron	Czecho-Slovak RSO, Leaper	Marco Polo	8.223446
The Children of Don	NSO of Ukraine, Penny	Marco Polo	8.223721
Birds of Rhiannon	NSO of Ukraine, Penny	Marco Polo	8.223721
Dylan	NSO of Ukraine, Penny	Marco Polo	8.223721

iv) Chamber

String Quartet No. 1	Rasumovsky Quartet	Dutton	CDLX 7124
String Quartet No. 2	Rasumovsky Quartet	Dutton	CDLX 7124
Clarinet Quintet in G	Rasumovsky Quartet; Hosford (clar)	Dutton	CDLX 7124
Violin Sonata No. 1	Peacock (violin); Stevenson, (piano)	Naxos	8.572649
Eilean Shona	Gould, Cooper (violins); Neary (cello); Plane (clar)	CPO	CPO 777 731-2

27. William Hurlstone (1876–1906)

Along with William Baines (1899–1922), George Butterworth (1885–1916) and Ernest Farrar (1885–1918), William Hurlstone was another highly promising English composer whose undoubted talents were nipped in the bud. As with Baines, pulmonary disease, not war, was the cause. Hurlstone had been an asthmatic from childhood. He was born in Fulham into a family of amateur musicians, and was the eldest of four children. His father was a surgeon and his mother taught the piano. It was with her that William had his first tuition. When he was seven, the family moved for a time to Bemerton, near Salisbury, where the great divine, George Herbert (1593–1633) had once been vicar. But it was a modern-day vicar in the village who recognised Hurlstone's remarkable talents, even inviting Hubert Parry and George Grove down from the RCM to informally assess him. Both men were suitably impressed.

To begin with, Hurlstone enjoyed a comfortable and happy upbringing. He began composing from an early age and wrote simple pieces for family entertainments. At the age of nine he composed a set of *Five Easy Waltzes for Piano* which so impressed his father that he had them published. Soon afterwards, however, Hurlstone Snr. caught smallpox from one of his patients and virtually lost his sight, resulting in the end of his job as a surgeon. From then on, the family lived in straitened circumstances.

In April 1894, William went up to the RCM where he studied composition with Stanford, among others. Stanford considered him to be the most brilliantly gifted student of a brilliant cohort[195] which, we must remember, included Vaughan Williams, Holst, Ireland, Dunhill and Coleridge-Taylor (a particular friend). It was during his time at the college that he composed some of the works for which he is best-remembered, including *Variations for*

195 The same accolade was applied by Stanford to Herbert Howells when his turn came to study at the RCM eighteen years later.

Orchestra on an Original Theme and the *Piano Concerto*, the latter being performed by the RCM Orchestra at St. James's Hall, with Hurlstone himself as soloist.

In 1896 his father died, leaving the family in potentially difficult financial circumstances. Fortunately, a wealthy family friend – a Captain Beaumont – offered support, and Hurlstone was able to offer his services as a piano teacher, so that penury was avoided.

On leaving the RCM in 1898, Hurlstone moved to Norwood and served as a teacher at the Croydon Conservatoire, involving himself in the life of the local community as much as possible. One of his most important ventures, in partnership with C.W. Nightingale, was the creation, in 1900, of the Croydon Centenary Concerts, devoted to the promotion of a wide variety of chamber music, Hurlstone's first love. Like Holbrooke, he used his position as a concert promoter to showcase the works of contemporary British composers, and various pieces by Frederic Cowen (1852–1935), Thomas Dunhill (1877–1946) and, not surprisingly, Samuel Coleridge-Taylor (1875–1912), among others, were aired.

In 1903, Hurlstone was appointed by Walford Davies (1869–1941) as accompanist to the Bach Choir, and in 1905 he had the distinction of winning the inaugural Cobbett Chamber Music Competition with his *Phantasie for String Quartet* (winners in later years included Vaughan Williams, Bridge, Howells and Ireland). In the same year, Parry appointed him to the staff of the RCM as Professor of Harmony and Counterpoint. He was not yet thirty years of age. At last, this post guaranteed him financial security, but tragically he had little time to enjoy it. In May 1906 he caught a chill which, given his chronic asthmatic condition, proved fatal. He lies in Croydon Cemetery where the words engraved on his tomb prove particularly apt: "Music hath here entombed fair treasures, but still fairer hopes".

As in the case of those other rising stars, mentioned above, whose careers were cut tragically short (and to whom we may add the name of Cecil Coles [1888–1918] and the "English" Australian Frederick Kelly [1881–1916]), the young William

Hurlstone provided a tantalising glimpse of his brilliance, causing us to wonder what might have been and how his music might have developed, had his promise come to fruition. He must have been one of Stanford's more compliant students, for they appear to have shared the same enthusiasms – for Brahms, for example, which is clearly reflected in the music he left behind. Vaughan Williams was thirty years old in 1902, at which time he was still very much under the influence of the nineteenth-century German composers prior to achieving a style all his own. It would have been interesting to see if the same might have been true of his fellow-student: but, alas, it was not to be. What he did possess was a developed sense of form and discipline, which is no doubt what endeared him to Stanford in addition to his love of Brahms.

To the two orchestral works noted above can be added the *Variations on a Swedish Air, Variations on a Hungarian Air* and the *Magic Mirror Suite,* all available on the Lyrita label. Other than these, Hurlstone's output consists of chamber works and piano music, which are now reasonably well represented on a range of recording labels, including Divine Art, Dutton, Naxos, Somm and Toccata. Between them these provide a fair impression of the character of Hurlstone's music across the board. The *Piano Concerto* is generally regarded as the pick of his orchestral corpus. Of the chamber works, the prize-winning *Phantasie for String Quartet* (1905) is as good as any, and represents some of the composer's last musical thoughts. It is no doubt an exaggeration to hail him as "the father of English chamber music", as one local newspaper did, but it is just as certain that he deserves to be ranked among the best English composers of his day.

a. Bibliography

Redwood, Christopher, *William Hurlstone* (Highbridge, Somerset: Sequoia Publishing, 2016)

b. Selected Discography

i) Orchestral

Piano Concerto	LPO, Braithwaite; Parkin (piano)	Lyrita	SRCD 2286
The Magic Mirror	LPO, Braithwaite	Lyrita	SRCD 208
Variations on an Original Theme	LPO, Braithwaite	Lyrita	SRCD 208
Variations on a Hungarian Air	LPO, Braithwaite	Lyrita	SRCD 208
Fantasie-Variations on a Swedish Air	LPO, Braithwaite	Lyrita	SRCD 208

ii) Chamber

Piano Quartet	Tunnell Piano Quartet	Lyrita	SRCD 2286
Piano Trio	Memebers of Tunnell Quartet	Lyrita	SRCD 2286
Piano Sonata	Bebbington (piano)	Somm	SOMMCD 097
Violin Sonata	Mitchell (violin); Ball (piano)	Somm	SOMMCD 031
Bassoon Sonata	Musson (bassoon); Emmerson (piano)	Continuum	

28. John Ireland (1879–1962)

In the judgement of many, the name of John Ireland ranks a little below the leading figures of English music. As one musician, the musicologist Barry March, said of Moeran in a radio broadcast in 1994, there is general agreement about the identity of the "first division" English composers, but if there was a second division, Moeran would be near the top of it. The same can be said of Ireland, and the fact that he was Moeran's composition teacher at the RCM is not without interest. Although Ireland turned out a small quantity of orchestral music, including what is arguably the best piano concerto of any English composer, he was more at home with solo piano music and art-song, although there are a few highly regarded chamber compositions, and some sacred pieces for choir and organ. In one sense, he is very much a musician's composer, and it is entirely fitting that he is commemorated in a memorial window in the Musician's Chapel in the Church of the Holy Sepulchre, London. Ireland's piano pieces and songs have always been rewarding to play and sing by the artists themselves, even though generally they may be regarded as caviare for the few.

As we shall see in more detail later, literature and a sense of place were both indispensable for Ireland as a creative artist. His literary awareness was instilled in him from the beginning, for both parents had literary connections. His favourite places were those with prehistoric associations, and included Neolithic sites in the Channel Islands, Dorset and, latterly, Sussex, all of which seemed remoter in Ireland's day than they are now. These two interests were combined in his discovery of the writings of the Welsh author Arthur Machen whose fascination with ancient lore and legend coincided with Ireland's own.

John Nicholson Ireland (Nicholson was his mother's maiden name) was born at Bowdon, now part of greater Manchester, on 13th August 1879. His father, Alexander, a publisher and proprietor of a local newspaper, the *Manchester Examiner*, was already sixty-nine years old when Ireland was born. His mother Annie, thirty years younger, was a biographer and played the piano. The family home was a comparatively extensive one and attracted leading figures from both literary and musical worlds. He was the youngest sibling out of five and, as his parents tended to leave him in their care, he was bullied and ill-used by them so that, although he did not want for anything materially, his home life was not a happy one, and the sense of inferiority that he carried throughout his life originated at that time. His early schooling he found equally unappealing. However, he worked diligently at music and at the tender age of fourteen (1893) was admitted to the RCM to study piano. This was the golden period of the college under Parry and Stanford, when his fellow students included Vaughan Williams, Holst, Dunhill, Hurlstone and Coleridge-Taylor, all of whom were a few years older than him, which made it unlikely that he would have been drawn into that particular circle. If he felt lonely in London, it must have been compounded by the death, in quick succession, of both parents, leaving Ireland orphaned at the age of fifteen. The legacy left to him was meted out in miserly fashion by the trustees, forcing him to find remuneration in any way he could. He made ends meet by hiring himself out as a church organist and as a pianist at a London restaurant.

He progressed well enough in his piano and organ studies, and must have secured a sufficient income from his legacy and paid work combined, since he was able to remain at college for a further spell of tuition (1897–1901), now in composition, under Stanford. Perhaps Ireland already knew enough about "the dust and ashes of things" to hold his own against his mentor's notorious barbs. Once, having presented a string quartet movement for his scrutiny, Stanford replied dismissively, "All Brahms and water, my boy – and more water than Brahms".[196] He certainly put Ireland through his paces, but he later remarked: "Stern discipline indeed – but I have since had every reason to bless him for it".

196 Lewis Foreman, ed., *The John Ireland Companion* (Woodbridge, Suffolk: Boydell Press, 2011), p. 400. The quotation derives from Ireland's own testimony to his experience of Stanford as a teacher, which makes for fascinating reading (pp. 399–401).

While still a student at the RCM, Ireland became Assistant Organist to Walter Alcock at the Church of the Holy Trinity, Sloane Street, Chelsea. One of the attractions, apart from the pay, was a particularly fine Walker organ which had only recently been installed. In addition, there were forty boy choristers who, under Alcock, had already reached a high standard. Further, Holy Trinity was "high church", which also suited Ireland. Bonding measures ensured a sense of unity. Ireland's first taste of the Channel Islands, for example, came through a holiday in Jersey organised for the choirboys by the staff of Holy Trinity. When Walter Alcock moved on to pastures new in 1902, Ireland had high hopes of succeeding him, but, still in his early twenties, he was considered too young for the post. A couple of years later he was appointed to St. Luke's, Chelsea, Holy Trinity's sister church, remaining there until 1926. Compared with Holy Trinity itself, this was considered by Ireland to be very much the consolation prize. He was unimpressed with the Nichols organ, and the boys choir needed a good deal of work lavished on it to bring it up to scratch. Naturally, Ireland set to work to make the necessary improvements, and left the standard of music-making in the church much better than he had found it. Still, even in old age, he lamented not having landed the post vacated by Alcock at Holy Trinity, sometimes even dreaming that he was still at the console there.

Like Benjamin Britten (soon to become a composition student of Ireland's at the RCM), Ireland was a bachelor and may have experienced a degree of sexual repression. In both cases, suggestive comment has frequently been made regarding their uncommonly friendly relations with some of the boys in their charge. In John Ireland's case, there appear to have been two favourites, namely Bobby Glassby and Charles Markes, both choirboys at St. Luke's. By all accounts Bobby was cherubic in appearance, but not especially talented, while Charles was very promising musically. In our cynical age many would raise eyebrows at the intimacy of these relationships, but they both seem to have been entirely innocent. Both boys continued into adulthood to hold Ireland in high esteem, and the relationships, so far as we can tell were purely professional. Ireland appears to have had a desire to help those boys in straitened circumstances. Glassby, for instance, like Ireland himself, lost his father while still an adolescent, and Ireland stepped in as a kind of father figure without any vulgar intrigue attached. Ireland acquired a bust of Bobby Glassby which he treasured to his dying day, but it had been made by his father, who was a sculptor, before Ireland became acquainted with the boy.[197]

Another aspect of Ireland's career was his role, from 1923, as Professor of Composition at his old *alma mater*, the RCM. His students over the years read like a Who's Who of English composers: Richard Arnell, Benjamin Britten, Alan Bush, Geoffrey Bush (no relation), E.J. Moeran and Humphrey Searle, among others. The comfortable, teddy-bear-like image depicted by the photographs taken in his later years somewhat masks the emotionally complex character that emerged in middle age when his teaching career was in full flow. Several of his students have left accounts of his teaching style, and all tend to comment on his unorthodox methods. Moeran opined that it was not really correct to call him a teacher of composition at all. Instead, he was "a very wise advisor and an astute critic, both of his own work and that of others, and [succeeded] in instilling in his pupils that blessed principle of self-criticism".[198] That may have been the case, but his plan of action, if there was one at all, seems to have been made up on the hoof. His advice may have struck home, either by luck or by judgement, but he would never have survived as a teacher by today's standards, with modern teaching requirements such as lesson plans, individual education plans (IEP's) – although he seems to have practiced this in principle – and regular inspections for performance management purposes. That being said, Ireland would certainly not have been the only composer-teacher who would have struggled with all this.

---

197 Charles Markes's account of his relationship with Ireland is told by George Dannatt in "John Ireland and Charles Markes: A Creative Relationship", *John Ireland Companion* (ed. L. Foreman), pp. 147–63.

198 Quoted in Foreman, *John Ireland Companion*, p. 344.

More serious were the clear breaches of professionalism, even by the standards of the day – Ireland's notorious lack of punctuality, for instance. Benjamin Britten's diary for the years that he was studying under him is riddled with comments of this kind: "Waiting for J. Ireland for 1½ [hours], & eventually he doesn't turn up"; "Have 1 hrs. lesson with John Ireland (after waiting ¾ hr) …". As Britten was travelling down from Lowestoft, it was hardly acceptable to be treated in that way. Along with many of Ireland's students, Britten also found that he was expected to attend sessions in Ireland's own home in Chelsea, and on one occasion found him drunk and urinating on the floor.

Still, it was not all bad news. Although Britten found Ireland equally as critical as his first mentor, Frank Bridge ("He is *terribly* critical and enough to take the heart out of anyone! …"), his diary entries often include comments such as: "have a topping lesson for nearly 2 hrs", "… have a v. nice lesson with Ireland".[199] It is clear that, despite the lack of punctuality and general unreliability, once he had a student in front of him, he was often prepared to go far beyond the call of duty. The picture painted by Britten and other students is that of a flawed individual with a kind and helpful nature. His criticisms may have seemed harsh, but were for the best (in any case, Ireland had received much the same treatment at the hands of Stanford), and generally his students made allowances for his weaknesses, given the benefits they derived from their lessons with him. Certainly, as time went by, Britten's diary comments became increasingly positive, and in their letters to one another in later years, they are fulsome in their praise of one another's works.

On occasion, the sexual repression apparently suffered by Ireland boiled over into liaisons with young female students. The first of these was with seventeen-year-old Dorothy Phillips who was thirty years Ireland's junior and who he actually married in

199 Extracts from Britten's diaries are quoted in Foreman, *John Ireland Companion*, pp. 337–40, who quotes in turn from J. Evans, ed., *Journeying Boy: The Diaries of the Young Benjamin Britten, 1928–38* (London: Faber & Faber, 2009, 2010), pp. 54–55.

December 1926. It was a disaster from the start, and within two years had been dissolved. The second, better-known affair was with Helen Perkin (1909–86) who was twenty at the time, and for whom he composed his *Piano Concerto* (1930). In the *finale* of this work, there is a covert quotation from a student string quartet by Perkin, which surely testifies to his feelings for her. This is evident also in his dedicating other works to her, including *Legend* for piano and orchestra, while she, in turn, championed his music in the concert hall. Having once had his fingers burned, however, it is unlikely that Ireland proposed marriage to her. Although they do seem to have been close for a while, for this talented young girl, the world was wide. She won a travelling scholarship to study abroad and in 1935 married an architect, George Adie, a man much closer to her own age, and emigrated with him to Australia. As a pianist and composer, Helen Perkin quickly faded from view[200], but her promotion of Ireland's piano works, especially the concerto, were most welcome at a time when his life, if not his career, had reached something of an impasse.

If some of Ireland's works were inspired by the various people with whom he was emotionally involved, and who, like Helen Perkin, served as a muse, others were inspired by place. Ireland was never a globe-trotter like Vaughan Williams and Holst; his favourite haunts were all in Britain – the Channel Islands, Dorset and Sussex. All these places were able to boast a prehistoric past which were evident in what had been left behind – Neolithic forts, barrows and tumuli, in particular. However, although he was irresistibly drawn to these places, his home for professional purposes was 14 Gunter Grove, Chelsea, with its studio attached, and London was not without its attractions. Although, as he grew older, he was regarded by some as a "glum bachelor", in his prime he was generally rather gregarious and amenable to the ambience of the pub. One favourite such haunt of both Ireland and his cronies was *The George*, on account of its being

200 A brief sample of Helen Perkin the composer can be found on the website of Gary O'Shea where two of her *Four Preludes* for piano can be heard (https://garyoshea.co.uk/2012/08/19helen-perkin-1909-1986-four-preludes).

adjacent to the Queen's Hall. Henry Wood dubbed it "The Gluepot", since so many of his musicians disappeared there during rehearsal breaks and had to be prised out again. Among the composers one was likely to spot there, apart from Ireland, were Bax, Alan Bush, Lambert, Elizabeth Lutyens, Moeran, Rawsthorne, Searle, Walton, Warlock and, during his rare visits to London, Delius. It was also frequented by poets such as Roy Campbell, Louis MacNeice, and Dylan Thomas.[201] There is no doubt, then, that he enjoyed a convivial occasion. The titles of one or two of his piano pieces – *Ballade of London Nights, Chelsea Reach, Solo Forenoons,* as well as his hymn tune *Chelsea* – testify to his affinity with the metropolis, as does his *London Overture* with its echo of the bus conductor's cry, "'Dilly, Piccadilly!"

The lure of the countryside, however, was never far away, and among his favourite haunts, as we have seen, were those with traces of a forgotten past. The Channel Islands had been a draw since he first visited Jersey with the choirboys of St. Luke's in 1900. As he grew older, London, whose noise and diesel fumes began at Leatherhead, according to Ireland himself, became less of an attraction, and in 1939 he sold up and moved with a friend, John Longmire, to Guernsey. The landscape was ideal for his artistic needs, although his relationship with Longmire, a much younger man than himself, was ambiguous ("Although Longmire is a good chap… and means well, too much of him gets on my nerves").[202] As it turned out, however, 1939 was an inauspicious time to be settling in the Channel Islands, and within a year of his arrival, Ireland found himself having to evacuate post-haste. He left on the SS Antwerp in June 1940, just eight days before the Germans invaded. Still, his brief sojourn there was enough to inspire some music, as the piano pieces *The Island Spell* (from *Decorations*) and

201 The Somm recording, *The Gluepot Connection* (SOMM CD 0180), presents a selection of choral music by various "Gluepot" composers, including Ireland's *The Hills.*

202 In a letter to Thomas Dunhill, dated September 1939. See Foreman, *John Ireland Companion*, p. 425.

Sarnia testify. As ever with Ireland, however, there is more in the music than is evident to the ear. According to Fiona Richards[203], the central movement of *Sarnia* concerns a nine-year-old boy, Michael Rayson, whose beauty Ireland remarked on more than once.

Perhaps the most influential and productive location of all was the Sussex downs, with Chanctonbury Ring as its crowning glory. He was introduced to it by a friend as early as 1920, and from then on, he was captivated by these ancient chalklands with their lore and legends, exploring them whenever he had the time. He even found himself a *pied a terre* in the village of Ashington, a few miles from Storrington where he could escape from London at weekends and for holidays. In 1953 he retired to Sussex on a permanent basis when he bought a converted windmill, Rock Mill, just outside the village of Washington, which boasted fine views of the South Downs, including Chanctonbury Ring. Back in 1947 he had hired a housekeeper to look after his daily needs at his London home, and managed to persuade her to accompany him to Rock Mill as his companion and personal secretary. During her fifteen years of service, she proved herself a loyal and devoted confidante, doing much to promote Ireland's interests. Without her he would probably have wasted away. He wrote little in the last decade of his life as it is – in part, at least, because his eyesight was beginning to fail, although he also realised that his best music was behind him. The music inspired by the Sussex Downs had all been written by the time he moved permanently to the area. The works normally regarded as the most evocative in this respect are *Legend* for piano and orchestra, and the solo piano piece *Amberley Wild Brooks*. However, we need to be careful in considering the names that Ireland accorded his works. He always said that he wrote the music he wanted to write, and that titles were of secondary importance, sometimes being added simply to please the publishers. It must be

203 F. Richards, "John Ireland's Personal World", in Foreman, *John Ireland Companion*, pp. 42–53 (50).

admitted, however, that the *Two Pieces* of 1929 is made to sound more interesting when the titles *For Remembrance* and *Amberley Wild Brooks* are added, and they distinguish these pieces from the earlier *Two Pieces* of 1925. *Amberley Wild Brooks,* named after an area of meadowland fed by a lattice of small streams, is a shimmering, impressionistic piece, widely regarded as one of his best works for solo piano. It certainly seems to catch the light on the water, but we should heed Ireland's caution that the title should not lead us to a programmatic interpretation of the work; rather, it is intended to evoke a particular range of moods.

A Downland Suite is not especially evocative of the South Downs and is not in any real sense nature music, any more than Vaughan Williams's hymn tune *Down Ampney* is evocative of his birth place.[204] It was written initially for brass band (hardly the forces appropriate to the South Downs), and only later arranged for strings.[205]

The one work on which there does hang something of a local tale is *Legend,* for we know that it was inspired by Harrow Hill (an outlier of the Downs between Storrington and Angmering) and its colourful ancient and medieval history. There are the scant remains of a medieval church which was once attended by local lepers who were allowed to observe the services through a squint, and of Neolithic flint mines and a fort – all of which would be overlooked by the casual observer today. According to Ireland, one day he had ventured to the top of the hill, and had just opened his packed lunch when he noticed some children wearing archaic clothing and dancing silently in front of him. He glanced away for a moment, and when he looked again, they had vanished. Perhaps he had been reading too much Arthur Machen! In any event, he reported

204 Vaughan Williams pointed out that the majority of his hymn tunes were somewhat randomly named after the villages around Dorking, and that, on one occasion, when he could not think of a name, he used the title *Sine Nomine* ("without name" – the hymn was "For all the saints").

205 Ireland himself rescored only two of the four movements (*Elegy* and *Minuet*); the task was completed by his former pupil Geoffrey Bush (*Prelude* and *Rondo*).

his experience to his author friend and received on a postcard the laconic reply: "So you've seen them too". A delicately scored dance in the middle of the work seems suggestive this event.

As noted above, orchestral music was not Ireland's preferred medium. He often complained about the difficulties of writing it, and sometimes passed on the task of orchestration to a favoured student, such as Alan Bush (the choral/ orchestral *These Things Shall Be* being a case in point). Some of the works familiar to us today as orchestral pieces actually began life in some other form. *A Downland Suite* and *A London Overture* both originated as test pieces for the National Brass Band Championships of 1932 and 1934 respectively, while *The Holy Boy*, now best-known as a piece for string orchestra, was conceived in 1913 for solo piano.[206] Other works were written for strings alone. One of these, the *Concertino Pastorale* was written in 1939 under the shadow of the approaching Second World War. It is a predominantly dark work with a central *Threnody*, and the title is rather misleading, and certainly not indicative of "lambkins frisking", as Vaughan Williams remarked about his *Pastoral Symphony*.

These Things Shall Be, on the other hand, although written during this same period of foreboding (1937), seems almost surreal in its optimistic tone, setting a poem by John Addington Symonds (1840–93) which envisages a utopia for future generations:

> These things – they are no dream – shall be
> For happier men when we are gone:
> Those golden days for them shall dawn,
> Transcending all we gaze upon.

206 *The Holy Boy* is perhaps Ireland's best-loved work, and he lost no time in promoting it by preparing several different versions – for string orchestra; voice and piano/ organ/ strings; unaccompanied chorus; violin & piano; solo organ. There are further arrangements by others – for cello & strings (Palmer); violin & strings (Parlett); brass (Stepp); solo viola (Tertis); cello & piano; and solo clarinet. See Foreman *John Ireland Companion*, pp. 431, 437.

In context, however, the mood suggested by Symonds and adopted (through gritted teeth) by Ireland, is appropriate to the occasion, for the work was commissioned by the BBC for the Coronation Concert to mark the accession of King George VI.

Once war had been declared, the BBC requested Ireland to write something equally patriotic, if not openly jingoistic. As usual the composer prevaricated, being reluctant to produce anything along the lines of *Land of Hope and Glory* (although there are shades of *Pomp & Circumstance No. 4* in the trio section of Ireland's piece, which he entitled *Epic March*). In the event, he managed to create something suitably uplifting at a time of national crisis without unwarranted bombast.

Two other orchestral conceptions deserve a brief mention. One is Ireland's only film score, *The Overlanders* (Ealing Studios, 1946), the real-life story of a group of Australian cattlemen threatened by the possibility of Japanese invasion who drive their herds more than 1,500 miles south to safety. The strong character of Ireland's music, exemplified by the stirring *Night Stampede* theme, makes one regret that he never produced scores for any other films. Until recently, this music could be heard only in the form of a five-movement suite prepared by Charles Mackerras, but it can now be enjoyed in full, thanks to a recording by Dutton (CDLX 7353) which also includes the complete score for a radio production of Shakespeare's *Julius Caesar*. As early as 1970, Ireland's ex-pupil Geoffrey Bush had edited the material to produce a viable two-movement suite, *Scherzo & Cortege*. The original score, edited by Graham Parlett in 2016, naturally does not have quite the same fluency, given its role in the play, but it does give us twice as much music as the suite.

The intimate nature of the chamber music medium suited Ireland's personality, yet, given a sixty-three year composing career, his output was fairly modest. There are two early string quartets, both dated 1897; a sextet for clarinet, horn & string quartet (1898); the ever-popular *Berceuse* (1903), *Cavatina* (1904), and *Bagatelle* (1911); cello and clarinet sonatas; and three piano trios. But it is the two violin sonatas which are the pick of his chamber works. The first of these, composed in 1908, was entered for the Cobbett Chamber Music Competition the following year, for which it was awarded first prize, and is regarded as an example of Ireland's early maturity as a composer. He thought highly enough of the work to revise it in 1917, and again in 1944. The Second Violin Sonata was a wartime composition (1917) and was premiered by Albert Sammons and William Murdoch in their army uniforms. Public reaction was sensational, and the work received nine performances within the first few months. After the first performance, the publisher Winthrop Rogers was on Ireland's doorstep before breakfast the following morning to request the publishing rights, and the first edition had sold out even before it had gone on general sale. It is difficult, after a hundred years, to appreciate what it was about the piece that so fired the public's imagination, but reaction to it was unprecedented for a chamber work. As Ireland himself later commented, it made him famous overnight.

Another area in which Ireland is well-represented is that of art-song, having written almost a hundred songs either in the form of song-cycles or as individual items. Having been born to literary parents, it was almost inevitable that his choice of texts would be wide-ranging, and so it proved – from little-known poets such as James Vila Blake and Ernest Blake to Shakespeare (although there seems to be only a single setting of the Bard). Among Ireland's favourite poets were Thomas Hardy, A.E. Housman, Christina Rossetti, and John Masefield whose *Sea Fever*, as set by Ireland, became hugely popular. In a BBC poll conducted in 1930 to find the most popular broadcast song, *Sea Fever* was a runaway winner. Masefield himself is said to have disliked the setting, but on investigation it appears that what irked him was not so much the song itself but rather the dirge-like manner in which it was generally performed. Ireland preferred a broad tempo. Certainly, this gives the song a sense of presence. The trick, of course, is to produce a mood of dignified solemnity without a descent into the dirge-like quality which the poet disliked.

In matters of religion, Ireland was ambivalent. His sacred works, including two Evening Services (Magnificat & Nunc dimittis), a Morning Service (Benedictus & Jubilate), and a Communion Service, are the equal of anything that other composers were producing at the time, and among his few hymn tunes is the ever-popular *My song is love unknown*. His preferred religion, for musical purposes, was high church Anglicanism, but there is little evidence of any doctrinal commitment, a stance shared by Vaughan Williams, Holst, Howells, Finzi, Walton, Bax, and many other leading English composers.

Ireland died at Rock Mill on 12th June 1962 at the age of eighty-two, and was buried in the churchyard of St. Mary the Virgin in the West Sussex village of Shipley. The epitaph on his tombstone reads: "Many waters cannot quench love", a quotation from Song of Solomon 8: 7 which Ireland had used in his motet *Greater Love Hath No Man*. His reputation as one of England's finest composers is secure.

a. Bibliography

Dannatt, George, "John Ireland and Charles Markes: A Creative Relationship", *British Music*, 28 (2006)

Foreman, Lewis, ed., *The John Ireland Companion* (Woodbridge, Suffolk: Boydell Press, 2012)

Longmire, John, *John Ireland: Portrait of a Friend* (John Baker, 1969)

Richards, Fiona, *The Music of John Ireland* (Aldershot, Hants.: Ashgate, 2000)

Scott-Sutherland, Colin, *John Ireland* (Triad Press, 1980)

Searle, Muriel V., *John Ireland: The Man and His Music* (London: Midas Books, 1979)

b. Selected Discography

i) Orchestral

Piano Concerto	LPO, Thomson; Parkin (piano)	Chandos	CHAN 8461
Legend	LPO, Thomson; Parkin (piano)	Chandos	CHAN 8461
Mai-Dun	LPO, Thomson; Parkin (piano)	Chandos	CHAN 8461
A Downland Suite	City of London Sinfonia, Hickox	Chandos	CHAN 9376
Concertino Pastorale	City of London Sinfonia, Hickox	Chandos	CHAN 9376
A London Overture	LSO, Hickox	Chandos	CHAN 7074
The Holy Boy	LSO, Hickox	Chandos	CHAN 7074
The Forgotten Rite	LPO, Boult	Lyrita	SRCD 240
The Overlanders Suite	LPO, Boult	Lyrita	SRCD 240
Epic March	LPO, Boult	Lyrita	SRCD 240

ii) Choral with Orchestra

These Things Shall Be	LSO & Chorus, Hickox; Terfel (bar)	Chandos	CHAN 7074
Greater Love Hath No Man	LSO & Chorus, Hickox; Bott (sop)	Chandos	CHAN 7074
Vexilla Regis	LSO & Chorus; soloists; Hickox	Chandos	CHAN 7074

iii) Chamber

Violin Sonata No. 1	Barritt (violin); Edwards (piano)	Helios	CDH 55164
Violin Sonata No. 2	Barritt (violin); Edwards (piano)	Helios	CDH 55164

iv) Solo Piano

Complete Solo Piano Music (3 vols.)	Parkin (piano)	Lyrita	SRCD 2277

v) Songs

Complete Songs	Milne (sop); Ainsley (ten); Maltmon (bar); Johnson (piano)	Hyperion	CDA 67261/2

c. Website

The John Ireland Trust (www.johnirelandtrust.org)

29. Gordon Jacob (1895–1984)

Gordon Jacob's reputation today rests largely on his orchestrations of other composers' music. He is perhaps best-remembered for his orchestration of Vaughan Williams's *English Folksong Suite*, which originated as a work for military band.[207] He also orchestrated Holst's works for military or brass band[208] and Elgar's Organ Sonata. Today some of these works are better-known in Jacob's orchestral versions than in their original form. Having such a facility for orchestration was perhaps a mixed blessing, since it tended to distract attention from his own compositions, and it was something he could be touchy about, as one of his students, Ruth Gipps, discovered when she attempted to compliment him on a particular orchestration he had made of another composer's piece.

In truth, Jacob was a compulsive composer in his own right, producing an estimated seven hundred items during his long career, in just about every conceivable instrumental combination.[209] His concertos alone include works for piano, violin, viola, cello, flute, oboe, clarinet, cor anglais, bassoon, trombone, tuba, and wind band, many of which were written to commission. Given such a large and varied output, it may be wondered why Jacob's original music is not better-known. One reason may be that he wrote most of it for particular use (something akin to Hindemith's *Gebrauchsmusik*, perhaps). In other words, it was written for a specific occasion and then laid aside once it had served its purpose. His concertos are generally of this kind. Most were written with specific performers in view, and sometimes for unfashionable instruments. Few are big-boned works, and are more concerned to challenge the soloist's technique.

---

207 Jacobs also transcribed the same work for brass band.

208 The *Suite No. 1 in E*; the *Suite No. 2 in F (A Hampshire Suite)*; and *A Moorside Suite*.

209 His Stainer & Bell publications alone run to over forty items, including piano transcriptions of orchestral works.

Then, too, there are no monumental works or show-stoppers which rely on orchestral pyrotechnics to fire the listener's interest. Jacob was not given to extravagant expression, nor was he an experimentalist. He wrote in a traditional tonal idiom which made for a satisfying, if not wholly memorable listening experience. It was with sound orchestral technique that Jacob was primarily concerned – he wrote two books on the subject[210] – and some listeners may have considered this a rather academic, strait-laced approach. Jacob wrote just the notes and used only those instruments he considered necessary for each composition, which for some may not have been quite enough.

What of Gordon Jacob the man? He was born in Upper Norwood, London, on 5th July 1895, the seventh son (hence his unusual middle name Septimus) and youngest of ten children. His father Stephen was an official in the Indian Civil Service, but died when Gordon was just three years old. The family was left financially comfortable, however, and he was educated at the prestigious Dulwich College. By this time, he was already composing and had several of his works performed by the school orchestra. At the age of eighteen, he left the college – only to walk straight into the First World War. He enlisted in the Queen's Royal Regiment, but after seeing action, was taken prisoner and interned in Ströhlen POW Camp. The régime there was relatively humane and Jacob was allowed to form a camp orchestra, composing music for whatever instruments were available. A year later he was transferred to Bad Kolberg Camp, but was allowed to continue with his musical activities. A favourite elder brother, Ansty, who had also enlisted, was not so lucky, having been killed during the Somme offensive.

Following his repatriation at the end of hostilities, Jacob enrolled as a student at the RCM where his composition teachers

210 Jacob, *Orchestral Technique: A Manual for Students* (London: Oxford University Press, 1931); idem., *The Elements of Orchestration* (London: October House, 1962). Among his other writings were several articles contributed to the *Grove Dictionary of Music and Musicians*, and he was for a decade the editor of Penguin Music Scores.

were Stanford and Vaughan Williams, whose respective teaching philosophies must have made for an interesting contrast. In 1924 Jacob himself joined the staff at the college, remaining in post for over forty years and teaching an entire generation of future composers, including Malcolm Arnold, Ruth Gipps, Imogen Holst, Joseph Horowitz, Elizabeth Maconchy and Bernard Stevens. He also taught the pianist Cyril Smith who was later to form a celebrated piano duo with his wife Phyllis Sellick. Later, when Smith lost the use of his right arm following a stroke, both Jacob and his former student Malcolm Arnold wrote a piano concerto for three hands so that the duo could carry on performing.

Remarkably, Jacob himself did not play any instrument to a professional standard. Although he had some ability on the piano, a hand injury put paid to his performing in public. Further, he had been born with a cleft palate on which he endured several operations in his childhood, so was unable to play any kind of wind instrument. Possibly this particular cloud had a silver lining, however, as it may have curtailed the likelihood of any instrumental bias. He was able to treat all instruments impartially and, as noted above, composed concertos and concertinos for virtually every instrument in the classical symphony orchestra, as well as a few others, including harmonica and, especially, recorder.[211]

Jacob retired from teaching at the RCM in 1966, but continued to compose until his death at Saffron Walden on 8th June 1984, just a month short of his eighty-ninth birthday. What sort of legacy did he leave? Certainly, in his own lifetime he was acclaimed as a master craftsman in the art of orchestration, a reputation which has deservedly endured down to the present. Most of his pieces are of modest proportions. There are no operas, but he contributed to nearly every other genre. His two full symphonies (there is also a *Little Symphony*) represent milestones in his achievement as a composer, but there are some very respectable chamber works, including two numbered string quartets (1929, 1931) as well as an

211 A selection of which is available on Naxos, CD 8.572364.

earlier effort in the medium, and a delightful oboe quartet (1938) which includes a meltingly beautiful slow movement, and was first recorded by Sarah Francis and the English String Quartet (minus second violin).[212] It was written originally for the legendary oboist Leon Goossens, and, as expected, Jacob's writing for the instrument is wonderfully idiomatic.

Like Vaughan Williams and Holst, Jacob turned his hand to composing for bands of various kinds. Examples of his work in this medium include *An Original Suite for Military Band* (1928); *Music for a Festival*, for concert band (1951); *York Symphony* for brass band(1970); *Concerto for Band* (1970); *Fantasia for Euphonium & Wind Band* (1974); *Symphony AD 78* (1978); and *Concerto for Timpani and Wind Band* (1984).

How might we characterise Jacob's style? The term "neo-classical" is perhaps the most accurate description in general. His music is readily approachable, tonal, and with well-defined themes. It is recognisably English in character, although his biographer, Eric Wetherell, detects French and Russian influences behind some of the music. Although not averse to the sounds emanating from the English folksong school of composers, he was not interested in folksong for its own sake, and certainly not a collector like Vaughan Williams, George Butterworth and Cecil Sharp, although he did occasionally weave a fantasia or a passacaglia around a traditional tune, as in the case of *Fantasia on an English Folk Song (Dashing Away with a Smoothing Iron)*. His music may not have quite the distinctive character of an Elgar, a Vaughan Williams or a Holst, but it does have an appeal of its own and is no doubt rewarding to play. Jacob was entirely versatile and adaptable, well capable of rising to any occasion. His chief aim was to write the kind of music that met the demands of whoever commissioned it. It is in the non-commissioned works that we are most likely to encounter Jacob's personal voice.

---

212 It was recorded again on the Dutton label (CDLX 7177) in 2006, with Sarah Francis again the oboe soloist.

a. Bibliography

Foreman, Lewis, "Gordon Jacob in Interview", *British Music*, 7 (1985), pp. 59–67

Jacob, Gordon, *Orchestral Technique: A Manual for Students* (London: Oxford University Press, 1931).

---------, *The Elements of Orchestration* (London: October House, 1962).

Potter, Tully, "Jacob's Ladder: How Gordon Jacob became a Composer (Part 1)", *British Music*, 36/1 (2014), pp. 5–23

----------, "Jacob's Ladder: How Gordon Jacob became a Composer (Part 2)", *British Music*, 37/1 (2015), pp. 6–32

Wetherell, Eric, *Gordon Jacob: A Centenary Biography* (London: Thames Publishing, 1995)

----------, "Gordon Jacob", *British Music*, 17 (1995)

b. Selected Discography

i) Symphonies

Symphony No. 1	LPO, Wordsworth	Lyrita	SRCD 315
Symphony No. 2	LPO, Wordsworth	Lyrita	SRCD 315
Little Symphony	Munich SO, Bostock	Classico	CLASSCD 204

ii) Concertos

Viola Concerto No. 1	BBC Concert O., Bell; Callus (viola)	Dutton	CDLX 7258
Viola Concerto No. 2	BBC Concert O., Bell; Callus (viola)	Dutton	CDLX 7258

iii) Orchestral

A Festival Overture	Munich SO, Bostock	Classico	CLASSCD 204
Concert Piece for Viola & Orchestra	BBC Concert O., Bell; Callus (viola)	Dutton	CDLX 7258
Three Pieces for Viola & Orchestra	BBC Concert O., Bell; Callus (viola)	Dutton	CDLX 7258

iv) **Chamber**

Quartet for Oboe & Strings	Tagore String Trio; Francis (oboe)	Dutton	CDLX 7177
Six Shakespearian Sketches	Tagore String Trio	Dutton	CDLX 7177
Sonata for Oboe & Piano	Francis (oboe); Dussek (piano)	Dutton	CDLX 7177
Suite for Recorder & String Quartet	Maggini Quartet; Knight (rec)	Naxos	8.572364

c. Website

The Gordon Jacob Homepage (www.gordonjacob.net)

30. John Jeffreys (1927–2010)

There is a gentle quality about much of John Jeffreys' music which seems to have befitted the man himself. Not for him the dramatic grand gestures of a Wagner or a Mahler. Indeed, the standard Austro-German tradition seems to have evaded him. Of the European composers, it was Scarlatti, Clementi and Grieg who appealed to him the most, while of the home-grown composers, Thomas Tallis and Philip Rosseter entered his bloodstream above all others. Thus, we can already detect a rich tapestry of musical influences on Jeffreys' own music; but we should also acknowledge the influence of his own Welsh mother who was a fine singer, and from whom he imbibed a fund of traditional Welsh folksongs. Yet the style that emerges is entirely Jeffreys' own, free of pastiche, and although there is a quintessential Englishness about the music, with its quiet understatement and reserve, it is not the Englishness of Vaughan Williams or Finzi, or even Milford – although Jeffreys does share Milford's gentle spirit.

John Jeffreys was born on 4th December 1927 at Cliftonville on the Isle of Thanet where his father was a Congregational minister. Jeffreys senior owned a large library to which his son had unrestricted access, and he soon became familiar with a wide range of Elizabethan and Jacobean poets. The family was an artistic one. A brother turned to painting and, as noted, Jeffreys' mother was a fine singer. He was at first uncertain as to the choice of his own career. He could have been an artist himself, but settled on music after studying the piano at Caterham School and, later, Exeter. He became a boy chorister at Minster-in-Thanet and, after the family had decamped to Devon, Exeter Cathedral. At the end of the Second World War, aged eighteen, he completed his statutory two-year National Service (in the RAF), and in 1951 went up to Trinity College of Music in London, where studies in philosophy of music and theory were added to his continuing piano studies. It was here that he met Pauline Ashley, a violinist, who was to become his wife.

Determined to become a full-time composer, Jeffreys wrote prolifically throughout the 1950s and 1960s, producing a symphony, three violin concertos, a cello concerto, a string quartet, and over two hundred songs. However, his unashamedly tonal and lyrical style did not curry favour with the musical establishment of that time, and he was almost entirely ignored. Deeply depressed by the situation, he severely culled his output during the seventies, destroying most of his orchestral music and many of his songs. The one substantial piece he did preserve was a beautiful violin concerto of 1951 which was probably saved from the flames by the fact that he had written it for his wife. Happily, it was recorded some years ago (Meridian CDE 84331).

During his exile from the world of music, Jeffreys turned his attention to other interests, becoming a sufficiently accomplished gardener to write books on the subject.[213] However, he had never been entirely forgotten as a composer and received particularly warm support from the conductor Kenneth Page and the violinists John Fry, André Mangeot (1883-1970) and René Soames. Together they ensured that Jeffreys' existing works were played, even during the darkest times. The support of these individuals and their subsequent deaths inspired some of Jeffreys' orchestral work. *Serenade for Strings* (1959), for example, was written as a gift for André Mangeot's seventy-sixth birthday (Jeffreys composed the entire piece the night before), while *Elegy for André Mangeot* (1984) is an *in memoriam* response to his death. Pieces of similar tenor include *Elegy for John Fry* (1986) and *Elegy for a Conductor* [Kenneth Page] (1999).[214]

If, on reflection, Jeffreys considered the destruction of so much of his early work to have been rash, the pain was somewhat

213 Jeffreys, *Hardy Plants for Small Gardens* (London: Ward Lock, 1974); idem., *Perennials for Cutting* (London: Faber, 1977). Another composer, George Lloyd, turned to market gardening when he faced similar rejection (see the entry below).

214 Another orchestral work, the *Exeter Fantasia*, for double string orchestra, is, to my knowledge, still awaiting its premiere.

mitigated by the chance discovery of a large number of his early songs on a forgotten tape. With the help of another valuable friend, the publisher Kenneth Roberton of The Windmill, Wendover, he was able to revive and publish these songs, revising them where necessary, the result being four beautifully calligraphed volumes containing some 120 songs in all.[215] This experience seemed to relight the muse, and Jeffreys added further songs to the corpus until shortly before 2005 when a serious illness prevented any further composition. In their later years, Jeffreys and his wife settled at Clare in Suffolk where he died on 3rd September 2010.

As I have noted, Jeffreys' limited number of orchestral compositions were often influenced by valued friends and supporters such as John Fry and André Mangeot. Others, however, were inspired by the places in which he settled. One favoured region, a stretch of the River Exe flowing through Bickleigh in Devon is depicted not only in the *Bickleigh Idyll,* but also in the sumptuous Violin Concerto, each movement of which represents a different aspect of the river and its surroundings. If music about a particular location can have the capacity to make the listener want to pay a visit to it, these works surely can.

It is as a song writer, however, that Jeffreys is best-remembered. The sensitivity of his settings, whatever the text and the mood, are the equal of most better-known song composers, and his choice of poets is more wide-ranging than most. Two of his particular enthusiasms were the Elizabethan and Jacobean poets (John Fletcher, Philip Rosseter, Thomas Ford, Thomas Nabbes and, of course, the great Bard himself), and the Georgian poets, especially Wilfrid Gibson (1878–1962). He was also attracted to the work of Ivor Gurney, his settings of whom include a relatively large-scale treatment of the *Poem for End* which Gurney almost certainly composed during his incarceration in the City of London Mental Hospital at Dartford. Jeffreys' setting uses an orchestral accompaniment. Other poets to

215 Roberton also published Jeffreys' study on Philip Rosseter – *The Life and Works of Philip Rosseter* (Wendover, Bucks: Roberton, 1990).

be set include A.E. Housman, Joseph Campbell, Francis Ledwidge, W.B. Yeats, and one or two of the composer's contemporaries, notably Barry Duane Hill (b. 1944) whose poem *The Fox,* a protest against foxhunting, is given a memorable treatment by Jeffreys using chamber forces, including a significant role for the French horn.

Happily, the majority of Jeffreys' songs have been commercially recorded, mainly on the Divine Art, Meridian, Somm and Sonic Market labels, using leading vocalists such as Ian Partridge, James Gilchrist and Jonathan Veira. There is, in addition, a recording of the composer's works for solo organ, including the seventeen-minute *Fantasia,* performed by Michel Bourcier on the organ of St. Antoine des Quinze-Vingts in Paris.

a. Selected Discography

i) Orchestral

Violin Concerto	Orchestra da Camera, Page; Jackson (violin)	Meridian	CDE 84331
The Fox	Orchestre Philharmonique des Pays de Loire, Colléau; Renshaw (ten)	Meridian	CDE 84331
Elegy for André Mangeot	Orchestre Philharmonique des Pays de Loire, Colléau	Meridian	CDE 84331
Serenade for Strings	Orchestre de Camera, Page	Meridian	CDE 84331
Bickleigh Idyll	Orchestre de Camera, Page	Meridian	CDE 84331
Elegy for John Fry	Orchestre de Camera, Page	Meridian	CDE 84331
Poem for End	Philharmonia O., Bateman; Veira (bar)	Divine Art	DDA 25082
Elegy for a Conductor	Philharmonia O., Bateman	Divine Art	DDA 25082

ii) Solo Songs

Of Fire and Dew (21 songs)	Veira (bar); Katz (piano)	Somm	SOMMCD 218
Who is at my window? (24 songs)	I. Partridge (ten); J. Partridge (piano)	Meridian	CDE 84343
Curlew Calling (41 songs)	Weir (ten); Hoffman (piano)	Sonic Mkt.	N 0203
The Far Country (26 songs)	Gilchrist (ten); Tilbrook (piano)	Divine Art	DDA 25049

31. Constant Lambert (1905–51)

Constant Lambert was very much a man of his time, a man in full creative vigour in the never-to-be-forgotten roaring twenties, and whose talent shone brighter than most, even in a decade of artistic talent. For this was the age of composers like Bax, Berkeley, Berners, Bliss, Tippett, Rawsthorne, Walton and Warlock, of artists like Michael Ayrton, Augustus John and Christopher Wood (not to mention Lambert's own father), and writers such as T.S. Eliot, D.H. Lawrence, the Sitwells, Virginia Woolf and W.B. Yeats – many of whom Lambert knew personally. The affinities between himself and Philip Heseltine (Peter Warlock) can hardly be ignored. Both came from well-heeled families; both were prodigious musical talents whose careers as composers were compromised by their interests in other fields such as writing, journalism, musical editing and, especially in Lambert's case, performing and conducting; both attracted a fund of stories about their outrageous behaviour; both were brilliant talkers and legendary drinkers; both possessed manic-depressive personalities; both exhibited a macabre interest in the occult; both could turn out an acerbic limerick; and both, alas, were among those brilliant lights whose luminosity fizzled out too soon. Indeed, Lambert's career lasted barely twenty-five years compared with the fifty-plus years of composers like Bliss, Tippett, Vaughan Williams and Walton. In comparing Lambert with Walton, Foreman[216] notes that, in his day, the former was the more brilliant of the two, while the latter's output has turned out to be the more enduring, thanks largely to the handful of masterpieces written in the decade 1925–35. Lambert's *The Rio Grande* is, of course, the work which stands out from the rest and with which he will always be associated first and foremost; but since the recording companies have recorded all his major ballet scores – and he was, above all, a composer for the ballet – the public has access to the music he was writing more generally.

216 Foreman, liner notes, Lambert, *Tiresias and Pomona*, Hyperion, CDA 67049, p. 3.

Leonard Constant Lambert was born on 23rd August 1905. His father, George Washington Lambert – despite the name – had been born in Russia, later emigrated to Australia, and had settled in London by the time Constant was born. He was an artist by profession, and there are several portraits by him of Constant and his brother Maurice as children, including a beautiful pencil drawing of Constant as a baby in his mother's arms, and an oil painting for which he sat at the age of eleven wearing the idiosyncratic uniform of the Bluecoat School (Christ's Hospital, Horsham), which he attended. Artistry ran in the blood, for brother Maurice became a noted sculptor, while later on Constant's own son, Kit (1935–81) became the manager for a number of pop groups, most notably The Who, and died, incidentally, at the same untimely age as his father.

Among Lambert's many interests, his talent for composition was obvious from the first, and he was composing credible orchestral scores from the age of thirteen. He enrolled with the RCM in 1922 where his composition teachers included Vaughan Williams and George Dyson, and he studied conducting with Malcolm Sargent. During this brief period, the major influences that were to shape Lambert's professional life were falling into place. The influences of jazz, which is generally associated with George Antheil (1900–59) and George Gershwin (1898–1937) in America, was also exerting itself on English composers too, none more so than Lambert, and can be detected at its most brilliant in *The Rio Grande*. Another modernist influence was the music being written at this time by *Les Six* (Auric, Durey, Honegger, Milhaud, Poulenc and Tailleferre), as well as Satie, in France. A third major influence, and surely the most enduring, was Diaghilev and his *Ballet Russes*. Lambert met the great man in 1925 and played him a dance suite, *Adam and Eve*. Diaghilev was impressed with the music and offered to stage the work as a ballet, on condition that the scenario was changed. Thus, *Adam and Eve* became *Romeo and Juliet*, one of only two ballets by English composers to be produced by Diaghilev (Berners' *The Triumph of Neptune* being the other) – some achievement considering that at the time of its premiere Lambert was just twenty years old and still studying at the RCM.

Controversy surrounded the production, as will always be the case when two or more temperamental, headstrong personalities are locked in a working relationship. Lambert considered that Diaghilev had taken too many liberties with his scenario and threatened to withdraw the score. Diaghilev retaliated by putting it under lock and key to prevent access, and in the end the ballet went ahead in Monte Carlo pretty much in the form Diaghilev had intended. Perhaps the precocious twenty-year old was unwise to make the scene he did, for it may well have deterred the Russian from working with him on future projects and, brilliant though Lambert may have been, he was still learning his trade. Still, it set the pattern and direction of his future career as a composer.

His next major ballet score was *Pomona* (1927) which was initially produced by Nijinska, but it was also the work which, from 1930, initiated a fruitful relationship with the British choreographer Frederick Ashton who, from this time, was associated with all Lambert's ballets. His third major effort in the genre was the one-act ballet *Horoscope* (1937) from which he extracted a suite of the best movements, the complete score having been lost during the Second World War. Lambert's final ballet, *Tiresias*, was one of his most extensive, and had been germinating in his mind for some twenty years. It was produced in the last year of his life when, for various reasons, he was in poor physical shape, and he had to enlist an army of fellow composers (including Dennis ApIvor, Christian Darnton, Robert Irving, Gordon Jacob, Elisabeth Lutyens, Alan Rawsthorne and Humphrey Searle) to orchestrate the various numbers. The first night, a Royal Gala performance, went ahead as planned, barely a month before the composer's death, but it was not well received. Despite Lambert's carefully-worded synopsis, the plot involving the Greek myth of Tiresias (who is able to swop sexes by striking one of two snakes, is struck blind by the goddess Hera when he declares that he prefers life as a woman against her prediction that he would not, but is given the boon of prophecy by Zeus in compensation), seems to have left the audience baffled. Still, it received over thirty performances at Covent Garden in the years following the composer's death. Indeed, the very existence of the Royal Ballet bears testimony to Lambert's commitment to the genre, for it was he who, in 1931, along with Frederick Ashton and Ninette de Valois, founded the company in its initial incarnation as the Vic-Wells, and remained the company's principal conductor until 1947.

There was much more to Lambert as a composer than ballet music. There are two piano concertos, each distinctive from the other in conception. The concerto of 1924 is scored for two trumpets, percussion and strings, and is cast in four short movements. It is a largely uplifting bravura work in contrast to the darker, more astringent *Concerto for Piano & Nine Players* (1931) which was dedicated to the memory of Philip Heseltine who had died in December 1930. The instrumental forces (flute, three different types of clarinet, trumpet, trombone, cello, bass and percussion [temple blocks, tam-tam and maracas]) are as particular as they are unusual.

The third piano-centred work is, of course, *The Rio Grande*, a choral setting of a poem by Lambert's friend Sacheverell Sitwell. Although the text deals with a Brazilian festival, the musical influences are as North American as South, and Lambert once expressed the wish that the chorus should ideally be a negro one. Certainly, there are suggestions of the young Delius in his Florida period.

Lambert's major choral work, extending for some fifty minutes, is *Summer's Last Will and Testament* (1932–36), a setting of some doleful texts by Thomas Nashe (1567–1601) which are informed by the plague which habitually ravaged the capital in those days, and may even have claimed the life of Nashe himself. This work, even more than *The Rio Grande*, is regarded by many critics as Lambert's true masterpiece. The orchestra plays a part equal to that of the chorus and baritone solo, and is not simply a supporting act. There are two purely orchestral movements. The texts, although given a specific role by the poet, are such that they can be applied to any natural catastrophe – be it AIDS, the Corona virus or climate change (none of which could have been in Lambert's mind).

After *Summer's Last Will and Testament*, Lambert composed relatively little. However, there was a brief foray into the world of film music, including the part-documentary *Merchant Seamen* (1941) and *Anna Karenina* (1948). The former, which he may have regarded as his contribution to the war-effort, was rescored as a five-movement suite, and shows the composer adapting his talents to film music as to the manor born. A stirring *Fanfare* and *March* envelop an eerie second movement (*Convoy in the Fog*), an alarming third (*Attack*), and a calm, assuring fourth (*Safe Convoy*). One other piece, also connected with the war, is *Aubade héroïque* (1942) which, although dedicated "to Ralph Vaughan Williams on his 70th birthday", alludes to a dramatic incident involving Lambert himself. During a visit of the Sadler's Wells Opera Company to Holland in 1940, he and everyone else found themselves stranded when the country was invaded by Germany. Eventually, they were able to get safe passage back to England, but it was touch-and-go for a few days.

As noted above, Lambert perhaps too freely dissipated his energies among a whole range of activities, not all of which were necessarily musical. One interest which is generally agreed to have been invaluable, however, was that of conducting. Unlike many conductor-composers, he did not restrict himself to conducting his own work, and his programmes were invariably imaginative. He introduced French and Russian music to British audiences which, at the time, were all too seldom heard, if at all. By all accounts, his manner on the podium inspired even the less talented musician to rise to the occasion.

Like his friend Philip Heseltine, Lambert's facility with language was excellent. Often, he used the medium as a vehicle for his caustic wit which can be found in full measure in his only book, *Music Ho!* (1934) which examines the place of music in the context of the other arts, sometimes in the most irreverent manner. As for the tales of his antics, which, like those of Heseltine, are the stuff of legend, one of the best-known (which does happen to be verifiable, having been related by one of the participants) will be sufficient to furnish the reader with a flavour:

Lambert and his friend, the artist Michael Ayrton, were boarding a train in London, deep in discussion. Lambert had claimed that he could draw fish better than Ayrton, while the other retorted that he could not hold a candle to him in the matter of drawing cats. To prove their respective points, they produced an envelope and proceeded to cover it with drawings of fish and cats. When this had been covered, they progressed to the walls of the compartment in which they were sitting and covered these also. Finally, only the ceiling remained in pristine condition, so they each climbed into a luggage rack, lay on their backs, and covered this, somewhat like Michelangelo in the Sistine Chapel. As they were hard at work, the train stopped at a station, and an elderly lady, thinking the compartment was empty, entered, sat down and took out her knitting. Suddenly, from above, came a mellow voice: "There will soon be no more room on the ceiling either". The lady fled from the carriage in alarm and back onto the platform. "One can only be thankful", said Michael Ayrton, in telling the tale, "that the train was still standing in the station."[217] They don't make 'em like that any more!

217 S. Lloyd, *Constant Lambert: Beyond the Rio Grande* (Woodbridge, Suffolk: Boydell Press, 2014), pp. 323–24.

a. Bibliography

Lambert, Constant, *Music Ho! A Study of Music in Decline* (London: Hogarth Press, 1985, orig. 1934)

Lloyd, Stephen, "The Constancy of Lambert, and Some Lesser-Known Aspects of the Man", *British Music*, 27 (1995)

----------, *Constant Lambert: Beyond the Rio Grande* (Woodbridge, Suffolk: Boydell Press, 2014)

Motion, Andrew, *The Lamberts: George, Constant and Kit* (London: Faber & Faber, 2018)

Mottershead, Tim, "Alan Rawsthorne: The Fish with an Ear for Music: A Concise Biography", *The Creel: Journal of the Rawsthorne Trust and the Friends of Alan Rawsthorne*, no. 19 (Winter 2005/06).

b. Selected Discography

i) Concertos

Piano Concerto	BBC Concert O., Wordsworth; Owen Norris (piano)	ASV	CD WHL 2122
Concerto for Piano and Nine Players	BBC Concert O., Wordsworth; Stott (piano)	ASV	CD WHL 2122

ii) Orchestral

Music for Orchestra	LPO, Wordsworth	Lyrita	SRCD 215
King Pest: Rondo Burlesca	RPO, Joly	Lyrita	SRCD 215
Romeo & Juliet (Ballet)	ECO, Del Mar	Lyrita	SRCD 215
Pomona (Ballet)	ECO, Del Mar	Lyrita	SRCD 215
Horoscope (Ballet)	BBC Concert O., Wordsworth	Decca	473 424-2

Tiresias (Ballet)	English Northern Phil., Lloyd-Jones	Hyperion	CDA 67049
Merchant Seamen Suite	BBC Concerto O., Wordsworth	ASV	CD WHL 2122
Aubade Héroique	English Northern Phil., Lloyd-Jones	Helios	CDH 55388

iii) **Chorus with Orchestra**

Summer's Last Will and Testament	English Northern Phil.; Chorus of Opera North; Leeds Festival Chorus; Shimell (bar); Burgess (mezz-sop); Lloyd-Jones	Helios	CDH 55388
The Rio Grande	English Northern Phil.; Choir of Opera North; Leeds Festival Chorus; Burgess (mezz-sop); Gibbons (piano); Lloyd-Jones	Helios	CDH 55388

32. Walter Leigh (1905–42)

Walter Leigh was born in the same year as Constant Lambert, but his personality and career could not have been more different. He seems to have been a well-balanced individual with a normal family life, who went about his work with a quiet assurance and responded with sensitivity to the many varied commissions he was given. There are no stories of histrionics or outrageous behaviour or heavy drinking as with Lambert. Yet they did have one thing in common: both men had the knack of choosing just the right instruments for the task with which they had been entrusted. Leigh, indeed, imposed strict limitations on himself, and knew how to get the most out of the resources at his disposal. He composed for the occasion. There are no self-indulgent symphonies, grand operas or cantatas.[218] The bulk of his small output (he was killed on active service, aged only thirty-six) consists of stage works, incidental music, film music, solo piano pieces and a handful of songs. Even most of the orchestral works were written with half an eye on the amateur player. There is little if any, angst in any of these pieces, which is remarkable in itself, given that most of them were composed in the shadow of Hitler's rise to power in the 1930s.

Leigh's interest in music ran in the family. His mother, a Prussian-born concert pianist, was his first teacher, but during his school days in Hampstead he studied with the distinguished organist Harold Darke (1888–1976) and later, at Christ's College, Cambridge, with Edward Dent. Thus, the young Leigh was in safe hands. After graduating, he spent a further two years studying with Paul Hindemith (1895–1963) at the Berlin Hochschule für Musik (1927–29), and it may have been his example of writing *Gebrauchtsmusik* (music for use) that instilled the same principle in

---

218 Roger Wimbush's prediction in 1938 that "one day the symphonies and operas will come" (quoted by Calum MacDonald in the liner notes to *Walter Leigh: Complete Chamber Works*, Dutton, CDLX 7143) never materialised. Had he had any inclination to compose such works, they would surely have shown signs of appearing by this time.

his pupil, for certainly, when he returned to England, this is what he determined to do, and the techniques he used to ensure that a work was suitable for amateur performers were probably imbibed – in part, at least – from Hindemith.

Leigh is best-remembered today for his delightful *Concertino for Harpsichord and Strings* (1934), a work in neo-classical vein and which, especially in his choice of solo instrument, glances back to an earlier age. Every work, however, is worthwhile. The substantial concert overture *Agincourt* was commissioned by the BBC for the coronation of King George VI in 1937, and he rose to the occasion with a blustery, celebratory piece containing moments of Elgarian grandeur. The dignified restraint at the heart of the overture is based around the traditional Agincourt tune which lends the work its title.

The incidental music to *A Midsummer Night's Dream* is really a masterpiece of its genre. Not a note seems out of place, and the magical effect of the music is entirely apt, given the character of the play. It was written in 1936 for an open-air performance in Weimar. In the same year Leigh also produced incidental music for the annual Cambridge Greek play which, in that year, was Aristophanes' *The Frogs*. Leigh wrote extensively for the chorus – music which has long-since been forgotten, even if it still exists. However, two numbers, *Overture* and *Dance*, do survive and were recorded in 1985 by Lyrita (SRCD 289).

Of his stage works, for which in his own day Leigh was best-known, the most successful and enduring was *Jolly Roger*, which he described as "a new musical burlesque". Opening on 13th February 1933, it ran for six months and 199 performances, first at the Opera House, Manchester, and subsequently at the Savoy and Lyceum Theatres in London. The lyrics were provided by V.C. Clinton-Baddeley (1900–70) with whom Leigh had already worked on a previous production, *The Pride of the Regiment* (1932). The breezy *Jolly Roger* overture is indicative of what the audience can expect throughout the production.[219]

---

219 It has now been recorded by Lyrita,

Leigh wrote a quantity of music for films and documentaries, including *His Lordship* (1932), *The Face of Scotland* (1938), *Man of the Alps* (1939), and *Squadron 992* (1939), all of which have long since been forgotten. Given Leigh's consummate craftsmanship, however, we can be confident that these scores would have been up to the mark. The most innovative of them was probably the one written for *Song of Ceylon*, which is said to have been distinguished by striking percussion effects.

Leigh seems to have reserved his most serious music for the chamber genre. His single string quartet (1929) was written while he was still a student under Hindemith, stylistic traces of whom are detectable. With becoming modesty, the composer referred to this piece as his Student String Quartet, and its four movements run for a total of just over ten minutes. However, this is no trivial work, for it contains some of the most intensely-felt music that he ever produced.

In the following year, now back in England, he wrote *Three Movements for String Quartet* in which there is a little more English lyricism and rather less of Hindemith. Once again, these movements are miniatures in the truest sense of the word. The final allegro is over almost before it has begun.

When we survey Leigh's output, it is striking how much of it was written in the 1930s. It includes all his substantial stage works, along with his orchestral pieces and some of his chamber and solo piano works. It was certainly a prolific decade for him, the majority of his 150 individual items being composed during that period. It is astonishing to realise that at the end of it he was not yet thirty-five years old.

Inevitably, when evaluating Leigh's tragically short life, the "what if?" factor is bound to arise. Did the musical world miss his talent as much as it missed George Butterworth after his equally tragic demise? To an extent, the answer depends on what is being sought. Butterworth has always been understood to be a composer of "serious" if entirely accessible music, and many expected great things following his early promise – extended works such as symphonies and concertos. In other words, he might have developed into a "complete" composer, not only stylistically, but with regard to the more extended canvases he would surely have produced, given time.

Walter Leigh, on the other hand, was six years older than Butterworth at the time of his death, yet showed little sign of ambition. He seems to have been content to work in miniature and to apply his exquisite craftsmanship to honing tiny, self-contained movements. Of course, the stage works were bound to be more extensive – that was the nature of the beast; but in a sense, having written one operetta, there is little more a composer can do beyond writing another. The only question of development in that case is whether the next can be made wittier or more entertaining. None of this mattered much to Leigh. His *raison d' être* was to serve the society of which he was a member rather than to write his name in history as a ground-breaker or leader of the *avant garde*. (Of course, it is doubtful that this would have been Butterworth's goal either). What we are left with, in both cases, is a body of finely-crafted music to enjoy, and in that regard, we should be grateful that it was written.

a. Selected Discography

i) Orchestral

Overture: Agincourt	NPO, Braithwaite	Lyrita	SRCD 289
Overture: Jolly Roger	NPO, Braithwaite	Lyrita	SRCD 289
Suite: A Midsummer Night's Dream	LPO, Braithwaite	Lyrita	SRCD 289
Music for Strings	LPO, Braithwaite	Lyrita	SRCD 289
The Frogs: Overture and Dance	LPO, Braithwaite	Lyrita	SRCD 289
Concertino for Harpsichord and Strings	LPO, Braithwaite; Pinnock (harps)	Lyrita	SRCD 289

ii) Musical Burlesque

Jolly Roger	BBC Concert O.; Ambrosian Singers; Lawrence	Lyrita	REAM 2116

iii) **Chamber**

Sonatina	Kiernan (violin); Rahman (piano)	Dutton	CDLX 7143
Trio	Noakes (flute); Anderson (oboe); Rahman (piano)	Dutton	CDLX 7143
Three Movements for String Quartet	Manning, Kiernan (violins); Pearson (cello)	Dutton	CDLX 7143

33. Kenneth Leighton (1929–88)

Although he spent almost half his life in Scotland, Kenneth Leighton was born in Wakefield, West Yorkshire, and always regarded himself as a true "Tyke". His parents were of modest means, but they recognised the academic potential of their son from an early age and were determined to encourage its development. With the help of a parish priest, they procured a piano on which young Kenneth was able to practice and take his first steps in composition. He spent a few years as a chorister at Wakefield Cathedral, which no doubt sparked his lifelong interest in writing choral music for the Church. His secondary schooling took place at Queen Elizabeth Grammar School where he accompanied the school assembly hymns on the piano and also played at school concerts. On leaving school he went up to Queen's College, Oxford, on a state scholarship to read Classics, but he soon immersed himself in the musical life of the university and, once settled, obtained permission to read for a BA in music concurrently with his Classics studies. His composition tutor, Bernard Rose, was so impressed with an early *Symphony for Strings*, written when Leighton was still only twenty years of age, that he showed it to Gerald Finzi. Soon afterwards, he received an invitation to attend a rehearsal of the work by Finzi's Newbury String Players, and the public premiere took place in Enborne Church in Newbury in December 1949.

Encouraged by this early breakthrough, Leighton next composed a piece specifically for Finzi and his players entitled *Veris Gratia* (1950), for cello, oboe and strings. Its four movements are generally pastoral in mood, and somewhat reminiscent of Finzi's own style as well as that of Vaughan Williams whose *Flos Campi* has been suggested as a model, whether consciously or otherwise.

The following year saw further progress when his overture *Primavera Romana* was performed by the RPO under no less a maestro than Leopold Stokowski, and he was awarded a Mendelssohn Scholarship which enabled him to study for a year with Goffredo Petrassi in Rome. He eagerly imbibed the serialism and neo-classicism of his teacher, and on his return to England in

1952 began to internalise these influences into his own technique, with the result that his music became more cosmopolitan. However, he did not abandon his home-grown lyricism and instinct for melody. His musical language may have broadened, but not at the expense of his personal integrity.

Leighton returned not only with an advanced understanding of compositional technique, but also with an Italian wife, Lydia Vignapiano, with whom he had two children. Family life necessitated financial security, and as he had no private source of income like Vaughan Williams and Bax, or rich patrons like Walton, he needed a job. This came initially with a post as Professor of Harmony at the Royal Marine School of Music at Deal in Kent. Thus began a fairly frantic period of teaching up and down the country. From Deal, he moved to the University of Leeds (1953–56), then Edinburgh (1956–68), then as Fellow in Music at Worcester College, Oxford (1968–70), and finally back to Edinburgh University (1970–88) where he remained for the remainder of his career. Among his students at various times were Donald Runnicles, Nicholas Cleobury, Nigel Osborne and James MacMillan, many of whom remember him with great affection and respect.

Although Leighton was proud of his Yorkshire roots, he fell in love with the Scottish landscape, especially the Western Isles. Although he cannot be regarded as a "landscape" composer in the sense of, say, Delius or Moeran, it did sometimes inspire him in his choice of subject material, as in the case of his opera *Columba* which is concerned with the life of the saint who evangelised parts of Scotland, including the Hebrides. A favourite haunt of Leighton's was the isle of Arran, which is where he was buried following his untimely death from cancer at the age of fifty-eight.

Despite his teaching workload and obligatory administrative duties, he found time to compose fairly prolifically, producing some large canvas works including three symphonies (the last two including settings for chorus), three piano concertos, and other concertos for organ, violin, viola, cello, oboe, harpsichord/ recorder, and strings. There is nothing frivolous about any of this music. It is always forthright and impassioned, with the timpani often used to add weight and gravitas. Several of his pieces, in fact, are scored for strings and timpani, sometimes with the addition of a solo instrument.

For more intimate expression Leighton used the chamber medium, composing two string quartets, three numbered piano sonatas, a piano quintet, and a piano trio, among others. Although he seems to have expressed little interest in art song, his Symphony No. 3, *Laudes Musicae*, is essentially a setting of texts by Sir Thomas Browne (1605–82), Shelley (1792–1822), and Elizabeth Barrett Browning (1806–61), while the Symphony No. 2, *Sinfonia Mistica*, sets a veritable florilegium of texts for chorus, including Donne (1572–1631), Traherne (1638–74) and Herbert (1593–1633). Most of his choral settings, however, are associated with the Church. In this regard, his style owes more than a passing nod to the English choral tradition as represented by Parry, Stanford, Elgar, Vaughan Williams, Howells and Finzi. There are several masses of one kind or another, the most substantial (and probably the best) being the *Mass for Double Choir* (1965), while another, the *Dublin Festival Mass* (1980), is scored for solo organ. Leighton's sacred works are indeed wide ranging – from the exquisite carol anthem *Lully, Lulla, Thou Tiny Little Child*, for chorus alone, written when he was just nineteen years of age, to the *Te Deum Laudamus* for solo soprano (or semi-chorus), chorus and orchestra (1964–66). Yet like many celebrated English composers writing sacred works, Leighton was never a church-going Christian. What attracted him were the challenges of writing music appropriate for the occasion.

Leighton's music cries out to be heard but, as I have said, it is serious, deeply-felt stuff, and the listener needs to give it time. It may not appeal to everyone on a first hearing, but once one becomes more familiar with it, one begins to appreciate just what powerful music it is. Luckily, all the most important works have now been recorded, so repeated hearings are on tap. Still, I wish the concert programmers would have the imagination to programme his most outstanding works in the concert hall. His Cello Concerto, for example, is a marvellous creation, worthy to be set alongside the Elgar, Finzi and Moeran concertos. We can always hope, I suppose.

a. Bibliography

Smith, Carolyn J., *Kenneth Leighton: A Bio-Bibliography* (Westport, CT: Praeger, 2004)

b. Selected Discography

i) Symphonies

Symphony No. 1	BBC NOW, Brabbins	Chandos	CHAN 10608
Symphony No. 2	BBC NOW & Chorus; Hickox	Chandos	CHAN 10495
Symphony No. 3 "Laudes Musicae"	Scottish NO, Thomson; Mackie (ten)	Chandos	CHAN 8741
Symphony for Strings	BBC NOW, Hickox	Chandos	CHAN 10461

ii) Concertos

Piano Concerto No. 1	Malta PO, Laus; Bainbridge (piano)	Cameo	CC 9046 CD
Piano Concerto No. 3	BBC NOW; Brabbins; Shelley (piano)	Chandos	CHAN 10608
Organ Concerto	BBC NOW, Hickox; Scott (org)	Chandos	CHAN 10461
Cello Concerto	Scottish NO, Thomson; Wallfisch (cello)	Chandos	CHAN 8741

iii) Choral with Orchestra

Te Deum Laudamus	BBC NOW & Chorus; Hickox; Fox (sop); Rhys-Davies (bar)	Chandos	CHAN 10495

iv) Chamber

Piano Trio	McAslan (violin); Fuller (cello); Dussek (piano)	Dutton	CDLX 7118
Partita	Fuller (cello); Dussek (piano)	Dutton	CDLX 7118

v) Choral

Choral Music	Finzi Singers, Spicer	Chandos	CHAN 9485

34. George Lloyd (1913–98)

George Lloyd's composing career falls conveniently into three distinct stages: an early period of uninterrupted success brought to a sudden halt by a shattering war experience; a period of post-war rehabilitation during which his work was largely ignored by the musical establishment of the Glock era; and finally, an Indian summer in which his music was restored to prominence.

George Lloyd is probably the most prominent composer to have emerged from Cornwall. He was born to musical parents in St. Ives on 28th June 1913. His father, William, was born in Rome and was greatly interested in opera as well as being a fine flautist, while his mother played the piano, violin and viola. It was no surprise, therefore, that the young George set himself to become a composer, taking his first steps at the age of ten. He had some formal schooling, but was not physically robust, and so was largely home-tutored by his father whose accomplishments extended well beyond the field of music.

By the time he was twenty-one years old, George had already written his First Symphony (1932) and an opera, *Iernin* (1934). He had a very close professional relationship with his father. They frequently played together in the various Cornish orchestras, and it was William Lloyd who provided the libretto for *Iernin*. After a week of sold-out performances in Penzance, the opera enjoyed a successful run at the Lyceum Theatre in London. Much encouraged, Lloyd composed a second opera, *The Serf*, which was staged at Covent Garden in 1938, by which time he had written two further symphonies. At this stage in his career the sky seemed to be the limit, and success bred success. For example, John Ireland happened to be present at the London premiere of *Iernin* and was so impressed with the work that he returned to hear further performances. He met the composer and invited him to his studio in Gunter Grove, Chelsea, and several other visits followed. Ireland became something of an unofficial mentor to Lloyd, introducing him to new music such as Stravinsky's *The Rite of Spring*, thereby broadening his musical education. It was through the good offices of Ireland that Lloyd's Third Symphony was premiered in 1935.

Among other important influences during his gestation period were Harry Farjeon (1878–1948), a composer with whom he took lessons on a private basis, and the acclaimed violinist Albert Sammons (1886–1957) with whom he studied for five years.

At the outbreak of the Second World War, Lloyd enrolled in the Royal Marines as a bandsman and entered service on HMS Trinidad, joining a close-knit group of twenty musicians. Their job was to entertain the crew, play ceremonial music as required when in port, and to man the transmission station when at sea. As a kind of composer-in-residence, Lloyd even wrote a march in honour of the ship, the *HMS Trinidad March*.[220] In 1942, while on convoy duties in the Arctic Ocean, the *Trinidad* was struck by a torpedo[221] which ruptured the ship's oil tanks, flooding the transmitting station and drowning all but three of the bandsmen in fuel oil. George Lloyd was the last man to escape before the hatch slammed shut on the rest. Having taken oil into his system, he was in very poor physical shape, but worse still was the shell-shock (or post-traumatic stress disorder, as we would call it today) caused by his terrible ordeal. He was hospitalised as soon as possible after the ship had limped into port,[222] but doctors gave him up as a hopeless case. Fortunately, he was given into the care of his Swiss wife, Nancy, who painstakingly nursed him back to health over a number of years, never losing hope

220 For Lloyd's own account of how his march came to be preferred to a rival march that had been commissioned from Vaughan Williams, and suggestions as to the fate of the latter, see William Lloyd's liner notes in *Havas*, EM Records, EMR CD026, on which the *HMS Trinidad March* can be heard.

221 Ironically, it was a malfunctioning torpedo belonging to the ship that caused the damage.

222 It is sometimes reported that the torpedo sunk the ship and that the survivors had to be pulled from the water. However, the *Trinidad* managed to limp back to port in Murmansk, from where Lloyd was transferred to hospital in Aberdeen. After the necessary repairs, the ship set out for Scapa Flow, but was bombed by enemy aircraft. This time it was irreparably damaged and, once the crew had abandoned ship, was scuttled.

that he would eventually recover a life of comparative normality. One important step in this process, after four years of convalescence, was the composition of his Fourth Symphony, *Arctic* (1946).

For a while, Lloyd managed to resume his musical career, composing his Fifth Symphony (1947) and the opera *John Socman*, which had been commissioned for the Festival of Britain in 1951 (alongside Vaughan Williams's *Pilgrims Progress* and Britten's *Billy Budd*). However, the musical climate began to change in the years following the war, and Lloyd's melodic style was no longer in vogue. Other tonalists, like Edmund Rubbra, William Alwyn and Malcolm Arnold, refused to be bullied into submission, simply battening down the hatches and sitting out the passing modernist storm. Others, such as Robin Milford and John Jeffreys, were more discouraged, culling their output, or, in Milford's case, committing suicide. Lloyd's solution was to withdraw to a remote cottage in Dorset and work as a market gardener, growing carnations and mushrooms. However, he did not abandon composition entirely. His routine was to rise at 4.00 a.m. and compose for three hours before beginning the day's work, the fruits of this regime including a further three symphonies (Nos. 6–8).

Eventually, the clouds lifted as the musical climate changed once more, now in the tonalists' favour. Lloyd sold his market garden business in 1972 and, now aged almost sixty, relocated to London to resume his music career. As the tide began to turn, the BBC "rediscovered" George Lloyd and began broadcasting his symphonies. The conductor Edward Downes became a champion of his music, and at last the Conifer and Albany record labels between them recorded the full cycle of Lloyd's twelve symphonies as well as other major works such as three piano concertos, two violin concertos, cello concerto, *Litany*, and the *Symphonic Mass*.

Lloyd's music is very much dependent on the creation and development of tunes, and if the listener finds these appealing, the same will be true of the work as a whole. There have been criticisms that his music fails to plumb the depths – that the statements it makes are not weighty enough. Of course, this is of no account in overtures and suites which are supposed to have a lightness of touch, but the symphonies are another matter. It is, perhaps, fair comment that the buoyancy in many of the symphonies is too easily won, but there are exceptions to this tendency. The Symphony No. 7, for example, is a tense, gritty affair with a good deal more dissonance than is usual for Lloyd. Its subtitle, *Proserpine* (the Greek goddess of death) may partly explain the mood of the music, and Paul Conway[223] has suggested that it is in this symphony, rather than in the earlier *Arctic* symphony, that all the angst of the composer's wartime experiences surfaces. By his own admission, Lloyd was feeling suicidal at the time the Seventh Symphony was being written, and was hospitalised for a time in the wake of it.

In his ability to swing between extremes of mood, it is possible to detect in Lloyd what is also characteristic of Malcolm Arnold, who also had to wrestle with the demons of mental trauma. In Arnold, however, these mood swings can occur within a few bars of a single work, often carrying an air of real menace, and they are not confined to his symphonic cycle. By comparison, the general tenor of Lloyd's symphonies is ebullient and vivacious, and the grinding dissonance found in his Seventh Symphony is thereby all the more conspicuous.

Lloyd's final work was the *Requiem*, unusually scored for countertenor, chorus and organ. It was written in memory of Diana, Princess of Wales, but as it was completed only three weeks before his own death at the age of eighty-five, it became a personal valediction, and was performed at the 2013 Proms to mark his centenary year.

---

223 Conway, liner notes, *Lloyd: Symphonies Nos. 6 & 7*, Lyrita, REAM. 1135, p. 11.

a. Bibliography

Gibbons, Alan, "George Lloyd: 'Out of the Depths'", *British Music*, 38/1 (2016)

b. Selected Discography

i) Symphonies

Symphony No. 1	Albany SO, Lloyd	Albany	TROY 032
Symphony No. 2	BBC PO, Lloyd	Conifer	CDCF 139
Symphony No. 3	BBC PO, Lloyd	Albany	TROY 090
Symphony No. 4 , "Arctic"	Albany SO, Lloyd	Albany	TROY 498
Symphony No. 5	BBC PO, Lloyd	Albany	TROY 022-2
Symphony No. 6	BBC Northern SO Downes	Lyrita	REAM 1135
Symphony No. 7 , "Proserpine"	BBC Northern SO Downes	Lyrita	REAM 1135
Symphony No. 8	Philharmonia O., Downes	Albany	TROY 230
Symphony No. 9	BBC PO, Lloyd	Conifer	CDCF 139
Symphony No. 10	BBC PO, Lloyd	Albany	TROY 015-2
Symphony No. 11	Albany SO, Lloyd	Conifer	CDCF 144
Symphony No. 12	Albany SO, Lloyd	Albany	TROY 032

ii) Concertos

Piano Concerto No. 3	BBC PO, Lloyd; Stott (piano)	Albany	TROY 019-2
Piano Concerto No. 4	LSO, Lloyd; Stott (piano)	Albany	AR 004
Violin Concerto No. 2	Philharmonia O., Parry; Anghelescu (violin)	Albany	TROY 316
Cello Concerto	Albany SO, Miller; Ross (cello)	Albany	TROY 458

iii) Orchestral

The Serf: Prelude	Bath Phil., Thornton	EM Records	EMR CD 026
In Memoriam	Bath Phil., Thornton	EM Records	EMR CD 026
Le Pont du Gard	Bath Phil., Thornton	EM Records	EMR CD 026
HMS Trinidad March	Bath Phil., Thronton	EM Records	EMR CD 026

iv) Choral with Orchestra

A Symphonic Mass	Bournemouth SO; Brighton Festival Chorus, Lloyd	Albany	TROY 100

A Litany	Philharmonia O.; Guildford Choral Society; Watson (sop), White (bar); Lloyd	Albany	TROY 200

b. Webpage

The George Lloyd Society (https://www.georgelloyd.com)

35. Elisabeth Lutyens (1906–83)

Of twentieth-century English women composers, no name is better-known than that of Elisabeth Lutyens. I say "no name" because the woman herself is difficult to pin down. She seems to have been a somewhat formidable person, and was certainly no blushing violet. But, as Ethel Smyth, Ruth Gipps and others discovered, in the early twentieth-century strength of character was necessary to succeed in a profession overwhelmingly dominated by men, and even in our more "enlightened times", few female composers have become household names. How many concert-goers can boast that they have ever heard a work by a woman live in the concert hall? (It *does* happen – occasionally).

However, if success is the measure of a composer, Lutyens had a distinct advantage. She came of aristocratic stock, being one of five children born to Lady Emily Bulwer-Lytton (1874–1964), and was the daughter of the world-famous architect Edwin Lutyens (1869–1944). No doubt she could have been a lady of leisure, but she aspired to be a composer from an early age. She knew what she wanted and her position helped her to realise her dream.

It was entirely in character that she was not prepared to follow meekly on a path that the previous generation of English composers had pioneered. Not for her the strains of Elgar, or of Vaughan Williams and his acolytes. Instead, she spent a year at the forward-looking École Normale de Musique in Paris, and then broadened her outlook still further by spending part of 1923 in India. On her return to Paris, she took lessons with fellow composer and theosophist John Foulds who was himself no stranger to new developments in music. Given her early background (we should remember that she was still only eighteen years old at this stage), it was almost inevitable that she would be drawn into the exciting world of serialism, which was still in its relative infancy.

Eventually, she returned to London where she consolidated her early studies with a more formal four-year spell at the RCM (1926–30), Harold Darke (1888–1976) being one of her teachers. One wonders whether he was much in sympathy with her European modernism, but, as he was only six years Lutyens's senior, he would have been well aware of the musical developments going on around him. At the college Lutyens became affectionately known as "twelve-tone Lizzie"

Like many women composers of the day, she found family life to be an inevitable impediment to her career. She was twice married, first to Ian Glennie, a singer (1933–38), with whom she had three children, and later to conductor Edward Clark (1941–62) with whom she had a son. Apart from any sexual chemistry, Clark had the attraction of having studied with Schoenberg (1874–1951). However, having had a steady job with the BBC, he resigned his post following an altercation, and despite some freelance work, earned little thereafter. Lutyens, therefore, found herself in the unenviable role as the family breadwinner, which meant writing to commission.

Back in 1929 Edward Clark had been involved with the premiere of Walton's Viola Concerto, and as Walton had more recently emerged as a successful composer of film music, she approached him for an introduction to Muir Mathieson with a view to getting some film work for herself. Walton happily obliged, and the commissions began to roll in. She soon found that her style, which depended very much on atmosphere rather than melody for its effect was perfectly suited to the spookiness often associated with horror films, and she was much in demand at the Hammer and Amicus studios writing scores for films such as *Paranoiac* (1963), *Dr. Terror's House of Horrors* (1965), *The Earth Dies Screaming* (1965), *The Skull* (1965), *The Psychopath* (1966), *Theatre of Death* (1967), and *The Terrornauts* (1967). One has only to glance at the dates to appreciate how much work she was being offered. Apparently, a favourite quip of hers at this time was: "Do you want it good, or do you want it Wednesday?"

The above-noted films and others of the same ilk were very much products of their day and would seem tame by modern standards. Unlike her friend Walton whose film scores have survived the films themselves, and are universally considered to be classics of the genre, Lutyens's music tended to die with the films, although a suite was extracted from the score for *The Skull* and later recorded.

Despite the heavy film-score workload, she did not neglect the more serious side of composition. She harboured a lifelong distrust of the kind of expansionism found in Mahler, and although she did turn to the orchestra on occasion – as in *Three Symphonic Preludes* (1942), the Violin Concerto (1947) and *Music for Orchestra* (1955) – she was more at home composing for chamber forces. Central to her output in this genre are the six Chamber Concertos from the 1940s which seem to have been conceived as a series, as they all share the same opus number (op. 8). Each concerto has a different instrumentation in mind. No. 2, for example, is scored for clarinet, tenor saxophone, piano & strings, No. 3 for bassoon & small orchestra, and No. 5 for string quartet & chamber orchestra. Lutyens was habitually meticulous about her choice of forces, using only those instruments she felt would create the precise effect she wanted. The *Six Bagatelles* (1976) are scored for six woodwind, four brass, percussion, harp, piano/ celeste, and five solo strings. Among other chamber works are several string quartets, quintets for strings and for wind, and trios, also for strings and for wind.

Lutyens wrote a quantity of music for chorus or vocal solo with various accompaniments. One of the best-known pieces in the genre is the cantata *Ô saisons, Ô châteux* for soprano and strings (1946) to a text by the French poet Rimbaud. When it was first written it was declined by the BBC on the grounds that it was too difficult for any soprano to sing. However, singers rose to the challenge to prove this judgement premature.

Unlike many tonal composers, Lutyens was fortunate in flourishing just as the taste for modernist, and in particular serialist music was beginning to take hold in Britain, and under Sir William Glock, much was being done to promote such music at the BBC. With fewer family commitments after her children had become independent, she found more freedom to work on her scores and was composing fairly prolifically until shortly before her death on 14th April 1983.

Lutyens was never a popularist composer and was more interested in developing her technique than being a crowd-pleaser. Her music will never be everyone's cup of tea, but for the music specialist who likes to engage with the academic problems which serious music may present, there is no doubt plenty of food for thought in Lutyens's output.

a. Bibliography

Harries, Meirion and Susie, *A Pilgrim Soul: The Life and Work of Elisabeth Lutyens* (Harmondsworth, Middlesex: Michael Joseph, 1989)

Mathias, Rhiannon, *Lutyens, Maconchy, Williams, and Twentieth Century British Music: A Blest Trio of Sirens* (London: Routledge, 2016)

b. Selected Discography

Six Bagatelles	Brunel Ensemble	Cala	CACD 77005
Nine Bagatelles for Cello & Piano	Handy (cello); Hughes (piano)	Lyrita	SRCD 383
Wind Trio	Endymion	NMC	
String Trio	Endymion	NMC	
Fantasie Trio	Endymion	NMC	
Magnificat & Nunc Dimittis	Exaudi, Weeks	NMC	
Chamber Concerto No. 1	Jane's Minstrels, Montgomery	NMC	

36. Robin Milford (1903–59)

For the entirety of his career, Robin Milford was a composer who lived in the shadow of other, better-known composers, notably Vaughan Williams and Finzi with whom he was on friendly terms and who generously supported Milford's own work. They did not do this out of charity, but because they genuinely believed in him and his music. In a letter to Adrian Boult, Vaughan Williams wrote: "If I wanted to show the intelligent foreigner something worth doing which could only possibly come out of England, I think I would show him some of the work of Milford".[224]

By all accounts, he was a gentle, sensitive individual who attracted a wide circle of friends, all of whom he could count on for help and encouragement, but his innate lack of self-esteem was a lifelong enemy that thwarted his development as a composer, and the fact that he is remembered, rightly, as a miniaturist bears testimony to the fact that he felt less secure in tackling the larger forms, although works like the Violin Concerto (now happily recorded – EM Records, EMR 023) and his oratorio *A Prophet in the Land* (which, sadly, is not), as well as a Symphony, all show that he made the attempt. Milford's life was tinged with tragedy with which his temperament did not allow him to deal very well, and he lived a semi-nomadic existence, drifting from place to place and from job to job, all in the quest to support his vocation as a composer. Yet even in his darkest hours – and there were many – the muse never deserted him.

Milford was born on 22nd January 1903 in Oxford where his father, Humphrey Milford (later to be knighted) had recently founded the music department at the Oxford University Press. Humphrey was a confident, slightly aloof, but generous man of the world. Another son, David, took after him as an outgoing active individual who enjoyed sport and seems to have made a success

224 Quoted in I. Copley, *Robin Milford* (London: Thames Publishing, 1984), p. 48.

of all he attempted. He was a world champion at racquets. Robin, by contrast, was left very much in the shadows. Perhaps he did not feel that he could live up to his father's expectations. Yet it is difficult to know why this insecurity developed, for he was given every encouragement from the first, especially by his doting mother, Martha.

Milford's schooling was of the kind that was expected of a boy of his privileged upbringing – preparatory school at West Downs near Winchester, and thence to Rugby. Peter Hunter of the Robin Milford Trust suggests that a boy of Milford's temperament, who showed no aptitude for sport, would have been mercilessly bullied at the latter establishment. No doubt he is correct, but, if so, it did not stop him from making considerable progress under music master A.H. Peppin – enough, certainly, to enable him to gain entry to the RCM. Milford went up to the college at the age of eighteen and remained for five years. He studied composition with both Vaughan Williams and Holst, counterpoint with R.O. Morris, and organ with Henry Ley, all of whom remained committed friends in later life and continued giving Milford encouragement.

During his college years Milford was already beginning to make his way as a composer and musician. By this time the family had moved to Epsom, and Milford set about enriching the musical life of the local community. He established a music group consisting largely of the members of two families – his own and that of the Sir John Stainer (of *The Crucifixion* fame). Milford's brother David and his sister Pippa, and occasionally his parents, participated as singers or players, while two daughters of Sir John Stainer (1840–1901) and a governess, Kirsty Newsom, also joined in. With these modest forces Milford organised concerts, some of which included his own works. The first of them to excite comment was his children's opera *The Shoemaker* (op. 3), and it says something about the esteem in which the young composer was held to note that Sir Hugh Allen (1869–1946), then Director of the RCM, attended the first performance.

Milford's relationship with the Stainers' governess soon became more than a working one and, following a seven-year engagement, they were married in 1927. Their devotion to one another was unimpeachable, which is just as well, for never was the marriage-vow clause "in sickness and in health" put to the test more than in this marriage. The fact that there was little money in composing forced Milford to earn his bread in other ways. Despite his privileged background, financial worries were ever-present. He began by working for the Aeolian Company, editing Duo Arte pianola rolls (a task long-since defunct), and then took on various teaching roles, usually at genteel preparatory schools. He moved around the country. At various times in his life there were addresses in London, Epsom, Cold Ash and Hermitage (both near Newbury), Guernsey, Butcombe near Bristol, and Lyme Regis. In all these locations there were part-time teaching appointments, sometimes dovetailing into one another – Ludgrove School at Cockfosters, Downe House Girls School at Cold Ash, Badminton School near Bristol, and Parrott Hill Preparatory School in Somerset. These were occasionally supplemented by other work. During his short spell on Guernsey during World War Two he was employed as a market gardener, and at Cold Ash worked for a time as a farm labourer.

The above sketch provides some idea of Milford's somewhat makeshift existence throughout his working life, but despite everything he continued to compose. One of his most prestigious and extensive commissions, his oratorio *A Prophet in the Land*, was performed at the Gloucester Three Choirs Festival in 1931. Even here, however, Milford was not entirely in luck, as his piece appeared at much the same time as Walton's *Belshazzar's Feast*. However, there were other successes at this time. His *Double Fugue for Orchestra* (op. 10) which, alas, has never been recorded, despite its having won a Carnegie Award, was performed at the Queen's Hall by the LSO with Vaughan Williams on the podium, while the better-known *The Darkling Thrush* (op. 17), inspired by Hardy's poem of that name, was heard at a Patrons' Fund Concert at the RCM under Malcolm Sargent, and *has* been recorded (Dutton CDLX 7320).

In 1929, Milford was introduced to fellow composer Gerald Finzi, and a lifelong friendship developed. Finzi was a man of generous spirit, as we have seen in relation to his championing of Gurney's music, and despite being only two years Milford's senior, took him under his wing, encouraging him during his all too frequent bouts of depression, and programming his works in concerts given by his own Newbury String Players, including Milford's best-known piece *Fishing By Moonlight*, which he premiered.

The years 1935–41 were a rollercoaster of emotions for Milford. One joyous occasion was the birth of his only son Barnaby over whom both parents doted. Another generous friend, Balfour-Gardiner, not only congratulated them on the happy event and agreed to become the child's godfather, but provided financially for the future of the child's education.

When war broke out in 1939, Milford dutifully signed up and joined the Pioneer Corps, but he was completely unsuited to army life and suffered a nervous collapse within a week of his enlisting. Although, once discharged, he recovered some degree of equilibrium, two other cruel hammer blows were in store for him. The first was the death of his mother at the end of 1939. Her love and support had been crucial, and losing her was a bitter blow. Then, more tragically still, in 1941 he lost his son Barnaby who was killed in a road accident a week before his sixth birthday. Both parents were, of course, devastated, but Milford, in particular, must have felt the loss all the more keenly, since it was he who had sent Barnaby on an errand to fetch some score paper from a hut down the road, which is when the accident happened.

Remarkably, however, none of these distressing and tragic events affected Milford's compulsion to compose. His catalogue of works suggests that at least fifteen compositions were either completed or in progress between 1939–41. True, many of these were solo songs or piano miniatures, so that the actual quantity of music may not have been substantial, but equally, it is clear that the muse had not deserted him. A glance at the dedications of his works at this time, too, does not reveal an obsession with the two bereavements in Milford's life. Two short pieces, the song *Daffodils* (1940) and a *Fantasia* for string quartet (1945), are dedicated to his mother, the latter specifically in her memory. Likewise, there are two dedications to Barnaby: a *Mass for Children's Voices* (1941), dedicated "For my son Barnaby and for my godchildren Julia, Jane and Pyers"; and the masque *The Summer Stars* (1946–57), simply headed "Barnaby Milford". The shared dedication of the first piece may suggest that it was made prior to Barnaby's death.

Nevertheless, these tragedies inevitably took their toll psychologically. The story of Milford's final fifteen years is one of clouds and shadows interspersed with brief periods of sunlight. Suicide was attempted by overdosing on aspirin, but he was found by his wife just in time. He was hospitalised, only to make a further attempt by jumping from a window while under medical supervision. Friends rallied round. His works were played, both by amateurs and professionally, and salaried work was found for him. His *Overture for a Celebration* was performed by the Hallé Orchestra under Barbirolli at the Cheltenham Festival. He moved to Butcombe near Bristol, where he was enthusiastically incorporated into the musical life of the community – teaching at Badminton School, working in various capacities for BBC West of England, and serving as organist at Butcombe Parish Church, among other duties. A number of his works were broadcast in the 1940s and 1950s. Photographs exist from as late as 1951 of Milford looking content alongside his wife, or surrounded by his extended family. The mix of teaching, organ-playing, broadcasting and choral work continued after he moved to his final home in Lyme Regis, and, of course, composition continued too.

From 1952, however, Milford suffered a series of further bereavements and reversals. In that year his father died, and although he had never been as close to Robin as his mother had been, he had been supportive and probably influential in getting his son's music published at the OUP (although Novello and Hindrichsen also took up some works). More devastating from the professional point of view were the deaths of Finzi and Vaughan Williams in 1956 and 1958 respectively. Milford had relied heavily on their advice and support and must have felt bereft for this reason alone as well as losing two staunch friends.

Three professional reversals in particular must have hit hard. In the last year of his life, he wrote a full four-act opera, *The Scarlet Letter*, based on Nathaniel Hawthorne's novel, which he entered for the John Lewis Competition, but it failed to achieve a place. Then, too, musical tastes were beginning to shift. During the Glock era at the BBC (1959–72), ears were attuned to modernism, and those in high places considered Milford's style *passé*. Finally, in December 1959 he received a letter from the OUP demanding that his remaindered works be removed from the catalogue. It was the final straw. Already being treated at hospital in Bristol for depression, and facing further unpleasant "shock" (ECT) therapy, he overdosed with aspirin on 29th December 1959 which this time proved fatal.

Milford was capable of some large-scale pieces, as already noted, but it is as a composer of exquisite miniatures, both for orchestra and for solo piano, that he is best remembered. The gentle, understated ambience of *Fishing by Moonlight* for piano & strings (op. 96a), with its slightly limping rhythm, perfectly captures the typical Milford mood. The work was inspired by a painting of the same title by the Dutch artist Aernout van der Neer (1603–77). A slightly more vivacious work, *Elegy for James Scott, Duke of Monmouth and Buccleugh* (op. 50), was also inspired by a painting – ostensibly a portrait of the subject mentioned in the title – which, however, was later confirmed to be of someone else, and not James Scott. Still, the music is what matters, and it demonstrates Milford's fine handling of the orchestra. Further orchestral works on record, apart from *The Darkling Thrush*, mentioned earlier, include: *Festival Suite* (op. 97) (Hyperion CDA 67444), and *Concertino* for piano & strings (op. 106) (Hyperion CDA 67316).

Some of Milford's works bear the kind of titles or sub-titles more commonly found in music of the Elizabethan and Jacobean periods – *My Lady's Pleasure, Mr. Ben Jonson's Pleasure, Sir Nicholas's Caper*, and so on, and it may not be too much of an exaggeration to say that the composer would not have felt out of place in that bygone age, even though his style was very much of the twentieth century.

Milford was acquainted with a wide range of literature, and Hardy and Bridges, in particular, inspired some of his best songs. However, there are settings of many lesser-known poets, with Ralph Hodgson's *The Moor* prompting a particularly fine treatment. It was composed as early as 1925 and served notice that melody was an accomplishment that Milford would retain throughout his career.

His output includes a wide range of choral works, with and without organ, and there is a quantity of solo organ music too. Like Vaughan Williams, he was particularly inspired by the Christmas season. There are two traditional carols (the *Coventry Carol* and the *Cherry Tree Carol*) taken from an early unperformed opera entitled *Vertue* (op. 13a); *Three Christmas Pieces*, with versions for piano duet, solo organ, and orchestra, and which includes one of RVW's favourite tunes, *On Christmas Night*; a Christmas Cantata, *Midwinter*; *A Christmas Tune* for solo organ; several carol arrangements; and *A Mass for Christmas Morning* (op. 84), the most substantial of the "Christmas" pieces which, however, was retitled *Mass for Five Voices* for its recording by Stone Records, as it appears to have no obvious musical association with Christmas. There is just as much music associated with the other great Christian festival, Easter, and some for Ascension Day.

A full catalogue of Milford's output is provided by Reg Pocock in Ian Copley's biography *Robin Milford*[225], and makes for interesting reading. Of the 115 opus numbers listed (some of which are sub-divided to take account of different forms or arrangements of specific works), roughly half the original manuscripts can no longer be located, either because they have been lost, destroyed or misplaced. In a few cases, later copies have been preserved[226], thus enabling the possibility of future performances and recordings. The *Double Fugue for Orchestra* (op. 10) exists as a two-piano reduction,

225 Copley, *Robin Milford*, pp. 85–112.

226 The Suite for Oboe & Strings (op. 8) is a case in point.

but the orchestral score is missing, as is a Concerto for Clarinet & Strings (op. 31). Many other manuscripts are accessible[227], including the Symphony (op. 34) and the major cantata *A Prophet in the Land*, although Milford left instructions that the Symphony was not to be published or performed. Still, it seems a pity that the public cannot be allowed to make up its own mind about it – and surely it is high time for a recording of the cantata, as well as a definitive recording of the composer's best twenty of thirty songs. As things stand, he has not fared too badly in the recording studio (Hyperion, Toccata, EM Records, Dutton, Cameo and Stone Records have all issued discs, and there are a couple of amateur recordings, one using mainly amateur performers issued under the auspices of the Robin Milford Trust). Still, there is plenty of scope for the further exposure of Milford's music.

227 The majority of these are housed in the Bodleian Library, Oxford, although at the time Pocock's catalogue was compiled in 1983, some were still lodged with Milford's widow or niece.

a. Bibliography

Copley, Ian, *Robin Milford* (London: Thames Publishing, 1984)

b. Selected Discography

i) Orchestral

Violin Concerto	BBC Concert O., Arwel Hughes Marshall-Luck (violin)	EMR	EMR CD023
The Darkling Thrush	RSNO; Lloyd-Jones; Graffin (violin)	Dutton	CDLX 7320
Fishing by Moonlight	Guildhall Strings, Salter; J. Milford (piano)	Hyperion	CDA 67444
Miniature Concerto	Guildhall Strings, Salter	Hyperion	CDA 67444
Elegiac Meditation	Guildhall Strings, Salter; Finnimore (viola)	Hyperion	CDA 67444
Two Orchestral Interludes	Guildhall Strings, Salter	Hyperion	CDA 67444
Suite: Go, Little Book	Guildhall Strings, Salter; Lane (sop)	Hyperion	CDA 67444
Elegy for James Scott	Guildhall Strings, Salter	Hyperion	CDA 67444
Interlude for Flute & Strings	Guildhall Strings, Salter; Sperry (flute)	Hyperion	CDA 67444
Festival Suite	Guildhall Strings, Salter	Hyperion	CDA 67444

Concertino for Piano & Strings	Guildhall Strings, Salter; Roscoe (piano)	Hyperion	CDA 67316

ii) Chamber

Phantasy Quintet	Gould, Cooper (violins); Adams (viola); Neary (cello); Plane (clar)	Toccata	TOCC 0244
Trio	Gould Piano Trio	Toccata	TOCC 0244
Threne	Neary (cello); Frith (piano)	Toccata	TOCC 0244
Lyrical Movement	Plane (clar); Frith (piano)	Toccata	TOCC 0244
Violin Sonata	Gould (violin); Frith (piano)	Toccata	TOCC 0244

iii) Songs

Selected Songs	Bannister (contr); Terroni (piano)	Toccata	TOCC 0009
If its ever spring again	Partridge (ten); Benson (piano)	Hyperion	CDA 66015

c. Website

The Robin Milford Trust (https://robinmilfordtrust.org.uk)

37. Ernest John Moeran (1894–1950)

E.J. ("Jack") Moeran was one of the last English composers to be heavily influenced by the folksong movement which reached its zenith in the first decade of the twentieth century and included figures like Vaughan Williams, Holst, Butterworth, Grainger and, of course, that folksong collector *par excellence*, Cecil Sharp. Moeran himself was a keen collector of folksong, both in Norfolk, where he grew up, and in County Kerry in Eire. His arrangements of these songs include *Six Songs from Norfolk*, *Six Suffolk Folksongs*, and *Songs from County Kerry*, but there are folksong inflections in many of his works, even when there are no direct quotations. The result is a sound-world which very much caught the mood of the times. Yet there is no doubt that Moeran developed his own distinctive voice from the outset. True, his later works are more finely honed than the earlier ones, but there seems to have been no lengthy gestation period under the influence of Wagner or Brahms such as we detect in the early music of Vaughan Williams and Holst, despite the fact that, like them, he sat at the feet of the notoriously conservative Stanford. His Anglo-Irish accent is evident from his earliest piano pieces.

Moeran was one of those composers whose life was surrounded by a kind of mystique, so that, although the broad outline of his life is clear, the details are often hazy. No doubt this is due in part to the various reminiscences of his many friends which sometimes coincided and sometimes diverged. The severity of a head wound sustained while on active service has been a matter for much conjecture and debate, as also the question of whether or not he was an alcoholic or simply over-fond of alcohol. His death, too, is shrouded in mystery. The plain facts are clear enough. Moeran was seen to fall from the pier at Kenmare into the water. But what was the cause of death – brain haemorrhage, heart attack or stroke? – for all three have been suggested. The more speculative have even suggested suicide.

There is no doubt that Moeran was a complex character whose geniality and generosity endeared him to many, and there is the suspicion that his friends used his virtues to disguise or excuse his weaknesses. He was easily led into bad habits by those with stronger personalities than his, and could be notoriously unreliable. There were dark periods, increasingly frequent in later life, which he tried to drown in alcohol, as a result of which his musical projects suffered. In particular, there is the mystery of the much-vaunted but never-completed Second Symphony.[228]

Moeran was born on New Year's Eve 1894 at Heston, now situated on the periphery of Heathrow Airport, where his Irish-born father, Joseph, was a Protestant clergyman. His mother, Ada, was a pianist and singer, and it was with her that Moeran had his first musical experiences. While he was still very young, his father moved to a new incumbency at Bacton, a remote village on the north Norfolk coast.[229] Here he enjoyed a typically comfortable parsonage upbringing. His initial education was with a governess, but in 1904, aged nine, he was sent a little way up the coast to Suffield Park Preparatory School as a boarder. Here he began studies in piano and violin, and heard the band playing on Cromer pier, another formative experience.

Four years later, he continued his education at the prestigious Uppingham School in Rutland, where Robert Sterndale Bennett (1880–1963), the grandson of composer William Sterndale Bennett (1816–75), was his music master. Years later, in an obituary notice, he wrote of his former pupil: "I doubt if any boy has grasped with more discernment and avidity or made better use of the opportunity

228 The mystery surrounding the Second Symphony is so intriguing that I have devoted a brief Appendix to it (see below, pp. 618–26).

229 Tim Rayborn (*A New English Music* [Jefferson, NC: McFarland & Co., 2016], p. 131) argues that the family actually moved to Salhouse, some twenty miles south of Bacton, citing an entry in Crockford's Clerical Directory for 1905, by which time Moeran would have been ten years old. However, it is known that Joseph Moeran was frequently on the move from parish to parish, and since Moeran himself testifies to an early association with Bacton, it may well be that the family's sojourn there preceded the Salhouse incumbency.

which school music has to offer".[230] It was at Uppingham that he took his first serious steps in composition, producing three string quartets and a lengthy cello sonata.

Moeran made sufficient progress at Uppingham to be admitted to the RCM as a piano student. After his first year there he switched to composition with Stanford, but his studies were interrupted by the outbreak of the First World War.[231] He was fascinated by all things mechanical, and a career in engineering had been considered before his all-consuming passion for composition took over. He was a great railway enthusiast and, according to Lionel Hill[232], could distinguish one class of locomotive from another merely by hearing the beat of its exhaust. Thus, in enlisting with the Royal Norfolk Regiment as a motorcycle dispatch rider, he must have been in his element. At first, he was based in Norfolk, guarding against a feared German invasion, but as this threat evaporated, his unit was eventually sent to France, and he saw action at the so-called Second Battle of Bullecourt where, on 3rd May 1917, he suffered a head wound, and was invalided back home. The usual story is that some fragments of shrapnel were lodged too near to the brain to be removed, and that a metal plate had to be inserted into his skull. His war wound has been blamed both for his apparent alcoholism and for his eventual death, assuming that it was caused by a brain haemorrhage.[233]

230 Robert Sterndale Bennett, "Obituary for Ernest John Moeran", *Uppingham School Magazine*, no. 631, March 1951; quoted in Geoffrey Self, *The Music of Ernest John Moeran* (London: Toccata Press, 1986), p. 18.

231 He later resumed his studies at the RCM (1920–23) with John Ireland during which time he was composing prolifically.

232 Hill, *Lonely Waters*, p. 18

233 Geoffrey Self (*E.J. Moeran*, pp. 19–20) is a firm advocate of the received opinion. However, Ian Maxwell ("A Composer Goes to War: E.J. Moeran and the First World War", *Journal of the Society for Musicology in Ireland*, 14 [2018–19], pp. 83–109) presents evidence to suggest that the damage was not as severe as has been suggested. Moeran was reportedly capable of performing a demanding piano solo at a London concert barely two months after sustaining his injury – this at a time when even minor operations required several weeks of recovery and rehabilitation.

One positive outcome of his ordeal is that he was able to spend the remainder of the war undertaking light duties in Boyle, County Roscommon, and so, for the first time, was able to experience something of his father's home country at first hand, and he began to steep himself in Ireland's lore, legend and music. Ever the countryman, whether in Norfolk, Ireland or, later, the Welsh Marches, he needed the inspiration of landscape to succeed.

In the same year as his discharge from the army in January 1919, Moeran produced his first mature work, a collection of three short solo piano movements unassumingly entitled *Three Pieces*. The individual items, *The Lake Island, Autumn Woods*, and *At the Horse Fair*, all testify to his new acquaintance with his Irish surroundings. This seemed to open the floodgates, and for the next five years he composed prolifically in a variety of forms – orchestral, chamber music, solo piano, songs with piano, and choral. The early twenties saw the orchestral Rhapsodies Nos. 1 & 2, and the symphonic impression *In the Mountain Country*, as well as the String Quartet No. 1, the String Trio, and the Viola Sonata.

Between the years 1926–28, however, there is an ominous hiatus in which, barring two minor exceptions[234], no music at all seems to have been forthcoming. This was due almost entirely to a three-year spell spent with Philip Heseltine (Peter Warlock) and his riotous friends who held court in a rented cottage in the village of Eynsford, Kent. The permanent residents, apart from Heseltine, were Moeran and Hal Collins, an artist hailing from New Zealand who seems to have been in charge of the cooking arrangements. Anybody who was anybody was likely to turn up for the weekend, including the composers Lord Berners, Constant Lambert and, occasionally, Bax; the singer John Goss; and the artists Augustus John and Nina Hamnett, as well as various girlfriends of Heseltine. The police were called on occasion when matters got out of hand.

234 These being a couple of traditional Irish folksong arrangements for piano solo, *Irish Love Song* and *The White Mountain*.

It was probably during this period that Moeran developed a taste for heavy alcohol consumption rather than as a result of his war wound. Heseltine was almost exclusively a small-scale composer, songs being his staple diet. A short inspirational burst would be sufficient to produce a song. Moeran, on the other hand, had begun producing larger canvas works which required sustained concentration, peace and quiet – none of which were available at Eynsford. As a result, he wrote hardly a note of music during his three years there. Certainly, Hamilton Harty's major commission for a symphony in 1924 had to be put on hold and did not see fruition until 1937. The suggestion that Moeran found that he had bitten off more than he could chew and came to realise that he was incapable of composing a symphony at that point, may have an element of truth to it, but any hope of getting the project underway was scotched by the Bohemian lifestyle he shared with the Heseltine menage.

Once liberated from the stultifying atmosphere of the Heseltine influence, Moeran began composing again, but not as prolifically as before. From the early thirties come the small orchestral piece *Wythorne's Shadow* (1931); *Nocturne* for baritone, chorus and orchestra (1934); the Sonata for Two Violins (1930), the String Trio (1931), and the *Songs of Springtime* for unaccompanied chorus (1930). *Wythorne's Shadow*, based on a theme by Elizabethan composer Thomas Wythorne (1528–96) bears witness to an enthusiasm shared with Philip Heseltine for the music of this composer[235] and others of the period. *Songs of Springtime* consists of seven settings of Elizabethan and Jacobean poets, again manifesting Moeran's fondness of setting such literature. His choral pieces, in fact, are almost exclusively settings of poets from that era, Shakespeare and Herrick being his particular favourites. By contrast, his solo songs tend to focus more on contemporary poets, with Housman, Joyce and O'Sullivan heading the list, and further examples from Bridges, Masefield, Yeats and Symons.

235 Heseltine transcribed several part-songs by Wythorne along with a pamphlet published by OUP in 1925 in order to draw attention to a composer who he felt had suffered undue neglect.

Throughout much of 1930, Moeran was laid up with what has been described as tuberculosis of the knee. He was also running short of funds, despite a regular allowance from his parents, so that a commission to write a full set of Morning (*Te Deum, Jubilate*) and Evening (*Magnificat, Nunc Dimittis*) Services for the Anglican Church proved welcome. Despite having a father and brother in holy orders, however, there is no indication that Moeran was in any sense committed to the Christian faith, and he spoke dismissively of these works as "tripe for the church" which he only did for the money. The church itself was probably blissfully unaware of his irreverent attitude, and his services and anthems (*Praise the Lord, O Jerusalem* [1930]; *Blessed are those Servants* [1938]) are sung to this day.

In 1937, the long-awaited Symphony in G minor was completed and given its premiere the following year at the Queen's Hall under Leslie Heward, who was the first to record it. It was certainly worth the wait – a brooding, full-blooded work in four movements lasting some three quarters of an hour. It appeared during the golden age of the English symphony and faced stiff competition from other ground-breaking works, including Vaughan Williams's Symphony No. 4, Walton's Symphony No. 1, and Bax's Symphony No. 6. Yet the consensus is that Moeran's own effort holds its own against these, and is considered by many to be his masterpiece. Moeran himself wrote a generous programme note for Heward's recording of the work in 1942[236], explaining that while most of the Symphony was conceived among the mountains and seaboard of County Kerry, the slow movement was inspired by "the sand-dunes and marshes of Norfolk". He aims for, and largely achieves, classical form with a traditional sonata form in the first movement, and a broad thematic unity. Over the years it has been recorded by Sir Adrian Boult, Neville Dilkes, Vernon Handley, and David Lloyd-Jones, as well as Heward, and is still occasionally aired in the concert hall, thereby testifying to the esteem in which this work is held.

236 Still available on Dutton, CDAX 8001 (along with Heward's recording of Ireland's Piano Concerto the same year. The programme note is reprinted in Self, *E.J. Moeran*, pp. 274–76.

For the next few years Moeran seems to have regained confidence as a composer and began to tackle other large-scale works, including two fine concertos for violin (1937–41) and cello (1945), the *Sinfonietta* (1944), and the *Rhapsody No. 3*, for piano and orchestra. The Violin Concerto is wholly Irish in its conception and was written there in its entirety. Its composition dates, however, testify to the composer's ponderous working methods. He was entering on the final phase of his career when his works were becoming more substantial but also more of a chore to complete. He complained that in order to give of his best he had to be in the right environment for sufficiently long periods – which at this time meant rural Ireland, and in particular County Kerry. Fortunately for him – and us – these conditions were met in the case of the Violin Concerto. The first movement was written in 1937–38 on Valentia Island, some forty miles west of Kenmare, and the last movement in Kenmare itself in 1941. Despite the *allegro moderato* marking of the first, both these movements are slow and reflective in mood, with plenty of meandering, dreamy passagework for the solo instrument. The critic Edwin Evans described the concluding passages as reflecting "the calm experienced in Southern Ireland at this [autumn] season, before the gales begin to burst in from the Atlantic".[237] By contrast, the middle movement is full of Irish dance rhythms, which fully reflects the sentiments he expressed in a letter from Kenmare: "... this time of year the whole countryside is on the dance round here. In the second movement I am planning to work some of the idiom into concerto form...".[238]Should further evidence for the Irishness of this concerto be required, it can be pointed out that there is a clear thematic relationship between the concerto and a phrase from Moeran's setting of James Joyce's poem *Now, O now in this brown land* (*Chamber Music*, XXXIII), which is quoted at the beginning of both the first and final movements.

237 E. Evans, *Musical Times* LXXXIV (1943), pp. 233–34.

238 Quoted by Lewis Foreman in the liner notes to the recording of the work by Chandos, CHAN 7078.

Geoffrey Self has advanced the intriguing hypothesis that there are close developmental relations between the Symphony in G minor and the Violin Concerto on which Moeran began work immediately afterwards:

> [This] point is of some importance, for I believe than the Symphony and the Concerto are complementary – possibly to the extent that the Violin Concerto may be considered as a completion of the Symphony. For the Symphony – noble, disturbed, elegiac and bitter by turns – is a questioning work. The Violin Concerto seeks to find and provide answers. Some of the "reference composers" noted in the Symphony carry over into the Violin Concerto.[239]

Although the concerto was intended for May Harrison and dedicated to her, it was Arthur Catterall who premiered the work at a Promenade Concert conducted by Henry Wood on 8th July 1942.[240]

There is some degree of Irishness in the Cello Concerto, but personal circumstances also had a hand in its creation. In 1943 Moeran renewed his acquaintance with the cellist Peers Coetmore (1905–76) whom he had first met in about 1930. A close friendship developed which led, eventually, to marriage. This took place on 26th July 1945 in Kington, Herefordshire, near to where his parents were then living. To some extent it was a marriage of convenience for both parties. Although there was certainly love on Moeran's side, she became his muse, inspiring not only the Cello Concerto, but

239 Self, *E.J. Moeran*, p. 135. Presumably the chief "reference composer" Self has in mind is Sibelius whose music influenced not only Moeran's Symphony, but those of many other English composers of the day.

240 Here is yet another anomaly. In contrast to the indication that Moeran intended his Violin Concerto for May Harrison, his frequent letters to his friend Lionel Hill over the period 1943–45 suggest that he had adopted Albert Sammons, Hill's father-in-law, as his violinist of choice. Writing to Hill on 27th December 1943, he declared, "Sammons is the only living violinist I would like to have interpret it" (Hill, *Lonely Waters*, p. 27).

also a fine Cello Sonata (1947), considered by many critics to be his masterpiece. The match from her side seems somewhat stranger. She was eleven years younger than Moeran, now entering on his fiftieth year, and was a career cellist engaged with ENSA and playing in concerts the world over. It has been suggested that she saw Moeran as her pet composer writing works specifically for her, which would certainly have enhanced her prestige. Moeran himself was complicit in this, stating at one point that, as long as he had control over the performing rights, he would not allow anyone other than Peers to perform the work. The relationship was certainly different from that between Bax and Harriet Cohen which, although often rocky, was bound by mutual love of a strong sexual character. By contrast, Lionel Hill reports a snatch of conversation between Peers and his wife in which she confided, "[It's] like living with an uncle – you don't know how frustrated I feel".[241] Whatever the truth of the matter, the marriage seems to have been doomed from the start. Moeran and Peers were not really personally compatible, and she was of little help in steering him away from his drink problem. They had separate careers which kept them apart for lengthy periods, and although Peers invited him to join her on tour in South Africa and Australia, it was never really a viable possibility for the diffident and country-loving Moeran who lived and breathed Anglo-Irish air. The marriage would almost certainly have folded had not Moeran's death intervened.

At the time the Cello Concerto was conceived, however, things looked more rosy. He wrote to her in 1943:

> Now please tell me you would like me to write a concerto specially for you, and I give you my promise that I will put my whole heart into it. I will be able to go one better than I did in the Violin Concerto; only give me your blessing on the project, and then I will be able to walk the Kerry mountains with a real happy object in view.

241 Hill, *Lonely Waters*, p. 73.

Still, it was not all plain sailing. As with the earlier Symphony and the later, unfinished Second, he had to grind away at composition as if it were a real chore:

> ... but with me the process of working it out bar by bar is so terribly slow – as it was with my Symphony, because I am putting into it the best of which I am at present capable. It is usually what sounds the most spontaneous that actually is the most laboured in the making.[242]

Ominous words. Still, on this occasion, the results were more than satisfactory, and the successful premiere took place at the Capitol Theatre in Dublin on 25th November 1945. The darkly passionate Cello Sonata was premiered by Coetmore in Dublin on 9th May 1947, with Charles Lynch as the pianist. It certainly shows some signs of technical development on Moeran's previous output, with even a hint or two of Bartok, and affords a tantalising glimpse of what might have been had Moeran lived his three score years and ten.

During the composition of the *Sinfonietta*, Moeran was certainly in Ireland at times, but he was now spending more time with his parents in Herefordshire, where Hergest Ridge and Radnor Forest became two of his favourite haunts. It is this landscape that most informs the music, although the final movement was written in County Kerry. It was commissioned by the BBC in 1944 and premiered under John Barbirolli the following year. The two lively outer movements frame a central one which takes the form of a theme and variations. Lewis Foreman has referred to this work as "really his *Second Symphony*". Technically-speaking this is perhaps true (what's in a name, after all?), but Moeran himself did not consider it as such, as we shall see.

And so we come at last to the final three sad years of Moeran's eventful life – years of steady decline into alcoholism and mental

242 Both quotations taken from the liner notes by Lewis Foreman in Chandos's recording of the work, CHAN 7078.

disintegration. With his attractive *Serenade*, the year 1948 found him still able to turn out an enjoyable orchestral suite, although two of the eight brief movements were lifted from the *Farrago Suite* of the early thirties which Moeran later withdrew. Both these works are loosely modelled on Warlock's *Capriol Suite*, with their use of antique dance forms, as the titles of the various movements – Galop, Minuet, Forlana, Rigadoon – demonstrate. The inner six movements are book-ended by a Prologue and Epilogue which make use of the same material. It proved very popular when it was premiered at the Proms on 2nd September 1948.

For the last two years of his life, Moeran's movements become increasingly difficult to trace. He would lose himself for weeks at a time and then re-emerge in Kenmare or elsewhere. However, he was an inveterate letter-writer, so some inkling of his whereabouts is possible. A glance at the letters published in Lionel Hill's book shows that Moeran's missives were sent from Kenmare (where he seems to have spent the winter of 1948), Ledbury, London, and Cheltenham (where in 1949 he was being treated for alcoholism). There were sojourns in Kington and Dublin, too, but he seems to have spent the final months of his life back in the place he loved best – Kenmare. He apparently did little by way of composition. In the end, death came suddenly on 1st December 1950 at the end of Kenmare pier. A large number turned out for his funeral, for he was a popular figure in the town, and it was said by the locals that if they could have elected a mayor, "Jacko" would have been everyone's first choice. He was buried in the cemetery just outside the town beneath a headstone whose inscription reads: "He rests in the mountain country he loved so well".

As noted earlier, Moeran was a complex character with a wide emotional range. He was gregarious, yet innately shy, generous and kind-hearted, as many were able to testify from personal experience. On the other hand, he possessed all the human foibles and frailties the rest of us have, which, in a sense, endeared him all the more to those who knew him. Professionally, he was held back by nagging self-doubt. Others might well have acclaimed whatever he wrote and flattered him, but, a man of integrity, he set himself the highest standards and rejected any work which he judged to fall below them. He worked slowly and meticulously, as a result of which his life's work was limited in quantity. His official catalogue yields just twelve completed orchestral works, including concertos, and ten chamber works, yet every one of them was deemed worthy of publication (chiefly by Novello). The solo piano pieces, songs and folksong arrangements are, of course, more numerous, since they took far less time to compose. In the final analysis, however, it is not quantity but quality that counts, and in that regard Moeran's output is of lasting value within the musical landscape of Britain.

a. Bibliography

Banfield, Stephen, "Moeran, Warlock and Song", *British Music*, 23 (2001), pp. 51-55

Bye, Chris, "E.J.Moeran: A Life and Death Beset by Controversy", *British Music*, 40/2 (2018)

Hill, Lionel, *Lonely Waters: Diary of a Friendship with E.J. Moeran* (London: Thames Publishing, 1986)

Maxwell, Ian, "The Moeran Myth", *British Music*, 32 (2010), pp. 26–49

Maxwell, Ian, "A Composer Goes to War: E.J. Moeran and the First World War", *Journal of the Society for Musicology in Ireland*, 14 (2018–19), pp. 83-109.

Self, Geoffrey, *The Music of E.J. Moeran* (London: Toccata Press, 1986)

Talbot, John, "Memories of Jack", *British Music*, 31 (2009), pp. 6–21

b. Selected Discography

i) Symphonies

Symphony in G minor	Ulster O., Handley	Chandos	CHAN 10169X
Symphony No. 2 (real. by Martin Yates)	RSNO, Yates	Dutton	CDLX 7281

ii) Concertos

Violin Concerto	Ulster O., Handley; Mordkovitch (violin)	Chandos	CHAN 7078
Cello Concerto	Ulster O., Handley; Wallfisch (cello)	Chandos	CHAN 7078

iii) Orchestral

Overture for a Masque	Ulster O., Handley	Chandos	CHAN 10169X

Rhapsody for Piano & Orchestra	Ulster O., Handley; Fingerhut (piano)	Chandos	CHAN 10169X
Lonely Waters	Ulster O., Handley	Chandos	CHAN 7078
Wythorne's Shadow	Ulster O., Handley	Chandos	CHAN 7078
Rhapsody No. 1	Ulster O., Handley	Chandos	CHAN 10235X
Rhapsody No. 2	Ulster O., Handley	Chandos	CHAN 10235X
In the Mountain Country	Ulster O., Handley	Chandos	CHAN 10235 X
Serenade in G	Ulster O., Handley	Chandos	CHAN 10235X
Nocturne	Ulster O., Handley; Mackey (bar)	Chandos	CHAN 10235X
Sinfonietta	Bournemouth SO, Lloyd-Jones	Naxos	8.555837

iv) Chamber

String Quartet in A minor	Maggini Quartet	Naxos	8.554079
String Quartet in E flat major	Maggini Quartet	Naxos	8.554079
String Trio in G major	Maggini Quartet (members)	Naxos	8.554079
Fantasy Quartet	English String Quartet; Francis (oboe)	Chandos	CHAN 10170X
Violin Sonata	Scotts (violin); Talbot (piano)	Chandos	CHAN 10170X

v) Piano Solo

Complete Solo Piano Music	Hunt (piano)	ASV	CD DCA 1138

vi) Choral

Choral Music	Finzi Singers, Spicer	Chandos	CHAN 9182

vii) Songs

Complete Solo Songs	McGreevy (sop); Thompson (ten); Williams (bar); Talbot (piano)	Chandos	CHAN 10596(2)

viii) Folksong Arrangements

Six Folksongs from Norfolk	Farnsworth (bar); Talbot (piano)	BMS	BMS438CD
Six Suffolk Folksongs	Farnsworth (bar); Talbot	BMS	BMS438CD
Songs from County Kerry	Thompson (ten); Talbot	BMS	BMS438CD

38. Roger Quilter (1877–1953)

There can be no doubt at all that Roger Quilter's enduring reputation rests entirely on his body of songs, of which there are 112 published individual items (Quilter frequently arranged his songs in opus-numbered sets ranging from two to seven items). There are, in addition, a few unpublished songs, and the so-called *Arnold Book of Old Songs*, which comprise arrangements of traditional tunes. Other than *A Children's Overture* (1914), extracted from the incidental music to a children's play, *Where the Rainbow Ends* (1911), and possibly the *Three English Dances* (1910), Quilter's music in other forms has been completely forgotten, probably because it lacked any distinctive character. The songs, too, can be uneven in quality, but they do generally boast an attractive fluency along with melodic invention, and Quilter was fortunate in that they were adopted by some of the leading singers of the day. More of that later.

Like Parry, Quilter was born into the aristocracy, his father being Sir William Quilter, 1st baronet, landowner, politician, businessman and art collector. Roger, the younger of two sons, first saw the light of day in Hove, Sussex, but the family owned an extensive estate in Suffolk, the centrepiece of which was Bawdsey Manor near Felixstowe, although Quilter spent most of his life at various residences in London. His route through education was initially typical for a boy of his upbringing: preparatory school (at Farnborough), followed by public school (Eton). However, the next projected stage, Oxbridge, did not materialise. Instead, on the advice of a friend, he chose to study at the Hoch Conservatorium at Frankfurt-am-Main in Germany, thus becoming one of the celebrated "Frankfurt Group" of mainly English composers studying there, the others being Cyril Scott, Norman O'Neill and Balfour Gardiner, along with the Australian, Percy Grainger. Quilter remained there for over four years, receiving a rigorous training from his composition teacher Ivan Knorr (1853–1916), whose method, though more to be endured than enjoyed, paid off in Quilter's own fastidious technique.

In the minds of many, Quilter cuts a pose as the quintessentially English gentleman, dapper and debonair, who never wanted for money, and simply wrote songs for pleasure rather than for a living. Indeed, he confessed to loving literature more than music, and even set his first published songs, *Four Songs of the Sea*, opus 1, to his own poems. These, however, are not particularly memorable and, according to Trevor Hold, always an astute and perceptive critic of English art-song[243], the settings follow suit. Hold regards them as "feeble stuff ... best regarded as juvenilia".[244] Nonetheless, it was with this set that Quilter arrived on the scene in 1900 when it was sung by Denham Price at Crystal Palace. Although these songs are uncharacteristic, according to Hold, it was not long before Quilter found his mature voice, after which there was no further appreciable development. He adhered to his tried and trusted formula of melody in the vocal line and fluency in the piano accompaniment. As regards quality, his choice of text was crucial. He needed words to inspire, and the better the poem, the better the song tended to be. A clear indication of this point can be found in the *Three Songs*, opus 3, of 1904–05 in which the mature Quilter is first evident. The songs in question are *Love's Philosophy* (Shelley). *Now Sleeps the Crimson Petal* (Tennyson), and *Fill a Glass with Golden Wine* (Henley), the first two of which are among Quilter's most enduring creations and always seem to find their way into any anthology of English songs, while the third has suffered comparative neglect. But why the contrast? What do the first two songs have that the other lacks? It will be instructive here to quote Hold:

> *Love's Philosophy* is still one of his most popular songs, and justifiably so. For sheer technical prowess there was nothing in English song at that time to compare with it. Its voluptuous harmonies and passionately-soaring vocal line are entirely in keeping with the sensuousness of Shelley's

243 T. Hold, *Parry to Finzi: Twenty English Song-Composers* (Woodbridge, Suffolk: Boydell Press, 2002)

244 Hold, *Parry to Finzi*, p. 147.

> verse. The rippling toccata-like figurations – reflecting the fountains, rivers and oceans of the poem – swirl around the *legato* phrases of the vocal line which is buffeted and buoyed up like a boat...[245]

Hold is normally extremely critical of repeated lines or phrases in song-settings, considering them to be superfluous, but here he fulminates: "The ... repetition of words at the end of the song are, in this instance, entirely appropriate". High praise indeed. But what of the Henley setting? Hold regards this as "vastly inferior" to the other two in the set. Quilter accords it a robust treatment which Hold feels betrays misjudgement of the intended mood. The poem itself seems to require an intimate and sensitive interpretation, which is exactly what it does receive in Butterworth's setting in his cycle *Love Blows as the Wind Blows*, and it is this interpretation, surely, which is closer to the heart of the poet, and which is enhanced by Butterworth's choice of string quartet as accompaniment. Quilter's setting is lovely music, but it would have been better lavished on a text of the outdoors.[246]

Henley, of course, does not match up to Shelley or Tennyson as a poet, and it is when he sets the great poets that Quilter seems to excel. Nowhere is this more evident than in his treatment of the Bard himself. He produced four sets of Shakespeare settings (opp. 6, 23, 30, 32) and a few individual songs, but the first of them, the *Three Shakespeare Songs* of 1905, is generally regarded as the best. It includes *Come away, death*; *O mistress mine*; and *Blow, blow, thou winter wind*, the upbeat treatment of the middle song making a

---

245 Hold, *Parry to Finzi*, p. 147

246 The reader may be better able to judge the pros and cons of the debate if he or she is aware of the text, the first verse of which runs:

Fill a glass with golden wine,
And the while your lips are wet,
Set their perfume unto mine,
And forget
Every kiss we take and give
Leaves us less of life to live.

satisfying foil for the weighty first one on the one hand, and the blustery final one on the other.

If Quilter is at his best in his settings of the greats – Shakespeare, Shelley, Herrick, and the like – one struggles to understand why so much of the verse he chooses to set is by minor poets, some of which is little more than doggerel. He devotes his opus 22 set to three Joseph Campbell poems, two of which (*Cherry Valley* and *I wish and I wish*) are banal in the extreme, while the other, *I will go with my father a-ploughing*, has slightly more merit, and was set also by Ivor Gurney, although the text is still slight. Of course, not all good poems necessarily deal with weighty matters, but if they are not intrinsically good, it is difficult to see how any composer can raise them to the status of fine art through music, and it can hardly be said that Quilter succeeds where others have failed.

It is generally felt that Quilter's best work was done in the few years between 1905–10, the period of his early maturity. Not only were his best songs composed during this period, but most of his other music, too. After this, there was no further advancement in his style or technique, and his output, although never very prolific at any stage, became even less so as he grew older. Nevertheless, he remained a force to be reckoned with for many years, since he had the happy knack of attracting the finest singers of the day to perform his work, often with himself providing the piano accompaniment. These performers included Gervase Elwes (until his untimely death in 1921), Harry Plunket Green, Muriel Foster, Clara Butt and Maggie Tate. After Elwes's demise, a new singer, Mark Raphael (1900–88) took up Quilter's cause. Thus, he was never without a worthy advocate.

Despite all the advantages his privileged upbringing provided, Quilter suffered later in life from bouts of deep depression, and the death of a favourite nephew, Arnold Guy Vivian (after whom the *Arnold Book of Traditional Songs* is named), hardly helped matters. By the 1950s, the Georgian drawing room songs, in which Quilter specialised, were no longer in fashion, and by the end of his life he had begun to suffer neglect. He died on 21st September 1953, in

London, and was buried in the family vault of St. Mary's Church, Bawdsey.

The kind of home music-making that was so popular in Quilter's heyday, and for which his songs provided, is now a thing of the past. However, all his published songs have been recorded, and the best of them – *Now sleeps the crimson petal*, *Love's Philosophy*, and *Go, lovely rose* – have frequently found their way into the many English song anthologies that have been released over the years.

a. Bibliography

Harrison, Nicola, "'Go, Lovely Rose': Roger Quilter – A Wordsmith's Guide", *British Music*, 38/2 (2016)

Hold, Trevor, *The Walled-In Garden: The Songs of Roger Quilter* (London: Thames Publishing, 1996)

Langfield, Valerie, *Roger Quilter: His Life and Music* (Woodbridge, Suffolk: Boydell Press, 2003)

b. Selected Discography

Songs

Three Shakespeare Songs, etc.	Ainsley (ten); Martineau (piano)	Hyperion	CDA 66878
Complete Songbook	Stone (bar); Barlow (piano)	Stone Rec.	
Selected Songs	Milne (sop); Rolfe Johnson (ten) Graham Johnson (piano); Duke Quartet	Naxos	8.557116

c. Website

Roger Quilter Homepage (www.valerielangfield.co.uk/Quilter/index.htm)

39. Alan Rawsthorne (1905–71)

Alan Rawsthorne was born in Haslingden, some ten miles south-west of Burnley in Lancashire, to professional parents, his father being a medical practitioner. His early education was rather piecemeal, for he was of somewhat delicate health, as a result of which he was home-tutored for a time, although he did eventually attend school in Southport. He developed an avid interest in music early on, but his story mirrors that of many other budding musicians of that time: it was all very well to have music as a recreation, but not as a profession. Thus, when the time came, he was sent to the University of Liverpool to study dentistry, but he had no enthusiasm for that enterprise, and so transferred to a course in architecture, in which he was equally disinterested. Wisely, his parents seem not to have forced the issue, and in 1925 he entered the Royal Manchester College of Music (later the RNCM) to study piano and cello. After some four years at the college, he continued his studies abroad with Egon Petri (1881–1962) in Poland. Of this early period of his life, his close friend Constant Lambert was later to say, with his characteristic wit: "Mr. Rawsthorne assures me that he has given up the practice of dentistry, even as a hobby". Among the Lambert set, Rawsthorne was affectionately known as "Fish Face".

Although his formal studies, both at home and abroad, seem to have been focused on his chosen instruments, he secured a brief spell as composer-in-residence at Dartington Hall, Devon (1932–34), after which he headed for London to try his luck as a freelance composer. His first significant success was his *Theme & Variations for Two Violins* (1938) which was performed at the ISCM Festival in London. This was followed the next year by a performance of his equally impressive *Symphonic Studies* at the same festival, this time in Warsaw. These promising beginnings were curtailed by the onset of the Second World War in which Rawsthorne served in the army. How much time he spent in the service of his country, however, is difficult to determine. Few of his major works were composed during that period, although he did revise his Piano Concerto No. 1 in 1942.

1940, however, saw Rawsthorne and his first wife (Jessie Hinchliffe, a violinist) occupying a flat in Bristol. Here he seems to have had a narrow escape during an air raid. At the time, Constant Lambert, Sidonie Goossens and other musical friends were visiting. Lambert, at first unaware that an air raid was going on, remarked on the "pretty lights" (flares) outside. Eventually, it was realised that the roof of their building was alight, but the gathering went on in a party atmosphere. Eventually it was deemed wise to decamp to the pub across the road where the group spent the night in the cellar with a furniture store blazing away next door. When they all emerged next morning, they found Rawsthorne's flat reduced to rubble. The score of his Violin Concerto No. 1, on which he had been working intermittently, was one of the casualties, along with several other manuscripts.[247] However, he was able to reconstruct the work in time for its premiere by John Barbirolli and the Hallé Orchestra in 1948, with Theo Olof as soloist.

Of the names associated with the Heseltine/ Warlock menage, or those on the periphery of it (Moeran, Lambert, Nina Hamnett, Augustus John, John Goss, Cecil Gray, Bruce Blunt, Lord Berners, and Walton), it was Lambert with whom Rawsthorne was most closely associated, and, perhaps through Lambert, he was acquainted with Walton. He would no doubt have revelled in the company of Heseltine had they been closer contemporaries, but by the time he came of age, the Eynsford years, in which Heseltine held court, were over, and Rawsthorne was still only twenty-five at the time of Heseltine's death. Lambert may have had some influence on Rawsthorne, personally if not professionally, and they had some shared influences. The latter's entertainment for speaker and orchestra, *Practical Cats* (1954), based on the poems of T.S. Eliot, would certainly have excited the interest of Lambert who (like Heseltine) was a noted lover of the feline species, but by the time of its composition he was dead, and Rawsthorne had taken Isobel Lambert, an artist, to be his second wife.

247 Lloyd, *Constant Lambert*, pp. 295–96. See also Tim Mottershead, "Alan Rawsthorne: The Fish with an Ear for Music: A Concise Biography", *The Creel*, no. 19 (Winter, 2005/06), pp. 46–47.

Rawsthorne certainly played his full part in activities at The George pub – or the Gluepot, as it had been facetiously dubbed by Sir Henry Wood – on the corner of Great Portland Street and Mortimer Street in London. As it was situated conveniently adjacent to the Queen's Hall, Langham Place, it became the focus of a loose-knit cabal of artists of all kinds, including – much to Wood's consternation – the members of the Queen's Hall Orchestra. Among the composers to be found there at various times of day and night, apart from Rawsthorne and Lambert, were Walton, Bax, Lutyens, Ireland, Moeran, Warlock, Alan Bush, Humphrey Searle, Denis ApIvor (for whom Rawsthorne provided some instruction in composition), and even Delius if he happened to be visiting from France. Among the poets on show were Louis MacNeice, Roy Campbell and Randall Swingler; and there were artists including Michael Ayrton and Isobel Nicholas, Lambert's wife. Despite Henry Wood's disapproval of the establishment, other conductors were not so sanctimonious, and both Hyam Greenbaum and Leslie Heward were to be found there from time to time. Elisabeth Lutyens reported a comment, perhaps not wholly tongue-in-cheek, to the effect that if a bomb had been dropped on The George a significant proportion of the literary and musical world would have been destroyed. Lutyens, along with Rawsthorne, Lambert and Walton, seem to have formed a clique within a clique (Gluepot relations were generally quite fluid). Michael Tippett regarded this particular quartet as an anti-Britten cabal. "They all had great chips on the shoulder and entertained absurd fantasies about a homosexual conspiracy in music led by Britten and Pears".

The heyday of The George's association with the artistic world was the 1940s. After the death of Lambert in 1951, the atmosphere was never the same, and the old cabal began to disintegrate. Bax and Ireland both retired to rural Sussex, settling within a couple of miles of one another, while Walton sought the sun in Ischia. Denis ApIvor movingly captures the mood in his and Rawsthorne's reaction to Lambert's death: "That night a sort of wake was held … at which only Jessie [Rawsthorne], Alan, Elisabeth Lutyens and myself were present. [Suddenly,] the enormity of what we were about to 'celebrate' – the total and permanent absence of Constant Lambert, suddenly struck us ... and we simultaneously gave vent to tears. It was the only time I ever observed the man whom Lambert had dubbed 'Old Fish-Face' openly moved".[248]

As a composer, Rawsthorne preferred the traditional forms – symphony, concerto, quartet and sonata, in particular. He also produced some significant film scores which no doubt helped him pay the bills. His style was broadly neo-classical, marked by directness of expression, conciseness and integrity, qualities he shared with Lennox Berkeley, although his voice remained distinctive. He came of age with his *Symphonic Studies* of 1938, but he was already forty-five years old when he tackled his first symphony. He was no latter-day Haydn, or even like his contemporary Havergal Brian, turning out one symphony after another. Three was his limit, for his was a comparatively laconic approach, never overstepping the bounds of classical propriety. Neither of the first two symphonies exceeds twenty-five minutes, even though they adopt the traditional four-movement form. The First Symphony (1950), for instance, launches straight in without ceremony, and a conciseness of which Arnold Cooke would have approved. All the essential material is laid out in the first minute of music, thereafter being worked out to its inevitable conclusion.

The Symphony No. 2 (1959) is entitled *A Pastoral Symphony*, and may have been inspired in part by the composer's settling in rural Essex. However, this is not the kind of landscape music more evident in Beethoven's *Pastoral Symphony*, nor does it contrive to throw the listener off the scent like Vaughan Williams's *Pastoral*. Rather, it reflects Rawsthorne's personal reaction to life in the country. The one concession to the descriptive element lies in the finale which is a setting of a pastoral poem by Henry Howard, Earl of Surrey (1516–47). Other than that, the musical argument is a wholly abstract one.

248 For this section, I have drawn liberally on Andrew Griffiths's liner notes in *The Gluepot Connection*, Somm, SOMMCD 0180.

The Third Symphony (1964), half-an-hour in performance, is regarded by John Belcher[249] as the culmination of Rawsthorne's purely symphonic writing, developing elements of both the previous symphonies. The same conciseness, craftsmanship and clarity of expression is evident throughout.

Rawsthorne made significant contributions to both the concerto and chamber music repertoire. The former includes two for piano (1939/42, 1951), two for violin (1948, 1956), and one each for cello (1966), clarinet (1937) and oboe (1947), as well as one for string orchestra (1949). His chamber pieces include three string quartets (1939, 1954, 1965), a piano quintet (1968), a clarinet quartet (1948), a quintet for piano, oboe, clarinet, horn and bassoon (1963), a piano trio (1962), two violin sonatas (1937/53, 1960) and one for cello (1949).

Rawsthorne applied the same careful craftsmanship to his film music of the 1940s–50s as he did to his "serious" work. Many of the films for which he wrote were very much of their time and have long been forgotten, but the one for which he is best-remembered, *The Cruel Sea* (1953) can still be recalled by persons of a certain age. Happily, not all Rawsthorne's film scores have sunk without trace, thanks to the enterprising decision of Chandos to issue recordings of some of them.[250]

Rawsthorne was a man of socialist rather than religious sympathies, but, following his death on 24th July 1971, he was interred in the churchyard in the Essex village of Thaxted, where, over thirty years earlier, Holst had been prominent in the musical life of the community. Rawsthorne had been working on an *Elegy* for solo guitar for Julian Bream, and on its completion by the intended soloist, it effectively became an elegy for Rawsthorne himself.

---

249 J. Belcher, liner notes, *Rawsthorne: Symphonies Nos. 1–3*, Naxos, 8.557480.

250 *The Film Music of Alan Rawsthorne*, Chandos, CHAN 9749. As well as music from *The Cruel Sea*, music from other films, as edited and/or orchestrated by Philip Lane or Gerard Schurmann, include *West of Zanzibar*, *The Captive Heart*, *Where No Vultures Fly*, *Uncle Silas*, and *Burma Victory*.

a. Bibliography

Dressler, John C., *Alan Rawsthorne: A Bio-Bibliography* (Westport, CT: Praeger, 2004)

McCabe, John, *Alan Rawsthorne: Portrait of a Composer* (Oxford: Oxford University Press, 1999)

Mottershead, Tim, "Alan Rawsthorne: The Fish with an Ear for Music – A Concise Biography", *The Creel*, 19 (Winter, 2005–6)

The Creel: Journal of the Rawsthorne Trust and the Friends of Alan Rawsthorne, vols. 1-13 (2008–20).

b. Selected Discography

i) Symphonies

Symphonies Nos. 1–3	Bournemouth SO, Lloyd-Jones	Naxos	8.557480

ii) Concertos

Piano Concerto No. 1	Ulster O., Yuasa; Donohoe, piano	Naxos	8.555959
Piano Concerto No. 2	Ulster O., Yuasa; Donohoe, piano	Naxos	8.555959
Violin Concerto No. 1	BBC Scottish SO, Friend; Hirsch (violin)	Naxos	8.554240
Violin Concerto No. 2	BBC Scottish SO; Friend; Hirsch (violin)	Naxos	8.554240
Cello Concerto	RSNO, Lloyd-Jones; Baillie (cello)	Naxos	8.553567
Concerto for Strings	Northern CO, Lloyd-Jones	Naxos	8.553567

Oboe Concerto	Northern CO, Lloyd-Jones;Rancourt (oboe)	Naxos	8.553567

iii) **Orchestral**

Overture: Street Corner	RLPO, Lloyd-Jones	Dutton	CDLX 7203
Coronation Overture	RLPO, Lloyd-Jones	Dutton	CDLX 7203
Madame Chrysanthème: Ballet Suite	RLPO, Lloyd-Jones	Dutton	CDLX 7203
Practical Cats	RLPO, Lloyd-Jones; Callow (narr)	Dutton	CDLX 7203
Theme, Variations & Finale	RLPO, Lloyd-Jones	Dutton	CDLX 7203
Medieval Diptych	RLPO, Lloyd-Jones; Williams (bar)	Dutton	CDLX 7203
Elegiac Rhapsody	Northern CO, Lloyd-Jones	Naxos	8.553567
Divertimento	Northern CO, Lloyd-Jones	Naxos	8.553567
Symphonic Studies	BBC Scottish SO, Friend	Naxos	8.554240

iv) Chamber

String Quartet No. 1	Maggini Quartet	Naxos	8.570136
String Quartet No. 2	Maggini Quartet	Naxos	8.570136
String Quartet No. 3	Maggini Quartet	Naxos	8.570136
Piano Quintet	Rogieri Trio; Messenger (violin), McCabe	Naxos	8.554352
Piano Trio	Rogieri Trio	Naxos	8.554352
Cello Sonata	Adams (cello); Endo (piano)	Naxos	8.554352
Viola Sonata	Outram (viola); Rolton (piano)	Naxos	8.554352

c. Website

Friends of Alan Rawsthorne (www.musicweb-international.com/index.htm)

40. Cyril Bradley Rootham (1875–1938)

Mention the cities of Bristol and Cambridge in the same breath, and it is likely that the name of Cyril Rootham will spring to the minds of English music enthusiasts, for he was born in the former city where his father held a prestigious position in its musical life, and was professionally associated with the latter for the best part of forty years. In his informative article on the composer, Kenneth Shenton[251] laments that "to the vast majority of music lovers the name Cyril Rootham will nowadays mean little". In general terms that may well be true, but in his lifetime he was a figure of some standing, not only in Cambridge, but well beyond. Like Patrick Hadley, who was first Rootham's student, and later his successor in many of his professional duties at the university, his progress in composition was somewhat impeded by his academic responsibilities, but he nevertheless managed to build a respectable corpus of works which included two symphonies, both written in the last decade of his life, and several large-scale choral/orchestral works, the best-known being *Ode on the Morning of Christ's Nativity* (1928), a setting of Milton's celebrated poem. There was also a small quantity of chamber music, several pieces for unaccompanied chorus, and for solo organ, and a few songs. An opera, *The Twa Sisters o' Binnorie*, although staged in 1922, has been completely forgotten. As a remembered composer, Hadley has perhaps fared better than his mentor, thanks largely to his masterpiece *The Trees So High* and a few short choral works like *I Sing of a Maiden* and *My Beloved Spake*, which remain in the repertoire.

Cyril Rootham was born on 5th October 1875, and from the beginning, both the city of his birth (which he never forgot) and Cambridge were in his blood. His grandfather, father and an uncle had all been associated in one capacity or another with the Choir of St. John's College, Cambridge, and after his father had

251 K. Shenton, "Cyril Bradley Rootham", *British Music*, 7 (1985), pp. 30–37.

moved to Bristol he became a well-known singing teacher in the city, with the renowned contralto Clara Butt being a star pupil, as well as conductor of the Bristol Madrigal Society for fifty years. The young Rootham attended Bristol Grammar School where he excelled in athletics and was head boy. Clearly, he was marked out for great things, and in 1895 went up to Cambridge on a Classics scholarship and a choral scholarship at the college of his forebears, St. John's. When the organist of the college, Dr. Garnett, fell ill, it was Rootham who was asked to deputise. He continued to excel in athletics and rowing (always an advantage in the Oxbridge environment of those days), but in order to extend his musical studies he enrolled at the RCM where his teachers included Parry, Stanford and Walter Parratt.

In 1901 he was appointed organist at St. Asaph Cathedral in North Wales, but the lure of Cambridge was ever-present, and when he was invited back to fill a position as organist and choir master, he jumped at the chance. Once settled, he set about raising the standards of both amateur and professional music-making in the city, particularly those of the Cambridge University Music Society (CUMS) which he conducted for almost a quarter of a century. He became celebrated for his innovative programming, introducing not only works by contemporary British composers like Vaughan Williams (*The Poisoned Kiss*), Holst, Bax (*Mater Ora Filium*), Hadley (*The Trees So High*), Moeran, and lesser-known lights like Gillies Whittaker and Arthur Warrell, but living European composers, including Kodaly (*Psalmus Hungaricus*), Honegger and Pizzetti. He also revived significant works by Mozart, Handel and Purcell which, but for his efforts, might not enjoy the popularity in Britain that they do today.

Stories abound about the ebullient and heavy-drinking Hadley who, in many ways, was not cut out to be a teacher. Although somewhat more staid and "proper", however, Rootham was not without a distinctiveness of character. Shenton[252] describes him as looking like "a guards officer on leave in civilian clothes, not

252 Shenton, "Cyril Bradley Rootham", p. 30.

a button, a hair or folded handkerchief out of place". He seems to have been popular among his students (who included, at various times, Arthur Bliss, Arnold Cooke, Christian Darnton, Cecil Armstrong Gibbs, Hadley, Walter Leigh, Robin Orr, and Bernard Stevens), breezing into lectures with typical athletic agility, and telling "freshers", "The name is pronounced *Root-ham*, as in Beethoven" – after which, with some inevitability, he was known among his charges as Dr. Roothoven (at least behind his back!).

If *Ode on the Morning of Christ's Nativity* is one of Rootham's finest works, the Second Symphony is undoubtedly a summation of his career as a composer, and the story of its creation is a poignant one. In 1935 he began to suffer from progressive muscular atrophy, an incurable condition which slowly and relentlessly robs the sufferer of his mobility and, once sufficiently advanced, his speech. As the illness progressed, he was obliged to relinquish most of his academic duties, but was initially still able to compose. When, finally, this also became too much, he engaged a number of devoted students and friends to take down the music at his dictation (one is reminded of the relationship between Eric Fenby and the ailing Delius). The work was all but completed just ten days before the composer's death on 18th March 1938 (a few pages of the final movement was left in short score and subsequently orchestrated by Hadley), and premiered by Adrian Boult with the BBC SO a year later. The score bears the following poignant dedication: "To R.M.R. [Rosemary, the composer's wife], J.St.J.R [Jasper St. John, his son], P.A.S.H. [Hadley], and those staunch friends whose devoted help made it possible that this music be heard. My gratitude goes to them always. C.B.R.".

By any standards, Rootham's Second Symphony is a fine work, but, given the circumstances of its creation, it is doubly impressive. The centrepiece of the Finale is a quotation from the book of Revelation (Rev. 21: 4; 22: 5). The first verse reads:

> Behold, there shall be no more death,
> Neither sorrow nor crying
> Neither shall there be any more pain;
> For the former things have passed away.

Given Rootham's circumstances at the time, it is difficult to believe that these were not very much in view as he wrote. Still, there is no impression of self-indulgence. The symphony is a work of art in itself, and a lasting legacy of his life's work.

Another piece very much associated with this same period is the choral/ orchestral *City in the West*. It was written in 1936 to a text by Rootham's son Jasper (1910–90) who decared: "I wrote the poem because I knew that my father was slowly dying of progressive muscular atrophy and I hoped to direct his energy into composition where he still had much to give".[253] The "city in the West" is, of course, Bristol, Rootham's birthplace, and it was premiered, appropriately enough, at the Colston Hall, since renamed the Bristol Beacon, by Bristol composer Arthur Warrell in 1937.

Although Rootham was generally a model of propriety, his strength of personality led, occasionally, to friction with others of a similar ilk. This was most evident in his working relationship with E.J. Dent at Cambridge, although, when it most mattered, the two men were usually able to co-operate. Another, better-known, spat occurred in regard to Rootham's choral/ orchestral piece, *For the Fallen* (1915), a setting of words from Binyon's *The Spirit of England*. A chance meeting with Elgar at the time revealed that the older composer was at work on a setting of verses from the same text, the only difference being that Elgar's setting was more extensive than that of Rootham who had chosen to set only lines from *For the Fallen*, with its final verse familiar to us from its use on Armistice Day. As Rootham's piece was nearing completion and Novello had provisionally arranged to publish it, Elgar felt obliged to withdraw his own work. There is no evidence of any overt ill-feeling between

253 Jasper Rootham, liner notes, EMI Classics, 5 05923, p. 6.

the composers themselves, but their respective acolytes took issue, with the Cambridge set – including E.J. Dent, who, as just noted, did not always see eye to eye with Rootham – backing their man, while Elgar's supporters urged him to bring his own setting to fruition, which he ultimately agreed to do. This seems to have led to a measure of antipathy towards Elgar's music in Cambridge circles which persisted for some years, but there is no suggestion that this was sanctioned or encouraged by Rootham. Indeed, the whole episode seems to have been a case of much ado about nothing. Elgar could be oversensitive at times, and seems to have felt on this occasion that the music world could not accommodate two settings of the same poem. In the event, both works saw the light of day, which could only be to the advantage of the music-lover. Sadly, neither work is much aired today.

What of Rootham's other works? Of his compositions for chorus and orchestra, *Brown Earth* (1921), to a text by Thomas Moult won a Carnegie Award, and has received some acclaim, but there seems to be little prospect of hearing it.[254] Another, *The Stolen Child* (1911), a setting of Yeats's poem, has been recorded and proves to be a very attractive piece. Among the solo songs, there is a set of four to texts by Siegfried Sassoon (*Morning Glory, South Wind, A Child's Prayer*, and *A Poplar and the Moon*) who Rootham got to know personally, but, again, no-one seems to take them up, despite the fact that performances, all with piano accompaniment, could easily be arranged. A *Magnificat & Nunc Dimittis* in E minor has found a place in the Anglican repertoire, but as he was obliged to conform to the requirements of the Anglican musical tradition, it is not the best work in which to find Rootham's distinctive voice. The major works – the *Ode on the Morning of Christ's Nativity*, both symphonies, *City in the West, For the Fallen* and *Psalm of Adonis*, have all been recorded, but his chamber music is grossly under-represented, only the Violin Sonata of 1925 having been recorded to date. Shenton's plea for the fiftieth anniversary of Rootham's

254 Shenton, "Cyril Bradley Rootham", p. 32

death (1988) to be recognised seems to have gone largely unheeded, although the EMI selection of orchestral and choral music was released the year before.

Unfortunately, Rootham's legacy as a university teacher has been more enduring than his legacy as a composer, but it would be sad indeed if his major works were to fall into neglect, for they represent an independent creative mind which eschewed fad and fashion and followed its own lights. Hearing his music is as satisfying an experience now as it was in his own day.

a. Bibliography

Shenton, Kenneth, "Cyril Bradley Rootham", *British Music*, 7 (1985), pp. 30–37

b. Selected Discography

i) Symphonies

Symphony No. 1	LPO, Handley	Lyrita	SRCD 269
Symphony No. 2	BBC Scottish SO, Handley	Lyrita	REAM 2118

ii) Choral with Orchestra

On the Morning of Christ's Nativity	BBC Concert O., BBC Singers, Trinity Boys' Choir; soloists; Handley	Lyrita	REAM 2118
The Stolen Child	Northern Sinfonia & Chorus, Hickox	EMI	5 05923 2
City in the West	Northern Sinfonia & Chorus, Hickox	EMI	5 05923 2
For the Fallen	Northern Sinfonia & Chorus, Hickox	EMI	5 05923 2
Miniature Suite	Northern Sinfonia, Hickox	EMI	5 05923 2
Psalm of Adonis	Northern Sinfonia, Hickox	EMI	5 05923 2

iii) Chamber

Violin Sonata	Roche (violin); Stevenson (piano)	Dutton	CDLX 7219

c. Website

Cyril Rootham Homepage (https://rootham.org)

41. Edmund Rubbra (1901–86)

The name Edmund Rubbra will conjure up in the minds of most aficionados of English music the image of a leading symphonist. And so he was. His cycle of eleven splendid examples of the genre is by any standards an impressive achievement, and Vaughan Williams – unofficially, at least – considered Rubbra to be his natural successor in the symphonic form. Of course, Rubbra was much more than a symphonist. His Symphony No. 1 (op. 44) did not see the light of day until 1937 (it was a couple of years in gestation), and it has been suggested that he came to the genre comparatively late – although this is not unusual among British composers.[255] Certainly it is true that, prior to the appearance of this symphony, he had produced little by way of orchestral music, the *Sinfonia Concertante* (op. 38) being his earliest significant orchestral work (an earlier piano concerto, opus 30, was later withdrawn). A glance at Rubbra's catalogue will show that a large proportion of his first thirty opus-numbered works were devoted to song – an interest which he maintained throughout his life. In fact, he produced work in most genres – concertos, chamber music, choral and solo piano. He had a keen, though not particularly conventional sense of the spiritual, which is reflected in his work generally, and not solely in his choral settings.[256]

Rubbra (like Malcolm Arnold, William Alwyn and Trevor Hold) was born in Northampton to parents of modest means on 23rd May 1901. They were not especially musical, although they soon recognised their son's flair for music and encouraged him in

255 Compare, for instance, Lennox Berkeley's First, completed when he was thirty-seven; Bax's First (aged 39); Havergal Brian's *Gothic* (aged 51); Arnold Cooke's First (aged 41); Dyson's Symphony in G (aged 54); Elgar's First (aged 51); Gunning's First (aged 58); Moeran's Symphony in G minor (aged 43); Vaughan Williams's *Sea Symphony* (aged 39); Tippett's First (aged 40); Walton's First (aged 33); Wordsworth's First (aged 36).

256 The Symphony No. 8, for instance, is entitled *Hommage à Teilhard de Chardin*, while Symphony No. 9, Rubbra's most substantial work in the genre, bears the title *Sinfonia Sacra*.

any way they could. An uncle owned a music shop and used the Rubbra household to install demonstration pianos in order to boost sales. The young Rubbra was engaged to play for clients, and if a sale went through, another demonstration piano arrived, and the Rubbra family received commission for the sale. His parents were so keen to help him succeed that when they moved house in order to facilitate the father's clock repair business, and found that the family piano would not fit through the door, they dismantled an upstairs window to get it in.

Young Edmund took piano lessons locally and became proficient enough not only to play hymn tunes at his local Congregational church, but Mozart piano sonatas. He was still at school when he took his first steps in composition. For a few years after he left school, aged fourteen, music had to take a back seat while he earned a living, first at a local boot and shoe factory (he did live in Northampton, after all!), and later as a railway clerk where his recently-acquired shorthand skills came in handy. Behind the scenes, however, he was continuing to work at composition, and occasionally met with another aspiring young composer of the town, William Alwyn. At some point, he became acquainted with the music of Cyril Scott (1879–1970), and at the age of seventeen decided to organise a local concert devoted entirely to Scott's work, in which Rubbra appeared as pianist. His church minister, who was present at the concert, sent Scott a copy of the programme, the result of which was that Scott offered to take Edmund under his wing, offering advice in composition.

Eventually, Rubbra was able to study music on a more formal basis when he gained a scholarship to Reading University to study composition with Holst. It was Holst who suggested to him that he should enrol at the RCM, and he spent the early 1920s there. At much the same time he befriended Gerald Finzi, another useful connection.

In 1941, now aged forty, he was called up for war service, but was wisely given administrative duties and, given his musical prowess, asked to form a trio for the entertainment of the troops which he did with William Pleeth (cello) and John Glazier (violin). The trio travelled widely, giving concerts up and down the country and, with the cessation of hostilities, in Germany, too.

As noted above, Rubbra was a religious man in an unconventional way. He was brought up conventionally enough in the Congregational (now United Reform) Church. However, after hearing a Chinese Christian missionary, his interests broadened to include Eastern spirituality. Among his works inspired by the Orient are *Fukagawa (Deep River)* for solo piano or harp, and the five-song set *The Jade Mountain*, which sets poems in translation from the T'ang Dynasty. There was also a one-act opera entitled *The Shadow*, the action of which takes place in a Kashmiri setting, which remains in manuscript. Christian spirituality, however, continued to be his main focus, and in 1947 he joined the Roman Catholic Church, apparently considering this to be a sufficiently significant turning-point in his life to compose a mass to mark the occasion – the spare but striking *Missa in honorem Sancti Dominici* (op. 66). This was one of several. There is a *Missa Cantauriensis* (op. 59) and a *Mass in Honour of St. Teresa of Avila*, as well as a *Missa á 3* and a *Missa Brevis*. He continued to write occasional pieces for the church (carols, motets and Evening Services, for instance) throughout his life.

By the end of the Second World War, Rubbra was established as one of Britain's leading composers. In 1942 he was one of a select trio of composers (Hadley and Lambert being the others) commissioned to write a short piece in honour of Vaughan Williams's seventieth birthday. Rubbra's contribution was entitled *A Tribute*. The older composer thought highly of his abilities, and when Rubbra received an honorary DMus from the University of Durham in 1949, he wrote to congratulate him with typical wit: "I am delighted to hear of the honour which Durham University is conferring on itself".[257] A year earlier he had been invited to take up the post of Lecturer in Music in the recently-formed Music Department at Oxford

257 Quoted in Ralph Scott Grover, *The Music of Edmund Rubbra* (Aldershot: Scolar Press, 1993), p. 2.

University, and became a Fellow of Worcester College, remaining in post until 1968. For some years after that, he continued teaching at the Guildhall School of Music and Drama, where the composer Christopher Gunning was one of his students.

Although somewhat luckless in matrimony (he was married three times), those who knew Rubbra generally present the impression of a quiet, unassuming man who was content to let his music do the talking. The conductor Vernon Handley (1930–2007) who went up to Baliol College, Oxford, in 1951, and had the conductorship of the university student orchestra, recalled that after one concert, in which a piece by Ravel had been on the programme, he was approached by a small, bearded man who commended him on the performance. It was Hadley's first meeting with Rubbra. Years later, in 1970, Hadley returned the compliment by conducting Rubbra's Second Symphony for a Lyrita recording.

Rubbra continued to compose high quality music until the end of his life, and died at Gerard's Cross on the 14th February 1986, at the advanced age of eighty-five.

Although Rubbra worked in a wide range of genres, there can be no doubt that the backbone of his mature work is the symphonic cycle. The term "cycle" is frequently used to denote the entire body of a composer's symphonic output, regardless of whether or not the symphonies were intended to have any relationship with one another in the manner of a genuine song-cycle. Occasionally, a composer premeditates such a relationship. Alwyn's first four symphonies, for example, were conceived as symphonies within a symphony, with each one representing one of the traditional four movements in a classical symphony. Other composers, a little less ambitiously, have introduced trilogies within their symphonic corpus. Shostakovich's so-called "war" symphonies (Nos. 7–9) are often regarded as such, while, closer to home, the same has been suggested of Bax's Symphonies Nos. 1–3, and of Havergal Brian's Symphonies Nos. 8–10. Along with these, we might add Rubbra's first four symphonies which, by his own admission, are similarly related, each successive symphony taking up where its predecessor left off. They were all written within a seven-year period between 1935–42, after which there was a six-year lull before the appearance of the Symphony No. 5 (1948), which stands alone. The remaining Symphonies (Nos. 6–11) appeared at intervals between 1968–79. A single page of manuscript found among Rubbra's papers after his death indicates that he was contemplating a twelfth symphony at the time.

His symphonic writing was always flexible in its use of form. There are both three (Nos. 1, 4, 7, 8) and four (Nos. 2, 3, 5, 6) movement works, and the expansive Symphony No. 9, *Sinfonia Sacra,* contrasts markedly with the compact single-movement Symphony No. 10. It all speaks of a restlessly searching symphonic mind.

Rubbra's approach to symphonic composition was one that applied to the majority of his mature works. It was one which involved exploration from a fixed point, and in which an intervallic interest was as important as key-relations. He wrote: "I never know where a piece is going to go next ... My method of working at a lengthy work is to continue steadily from the opening idea. The excitement of discovery would be lost if I 'graphed out' where certain climaxes, etc., would be. When I begin, my only concern is with fixing a starting point that I can be sure of".[258]

Rubbra made some significant contributions to the chamber music genre, inspired to some extent by his lifelong cellist friend William Pleeth, who became a kind of muse. At the core of Rubbra's output are the four string quartets (opp. 25, 73, 112, 150) which were composed over a period of more than forty years. There is also a striking trio of violin sonatas, the second of which made Rubbra's reputation as a composer, in much the way that Ireland's Violin Sonata No. 2 did in his case back in 1917. The first two sonatas, of 1925 and 1931 respectively, were comparatively early compositions, while the third was composed in 1968, over thirty-

258 Quoted by John Pickard in the liner notes to *Rubbra: String Quartets Nos. 2 & 4*, Dutton, CDLX 7114, p. 4.

five years later. The early sonatas were inspired by another muse, the French violinist Antoinette Chaplin, who later became Rubbra's second wife.

The composer's wartime experience as a leading member and pianist of the Army Classical Music Group gave him the opportunity to write for the trio, or members thereof. This led to the composition of the cello sonata (1946), which was dedicated to William Pleeth who premiered the work early in 1947, and is considered to be one of Rubbra's finest creations. Surprisingly – or perhaps not so surprisingly, given Rubbra's typically self-effacing personality – the Piano Trio No. 1 (1950) was the only work he wrote specifically for the Army Classical Music Group. The staple diet of the trio consisted of trios by Mozart, Haydn and Beethoven. Rubbra's Piano Trio No. 2 (op. 138) was composed some twenty years later. For its premiere, Rubbra and another member of the old wartime trio, William Pleeth, joined forces again, with the violinist Erich Gruenberg who had been Joshua Glazier's successor. It must have been a nostalgic occasion.

Rubbra was prolific in most of the main genres, but he was ever a "serious" composer. The more dramatic forms – opera, ballet, film music, incidental music – did not greatly attract him. Similarly, the listener should not expect memorable tunes. Only those boasting a professional intimacy with the music are likely to be able to hum a phrase or two from any of the symphonies. This is because, as noted earlier, his method of composition was linear. He fixed an initial idea and ran with it, not knowing himself where it would lead until it had taken him there. One might say he composed from hand to mouth. Yet he was highly respected by fellow composers whose methods were more traditional. Tunes meant everything to Vaughan Williams, yet, as noted above, he considered Rubbra to be his symphonic heir, and it is evident that there existed a warm mutual respect between them. Moreover, regardless of the manner in which he composed, Rubbra's music always provides a satisfying listening experience for those who make the effort to follow his line of thought and share his musical journey. John Pickard tells us that at the Cheltenham Festival of 1964, Rubbra's String Quartet No. 3 was programmed in the same concert as Stockhausen's *Zyklus* for solo percussion, but to suggest that there is any note of resemblance would be to completely misrepresent Rubbra's music.[259] If it is a thoughtful, often deeply spiritual experience that the listener requires, he/ she could do a lot worse than turn to the sound-world of this composer.

259 Pickard himself considered the programming bizarre (liner notes, *String Quartets Nos. 1–3*, Dutton, CDLX 7123, p. 8.

a. Bibliography

Black, Leo, *Edmund Rubbra: Symphonist* (Woodbridge, Suffolk: Boydell Press, rpr. 2014)

Blois, Louis, "The Symphonies of Edmund Rubbra", *British Music*, 6 (1984)

Grover, Ralph Scott, *The Music of Edmund Rubbra* (Scolar Press, 1993)

Ottoway, Hugh, *Edmund Rubbra: An Appreciation* (London: Lengnick, 1981)

b. Selected Discography

i) Symphonies

Symphonies Nos. 1–11	BBC NOW, Hickox	Chandos	CHAN 9944(5)

(Chandos set also available separately, Symphonies Nos. 2, 3, 4, 6, 7 & 8 are also available on Lyrita)

ii) Concertos

Piano Concerto	Philharmonia O., Menges; Abram (piano)	EMI	5 74781 2
Violin Concerto	Ulster O., Yuasa; Osostowicz (violin)	Naxos	8.557591

iii) Orchestral

A Tribute	Philharmonia O., Del Mar	Lyrita	SRCD 202
Overture: Resurgam	Philharmonia O., Del Mar	Lyrita	SRCD 202
Festival Overture	NPO, Handley	Lyrita	SRCD 235

Sinfonia Concertante	BBC NOW, Hickox; Shelley (piano)	Chandos	CHAN 9538
Improvisation for Violin & Orchestra	Ulster O., Yuasa; Osostowicz (violin)	Naxos	8.557591
Sinfonietta	City of London Sinfonia, Schönzeler	EMI	5 66936 2

iv) Choral/ Voice with Orchestra

Four Medieval Latin Lyrics	City of London Sinfonia, Schönzeler; Wilson-Johnson (bar)	EMI	5 66936 2
Five Spenser Sonnets	City of London Sinfonia, Schönzeler; Hill (ten)	EMI	5 66936 2

v) Chamber

String Quartet Nos. 1-4	Danté Quartet	Dutton	CDLX 7114/23
Cello Sonata	Doumenge (cello); Dussek (piano)	Dutton	CDLX 7123
Violin Sonata Nos. 1–3	Osostowicz (violin); Dussek (piano)	Dutton	CDLX 7101

vi) Choral

Five Motets	Voces Sacrae, Martin	ASV	CD DCA 1093

Mass in Honour of St. Teresa of Avila	Voces Sacrae, Martin	ASV	CD DCA 1093
Missa in Honorem Sancti Dominici, etc.	Choir of St. John's Coll., Camb., Robinson	Naxos	8.555255

42. Cyril Scott (1879–1970)

When we come to consider Cyril Scott, there is as much to be said about the man as the musician. Although composing was an abiding interest, and one in which he excelled, his interests as a whole were staggeringly wide-ranging, and his beliefs truly esoteric. Nowhere is this more apparent than in the brief bibliographical account left by his son Desmond. Childhood memories of his father are few, because Scott seems to have been a somewhat remote and distracted individual, and Desmond was dispatched to a boarding school from an early age. It was only after Scott's death, when his papers came into his son's possession, that he came to realise what a multi-talented man of many parts his father had been. The following extract from Desmond's memoir paints a vivid portrait of a man of huge vitality. Naturally, his standing as a composer takes pride of place.

> But then there are the books. He published over twenty, not counting two autobiographies, on a variety of subjects ranging from esoteric aspects of music to health matters and from a book on humour to several on Christianity and an occult trinity [sic], *The Initiate* [again, with autobiographical overtones]. He published pamphlets on cider vinegar and black molasses that in 1960 were selling over a thousand copies a week in England alone, and I've been in health food stores all over the world and found booklets sold by people who had no idea he was a composer of music. Going through his correspondence, we found literally hundreds and hundreds of letters from people with health problems ... all of which he dealt with individually ... He was also a poet, published four volumes of poetry and wrote libretti for two of his operas and many of his choral works. He spoke German and French fluently and translated into English the poems of Stefan George and Baudelaire's *Les Fleurs du Mal*... [H]e wrote plays, at least

> ten original scripts, and adaptions of *The Moonstone* and *Barchester Towers* ... As alive to colour as he was to sound, he painted. Using oil pastels, he produced a large number of vibrant landscapes...[260]

As if all this were not enough, he designed his own furniture, and his London home boasted two Burne-Jones-designed stained-glass windows. He was a devoted theosophist and occultist, and a key advocate of alternative medicine long before it became fashionable. He regularly practiced meditation and yoga, and smoked through a hookah. In matters of spirituality, in fact, he had much in common with John Foulds, a fellow theosophist and lover of all things Oriental, and like him believed that his music was channelled through him from beyond. In Scott's case, he believed that this happened with the aid of various "Adepts" belonging to the so-called Great White Brotherhood.[261]

Such was the weird and wonderful life of Cyril Meir Scott, who was born on 27th September 1879 at Oxton on the Wirral. His father, a shipper by trade, was a cultured man who had some scholarly ability in both Greek and Hebrew, while his mother, Mary, was an amateur pianist. His musical talent was recognised from

---

260 Desmond Scott, "Cyril Scott, A Personal Portrait", http://www.bmic.co.uk/cyril_scott.htm. A more extensive personal portrait of Scott by his son can be found in "Memories of the Man I Barely Knew", *The Cyril Scott Companion: Unity in Diversity* (eds. Desmond Scott, Lewis Foreman and Leslie De'ath; Woodbridge, Suffolk: Boydell Press, 2018), pp. 101–11.

261 On Cyril Scott as occultist, see David Tame, "Cyril Scott: 'The Father of British Modern Music'", in *The Secret Power of Music* (Rochester, VT: Destiny Books, 1984), pp. 263–71. The author of this article is clearly enthusiastic about the idea that music can be channelled from higher powers through sufficiently sensitive composers, mentioning the case of Robert Schumann, who was convinced that his music was transmitted to him by angels. Of course, it is one thing to be sympathetic to this kind of view; it is quite another to verify its validity. The fact remains that the music of Scott, Foulds, Schumann and others who entertain such claims, does not sound sufficiently distinctive from that of other composers who do not claim to be influenced by supernatural forces.

an early age, and when he was twelve years old, he was dispatched to Frankfurt-am-Main to study at the Hoch Conservatory with Englebert Humperdinck (1854–1921) for music theory and Lazarro Uzielli (1861–1943) for piano. After his first spell there, he returned some years later, now in his mid-twenties, studying composition with Ivan Knorr (1853–1916) who described his student as "brilliant and revolutionary". His peers included fellow Englishmen Balfour Gardiner, Roger Quilter and Norman O'Neill, with the Australian Percy Grainger, and together they became known as the Frankfurt Gang. He met and befriended the German poet Stefan George (1868–1933) whose poetry he translated into English. In return, George assisted Scott in securing a performance of his First Symphony (1899) when he was still only twenty years old. In 1903 his Piano Quartet (1899) was performed at St. James's Hall with no less a star than Fritz Kreisler as the violinist with himself at the piano. At this stage, Scott certainly seemed to have a stellar career in front of him. He was being feted as an English modernist, and his style at the time looked across the Channel to developments in Europe (Schoenberg, Stravinsky and Debussy[262] have all been mentioned as influences) rather than to those in England. There is little evidence of any interest in folksong during these years, although an orchestral piece based on *Early One Morning* and bearing that title appeared in 1931.

Domestically, Scott seems to have lived an off-beat kind of existence. His first marriage, to Rose Allatini, a novelist whose literature was as revolutionary as his music, lasted from 1921 up until the Second World War, producing two children, including Desmond (see above). Soon afterwards he took up with a clairvoyante, Marjorie Hartson, with whom he remained until his death, although they never married. Perhaps there is a degree of irony in the fact that one of his books, published in 1928, was entitled *The Art of Making a Perfect Husband*.

262 The popular description as "the English Debussy", however, is somewhat misleading.

Scott's twilight years were spent in a rambling house in Eastbourne amidst his exotic treasures. He had contemplated retiring from composition at the age of sixty-five, but was allegedly dissuaded by one of the "Adepts" of the Great White Brotherhood. Had he not obeyed higher authority (as he believed), his Symphony No. 4, the Piano Concerto No. 2, and fifteen or more chamber works would never have seen the light of day. He was still composing just three weeks before his death on New Year's Eve 1970, at the age of ninety-one.

If we include the 170 songs and 107 solo piano pieces, Scott built a catalogue of some four hundred works, including four operas (only one of which has ever been staged); three ballets; four symphonies (only two of which were performed in his lifetime); concertos for piano, violin, cello, harpsichord and oboe; various other orchestral works and a quantity of incidental music; four numbered string quartets, two piano quintets, a clarinet quintet, a sextet for piano & strings, two string trios, three piano trios, four violin sonatas, a viola sonata, and a cello sonata; and among the solo piano pieces, three piano sonatas.

During the 1920s–30s, Scott developed a close professional relationship with the talented Harrison sisters, May and Beatrice, respectively concerto violinist and cellist. He wrote a double concerto for them to play, and they each championed Scott's solo violin/ cello concertos and instrumental pieces. One particularly engaging work, written in 1929 for Beatrice, was *The Melodist and the Nightingales*, for cello and orchestra. The inspiration for this was a series of BBC broadcasts, from around 1924, of Beatrice playing solo cello works in her garden accompanied by the singing of a nightingale in the background. As Lewis Foreman has noted[263], the piece naturally invites comparison with Vaughan Williams's *The Lark Ascending* and the lesser-known work by Robin Milford, *The Darkling Thrush*. There is no actual nightingale's song, as in the BBC

263 Liner notes to Scott's *The Melodist and the Nightingales*, Dutton, CDLX 7326, p. 3

recording from 1924, when Beatrice Harrison often played music by Rimsky-Korsakov, or in the more celebrated third movement of Respighi's *The Pines of Rome*. Instead, the birds are represented in the woodwind, with which the solo cello engages in conversation.

Scott's books reveal an enquiring mind, but were written largely as a means of sharing his personal enthusiasms with a wider public rather than to impart authoritative knowledge. Indeed, his books on alternative medicine could, with hindsight, perhaps be regarded as more of a hindrance than a help. His title *Victory Over Cancer*, written in 1939, was hopelessly premature, as it turned out, and *Simpler and Safer Remedies for Grievous Ills* (1953) might well have had the effect of luring people away from scientifically-proven remedies in favour of quack solutions. Less potentially harmful and more instructive were Scott's two autobiographies, written forty-five years apart – *My Years of Indiscretion* (1924), and *Bone of Contention* (1969). There were, in addition, eight volumes of poetry, all written prior to 1915, apart from the last, which was somewhat enticingly entitled *The Poems of a Playboy* (1943). Stylistically, his verse was far less adventurous than his music. Scott's translations of a selection of the works of Stefan George (1910) were complemented over forty years later in a book, written in German, entitled *Die Tragoedie Stefan George* (1952). No fewer than four of Scott's books were written between 1938–39, and a further four between 1952–53 – periods during which he seems to have eased up on musical composition.

In his day, Scott was admired by musical personalities as diverse as Ivan Knorr, Debussy, Ravel, Stravinsky, Richard Strauss, Eugene Goossens (who labelled him "the father of modern British music"), Edmund Rubbra (who, as noted above, organised a concert of his music in his home town of Northampton when he was just seventeen years old), and Sir Thomas Armstrong, Principal of the RAM, who provided a balanced assessment of his achievement. In his early years, certainly, he seems to have been the great white hope of English music, but, although the twenty-first century has seen something of a revival, at least in the recording studio, he later suffered the fate of so many others – Richard Arnell, Stanley Bate and Havergal Brian, to name but three from the beginning of the alphabet. What were the reasons for such neglect in Scott's case? Some were down to circumstances beyond Scott's control, and others to Scott himself.

The most publishable of Scott's works were the many songs and solo piano miniatures he composed for public consumption. These were readily available to sing and play, and thus were saleable. The pianist Evelyn Suart, who played many of his works, introduced him to the publisher Elkin with whom he thereafter had a lifelong association. They happily published the kind of pieces just mentioned, which brought Scott some welcome revenue, but there was less enthusiasm for publishing his many more substantial works. Even today, where Scott is remembered at all, it is usually for his solo piano piece, *Lotus Land*.

Another factor dictated largely by circumstances is that the modernist approach of Scott's early music, which so intrigued people during the first two decades of the twentieth century, had become passé by the time of the Glock era in the 1950s-60s, when Scott's style was no longer in demand. By then the *avant garde* was in the hands of young guns like Peter Maxwell Davies, Harrison Birtwistle, Alexander Goehr and Colin Matthews.

There are a couple of other factors, however, for which Scott himself was responsible. Although his position as a compulsive creative artist in many forms is unquestionable, he was much less adept at promoting his works. His business was the impulse to create, but, as in the case of Havergal Brian, the fruits of his labours were left to languish. The bulk of his most substantial works went unplayed, and it is only in recent times, thanks to the efforts of recording companies like Chandos and Dutton, that it has been possible to hear and assess them. Ironically, his books, on subjects covering anything from music to constipation (yes – really!), were regularly published, and his pamphlets on alternative medicine sold widely.

There is no doubt that Scott was a multi-talented individual with a huge range of interests, but here again, this seems to have presented a problem for the creation and promotion of his more extensive compositions. He was so busy attending to these other enthusiasms

– writing, painting, the promotion of occultism, and so on – that he must have found it difficult to focus on music without distraction. As we have seen, he did produce a huge amount of music, but one does wonder whether, for him, quantity mattered more than quality. In the period 1900–02, to take a random example, he wrote four orchestral overtures, two orchestral suites, the Symphony No. 2, a piano concerto, a cello concerto, the *Ballad of Fair Helen of Kirkonnel*, for baritone, chorus & orchestra, a string quartet, and various songs – all to be fitted in to his other activities. How much quality control was he able to extend to each of these works, given the time at his disposal? Sadly, not one of his more substantial pieces has stood the test of time in the concert hall. It is a fate which has befallen the majority of overly-prolific composers in the modern era.[264]

Scott became a largely forgotten composer even in his own lifetime, a trend which continued for some thirty years after his death, and still does to some extent, despite the recordings. The huge amount of music he wrote makes it inevitable that the vast majority of it will be consigned to gathering dust on the shelves of academic libraries well beyond the public gaze – and out of sight is out of mind. The recordings, at least, should ensure that his name is not entirely obliterated. Chandos and Dutton seem to have dovetailed their efforts in this regard, the former having focused on the orchestral works (including all four symphonies)[265] and the

264 It would be interesting to know how many of Finnish composer/ conductor Leif Segerstam's 342 (!) symphonies have been performed (there is also the small matter of 30 string quartets, 13 violin concertos, 8 cello concertos, 4 viola concertos and 4 piano concertos). Closer to home, although all of Havergal Brian's thirty-two symphonies have been recorded, it is a rare treat to find one in a concert programme.

265 It may be questioned how far the recording of the First Symphony and the *Three Symphonic Dances* will advance Scott's cause. The first piece was composed in 1899 when he was barely twenty years old, and prior to his second period of study in Frankfurt under Knorr. It is, therefore, very much a prentice work. The same can be said of the Symphony No. 2 which followed hard on its heels (1901–02), and which Scott withdrew after the premiere and revised as *Three Symphonic Dances* (c. 1907), which may indicate that he harboured doubts about its working as a symphony.

latter on the chamber music and solo piano pieces. It is perhaps too early to discover whether or not this will spark a revival of interest in the work of one of the most remarkable and diverse creative minds of the twentieth century.

a. Bibliography

Collins, Sarah, *The Aesthetic Life of Cyril Scott* (Woodbridge, Boydell Press, Suffolk, 2013)

Sampsel, Laurie J., *Cyril Scott: A Bio-Bibliography* (Westport, CT: Greenwood Press, 2000)

Scott, Cyril, *Bone of Contention: The Autobiography of Cyril Scott* (London: HarperCollins, 1969)

Scott, Desmond, Lewis Foreman and Leslie De'Ath, eds., *The Cyril Scott Companion* (Woodbridge, Suffolk: Boydell Press, 2018)

Scott, Desmond, "Memories of the Man I Barely Knew", *Cyril Scott Companion*, pp. 101–11

Tame, David, "Cyril Scott: 'The Father of British Modern Music'", *The Secret Power of Music* (Rochester, VT: Destiny Books, 1984), pp. 263–71.

b. Selected Discography

i) Symphonies

Symphony No. 1	BBC Phil., Brabbins	Chandos	CHAN 10452
Symphony No. 3, "The Muses"	BBC Phil., Brabbins; Huddersfield Choral Society	Chandos	CHAN 10211
Symphony No. 4	BBC Phil., Brabbins	Chandos	CHAN 10376

ii) Concertos

Piano Concerto No. 1	BBC Phil., Brabbins; Shelley (piano)	Chandos	CHAN 10376
Piano Concerto No. 2	BBC Phil., Brabbins; Shelley (piano)	Chandos	CHAN 10211

Harpsichord Concerto	Malta P, Laus (dir. & harps.)	Cameo	CC 9041 CD
Violin Concerto	BBC Phil., Brabbins; Charlier (violin)	Chandos	CHAN 10407
Cello Concerto	BBC Phil., Brabbins Watkins (cello)	Chandos	CHAN 10452
Oboe Concerto	RLPO, Yates; Small (oboe)	Dutton	CDLX 7249

iii) **Orchestral**

Early One Morning	BBC Phil., Brabbins	Chandos	CHAN 10376
The Melodist and the Nightingales	BBC Phil., Yates; Kiseliev (cello)	Dutton	CDLX 7326
Neptune: Poem of the Sea	BBC Phil., Brabbins	Chandos	CHAN 10211
Festival Overture	BBC Phil., Brabbins Sheffield Philharmonic Chorus	Chandos	CHAN 10407
Three Symphonic Dances	BBC Phil., Brabbins	Chandos	CHAN 10407
Aubade	BBC Phil., Brabbins	Chandos	CHAN 10407

iv) **Chamber**

String Quartet No. 1	Archaeus Quartet	Dutton	CDLX 7138
String Quartet No. 2	Archaeus Quartet	Dutton	CDLX 7138

String Quratet No. 4	Archaeus Quartet	Dutton	CDLX 7138
Piano Trio No. 1	Gould Piano Trio	Chandos	CHAN 10575
Piano Trio No. 2	Gould Piano Trio	Chandos	CHAN 10575
Piano Quintet	Bingham String Quartet; Terroni (piano)	Naxos	8.571355
Clarinet Quintet	Gould Piano Trio; Adams (viola); Plane (clar)	Chandos	CHAN 10575

v) **Piano Solo**

Lotus Land	Guinery (piano)	Stone Rec.	
Consolation	Rubbra (piano)	Lyrita	REAM 1134

43. Robert Simpson (1921–97)

Robert Simpson's music is not of the kind that one can have on in the background while attending to something else; it is uncompromising, gritty music that demands to be heard and grappled with. Perhaps that is why Simpson was so keen to promote the music of Havergal Brian, which, in its own distinctive way, has qualities similar to his own. "Honesty" and "integrity" are the two words which spring most readily to mind in respect of Simpson's compositions.

Robert Levick Simpson was born on 2nd March 1921 in Leamington, Warwickshire. On his father's side, medical science ran in the family. One of his forebears, Sir James Young Simpson (1811–70), was a pioneer of anaesthetics. He was himself briefly destined for a medical career until his passion for music prompted a change of course, but his interest in science persisted in his lifelong fascination with astronomy. He was a keen amateur in the field, and was knowledgeable enough to eventually be elected Fellow of the Royal Astronomical Society, a rare honour for an amateur.

Simpson's statutory education took place at Westminster School, and shortly after the end of his studies there the Second World War broke out. He was a highly principled young man, and was a conscientious objector, but he made good use of his medical knowledge by joining the ARP mobile surgical unit and serving through the Blitz, a perilous occupation in itself. During these war years he also availed himself of the opportunity to study with Herbert Howells on an informal basis. Howells suggested that Simpson formalise his studies by enrolling on a BA course, which he did at the University of Durham where he was eventually awarded not only the BA, but, in 1952, a PhD, his chief submission for the latter being his Symphony No. 1. The fact that he always regarded this work as a part of his mature output rather than a prentice piece says a good deal about its quality.

In 1951, at the age of thirty, Simpson joined the music department of the BBC where he became one of its most valued producers, remaining in post for almost thirty years before resigning on a matter of principle. During his tenure at the BBC he was sometimes an outspoken critic of management policy and in the 1970s opposed the plan to create separate networks for different genres. A more justifiable protest, perhaps, was against the BBC's cost-cutting programme which included the axing of almost half the corporation's orchestras. It was on this occasion that Simpson chose to go public with his views, against his contractual obligations. He thereafter resigned (he would probably have been dismissed for breach of contract in any case). During his tenure, however, he was noted as an efficient, effective and visionary producer. One of the beneficiaries of his work was Havergal Brian who at that time was languishing in retirement in a bungalow in Shoreham-by-Sea, writing symphony after symphony without the slightest hope of a public hearing. The extent of Simpson's promotion of Brian's work was incalculable. It was he who encouraged Bryan Fairfax to put on a semi-professional performance of Brian's great *Gothic Symphony* at Westminster Hall, London, in 1961, and he was again one of the leading movers behind the first fully-professional performance of the symphony by the BBC SO, massed choirs and soloists under Adrian Boult in 1966. Boult speaks glowingly of all the administrative work done behind the scenes, much of it undertaken by Simpson, leaving the impression that without him the project could never have been as successful as it proved to be.[266] For example, he took charge of publicity for the event, ensuring that it would attract an audience sufficient to pack the Royal Albert Hall.

Simpson's promotion of Brian did not stop there. In the same year as the *Gothic*'s performance, he also secured performances of the Symphony No. 6 (*Sinfonia Tragica*) and the Symphony No. 10, and in the 1970s several more symphonies were broadcast by the BBC as a result of Simpson's advocacy. He was also a driving force behind the first commercial recording of any of Brian's symphonies – Nos. 10 and 21, played by the Leicestershire Schools Symphony

266 Boult's appreciation is quoted at length by Reginald Nettel, *Havergal Brian: The Man and His Music* (London: Dennis Dobson, 1976), pp. 142–44.

Orchestra, conducted by James Loughran and Eric Pinkett respectively. This was followed by a further LSSO recording of Brian's music, including the *Sinfonia Brevis* (Symphony No. 22), *Psalm 23*, and the *English Suite No. 5*[267], the production of which was again left in Simpson's capable hands.

Simpson had other enthusiasms, notably the music of Haydn, Beethoven, Bruckner and Nielsen. His own symphonies pay conscious homage to the Beethoven cycle, and his String Quartet No. 9 is subtitled *32 Variations and Fugue on a Theme of Haydn*, while his admiration for Nielsen is evident in both his incidental music to the play *Ebbe Skamulsen* and in a scholarly study of the six symphonies[268], for which he received the Carl Nielsen Gold Medal in 1956.

He was twice married, initially to Bessie Fraser in 1946 until her death in 1981, and subsequently to Angela Musgrave, a colleague in the BBC music department, who also happened to be a relative of the Scottish composer Thea Musgrave. Following his resignation from the BBC, they moved to the peace and solitude of Tralee Bay in County Kerry, where he continued to compose, the fruits of which included his three final symphonies (Nos. 9–11), his final four string quartets (Nos. 12–15), and two late string quintets. In 1991 he suffered a debilitating stroke from which he never fully recovered, although he continued to write music as best he could. His final work, the String Quintet No. 2, was completed in 1994, the final coda by dictation to his wife. He died on 21st November 1997 at the age of seventy-six.

Like Shostakovich, the core of Simpson's oeuvre consists of important cycles of symphonies and string quartets. There are also other important chamber works, including two string quintets, a clarinet quintet, a string trio and a violin sonata. More surprisingly,

---

267 The original LP appeared on the Unicorn label (RHS 313) in 1973, and has since been transferred to CD along with the later LSSO recording of Brian's music (Heritage HTGCD 256/57).

268 R. Simpson, *Carl Nielsen: Symphonist* (2nd edn; London: Kahn & Averill, 1979; orig. 1952).

perhaps, for one so committed to the classical orchestra and chamber forces, there is also a small quantity of music for brass band.

Simpson's abiding interest from the outset seems to have been to explore the possibilities of the symphonic form and the string quartet, and to pursue them to their logical conclusion. Although he was always a tonal composer, he explored that tonality in unconventional ways. In particular, there is evidence in some of his symphonies of his working through a conflict between different tonal centres which may or may not be resolved. Another characteristic, which can be detected as far apart as the First and Ninth Symphonies, is the use of a single pulse throughout, and the latter work, at almost fifty minutes duration, is widely considered to be the longest anywhere to maintain the same pulse without change.

Simpson's profound knowledge of earlier composers' symphonies – those of Mozart, Haydn, Bruckner, Beethoven and Nielsen, in particular – feeds into his own. Some of his scherzos, for example, seek to emulate the relentless energy found in Beethoven's scherzos which he believed had been lost by the beginning of the twentieth century. Certainly, there is an insistent, breathless quality to many of Simpson's own examples. He seems to have learned, too, from various contemporaries, including Havergal Brian. The opening of Simpson's Fifth Symphony (1972), for instance, consists of a soft, sustained chord which the composer describes as representing "the part of the mind that quietly watches you, regardless of the sort of experiences you are having" – the very quality which arrested him in a particular passage in Brian's Symphony No. 10, for which he was the record producer at precisely the time that his own Fifth Symphony was being written.

Regarding the chamber music, the fifteen string quartets (the same number as Shostakovich composed) are formally diverse, ranging from single movement works (Nos. 2, 7, 9, 15), through two movement (Nos. 1, 3, 12) and three movement (No. 10) to traditional four movement works. Similarly, the quartets range widely in length, from the fifteen-minute String Quartet No. 2 (1953) to the huge one-movement String Quartet No. 9 (1982), which lasts for almost an hour. The first three form a loose sequence regarding tonality and symmetry, as Simpson acknowledged, and although they were not formally intended as a threesome, they were written in quick succession (1952–54). The next three quartets (Nos. 4–6) are linked in some respects to Beethoven's Rasumovsky Quartets, opus 59, particularly with regard to layout, while Nos. 7 (1977) and 8 (1979) exhibit certain technical similarities. The Quartet No. 9 is a set of variations on a theme of Haydn with concluding fugue, while the following two form a contrasting pair. No. 10 (1983) is subtitled *For Peace* (as already noted, Simpson was a pacifist), while, by contrast, No. 11 (1984), although sharing some of its material with the previous quartet, is much more turbulent and edgy, on the whole. No. 12 (1987) consists of two substantial movements, the first slow and deeply meditative, the second a huge scherzo boiling with relentless energy. In formal terms, No. 13 (1989) is almost an antithesis of No. 12, consisting of four concentrated movements (fast–slow–fast–slow) played without a break and lasting a mere fifteen minutes in total. No. 14, a four-movement work, is characterised by one of Simpson's favourite Beethovenian scherzos, and an Andante which Matthew Taylor has described as "one of the most beautifully transparent quartet slow movements [of the] twentieth century".[269] The final quartet (No. 15, 1991), like most of the others, guides the listener through a range of moods, but the general impression is one of turbulence. Although this was not quite Simpson's last musical thought (the String Quintet No. 2 was to follow), there is something fitting about the way the work melts into silence, as if dissolving into the outer space which so fascinated the composer.

Simpson's music is not the kind that can be appreciated without sustained concentration on the part of the listener. In a recorded talk about his Ninth Symphony[270], he pointed out that it would mean nothing to anyone not prepared to engage with it in a positive

269 M. Taylor, liner notes, *Robert Simpson: String Quartet No. 14*, Hyperion, CDA 66626, p. 3.

270 Recorded on *Simpson: Symphony No. 9*, Hyperion, GAW 21299, track 18.

manner. In the body of his talk, Simpson then provided some pointers towards arriving at an understanding of the work, but they were concerned largely with technical issues involving structure, key relations, and so on. These comments might have been applied equally to any of his symphonies, concertos and chamber works. Simpson's music is hard work for the listener. On the other hand, it is not drily academic; there is an emotional heart to it, too, and it expresses a wide range of moods. Repeated listening is likely to reap rewards not only for the professional musician and the proficient amateur, but for the general listener too.

a. Bibliography

Macauley, Donald, *The Power of Robert Simpson: A Biography* (Bloomington: Xlibris, 2013)

Schaarwächter, Jürgen, *Robert Simpson, Composer: Essays, Interviews, Recollections* (Hildesheim: Georg Olms Verlag, 2013)

b. Selected Discography

i) Symphonies

Symphonies Nos. 1–10 (Boxed set)	RLPO/ RPO/ Bournemouth SO, Handley	Hyperion	
Symphony No. 11	City of London Sinfonia, Taylor	Hyperion	CDA 67500

ii) Chamber

String Quartets Nos. 1–15	Delmé/ Coull/ Vanbrugh Quartets	Hyperion	
String Quintet No. 1	Coull String Quartet	Hyperion	CDA 66503
String Quartet No. 2	Delmé Quartet	Hyperion	CDA 66905
Clarinet Quintet	Delmé Quartet; King (clar.)	Hyperion	CDA 66905
String Trio	Delmé Quartet	Hyperion	CDA 66376

c. Website

The Robert Simpson Society (https://robertsimpson.org.uk)

44. Dame Ethel Smyth (1858–1944)

The name Ethel Smyth most commonly conjures up two images in the minds of those acquainted with it – first, that of her position as a female composer in an age when the general assessment was that women could not compose, and at any rate lacked the masculine qualities required for "serious" composition; and second, her role in actively supporting women's suffrage. In any assessment of the life and work of Ethel Smyth, both factors must inevitably be taken into account, but if they are allowed to dominate, they are apt to skew our understanding of one who, by any standards, was a remarkable person. It is now recognised that we must not allow Victorian prejudices about women and their traditional roles in society to be imported into the twenty-first century in such a way as to jaundice our view of Smyth as a composer. And with regard to the political factor, it should be noted that her involvement with the suffrage movement, although fully committed at the time, lasted only a few years. So, although these factors are of significance, they must be viewed in the context of her life as a whole.

Ethel Mary Smyth was born in Sidcup, Kent, on April 22nd 1858, the fourth of eight children. Her father, John Hall Smyth, was a major general in the Royal Artillery, and the army was in the family blood more generally. As was typical for offspring brought up in prosperous Victorian families, young Ethel was home-educated by various governesses, one of whom instilled in her the music-bug by introducing her to the works of Beethoven. This filled her with the desire to become a composer herself, and her father indulged her fancy by employing the services of Alexander Ewing (1830–95) to teach her the rudiments of composition – harmony and counterpoint. He also introduced her to the operas of Wagner. Of course, the family had no intention of allowing her to take up composition in a professional capacity, but she was a headstrong individual and resisted the pressure exerted on her to take up a more seemly profession, such as that of governess. Finally, her father conceded defeat and allowed her to study music at the conservatory in Leipzig for a year. She considered the teaching standards there to be unsatisfactory, but stayed on in the city to study privately with Heinrich von Herzogenberg (1843–1900) and remained there for the next decade. During that period Smyth probably learned as much from the cultural rewards that Leipzig had to offer as from her formal music studies. It was there that she met some of the leading composers of the day, including Brahms, Dvorak, Tchaikovsky, and Clara Schumann.

Despite her formidable temperament, Smyth had the knack of forming deep relationships with both men and women. Her first love was Elisabeth von Herzongenberg (1847–92), her mentor's wife. It was through her good offices that she later met another influential personality, Henry Brewster (1850–1908), Elisabeth's brother-in-law, who lived with his family in Florence. The relationship became a close, probably passionate one, and Smyth began wintering with him in Florence (another important cultural city). The liaison caused a souring of relations between herself and Elisabeth.

As to her recognition as a composer, Smyth was fortunate to be living on the continent at just the right moment. She wrote first in the more modest forms – songs and chamber music genres which tended to be favoured in the drawing rooms of influential people, and when she did turn her attention to the orchestra, at the instigation of Tchaikovsky, she managed to garner the patronage of continental conductors such as Bruno Walter. Thus, by the time she attracted the attention of the more conservative musical establishment in Britain, her earlier compositions had already gained a foothold in the repertoire, and it was on this basis that her late-flowering celebrity was established. In celebration of her seventy-fifth birthday, Thomas Beecham organised a festival which was concluded by a concert at the Royal Albert Hall with royalty in attendance. Even in those comparatively more enlightened times, this was a remarkable achievement for a female composer.

Smyth's first orchestral venture occurred in 1890 with the substantial four-movement *Serenade in D* which was performed at a Crystal Palace concert under Augustus Manns and was well-received. Although it bears the stamp of the composer's Teutonic training and is clearly Brahmsian in conception, her handling of the orchestra is remarkably confident for a first effort, and the success of the work spurred her on to produce other large-scale works. Her first opera (of six), *Fantasio*, was premiered in 1898 (although this time to mixed reviews), followed in 1902 by *De Wald* which enjoyed performances not only at Covent Garden, but at the Metropolitan Opera in New York. Her third opera, *The Wreckers,* was a collaboration between Smyth and her friend Henry Brewster who provided a French libretto. However, as the work was premiered in Leipzig in 1906, a German translation was provided. The plot, set on the rugged Cornish coast, tells the story of criminal gangs or smugglers of the eighteenth century who plunder ships by luring them onto the rocks. The opera became one of Smyth's best-known works, and was regarded by some at the time as one of the best English operas since the days of Purcell.[271] Although the work has been recorded in full[272], it tends to be remembered today only for its lively overture.

A further substantial work from these early decades of Smyth's career was her *Mass in D,* of 1889–91. Lasting an hour in performance, it is scored for chorus, soloists and orchestra, and was conceived as a concert work rather than a sacred piece, although it sets the Mass in ordinary and reflects Smyth's engagement with the Anglican Church. Although the music is very much of its time, there are some stirring moments, particularly in the Gloria, and Smyth's connections on the continent ironically ensured its reception in England at the highest level. Having composed much of it while she was a guest of Princess Eugenie in Monaco, the latter was impressed enough to arrange a taster (in piano reduction) of the piece to be played before Queen Victoria at Balmoral, and it was through her good offices and those of Alfred, the then Duke of Edinburgh, that the premiere of the complete work was arranged to be performed

271 An accolade later awarded to Britten's *Peter Grimes.*

272 *Ethel Smyth: The Wreckers,* Conifer, CFCD 250/51.

in the Royal Albert Hall in 1893. A second performance had to wait until 1924 when Adrian Boult with the Birmingham Festival Choral Society did the honours, and it was included in Thomas Beecham's seventy-fifth birthday tribute to the composer in 1934.

In the first decade of the twentieth century, Smyth reverted principally to the genres with which she had begun her career – songs and chamber music – but, ever a woman of principle, for two or three years at the beginning of the Georgian era she became a prime mover for the suffragist cause, forming a close relationship with Emmeline Pankhurst, founder of the Women's Social and Political Union (WSPO). She even wrote an anthem, *March of the Women*, which became the movement's clarion call. Members of the WSPO began targeting the homes of anti-suffragist politicians, and among the ensuing arrests for criminal damage was that of Ethel Smyth who was sentenced to two months internment in Holloway Prison. According to Thomas Beecham, who visited her there, he found the suffragettes marching around the quadrangle singing Smyth's anthem, with the composer conducting with a toothbrush from the window of her cell.

Smyth's last substantial composition to be completed before the outbreak of the First World War was the first of her light operas, *The Boatswain's Mate* (1914). The war itself, however, brought an abrupt end to this stage of her development, and, as it turned out, to the greater part of her career as a composer (in 1914 she was already fifty-six years old). She trained as a radiographer and volunteered for work at a military hospital in Vichy. Musical performances were not exactly a priority in the public consciousness at the period, but Smyth was doubly unfortunate in that much of her success to date had been in Germany, and now the opportunities for performances there, or even under German conductors like August Manns in Britain, were severely curtailed, as was the publication of her works by German publishing houses. Further, she began to experience a progressive loss of hearing which would eventually result in a state of profound deafness that would prevent effective composition and make the conducting of her own works impossible. With the few productive years she had left to her, she composed two further light operas and other choral and symphonic works.

Her final major composition, dating from 1930, was her choral symphony, *The Prison*, to a text by her old friend, the late Henry Brewster. The text takes the form of a Platonic-style dialogue on the nature of immortality, and the prisoner is really the soul. The two aspects of man are represented by a baritone and a soprano respectively, while the "immortal ones" or "voices" are represented by the chorus.[273]

Although *The Prison* may form a fitting end to her composing career, it was not the end of Smyth's creative output. Unable to compose any longer owing to her deafness, she turned instead to the written word, in which capacity she met and befriended the novelist Virginia Woolf, although the intensity of the relationship appears to have been all on Smyth's side, for Woolf described it as "like being caught by a giant crab". Her own books (there were ten of them) included some autobiographical material, and since she had travelled widely, these no doubt made for interesting reading.[274]

Comment has often been passed on the vigour and masculinity of Smyth's music, but, given her character, perhaps this is hardly surprising. She was no shrinking violet, as we have seen, and her leisure interests included horse riding, golf and (in her younger days) tennis. One can easily imagine her being one of the first women to wear bloomers! Her passion for golf is reflected in the fact that after her death at the age of eighty-six, on 8th May 1944, and subsequent cremation, her ashes were scattered, at her own request, on land adjacent to Woking Golf Club, where she had been a member.

As a composer, Smyth enjoyed greater acclaim, even in conservative Britain, than any female composer before her time, and very largely since. She received a DBE in 1922 in recognition

273 Happily, this long-forgotten work has now been recorded by Chandos (CHSA 5279).

274 This is still available today, both in full (over 500 pages) as *Impressions That Remained: Memoirs of Ethel Smyth* (Brousson Press, 1919), and abridged as *The Memoirs of Ethel Smyth* (London: Faber & Faber, 1987).

of her work, despite (or because of?) her active support for the suffrage movement, and was awarded honorary doctorates from the universities of Oxford and Durham. Her example, however, does not seem to have set a precedent for official and public recognition of female composers in more recent times, as some of the cases noted in this book have shown.

a. Bibliography

St. John, Christopher, V. Sackville-West, et al., *Ethel Smyth: A Biography* (London: Longmans, Green & Co., 1959)
Crichton, R., ed., *The Memoirs of Ethel Smyth* (London: Faber & Faber, 1987)

b. Selected Discography

i) Orchestral

Overture: The Wreckers	BBC SO, Oramo	Chandos	CHSA 5240
Serenade	BBC Phil., Martinez	Chandos	CHAN 9449
Concerto for Violin, Horn & Orchestra	BBC Phil., Martinez; Langdon (violin); Watkins (horn)	Chandos	CHAN 9449

ii) Choral with Orchestra

Mass	BBC SO & Chorus; Huddersfield Choral Society; Soloists; Martinez	Chandos	CHSA 5240
The Prison	Experiential Orchestra & Chorus; Brailey (sop); Burton (bass-bar); Blachly	Chandos	CHSA 5279

iii) Opera

The Wreckers	BBC Phil., Huddersfield Choral Society; soloists; Martinez	Conifer	CDCF 250/1
The Boatswain's Mate	Lontano Ensemble; soloists; Martinez	Retrospect	RO 001

iv) Chamber

Cello Sonata	Handy (cello); Hughes (piano)	Lyrita	SRCD 383

c. Website

Dame Ethel Smyth Website (https://www.ethelsmyth.org)

45. Sir Arthur Somervell (1863–1937)

Today, Arthur Somervell tends to be remembered only for his song-cycles *Maud* (1898) and *A Shropshire Lad* (1904), but in fact he composed in a wide range of genres. Apart from further song-cycles (*James Lee's Wife, A Broken Arc, Love in Springtime*), there were individual songs, operettas, orchestral works including a symphony, concertos, choral music including a mass, and a quantity of chamber music – not bad, given that much of his professional life was given to administrative duties associated with his position (from 1901) as Inspector of Music at the Board of Education.

Somervell was born of well-to-do parents in Windermere on 5th June 1863. The Somervells were an influential family locally. Arthur's father was the founder of the well-known shoe manufacturer, K Shoes, and a JP, while a brother, Colin, became High Sheriff of Westmorland in 1916, followed by others in the Somervell family. Given Arthur's musical proclivities, his education was pretty much par for the course – public school (Uppingham), followed by Cambridge (King's College), a couple of years at the Musikhochschule in Berlin (1883–85), and a finishing period at the RCM (1885–87), where one of his teachers was Sir Hubert Parry. In 1903 he was awarded a PhD in music from Cambridge University, having been taught there by Stanford. With a grounding as thorough as this, the music world was his oyster, but he chose to devote his professional life to the musical education of others[275], fitting in his composing as and when he was able. Despite his heavy workload, however, works of quality flowed steadily from his pen – from his *Six Songs of Robert Burns* (1885–86) to the Violin Concerto (1930).

Somervell was as much a pioneer in composition as he was in music education. Although by today's assessment his style was

275 Somervell's work as a music educator is documented in Gordon Cox, et al, eds., *Sir Arthur Somervell on Music Education: His Writings, Speeches and Letters* (Classic Texts on Music Education; Woodbridge, Suffolk: Boydell Press, 2003).

conservative and redolent of Brahms and Mendelssohn, he was one of the first – probably *the* first – in Britain to introduce the concept of the song cycle as a distinct genre. Creating a song-cycle requires much more than simply collecting a number of songs on the same or similar themes under one title, even if the texts are provided by a single poet. A song-cycle should tell a story, or at least display a thematic unity in the texts, underscoring it with a commensurate thematic unity in the music. A good example of the latter is George Butterworth's song-cycle *Love Blows as the Wind Blows,* for baritone and string quartet. The unity of the cycle is established by a six-note motif played at the outset and reappearing in three out of the four songs in one way or another. All the texts are taken from W.E. Henley's volume *Echoes,* and treat different aspects of love, but in Butterworth's piece they are carefully arranged to provide a kind of temporal journey. The first song, *In the year that's come and gone,* speaks of the constancy of love and looks forward to a new year of continued devotion. *Life in her creaking shoes* recognises the mystery of love: it "blows as the wind blows", and is certainly not all plain-sailing. The exquisitely intimate *Fill a glass with golden wine* seems to stop the clock in a moment of pure ecstasy where nothing, not even death, matters, except that moment. In reality, however, time does not stand still, and the final song, *On the way to Kew,* introduces a note of nostalgia: love may pass away, as all things do, but at least there remains gratitude for the experience itself, and perhaps the hope that it can be experienced again ("Not in vain, not in vain, shall I look for you again").

Now, in Somervell's major song-cycle *Maud,* thematic unity is maintained largely by strict adherence to the textual sequence of Tennyson's mawkish melodrama in which the protagonist, having suffered the suicide of his father owing to financial ruin, and unable to be matched with the daughter of his closest friend, falls in love with her anyway. Maud's brother learns of the tryst and breaks in to prevent it, but is killed in a dual with Maud's lover. He flees into exile, and Maud dies in his absence, after which he seeks his fate in military service. Somervell condenses the story into thirteen songs. It became one of his most popular works, probably because Tennyson himself was the pre-eminent poet of the Victorian age, and a story like that of Maud had a direct appeal to the populace of that time. Somervell was faithful to the story, and the fluency of his writing was in complete harmony with the nature of the text.

Equally as popular was Somervell's song-cycle *A Shropshire Lad*. It was published in 1902 when, once again, the composer seemed to catch the mood of the hour. Sales of Housman's famous poem collection, published in 1896, only eight years prior to the song-cycle, had been sluggish, but were beginning to pick up by the turn of the century, and by 1916 its popularity among the British Tommies on the Western Front was probably second only to that of the Bible. As far as can be ascertained, Somerville's song-cycle was the first full setting of Housman's verse, and he seems to have started a trend, with a host of others – Berkeley, Butterworth, Gurney, Ireland, Moeran, C.W. Orr, Vaughan Williams, and many others following suit, even down to the present day.[276] Housman always gave permission for his poems to be set, arguing that it was his road to immortality, although he did take issue with Vaughan Williams's decision to omit two verses from *Is my team ploughing?*

As in *Maud*, Somervell largely (but not entirely) follows the sequence as set out by Housman whose poems trace the story of a young man, an idealised *Shropshire Lad*, who first rejoices in the ecstasy of spring with its intimations of love (Poem I), but by the time he is one-and-twenty (Poem XIII) has already learned something of love's bittersweetness. By the time we reach *Bredon Hill* (Poem XXI), the tragedy of love is all too evident, not least, perhaps, because his fiancé had died giving birth to his child. In order to mask his grief, the protagonist contemplates leaving his beloved Shropshire and enlisting in the army (poems XXII, XXXV). In the meantime, at least he can drown his sorrows in drink (Poem XLIX).

276 For example, Michael Csányi-Wills, *Six A.E. Housman Songs* [2009–13], Toccata, TOCC 0329. Three of the songs are for baritone, and three for tenor, with orchestral accompaniment. This is a substantial work, lasting some forty minutes in performance.

Up to this point, Somervell has followed Housman's sequence, but now he reverts to the earlier Poem XL, *Into my heart an air that kills*, in which the "blue remembered hills" of Shropshire are far off. In order to effect the appropriate mood, the composer reintroduces the melody of the initial song (Poem I), as if the protagonist is looking back longingly to his ecstatic beginnings. The final song, *The lads in their hundreds* (Poem XXIII), is again out of sequence, but here the poem seems to foreshadow the ultimate fate of one who will "die in his glory and never be old". In this cycle everything seems to click and, like *Maud*, it was immediately taken up by Harry Plunket Greene, one of the foremost baritones of the day.

Two further song-cycles by Somervell draw on the poetry of Robert Browning (1812–89). *James Lee's Wife* (1907), written first with orchestral accompaniment, was later provided with an alternative piano quintet version, possibly with an eye to facilitating more performances. As in the case of *Maud*, the five poems that Somervell chooses to set retain Browning's original order, but the narrative impact is less obvious. The work as a whole is more of a meditation on the vagaries of love – the kind of bittersweetness, perhaps, that attracted the composer to Housman's poems – than on the unfolding story in linear terms.

Somervell's final cycle, *The Broken Arc* (1923), on the other hand, is more in the style of *Maud*. Here, however, texts are taken from various Browning poems rather than from a single work. Nevertheless, a narrative of sorts does emerge. A man falls in love, the idyllic nature of which is outlined in the first four songs (taken primarily from Browning's *Dramatic Lyrics*). In the fifth song, the woman proves false, preferring the love of her fiancé's best friend. In the sixth song the two friends quarrel, ending in a duel in which the friend is killed. Looking down on the lifeless body, the protagonist expresses remorse for the deed: "I would we were boys as of old, in field, by the fold". In the penultimate song he resolves to face the future alone, and further tragedy is avoided as the final item, *The year's at the spring*, envisages a fresh start. This verse includes the most celebrated of all Browning's lines: "God's in his heaven – all's right with the world".

Although Somervell is best-known today as an art-song composer, he was much more. His four-movement symphony *Thalassa* (1913) is an impressive work, notable for the composer's skilful handling of the orchestra and its attractive melodic content. It is, in effect, Somervell's "sea symphony", as the Greek title makes plain, and the second movement, *Elegy*, reflects on the tragic death of Robert Falcon Scott and his colleagues on their trek back from the South Pole in 1912. It may have been this event that inspired the symphony as a whole. On the other hand, Somervell cannot have been oblivious to the success in 1910 of Vaughan Williams's *Sea Symphony* and may possibly have wanted to emulate him. Comparison of the two works – if that is legitimate – shows Vaughan Williams to have been the more adventurous and forward-looking. The ghost of Brahms, perhaps, still underlies *Thalassa*, but it is nevertheless a worthy achievement.[277] Among the other works were a Violin Concerto (1930);[278] five operettas, including *Thomas the Rhymer*, the subject on which Vaughan Williams left an unfinished opera at his death; further orchestral pieces, including *Helen of Kirconnel* and a suite, *Arcady*; various pieces for chorus and orchestra, including a setting of Tennyson's *The Charge of the Light Brigade*; a clarinet quintet; and various solo piano works. There was also a *Mass in D minor*. Sadly, most of this output has suffered terminal neglect.

Although some modern listeners may consider Somervell's music a product of it time, we should remember that at the turn of the last century it would have been regarded as rather up to date. Occasionally he chose poets from a more distant past for his song settings – Shakespeare, Philip Sidney, and Blake, for instance – but his three favourites, Browning, Tennyson and Housman, were broadly contemporary, with Somervell outliving the last-named by

277 This work was recorded some years ago by Campion for its five-volume British Composers Premiere Collection series (CC 9034 CD), which was more recently re-released as a full package by Lyrita (REAM.2139). The symphony can also be accessed on YouTube.

278 Recorded on Hyperion CDA 67420.

just a year. Thus, he kept himself fully up to date with his reading, and was not beyond setting his own verse, as in his song of 1904, *When spring returns* – an effort which, although not quite out of the top drawer in poetic terms, exceeds some of the verse that Elgar chose to set.

a. Bibliography

Cox, Gordon, et al, eds., *Sir Arthur Somervell on Music Education: His Writings, Speeches and Letters*, Classic Texts on Music Education (Woodbridge, Suffolk: Boydell Press, 2003)

b. Selected Discography

i) Orchestral

Symphony in D minor, "Thalassa"	Malta PO, Laus	Lyrita	REAM.2139
Violin Concerto	BBC Scottish SO, Marwood; Brabbins	Hyperion	CDA 67420

ii) Song Cycles

A Shropshire Lad	Wilson-Johnson (bar); Owen Norris (piano)	Helios	CDH 55089
Maud	Wilson-Johnson (bar); Owen Norris (piano)	Helios	CDH 55089
James Lee's Wife	Wyn-Rogers (mezz-sop); Duke Quartet	Naxos	8.557113
Songs of Innocence	Wyn-Rogers (mezz-sop); Johnson (piano)	Naxos	8.557113

46. Bernard Stevens (1916–83)

One of England's more underrated composers was Bernard Stevens. Although the centenary of his birth fell on 2nd March 2016, little seems to have been organised by way of celebration, other than his appearance as BBC Radio 3's Composer of the Week in July of that year. He appears to have been consigned to a footnote in English musical history, yet his works are finely-crafted and always marked by integrity.

Born in London, he studied music at Cambridge University under E.J. Dent and Cyril Rootham, furthering his studies at the RCM with R.O. Morris and Gordon Jacob. He thus received a thorough grounding in counterpoint and orchestration from some of the best minds in the business. Leaving the RCM in 1940, Stevens entered war service with the army, but still found time to compose a violin sonata, his first opus-numbered work, on the basis of which the concert violinist Max Rostal commissioned a violin concerto (1943).

At the end of the war, the *Daily Express* newspaper sponsored a competition for a "Victory Symphony" to celebrate the cessation of hostilities, which Stevens won with his *Symphony of Liberation* (1946). Naturally, the celebratory mood is paramount, but symphonic form is not neglected, and Stevens's ability to apply relentless logic to the process of composition, imbibed to some extent from Schoenberg, has been one of his fortes. The symphony enjoyed a high-profile performance at the Royal Albert Hall, but this did not lead immediately to further exposure, the reasons for which were probably political. A committed communist (he was a party member until he resigned in response to the Soviet reaction to the Hungarian uprising of 1956), he incurred the suspicions of the establishment, musical and otherwise, and like other composers with similar left-wing views – notably Alan Bush – performances of his music were discouraged. Bush himself was a close friend, as was the poet Randall Swingler (some of whose work was set by Stevens) and the librettist Montagu Slater, who also shared his socialist views.

Despite Stevens's political proclivities, however, he was appointed Professor of Composition at the RCM in 1948, a post he held for thirty-three years. From 1967 he combined this role with a professorship at the University of London. Thus, a whole generation of aspiring composers passed through his hands, including such celebrated names as Michael Finnissy (b. 1946). He retired from teaching in 1981, and died at Colchester on 6th January 1983 at the age of sixty-six.

Teaching and administration took up much of Stevens's time, so his output is not huge, extending to some fifty opus numbers, but he did compose steadily over a period of forty years, and his meticulous technique, along with his penchant for self-criticism, meant that every work he produced was worthwhile. Unlike many composers who subject their works to revision once they have heard them in performance, Stevens's careful approach to the composition process meant that in his case this was largely unnecessary. The one obvious exception is the Piano Concerto, written in 1955, but extensively revised in 1981, and here the revision did not do the work any favours. The original was an uncompromising, demanding work which was never taken up, and the revision, which weakens the original conception, was done with a view to making a performance more likely, but still Stevens never heard one. Fortunately, a recording of the original version was released on the Marco Polo label in 1993[279], ten years after the composer's death, with the pianist Martin Roscoe and the National Symphony Orchestra of Ireland conducted by Adrian Leaper.

Beginning with the Violin Concerto, Stevens began to develop a distinctive application of Schoenberg's serialist technique in which he maintained a tonal approach as opposed to the atonalism of Schoenberg and his devotees. It was developed further in key works of the sixties, notably the String Quartet No. 2 (1962), the Symphony No. 2 (1964) and the *Variations* for orchestra (1964). All

279 Marco Polo, 8.223480. Other works on the same disc include the *Dance Suite* (op. 28) and the orchestral *Variations* (op. 36).

these works are stylistically distinct from *A Symphony of Liberation* of almost twenty years earlier.

Although, as noted, Stevens's output was limited, he tried his hand at all the main genres – opera, symphonies, concertos, orchestral, choral, chamber, solo organ, solo piano, film music and art-song. Apart from the two concertos already mentioned, there was a Cello Concerto (1952), and among the orchestral works was the *Fugal Overture* (1947), the *Sinfonietta* for string orchestra (1948), and the overture *East and West* (1950). Among his small body of chamber works, the String Quartet No. 2 is generally acknowledged to be the most significant, although there was also a string trio (*Lyric Suite*) (1958), a piano trio (1942) and a horn trio (1966).

Stevens's earliest surviving *a capella* choral work was his *Mass* for double choir (1938–39). At first blush this may seem a strange choice for a composer with Marxist sympathies, and although it was found among his papers after his death, as if, perhaps, he never intended it for performance, the fact remains that he did preserve it, suggesting that some spiritual sense inspired him to proceed with the work at the time. Like Vaughan Williams, Howells, and many other composers who could best be described as agnostic, he seems to have found no incongruity in the idea of agnostics writing religious music. In fact, the *Mass* is untypical of Stevens's personal style. It conforms perfectly well with what is expected in Christian musical tradition, and sits comfortably alongside the masses of other English composers of the twentieth century – in addition to those just mentioned, Leighton, Rubbra and Berkeley.[280] Stevens's interest in religious tradition as a whole is maintained in later works such as *Et Resurrexit* (1969), a cantata for soloists, choir and orchestra, in which the book of Ecclesiastes is mined for part of the text. The spiritual dimension is found more broadly in two works based on the writings of Rabindranath Tagore (1861–1941), the

280 Stevens's *Mass* complements Howells's *Mass in the Dorian Mode* perfectly well on the Chandos recording of the two works (CHAN 9021).

great Indian sage: *Thanksgiving* (1965), a motet for mixed choir and string orchestra; and *Hymn to Light* (1970), an anthem for choir, organ, brass and percussion.

Several settings draw on the work of Stevens's close friend, the poet Randall Swingler (1909–67), including *Ex Resurrexit*; the cantata *Harvest of Peace* (1952), for speaker, soprano, baritone, choir and string orchestra; *The Turning World* (1971), a motet for baritone, choir and orchestra; and *The True Dark* (1974), a song-cycle for baritone and piano.

Between 1947–48, Stevens made a brief foray into the world of film-music, although none of the films – *The Upturned Glass* (1947), *The Mark of Cain* (1947), and *Once a Jolly Swagman* (1948) – are particularly remembered today. From what can still be recovered of the music (the films can be accessed on YouTube), it was just what the doctor ordered for the kind of films being made in Britain at that time. In *The Mark of Cain,* he shows he can turn out a lush, romantic tune, while in *Once a Jolly Swagman,* he captures all the excitement of the speedway.

Among Stevens's varied output is a single one-act opera, *The Shadow of the Glen* (1978–79), in fact the penultimate work of his career. He had attempted a full-length opera, *Mimosa,* back in 1950, with Montagu Slater as the librettist, but this was never completed. At around forty-five minutes in performance, *The Shadow of the Glen* is ideal as one half of a double bill. The libretto is an abridged version of J.M. Synge's play of the same name, and is very much in line with the earlier one-act operas of Vaughan Williams (*Riders to the Sea*) and Holst (especially *The Wandering Scholar*)[281] in which

281 The Vaughan Williams connection lies in the choice of playwright, J.M. Synge (1871–1909). In effect, Vaughan Williams simply sets *Riders to the Sea* to music, as Stevens does in *The Shadow of the Glen*. The story-line of the latter, however, is much closer to that of Holst's *The Wandering Scholar* (1929–30). Holst's libretto was by Clifford Bax, brother of Arnold, which in turn was based on one of Helen Waddell's *Wandering Scholar* tales (*Le Pauvre Clerc*), set in a thirteenth-century farmhouse. Stevens would no doubt have been aware of these earlier examples of the genre.

resources are pared to the bone, using a chamber-sized orchestra, and just the essential characters.

In Stevens's opera, as in Holst's, there are just four – a young wife, Nora (mezzo-soprano), her much older husband, Dan (baritone), a passing tramp (bass), and a young herdsman, Michael Dara (tenor). At the start of the action the tramp arrives at Nora's lonely cottage on a stormy night, seeking food and shelter. As she opens the door, he looks in to find her husband apparently dead, and a cake and whiskey prepared for the wake. However, Nora must venture out through the storm to seek help from the local sheep herder, Michael Dara, and while she is absent, husband Dan rises from his sheet, giving the tramp a start. It transpires that he had been feigning death in order to try his young wife's fidelity by listening to how she speaks of him to others. As she returns with Michael, Dan reverts to being dead. He hears all that is going on, including the sheep herder's marriage proposal to Nora. As she prevaricates, Dan rises with a loud sneeze, catches her in what he takes to be her infidelity, and evicts her with immediate effect. When she leaves, however, it is with the tramp, who extols the virtues of the open road (shades of *Hugh the Drover*). Although Dan had been intending to beat Michael with a stick, he relents, throws the stick into a corner, and embarks with his "rival" on a drinking session, now on the friendliest of terms. The opera has never been fully-staged (there has been a semi-staged performance), but it was recorded by the BBC for a studio performance shortly before the composer's death and aired a few months later. It is that performance that is available on CD[282], along with the work that immediately preceded it in Stevens's catalogue, the song-cycle *The True Dark*, written in memory of Randall Swingler whose poems provide the text.

The True Dark is taken from a long poem entitled *The Map*, which is essentially a meditation on "the loss of old religious and intellectual certainties, and the alternative consolation offered by the

282 *The Shadow of the Glen*, Albany, TROY 418.

vastness of the cosmos now opened up to human minds".[283] Stevens sets ten sections of the poem which are meant to take their place as part of a genuine cycle; in other words, they would not make much sense if sung independently. An invocation to *Comet Silence* and an *Envoi* in which the same heavenly body appears, envelop the remaining songs, except for a brief coda.

Other than the aforementioned thorough revision of his earlier Piano Concerto, the two works just discussed were the last he completed. His slow production rate over this period was probably due not only to his professional commitments, but to the onset of the cancer that eventually killed him. These pieces are, however, monuments to the work of a meticulously careful composer who valued quality over quantity, and whose hold on the repertoire is unjustifiably precarious. His revival in the concert hall is long overdue, but judging by the lack of any widespread response to his centenary in 2016, it is a vain hope.

283 Malcolm MacDonald, liner notes, Albany, TROY 418, p. 2.

a. Bibliography

Bush, Alan and Bertha Stevens, *Bernard Stevens and His Music: A Symposium* (London: Kahn & Averill, 2006)

Stevens, Catherine, "Memories of Bernard Stevens, My Dad", *British Music*, 38/2 (2016)

b. Selected Discography

i) Symphonies

Symphony No. 1, "Symphony of Liberation"	BBC Philharmonic, Downes	Meridian	CDE 84124
Symphony No. 2	BBC Philharmonic, Downes	Meridian	CDE 84174

ii) Concertos

Piano Concerto	National SO of Ireland, Roscoe (piano); Leaper	Marco Polo	8.223480
Violin Concerto	BBC Philharmonic, Kovacic (violin); Downes	Meridian	CDE 84174
Cello Concerto	BBC Philharmonic, Baillie (cello); Downes	Meridian	CDE 84124

iii) Orchestral

Dance Suite	National SO of Ireland, Leaper	Marco Polo	8.223480

Orchestral Variations	National SO of Ireland, Leaper	Marco Polo	8.223480
Sinfonietta	Boyd Neel Orchestra, Neel	Lyrita	REAM.1117

iv) Opera

Shadow of the Glen	Divertimenti O., soloists, Williams	Albany	TROY 418

v) Choral

Mass for Double Choir	Finzi Singers, Spicer	Chandos	CHAN 9021

vi) Chamber

String Quartet No. 2	Delmé String Quartet	Albany	TROY 455
Theme & Variations	Delmé String Quartet	Albany	TROY 455
Lyric Suite	Delmé String Quartet	Albany	TROY 455
Violin Sonata	Academy of St. Martin-in-the-Fields Chamber Ensemble	Albany	TROY 572
Piano Trio	Academy of St. Martin-in-the-Fields Chamber Ensemble	Albany	TROY 572
Horn Trio	Academy of St. Martin-in-the-Fields Chamber Ensemble	Albany	TROY 572

47. Sir John Tavener (1944–2013)

At the funeral of Princess Diana on 6th September 1997, the coffin was borne into Westminster Abbey to the strains of John Tavener's *Song for Athene.* To the majority of those present, or watching on television, it was a first hearing, and many had never heard of the composer. Afterwards, record sales of the piece soared and Tavener became a household name. Yet, as the title implies, *Song for Athene* had not originally been intended for this event, but for the daughter of a family friend who had been killed in a road accident a few years earlier. Tavener had been approached for a piece especially for Princess Di's funeral, but felt that the existing work was more appropriate than anything else.

This was not the first time that Tavener's music had caused a stir. He had made a splash in 1968 with the premiere of his cantata *The Whale* (1965–66) which sounded unlike anything that had been written up to that time. In this instance, however, the impact was felt chiefly by the concert-going public – it caused a sensation when it was aired at the Proms – and once the novelty had worn off, the tsunami abated, and classical buffs were able to settle back to their traditional fayre. Meanwhile, Tavener continued to compose, now out of the spotlight. There were to be other popular successes – notably *The Protecting Veil* – but much of his music is not generally well-known, especially the more extensive pieces with their demands for stamina on the part of the listener.

John Kenneth Tavener was born in Wembley, London, on 28th January 1944, to reasonably affluent parents with an interest in music. His father ran the family building firm, but also served as organist at St. Andrew's Presbyterian Church in Hampstead. His son's early musical memories were recordings of Handel's *Samson* and Humperdinck's *Hansel and Gretel.* Two pieces which he heard at the age of twelve, however, made a lasting impression on him: Mozart's *Magic Flute,* which he heard live at Glyndebourne, and Stravinsky's *Canticum Sacrum.* Of the first piece, he was later to say that its true greatness lay in the fact that it could be universally understood, and not only by a musical elite. The latter work possessed a spiritual quality which first instilled in Taverner the desire to be a composer.

At the age of thirteen he won a music scholarship to Highgate School. Although music was supposed to be part of a balanced curriculum, as soon as his talent was recognised, he was excused most lessons in order to devote himself to music and was allowed full access to facilities including organ and piano. Fellow music students included John Rutter and the concert pianist Howard Shelley. It was at Highgate that he began to compose in earnest, producing a work for piano and trombone which he dedicated to his headmaster who was a trombone player. Although his mind was set on composition, he became proficient enough on the piano to perform concert works, including Shostakovich's Piano Concerto No. 2 with the National Youth Orchestra. At the same time, still only seventeen years of age, he became organist and choirmaster of St. John's Church, Kensington. A year later, he entered the RAM where Sir Lennox Berkeley was one of his teachers.

As already noted, Tavener's breakthrough work as a composer was his cantata *The Whale*. By his own admission, it was the work of an angry young man – angry because the world did not see things the way he did, and in particular because the music of the day did not satisfy him, and left him feeling cold. He eschewed what he described as the po-faced serialism emanating from Darmstadt and Manchester, but, with a desultory waft of his hand, also dismissed three centuries of the Western musical tradition. Among the very few exceptions he allowed were some of Webern's later pieces and some Stravinsky. Later, he was to find succour in the musical traditions of the Russian Orthodox Church.

Perhaps this ultra-dismissive attitude, however, is apt to tell us more about Tavener himself than about the state of Western musical tradition. Some of his comments seem to suggest that he fancied himself as the one fixed point at the centre of a revolving musical universe, a position which did not endear him to everyone. Still, it is true that *The Whale* is a striking piece. It is a kind of symbolic re-telling of the biblical story of Jonah, in which colour is brought to the fore by means of the unusual forces used, including not only the standard orchestra, soloists and chorus expected of a cantata, but two organs (one a Hammond), a wide range of percussion, including football rattle and whip, and pre-recorded electronics. At one point, in the section entitled *In the Belly*, the vocal performers are instructed to "clap, neigh, grunt, snort, yawn, make vomiting noises, whisper, cough, shuffle, hum and talk to each other" ad lib. The work begins with a narrator reading, in the best Oxford English, an encyclopaedia entry about the whale. After a couple of minutes, the music enters softly, as if from the depths, increasing in volume until, at the point at which it is about to drown out the reader, there is a sudden pause. What follows then is an eclectic mix of styles, including jazz and pop elements, while still retaining the character of a classical work, including serialist features. No doubt it appalled many traditionalists, but with the younger, anti-establishment generation who were looking to break free, it struck a chord.

The wider dissemination of the piece, following its initial live performances, arrived somewhat fortuitously. Tavener's brother, Roger, had begun to take an important role in the family building firm, and at the time was undertaking work at the home of Beatles drummer Ringo Starr in Highgate. He took the opportunity to pass on some tapes of *The Whale* which Ringo played and found impressive. Another of the Beatles, John Lennon, was called in for a second opinion, the upshot being that John Tavener was offered a contract with the Beatles' recording company, Apple, to record the piece. Others followed, the most substantial being *Celtic Requiem* (1969) for chamber ensemble, choir, children's choir and vocal soloists.

Although the subject matter of *Celtic Requiem* is distinctive, the work shares with *The Whale* the same unusual orchestration (whip, dinner gongs, Aeolian bagpipes, electric and bass guitars, and organ), and an eclectic mix of texts (Requiem Mass, Henry Vaughan, Cardinal Newman, and children's chants and singing games). Not everyone felt comfortable with such a heady mix. The critic Ates Orga opined: "Profusion of styles is no substitute for artistic integrity".[284]

The most substantial work of 1972, and of Tavener's entire oeuvre up to that time, was *Ultimos Ritos* (Last Rites) which had germinated through two earlier works, *Nomine Jesu* and *Copas* (both 1970). Dripping with religious symbolism, its architecture was based on a five-movement arrangement in which the central "Jesus" movement is surrounded by the others in a kind of cruciform shape. Even the instruments are given symbolic significance (trumpets = royalty; flutes = love, for instance). As the title implies, the work is a meditation on death and death's significance. Tavener harboured an obsession with death throughout his career, which seems to have been informed by personal circumstances. As early as 1980, aged only thirty-six, he suffered a stroke, and in his forties two heart attacks which were eventually traced to a congenital condition called Marfan's syndrome. Typically, for Tavener, he considered death as a kind of muse.[285] However, *Ultimos Ritos* also presages other interests which were to blossom in later works such as *The Veil of the Temple* (2003) and *Lament for Jerusalem* (2004) in which the monumentalism, religious eclecticism, and multi-lingual settings of the earlier piece reach their zenith.

1974 was the year of Tavener's disastrous marriage to a young Greek dancer, Victoria Maragopoulou. His father, Kenneth, spent a good deal of time and money buying and fitting out a house for the newlyweds, which happened to be fairly close to the Tavener family home. But Tavener had an abnormally close relationship with his mother (shades of Paul Morel and his mother in Lawrence's *Sons and Lovers*), and after the wedding celebrations, instead of retiring with his wife to the new abode, he went home to his parents, leaving

---

284 Quoted in Piers Dudgeon, *Lifting the Veil: The Biography of John Tavener* (London: Portrait, 2003), p. 49.

285 But then, so was the Russian Orthodox rite, and a bevy of women ranging from his mentor Mother Thekla to Mia Farrow who was at the time in transit between Frank Sinatra and Andre Previn, to the Icelandic pop singer Björk.

the wedding gifts unopened in the new house, since he could not make the transition between mother and wife. Little wonder, then, that just eight short months after the wedding, the marriage was effectively over.

The next milestone in Tavener's life was his well-publicised admission to the Russian Orthodox Church. The word "conversion" would be misplaced here, because this was not a Damascus experience of the heart, but a rational decision in the interests of his art. Tavener's continued extravagant – and sometimes dubious – behaviour suggests that he felt no sense of moral obligation. Lennox Berkeley, himself a member of the Roman Catholic Church, urged Tavener to join him, but he refused to do so on the grounds that Catholicism was rooted in the negative, condemning mankind as essentially sinful, with no hope of salvation other than through divine grace alone, whereas Orthodoxy began with the affirmation that mankind was essentially good, but flawed by his own wilfulness. So, in 1977, Tavener joined the Russian Orthodox Church as one might join a political party. He even bent the ear of Metropolitan Anthony of Zorazh, the head of the Orthodox Church in the West. But despite this, he soon found that he had much to learn. One of his first works for the Orthodox Church was the *Liturgy of John Chrysostom* (1977), but it was not well-received because it neglected the tone systems of traditional Orthodox music. Only when he incorporated these into his works for the Church were they considered acceptable for the liturgy. Tavener's rather exalted claim that his music was the sound of God, since God was essentially dictating the notes, also raised eyebrows, especially as the suggestion was based on a theologically dubious interpretation of Paul's famous statement, "It is no longer I who live, but Christ lives in me" (Gal. 2: 20). Although claims of divine inspiration are common among composers, the obvious question to ask would be how anyone could distinguish between a work that had been divinely inspired or dictated, from one that had not. Inspiration may not be a figment of the imagination, but persuasive explanations are more likely to be found in the natural world than in the ether.

What we do know of Tavener is that he was constantly in need of muses of various kinds in order to produce his finest work, be they persons, concepts, objects or institutions. One of the most potent and long-serving was Mother Thekla, a Russian Orthodox nun who operated from a monastery on the edge of the North Yorkshire Moors. She met the composer after he had rung her to ask her permission to set a particular text that had been published by the monastery. From their first meeting in 1981 they became friends, and for the next twenty years he sought her advice on anything from choices of text to the intricacies of Orthodox musical tradition. One of their most substantial collaborations was the opera *Mary of Egypt* (1986–91), for which Mother Thekla produced most of the libretto. On this, she required the patience of Job, as Tavener rejected draft after draft until, on the fifth attempt, she insisted it would be her last. She also had a considerable hand in the production of another substantial work, *Resurrection* (1988–89), and at one point was alternating between this and the opera.[286]

From 1980 onwards, Tavener began producing his popular shorter pieces for unaccompanied choir: *Funeral Ikos* (1981), *Love Bade me Welcome* (1985), *Two Hymns to the Mother of God* (1985), *The Lamb* (1985), *God is with Us* (1987), and *The Tyger* (1987). Although written a couple of years apart, *The Lamb* and *The Tyger* are often paired in performance because they are thematically linked. Both take their texts from William Blake (1757–1827). The former was written for the third birthday of Tavener's nephew, and was completed in fifteen minutes.

In 1985, Tavener suffered a devastating blow when his mother, Muriel, died. Yet, unlike Herbert Howells, who fell musically silent for almost two years following the death of his son, Tavener was composing again within a few weeks. He seems to have dealt with this tragedy, in part at least, by writing *Eis Thanaton* (To

286 An insightful chapter on Mother Thekla's contribution to Tavener's works at this time can be found in Dudgeon, *Lifting the Veil*, pp. 172–92.

Death), a setting of a lengthy poem by the Greek poet Andreas Kalvos (1792–1869) in which a son visits his mother's grave to pray for her soul and receives assurance that she is at peace with God. Tavener divides his instrumental forces into two groups set spacially apart, one (including timpani, bass trombones and lower strings) to represent the son, and the other (violins and violas) the mother.

The composition of *Eis Thanaton* certainly helped him to work through his bereavement, and at much the same time he was further helped when he met a young Cambridge University student, Maryanna Shaefer, who was to become yet another muse and eventually (a decade later) his wife. Her practical and organisational skills seem to have been superior to those of his first wife, and his second marriage was to endure.

By the late eighties, Tavener was drawing away from the compositional techniques used in mainstream Western secular music with its harmony, counterpoint and key relations. The new Eastern-influenced style was immediately evident not only in choral works such as the *Ikon of St. Cuthbert of Lindisfarne* and the *Akathist of Thanksgiving* (1986–87), but also in instrumental ones, notably *The Protecting Veil* for cello and orchestra (1987). All Tavener's works now were imbued with religious significance.[287] Mother Thekla had more than a hand in both these pieces. Her translation of the Russian text of Archbishop Gregory Petrov, who died in a Siberian labour camp in the 1940s underlie the *Akathist*, while her voluminous understanding of Orthodox religious imagery and symbolism inform *The Protecting Veil*. The latter became an instant hit, topping the classical record charts as soon as it was issued on CD. Today, there are at least ten recordings of that work.

Another substantial Russian Orthodox-influenced work, written in 1990 as a commission for the 900th anniversary of

287 "In everything I do, I aspire to the sacred ... music is a form of prayer, a mystery"; cited by Andrew Burn in *Tavener: we shall see Him as He is*, liner notes, Chandos, CHAN 9128, p. 3

Chester Cathedral is *We Shall See Him as He Is*, for massed choirs, soprano and tenor soloists, and orchestra. Despite the hour-long duration of the piece, its structure is clear and easy to follow. It consists of eleven "ikons" interspersed with a refrain for cellos which becomes richer with each repetition. Mother Thekla provided the text and advised Tavener on the appropriate symbolism. The text is based on the ministry of Jesus as presented in John's Gospel, but is pared down to an absolute minimum. Ikon III, for instance, which concerns the turning of water into wine (John 2: 1–11), is reduced to:

> I saw:
> The marriage feast.
> They wanted wine.
> Six water-pots of stone.
> Water to wine.
> The good wine at the end.

The term "ikon" (or icon) is musically significant for Tavener.[288] The term normally refers to the picture-images of Jesus, Mary or the saints, found in Russian and Greek Orthodox churches, often on a large screen called the *iconostasis* (the place where icons stand). The use of the word by the composer, as in the work under discussion, signifies his attempt to recreate the spiritual effect which an icon is meant to exert on the viewer in terms of music – the musical equivalent of what is normally seen.

We Shall See Him as He Is may not have become one of Tavener's best-known works, but it probably constitutes the most accessible introduction to the Orthodox-inspired works that dominated his output during the 1980s–90s.

This period of Tavener's life was blighted by both mental and physical illness. He suffered badly from depression, underwent an

288 It appears, for example, in the titles of *Funeral Ikos* (1981) and *Ikon of Light* (1984).

operation for a possibly malignant cyst on his jaw, and was diagnosed with Marfan's syndrome, for which a tricky heart operation was necessary. He was very much indebted to his wife Maryanna for nursing him through these crises, and considered that without her he may not have survived.

1991 saw the completion of Tavener's five-act opera *Mary of Egypt*, a highly stylised work which explores the parallel paths to salvation for Mary, a notorious prostitute, and Zossima, a novice monk whose way is barred by a lack of humility. The only other soloist required is a soprano to sing the part of the disembodied voice of the Mother of God. Otherwise, there is a chorus and a body of cathedral choristers, along with a chamber-sized ensemble which includes the usual exotic instruments, including handbells and a simantron – a long wooden plank struck by a mallet as a means of calling Greek Orthodox monks to prayer. Various instruments have symbolic significance, the flute representing Mary and the trombone Zossima. The ever-obliging Mother Thekla provided the stylised libretto, which she had to rewrite four times before the composer was satisfied. Much of the music revolves around a so-called eternity note in F which is sustained in the form of a drone (perhaps somewhat akin to the "om" sound of divinity in Hinduism). *Mary of Egypt*, which runs for just short of two hours, does not have the immediate appeal of shorter works like *The Lamb* or *Song for Athene*, and one really needs to be in sympathy with the Orthodox mindset in order to appreciate it to the full. However, if nothing else, it did provide Tavener with another of his muses, the Indian-born soprano Patricia Rozario, who sang the demanding role of Mary. She proved ideal for the part because, being Indian, she could effortlessly sing the microtones which the piece required at times. From this point, Tavener offered first refusal to Rozario for all future soprano roles.

Another major work which confirmed Tavener's drift towards monumentalism was *Fall and Resurrection* (not to be confused with *Resurrection* [1989]) which was recorded by Chandos on the occasion of its premiere on 4th January 2000.[289] All the ingredients of the earlier large-scale pieces are present, including the symbolic architecture (it was intended for performance in a large religious space such as a cathedral), the exotic instruments, including the *kaval* (a kind of ney flute), shofar (ram's horn), and Tibetan temple bowls, and the characteristic spare libretto provided by Mother Thekla.

Tavener received advice from some unexpected quarters, including that of HRH, the Prince of Wales, who took a personal interest in the project and, in some odd way, made it his own. It was he who urged Tavener to push the thematic matter back beyond the Fall itself (the story in Genesis 2–3) to the primordial chaos of the universe. HRH had spoken; he was bound to obey! Meanwhile, it had been Mother Thekla's idea to push the matter *forward* to the event of Christ's resurrection, rather than focusing chiefly on Eden and the Fall as he had intended. His original conception had thus largely been taken out of his hands. At least Prince Charles's involvement reaped rewards for Tavener personally. The two men became close friends, and after writing a short piece for the Prince's fiftieth birthday entitled *Many Years*, his name was included among the knighthoods on the Millennium Honours list.

A shorter piece of this period, which became something of an icon in itself, was *Prayer of the Heart* (1999), a multi-lingual setting of the so-called Jesus Prayer, "Lord Jesus, have mercy on me". Apart from English, the other languages used are Greek and Coptic, representing the Orthodox and Coptic Churches. He wrote the piece for the Icelandic pop-star Björk, being attracted to the untrained, primordial quality of her voice. The accompaniment was for string quartet, with a taped heartbeat serving as a kind of ostinato throughout. The work has a hypnotic, mantra-like quality.

289 Tavener, *Fall and Resurrection*, Chandos, CHAN 9800. The forces used at the premiere included soprano soloist (Patricia Rozario), counter-tenor (Michael Chance), psaltis (Martyn Hill), bass (Stephen Richardson), the BBC Singers, St. Paul's Cathedral Choir, City of London Sinfonia, with Richard Hickox conducting. The venue was St. Paul's Cathedral.

Although, at the end of the twentieth century, Tavener was still committed to the Orthodox tradition, both personally and musically, there were signs, even in works like *Fall and Resurrection,* that he was contemplating an expansion of his spiritual alliances, a tendency that had already been spotted by the perceptive Mother Thekla. The *Ikon of Eros* (2000), for violin, orchestra and chorus, included a setting of Hindu Vedic texts which used the rhythmic language of Samavedic music, and was the firstfruits of this new direction taken by Tavener. At the same time, he became infatuated with the work of a Swiss Sufi poet called Frithjof Schuon (1907–98) whose eclectic philosophy led to the suggestion that all religious traditions are attempts to express universal divine truth in different ways. All religions lead to God. Tavener even claimed to have had visionary encounters of Schuon, who had died a few years previously. In short, even as Mother Thekla was fading from the scene, he was acquiring a new muse.

What Tavener was inexorably working towards was a completely universalist spirituality in which all religions are ultimately subsumed under the grandeur of God. This view, which represents Tavener's final position on God and the universe, finds ultimate expression in the mammoth seven-hour long All Night Vigil, *The Veil of the Temple.* The veil itself represents that which separates one faith or denomination from another – Judaism from Christianity, Christianity from Islam, Shia from Sufi, and so on. From this perspective, Mother Thekla represented what Tavener had outgrown, namely denominational division. His guides now were the various Sufi teachers like Jalaluddin Rumi and Frithjof Schuon who were open to the universalist approach, and the rending of the veil, as in the Gospel accounts (Mark 15: 38), represents a uniting of what was formerly separate. Tavener drives home this message by blending the world's various religious traditions through the media of his texts and music. For example, at the point at which the veil of the Temple is torn, Mary Magdalene, in the Gospels one of Jesus's most devoted disciples, sings, *in Sanskrit,* "Maya Atma" – reality, illusion – to signify that this event denotes the triumph of one over the other in the revelation that God is one, and in all things. The illusion lies in human division.

In order to achieve this great universalist vision, Tavener divides his work into eight cycles, each successive cycle being lifted an octave higher than its predecessor, on which it builds thematically. The music begins in the depths, as if out of the primordial chaos, then grows inexorably in dynamic force to reach a great climax in the final cycle, which also contains completely fresh thematic material, as if to suggest that the old order has vanished and the new has begun.

In our increasingly materialistic world, where science is king, many will regard Tavener's universalist creed as pretentious nonsense with little practical meaning; but it is precisely his spiritual eclecticism which has inspired music that even the composer's detractors admit to being impressive. Tavener was well-aware that a seven-hour long work was unlikely to attract many performances, if only because of the logistical problems involved in mounting them, so he prepared a much-abridged version which retained the general architecture of the piece, but reduced performance length to around two-and-a-half hours, a version which has been recorded.[290]

Another work, *Lament for Jerusalem*, written at much the same time, has much in common with *The Veil*. It is structurally similar, being cast in seven cycles, each with a "stanza" followed by a "cosmic lament", and the subject matter, which is concerned with unity out of division, is also similar. However, although it lasts almost an hour in performance, which is lengthy by ordinary standards, it is only a seventh of the length of *The Veil*, and the forces required are comparatively modest: soprano and counter-tenor, a small choir, and a chamber-sized orchestra, devoid of exotic instruments. The texts are largely biblical, taken from Psalm 137 ("By the waters of Babylon") sung in English, and Matthew 23: 37–39 (Jesus's lament over Jerusalem) sung in Greek; but there are contributions, too, from the Sufi mystic, Rumi, whose words are given to the counter-tenor, and these offer a way out of the pit of desolation, although it is one

290 RCA Red Seal, 82876661542.

that demands the initiative of the individual: "Love desires that this secret should be revealed ... For if a mirror does not reflect, how is that? ... Dost thou not know why the mirror does not reflect? ... Because the dust is not cleared from its face".

Tavener continued to explore other religions in musical terms in works such as *The Beautiful Names*, a setting of the traditional ninety-nine names of Allah. He had gone as far as he could in exploring the possibilities of Orthodox music, but, despite Mother Thekla's distaste for his eclecticism, he maintained to the end of his life that he had never abandoned the Orthodox faith, but had simply broken away from the musical traditions which he felt had, in the end, exerted a constricting influence on his freedom of development in musical terms.

In December 2007, Tavener suffered a major heart attack which left him comatose for some time and required urgent surgery. On being restored to consciousness, he found that the fervour of his faith had diminished and that his desire to compose had deserted him for the first time in his life. Little by way of productivity emerged over the next three years, although his forty-five minute *Requiem*, written to commission for the City of Liverpool's tenure as the European Capital of Culture for 2008, was an obvious exception. In a sense, this work carried forward the objectives of *The Veil* and *Lament*, and used a heady mix of texts, including the Roman Catholic Mass, the Bible, the Qu'ran, the Upanishads, and various Hindu sages and Sufi mystics. These are set partly in translation, and partly in the original languages – Latin, Greek, Hebrew, Arabic and Sanskrit.

On the whole, however, the works of Tavener's final years, when he continued to be dogged by ill-health, were succinct, austere compositions, "stripped of all superfluous ornament and excess".[291] Typical of this late flowering of his art is *Missa Wellensis*, composed to a commission from Wells Cathedral for a setting of the Latin Mass. Written for unaccompanied double choir, it was to be one of his last substantial works.

291 Andrew Stewart, liner notes, *John Tavener: Missa Wellensis*, Signum, SIGCD 442, p. 3.

For much of his professional life, Tavener had been a globe-trotter, and in particular had fallen under the spell of Greece with its ancient Classical culture and philosophy. He eventually established a *pied a terre* on the island of Aegina where, at one time, he spent several months each year. In 2000, however, he exchanged this lifestyle for life in the quiet rural setting of Child Okeham in Dorset where he spent his remaining years. He died at his home on 12th November 2013, aged sixty-nine. Tributes rained in, including one from his old friend Prince Charles.

As a personality, Tavener was a mass of contradictions. In religious terms he was totally ambivalent. Brought up in the Presbyterian tradition, he eventually joined (conversion would be the wrong word) the Russian Orthodox Church and steeped himself in its traditions, but later seemed to favour an eclectic approach which embraced Sufi mysticism and Hinduism – a kind of pantheism, all told. He had a passion for the divine and the spiritual, even believing himself to be writing God's music, yet on the earthly plane was at times a heavy drinker with a passion for classic cars, owning a Rolls Royce Silver Shadow, a Jaguar XJ6, and a Bentley Mulsanne Turbo, among others. Ultimate love, for him was the divine Eros, yet in earthly terms he seems to have experienced difficulty in distinguishing between love and lust.

Musically, he continued to maintain his mistrust of the Western tradition from Bach onwards, but many of his own compositions, although searingly beautiful, clearly draw on the very tradition he sought to disown. On the personal level, he maintained that in order to find one's true self, one needed to abandon the ego, a theme which is explored in his major work of 1972, *Ultimos Ritos*, and considered that the ego proved to be an impediment in the later works of Stravinsky. Yet Tavener himself seems to have been a somewhat narcissistic character, cultivating an image of himself as supreme artist in his manner of dress and bohemian lifestyle which was sharply at odds which the Orthodox tradition to which he claimed allegiance. He was certainly not beyond using others for the sake of his precious art. Mother Thekla, for example, collaborated with him on several important works, yet he was prepared to break with her when his evolving art demanded it. Indeed, his relationship with those around him, and even with certain concepts, such as death, was dictated largely by whether or not they could serve as a muse for the advancement of his work.

a. Bibliography

Dudgeon, Piers, *Lifting the Veil: The Biography of Sir John Tavener* (London: Portrait, 2003)

Haydon, Geoffrey, *John Tavener: Glimpses of Paradise* (Phoenix, 1998)

Tavener, John, *The Music of Silence: A Composer's Testament* (London: Faber & Faber, 1999)

b. Selected Discography

i) Orchestral

Eternal Memory	RLPO, Petrenko; Knight (cello) Gould (violin)	EMI	2 35134 2
Song for Athene	LPO, Litton; Benedetti (violin)	Deutsche Grammaphon	476619-8
The Repentant Thief	LSO, Tilson Thomas; Marriner (clar)	RCA	88697217612

ii) Choral with Orchestra

The Whale	London Sinf. & Chorus, Liddell (speaker); Reynolds (mezz-sop); Herincx (bar); Atherton	Apple	CD SAPCOR 15
Celtic Requiem	London Sinf. & Chorus, soloists; Atherton	Apple	CDP 0777 781258

We Shall See Him as He Is	BBC Welsh SO; Britten Singers; Chester Festival Chorus; soloists; Hickox	Chandos	CHAN 9128
Fall & Resurrection	City of London Sinf.; BBC Singers; St. Paul's Cathedral Choir; soloists; Hickox	Chandos	CHAN 9800
Eis Thanaton	City of London Sinf.; Rozario (sop) Richardson (bass); Hickox,	Chandos	CHAN 9440
Requiem	RLPO & Choir; soloists; Petrenko	EMI	2 35134 2
Mary of Egypt	Aldeburgh Festival Ensemble; Britten-Pears Chamber Choir; Choristers of Ely Cathedral; Rozario (Mary), Varcoe (Zossima); Friend	Regis	RRC 2026
Lament for Jerusalem	Choir of London & Orchestra; Jones (sop), Crawford (counterten); Summerley	Naxos	8.557826
The Veil of the Temple	ECO, Holst Singers, Choir of the Temple Church; Rozario (sop); Layton	RCA	

Eternity's Sunrise	Choir & Orchestra of the Academy of Ancient Music; Rozario (sop); Goodwin	Harmonia	HMU 907231
Funeral Canticle	Choir & Orchestra of the Academy Of Ancient Music; Mosley (bar); Goodwin	Harmonia	HMU 907231

iii) **Choral**

Ex Maria Virgine	Choir of Clare Coll., Camb., Brown	Naxos	8.572168
Birthday Sleep	Choir of Clare Coll., Camb., Brown	Naxos	8.572168
Song for Athene, etc.	Choir of St. John's Coll., Camb., Robinson	Naxos	8.555256

iv) **Solo Vocal**

To a Child Dancing in The Wind	Rozario (sop); instrumentalists	Collins	14282
A Mini Song Cycle for Gina	Rozario (sop); instrumentalists	Collins	14282
Akhmatova Songs	Rozario (sop); Vanbrugh Quartet	Hyperion	CDA 67217

v) **Chamber**

Diódia	Vanbrugh Quartet	Hyperion	CDA 67217
Towards Silence	Medici, Finzi, Cavaleri Quartets	Signum	SIGCD 221

48. Ian Venables (b. 1955)

Ian Venables may not be a household name, but he has been hailed as one of the most significant English composers of art-song since Finzi. The lyrical and harmonic qualities of his music, the sensitivity of his settings, and his undoubtedly deep knowledge and love of the wide range of literature from which he chooses his texts, make him a worthy contributor to a tradition stretching back to the Elizabethans, and including, since the onset of the English musical renaissance, such exalted names as Bridge, Butterworth, Finzi, Gurney, Ireland and Warlock. Although the piano is often regarded as the bread-and-butter instrument for art-song accompaniment, Venables has clearly learned from Vaughan Williams in his exploration of other instrumental possibilities. His song-cycles *Invite to Eternity* and *Song of the Severn*, for example, make use of the string quartet, while *On the Wings of Love* and the solo song *Acton Burnell* provide a role for clarinet and viola respectively.

Ian Venables was born in Liverpool in 1955 and was educated at the Collegiate Grammar School there. Although he was a budding musician from an early age, he seems to have been in no hurry to consolidate his interest on a formal basis. He spent three years at Liverpool University (1974–77), graduating with a BA degree, not in music, but in social science, and spent a further period at his local teacher training college studying for his PGCE. He began his teaching career in 1978 as an economics teacher at the Royal Russell School in Croydon, concurrently studying composition with Richard Arnell at Trinity College of Music. In 1983 he moved to Sherbourne School in Dorset, and then, in 1986, on to the Royal Grammar School in Worcester, taking the opportunity to study with Andrew Downes, and later with John Joubert, at the nearby Royal Birmingham Conservatoire. He continues to live in Worcester, and is inspired artistically by the surrounding countryside, especially Severn side and the Malverns.

To date, Venables has composed some eighty individual songs (many in the form of song-cycles), mainly, but not solely, for male voice, and there is little doubt that this is his chief métier. However, he has produced a quantity of chamber music, including an impressive piano quintet and an equally fine string quartet, as well as shorter pieces for violin or cello and piano, and several early solo piano works, his first opus-numbered piece being the ambitious *Sonata (1975): In Memoriam D.S.C.H.* (the musical initials of Shostakovich, who had died earlier in the year). In addition, there are a few choral works with organ accompaniment, including a substantial forty-minute *Requiem* (2020), and an organ *Rhapsody* (1996). Venables has not so far been greatly attracted by the orchestra. He did, however, join forces with Philip Lancaster in preparing performing versions of Gurney's two surviving orchestral works, *War Elegy* and *A Gloucestershire Rhapsody* which, in their original chaotic state, had been unplayable, but which, thanks to the painstaking efforts of Lancaster and Venables, have now been recorded.[292]

Venables' love of Ivor Gurney's poetry is evident from his chairmanship of the Ivor Gurney Society, and his song-cycle *The Pine Boughs Past Music*, written for the Gloucester Music Society's eightieth anniversary celebrations in 2010, which includes settings of three Gurney poems – *Songs on Lonely Roads*, *Soft Rain*, and *The Wind* – with Leonard Clark's *In Memoriam: Ivor Gurney* as an epilogue. Further song-cycles include *Invite to Eternity*, setting the poetry of John Clare (1793–1864), and *Love's Voice*, setting John Addington Symonds (1840–93) on whom Venables is an acknowledged authority. There are settings, too, of a wide range of other English poets – Ernest Dowson, John Drinkwater, Robert Graves, A.E. Housman, John Masefield, Harold Monro, Wilfred Owen, Isaac Rosenberg, Siegfried Sassoon, Geoffrey Scott, and Alfred Lord Tennyson. Others, from further afield, include the Greek poet Constantine Cavafy, the Spaniard Federico García, and the Americans Edna St. Vincent Millay and Theodore Roethke.

292 *War Elegy* on Dutton, CDLX 7172, and *A Gloucestershire Rhapsody* on Chandos, CHAN 10939.

The Piano Quintet and String Quartet are impressive accomplishments which demonstrate that Venables has more than one string to his bow. The first of these was itself first conceived as a string quartet before the piano was deemed a necessary addition. In fact, the piano does not enter until two minutes into the piece. When it does, it initiates a simple, uplifting and memorable theme which dominates the remainder of the movement. The second movement, the emotional heart of the work, takes the form of a deeply-felt elegy, somewhat redolent of Finzi in similar vein, and probably influenced by the recent death of Venables' mother. An intense passage for piano solo leads to a lightening of mood, even more Finzian in nature, before the return of the elegiac feeling. The finale begins with a good-natured romp reminiscent of Malcolm Arnold at his most extrovert, before some later reference back to the earlier movements leads to a serene coda.

Venables' desire to compose a string quartet must still have been there, because he began work on one soon after finishing the quintet. The moods treated in this work are, if anything, more starkly diverse than in its companion piece. It opens with a gritty, uncompromising passage set against a strident, staccato rhythm in the cello, but soon this leads to a much more expansive, lyrical theme with suggestions of Howellsian rapture in its soaring, melodic lines. The more strident music, by contrast, demonstrates that Venables is more than capable of deploying dissonance for dramatic effect. The brief central movement lightens the mood, providing a kind of sorbet to cleanse the ear prior to the extensive finale, the emotional heart of the work. The moods here range from intense passionate feeling to the blustery optimism with which the work concludes.

At a little over fifty opus-numbered works to date, it cannot be said that Venables is a particularly prolific composer, and he has never yet been tempted by the larger canvas; but neither of these observations makes him any less of a composer. Indeed, the opposite may well be true, for it is all too easy to write too much and in so doing compromise on quality. Venables pays meticulous attention to detail in every work, and his sensitivity to the words he sets is perhaps more finely tuned than that of any other art-song composer since Finzi. Still only sixty-five years of age (as at 2020), it is to be hoped that the fires of his creative imagination will remain alight for many years to come.

a. Select Discography

i) Chamber

Piano Quintet	Coull Quartet; Bebbington (piano)	Somm	SOMMCD 0101
String Quartet	Danté Quartet	Signum	SIGCD 204
Three Pieces for Violin & Piano	Coull (violin); Lloyd (piano)	Somm	SOMMCD 0101
Elegy for Cello & Piano	Roberts (cello); Lloyd (piano)	Somm	SOMMCD 0101

ii) Piano Solo

The Stourhead Follies	Lloyd (piano)	Naxos	8.573156
Sonata: In Memoriam D.S.C.H.	Lloyd (piano)	Naxos	8.573156
Impromptu: The Nightingale & the Rose	Lloyd (piano)	Naxos	8.573156

iii) Song Cycles

Invite to Eternity	Kennedy (ten); Danté Quartet	Signum	SIGCD 204
Love's Voice	McLean-Mair (ten); Lloyd (piano)	Enigma	ED10045
On the Wings of Love	Kennedy (ten); Horsford (clar); Burnside (piano)	Naxos	8.572514
The Pine Boughs Past Music	Williams (bar); Lloyd (piano)	Signum	SIGCD 424

The Song of the Severn	Williams (bar); Carducci String Quartet; Lloyd (piano)	Signum	SIGCD 424
Through These Pale, Cold Days	Clayton (ten); Schmidt-Martin (viola); Lloyd (piano)	Signum	SIGCD 617

iv) **Solo Songs**

Flying Crooked	Williams (bar); Carducci String Qt.	Signum	SIGCD 424
A Kiss	Williams (bar); Carducci String Qt.	Signum	SIGCD 424
The Night has a Thousand Eyes	Williams (bar); Carducci String Qt.	Signum	SIGCD 424
Midnight Lamentation	Kennedy (ten); Burnside (piano)	Naxos	8.572514
At Malvern	Kennedy (ten); Burnside (piano)	Naxos	8.572514
At Midnight	McLean-Mair (ten); Lloyd (piano)	Enigma	ED 10045
Love Lives Beyond the Tomb	Bevan (sop); Lloyd (piano)	Signum	SIGCD 617

49. Peter Warlock (Philip Heseltine) (1894–1930)

Not many people can boast of having been born in London's exclusive Savoy Hotel, but Philip Heseltine can. It is just one strange fact among many about a man who was a mass of contradictions. Even his name excites comment. He was christened Philip Arnold Heseltine, but in adult life he came to refer to himself as Peter Warlock. The reason for the alias is not absolutely clear. In the main it seems to have been adopted as a result of his desire to separate Peter Warlock the composer from Philip Heseltine the acerbic music critic and scholar. The underlying motive may have been a perfectly common sense one. As just mentioned, his dismissive attitude towards fellow music critics – Ernest Newman, Winthrop Rogers and Edwin Evans, especially – made him their *béte noire*, and he seems to have thought it expedient to compose under an alias in order to avoid critical assaults on his own compositions. He also found that attempts to publish his work were more successful when he submitted it under a pseudonym.

But why "Peter Warlock"? The word "warlock" refers to a male witch, particularly one with malevolent intent. It derives from the Old English *wærloga*, meaning "scoundrel" or "monster", and if we cannot venture as far as the latter, Heseltine's behaviour could certainly extend to the scandalous. Again, "warlock" is associated with the dark arts – of being in league with the devil, and Heseltine had a macabre side to him, dabbling in the occult and witchcraft, and sometimes dressing the part. So perhaps the name Warlock was well-chosen. As he turned out to be a manic-depressive character, with two sharply contrasting sides to his nature, it seems natural that he should operate under two different names, even if these tended to correspond to his working practices more than to his manic psyche. *Having explained all this, my own procedure from hereon will be to adopt the assumed name throughout, which is the one by which he is generally recognised. At times, it is difficult to separate man from music, and it would be tiresome to be switching names at such frequent intervals.*

Peter Warlock was born on 30th October 1894. The family's financial circumstances can be guessed from the fact that, as noted above, his parents were using rooms at the Savoy as their personal London residence. His father, Arnold Heseltine, was a well-respected solicitor, and his wife Edith was the daughter of a Welsh doctor. Soon after Warlock's birth, his parents moved to more permanent lodgings in fashionable Chelsea, but, when he was only two years old, his father died suddenly, aged only forty-five. In 1903, Edith remarried, her new husband being Walter Buckley Jones who owned the imposing Cefn Bryntalch estate near Montgomery. Although retaining the Chelsea residence as a town house, they moved to Jones's estate, but for the moment young Warlock had little time to enjoy its spaciousness, for he was dispatched to prep school in Broadstairs. He seems to have done well academically in his five-year spell there, carrying off a number of prizes. In 1908, now aged thirteen, he was sent to Eton where he grew to abhor the colonial traditionalism, military-style training and systemic bullying. However, the inevitable piano lessons were continuing apace, and in Edward Mason (1878–1915) and Colin Taylor (1881–1973), he found teachers of music who took a general interest in his development and introduced him to new musical trends which were a far cry from the stodgy Victorian hymns served up in chapel. It was here, with the full encouragement of Mason and Taylor, that the young Warlock discovered the music of Delius.

His infatuation with Delius's music developed over a few years. The first glimmerings emerged while he was still at prep school. He had an uncle who lived very close to Delius's home at Grez-sur-Loing, and through him succeeded in obtaining the great man's autograph as a favour to his prep school teacher W.E. Brockway who wished to add it to his autograph collection. In Edward Mason, however, Warlock came across someone who had a genuine enthusiasm for Delius's music and was eager to pass it on to him. Given the earlier connections, he soon caught the Delius bug and began to idolise his new hero. In letters to his mother, dated 1910, we hear something of these effusions:

> [Mason] is an enthusiast in the cause of that really great and (here in his native land only) much neglected composer Frederick Delius, whose works I positively adore; I am studying his operas and songs now with very great pleasure ... And although I have heard nothing of his music, yet from what I can discover at the piano, I may say that so far as I have yet found, Delius comes the nearest to my own perfect ideal of music, though when I say nearest I mean "*one* of *the* nearest", as I could not say I like him better than Elgar or Wagner, but I still think he is wonderful. There is one little work of his ... *On Craig Ddu*: I think that [part-] song appeals to me almost as much as almost anything I have ever heard ... I would give anything to hear it sung, as it seems to me nothing short of wonderful.[293]

This extract is most revealing in a number of ways. First, it provides some insight into the nature of Warlock's enthusiasms. His effusive comments show that at this stage, he had yet to master the art of genuine musical appreciation. There is no sense of equilibrium, although he does acknowledge the greatness of Wagner and Elgar, as if Delius was now to be admitted as the third Person of the Trinity. However, this adulation was based solely on what he had read of the scores he had managed to obtain. Presumably he had found some of these in the music department at Eton, and we do know that Mason had lent him his personal copy of the score of *Sea Drift*, after which Warlock gushed: "It is absolutely heavenly and, to my mind, as near perfect almost as any music I have ever seen. What it must be with the proper orchestral colour! O that I could *hear* some Delius!"[294]

---

293 Heseltine to his mother, 7th October 1910; cited by Barry Smith, *Peter Warlock: The Life of Philip Heseltine* (Oxford: Oxford University Press, 1994), p. 18.

294 Heseltine to his mother, 12th February 1911, cited by Smith, *Peter Warlock*, p. 18.

We also learn from these comments how perceptive he was about the music for a young man who was still only sixteen years old at this time. The works he mentions – *On Craig Ddu* and *Sea Drift* – are generally acknowledged by music critics to be among Delius's finest works – and Warlock was able to form his judgement simply by reading the scores.

A few months later, in June 1911, his greatest wish, to actually *hear* some Delius, was to be gloriously fulfilled. An all-Delius concert at the Queen's Hall, conducted by Thomas Beecham, was scheduled, at which Delius himself planned to be there. There seemed little chance of Warlock's being allowed from Eton to be in attendance, but, thanks to the timely intervention of Colin Taylor, permission was granted, as Taylor himself would be present to keep an eye on him. The items included *Appalachia*, *Paris – Song of a Great City*, the *Dance Rhapsody*, and the premiere of *Songs of Sunset*. This concert was not only a milestone for Delius, but for Warlock, too. He even had the honour of being introduced to his idol during the interval, and was suitably overwhelmed. The next day he sent Delius a letter of appreciation – in effect, a fan letter – and received a reply. Further exchanges followed, along with a warm friendship which was crowned with Warlock's composition in 1922 of the *Serenade for Strings* to mark Delius's sixtieth birthday, which is stylistically so close to that of Delius that it might have been written by him.

However, although this relationship endured until Warlock's death, his adolescent crush on Delius's music gradually faded until there developed a more objective assessment which recognised a distinction between the top quality works and those of a lower order. It should be remembered that as a youth, Warlock lacked the ability to discriminate. In one letter to Delius, he wrote: "... your works appeal to me so strongly – so much more than any other music I have ever heard ..."[295] – words that are redolent of a music-intoxicated youth. Throughout his life, in fact, Warlock was prone

295 Cited in Smith, *Peter Warlock*, p. 21.

to flashes of enthusiasm, some of which lasted longer than others. His patronage of the Dutch composer Van Dieren (1887–1936), for instance, later became as important to him as that of Delius, if not more so.

While still in his teens, Warlock showed signs of the traits that would come to characterise him throughout his life. He imbibed what Eton had to offer, and then tired of it, persuading his mother to let him leave a year early, despite the positive influences of Edward Mason and Colin Taylor. A young man with his privileged background would have been expected to progress to Oxbridge, but he pleaded to be allowed to spread his wings abroad. Again, his mother relented, on condition that, after a year, he return to take up a degree course at Oxford. He spent his gap year, as we would call it now, in Cologne, imbibing the culture, and half-heartedly studying the piano at the conservatory there. He returned to England on cue, spending time in London preparing for his university entrance examinations and dabbling in music journalism. His mother's expectation was that, having passed through Oxford, he would take up a respectable career in the City or the civil service, but having had his eyes opened to the allurements of music, especially composition, there was little chance of that. He did attend Christ Church, Oxford, to study Classics, but was restless and unhappy there. At the end of his second term, he visited Delius at his home in Grez where he was told what he wanted to hear – that he should set his heart on what most interested him in life and focus on that alone. In Warlock's case, as in Delius's own, that interest was music.

Buoyed by this advice, he left Oxford at the end of the academic year, moving to London to study language, literature and philosophy at University College. Why he should have chosen this option, which had nothing to do with the real love of his life, is a mystery, unless he regarded it as an excuse to evade the stultifying influence (as he saw it) of his mother. In any event, he spent only a term there, and with the help of Lady Maud "Emerald" Cunard (1872–1948), a fabulously rich American socialite, secured a job as music critic for the *Daily Mail*.

There is no doubt that he was an expressive writer in a range of genres. His letters, which he wrote copiously to all and sundry, are works of art, and he became legendary for the witticism of his limericks. His journalistic notices and articles certainly drew the public's attention, but they were also highly self-opinionated and devoid of all restraint. If he decided something was good, it received his total adulation; if he thought it mediocre, he could be damning, as even many of his fellow music critics were later to discover. This is not to say that he did not have anything useful or important to contribute, but his well-reasoned and temperate comments were too often interspersed with excesses. On one occasion, for example, he hailed Delius, during a review of his Piano Concerto, as "the greatest composer England has produced for two centuries" (since Purcell, presumably – notwithstanding Elgar and Vaughan Williams). When his employers insisted on vetting his work with a view to culling the more outlandish comments, he promptly resigned – after just two months on the paper.

From this point on, Warlock began to live the wayward, nomadic existence for which he became notorious. Despite his disregard of his mother's wishes for his future, she kept him afloat financially by granting him a monthly allowance which helped keep the wolf from the door, although it was certainly not sufficient to fund his extravagances. Much has been written about his dissolute lifestyle, and at least some of it can be verified – his dervish dancing on Charing Cross station, and his riding naked through the countryside on his motorcycle are just a couple of his escapades. No doubt some of the tales grew in the telling, but that such behaviour took place, if only spasmodically, can hardly be denied. Warlock's son, Nigel, who was sired by him through a model, Minnie Channing (known to all as Puma), briefly his lawful wife, pointed the finger of blame at his unsavoury friends who are supposed to have led him astray; but some of his outrageous behaviour occurred before he had met many of them. It began as early as the summer of 1915 when he and Puma, with two friends, the pianist Adrian Allison and the novelist Jean Rhys (1890–1979) rented a holiday cottage in the

Vale of Evesham where the generally riotous behaviour aroused the censure of the locals, and at least one naked motorcycle ride took place down Crickley Hill. All this happened a decade before he set up his menagerie at Eynsford in Kent, much to the despair of the locals there. By then, the members of the Warlock set were almost unrecognisable from what they had been in 1915.

But the story is not entirely one of dissolution. The excesses tended to be spasmodic. In between times, Warlock was capable of some useful work. He began spending time, on his own account, studying in the British Museum with a view to transcribing the neglected music of Elizabethan composers such as Byrd, Farnaby, Gibbons, Tomkins, and Whythorne, who he felt had been ill-served by other musicologists such as the well-meaning but inept Reverend Edmund Horace Fellowes (1870–1951). Over the next few years, Warlock transcribed, for piano, hundreds of lute songs, just as they appeared in the original score, and without the "Victorian" embellishments applied by Fellowes.

As ever, though, his initial foray into this work, was intermittently interrupted by the latest distraction. In November 1915 he met in London D.H. Lawrence (1885–1930) who already had a body of ground-breaking work under his belt, notably *The White Peacock* and *Sons and Lovers*. The two men warmed to each other immediately, each recognising the other's talent. Naturally, this new relationship drew forth from Warlock one of his gushing assessments, Lawrence being described as "the greatest literary genius of his generation". Lawrence, in turn, spoke warmly, if less effusively, of Warlock. In December 1915, Lawrence and his wife Frieda moved from London to a remote rented cottage in Cornwall, where they were soon joined by Warlock. Whatever else their motives were, it was a good place to avoid conscription and to sit out the war in peace. Warlock declared himself to be a conscientious objector, though just how much integrity lay behind it is debatable. Anyhow, this idyllic existence, with the war raging around them, was not to last. How could it, with two such imposing personalities under one roof? Any particular reason for the rift has been lost in the mists of time, but the fact remains that the friendship cooled to the point of mutual dislike, and those who Lawrence disliked usually ended up being unflatteringly portrayed in his novels. So it was with Warlock, who appears in *Women in Love* in the guise of Halliday, along with Puma (called Pussum in the novel). Lawrence never disguised his characters to the extent that they would not recognise themselves, and threats of legal action were fairly common.

By February 1916 Warlock was back in London, spending a good deal of time at the Café Royal in Regent Street, the artistic hub of the capital where leading musicians, writers and painters were to be found in lively discussion over the latest trends and ideas. Here, he surrounded himself with various artists of all kinds, including the sculptor Jacob Epstein (1880–1959), the artist Augustus John (1878–1961), and the composers Cecil Gray (1895–1951), and Bernard van Dieren (1880–1936). Together they dreamed up all kinds of grandiose schemes, from inaugurating new music journals to establishing a season of operas and concerts. Most of these projects were stillborn. Warlock and his friends had neither the expertise nor the capital to make a success of them, yet when Thomas Beecham offered him a steady position with his English Opera Company he turned it down, supposedly on the grounds that he found Beecham's programmes too unadventurous. In reality, he had become addicted to his Bohemian do-it-my-way lifestyle, and probably had no intention of working for anyone else.

Warlock was introduced to Bernard van Dieren by Epstein late in 1916. The Dutchman was a rather shadowy figure, yet for the next few years he became one of the most important influences in Warlock's life. A Dutch composer living in London, he was largely self-taught, and specialised in writing songs and chamber music, although he produced a number of orchestral pieces, too, including the substantial *Chinese Symphony* (op. 6, 1914). Publishers, however, were dubious about the quality of his work, and Herbert Howells, whose compositional technique was beyond reproach, commented that he "was not a composer at all, it was all make believe, and the Oxford Press took him up and gave him a sort of smear of respectability".[296] It should be said, in fairness, that Howells was no admirer of the Warlock set, and blamed him for impeding the development of E.J. Moeran as a composer (which is probably true), and the reports of others, including Cecil Gray, paint a glowing picture of van Dieren as a veritable polymath who knew a great deal about most of the natural sciences, could write fluently in four languages, and speak fluently in four others. He also displayed practical skills in carpentry and book-binding, for example. By all accounts he had a magnetic personality that might have made him the centre of his own menage, had not Warlock been in town.

Almost immediately following their introduction, van Dieren invited Warlock to his home in Hampstead where he played him some of his compositions, including the *Chinese Symphony* in piano reduction, according to Warlock's own account. The importance of this occasion is not to be underestimated, as his letter of appreciation makes clear:

> I was so utterly overwhelmed by your music this afternoon, that all words fail me. And so I feel I have to write and tell you ... what a profound impression my visit to you has had upon me. It has brought me to a turning point, opened out a vista of a new world ... Your music ... is nothing short of a revelation to me. I have been groping about aimlessly in the dark for so long, with ever growing exasperation – and at last you have shown a light, alone among composers who I have met; for neither Delius nor any other has even so much as suggested a practical solution of the initial difficulties of musical composition ...[297]

No doubt van Dieren was flattered by such glowing remarks, but they tell us rather less about him than about Warlock's own personality. Initially, the saviour of English music had been Delius, but now his position in Warlock's pantheon was about to be usurped by another. The music of the two men, admittedly reveals some

296 C. Palmer, *Herbert Howells: A Centenary Celebration* (London, 1992), p. 354; cited in Smith, *Peter Warlock*, p. 98.

297 Cited in Smith, *Peter Warlock*, p. 99.

superficial similarities, notably its use of chromatic harmonies, but there may have been more practical reasons for the shift in allegiances. After all, van Dieren was on the spot, while Delius was located in far-off Grez and could only be consulted by letter. Warlock never abandoned Delius; as late as 1929 he was helping Beecham to organise the Delius Festival in London. But van Dieren was the man of the moment, and Warlock was full of grandiose ideas for trumpeting his cause. However, with Warlock everything was done on impulse rather than on the basis of rationale, and many items on his wish list were utterly impracticable. For instance, he suggested setting up a conservatorium devoted to van Dieren's musical ideals. Other ideas, however, were acted upon. An attempt was made, unsuccessfully, as it turned out, to gather funds for the publication of van Dieren's *Chinese Symphony*, and for a concert consisting entirely of his works – a project which *was* realised. However, the patronage of the concert by Warlock and Cecil Gray, although in earnest, turned out to be more of a curse than a blessing. The pre-concert marketing material, presenting van Dieren's work as a kind of Hegelian synthesis of Palestrina, Bach and Beethoven, was frankly preposterous, and the decision to include the highly complex and contrapuntal hour-long *Diaphony*, complete with the inclusion of its two-and-a-half Shakespeare sonnets, was surely ill-advised. Heavy financial losses were incurred, and a planned second concert had to be cancelled. A much lower-key introduction of van Dieren's music to the public – perhaps a concert of short chamber music pieces and songs – would have done far more for the cause.

Such were the diverse activities of Warlock in 1916 – when half the flower of England was being slaughtered or maimed on the Somme and other notorious hell-holes – that it seems almost trite to mention that, prior to his ill-starred marriage to Puma at the end of the year, she gave birth to his son, Nigel, although even in this, matters are not straightforward. A Nigel Heseltine appeared on a BBC Radio 3 programme in 1992. He was aged seventy-five at the time, which would certainly correspond to the date on which Puma gave birth to Warlock's son. However, in a memoir, Nigel claimed that his mother was *not* Puma, but a Swiss girl with whom Philip was having a liaison at the same time (he was notoriously promiscuous). Ian Parrott[298] suggests that Puma's child was named Peter and died in infancy, while Barry Smith[299], perhaps less plausibly, opines that "for reasons which have not yet satisfactorily been explained", the baby was christened Peter, but later renamed Nigel. Smith's view is perhaps based on a misunderstanding, and Parrott's suggestion best fits the available evidence. Warlock himself refers to a son named Peter in a letter dated 13th May 1917, at which time *Nigel*, had he been Puma's son, would have been five months old. But he could have been this age in any case, regardless of who his mother was. What we do know is that Nigel was raised by Warlock's mother, Edith, whereas nothing more is heard of Peter. Many of Warlock's friends, incidentally, regarded Edith as a formidable, domineering woman, but in the abovementioned BBC Radio broadcast, Nigel affirmed her finer qualities, calling her a "wonderful woman", and saying that he felt fortunate to have been raised by her.

In the summer of 1917, when the war was not going well for the Allies, Warlock, who had somehow wangled exemption from military service, learned that his case was under review and was ordered to attend a medical. His reaction to this was to flee the country, taking Puma with him. He ended up in Dublin – not exactly the best place for a heavy drinker. However, it did provide the opportunity for him to meet some influential people, including W.B. Yeats (1865–1939) and the medium Hester Dowden (1868–1949). The latter became a close friend, and also stimulated Warlock to serious composition, for he found in her a kindred spirit, and it was in her house, sitting at her piano, that he suddenly found himself as a composer. The handful of songs he had written before this had been somewhat derivative – first of Delius and then of Van Dieren – but now he became prolific (at one point, he completed ten songs in a fortnight), developing his own distinctive style. *My*

298 Ian Parrott, *The Crying Curlew. Peter Warlock: Family and Influences* (Llandysul, Dyfed, Gomer Press 1994), pp. 24–25.

299 Smith, *Peter Warlock*, pp. 106–07.

gostly fader; Take, O, take those lips away; The bayley berith the bell away; As ever I saw; Lullaby – these are the songs that made him as a composer. As for making the acquaintance of Yeats, this may well have sown the seed for what was to become arguably Warlock's masterpiece, *The Curlew*, which was completed in 1922, using Yeats's poems, principally from his collection, *The Wind Among the Reeds*.

Two months of Warlock's sojourn in Ireland were spent on the remote Achill Island, just off the west coast, where he steeped himself in the Erse language. His son Nigel was of the view that this brief period, like his association with Hester Dowden, had an invigorating effect on him. However, after a year avoiding conscription, he deemed it safe enough to return to mainland Britain, and settled back in London at the end of August 1918, just as the war was drawing to a close. The next three years were marked by musical journalism, and although the occasional song appeared (*My lady is a pretty one; There is a lady sweet and kind; Late Summer; The Singer* were all written in 1919), the muse of fire was not burning as brightly as it had done in Ireland.

The chief venture of these years was the inauguration of a new music journal, *The Sackbut*. It had been mooted by Beecham as early as 1915 but kept on the back-burner. Now it had been taken up and financed by the publisher Winthrop Rogers, and, despite their love-hate relationship, he appointed Warlock as its editor. Naturally, he immediately stamped his own prejudices and enthusiasms on the journal. The style was combative, and those antagonistic to the Warlock circle or its cause came in for some stick. Concerts featuring Warlock's pet composers – Delius, Van Dieren and Sorabji (1892–1988)[300] – were, of course, well-publicised.

300 Kairosru Sorabji, also known as Dudley Sorabji Sharpurgi, became noted for his vast and highly complex piano scores, and in many ways was Warlock's mirror image. He was born of a Parsee father, and his mother, of Spanish-Sicilian stock, was an operatic singer. He was something of a polymath, and like Warlock was not shy in expressing his views regarding his pet loves and hates ("... it is in the ultra-moderns that I am in my musical element ... much of Beethoven's music is absolutely repellent to me" [Smith, *Peter Warlock*, p. 47]). After some correspondence, the two of them finally met in 1914, remaining on friendly terms until Warlock's death.

It is hardly surprising that Delius became a cheerleader for *The Sackbut*, as it served his interests, and Warlock was able to use his editorial privilege to attack critics who were hostile – or even lukewarm – to the music of Delius and his other favourites. However, away from the ferment of London's music scene, Delius had time for reflection and was able to make some well-judged comments on the course of his protégé's career. He saw that Warlock was lacking in direction, dabbling in this and that, but never focusing on one thing:

> You would succeed at anything you take up if you would concentrate on it & not diffuse your energies on so many things ... Stick to one thing just for fun for 2 or 3 years & see if I am not right. I think you are admirably gifted as a writer – you would succeed as a writer on music or as a composer if *you stick to one* & push it thro' regardless of everything.[301]

Of course, this is precisely what Delius himself could do, but then he was tucked away in the quiet village of Grez, deep in the French countryside, and far from the dazzling allurements of London which a man of Warlock's temperament could hardly resist. Thus, Delius's advice was never heeded.

After only five issues of *The Sackbut*, Winthrop Rogers withdrew his financial support, and for the next few months Warlock struggled to keep the venture alive until, in September 1921, it was taken over by a new publisher, John Curwen, who promptly dismissed Warlock as editor, replacing him with a young twenty-something by the name of Ursula Greville.[302]

At this point, Warlock was out of luck and out of money, and so he did the only thing left to him and returned to the family estate. Although it might be thought that this was the last place he would

301 Delius to Warlock, cited in Smith, *Peter Warlock*, p. 160.

302 He poured out his frustrations in a typically forthright limerick commencing: "One evening, Miss Ursula Greville ..." – the rest being too risqué to print (which did not stop Barry Smith [*Peter Warlock*, p. 185] from doing so).

want to be, it was really a blessing in disguise, for it removed at a stroke all the distractions of living in London, surrounded by his Bohemian friends and fuelled by drink. We have already noticed that during his year in Ireland his capacity to compose improved markedly, and so it proved in Wales where he spent much of the next three years. He himself acknowledged the benefits:

> Wild Wales alone holds an enchantment for me stronger than wine or woman and intimately associated with music. In these admirable and tranquil surroundings I can work more quietly and steadily than I have ever been able to before … Congenial companionship alone is lacking – but I console myself with the reflection that if I had that also there would be more drinking and less working – and I have a great deal of lost time to make up.[303]

In the event, his output during this period included some of his best-known songs, including *Sleep*, one of his most inspired creations, and some settings for unaccompanied chorus, such as *Adam lay ybounden*, *Three Carols*, and *All the flowers of spring*. But the most significant work to be completed at this time was *The Curlew*, scored for tenor, string quartet, flute and cor anglais – an unusual but strikingly effective combination. Warlock had been engaged on the work since 1920 when a first version had been performed, but, dissatisfied, he substantially revised it, producing the form known to listeners today. The poems of Yeats chosen by the composer for the piece speak of unrequited or cancelled love – they are the poems of a young man (Yeats was thirty-four when they were published) that would have appealed to Warlock's personal outlook. Rarely has the desolation of such verse been so clearly reflected in the sparsity of the scoring. The final movement, "I wander by the edge of this desolate lake", for instance, is taken up by the tenor unaccompanied by the instruments, until the dark colours of the viola and cello steal in towards the end.

303 Warlock to Cecil Gray, cited in Smith, *Peter Warlock*, p. 188.

There is no doubt that Warlock's three-year sojourn in Wales was good for him professionally, but this is not to say that he did not get out and about. In the autumn of 1923, he joined his composer friend E.J. Moeran on a folksong-collecting expedition in Norfolk, attracted, no doubt, by the pubs in which some of the songs were likely to have been collected. Moeran was a keen collector, Warlock much less so. He did compose a brief set of piano preludes on folksongs, although these were of Celtic origin, and by all accounts were limited in quality. Another excursion which took place immediately afterwards was to Grez-sur-Loing to visit Delius, when he had Cecil Gray in tow. Heseltine was becoming restless again, and in June 1924 he returned to London, renting a flat in Chelsea. The Welsh idyll was at an end, and the wild parties with old friends became a feature of his life once more. After spending Christmas in Majorca, he returned, not to London, but to a cottage in Eynsford in Kent, and so began the next riotous stage in his life.

He had leased the cottage from Hubert Foss (1899–1953), head of the Music Department of the Oxford University Press – perhaps one reason why he did not receive the outrageous treatment Warlock doled out to most other publishers and critics. The location was ideal in that it was close enough to London to allow him to stay in touch with musical life in the metropolis, but distant enough to get away from the stultifying atmosphere of the city. Eynsford, in those days, was still very much a village out in the country. Warlock did not stay there alone; he was joined by Moeran and a Maori factotum called Hal Collins (birth name Te Akau) (1885–1929), who was a good practical man to have around, but an artist in his own right, graphic design being a speciality. These were the permanent residents. However, Warlock's girlfriend of the moment, Barbara Peache (b. 1900), was also present for much of the time. Weekends, on the other hand, were open house when anyone who was anyone might turn up. The regulars included Augustus John, and the singer John Goss who regularly performed Warlock's songs. Among others who were likely to appear from time to time were composers Lord Berners (1883–1950), Walton, Lambert, and Patrick Hadley, and the artist Nina Hamnett (1890–1956).[304]

Not everyone approved. The poet Robert Nichols (1893–1944), after visiting the cottage, remarked on its oppressive atmosphere, and we have already noted that Herbert Howells considered the Eynsford years to be the ruin of Moeran. It is certainly true that Warlock was a domineering personality (taking after his mother, perhaps) who cast a spell over people, and not always for their good. Unlikely as it may seem, however, it was not all play and no work at Eynsford. The weekend was party-time, but during the week Warlock was capable of producing some useful work. Apart from a book on the Italian madrigalist Gesualdo, written jointly by himself and Cecil Gray, he composed some of his most characteristic songs, including *My Own Country, Ha'nacker Mill, Passing By, Jillian of Berry, The First Mercy,* and others, as well as the beautiful choral carol *Bethlehem Down.*

The most celebrated piece to be written during this period, however, was his *Capriol Suite,* based on sixteenth century dance tunes taken from Thoinot Arbeau's[305] *Orchésographie,* a kind of dance manual. Although the tunes came ready-served, Warlock did a grand job of weaving them into a suite for string orchestra, which appeared in 1927, following this with a version for full orchestra. It has been noticed that the harmonic language of the final movement is redolent of Bartok, a composer who Warlock came to know personally, and who even stayed for a couple of days at the family home in Wales on his way back to London from a concert in Aberystwyth. For a time, at least, Bartok became one of Warlock's all-embracing enthusiasms.

304 Nina Hamnett was quite a regular, and provided an entertaining account of the riotous living that characterised weekends at the cottage (Hamnett, *Is She a Lady?* [London, 1955], pp. 23–33; abridged in Smith, *Peter Warlock,* pp. 223–26).

305 His real name was Jehan Tabourot, of which Thoinot Arbeau is an anagram (J = I), which he thought politic to use of his secular works, since he was a practicing cathedral canon.

The chief loser from the Eynsford years was poor old Moeran. When Warlock had the bit between his teeth, he could be as tenacious as Delius at seeing a job through, whereas Moeran, who always found composition something he had to grind at, had to be in the right place at the right time to produce of his best – which usually meant Ireland or Norfolk, and to some degree the Welsh Marches. He also needed to be alone, which he never was in Eynsford. He was a gregarious character, easily led, and Warlock was all he needed as an excuse to set all thought of work aside. Thus, for three years he produced nothing of significance.

By the summer of 1928, however, funds had become so depleted that continued occupation of the Eynsford cottage was no longer viable, and the whole aimless idyll came to an end – much to the relief of the locals, no doubt. Warlock repaired to the family mansion once more, and had he remained there all might have been well; but by the November of that year, he was back in London where he reverted to his old self-destructive habits. Most alarming were the signs that the muse was beginning to desert him, and the outlook seemed bleak. His "grisly" moods, as he called them, became deeper and more frequent, and his lack of purpose more obvious. Beecham tried to help in various ways. Having founded the Imperial League of Opera in 1927, he invited Warlock to edit the company journal, and so, for a while, he enjoyed a salaried position; but Beecham's venture was short-lived, and the journal ceased publication at the end of 1929. Another short-term project of Beecham's, in which Warlock proved an able assistant, was the Delius Festival projected for that autumn. Here he was in his element, marketing the event, and producing programme notes and a biographical sketch. In this, Warlock was eminently qualified, as he had been the first person to write a biography of the composer.[306] He travelled to Grez to make arrangements with Delius himself, and to see if he had any new work that might be premiered at the festival, and was rewarded with the discovery of *Cynara*, which had been intended

306 P. Heseltine, *Frederick Delius* (London: John Lane, 1923). Even this work, however, took a great deal of hand-wringing, and was almost ten years in the germination.

as one of the *Songs of Sunset* back in 1907, but had been laid aside at that time. Now it had been completed and orchestrated with the help of his amanuensis, Eric Fenby (1906–97).

The Delius Festival was a great success, but in its aftermath, without any other meaningful employment on the cards, Warlock must have felt overlooked and neglected. In fact, he seems to have spent his final few months campaigning on behalf of friends such as van Dieren, whose music he promoted to the bitter end. By this time, the age of the ribald songs – *Captain Stratton's Fancy, Mr. Belloc's Fancy, Peter Warlock's Fancy* – were well behind him, and the motivation to write any songs at all was hardly encouraged by the slump in demand for this kind of music in the later twenties. His final efforts in the genre were occasional pieces written to texts by a journalist friend he had met in 1927, Bruce Blunt (1899–1957). Blunt was just Warlock's cup of tea, sharing his taste in drink (they had both been fined for being found drunk and disorderly together on London's Cadogan Street), but also having the knack of writing the kind of verse that inspired Warlock to translate into song. The outer image of the pair as disreputable topers could hardly be further from the dark beauty of Blunt's best poems and Warlock's sensitive response to them. Three of these collaborations – *Bethlehem Down, The Frostbound Wood* and *The Fox* – resulted in some of Warlock's finest settings. The first of them, written for chorus in 1927, and adapted for baritone and piano in 1930, drew from Warlock a melody whose beauty he never surpassed. *The Frostbound Wood,* another carol, but one with a troubling message, appeared in 1929 at a time when the dark periods in Warlock's life were becoming longer and deeper, and something of his desolation is evident in the music's bleak, heavy tones. The poem tells of the Virgin Mary's pain at the loss of her Son, and the poignancy can be felt in the following verses:

> Bethlehem could hear sweet singing,
> "Peace on earth, a Saviour's come".
> Here the trees were dark, the heavens
> Without stars, and dumb.

Past she went with no word spoken,
Past the grave of him I slew,
Myself the sower of the woodland
And my heart the yew.

Of the three songs abovementioned, *The Fox* can boast the most unusual origin. It was written in the village of Bramdean in Hampshire where Bruce Blunt owned a cottage to which he had invited Warlock to stay for a few days. Naturally, there were regular forays to the local pub, *The Fox Inn,* in which the mask of an actual fox was hung on the wall. This drew a poem from Blunt which he penned after his guest had retired for the night. He left it out on the table and when he came down next morning, found Warlock setting it to music. The fruits of this collaboration were duly celebrated at *The Haunch of Mutton* in Salisbury. Despite the circumstances surrounding the song, however, both words and music are predominantly dark in tenor, and had Warlock been in his more manic mood, he could not have written it. As it happened, it was his penultimate original composition.

The circumstances surrounding Warlock's death in the early morning of 17th December 1930 are as mystifying as the man himself. In September of that year, he had moved with his long-time girlfriend Barbara Peache into a basement flat at 12A Tite Street, Chelsea. He was known to have been suffering from bouts of depression at the time which may – or may not – have been in the nature of a winter affective disorder. On the eve of his death, however, he appeared to friends to be his normal self, with no sign of depression. That evening he met Bernard van Dieren and his wife for a drink and invited them back to the flat, apologising for the fact that he hadn't a bottle beer to offer them. They were the last people to see him alive. They left him, no worse for wear, just after midnight. There has been a suggestion made by some that he and Barbara had a tiff, and that she had flounced out of the house to attend a dance and stayed out all night. At the inquest following Warlock's death, however, she deposed that they were on the best of terms, and that her dance date had been prearranged with a female friend. When she returned early next morning, she found the windows locked and bolted, and smelt gas. Warlock's kitten was in the yard with a bowl of food. The police were called and broke in to find the gas tap full on and Warlock lying unconscious on the sofa. He was pronounced dead on arrival at hospital. An autopsy found no alcohol or drug intake – although during his lifetime his alcohol consumption was known to have been legendary, if sporadic, and he had not been averse to taking cocaine. A friend of Warlock's, Judge Lionel Jellineck (1898–1979), claimed that when he had visited the flat a few days before Warlock's death, he noticed how loose the gas tap was, a fact confirmed by the coroner, who returned an open verdict. The likelihood is that Warlock intentionally turned on the gas tap and lay down to await the end. The locked and bolted doors and windows, and the kitten in the yard would support this, as would the fact that he had already contemplated suicide by gas poisoning, as witnessed by Barbara Peache, and again on the occasion when Lionel Jellineck pointed out the loose tap.[307]

Given the circumstances and the personality involved in them, it was inevitable that various conspiracy theories would emerge. In a controversial book, his son Nigel[308] went as far as to suggest that he was murdered by van Dieren. The pretext for this outlandish claim is that in his original will, Warlock had left his entire estate to his fellow composer, but in a new, unsigned will, found among his papers after his death, all his worldly goods had been left to a certain Winifred Baker who seems to have been on the fringe of his affairs while he lived. The suggestion is that van Dieren had the motive to dispose of Heseltine because he stood to gain from it, and clandestinely flicked on the loose gas tap just before he left. None of this stands up to scrutiny. The evidence for suicide is substantial (the coroner probably returned an open verdict to spare his respectable family the stigma of a suicide verdict), and a gas board official called

307 Of this, Warlock is supposed to have told Jellineck, "It may come in very useful" (Smith, *Peter Warlock*, p. 283).

308 Nigel Heseltine, *Capriol for Mother* (London: Thames Publishing, 1992).

at the inquest stated that, in the "on" position, the gas tap would have made a hissing noise too loud to have been overlooked by anyone with normal hearing. Moreover, sounds were heard emanating from Warlock's flat as late as six o' clock next morning, suggesting that he was still alive at that time. Van Dieren himself testified that he had been unaware that Warlock had made him his sole heir and executor in his will until the day of the inquest.

The fact that, at the last minute, Warlock had considered leaving everything to Winifred Baker instead, and nothing to other friends and family, may well testify to his state of mind that fateful evening. What part did she play in his life? Barry Smith[309] describes her as "a nurse with whom he had a long and close relationship from about 1919 to the end of his life", but he adds that she was a shadowy figure. Still, there exists a long, passionate letter to her from Warlock, which really does seem to have the seal of sincerity[310], in which he reveals to her how much she means to both his personal and creative life, while she disbursed her feelings for him in a letter to van Dieren in early January 1931, writing, "... anything that concerned Philip is of great worth to me".[311] And it was she who found just the right words to pronounce a suitable benediction on his life: "I can feel almost gladness now that it is over – that he has at last found the peace and quietude he so loved and never – or seldom – could find in the world".[312]

There is little doubt that for most of his adult life Warlock suffered from manic depression, and that this was exacerbated by the winter months. In his manic phases he was the life and soul of the party, while in his depressive moods he suffered the extremes of "grisliness", as he called it. It is hardly surprising, then, that he was a man of contradictions who, according to the composer Elizabeth Poston (1905–87), another of his female admirers, had no difficulty

309 Smith, *Peter Warlock*, pp. 213–14.

310 Quoted in Smith, *Peter Warlock*, pp. 271–72. He was dedicating songs to her from the time of their first meeting.

311 Smith, *Peter Warlock*, p. 284.

312 Smith, *Peter Warlock*, p. 284.

in giving vent to them all. He seems to have been loved and loathed in equal measure. Herbert Howells was definitely not one of his admirers, accusing him of leading others astray, and fellow composer Frederic Austin (1872–1952) went even further, raging to Warlock: "There are blackguards of so offensive a type that contact with them is so distasteful to the point of nausea. You are one of them".[313] On the other hand, he was idolised by others, not least Bernard van Dieren, Cecil Gray, Bruce Blunt, E.J. Moeran, and, of course, a galaxy of women, while Delius regarded him as the son he never had.

However, Warlock was to a large extent his own worst enemy. He all too easily alienated the critics and other figures in the music establishment, and championed composers whose value was, to say the least, debatable. He himself was an acerbic, if perceptive critic, and might have made a career out of it, but he never heeded Delius's sound advice to focus his attention on one activity. His whole professional life was spent in dabbling in one thing or another – music criticism, scholarship, promotional activities, composition – without concentrating on any one of them. In the final analysis, he regarded himself as a composer, but his resources were limited because he lacked both the formal academic training and the patience that would have allowed him to produce larger canvas works. He wrote nothing more substantial than the *Capriol Suite* and *The Curlew*, yet these are rightly regarded as ranking among his most celebrated works. They reveal a fine harmonist with a sensitivity to the musical possibilities of any theme on which he has a mind to elaborate, whether that is the transposition of an Elizabethan lute song or dance tune, a rollicking drinking song, or the bittersweetness of love. Apart from the abovementioned works, his reputation today rests on a handful of individual songs, but the best of them – *Sleep, The Fox, The Frostbound Wood, My Gostly Fadir, The Cloths of Heaven, Bethlehem Down* – are so exquisite and finely judged, that they will surely keep his music alive long into the future. Perhaps the essence of the man can be summed up in his own quirky epitaph:

313 Cited in Smith, *Peter Warlock*, p. 270.

Here lies Warlock, the composer,
Who lived next door to Munn, the grocer.
He died of drink and copulation,
A great discredit to this nation.

a. Bibliography

Chisholm, Alastair, *Bernard van Dieren: An Introduction* (London: Thames Publishing, 1984)

Copley, Ian, *The Music of Peter Warlock* (London: Dennis Dobson, 1979)

Gray, Cecil, et al., *Peter Warlock: A Memoir of Philip Heseltine* (London: Jonathan Cape, 1934)

Heseltine, Nigel, *Capriol for Mother: A Memoir for Peter Warlock and His Family* (London: Thames Publishing, 1992)

Parrott, Ian, *The Crying Curlew: Family and Influences* (Llandysul, Ceredigion: Gomer Press, 1994)

Reynolds, Peter J., "Peter Warlock, His Friends and Their Influence", *British Music*, 7 (1985), pp. 48–58

Smith, Barry, *Peter Warlock: The Life of Philip Helseltine* (Oxford: Oxford University Press, 1994)

Smith, Barry, *Frederick Delius and Peter Warlock: A Friendship Revealed* (Oxford: Oxford University Press, 2000)

b. Selected Discography

i) Orchestral

Capriol Suite	LFO, Pople	Arte Nova	74321 37868 2
Serenade	LFO, Pople	Arte Nova	74321 37868 2

ii) Choral

Corpus Christi, etc.	The Carice Singers, Parris	Naxos	8.573227

iii) Songs with Quartet

The Curlew	Ainsley (ten); Phillips, Wexler (violins); Chase (viola); van Kampen (cello); Davies (flute); Hulse (cor ang.)	Hyperion	CDA 66938
Sleep	Ainsley (ten); Phillips, Wexler (violins); Chase (viola); van Kampen (cello)	Hyperion	CDA 66938
My gostly fader	Artists as above	Hyperion	CDA 66938
Take, O take those lips away	Artists as above	Hyperion	CDA 66938
My lady is a pretty one	Artists as above	Hyperion	CDA 66938
Mourn no moe	Artists as above	Hyperion	CDA 66938

iv) Songs with Piano

Song selection (34 songs)	Ainsley (ten); Vignoles (pi.)	Hyperion	CDA 66736
The Frostbound Wood	Bailey (bass-bar); Parsons	Decca	470 199-2
Twelve Oxen	Bailey (bass-bar); Parsons	Decca	470 199-2
Cricketers of Hambledon	Bailey (bass-bar); Parsons	Decca	470 199-2
Captain Stratton's Fancy	Maltman (bar); Constable	Naxos	8.557115

Sweet and Twenty	Thompson (ten); Constable	Naxos	8.557115

c. DVD

Peter Warlock: Some Little Joy (Tony Britten, Signum Vision, 2008). SIGDVD002

d. Website

The Peter Warlock Society (www.peterwarlock.org)

50. William Wordsworth (1908–88)

When people hear the name William Wordsworth, most will think immediately of the famous Lakeland poet, not of the twentieth century composer. But although the name is common enough, as irony would have it, the two really are linked in that the musician was a descendant of the poet's brother Christopher (1774–1846). William was born in London on 17th December 1908. His early education was conducted by his father, an Anglican priest, and while still very young, he moved with his family to Hindhead in Surrey. His taste for music was encouraged by a local woman who gave him his first piano lessons, and was astute enough to realise his talent and recognise that he needed a broader musical education than she was able to provide. She therefore recommended him to the composer George Olroyd who was organist and choirmaster of St. Michael's Church, Croydon, with whom Wordsworth enjoyed a fruitful, decade-long relationship, learning the essentials of counterpoint and harmony, and adding organ and viola to his piano studies. At the end of this period (1921–31) he might have been expected to progress to one of the London music colleges, the RAM or RCM, but he decided to send one of his early works to Sir Donald Tovey (1875–1940), one of the leading musicologists of the day and a composer in his own right, who was impressed enough to take him on as a student in Edinburgh. He imbibed what Tovey had to offer without formalising it in a university degree, and in due course returned to Hindhead. His first taste of Scotland, however, impressed itself upon him and was to have lasting repercussions.

Wordsworth was fortunate enough to have as his immediate neighbour a professional violinist, Nellie Gill, who held regular chamber concerts in her home, and it was there, among approving friends, that the diffident young composer was able to try out some of his own early chamber pieces. It was at this time, in the mid-thirties, that he formalised his pacifist disposition by joining the Peace Pledge Union, and when the Second World War broke out, he declared himself a conscientious objector, and was set to work as a farm labourer. In his spare time, however, he continued to compose, producing his First Symphony (1944), and his first two string quartets (1941, 1944), along with a substantial oratorio, *Dies Domini*, for soloists, chorus and orchestra (1942–44), which still awaits its premiere. It was at this time, too, that he met a fellow pacifist, Frieda Robson, with whom he fell in love and married.

Wordsworth's natural reticence[314] did not prevent him from moving in distinguished musical circles and serving on – or sometimes chairing – various committees. These included the Executive Committee of the Composers' Guild of Great Britain, of which he eventually became Chairman. As a result of this, he was selected in 1961 to tour the Soviet Union at the invitation of the Union of Soviet Composers, during which he met both Shostakovich and Khachaturian, and gave a characteristically self-deprecating speech:

> I believe I share with your most famous composer, Shostakovich, one characteristic – an extreme distaste for speaking in public. For an occasion such as this, I could wish that the floor would open and I could disappear. I could wish also that the resemblance between me and Shostakovich did not end there, but I cannot be so arrogant as to pretend that my own compositions are on a level with his![315]

Wordsworth had a lifelong affinity with nature, and in 1961 he moved with his family (he claimed that the birth of his children tended to coincide with the production of his symphonies!) to Kincraig in the Scottish Highlands whose landscape became something of a muse.

314 For a typical example, see C.M. Maclean,"William Wordsworth (1908–88)", *Music Current*, No. 1 (September 1988), p. 1; cited by Paul Conway, liner notes, *William Wordsworth: Orchestral Music, Volume 1*, Toccata, TOCC 0480, p.2.

315 Cited by Paul Conway, liner notes, *William Wordsworth: Orchestral Music, Volume 1*, Toccata, TOCC 0480, p.5.

Once again, he flung himself into administrative duties, this time with the Composers' Guild for Scotland. Perhaps he became rather comfortable in his day-to-day routine, for he became less prolific as a composer and produced fewer large-scale works. Further, there were several other interests to distract him. He was a voracious reader, and enjoyed a number of hobbies, including golf, chess, gardening, bee-keeping, fishing and carpentry. He would have been perfectly content living the life of a country squire.

In Wordsworth's later years, the clouds began to gather. One of his sons, Tim, died in a car accident in 1971, a tragedy which underlies both the Symphony No. 6, "Elegiaca", and *Adonais* for mixed voices. In 1982, his wife, Frieda, passed away, invoking another musical response in the form of *Elegy for Frieda* for string quartet (later rescored for string orchestra). Wordsworth himself suffered in his final years with ill health and died on 10th March 1988, aged seventy-nine.

His oeuvre amounts to well over one hundred opus-numbered works in most of the traditional forms. There are eight symphonies, three concertos (for piano, violin and cello), along with other orchestral works; six string quartets and other chamber pieces; solo piano works, including an early sonata (1939); a few choral works, usually with instrumental accompaniment of some sort; and contributions to the art-song repertoire.[316] The symphonies lie at the heart of his output and account for some of his most powerful and expressive work. They are tonal in idiom and, like the symphonies of Rubbra, maintain the symphonic tradition in the line of Vaughan Williams, if in a more contemporary stylistic language. Formally, they are quite inventive, ranging from the traditional four-movement form (Symphonies Nos. 1 and 2), through three (Nos. 3 and 5), and two (No. 8) to just a single movement (No. 4). The latter may have been suggested by Sibelius's Symphony No. 7, and there may be a smidgeon of the Master's style, too. Sibelius strode like a colossus

316 Three of his songs – *Red Skies*, *The Wind*, and *Clouds* – were recorded by Kathleen Ferrier, no less (on *Kathleen Ferrier: Song Recital*, London [Decca], 430 061-2).

through the symphonic world of the mid-twentieth century, and his influence can be detected to some degree in the symphonic works of other English composers of the period, including those of Vaughan Williams, Bax, Walton and Moeran. Another work, which aspires to be a symphony but was never so labelled, is the *Divertimento* which impressed Vaughan Williams enough to suggest that, suitably "beefed up", it could easily pass as a symphony.

All but two of Wordsworth's symphonies have now been recorded, and it is to be hoped that the outstanding ones – Nos. 6 and 7 – will follow in due course. Likewise, two of the three concertos (piano and violin) are available on the Toccata label. Less fortunate is the small but significant body of chamber works. I say "significant", but it is difficult to assess the quality of these pieces if they are not widely disseminated which, unfortunately, has been the case so far. None of the six quartets have, to my knowledge, ever reached the recording studio. Paul Conway shares this concern about Wordsworth's music generally. Towards the end of his essay on the composer[317], he writes:

> It is to be hoped that this release [Toccata, TOCC 0480] will renew interest in the music of a composer whose body of work is still a largely untapped resource. His scores must be performed to give them life. In his own words, "My music is what you hear. It is not a set of dots and lines on a piece of paper; it does not exist until the written symbols are translated into an aural experience which matches that imagined by the composer in the first place".[318]

I am sure we can all say "Amen" to that.

---

317 P. Conway, *William Wordsworth: Orchestral Music, Volume 1*, Toccata, TOCC 0480, pp. 2–15 (15).

318 William Wordsworth, "Music in the Dark", *The Times*, 6th March 1961, p. 13; cited by Conway.

a. Bibliography

Dodd, John, "William Wordsworth: A 75th Anniversary Tribute", *British Music*, 5 (1983)

Maclean, C.M., "William Wordsworth (1908–88)", *Music Current*, no. 1 (Sept. 1988)

b. Selected Discography

i) Symphonies

Symphony No. 1	BBC Scottish SO, Loughran	Lyrita	REAM 1121
Symphony No. 2	LPO, Braithwaite	Lyrita	SRCD 207
Symphony No. 3	LPO, Braithwaite	Lyrita	SRCD 207
Symphony No. 4	Liepāja SO, Gibbons	Toccata	TOCC 0480
Symphony No. 5	BBC Scottish SO, Robertson	Lyrita	REAM 1121
Symphony No. 8	Liepāja SO, Gibbons	Toccata	TOCC 0480

ii) Concertos

Piano Concerto	Liepāja SO, Gibbons; Arnicane (piano)	Toccata	TOCC 0526
Violin Concerto	Liepāja SO, Gibbons; Bydlowska (violin)	Toccata	TOCC 0526

iii) **Orchestral**

Overture: Conflict	BBC Scottish SO, Loughran	Lyrita	REAM 1121
Three Pastoral Sketches	Liepāja SO, Gibbons	Toccata	TOCC 0526
Divertimento	Liepāja SO, Gibbons	Toccata	TOCC 0480
Variations on a Scottish Theme	Liepāja SO, Gibbons	Toccata	TOCC 0480

iv) **Chamber**

Cello Sonata No. 2	Wallfisch (cello); Terroni (piano)	Naxos	8.571352

v) **Songs**

Red Skies	Ferrier (contr); Lush (piano)	Decca	430 061-2
The Wind	Ferrier (contr); Lush (piano)	Decca	430 061-2
Clouds	Ferrier (contr); Lush (piano)	Decca	430 061-2

Three

Accessing the Music

Essentially, there are four ways of accessing the music of the composers included in this volume: CD, MP3, YouTube and, of course, live concerts.

1. Compact Disc (CD)

Older readers will remember the good old days when vinyl records (LPs) reigned supreme, and for those cherished LP collections there are still machines available on which to play them. With repeated playing LPs soon began to show signs of wear and tear, and the old "snap, crackle and pop", which some listeners found endearing, became evident. Towards the end of the LP era came a brief flirtation with the magnetic tape. These tape recordings avoided the extraneous noise of LPs, but replaced it with some of their own in the form of a continuous "hiss" which the best (i.e. most expensive) tape recorders claimed to eradicate, but never quite did. Moreover, even so-called quality tapes were susceptible to being chewed by the machine, after which they became unplayable.

Thus, the stage was set for a genuine sound revolution in the form of the CD which burst onto the scene in the mid-1980s. As with any innovation, people had mixed feelings initially. I remember reading a newspaper article entitled "Why the CD will remain an expensive luxury" – or words to that effect – a claim which must certainly have come back to haunt the author. The only significant expense, as it turned out, was the initial outlay on the required CD player. With its ability to transcend the shortcomings of the LP and tape recordings alike, the CD soon gained popularity, and for a time became the only medium available. Any problems now lay not with the medium itself, but with the recording engineer and the performers of the works being recorded. These, of course, are ever with us, whatever the format, but most recording companies now employ highly experienced engineers and producers, and the standard of performances by artistes at the top of their profession can hardly be exceeded.

Today, the default means of listening for an ever-growing number is the MP3 format – or possibly YouTube, and of course many prefer listening to music on the move. What, then, has the humble CD to offer against this onrushing tide? One essential asset is the CD case with its liner notes. Although these can vary in both length and quality, most recording companies engage the services of highly-respected music critics whose notes are well-researched and admirably thorough. Along with many others, I find that having some prior knowledge of a composer, and of the particular work to which I am listening, considerably enhances both my appreciation of the music and the overall pleasure of the listening experience.

Some might object that the CD has the potential to restrict mobility; one must remain in the room where the CD player (or the speakers, at least) is located. But surely this is precisely the point. Quality music is intended as a listening experience, not as mere background noise to accompany some other activity as is the case with most pop music. What better on a winter's evening than to relax in the comfort of one's sitting room with the lights turned low and a glass of claret to hand while appreciating the glories of Elgar, Vaughan Williams, Delius – or any other of our home-grown composers? Music on the move may be convenient, but it surely cannot provide the sound quality of the at-home CD experience, especially given the high-quality sound systems now available.

2. The MP3 Format

Many people these days prefer to listen in MP3 format – that is, directly through the speakers on their computer. The economy-conscious listener may welcome MP3 in that it enables him or her to target the pieces s/he wishes to hear, and to purchase those alone, whereas with a CD one must buy the entire package. Not only is it possible to invest in specific works, but even in individual movements of more extensive pieces. The ravishingly beautiful third movement of Vaughan Williams's Symphony No. 5, for instance, can be bought separately from the remainder of the work.

There is no doubt that MP3 sound quality rivals that of the CD, and it is a convenient way of accessing the music. Yet composers who write multi-movement symphonies, concertos and other pieces do so because they intend these works to be heard *in toto*. Of course, selecting an individual movement is hardly a crime, but the listening experience is generally more fulfilling when it is heard in the context of the work as a whole.

3. YouTube

Vast quantities of classical music can now be accessed entirely free on YouTube. The sound quality is very often (though not always) as high as in any other format, largely because much of the repertoire on offer is uploaded CD material. But there is much more to YouTube than this. One can find old radio broadcasts of works that have never been released on commercial recordings. My own introduction to Ina Boyle's beautiful Violin Concerto was via YouTube at a time when the prospects of a CD release seemed remote (Dutton has since done the honours). The sound quality in this case was indifferent, but at the time there was no other means of hearing the work. In addition, one can find live performances of the better-known English repertoire, such as Andrew Manze's Vaughan Williams symphonic cycle which he conducted at the Proms in 2013.

The great advantage of YouTube is that it allows the intrepid Anglophile to explore a vast range of English music, much of it rarely-heard and little-known, without having to invest financially. But there lies the rub! In the case of – let us say – Ruth Gipps's Symphony No. 3, a work given some critical acclaim at the time of its premiere, YouTube provides the listener with the only means of access today. However, YouTube is also stacked to the gunnels with commercially recorded material, thereby allowing the listener access to the music without the expense of purchasing the CD. But, obviously, the success of important recording companies depends heavily on revenue from sales, without which future recordings cannot be undertaken, or must be drastically curtailed. Stories of aborted or scaled-back projects are legion. Let me outline three:

Chandos, one of the most respected of English independent record companies, is highly regarded for its championing all the major works of Elgar, Vaughan Williams, Holst, Howells and Bax, as well as younger contemporaries like Kenneth Leighton, and "one-offs" such as Margaret Hubicki. In its heyday, Chandos produced some twelve recordings per month, and for just £20.00 provided the listener with a monthly sampler. Today, financial constraints have led to the production being pared down to about half, and the present output includes repackaged material. Given that Chandos is committed to exploring the international repertoire as well as English music, it is hardly surprising that the latter is now at a premium.

The Dutton Epoch label has for many years had a well-deserved reputation for spotlighting both the unjustly neglected works of lesser-known English composers, and the lesser-known works of well-known ones. Alongside the greats – Elgar, Vaughan Williams, Delius – stand others who have suffered shameful neglect for one reason or another, or maybe no reason at all: Richard Arnell, Stanley Bate, York Bowen, Alan Bush, Benjamin Dale, Thomas Dunhill, Lillian Elkington, Armstrong Gibbs, Michael Hurd, Walter Leigh, Celia McDowall, and Cyril Rootham, to name but a few. At one time, the output amounted to four or five new recordings every three months, whereas now this refreshing enterprise has virtually ground to a halt.

At the beginning of the 1990s, Marco Polo set out its ambitious, but highly laudable aim of recording the entire symphonic cycle of Havergal Brian (32 symphonies, no less!), including the vast Gothic Symphony. The project faltered, however, when only a third complete, presumably for lack of capital. Other recording companies took up the strain, while Naxos, originally the budget arm of Marco Polo, not only reissued the existing recordings, but added new ones. Eventually, all the symphonies were recorded, though by several different recording companies using different orchestras and conductors, so that the outcome is not a symphonic cycle in the strictest sense – although we must be grateful for small mercies.

The problem before us is clear: in order to undertake interesting and rewarding projects involving the recording of lesser-known English composers, the participating companies require capital which will be much diminished if potential customers choose to access the music for free on YouTube. It is a problem the solution of which calls for public-spiritedness and personal discipline. After all, the lure of YouTube is difficult to resist when it offers for free what otherwise would incur a cost – perhaps of £10.00 or more. The alternative, however, is to stand by and watch the demise of the very recording companies we seek to promote.

4. Live Concerts

For sheer atmosphere, nothing can beat a live concert. The acoustic quality may vary from venue to venue, and may even depend on the location of the listener inside the auditorium, or the arrangement of the orchestra on stage. No recording engineer and his staff are required to facilitate the desired auditory experience. The orchestra speaks directly to the listener without any mechanical intervention, and the dynamics are as true and direct as they can be. One is also caught up in the thrill and the passion of the experience, and in the knowledge that hundreds and sometimes thousands of others are sharing in the same experience. There is the sense of anticipatory hush before a work begins, and of fulfilment after the final bar.

None of this really applies to any other form of listening. The celebrated performance of Havergal Brian's Gothic Symphony at a Proms concert on 11th July 2011, with nine hundred performers, thousands of "Promers", including myself, in attendance, can only be described as a phenomenon which far transcended the listening experiences of the performances of the work on record which I already possessed at that time.

On the debit side, there is the deplorable reluctance of conductors and programmers to select all but the best-known works of the English orchestral repertoire for performance. London, with its cosmopolitan scene, fares better in this regard than the provinces where we are all too frequently starved of anything "new" or adventurous. Part of the abovementioned reluctance is attributable to the conservative tastes of concert-goers. Sheffield, for example, is notorious for it. Adventurous programming and unfamiliar works result in a more than half-empty auditorium. Even traditional concerts comprising traditional mainstream European fayre do not guarantee full houses these days. Any "strange" work must be surreptitiously smuggled in between the Mozart and the Beethoven if the audience is not to vote with its feet. Psychologically, the spirit of adventure is, more often than not, absent. We tend to seek sanctuary in the familiar because it provides a measure of certainty in our lives. Yet there must have been an occasion when each one of us heard Beethoven's Fifth for the first time, and for some, that has become part of their identity. Why not Arthur Butterworth's Third, or Ruth Gipps's Second (a beautiful work)? No doubt some will think I am over-egging the pudding, but my point is clear: How do we know what we are missing if we never have the chance to hear such works or – worse still – choose not to do so?

Appendix

Moeran's Unfinished Symphony

The saga of Moeran's unfinished Symphony in E flat is so intriguing that I consider it worthy of a separate appendix. Its mystique has attracted several scholarly articles[319], book chapters[320] and web-site contributions.[321] The one certainty about it is that the symphony – or part of it – did reach the manuscript stage; it did not simply remain a conception inside the composer's head. He frequently reports progress on it – or the lack of it – in correspondence with his wife, the cellist Peers Coetmore, and others, such as his close friend Lionel Hill. In 1946 he announced in the *Daily Sketch* that he was at work on the symphony, and again in a radio broadcast in 1948, in which he said that he had been commissioned to write it by Sir John Barbirolli. And in the summer of 1949, he discussed it with

319 Rhoderick McNeill, "Moeran's Unfinished Symphony", *Musical Times*, 121, no. 1654 (December 1980), pp. 771–77; Fabian Huss, "E.J. Moeran's Symphony No. 2 in E flat", *Journal of the Society for Musicology in Ireland*, 6 (2010–11), pp. 67–85.

320 Self, *E.J. Moeran*, pp. 221–30.

321 *The Worldwide Moeran Database*, http://www.moeran.net/Orchestral/SecondSymphony.html; Ian Maxwell, *The Importance of Being Ernest John: Challenging the Misconceptions about the Life and Works of E.J. Moeran*, PhD Thesis, University of Durham, 2014; http://www.etheses.dur.ac.uk/10752.

the Hallé Orchestra's principal clarinettist Pat Ryan in Kenmare, County Kerry. Thus, there can be no doubt of its existence.

It is often stated that Moeran must have begun work on the Second Symphony in about 1945, while Geoffrey Self[322] traces its first mention to a letter from Moeran to his wife, dated 7th January 1946. But in fact, the seeds seem to have been sown as early as 1939, almost immediately following the premiere of the G minor Symphony. In a letter to the violinist May Harrison, he writes:

> My other musical activity [he was working on the Violin Concerto at the time] consists of going up the mountain & filling pages of notebooks with ideas I am working out for another symphony. I might actually commence the composition thereof during the winter when the concerto & also the short pfte [piano] and orchestra work are, I hope, finished. It will be entirely different to No. 1. I may say I think I have hit on a winner for my opening subject, thanks to the view from Moll's Gap looking across to the Reeks & Killarney Lakes 1000 ft below on a brilliant spring morning. There will be no gloom or Atlantic winter in No. 2.[323]

This quotation tells us a good deal about Moeran's approach to the composition of his projected new symphony, and one of the reasons why it proved so problematic. By his own admission, his working methods were painstakingly slow, and although the success of the G minor Symphony (itself thirteen years in the making) may have prompted thoughts of a second symphony, he was already engaged on two other major works, neither of which was completed within the timescale envisaged. Once they were finished, other projects intervened: *Overture for a Masque* (1944); the Six Poems of Seamus O'Sullivan (1944); *Sinfonietta* (1944); the Cello Concerto (1945);

322 Self, *E.J. Moeran*, p. 221.

323 Quoted in Huss, "E.J. Moeran's Symphony No. 2", pp. 67–68. To be fair to Geoffrey Self, this letter had not come to light at the time he was at work on his book in 1986.

the Cello Sonata (1947); and *Serenade* (1948). As if this were not enough, there was a *Prelude* for cello & piano (1943); the *Irish Lament* for cello & piano (1944); the *Fantasy Quartet* for oboe & strings (1946); and various songs and short choral works. If Moeran was fighting alcoholism and mental disintegration during the latter stages of this period, he was certainly not idle.

Yet his most ambitious project, the new symphony, was frozen out by all these other activities. Perhaps he consciously used this general busyness as an excuse to avoid serious work on the symphony in order to mask his sense of insecurity in tackling the project. After all, as noted above, he was under obligation to deliver, and a performance had provisionally been pencilled in for the 1947 concert season. But, as Moeran struggled to meet his commitments, postponements began to mount. Meanwhile, the Cello Concerto had been written *con amore* for Peers Coetmore, as were all the other cello works listed above. Barry Marsh's reference to the symphony becoming "a victim of its composer's misdirected creativity"[324] is surely not far short of the mark. Moeran, too, frittered away much of the time he might have been working on the symphony, pouring out his angst about it in frequent letters, addressed chiefly to his longsuffering wife. Thus, following earlier missives in which he expressed satisfaction and optimism, he wrote to her in May 1949: "I am sorry to say that I am by no means satisfied with my $E^{\flat}$ Symphony; well on towards the finish. I am terribly depressed about it as I fear it may have to scrapped in toto".[325] At this time he was residing in Cheltenham where he was undergoing treatment for alcoholism, and could have availed himself of walks in the adjacent Cotswolds, but he insisted that his symphony required a wholly Irish landscape: "If I were in Southern Ireland, I could work it out and finish it, but it is absolutely and irreconcilably impossible to do it here. It started by being Irish, and if I try to put it right here, it

324 B. Marsh, liner notes to *E.J. Moeran, Symphony No. 2 (Realised and Completed by Martin Yates)*, Dutton, CDLX 7281, p. 4.

325 Quoted in Self, *E.J. Moeran*, p. 222.

only ends up by being pastiche Irish".[326] However, despite eventually returning to Ireland and spending the greater part of 1950 there, first near Dublin, but ultimately in his county of preference, Kerry, he was no nearer to applying himself than he had been in Cheltenham.

Although Moeran's many references to the symphony, taken in chronological order, paint a picture of steadily growing disillusionment, within this trend his attitude fluctuated markedly in accordance with his sudden mood swings. As early as 1945, Moeran had apparently confessed to Lionel Hill that he was having trouble with the work.[327] Hill claims to have suggested turning its projected three-movement form into a single movement, *a la* Sibelius's Symphony No. 7, which, he says, left Moeran deep in thought. A few months later, he heard Moeran play through the symphony on the piano and was impressed. In his recollection of these events in his book thirty-five years later, and later still in a radio interview given in 1992, however, one must wonder about the accuracy of detail after such a long time-lapse. In the book he admits to not being sure how much of the symphony had been completed at the time he heard it, whereas in the interview of 1992, he gave the impression of having heard the work in full, even suggesting that it was as long as the G minor Symphony. It is always possible, of course, that the manuscript was substantial at that stage, and that Moeran later had second thoughts and did what he periodically threatened to do by scrapping most of it.

One point of interest which does seem to testify to the accuracy of Lionel Hill's memory in one respect concerns the opening of the symphony: "It began vigorously with high-flying trumpets, followed by strings *divisi* – the instrumentation was visible on the score."[328] This description certainly corresponds with Geoffrey Self's music example[329], and can be heard at the outset of Yates's realisation, based on the sketches he accessed in the Victorian College, Melbourne.

326 Quoted in Self, *E.J. Moeran*, p. 223.

327 Hill, *Lonely Waters*, p. 71.

328 Hill, *Lonely Waters*, p. 71.

329 Self, *E,J. Moeran*, p. 227, Ex. 97.

We can be confident, therefore, that the opening bars we hear on the Dutton recording are those which Moeran himself wrote, and which Lionel Hill heard back in 1945. It is unlikely, in any case, that Moeran would have discarded this opening, regardless of the changes he made to the rest of the symphony, because in a letter to his wife, dated 14th June 1949, in which he contemplates scrapping the symphony in its then current form, he laments: "It's a pity, because the first part of the symphony is so good...".[330]

Even so, disagreement persists about the quality of those opening bars. Lionel Hill thought that what he heard, even on the piano, had the makings of a masterpiece, commenting: "It was breathtaking in its sweep, and I thought. 'This will out-do the First Symphony if it continues like this'".[331] Geoffrey Self, however, is more circumspect: "The opening is brash..., and does not compare in grip and originality with the opening of the Symphony in G minor".[332] One possible reason for this sharp difference of opinion is that Hill, unlike Self, had been personally involved with Moeran for several years. He was clearly flattered by the fact that, having idolised the composer from the moment he first heard some of his music (*Lonely Waters*, in his case), the great man responded by actually befriending him, just as Delius had done with Philip Heseltine. After all, Hill was much younger than Moeran, and only a musical amateur. It must have been gratifying for him to have been taken into the composer's confidence to the extent of his being asked for his advice on the nature of the Symphony. There are clearly times when he saw Moeran worse for drink, but he made allowances for such defects for the sake of his virtues, and was always ready to defend his friend's reputation as a generous, genial man with an outstanding talent for composition.

As far as can be ascertained, no further work was done on the Symphony after March 1950. Moeran settled for the last six

330 Quoted in Self, *E.J. Moeran*, p. 223.

331 Hill, *Lonely Waters*, p. 71.

332 Self, *E.J. Moeran*, pp. 227–28.

months of his life in his beloved Kenmare, but seems to have spent most of his time pottering around the area, possibly giving some music tuition to the locals, and visiting the local hostelries, although Michael Bowles contradicts the latter suggestion.[333] Be that as it may, Moeran's general physical and mental health continued to deteriorate, and he met his sudden end in the Kenmare River (actually an estuary) on a stormy afternoon on 1st December 1950.

After Moeran's death, efforts were made to recover his remaining manuscripts, but these were somewhat uncoordinated and haphazard. Both his brother Graham and his wife Peers were involved in this quest, and they made some effort to keep in touch. Nothing of any value, it seems, was discovered at Kenmare.[334] Piecing together events from the correspondence produced by Moeran's relatives and acquaintances subsequent to his death, and reproduced by Lionel Hill[335], it seems that affairs relating to the remaining manuscripts can be described as follows: Before his death, Moeran had appointed Sir Arnold Bax as his literary executor. Subsequently, Moeran's brother Graham managed to retrieve a bundle of manuscripts from Moeran's *pied à terre* near Dublin[336], and despatched these to Bax in accordance with his brother's will. Bax seems to have done little but hold them in safe-

333 "Actually, as far as I know, he had stopped taking any alcohol at all for six months before he died" (quoted in Self, *E.J. Moeran*, p. 229).

334 Pat Ryan, the Hallé Orchestra's principal clarinettist, testifies to having visited Moeran at Kenmare during the summer of 1950 where he discussed the Symphony with him in detail (Self, *E.J. Moeran*, p. 226), but he never claims that they had the score or sketches in front of them, which, in the end, were retrieved from Moeran's *pied à terre* near Dublin after his death. Thus, Ryan's conjecture that the Symphony was virtually complete at that stage must ever remain that – speculation. Of course, Ryan's further speculation that much of the manuscript was subsequently destroyed by Moeran himself cannot be discounted.

335 Hill, *Lonely Waters*, pp. 111–13.

336 The story that a cleaning lady came across them and, finding that they were in poor condition, threw them out "for decency's sake", is entirely hearsay.

keeping until his own death in Cork in 1953[337], after which they passed into the hands of the then editor of *BBC Music Magazine*, Julian Herbage (1904–76), and ultimately to Peers Coetmore who deposited them with the Victorian College, Melbourne. Among the works, wholly or partially complete, were an overture[338], a string quartet, and a substantial piece of 550 bars which was assumed to be what remained of the Symphony.

Soon after Moeran's death, the contents of the package had been examined by his former composition teacher at the RCM, John Ireland, who considered nothing in it to be in a sufficiently developed state to merit an attempt at completion. Barry Marsh concurs:

> Sadly there can be no "realisation" or "completion", whatever the word for it these days. 550 bars of music exists [sic] in short score, but after only nine pages the sketches become disjointed with little or no fragments to point a further way. The MSS which is [sic] now in the Victorian College of Arts, Melbourne arrived there after a series of blunders and misfortunes...[339]

Yet when conductor Martin Yates examined the sketches some time prior to 2011, he not only saw their potential, but realised a performing version of the Symphony based on them, which was

---

337 He must have glanced at them briefly, however, because he pronounced the contents "rubbish".

338 Presumably, this is the work that Rodney Newton orchestrated from short score, and which was recorded under the title *Overture for a Festival* by Martin Yates and the RSNO (Dutton CDLX 7281).

339 "Symphony No. 2 in E Flat (unfinished)", *Worldwide Moeran Database*, http://www.moeran.net/Orchestral/SecondSymphony.html. As noted above, however, this site appears to be no longer accessible. According to Huss ("E.J. Moeran's Symphony No. 2", p. 80), the Melbourne sketches amount to only seventeen pages *in toto*, which is a far cry from the "great thick manuscript" that Hill claims to have seen propped up on the piano on the occasion of his hearing the Symphony (comment made in his 1992 interview).

subsequently recorded by Dutton (CDLX 7281). The liner notes for the recording include an explanation by Yates of how he went about the task, and a comment by Barry Marsh who had previously declared such realisation impossible. Tactfully, he reserves judgement on Yates's effort.

We have already considered the pros and cons of "realising" the unfinished works of deceased composers in respect of Elgar's Symphony No. 3, and Yates frankly admits that, in the present case, he would be "the first person to admit that this symphony cannot be the one that Moeran would ultimately have written". However, he goes on, "I do unreservedly say that the music deserves to be heard within the symphonic context that Moeran was attempting, and by undertaking the realisation and completion I hope I have helped that happen."[340] It must be admitted that the results of Yates's work are impressive and could easily be mistaken for that of Moeran himself. He achieves the Moeran idiom not only by using the sketches he left behind, but by employing the kind of technique and orchestration he was using in works composed at the same time as the Symphony was under consideration – the *Sinfonietta*, in particular. Perhaps the most fruitful way to approach the Symphony is to acknowledge it as a work by Martin Yates using the material from the Moeran sketches.

340 Yates, liner notes, *Moeran Symphony No. 2*, Dutton, CDLX, 7281, p. 8.

a. Bibliography

Hill, Lionel, *Lonely Waters* (London: Thames Publishing, 1985)

Huss, Fabian, "E.J. Moeran's Symphony No. 2 in E flat", *Journal of the Society for Musicology in Ireland*, 6 (2010–11), pp. 67–85.

Maxwell, Ian, *The Importance of Being Ernest John: Challenging the Misconceptions about the Life and Works of E.J. Moeran*, PhD Thesis, University of Durham, 2014; http://www.etheses.dur.ac.uk/10752.

McNeill, Rhoderick, "Moeran's Unfinished Symphony", *Musical Times*, 121, no. 1654 (December 1980), pp. 771–77.

Self, Geoffrey, *The Music of E.J. Moeran* (London: Toccata Press, 1986), pp. 221–30.

General Bibliography

Ackroyd, P., *English Music* (London: Hamish Hamilton, 1992)

Aldritt, Keith, *England Resounding: Vaughan Williams, Britten and the English Musical Renaissance* (London: Robert Hale, 2019)

Bacharach, A.L., *British Music of our Time* (Harmondsworth: Penguin, 1946)

Banfield, Stephen, ed., *Music in Britain in the Twentieth Century* (Oxford: Blackwell, 1995)

Blackwood, Alan, *Sir Thomas Beecham: The Man and the Music* (London: Ebury Press, 1994)

Blom, E., *Music in England* (Harmondsworth: Penguin, 1942)

Cardus, Neville, *Sir Thomas Beecham* (London: Collins, 1961)

Ferguson, Howard, *Music, Friends and Places: A Memoir* (London: Thames Publishing, 1996).

Foreman, Lewis, ed., *From Parry to Britten: British Music in Letters, 1900-1945* (London: Batsford, 1987)

France, John, "The Music of Janet Hamilton: A Preliminary Survey", *British Music*, 32 (2010), pp. 78–81

Frank, A. *Modern British Composers* (London: Dennis Dobson, 1953)

Geraghty, Tony, *Rendezvous with Death: Artists and Writers in the Thick of it* (Barnsley: Pen & Sword, 2017)

Hadow, W.H., *English Music* (London: Longman, 1931)

Hamnett, Nina, *Is She a Lady?* (London: Wingate, 1955)

Harker, D., *Fakesong: The Manufacturing of British "Folksong", 1700 to the Present Day* (Milton Keynes: Open University Press, 1985).

Hiscock, Terry, *Composing Mortals: Twentieth Century British Classical Composers* (London: Thames Publishing, 1998)

Holbrook, Joseph, *Contemporary British Composers* (Cecil Palmer, 1925)

Hold, Trevor, *Parry to Finzi: Twenty English Song Composers* (Woodbridge, Suffolk: Boydell, 2005)

Howes, Frank, *The English Musical Renaissance* (London: Secker & Warburg, 1966)

Hughes, Meirion and Robert Stradling, *The English Musical Renaissance 1840–*

1940: Constructing a National Music (Manchester: Manchester University Press, 2nd edn, 2001)

Jefferson, A., *Sir Thomas Beecham – A Centenary Tribute* (MacDonald & Jane's, 1979)

Jeffreys, John, *The Life and Works of Philip Rosseter* (Wendover, Bucks.: Roberton, 1990)

Jordan, Rolf, "The Life and Works of Janet Hamilton", *British Music*, 32 (2010), pp. 62–76

Karpeles, Maud, *Cecil Sharp: His Life and Work* (London: Routledge & Kegan Paul, 1967)

----------, *An Introduction to English Folksong* (Oxford: Oxford University Press, 1987)

Kennedy, Michael, *Barbirolli: Conductor Laureate* (London: MacGibbon & Kee, 1971)

----------, *Adrian Boult* (London: Macmillan, 1989)

King, Richard, *The Lark Ascending: People, Music and Landscape in Twentieth Century Britain* (London: Faber & Faber, 2020)

Lloyd, S., *Sir Dan Godfrey – Champion of British Composers* (London: Thames Publishing, 1995)

Marshall, Em, *Music in the Landscape* (London: Robert Hale, 2011)

McVeagh, Diana, *The New Grove Twentieth Century English Masters* (London: W.W. Norton, 1986)

Norris, G., *A Musical Gazetteer of Great Britain and Ireland* (Newton Abbot: David & Charles, 1981)

Northcote, S., *Byrd to Britten: A Survey of English Song* (London: Baker, 1966)

Palmer, R., *British Music* (London: Skelton Robinson, 1947)

Pirie, Peter, *The English Musical Renaissance* (London: Gollancz, 1979)

Rayborn, Tim, *A New English Music* (Jefferson, NC: McFarland & Co. 2016)

Reid, C., *Thomas Beecham: An Independent Biography* (London: Gollancz, 1962)

----------, *Malcolm Sargent* (London: Hamish Hamilton, 1968)

Robinson, S., *Peggy Glanville-Hicks: Composer and Critic*, Music in American Life (Chicago: University of Illinois Press, 2019)

Roud, Steve, *Folk Song in England* (London: Faber & Faber, 2017)

Simpson, Robert, *Carl Nielsen: Symphonist* (2nd edn: London: Kahn & Averill, 1979, orig. 1952)

Tame, David, *The Secret Power of Music: The Transformation of Self and Society through Musical Energy* (Rochester, VT: Destiny Books, 1984)